Lecture Notes in Computer Science 7253

Commenced Publication in 1973
Founding and Former Series Editors:
Gerhard Goos, Juris Hartmanis, and Jan van Leeuwen

Editorial Board

David Hutchison
Lancaster University, UK

Takeo Kanade
Carnegie Mellon University, Pittsburgh, PA, USA

Josef Kittler
University of Surrey, Guildford, UK

Jon M. Kleinberg
Cornell University, Ithaca, NY, USA

Alfred Kobsa
University of California, Irvine, CA, USA

Friedemann Mattern
ETH Zurich, Switzerland

John C. Mitchell
Stanford University, CA, USA

Moni Naor
Weizmann Institute of Science, Rehovot, Israel

Oscar Nierstrasz
University of Bern, Switzerland

C. Pandu Rangan
Indian Institute of Technology, Madras, India

Bernhard Steffen
TU Dortmund University, Germany

Madhu Sudan
Microsoft Research, Cambridge, MA, USA

Demetri Terzopoulos
University of California, Los Angeles, CA, USA

Doug Tygar
University of California, Berkeley, CA, USA

Gerhard Weikum
Max Planck Institute for Informatics, Saarbruecken, Germany

T0223497

Farhad Arbab   Peter Csaba Ölveczky (Eds.)

Formal Aspects of Component Software

8th International Symposium, FACS 2011
Oslo, Norway, September 14-16, 2011
Revised Selected Papers

 Springer

Volume Editors

Farhad Arbab
Centre for Mathematics
and Computer Science (CWI)
Science Park 123
1098 XG Amsterdam, The Netherlands
E-mail: farhad@cwi.nl

Peter Csaba Ölveczky
University of Oslo
Department of Informatics
Postboks 1080 Blindern
0316 Oslo, Norway
E-mail: peterol@ifi.uio.no

ISSN 0302-9743   e-ISSN 1611-3349
ISBN 978-3-642-35742-8   e-ISBN 978-3-642-35743-5
DOI 10.1007/978-3-642-35743-5
Springer Heidelberg Dordrecht London New York

Library of Congress Control Number: 2012954139

CR Subject Classification (1998): D.2.4, D.2, F.4, F.3, H.3.5, D.3, D.1, K.6.3

LNCS Sublibrary: SL 2 – Programming and Software Engineering

© Springer-Verlag Berlin Heidelberg 2012

This work is subject to copyright. All rights are reserved, whether the whole or part of the material is
concerned, specifically the rights of translation, reprinting, re-use of illustrations, recitation, broadcasting,
reproduction on microfilms or in any other way, and storage in data banks. Duplication of this publication
or parts thereof is permitted only under the provisions of the German Copyright Law of September 9, 1965,
in its current version, and permission for use must always be obtained from Springer. Violations are liable
to prosecution under the German Copyright Law.
The use of general descriptive names, registered names, trademarks, etc. in this publication does not imply,
even in the absence of a specific statement, that such names are exempt from the relevant protective laws
and regulations and therefore free for general use.

Typesetting: Camera-ready by author, data conversion by Scientific Publishing Services, Chennai, India

Printed on acid-free paper

Springer is part of Springer Science+Business Media (www.springer.com)

Preface

This volume contains the revised versions of accepted regular papers presented at the 8th International Symposium on Formal Aspects of Component Software (FACS 2011), held at the Department of Informatics, University of Oslo, on September 14–16, 2011. It also contains contributions by the three invited speakers at this event: José Meseguer, John Rushby, and Ketil Stølen.

FACS 2011 was the eighth event in a series founded by the International Institute for Software Technology of the United Nations University (UNU-IIST). The objective of FACS is to bring researchers and practitioners of component software and formal methods together in order to foster a deeper understanding of reliable component-based systems development and their applications, using formal methods. The component-based software development approach has emerged as a promising paradigm to cope with the complexity of present-day software systems by bringing sound engineering principles into software engineering. However, many challenging conceptual and technological issues still remain in the theory and practice of component-based software development. Moreover, the advent of service-oriented computing has brought to the fore new dimensions, such as quality of service and robustness to withstand inevitable faults, that require revisiting established component-based concepts in order to meet the new requirements of the service-oriented paradigm.

We received 46 submissions from 26 countries, out of which the Program Committee accepted 16 as regular papers, and, furthermore, conditionally accepted 4 additional papers. The revised versions of 18 of these papers appear in this volume. Each submission to FACS 2011 was reviewed by at least three referees.

Many colleagues and friends contributed to FACS 2011. First, we thank the authors who submitted their work to FACS 2011 and who, by their contributions and participation, made this symposium a high-quality event. We thank the Program Committee members and their sub-reviewers for their timely and insightful reviews as well as for their involvement in the post-reviewing discussions. We are also grateful to the FACS Steering Committee for its guidance, to the invited speakers, and to Lucian Bentea for all his assistance in organizing this event. Finally, we thank Andrei Voronkov for the excellent EasyChair conference system, and the Research Council of Norway and the Department of Informatics at the University of Oslo for financially supporting the symposium.

April 2012

Farhad Arbab
Peter Ölveczky

Organization

Program Chairs

Farhad Arbab   CWI and Leiden University, The Netherlands
Peter Csaba Ölveczky   University of Oslo, Norway

Steering Committee

Zhiming Liu (Coordinator)   IIST UNU, Macau
Farhad Arbab   CWI and Leiden University, The Netherlands
Luís Barbosa   University of Minho, Portugal
Carlos Canal   University of Málaga, Spain
Markus Lumpe   Swinburne University of Technology, Australia
Eric Madelaine   INRIA, Centre Sophia Antipolis, France
Peter Csaba Ölveczky   University of Oslo, Norway
Corina Păsăreanu   NASA Ames, USA
Bernhard Schätz   fortiss GmbH, Germany

Program Committee

Erika Ábrahám   RWTH Aachen University, Germany
Farhad Arbab   CWI and Leiden University, The Netherlands
Christel Baier   Technical University of Dresden, Germany
Luís Barbosa   Universidade do Minho, Portugal
Mihaela Bobaru   NASA/JPL, USA
Christiano Braga   Universidade Federal Fluminense, Brazil
Roberto Bruni   University of Pisa, Italy
Carlos Canal   University of Málaga, Spain
Frank De Boer   CWI, The Netherlands
Francisco Duran   University of Málaga, Spain
Rolf Hennicker   Ludwig-Maximilians-Universität München, Germany
Alexander Knapp   Augsburg University, Germany
Zhiming Liu   IIST UNU, Macau
Markus Lumpe   Swinburne University of Technology, Australia
Eric Madelaine   INRIA, Centre Sophia Antipolis, France
Sun Meng   Peking University, China
Peter Csaba Ölveczky   University of Oslo, Norway
Corina Păsăreanu   NASA Ames, USA
František Plášil   Charles University, Czech Republic

Gwen Salaün	Grenoble INP - INRIA, France
Bernhard Schätz	fortiss GmbH, Germany
Wolfram Schulte	Microsoft Research, USA
Nishant Sinha	NEC Labs, Princeton, USA
Marjan Sirjani	Reykjavik University, Iceland
Volker Stolz	University of Oslo, Norway
Carolyn Talcott	SRI International, USA
Emilio Tuosto	University of Leicester, UK

Additional Reviewers

Adam, Ludwig
Ardourel, Gilles
Bauer, Sebastian
Baumeister, Hubert
Bertolini, Cristiano
Blech, Jan Olaf
Chen, Zhenbang
Choppy, Christine
Corzilius, Florian
Dan, Li
Faber, Johannes
Guanciale, Roberto
Helvensteijn, Michiel
Henrio, Ludovic
Hölzl, Florian
Jaghoori, Mohammad Mahdi
Jansen, Nils
Jezek, Pavel
Jongmans, Sung
Kemper, Stephanie
Keznikl, Jaroslav
Khakpour, Narges
Khalil, Maged

Khamespanah, Ehsan
Khosravi, Ramtin
Kofron, Jan
Komuravelli, Anvesh
Lang, Frédéric
Lepri, Daniela
Lluch Lafuente, Alberto
Loup, Ulrich
Malohlava, Michal
Melgratti, Hernan
Morisset, Charles
Nellen, Johanna
Ouederni, Meriem
Pfaller, Christian
Poch, Tomas
Ramalho, Franklin
Rodrigues, Genaina
Sabouri, Hamideh
Schlatte, Rudolf
Schäf, Martin
Verdejo, Alberto
Vogler, Walter

Table of Contents

Taming Distributed System Complexity through Formal Patterns*

José Meseguer

University of Illinois at Urbana-Champaign

Many current and future distributed systems are or will be:

- real-time and cyber-physical
- probabilistic in their operating environments and/or their algorithms
- safety-critical, with strong qualitative and quantitative formal requirements
- reflective and adaptive, to operate in changing and potentially hostile environments.

Their distributed features, their adaptation needs, and their real-time and probabilistic aspects make such systems quite complex and hard to design, build and verify, yet their safety-critical nature makes their verification essential. One important source of complexity, causing many unforeseen design errors, arises from ill-understood and hard-to-test interactions between their different distributed components.

Methods to tame and greatly reduce system complexity are badly needed. System complexity has many aspects, including the complexity and associated cost of:

- designing
- verifying
- developing
- maintaining and
- evolving

such systems.

The main goal of this talk is to propose the use of formal patterns as a way of drastically reducing all the above system complexity aspects. By a "formal pattern" I mean a solution to a commonly occurring problem that is:

- as generic as possible, with precise semantic requirements for its parameters
- formally specified
- executable, and
- comes with strong formal guarantees.

* Partially supported by NSF Grant CCF 09-05584, AFOSR Grant FA8750-11-2-0084, and Boeing Grant C8088.

F. Arbab and P.C. Ölveczky (Eds.): FACS 2011, LNCS 7253, pp. 1–2, 2012.
© Springer-Verlag Berlin Heidelberg 2012

This means that a formal pattern can be applied to a potentially infinite set of concrete instances, where each such instance is correct by construction and enjoys the formal guarantees ensured by meeting the semantic requirements of the pattern's parameters.

The overall vision is that distributed systems should be designed, verified, and built by composing formal patterns that are highly generic and reusable and come with strong formal guarantees. A large part of the verification effort is spent in an up-front, fully generic manner, and is then amortized across a potentially infinite number of instances. As I show through concrete examples, this can achieve very drastic reductions in all aspects of system complexity, including the formal verification aspect. It can lead to high-quality, highly reliable distributed systems at a fraction of the cost required when not using such patterns.

To develop formal patterns for distributed systems with features such as those mentioned above an appropriate semantic framework is needed, one supporting:

- concurrency
- logical reflection
- distributed reflection and adaptation
- real time and probabilities
- executability, and
- formal verification methods.

I use rewriting logic as such a semantic framework, and illustrate with several examples its adequacy to specify and verify formal patterns of this nature.

Composing Safe Systems*

John Rushby

Computer Science Laboratory
SRI International
333 Ravenswood Avenue
Menlo Park, CA 94025 USA

Abstract. Failures in component-based systems are generally due to unintended or incorrect interactions among the components. For safety-critical systems, we may attempt to eliminate unintended interactions, and to verify correctness of those that are intended. We describe the value of partitioning in eliminating unintended interactions, and of assumption synthesis in developing a robust foundation for verification. We show how model checking of very abstract designs can provide mechanized assistance in human-guided assumption synthesis.

1 Introduction

We build systems from components, but what makes something a *system* is that its properties and behaviors are distinct from those of its components. As engineers and designers, we wish to predict and calculate the properties of systems from those of their interconnected components, and we are quite successful at doing this, *most of the time*. For many systems and properties, "most of the time" is good enough: we can live with it if our laptop occasionally locks up, our car doesn't start, or our music player seems to lose our playlists. But we will be considerably more aggrieved if our laptop catches fire, our car fails to stop, or our music player loses the songs that we purchased. As we move from personal systems to those with wider impact and from properties about normal function to those that concern safety or security, so "most of the time" becomes inadequate: we want those properties to be true *all the time.*

Often, properties that we want to be true "all the time" fail to be so, and subsequent investigations generally reveal some unexpected interaction among the system's components. Thus, attempts to reason about the properties of systems by combining or *composing* the properties of their components, while generally successful for "most of the time" properties, are less successful for "all the time" properties. It is for this reason that regulatory bodies examine only complete systems (e.g., the FAA certifies only airplanes and engines) and not components: they need to consider the behaviors and possible interactions of multiple components in the context of a specific system.

---

* This work was supported by National Science Foundation Grant CNS-0720908. The content is solely the responsibility of the author and does not necessarily represent the official views of NSF.

F. Arbab and P.C. Ölveczky (Eds.): FACS 2011, LNCS 7253, pp. 3–11, 2012.
© Springer-Verlag Berlin Heidelberg 2012

Now, although it is generally infeasible at present to guarantee critical "all the time" properties by compositional (or "modular") methods, it is a good research topic to investigate why this is so, and how we might extend the boundaries of what is feasible in this area. Safety, in the sense of causing no harm to the public, is one of the most demanding properties, and so the motivation for the title of this paper is to indicate a research agenda focused on methods that might allow certification of safety for complex systems by compositional means.

As mentioned, system safety failures and the attendant flaws in compositional reasoning are generally due to unanticipated interactions among components. These interactions can be classified into those that exploit a previously unanticipated pathway for interaction, and those that are due to unanticipated behavior along a known interaction pathway. One way to control the first class of unanticipated interactions is to use integration frameworks that restrict the pathways available for component interactions; in avionics, this approach is called "partitioning" and it is the topic of Section 2.

There are two complementary ways to deal with the second class of unanticipated interactions: one is to augment components with wrappers, monitors, or other mechanisms that attempt to limit interactions to those that are needed to accomplish the purpose for which the interaction pathway was established; the other is to actually verify correctness of some interactions. Ideally, the verification should be done compositionally: that is, we verify properties of components considered separately, then from those properties we derive properties of their interaction. The verification of each component has to consider the environment in which it will operate, and that environment is composed of the other components with which it interacts. This seems contrary to a pure conception of component-based design, because it looks as if each component needs to consider the others during its design. One way to avoid this is to calculate the weakest environment in which a component can perform its task; this is among the topics of Section 3, which mainly focuses on assume/guarantee and methods for assumption synthesis. Brief conclusions are provided in Section 4.

2   Partitioning

Aircraft are safe, yet employ many interacting subsystems, so the techniques they employ are worthy of interest. Traditionally, the various avionics functions on board aircraft were provided by fairly independent subsystems loosely integrated as a "federated" system. This meant that the autopilot, for example, had its own computers, replicated for redundancy, and so did the flight management system. The two system would communicate though the exchange of messages, but their relative isolation provided a natural barrier to the propagation of faults: a faulty autopilot might send bad data to the flight management system, but could not destroy its ability to calculate or communicate.

Modern aircraft employ Integrated Modular Avionics (IMA) where many critical functions share the same computer system and communications networks, and so there is naturally concern that a fault in one function could propagate to others sharing the same resources. Hence, the notion of "robust partitioning" has developed [1]: the idea is that applications that use the shared resources should be protected from each other as if they were not sharing and each had their own private resources.

The primary resources that require partitioning are communication and computation: i.e., networks and processors. For networks, the concern is that a faulty or malicious component will not adhere to the protocol and will transmit over other traffic, or will transmit constantly, thereby denying good components the ability to communicate. The only way to provide partitioning in the face of these threats is to employ redundancy, so that components' access to the network is mediated by additional components that limit the rate or the times at which communication can occur. Of course, these additional components and the mechanisms they employ may themselves be afflicted by faults (e.g., transient hardware upsets caused by ambient radiation), and so the design and assurance of these partitioning network technologies are very demanding [2], but they are now reasonably well understood and available "off the shelf."

For processors, the concerns are that faulty or malicious processes will write into the memory of other processes, monopolize the CPUs, or corrupt the processor's state. Partitioning against these threats can be provided by a strong operating system or, more credibly, by a hypervisor or virtual machine environment; minimal hypervisors specialized to the partitioning function are known as "separation kernels" [3] and, like partitioning networks, efficient and highly assured examples are now available "off the shelf."

Partitioning for the basic resources of communication and computation can be leveraged to provide partitioning for additional resources synthesized above them, such as file systems. A collection of partitioning resources may be configured to specify quite precisely what software components are allocated to each partition and what interactions are allowed with other components (the configuration for an IMA is many megabytes of data). Such configurations, which may be portrayed as box and arrow diagrams and formalized as "policy architectures" [4], eliminate undesired paths for interaction and provide direct assurance for certain system-level properties, such as some notions of security.

Fig. 1. A Partitioned System Configured to Support the System Purpose

The properties for which partitioning, on its own, provides adequate enforcement and assurance are those that can be stated in terms of the absence of information flow. As mentioned, certain security concerns are of this kind (e.g., "no flow from secret to unclassified"), but most properties also concern the computations that take place in (some of) the partitions. For example, many secure systems *do* allow flow from secret to unclassified provided the information concerned is suitably "sanitized" by some function interposed in the flow, as portrayed by the minimal policy architecture of Figure 1. The partitioning configuration ensures the sanitizer cannot be bypassed, but we still require assurance that the sanitizer does its job. More complex properties, such as most notions of safety, cannot be ensured by individual components; instead, they emerge from the interactions of many—but partitioning eliminates unintended interactions and allows us to focus on correctness of the intended interactions, which is the topic of the next section.

3   Assumption Synthesis

If we suppose that "traditional software engineering" is able to develop systems that work "most of the time" then it might be possible to turn these into systems that work "all the time" by simply blocking untanticipated events and interactions that might lead to failure, or by controlling the propagation of any failures that are precipitated. These topics are addressed by a variety of techniques such as systematic exception handling [5], anomaly detection [6], safety kernels [7] and enforceable security [8], and runtime monitoring [9]. All these techniques merely reduce the frequency or severity of failures (e.g., by turning "malfunction" or "unintended function" into "loss of function") rather than eliminate them. However, they can be very valuable in systems with many layers of redundancy or fault management, since these often cope very well with the "clean" failure of subsystems, but less well with their misbehavior. Some aircraft systems employ "monitored architectures," where a very simple component monitors the system safety property and shuts down the operational component if this is violated; these architectures can support rather strong assessments of reliability [10].

To get from clean failures to true "all the time" systems by compositional means, we need to be able to calculate the properties of the composed system from those of its components; if the calculation is automated, then it can support an iterative design loop: if the composed system does not satisfy the properties required, then we modify some of the components and their properties and repeat the calculation.

The established way to calculate the properties of interacting components is by assume/guarantee reasoning [11]: we verify that component A delivers (or guarantees) property p on the assumption that its environment delivers property q, and we also verify that B guarantees q assuming p; then when A and B are composed, each becoming the environment of the other, we may conclude (under various technical conditions) that their composition $A||B$ guarantees both p and q. There is, however, a practical difficulty with this approach: if A and B are intended for general use, they are presumably developed in ignorance of each other, and it will require good fortune or unusual prescience that they should each make just the right assumptions and guarantees that they fit together perfectly.

Shankar proposes an alternative approach [12] that treats assumptions as abstract components; here, we establish that p is a property of A in the context of an ideal environment E; if we can then show that B as a refinement of E, then

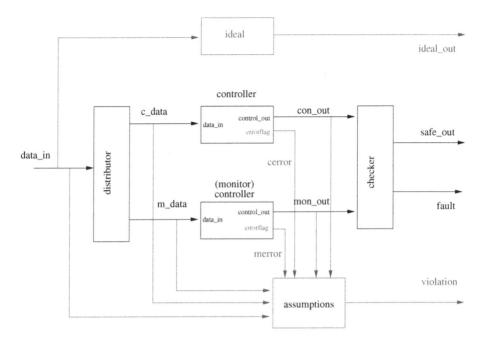

Fig. 2. A Self-Checking Pair, and Additional Components Used in Analysis

the composition of A and B also delivers p. This requires less prescience because we do not need to know about B at the time we design A; we do, however, need to postulate a suitable E.

One interesting idea is to design A, then *calculate* E as the weakest environment under which we can guarantee that A delivers p. When A is a concrete state machine, this can be done using L^* learning [13]. Early in the design process, however, we are unlikely to have developed A to the point where it is available as a fully concrete design; in this case we can often perform assumption synthesis interactively using infinite bounded model checking (inf-BMC).

Inf-BMC performs bounded model checking on state machines defined over the theories supported by an SMT solver (i.e., a solver for *Satisfiability Modulo Theories*) [14]; these theories include equality over uninterpreted functions, possibly constrained by axioms, so it is possible to specify very abstract state machines. An example, taken from [15], is illustrated in Figure 2. Here, the goal is to deduce the assumptions under which a self-checking pair works correctly.

Self-checking pairs are used quite widely in safety-critical systems to provide protection against random hardware faults: two identical processors perform the same calculations and their results are compared; if they differ the pair shuts down (thereby becoming a "fail-stop" processor [16]) and some higher-level fault management activity takes over. Obviously, this does not work if both processors become faulty and compute the *same* wrong result. We would like to learn if there are any other scenarios that can cause a self-checking pair to deliver the wrong result; we can then assess their likelihood (for example, the double fault scenario just described may be considered extremely improbable) and calculate the overall reliability of this architecture.

The scenarios we wish to discover are, on one hand, the *hazards* to the design and, on the other (i.e., when negated), its assumptions. At the system level, hazard analysis is the cornerstone of safety engineering [17]; in component-based design, assumption discovery—its dual—could play a similar rôle: it helps us understand when it is safe for one component to become the environment for another.

Because of its context (the environment of a self-checking pair really is the natural environment, rather than another system), this example is closer to hazard discovery than assumption synthesis—but since these are two sides of the same coin, it serves to illustrate the technique. The idea is that the `controller` and the `monitor` are identical fault-prone processors that compute some uninterpreted function $f(x)$; a `distributor` provides copies of the input x to both processors and the results are sent to a `checker`; if the results agree, the checker passes one of them on as `safe_out`, otherwise it raises a `fault` flag. The `distributor` as well as the two processors can deliver incorrect outputs, but for simplicity of exposition the checker is assumed to be perfect (the checker can be eliminated by having the `controller` and `monitor` cross-check their results). An `ideal` processor, identical to the others but not subject to failures, serves as the correctness oracle, and an `assumptions` module, which operates as a *synchronous observer*, encodes the evolving assumptions. In the figure, the `ideal` and `assumptions` modules and their associated data are shown in red to emphasize that these are artifacts of analysis, not part of the component under design.

Initially, the assumptions are empty and we use inf-BMC to probe correctness of the design (i.e., we attempt to verify the claim that if the `fault` flag is down, then `safe_out` equals `ideal_out`). We obtain a counterexample that alerts us to a missing assumption; we add this assumption and iterate. The exercise terminates after the following assumptions are discovered.

1. When both members of the self-checking pair are faulty, their outputs should differ (this is the case we already thought of).
2. When the members of the pair receive different inputs[1] (i.e., when the distributor is faulty), their outputs should differ. There are two subcases here.

   (a) Neither member of the pair is faulty. The scenario here is that instead of sending the correct value x, the distributor sends y to one member of the pair and z to another, but $f(y) = f(z)$ (and $f(y) \neq f(x)$).
   (b) One or both of the pair are faulty. Here, the scenario is the distributor sends the correct value x to the faulty member, and an incorrect value y to the nonfaulty member, but $f(y) = f'(x)$, where f' is the computation of the faulty member.

---

[1] Readers may wonder how a distributor, whose implementation could be as simple as a solder joint connecting two wires, can alter the values it delivers to the processors; one possibility is it adds resistance and drops the voltage: one processor may see a weak voltage as a 1, the other as a 0.

3. When both members of the pair receive the same input, it is the correct input (i.e., the distributor should not create a bad value and send it to both members of the pair).

Inf-BMC can verify that the self-checking pair works, given these four assumptions, so our next task is to examine them.

Cases 1 and 2(b) require double faults and may be considered improbable for that reason. Case 2(a) is interesting because it probably would not be discovered by finite state model checking, where we do not have uninterpreted functions: instead, the usual way to analyze an "abstract" design is to provide a very simple "concretization," such as replacing $f(x)$ by $x + 1$, which masks any opportunity to find the fault. This case is also interesting because, once discovered, it can be eliminated by modifying the design: simply cause each member of the pair to pass its input as well as its output to the checker; since both processors are nonfaulty, the inputs will be passed correctly to the checker, which will then raise the fault flag because it sees that the inputs differ. That leaves case 3 as the one requiring further consideration (which we do not pursue here) by those who would use a self-checking pair.

This example has illustrated, I hope, how automated methods such as inf-BMC can be used to help calculate the weakest assumptions required by a component, and thereby support the design of systems in which components' assumes and guarantees are mutually supportive, without requiring prescience.

4 Conclusions

All fields of engineering build on components, and it is natural that computer science should do the same. However, component-based systems can be rather more challenging in computer science than in other fields because of the complexity of interaction—unintended as well as in intended—that is possible. This complexity of interaction becomes even more vexatious when we aim to develop safety-critical and other kinds of system that must work correctly all the time. (Perrow [18] argues that unintended interactions and their enablers, "interactive complexity" and "tight coupling," are the primary causes of disasters in all engineering fields; however, computer systems generally have more complexity of these kinds, even in normal operation, than those of other fields.)

A plausible way to develop safe systems from components begins by eliminating unintended interactions, then ensures that the intended interactions are correct.

Unintended interactions can be divided into those that deliver unintended behavior along intended pathways, and those that employ unintended pathways. I have outlined techniques that can ameliorate these concerns. *Partitioning* aims to eliminate unintended pathways for interaction in networks and processors and higher-level resources built on these. Partitioning guarantees "preservation of prior properties" when new components are added to an existing system; it also seems sufficient, on its own, to guarantee certain kinds of information flow security properties, and to simplify the assured construction of more complex properties of this kind [19].

With unintended pathways controlled by partitioning, we can turn to interactions along known pathways; we need to ensure that unintended interactions are eliminated and the intended ones are correct. Various techniques related to wrapping and monitoring can be used to control faulty inputs and outputs; suitable wrappers or monitors can often be generated automatically by formal synthesis from component assumptions and high-level system requirements.

These techniques can eliminate, or at least reduce, the incidence of unintended and faulty interactions, but ultimately we need to calculate the composed behaviors of interacting components and verify their correctness. Traditional methods for compositional verification by assume/guarantee reasoning demand a degree of prescience to ensure that the assumes of one component are met by the guarantees of another that was designed in ignorance of it. One way to lessen this need for prescience is to derive the weakest assumptions under which a component can deliver its guarantees, and I sketched how inf-BMC can be used to provide automated assistance in this process (which is closely related to hazard analysis) very early in the design cycle.

Compositional design and assurance for critical systems that must function correctly, or at least safely, all the time, are challenging and attractive research topics. Further systematic examination and study of the methods and directions I described could be worthwhile, but fresh thinking would also be welcome.

References

1. Requirements and Technical Concepts for Aviation Washington, DC: DO-297: Integrated Modular Avionics (IMA) Development Guidance and Certification Considerations (2005), Also issued as EUROCAE ED-124 (2007)
2. Rushby, J.: Bus Architectures for Safety-Critical Embedded Systems. In: Henzinger, T.A., Kirsch, C.M. (eds.) EMSOFT 2001. LNCS, vol. 2211, pp. 306–323. Springer, Heidelberg (2001)
3. Rushby, J.: The design and verification of secure systems. In: Eighth ACM Symposium on Operating System Principles, Asilomar, CA, pp. 12–21 (1981); ACM Operating Systems Review 15(5)
4. Boettcher, C., DeLong, R., Rushby, J., Sifre, W.: The MILS component integration approach to secure information sharing. In: 27th AIAA/IEEE Digital Avionics Systems Conference, St. Paul, MN. The Institute of Electrical and Electronics Engineers (2008)
5. Cristian, F.: Exception handling and software fault tolerance. IEEE Transactions on Computers C-31, 531–540 (1982)
6. Chandola, V., Banerjee, A., Kumar, V.: Anomaly detection: A survey. ACM Computing Surveys 41 (2009)
7. Rushby, J.: Kernels for safety? In: Anderson, T. (ed.) Safe and Secure Computing Systems, pp. 210–220. Blackwell Scientific Publications (1989)
8. Schneider, F.: Enforceable security policies. ACM Transactions on Information and System Security 3, 30–50 (2000)
9. Havelund, K.: Program Monitoring; Course material for part II of Caltech CS 119 (May), http://www.runtime-verification.org/course/

10. Littlewood, B., Rushby, J.: Reasoning about the reliability of fault-tolerant systems in which one component is "possibly perfect". IEEE Transactions on Software Engineering (2011) (accepted for publication)
11. Jones, C.B.: Tentative steps toward a development method for interfering programs. ACM Transactions on Programming Languages and Systems 5, 596–619 (1983)
12. Shankar, N.: Lazy Compositional Verification. In: de Roever, W.-P., Langmaack, H., Pnueli, A. (eds.) COMPOS 1997. LNCS, vol. 1536, pp. 541–564. Springer, Heidelberg (1998)
13. Giannakopoulou, D., Pasareanu, C.S., Barringer, H.: Component verification with automatically generated assumptions. International Journal on Automated Software Engineering 12, 297–320 (2005)
14. Rushby, J.: Harnessing disruptive innovation in formal verification. In: Hung, D.V., Pandya, P. (eds.) Fourth International Conference on Software Engineering and Formal Methods (SEFM), Pune, India, pp. 21–28. IEEE Computer Society (2006)
15. Rushby, J.: A safety-case approach for certifying adaptive systems. In: AIAA Infotech@Aerospace Conference, Seattle, WA. American Institute of Aeronautics and Astronautics (2009); AIAA paper 2009-1992
16. Schlichting, R.D., Schneider, F.B.: Fail-stop processors: An approach to designing fault-tolerant computing systems. ACM Transactions on Computer Systems 1, 222–238 (1983)
17. Leveson, N.G.: Safeware: System Safety and Computers. Addison-Wesley (1995)
18. Perrow, C.: Normal Accidents: Living with High Risk Technologies. Basic Books, New York (1984)
19. Chong, S., van der Meyden, R.: Using architecture to reason about information security. Technical report, University of New South Wales (2009)

A Denotational Model for Component-Based Risk Analysis

Gyrd Brændeland[1,2,*], Atle Refsdal[2], and Ketil Stølen[1,2]

[1] Department of Informatics, University of Oslo, Norway
[2] SINTEF, Norway

Abstract. Risk analysis is an important tool for developers to establish the appropriate protection level of a system. Unfortunately, the shifting environment of components and component-based systems is not adequately addressed by traditional risk analysis methods. This paper addresses this problem from a theoretical perspective by proposing a denotational model for component-based risk analysis. In order to model the probabilistic aspect of risk, we represent the behaviour of a component by a probability distribution over communication histories. The overall goal is to provide a theoretical foundation facilitating an improved understanding of risk in relation to components and component-based system development.

1   Introduction

The flexibility offered by component-based development facilitates rapid development and deployment, but causes challenges for security and safety as upgraded sub-components may interact with a system in unforeseen ways. The difficulties faced by Toyota in explaining what caused the problem with the sticky accelerators [1] illustrate this problem. Due to their lack of modularity conventional risk analysis methods are poorly suited to address these challenges. A modular understanding of risks is a prerequisite for robust component-based development and for maintaining the trustworthiness of component-based systems.

There are many forms and variations of risk analysis, depending on the application domain, such as finance, reliability and safety, or security. Within reliability/safety and security, which are the most relevant for component-based development, risk analysis is concerned with protecting assets. This is the type of risk analysis we focus upon in this paper, referred to as defensive risk analysis. The purpose of defensive risk analysis is to gather sufficient knowledge about vulnerabilities, threats, consequences and probabilities, in order to establish the appropriate protection level for assets. It is important that the level of protection matches the value of the assets to be protected. A certain level of risk may be acceptable if the risk is considered to be too costly or technically impossible to rule out entirely. Hence, a risk is part of the behaviour of a system that is implicitly allowed but not necessarily intended. Based on this observation we

---

* Contact author: email: gyb@sintef.uio.no

F. Arbab and P.C. Ölveczky (Eds.): FACS 2011, LNCS 7253, pp. 12–41, 2012.
© Springer-Verlag Berlin Heidelberg 2012

have defined a component model that integrates the explicit representation of risks as part of the component behaviour and provides rules for composing component risks. We also explain how the notion of hiding can be understood in this component model. We define a hiding operator that allows partial hiding of internal interactions, to ensure that interactions affecting the component risk level are not hidden. We are not aware of other approaches where the concept of risk is integrated in a formal component semantics.

An advantage of representing risks as part of the component behaviour, is that the risk level of a composite component, as well as its behaviour, is obtained by composing the representations of its sub-components. That is, the composition of risks corresponds to ordinary component composition. The component model provides a foundation for component-based risk analysis, by conveying how risks manifests themselves in an underlying component implementation. By component-based risk analysis we mean that risks are identified, analysed and documented at the component level, and that risk analysis results are composable.

1.1   Outline of paper

The objective of Section 2 is to give an informal understanding of component-based risk analysis. Risk is the probability that an event affects an asset with a given consequence. In order to model component risks, we explain the concept of asset, asset value and consequence in a component setting. In order to represent the *behavioural* aspects of risk, such as the probability of unwanted incidents, we make use of an asynchronous communication paradigm. The selection of this paradigm is motivated as part of the informal explanation of component-based risk analysis. We also explain the notions of observable and unobservable behaviour in a component model with assets. The informal understanding introduced in Section 2 is thereafter formalised in a semantic model that defines:

- The denotational representation of interfaces as probabilistic processes (Section 3).
- The denotational representation of interface risks including the means to represent risk probabilities (Section 4). Interface risks are incorporated as a part of the interface behaviour.
- The denotational representation of a component as a collection of interfaces or sub-components, some of which may interact with each other (Section 5). We obtain the behaviour of a component from the probabilistic processes of its constituent interfaces or sub-components in a basic mathematical way.
- The denotational representation of component risks (Section 6).
- The denotational representation of hiding (Section 7).

We place our work in relation to ongoing research within related areas in Section 8. Finally we summarise our findings and discuss possibilities for future work in Section 9. Formal proofs of all the results presented in this paper is available in a technical report [2][1].

---

[1] http://heim.ifi.uio.no/ ketils/kst/Reports/2011-02.UIO-IFI-363.
    A-Denotational-Model-For-Component-Based-Risk-Analysis.pdf

2   An Informal Explanation of Component-Based Risk Analysis

In order to provide a foundation for component-based risk analysis, we first explain informally how concepts from risk analysis can be understood at the component level. Concepts to consider in defensive risk analysis [31,14] include: A *stakeholder* refers to a person or organisation who is affected by a decision or activity. An *asset* is something to which a stakeholder directly assigns value and, hence, for which the stakeholder requires protection. An *incident* is an event that reduces the value of one or more assets. A *consequence* is the reduction in value caused by an incident to an asset. A *vulnerability* is a weakness which can be exploited by one or more threats to harm an asset. A *threat* is a potential cause of an incident. *Probability* is a measure of the chance of occurrence of an event, expressed as a number between 0 and 1. A *risk* is the combination of the probability of an incident and its consequence with regard to a given asset. There may be a range of possible outcomes associated with an incident. This implies that an incident may have consequences for several assets. Hence, an incident may be part of several risks.

2.1   Component-Based Risk Analysis

We explain the concepts of component-based risk analysis and how they are related to each other through a conceptual model, captured by a UML class diagram [22] in Figure 1. The associations between the elements have cardinalities specifying the number of instances of one element that can be related to one instance of the other. The hollow diamond symbolises aggregation and the filled composition. Elements connected with an aggregation can also be part of other aggregations, while composite elements only exist within the specified composition.

An *interface* is a contract describing both the provided operations and the services required to provide the specified operations. To ensure modularity of our component model we represent a stakeholder by the component interface, and identify assets on behalf of component interfaces. Each interface has a set of assets. A vulnerability may be understood as a property (or lack thereof) of

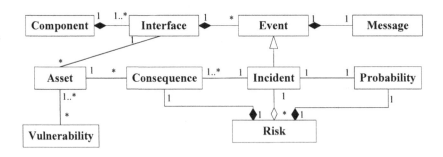

Fig. 1. Conceptual model of component-based risk analysis

an interface that makes it prone to a certain attack. It may therefore be argued that the vulnerability concept should be associated to the interface concept. However, from a risk perspective a vulnerability is relevant to the extent that it can be exploited to harm a specific asset, and we have therefore chosen to associate it with the asset concept. The concept of a threat is not part of the conceptual model, because a threat is something that belongs to the environment of a component. We cannot expect to have knowledge about the environment of the component as that may change depending on the where it is deployed.

A *component* is a collection of interfaces some of which may interact with each other. Interfaces interact by the transmission and consumption of messages. We refer to the transmission and consumption of messages as *events*. An event that harms an asset is an incident with regard to that asset.

2.2   Behaviour and Probability

A probabilistic understanding of component behaviour is required in order to measure risk. We adopt an asynchronous communication model. This does not prevent us from representing systems with synchronous communication. It is well known that synchronous communication can be simulated in an asynchronous communication model and the other way around [13].

An interface interacts with an environment whose behaviour it cannot control. From the point of view of the interface the choices made by the environment are non-deterministic. In order to resolve the external non-determinism caused by the environment we use queues that serve as schedulers. Incoming messages to an interface are stored in a queue and are consumed by the interface in the order they are received. The idea is that, for a given sequence of incoming messages to an interface, we know the probability with which the interface produces a certain behaviour. For simplicity we assume that an interface does not send messages to itself.

A component is a collection of interfaces some of which may interact. For a component consisting of two or more interfaces, a queue history not only resolves the external non-determinism, but also all internal non-determinism with regard to the interactions of its sub-components. The behaviour of a component is the set of probability distributions given all possible queue histories of the component.

Figure 2 shows two different ways in which two interfaces n_1 and n_2 with queues q_1 and q_2, and sets of assets a_1 and a_2, can be combined into a component. We may think of the arrows as directed channels.

- In Figure 2 (1) there is no direct communication between the interfaces of the component, that is, the queue of each interface only contains messages from external interfaces.
- In Figure 2 (2) the interface n_1 transmits to n_2 which again transmits to the environment. Moreover, only n_1 consumes messages from the environment.

Initially, the queue of each interface is empty; its set of assets is fixed throughout an execution. When initiated, an interface chooses probabilistically between a number of different actions. An action consists of transmitting an arbitrary

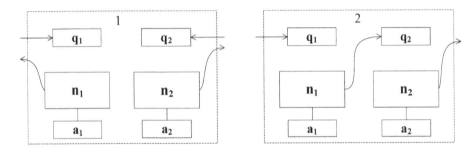

Fig. 2. Two interface compositions

number of messages in some order. The number of transmission messages may be finite, including zero which corresponds to the behaviour of skip, or infinite. The storing of a transmitted message in a queue is instantaneous: a transmitted message is placed in the queue of the recipient, without time delay. There will always be some delay between the transmission of a message and the consumption of that message. After transmitting messages the interface may choose to quit or to check its queue for messages. Messages are consumed in the order they arrive. If the queue is empty, an attempt to consume blocks the interface from any further action until a new message arrives. The consumption of a message gives rise to a new probabilistic choice. Thereafter, the interface may choose to quit without checking the queue again, and so on.

A probabilistic choice over actions never involves more than one interface. This can always be ensured by decomposing probabilistic choices until they have the granularity required. Suppose we have three interfaces; die, player1 and player2 involved in a game of Monopoly. The state of the game is decided by the position of the players' pieces on the board. The transition from one state to another is decided by a probabilistic choice "Throw die and move piece", involving both the die and one of the players. We may however, split this choice into two separate choices: "Throw die" and "Move piece". By applying this simple strategy for all probabilistic choices we ensure that a probabilistic choice is a local event of an interface.

The probability distribution over a set of actions, resulting from a probabilistic choice, may change over time during an execution. Hence, our probabilistic model is more general than for example a Markov process [32,21], where the probability of a future state given the present is conditionally independent of the past. This level of generality is needed to be able to capture all types of probabilistic behaviour relevant in a risk analysis setting, including human behaviour.

The behaviour of a component is completely determined by the behaviour of its constituent interfaces. We obtain the behaviour of a component by starting all the interfaces simultaneously, in their initial state.

2.3   Observable Component Behaviour

In most component-based approaches there is a clear separation between external and purely internal interaction. External interaction is the interaction

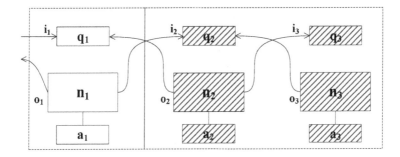

Fig. 3. Hiding of unobservable behaviour

between the component and its environment; while purely internal interaction is the interaction within the components, in our case, the interaction between the interfaces of which the component consists. Contrary to the external, purely internal interaction is hidden when the component is viewed as a black-box.

When we bring in the notion of risk, this distinction between what should be externally and only internally visible is no longer clear cut. After all, if we blindly hide all internal interaction we are in danger of hiding (without treating) risks of relevance for assets belonging to externally observable interfaces. Hence, purely internal interaction should be externally visible if it may affect assets belonging to externally visible interfaces. Consider for example the component pictured in Figure 3. In a conventional component-oriented approach, the channels i_2, i_3, o_2 and o_3 would not be externally observable from a black-box point of view. From a risk analysis perspective it seems more natural to restrict the black-box perspective to the right hand side of the vertical line. The assets belonging to the interface n_1 are externally observable since the environment interacts with n_1. The assets belonging to the interfaces n_2 and n_3 are on the other hand hidden since n_2 and n_3 are purely internal interfaces. Hence, the channels i_3 and o_3 are also hidden since they can only impact the assets belonging to n_1 indirectly via i_2 and o_2. The channels i_2 and o_2 are however only partly hidden since the transmission events of i_2 and the consumption events of o_2 may include incidents having an impact on the assets belonging to n_1.

3   Denotational Representation of Interface Behaviour

In this section we explain the formal representation of interface behaviour in our denotational semantics. We represent interface behaviour by sequences of events that fulfil certain well-formedness constraints. Sequences fulfilling these constraints are called traces. We represent probabilistic interface behaviour as probability distributions over sets of traces.

3.1   Sets

We use standard set notation, such as *union* $A \cup B$, *intersection* $A \cap B$, *set difference* $A \setminus B$, *cardinality* $\#A$ and *element of* $e \in A$ in the definitions of our basic concepts and operators. We write $\{e_1, e_2, e_3, \ldots, e_n\}$ to denote the set consisting of n elements $e_1, e_2, e_3, \ldots, e_n$. Sometimes we also use $[i..n]$ to denote a totally ordered set of numbers between i and n. We introduce the special symbol $\mathbb{N}$ to denote the set of natural numbers and $\mathbb{N}_+$ to denote the set of strictly positive natural numbers.

3.2 Events

There are two kinds of events: transmission events tagged by ! and consumption events tagged by ?. $\mathcal{K}$ denotes the set of kinds $\{!, ?\}$. An event is a pair of a kind and a message. A message is a quadruple $\langle s, tr, co, q \rangle$ consisting of a signal s, a transmitter tr, a consumer co and a time-stamp q, which is a rational number. The consumer in the message of a transmission event coincides with the addressee, that is, the party intended to eventually consume the message. The *active* party in an event is the one performing the action denoted by its kind. That is, the transmitter of the message is the active party of a transmission event and the consumer of the message is the active party of a consumption event.

We let $\mathcal{S}$ denote the set of all signals, $\mathcal{P}$ denote the set of all parties (consumers and transmitters), $\mathcal{Q}$ denote the set of all time-stamps, $\mathcal{M}$ denote the set of all messages and $\mathcal{E}$ denote the set of all events. Formally we have that:

$$\mathcal{E} \stackrel{\text{def}}{=} \mathcal{K} \times \mathcal{M}$$

$$\mathcal{M} \stackrel{\text{def}}{=} \mathcal{S} \times \mathcal{P} \times \mathcal{P} \times \mathcal{Q}$$

We define the functions

$$k._{\text{-}} \in \mathcal{E} \to \mathcal{K} \quad tr._{\text{-}}, co._{\text{-}} \in \mathcal{E} \to \mathcal{P} \quad q._{\text{-}} \in \mathcal{E} \to \mathcal{Q}$$

to yield the kind, transmitter, consumer and time-stamp of an event. For any party $p \in \mathcal{P}$, we use $\mathcal{E}_p$ to denote the set of all events in which p is the active part. Formally

(1) $\mathcal{E}_p \stackrel{\text{def}}{=} \{e \in \mathcal{E} \mid (k.e =! \wedge tr.e = p) \vee (k.e =? \wedge co.e = p)\}$

For a given party p, we assume that the number of signals assigned to p is a most countable. That is, the number of signals occurring in messages consumed by or transmitted to p is at most countable.

We use $\mathcal{E}_p^{\downarrow}$ to denote the set of transmission events with p as consumer. Formally

$$\mathcal{E}_p^{\downarrow} \stackrel{\text{def}}{=} \{e \in \mathcal{E} \mid k.e =! \wedge co.e = p\}$$

3.3 Sequences

For any set of elements A, we let A^ω, A^∞, A^* and A^n denote the set of all sequences, the set of all infinite sequences, the set of all finite sequences, and the set of all sequences of length n over A. We use $\langle \rangle$ to denote the empty sequence of length zero and $\langle 1, 2, 3, 4 \rangle$ to denote the sequence of the numbers from 1 to 4. A sequence over a set of elements A can be viewed as a function mapping positive natural numbers to elements in the set A. We define the functions

$$(2) \qquad \#_- \in A^\omega \to \mathbb{N} \cup \{\infty\} \quad _-\sqsubseteq_- \in A^\omega \times A^\omega \to \mathbb{Bool}$$

to yield the length, the nth element of a sequence and the prefix ordering on sequences[2]. Hence, $\#s$ yields the number of elements in s, $s[n]$ yields s's nth element if $n \le \#s$, and $s_1 \sqsubseteq s_2$ evaluates to true if s_1 is an initial segment of s_2 or if $s_1 = s_2$.

For any $0 \le i \le \#s$ we define $s|_i$ to denote the prefix of s of length i. Formally:

$$(3) \qquad _-|_- \in A^\omega \times \mathbb{N} \to A^\omega$$

$$s|_i \stackrel{\text{def}}{=} \begin{cases} s' \text{ if } 0 \le i \le \#s, \text{ where } \#s' = i \wedge s' \sqsubseteq s \\ s \text{ if } i > \#s \end{cases}$$

Due to the functional interpretation of sequences, we may talk about the *range* of a sequence:

$$(4) \qquad \mathsf{rng}._- \in A^\omega \to \mathbb{P}(A)$$

For example if $s \in A^\infty$, we have that:

$$\mathsf{rng}.s = \{s[n] \mid n \in \mathbb{N}_+\}$$

We define an operator for obtaining the sets of events of a set of sequences, in terms of their ranges:

$$(5) \qquad ev._- \in \mathbb{P}(A^\omega) \to \mathbb{P}(A)$$

$$ev.S \stackrel{\text{def}}{=} \bigcup_{s \in S} \mathsf{rng}.s$$

We also define an operator for concatenating two sequences:

$$(6) \qquad _-\frown_- \in A^\omega \times A^\omega \to A^\omega$$

$$s_1 \frown s_2[n] \stackrel{\text{def}}{=} \begin{cases} s_1[n] \text{ if } 1 \le n \le \#s_1 \\ s_2[n - \#s_1] \text{ if } \#s_1 < n \le \#s_1 + \#s_2 \end{cases}$$

Concatenating two sequences implies gluing them together. Hence $s_1 \frown s_2$ denotes a sequence of length $\#s_1 + \#s_2$ that equals s_1 if s_1 is infinite and is prefixed by s_1 and suffixed by s_2, otherwise.

---

[2] The operator $\times$ binds stronger than $\to$ and we therefore omit the parentheses around the argument types in the signature definitions.

The filtering function $\circledS$ is used to filter away elements. By $B \circledS s$ we denote the sequence obtained from the sequence s by removing all elements in s that are not in the set of elements B. For example, we have that

$$\{1,3\} \circledS \langle 1, 1, 2, 1, 3, 2 \rangle = \langle 1, 1, 1, 3 \rangle$$

We define the filtering operator formally as follows:

(7)
$$\_\circledS\_ \in \mathbb{P}(A) \times A^\omega \to A^\omega$$

$$B \circledS \langle\rangle \stackrel{\text{def}}{=} \langle\rangle$$

$$B \circledS (\langle e \rangle \frown s) \stackrel{\text{def}}{=} \begin{cases} \langle e \rangle \frown B \circledS s & \text{if } e \in B \\ B \circledS s & \text{if } e \notin B \end{cases}$$

For an infinite sequence s we need the additional constraint:

$$(B \cap \text{rng}.s) = \emptyset \Rightarrow B \circledS s = \langle\rangle$$

We overload $\circledS$ to filtering elements from sets of sequences as follows:

$$\_\circledS\_ \in \mathbb{P}(A) \times \mathbb{P}(A^\omega) \to \mathbb{P}(A^\omega)$$

$$B \circledS S \stackrel{\text{def}}{=} \{B \circledS s \mid s \in S\}$$

We also need a projection operator $\Pi_i.s$ that returns the ith element of an n-tuple s understood as a sequence of length n. We define the projection operator formally as:

$$\Pi_{\_\cdot\_} \in \{1 \ldots n\} \times A^n \to A$$
$$\_[\_] \in A^\omega \times \mathbb{N}_+ \to A$$

The projection operator is overloaded to sets of index values as follows.

$$\Pi_{\_\cdot\_} \in \mathbb{P}(\{1 \ldots n\}) \setminus \emptyset \times A^n \to \bigcup_{1 \leq k \leq n} A^k$$

$$\Pi_I.s \stackrel{\text{def}}{=} s'$$
$$\text{where } \forall j \in I : \Pi_j.s = \Pi_{\#\{i \in I \mid i \leq j\}}.s' \wedge \#s' = \#I$$

For example we have that:

$$\Pi_{\{1,2\}}.\langle p, q, r \rangle = \langle p, q \rangle$$

For a sequence of tuples s, $\Pi_I.s$ denotes the sequence of k-tuples obtained from s, by projecting each element in s with respect to the index values in I. For example we have that

$$\Pi_{\{1,2\}}.\langle\langle a, r, p\rangle, \langle b, r, p\rangle\rangle = \langle \Pi_{\{1,2\}}.\langle a, r, p\rangle\rangle \frown \langle\Pi_{\{1,2\}}.\langle b, r, p\rangle\rangle = \langle\langle a, r\rangle, \langle b, r\rangle\rangle$$

We define the projection operator on a sequence of n-tuples formally as follows:

$$\Pi_{\_.\_} \in \mathbb{P}(\{1\ldots n\}) \setminus \emptyset \times (A^n)^\omega \to \bigcup_{1 \leq k \leq n} (A^k)^\omega$$

$$\Pi_I.s \overset{\text{def}}{=} s'$$

where

$$\forall j \in \{1\ldots \#s\} : \Pi_I.s[j] = s'[j] \wedge \#s = \#s'$$

If we want to restrict the view of a sequence of events to only the signals of the events, we may apply the projection operator twice, as follows:

$$\Pi_1.(\Pi_2.\langle !\langle a, r, p, 3\rangle, !\langle b, r, p, 5\rangle\rangle) = \langle\langle a\rangle, \langle b\rangle\rangle$$

Restricting a sequence of events, that is, pairs of kinds and messages, to the second elements of the events yields a sequence of messages. Applying the projection operator a second time with the subscript 1 yields a sequence of signals.

3.4 Traces

A trace t is a sequence of events that fulfils certain well-formedness constraints reflecting the behaviour of the informal model presented in Section 2. We use traces to represent communication histories of components and their interfaces. Hence, the transmitters and consumers in a trace are interfaces. We first formulate two constraints on the timing of events in a trace. The first makes sure that events are ordered by time while the second is needed to avoid Zeno-behaviour. Formally:

(8) $$\forall i, j \in [1..\#t] : i < j \Rightarrow q.t[i] < q.t[j]$$
(9) $$\#t = \infty \Rightarrow \forall k \in \mathcal{Q} : \exists i \in \mathbb{N} : q.t[i] > k$$

For simplicity, we require that two events in a trace never have the same time-stamp. We impose this requirement by assigning each interface a set of time-stamps disjoint from the set of time-stamps assigned to every other interface. Every event of an interface is assigned a unique time-stamp from the set of time-stamps assigned to the interface in question.

The first constraint makes sure that events are totally ordered according to when they take place. The second constraint states that time in an infinite trace always eventually progress beyond any fixed point in time. This implies that time never halts and Zeno-behaviour is therefore not possible. To lift the assumption that two events never happen at the same time, we could replace the current notion of a trace as a sequence of events, to a notion of a trace as a sequence of sets of events where the messages in each set have the same time-stamp.

We also impose a constraint on the ordering of transmission and consumption events in a trace t. According to the operational model a message can be transmitted without being consumed, but it cannot be consumed without having been transmitted. Furthermore, the consumption of messages transmitted to the same

party must happen in the same order as transmission. However, since a trace
may include consumption events with external transmitters, we can constrain
only the consumption of a message from a party which is itself active in the
trace. That is, the ordering requirements on t only apply to the communication
between the internal parties. This motivates the following formalisation of the
ordering constraint:

(10)   let $N = \{n \in \mathcal{P} \mid \mathsf{rng}.t \cap \mathcal{E}_n \neq \emptyset\}$

     in $\forall n, m \in N$:

        let $i = (\{?\} \times (\mathcal{S} \times n \times m \times \mathcal{Q})) \circledS t$

           $o = (\{!\} \times (\mathcal{S} \times n \times m \times \mathcal{Q})) \circledS t$

        in $\Pi_{\{1,2,3\}}.(\Pi_{\{2\}}.i) \sqsubseteq \Pi_{\{1,2,3\}}.(\Pi_{\{2\}}.o) \wedge \forall j \in \{1..\#i\} : q.o[j] < q.i[j]$

The first conjunct of constraint (10) requires that the sequence of consumed
messages sent from an internal party n to another internal party m, is a prefix
of the sequence of transmitted messages from n to m, when disregarding time.
We abstract away the timing of events in a trace by applying the projection
operator twice. Thus, we ensure that messages communicated between internal
parties are consumed in the order they are transmitted. The second conjunct of
constraint (10) ensures that for any single message, transmission happens before
consumption when both the transmitter and consumer are internal. We let $\mathcal{H}$
denote the set of all traces t that are well-formed with regard to constraints (8),
(9) and (10).

3.5   Probabilistic Processes

As explained in Section 2.2, we understand the behaviour of an interface as
a probabilistic process. The basic mathematical object for representing probabilistic processes is a *probability space* [11,30]. A probability space is a triple
$(\Omega, \mathcal{F}, f)$, where Ω is a sample space, that is, a non-empty set of possible outcomes, $\mathcal{F}$ is a non-empty set of subsets of Ω, and f is a function from $\mathcal{F}$ to $[0, 1]$
that assigns a probability to each element in $\mathcal{F}$.

    The set $\mathcal{F}$, and the function f have to fulfil the following constraints: The set
$\mathcal{F}$ must be a σ-field over Ω, that is, $\mathcal{F}$ must be not be empty, it must contain Ω
and be closed under complement[3] and countable union. The function f must be a
probability measure on $\mathcal{F}$, that is, a function from $\mathcal{F}$ to $[0, 1]$ such that $f(\emptyset) = 0$,
$f(\Omega) = 1$, and for every sequence ω of disjoint sets in $\mathcal{F}$, the following holds:
$f(\bigcup_{i=1}^{\#\omega} \omega[i]) = \sum_{i=1}^{\#\omega} f(\omega[i])$ [10]. The last property is referred to as countably
additive, or σ-additive.

    We represent a probabilistic execution H by a probability space with the set
of traces of H as its sample space. If the set of possible traces in an execution is
infinite, the probability of a single trace may be zero. To obtain the probability

---

[3] Note that this is the relative complement with respect to Ω, that is if $A \in \mathcal{F}$, then
$\Omega \setminus A \in \mathcal{F}$.

that a certain sequence of events occurs up to a particular point in time, we can look at the probability of the set of all *extensions* of that sequence in a given trace set. Thus, instead of talking of the probability of a single trace, we are concerned with the probability of a set of traces with common prefix, called a *cone*. By $c(t, D)$ we denote the set of all continuations of t in D. For example we have that

$$c(\langle a \rangle, \{\langle a, a, b, b \rangle, \langle a, a, c, c \rangle\}) = \{\langle a, a, b, b \rangle, \langle a, a, c, c \rangle\}$$
$$c(\langle a, a, b \rangle, \{\langle a, a, b, b \rangle, \langle a, a, c, c \rangle\}) = \{\langle a, a, b, b \rangle\}$$
$$c(\langle b \rangle, \{\langle a, a, b, b \rangle, \langle a, a, c, c \rangle\}) = \emptyset$$

We define the cone of a finite trace t in a trace set D formally as:

Definition 1 (Cone). *Let D be a set of traces. The cone of a finite trace t, with regard to D, is the set of all traces in D with t as a prefix:*

$$c \_\_ \in \mathcal{H} \times \mathbb{P}(\mathcal{H}) \rightarrow \mathbb{P}(\mathcal{H})$$

$$c(t, D) \stackrel{\text{def}}{=} \{t' \in D \mid t \sqsubseteq t'\}$$

We define the *cone set* with regard to a set of traces as:

Definition 2 (Cone set). *The cone set of a set of traces D consists of the cones with regard to D of each finite trace that is a prefix of a trace in D:*

$$C\_ \in \mathbb{P}(\mathcal{H}) \rightarrow \mathbb{P}(\mathbb{P}(\mathcal{H}))$$

$$C(D) \stackrel{\text{def}}{=} \{c(t, D) \mid \#t \in \mathbb{N} \wedge \exists t' \in D : t \sqsubseteq t'\}$$

We understand each trace in the trace set representing a probabilistic process H as a complete history of H. We therefore want to be able to distinguish the state where an execution stops after a given sequence and the state where an execution may continue with different alternatives after the sequence. We say that a finite trace t is complete with regard to a set of traces D if $t \in D$. Let D be a set of set of traces. We define the *complete extension* of the cone set of D as follows:

Definition 3 (Complete extended cone set). *The complete extended cone set of a set of traces D is the union of the cone set of D and the set of singleton sets containing the finite traces in D:*

$$C_{E}\_ \in \mathbb{P}(\mathcal{H}) \rightarrow \mathbb{P}(\mathbb{P}(\mathcal{H}))$$

$$C_E(D) \stackrel{\text{def}}{=} C(D) \cup \{\{t\} \subseteq D \mid \#t \in \mathbb{N}\}$$

We define a probabilistic execution H formally as:

Definition 4 (Probabilistic execution). *A probabilistic execution H is a probability space:*

$$\mathbb{P}(\mathcal{H}) \times \mathbb{P}(\mathbb{P}(\mathcal{H})) \times (\mathbb{P}(\mathcal{H}) \rightarrow [0, 1])$$

whose elements we refer to as D_H, $\mathcal{F}_H$ and f_H where D_H is the set of traces of H, $\mathcal{F}_H$ is the σ-field generated by $C_E(D_H)$, that is the intersection of all σ-fields including $C_E(D_H)$, called the cone-σ-field of D_H, and f_H is a probability measure on $\mathcal{F}_H$.

If D_H is countable then $\mathbb{P}(D_H)$ (the power set of D_H) is the largest σ-field that can be generated from D_H and it is common to define $\mathcal{F}_H$ as $\mathbb{P}(D_H)$. If D_H is uncountable, then, assuming the continuum hypothesis, which states that there is no set whose cardinality is strictly between that of the integers and that of the real numbers, the cardinality of D_H equals the cardinality of the real numbers, and hence of $[0, 1]$. This implies that there are subsets of $\mathbb{P}(D_H)$ which are not measurable, and $\mathcal{F}_H$ is therefore usually a proper subset of $\mathbb{P}(D_H)$ [8]. A simple example of a process with uncountable sample space, is the process that throws a fair coin an infinite number of times [23,9]. Each execution of this process can be represented by an infinite sequence of zeroes and ones, where 0 represents "head" and 1 represents "tail". The set of infinite sequences of zeroes and ones is uncountable, which can be shown by a diagonalisation argument [5].

3.6   Probabilistic Interface Execution

We define the set of traces of an interface n as any well-formed trace consisting solely of events where n is the active party. Formally:

$$\mathcal{H}_n \stackrel{\text{def}}{=} \mathcal{H} \cap \mathcal{E}_n{}^\omega$$

We define the behavioural representation of an interface n as a function of its queue history. A queue history of an interface n is a well-formed trace consisting solely of transmission events with n as consumer. That a queue history is well formed implies that the events in the queue history are totally ordered by time. We let $\mathcal{B}_n$ denote the set of queue histories of an interface n. Formally:

$$\mathcal{B}_n \stackrel{\text{def}}{=} \mathcal{H} \cap \mathcal{E}_n^{\downarrow\omega}$$

A queue history serves as a scheduler for an interface, thereby uniquely determining its behaviour [27,6]. Hence, a queue history gives rise to a probabilistic execution of an interface. That is, the probabilistic behaviour of an interface n is represented by a function of complete queue histories for n. A *complete queue history* for an interface n records the messages transmitted to n for the whole execution of n, as opposed to a *partial queue history* that records the messages transmitted to n until some (finite) point in time. We define a probabilistic interface execution formally as:

Definition 5 (Probabilistic interface execution). *A probabilistic execution of an interface n is a function that for every complete queue history of n returns a probabilistic execution:*

$$I_{n-} \in \mathcal{B}_n \to \mathbb{P}(\mathcal{H}_n) \times \mathbb{P}(\mathbb{P}(\mathcal{H}_n)) \times (\mathbb{P}(\mathcal{H}_n) \to [0,1])^4$$

Hence, $I_n(\alpha)$ denotes the probabilistic execution of n given the complete queue history α. We let $D_n(\alpha), \mathcal{F}_n(\alpha)$ and $f_n(\alpha)$ denote the projections on the three elements of the probabilistic execution of n given queue history α. I.e. $I_n(\alpha) = (D_n(\alpha), \mathcal{F}_n(\alpha), f_N(\alpha))$.

In Section 2 we described how an interface may choose to do nothing. In the denotational trace semantics we represent doing nothing by the empty trace. Hence, given an interface n and a complete queue history α, $D_n(\alpha)$ may consist of only the empty trace, but it may never be empty.

The queue history of an interface represents the input to it from other interfaces. In Section 2.2 we described informally our assumptions about how interfaces interact through queues. In particular, we emphasised that an interface can only consume messages already in its queue, and the same message can be consumed only once. We also assumed that an interface does not send messages to itself. Hence, we require that any $t \in D_n(\alpha)$ fulfils the following constraints:

(11) let $i = (\{?\} \times \mathcal{M}) \circledS t$

in $\Pi_{\{1,2\}}.(\Pi_{\{2\}}.i) \sqsubseteq \Pi_{\{1,2\}}.(\Pi_{\{2\}}.\alpha) \land \forall j \in \{1..\#i\} : q.\alpha[j] < q.i[j]$

(12) $\forall j \in [1..\#t] : k.t[j] \neq co.t[j]$

The first conjunct of constraint (11) states that the sequence of consumed messages in t is a prefix of the messages in α, when disregarding time. Thus, we ensure that n only consumes messages it has received in its queue and that they are consumed in the order they arrived. The second conjunct of constraint (11) ensures that messages are only consumed from the queue after they have arrived and with a non-zero delay. Constraint (12) ensures that an interface does not send messages to itself.

A complete queue history of an interface uniquely determines its behaviour. However, we are only interested in capturing time causal behaviour in the sense that the behaviour of an interface at a given point in time should depend only on its input up to and including that point in time and be independent of the content of its queue at any later point in time.

In order to formalise this constraint, we first define an operator for truncating a trace at a certain point in time. By $t\!\downarrow_k$ we denote the timed truncation of t, that is, the prefix of t including all events in t with a time-stamp lower than or equal to k. For example we have that:

$$\langle ?\langle c,q,r,1\rangle, !\langle a,r,p,3\rangle, !\langle b,r,p,5\rangle \rangle\!\downarrow_4 = \langle ?\langle c,q,r,1\rangle, !\langle a,r,p,3\rangle \rangle$$
$$\langle ?\langle c,q,r,1\rangle, !\langle a,r,p,3\rangle, !\langle b,r,p,5\rangle \rangle\!\downarrow_8 = \langle ?\langle c,q,r,1\rangle, !\langle a,r,p,3\rangle, !\langle b,r,p,5\rangle \rangle$$
$$\langle ?\langle c,q,r,\tfrac{1}{2}\rangle, !\langle a,r,p,\tfrac{3}{2}\rangle, !\langle b,r,p,\tfrac{5}{2}\rangle \rangle\!\downarrow_{\frac{3}{2}} = \langle ?\langle c,q,r,\tfrac{1}{2}\rangle, !\langle a,r,p,\tfrac{3}{2}\rangle \rangle$$

---

[4] Note that the type of I_n ensures that for any $\alpha \in \mathcal{B}_n : \mathsf{rng}.\alpha \cap ev.D_n(\alpha) = \emptyset$.

The function $\downarrow$ is defined formally as follows:

(13) $\downarrow_- \in \mathcal{H} \times \mathcal{Q} \to \mathcal{H}$

$$t\downarrow_k \overset{\text{def}}{=} \begin{cases} \langle\rangle \text{ if } t = \langle\rangle \vee q.t[1] > k \\ r \text{ otherwise where } r \sqsubseteq t \wedge q.r[\#r] \leq k \\ \qquad \wedge \ (\#r < \#t \Rightarrow q.t[\#r + 1] > k) \end{cases}$$

We overload the timed truncation operator to sets of traces as follows:

$$\downarrow_- \in \mathbb{P}(\mathcal{H}) \times \mathcal{Q} \to \mathbb{P}(\mathcal{H})$$

$$S\downarrow_k \overset{\text{def}}{=} \{t\downarrow_k \mid t \in S\}$$

We may then formalise the time causality as follows:

$$\forall \alpha, \beta \in \mathcal{B}_n : \forall q \in \mathcal{Q} : \alpha\downarrow_q = \beta\downarrow_q \Rightarrow (D_n(\alpha)\downarrow_q = D_n(\beta)\downarrow_q) \wedge$$
$$((\forall t_1 \in D_n(\alpha) : \forall t_2 \in D_n(\beta)) : t_1\downarrow_q = t_2\downarrow_q) \Rightarrow$$
$$(f_n(\alpha)(c(t_1\downarrow_q, D_n(\alpha))) = f_n(\beta)(c(t_2\downarrow_q, D_n(\beta))))$$

The first conjunct states that for all queue histories α, β of an interface n, and for all points in time q, if α and β are equal until time q, then the trace sets $D_n(\alpha)$ and $D_n(\beta)$ are also equal until time q. The second conjunct states that if α and β are equal until time q, and we have two traces in $D_n(\alpha)$ and $D_n(\beta)$ that are equal until time q, then the likelihoods of the cones of the two traces truncated at time q in their respective trace sets are equal. Thus, the constraint ensures that the behaviour of an interface at a given point in time depends on its queue history up to and including that point in time, and is independent of the content of its queue history at any later point.

4   Denotational Representation of an Interface with a Notion of Risk

Having introduced the underlying semantic model, the next step is to extend it with concepts from risk analysis according to the conceptual model in Figure 1. As already explained, the purpose of extending the semantic model with risk analysis concepts is to represent risks as an integrated part of interface and component behaviour.

4.1   Assets

An *asset* is a physical or conceptual entity which is of value for a stakeholder, that is, for an interface (see Section 2.1) and which the stakeholder wants to protect. We let $\mathcal{A}$ denote the set of all assets and $\mathcal{A}_n$ denote the set of assets of interface n. Note that $\mathcal{A}_n$ may be empty. We require:

(14) $\forall n, n' \in \mathcal{P} : n \neq n' \Rightarrow \mathcal{A}_n \cap \mathcal{A}_{n'} = \emptyset$

Hence, assets are not shared between interfaces.

4.2 Incidents and Consequences

As explained in Section 2.1 an *incident* is an event that reduces the value of one or more assets. This is a general notion of incident, and of course, an asset may be harmed in different ways, depending on the type of asset. Some examples are reception of corrupted data, transmission of classified data to an unauthorised user, or slow response to a request. We provide a formal model for representing events that harm assets. For a discussion of how to obtain further risk analysis results for components, such as the cause of an unwanted incident, its consequence and probability we refer to [3].

In order to represent incidents formally we need a way to measure harm inflicted upon an asset by an event. We represent the *consequence* of an incident by a positive integer indicating its level of seriousness with regard to the asset in question. For example, if the reception of corrupted data is considered to be more serious for a given asset than the transmission of classified data to an unauthorised user, the former has a greater consequence than the latter with regard to this asset. We introduce a function

$$(15) \qquad cv_{n\text{--}} \in \mathcal{E}_n \times \mathcal{A}_n \to \mathbb{N}$$

that for an event e and asset a of an interface n, yields the consequence of e to a if e is an incident, and 0 otherwise. Hence, an event with consequence larger than zero for a given asset is an incident with regard to that asset. Note that the same event may be an incident with respect to more than one asset; moreover, an event that is not an incident with respect to one asset, may be an incident with respect to another.

4.3 Incident Probability

The *probability* that an incident e occurs during an execution corresponds to the probability of the set of traces in which e occurs. Since the events in each trace are totally ordered by time, and all events include a time-stamp, each event in a trace is unique. This means that a given incident occurs only once in each trace.

We can express the set describing the occurrence of an incident e, in a probabilistic execution H, as $occ(e, D_H)$ where the function occ is formally defined as:

$$(16) \qquad occ_{\text{--}} \in \mathcal{E} \times \mathbb{P}(\mathcal{H}) \to \mathbb{P}(\mathcal{H})$$

$$occ(e, D) \overset{\text{def}}{=} \{t \in D \mid e \in \text{rng}.t\}$$

(rng.t yields the range of the trace t, i.e., the set of events occurring in t). The set $occ(e, D_H)$ corresponds to the union of all cones $c(t, D_H)$ where e occurs in t (see Section 3.5). Any union of cones can be described as a disjoint set of cones [26]. As described in Section 3, we assume that an interface is assigned at most a countable number of signals and we assume that time-stamps are rational numbers. Hence, it follows that an interface has a countable number of events.

Since the set of finite sequences formed from a countable set is countable [18], the union of cones where e occurs in t is countable. Since by definition, the cone-σ-field of an execution H, is closed under countable union, the occurrence of an incident can be represented as a countable union of disjoint cones, that is, it is an element in the cone-σ-field of H and thereby has a measure.

4.4   Risk Function

The *risk function* of an interface n takes a consequence, a probability and an asset as arguments and yields a risk value represented by a positive integer. Formally:

(17) $rf_{n\,\text{---}} \in \mathbb{N} \times [0,1] \times \mathcal{A}_n \to \mathbb{N}$

The risk value associated with an incident e in an execution H, with regard to an asset a, depends on the probability of e in H and its consequence value. We require that

$$rf_n(c,p,a) = 0 \Leftrightarrow c = 0 \vee p = 0$$

Hence, only incidents have a positive risk value, and any incident has a positive risk value.

4.5   Interface with a Notion of Risk

Putting everything together we end up with the following representation of an interface:

Definition 6 (Semantics of an interface). *An interface n is represented by a quadruple*

$$(I_n, \mathcal{A}_n, cv_n, rf_n)$$

consisting of its probabilistic interface execution, assets, consequence function and risk function as explained above.

Given such a quadruple we have the necessary means to calculate the risks associated with an interface for a given queue history. A *risk* is a pair of an incident and its risk value. Hence, for the queue history $\alpha \in \mathcal{B}_n$ and asset $a \in \mathcal{A}_n$ the associated risks are

$$\{rv \mid rv = rf_n(cv(e,a), f_n(occ(e, D_n(\alpha))), a) \wedge rv > 0 \wedge e \in \mathcal{E}_n\}$$

5   Denotational Representation of Component Behaviour

A component is a collection of interfaces, some of which may interact. We may view a single interface as a basic component. A composite component is a component containing at least two interfaces (or basic components). In this section we lift the notion of probabilistic execution from interfaces to components. Furthermore, we explain how we obtain the behaviour of a component from the behaviours of its sub-components. In this section we do not consider the issue of hiding; this is the topic of Section 7.

In Section 5.1 we introduce the notion of conditional probability measure, conditional probabilistic execution and probabilistic component execution. In Section 5.2 we characterise how to obtain the trace set of a composite component from the trace sets of its sub-components. The cone-σ-field of a probabilistic component execution is generated straightforwardly from that. In Section 5.3 we explain how to define the conditional probability measure for the cone-σ-field of a composite component from the conditional probability measures of its sub-components. Finally, in Section 5.4, we define a probabilistic component execution of a composite component in terms of the probabilistic component executions of its sub-components. We sketch the proof strategies for the lemmas and theorems in this section and refer to Brændeland et al. [2] for the full proofs.

5.1   Probabilistic Component Execution

The behaviour of a component is completely determined by the set of interfaces it consists of. We identify a component by the set of names of its interfaces. Hence, the behaviour of the component $\{n\}$ consisting of only one interface n, is identical to the behaviour of the interface n. For any set of interfaces N we define:

$$(18) \qquad \mathcal{E}_N \overset{\text{def}}{=} \bigcup_{n \in N} \mathcal{E}_n$$

$$(19) \qquad \mathcal{E}_N^{\downarrow} \overset{\text{def}}{=} \bigcup_{n \in N} \mathcal{E}_n^{\downarrow}$$

$$(20) \qquad \mathcal{H}_N \overset{\text{def}}{=} \mathcal{H} \cap \mathcal{E}_N{}^{\omega}$$

$$(21) \qquad \mathcal{B}_N \overset{\text{def}}{=} \mathcal{H} \cap \mathcal{E}_N^{\downarrow}{}^{\omega}$$

Just as for interfaces, we define the behavioural representation of a component N as a function of its queue history. For a single interface a queue history α resolves the external nondeterminism caused by the environment. Since we assume that an interface does not send messages to itself there is no internal non-determinism to resolve. The function representing an interface returns a probabilistic execution which is a probability space. Given an interface n it follows from the definition of a probabilistic execution, that for any queue history $\alpha \in \mathcal{B}_n$, we have $f_n(\alpha)(D_n(\alpha)) = 1$.

For a component N consisting of two or more sub-components, a queue history α must resolve both external and internal non-determinism. For a given queue history α the behaviour of N, is obtained from the behaviours of the sub-components of N that are possible with regard to α. That is, all internal choices concerning interactions between the sub-components of N are fixed by α. This means that the probability of the set of traces of N given a queue history α may be lower than 1, violating the requirement of a probability measure. In order to formally represent the behaviour of a component we therefore introduce the notion of a *conditional probability measure*.

Definition 7 (Conditional probability measure). *Let D be a non-empty set and $\mathcal{F}$ be a σ-field over D. A conditional probability measure f on $\mathcal{F}$ is a function that assigns a value in $[0,1]$ to each element of $\mathcal{F}$ such that; either $f(A) = 0$ for all A in $\mathcal{F}$, or there exists a constant $c \in \langle 0,1]$[5] such that the function f' defined by $f'(A) = f(A)/c$ is a probability measure on $\mathcal{F}$.*

We define a conditional probabilistic execution H formally as:

Definition 8 (Conditional probabilistic execution). *A conditional probabilistic execution H is a measure space [11]:*

$$\mathbb{P}(\mathcal{H}) \times \mathbb{P}(\mathbb{P}(\mathcal{H})) \times (\mathbb{P}(\mathcal{H}) \to [0,1])$$

whose elements we refer to as D_H, $\mathcal{F}_H$ and f_H where D_H is the set of traces of H, $\mathcal{F}_H$ is the cone-σ-field of D_H, and f_H is a conditional probability measure on $\mathcal{F}_H$.

We define a probabilistic component execution formally as:

Definition 9 (Probabilistic component execution). *A probabilistic execution of a component N is a function I_N that for every complete queue history of N returns a conditional probabilistic execution:*

$$I_{N\_} \in \mathcal{B}_N \to \mathbb{P}(\mathcal{H}_N) \times \mathbb{P}(\mathbb{P}(\mathcal{H}_N)) \times (\mathbb{P}(\mathcal{H}_N) \to [0,1])$$

Hence, $I_N(\alpha)$ denotes the probabilistic execution of N given the complete queue history α. We let $D_N(\alpha), \mathcal{F}_N(\alpha)$ and $f_N(\alpha)$ denote the canonical projections of the probabilistic component execution on its elements.

5.2   Trace Sets of a Composite Component

For a given queue history α, the combined trace sets $D_{N_1}(\mathcal{E}^{\downarrow}_{N_1} \circledS \alpha)$ and $D_{N_2}(\mathcal{E}^{\downarrow}_{N_2} \circledS \alpha)$ such that all the transmission events from N_1 to N_2 are in α and the other way around, constitute the legal set of traces of the composition of N_1 and N_2. Given two probabilistic component executions I_{N_1} and I_{N_2} such that $N_1 \cap N_2 = \emptyset$, for each $\alpha \in \mathcal{B}_{N_1 \cup N_2}$ we define their composite trace set formally as:

(22) $D_{N_1} \otimes D_{N_2\_} \in \mathcal{B}_{N_1 \cup N_2} \to \mathbb{P}(\mathcal{H}_{N_1 \cup N_2})$

   $D_{N_1} \otimes D_{N_2}(\alpha) \stackrel{\text{def}}{=}$

   $\{t \in \mathcal{H}_{N_1 \cup N_2} | \mathcal{E}_{N_1} \circledS t \in D_{N_1}(\mathcal{E}^{\downarrow}_{N_1} \circledS \alpha) \wedge \mathcal{E}_{N_2} \circledS t \in D_{N_2}(\mathcal{E}^{\downarrow}_{N_2} \circledS \alpha) \wedge$

   $(\{!\} \times \mathcal{S} \times N_2 \times N_1 \times \mathcal{Q}) \circledS t \sqsubseteq (\{!\} \times \mathcal{S} \times N_2 \times N_1 \times \mathcal{Q}) \circledS \alpha \wedge$

   $(\{!\} \times \mathcal{S} \times N_1 \times N_2 \times \mathcal{Q}) \circledS t \sqsubseteq (\{!\} \times \mathcal{S} \times N_1 \times N_2 \times \mathcal{Q}) \circledS \alpha\}$

---

[5] We use $\langle a, b \rangle$ to denote the open interval $\{x \mid a < x < b\}$.

The definition ensures that the messages from N_2 consumed by N_1 are in the queue history of N_1 and vice versa. The operator $\otimes$ is obviously commutative and also associative since the sets of interfaces of each component are disjoint.

For each $\alpha \in \mathcal{B}_{N_1 \cup N_2}$ the cone-σ-field is generated as before. Hence, we define the cone-σ-field of a composite component as follows:

$$(23) \qquad \mathcal{F}_{N_1} \otimes \mathcal{F}_{N_2}(\alpha) \stackrel{\text{def}}{=} \sigma(C_E(D_{N_1} \otimes D_{N_2}(\alpha)))$$

where $\sigma(D)$ denotes the σ-field generated by the set D. We refer to $C_E(D_{N_1} \otimes D_{N_2}(\alpha))$ as the *composite extended cone set* of $N_1 \cup N_2$.

5.3   Conditional Probability Measure of a Composite Component

Consider two components C and O such that $C \cap O = \emptyset$. As described in Section 2, it is possible to decompose a probabilistic choice over actions in such a way that it never involves more than one interface. We may therefore assume that for a given queue history $\alpha \in \mathcal{B}_{C \cup O}$ the behaviour represented by $D_C(\mathcal{E}_C^\downarrow \circledS \alpha)$ is independent of the behaviour represented by $D_O(\mathcal{E}_O^\downarrow \circledS \alpha)$. Given this assumption the probability of a certain behaviour of the composed component equals the product of the probabilities of the corresponding behaviours of C and O, by the law of statistical independence. As explained in Section 3.5, to obtain the probability that a certain sequence of events t occurs up to a particular point in time in a set of traces D, we can look at the cone of t in D. For a given cone $c \in C_E(D_C \otimes D_O(\alpha))$ we obtain the corresponding behaviours of C and O by filtering c on the events of C and O, respectively.

The above observation with regard to cones does not necessarily hold for all elements of $\mathcal{F}_C \otimes \mathcal{F}_O(\alpha)$. The following simple example illustrates that the probability of an element in $\mathcal{F}_C \otimes \mathcal{F}_O(\alpha)$, which is not a cone, is not necessarily the product of the corresponding elements in $\mathcal{F}_C(\mathcal{E}_C^\downarrow \circledS \alpha)$ and $\mathcal{F}_O(\mathcal{E}_O^\downarrow \circledS \alpha)$. Assume that the component C tosses a fair coin and that the component O tosses an Othello piece (a disk with a light and a dark face). We assign the singleton time-stamp set $\{1\}$ to C and the singleton time-stamp set $\{2\}$ to O. Hence, the traces of each may only contain one event. For the purpose of readability we represent in the following the events by their signals. The assigned time-stamps ensure that the coin toss represented by the events $\{h, t\}$ comes before the Othello piece toss. We have:

$$D_C(\langle \rangle) = \{\langle h \rangle, \langle t \rangle\}$$
$$\mathcal{F}_C(\langle \rangle) = \{\emptyset, \{\langle h \rangle\}, \{\langle t \rangle\}, \{\langle h \rangle, \langle t \rangle\}\}$$
$$f_C(\langle \rangle)(\{\langle h \rangle\}) = 0.5$$
$$f_C(\langle \rangle)(\{\langle t \rangle\}) = 0.5$$

and

$$D_O(\langle \rangle) = \{\langle b \rangle, \langle w \rangle\}$$
$$\mathcal{F}_O(\langle \rangle) = \{\emptyset, \{\langle b \rangle\}, \{\langle w \rangle\}, \{\langle b \rangle, \langle w \rangle\}\}$$
$$f_O(\langle \rangle)(\{\langle b \rangle\}) = 0.5$$
$$f_O(\langle \rangle)(\{\langle w \rangle\}) = 0.5$$

Let $D_{CO} = D_C \otimes D_O$. The components interacts only with the environment, not with each other. We have:

$$D_{CO}(\langle\rangle) = \{\langle h, b\rangle, \langle h, w\rangle, \langle t, b\rangle, \langle t, w\rangle\}$$

We assume that each element in the sample space (trace set) of the composite component has the same probability. Since the sample space is finite, the probabilities are given by discrete uniform distribution, that is each trace in $D_{CO}(\langle\rangle)$ has a probability of 0.25. Since the traces are mutually exclusive, it follows by the laws of probability that the probability of $\{\langle h, b\rangle\} \cup \{\langle t, w\rangle\}$ is the sum of the probabilities of $\{\langle h, b\rangle\}$ and $\{\langle t, w\rangle\}$, that is 0.5. But this is not the same as $f_C(\langle\rangle)(\{\langle h\rangle, \langle t\rangle\}) \cdot f_O(\langle\rangle)(\{\langle b\rangle, \langle w\rangle\})^6$, which is 1.

Since there is no internal communication between C and O, there is no internal non-determinism to be resolved. If we replace the component O with the component R, which simply consumes whatever C transmits, a complete queue history of the composite component reflects only one possible interaction between C and R. Let $D_{CR} = D_C \otimes D_R$. To make visible the compatibility between the trace set and the queue history we include the whole events in the trace sets of the composite component. We have:

$$D_{CR}(\langle !\langle h, C, R, 1\rangle\rangle) = \{\langle !\langle h, C, R, 1\rangle, ?\langle h, C, R, 2\rangle\rangle\}$$
$$D_{CR}(\langle !\langle t, C, R, 1\rangle\rangle) = \{\langle !\langle t, C, R, 1\rangle, ?\langle t, C, R, 2\rangle\rangle\}$$

For a given queue history α, the set $\mathcal{E}_C \circledS D_{CR}(\alpha)$ is a subset of the trace set $D_C(\mathcal{E}_C^{\downarrow} \circledS \alpha)$ that is possible with regard to α (that $\mathcal{E}_C \circledS D_{CR}(\alpha)$ is a subset of $D_C(\mathcal{E}_C^{\downarrow} \circledS \alpha)$ is shown in [2]). We call the set of traces of C that are possible with regard to a given queue history α and component R for $CT_{C-R}(\alpha)$, which is short for *conditional traces*.

Given two components N_1 and N_2 and a complete queue history $\alpha \in \mathcal{B}_{N_1 \cup N_2}$, we define the set of conditional traces of N_1 with regard to α and N_2 formally as:

$$(24) \quad CT_{N_1-N_2}(\alpha) \stackrel{\text{def}}{=} \{t \in D_{N_1}(\mathcal{E}_{N_1}^{\downarrow} \circledS \alpha) \mid (\{!\} \times \mathcal{S} \times N_1 \times N_2 \times \mathcal{Q}) \circledS t \sqsubseteq$$
$$(\{!\} \times \mathcal{S} \times N_1 \times N_2 \times \mathcal{Q}) \circledS \alpha\}$$

Lemma 1. *Let I_{N_1} and I_{N_2} be two probabilistic component executions such that $N_1 \cap N_2 = \emptyset$ and let α be a queue history in $\mathcal{B}_{N_1 \cup N_2}$. Then*

$$CT_{N_1-N_2}(\alpha) \in \mathcal{F}_{N_1}(\mathcal{E}_{N_1}^{\downarrow} \circledS \alpha) \wedge CT_{N_2-N_1}(\alpha) \in \mathcal{F}_{N_2}(\mathcal{E}_{N_2}^{\downarrow} \circledS \alpha)$$

PROOF SKETCH: The set $CT_{N_1-N2}(\alpha)$ includes all traces in $D_{N_1}(\mathcal{E}_{N_1}^{\downarrow} \circledS \alpha)$ that are compatible with α, i.e., traces that are prefixes of α when filtered on the transmission events from N_1 to N_2. The key is to show that this set can be constructed as an element in $\mathcal{F}_{N_1}(\mathcal{E}_{N_1}^{\downarrow} \circledS \alpha)$. If α is infinite, this set corresponds

---

[6] We use $\cdot$ to denote normal multiplication.

to (1) the union of all finite traces in $D_{N_1}(\mathcal{E}_{N_1}^\downarrow \circledS \alpha)$ that are compatible with α and (2) the set obtained by constructing countable unions of cones of traces that are compatible with finite prefixes of $\alpha|_i$ for all $i \in \mathbb{N}$ (where $\alpha|_i$ denotes the prefix of α of length i) and then construct the countable intersection of all such countable unions of cones. If α is finite the proof is simpler, and we do not got into the details here. The same procedure may be followed to show that $CT_{N_2-N_1}(\alpha) \in \mathcal{F}_{N_2}(\mathcal{E}_{N_2}^\downarrow \circledS \alpha)$.

As illustrated by the example above, we cannot obtain a measure on a composite cone-σ-field in the same manner as for a composite extended cone set. In order to define a conditional probability measure on a composite cone-σ-field, we first define a measure on the composite extended cone set it is generated from. We then show that this measure can be uniquely extended to a conditional probability measure on the generated cone-σ-field. Given two probabilistic component executions I_{N_1} and I_{N_2} such that $N_1 \cap N_2 = \emptyset$, for each $\alpha \in \mathcal{B}_{N_1 \cup N_2}$ we define a measure $\mu_{N_1} \otimes \mu_{N_2}(\alpha)$ on $C_E(D_{N_1} \otimes D_{N_2}(\alpha))$ formally as follows:

$$(25) \quad \mu_{N_1} \otimes \mu_{N_2} \text{--} \in \mathcal{B}_{N_1 \cup N_2} \to (C_E(D_{N_1} \otimes D_{N_2}(\alpha)) \to [0,1])$$

$$\mu_{N_1} \otimes \mu_{N_2}(\alpha)(c) \stackrel{\text{def}}{=} f_{N_1}(\mathcal{E}_{N_1}^\downarrow \circledS \alpha)(\mathcal{E}_{N_1} \circledS c) \cdot f_{N_2}(\mathcal{E}_{N_2}^\downarrow \circledS \alpha)(\mathcal{E}_{N_2} \circledS c)$$

Theorem 1. *The function $\mu_{N_1} \otimes \mu_{N_2}(\alpha)$ is well defined.*

PROOF SKETCH: For any $c \in C_E(D_{N_1} \otimes D_{N_2}(\alpha))$ we must show that $(\mathcal{E}_{N_1} \circledS c) \in \mathcal{F}_{N_1}(\mathcal{E}_{N_1}^\downarrow \circledS \alpha)$ and $(\mathcal{E}_{N_2} \circledS c) \in \mathcal{F}_{N_2}(\mathcal{E}_{N_2}^\downarrow \circledS \alpha)$. If c is a singleton (containing exactly one trace) the proof follows from the fact that (1): if $(D, \mathcal{F}, f)$ is a conditional probabilistic execution and t is a trace in D, then $\{t\} \in \mathcal{F}$ [23], and (2): that we can show $\mathcal{E}_{N_1} \circledS t \in D_{N_1}(\mathcal{E}_{N_1}^\downarrow \circledS \alpha) \land \mathcal{E}_{N_2} \circledS t \in D_{N_2}(\mathcal{E}_{N_2}^\downarrow \circledS \alpha)$ from Definition 3 and definition (22).

If c is a cone $c(t, D_{N_1} \otimes D_{N_2}(\alpha))$ in $C(D_{N_1} \otimes D_{N_2}(\alpha))$, we show that $CT_{N_1-N_2}(\alpha)$, intersected with $c(\mathcal{E}_{N_1} \circledS t, D_{N_1}(\mathcal{E}_{N_1}^\downarrow \circledS \alpha))$ and the traces in $D_{N_1}(\mathcal{E}_{N_1}^\downarrow \circledS \alpha)$ that are compatible with t with regard to the timing of events, is an element of $\mathcal{F}_{N_1}(\mathcal{E}_{N_1}^\downarrow \circledS \alpha)$ that equals $(\mathcal{E}_{N_1} \circledS c)$. We follow the same procedure to show that $(\mathcal{E}_{N_2} \circledS c) \in \mathcal{F}_{N_2}(\mathcal{E}_{N_2}^\downarrow \circledS \alpha)$.

Lemma 2. *Let I_{N_1} and I_{N_2} be two probabilistic component executions such that $N_1 \cap N_2 = \emptyset$ and let $\mu_{N_1} \otimes \mu_{N_2}$ be a measure on the extended cones set of $D_{N_1} \otimes D_{N_2}$ as defined by (25). Then, for all complete queue histories $\alpha \in \mathcal{B}_{N_1 \cup N_2}$*

1. $\mu_{N_1} \otimes \mu_{N_2}(\alpha)(\emptyset) = 0$
2. $\mu_{N_1} \otimes \mu_{N_2}(\alpha)$ is σ-additive
3. $\mu_{N_1} \otimes \mu_{N_2}(\alpha)(D_{N_1} \otimes D_{N_2}(\alpha)) \leq 1$

PROOF SKETCH: We sketch the proof strategy for point 2 of Lemma 2. The proofs of point 1 and 3 are simpler, and we do not go into the details here. Assume ϕ is a sequence of disjoint sets in $C_E(D_{N_1} \otimes D_{N_2}(\alpha))$. We construct a sequence ψ of length $\#\phi$ such that $\forall i \in [1..\#\phi] : \psi[i] = \{(\mathcal{E}_{N_1} \circledS t, \mathcal{E}_{N_2} \circledS t) \,|\, t \in$

$\phi[i]\}$ and show that $\bigcup_{i=1}^{\#\psi} \psi[i] = \mathcal{E}_{N_1} \circledS \bigcup_{i=1}^{\#\phi} \phi[i] \times \mathcal{E}_{N_2} \circledS \bigcup_{i=1}^{\#\phi} \phi[i]$. It follows by Theorem 1 that $(\mathcal{E}_{N_1} \circledS \bigcup_{i=1}^{\#\phi} \phi[i]) \times (\mathcal{E}_{N_2} \circledS \bigcup_{i=1}^{\#\phi} \phi[i])$ is a measurable rectangle [11] in $\mathcal{F}_{N_1}(\mathcal{E}_{N_1}^{\downarrow} \circledS \alpha) \times \mathcal{F}_{N_2}(\mathcal{E}_{N_2}^{\downarrow} \circledS \alpha)$. From the above, and the product measure theorem [11] it can be shown that $f_{N_1}(\mathcal{E}_{N_1}^{\downarrow} \circledS \alpha)(\mathcal{E}_{N_1} \circledS \bigcup_{i=1}^{\#\phi} \phi[i]) \cdot f_{N_2}(\mathcal{E}_{N_2}^{\downarrow} \circledS \alpha)(\mathcal{E}_{N_2} \circledS \bigcup_{i=1}^{\#\phi} \phi[i]) = \sum_{i=1}^{\#\phi} f_{N_1}(\mathcal{E}_{N_1}^{\downarrow} \circledS \alpha)(\mathcal{E}_{N_1} \circledS \phi[i]) \cdot f_{N_2}(\mathcal{E}_{N_2}^{\downarrow} \circledS \alpha)(\mathcal{E}_{N_2} \circledS \phi[i])$.

Theorem 2. *There exists a unique extension of* $\mu_{N_1} \otimes \mu_{N_2}(\alpha)$ *to the cone-σ-field* $\mathcal{F}_{N_1} \otimes \mathcal{F}_{N_2}(\alpha)$.

PROOF SKETCH: We extend $C_E(D_{N_1} \otimes D_{N_2}(\alpha))$ in a stepwise manner to a set obtained by first adding all complements of the elements in $C_E(D_{N_1} \otimes D_{N_2}(\alpha))$, then adding the finite intersections of the new elements and finally adding finite unions of disjoint elements. For each step we extend $\mu_{N_1} \otimes \mu_{N_2}(\alpha)$ and show that the extension is σ-additive. We end up with a finite measure on the field generated by $C_E(D_{N_1} \otimes D_{N_2}(\alpha))$. By the extension theorem [11] it follows that this measure can be uniquely extended to a measure on $\mathcal{F}_{N_1} \otimes \mathcal{F}_{N_2}(\alpha)$.

Corollary 1. *Let* $f_{N_1} \otimes f_{N_2}(\alpha)$ *be the unique extension of* $\mu_{N_1} \otimes \mu_{N_2}(\alpha)$ *to the cone-σ-field* $\mathcal{F}_{N_1} \otimes \mathcal{F}_{N_2}(\alpha)$. *Then* $f_{N_1} \otimes f_{N_2}(\alpha)$ *is a conditional probability measure on* $\mathcal{F}_{N_1} \otimes \mathcal{F}_{N_2}(\alpha)$.

PROOF SKETCH: We first show that $\forall \alpha \in \mathcal{B}_{N_1 \cup N_2} : f_{N_1} \otimes f_{N_2}(\alpha)(D_{N_1} \otimes D_{N_2}(\alpha)) \leq 1$. When $f_{N_1} \otimes f_{N_2}(\alpha)$ is a measure on $\mathcal{F}_{N_1} \otimes \mathcal{F}_{N_2}(\alpha)$ such that $f_{N_1} \otimes f_{N_2}(\alpha)(D_{N_1} \otimes D_{N_2}(\alpha)) \leq 1$ we can show that $f_{N_1} \otimes f_{N_2}(\alpha)$ is a conditional probability measure on $\mathcal{F}_{N_1} \otimes \mathcal{F}_{N_2}(\alpha)$.

5.4   Composition of Probabilistic Component Executions

We may now lift the $\otimes$-operator to probabilistic component executions. Let I_{N_1} and I_{N_2} be probabilistic component executions such that $N_1 \cap N_2 = \emptyset$. For any $\alpha \in \mathcal{B}_{N_1 \cup N_2}$ we define:

$$(26) \qquad I_{N_1} \otimes I_{N_2}(\alpha) \stackrel{\text{def}}{=} (D_{N_1} \otimes D_{N_2}(\alpha), \mathcal{F}_{N_1} \otimes \mathcal{F}_{N_2}(\alpha), f_{N_1} \otimes f_{N_2}(\alpha))$$

where $f_{N_1} \otimes f_{N_2}(\alpha)$ is defined to be the unique extension of $\mu_{N_1} \otimes \mu_{N_2}(\alpha)$ to $\mathcal{F}_{N_1} \otimes \mathcal{F}_{N_2}(\alpha)$.

Theorem 3. $I_{N_1} \otimes I_{N_2}$ *is a probabilistic component execution of* $N_1 \cup N_2$.

PROOF SKETCH: This can be shown from definitions (22) and (23) and Corollary 1.

6   Denotational Representation of a Component with a Notion of Risk

For any disjoint set of interfaces N we define:

$$A_N \overset{\text{def}}{=} \bigcup_{n \in N} A_n$$

$$cv_N \overset{\text{def}}{=} \bigcup_{n \in N} cv_n$$

$$rf_N \overset{\text{def}}{=} \bigcup_{n \in N} rf_n$$

The reason why we can take the union of functions with disjoint domains is that we understand a function as a set of *maplets*. A maplet is a pair of two elements corresponding to the argument and the result of a function. For example the following set of three maplets

$$\{(e_1 \mapsto f(e_1)), (e_2 \mapsto f(e_2)), (e_2 \mapsto f(e_2))\}$$

characterises the function $f \in \{e_1, e_2, e_3\} \to S$ uniquely. The arrow $\mapsto$ indicates that the function yields the element to the right when applied to the element to the left [4].

We define the semantic representation of a component analogous to that of an interface, except that we now have a set of interfaces N, instead of a single interface n:

Definition 10 (Semantics of a component). *A component is represented by a quadruple*

$$(I_N, A_N, cv_N, rf_N)$$

consisting of its probabilistic component execution, its assets, consequence function and risk function, as explained above.

We define composition of components formally as:

Definition 11 (Composition of components). *Given two components N_1 and N_2 such that $N_1 \cap N_2 = \emptyset$. We define their composition $N_1 \otimes N_2$ by*

$$(I_{N_1} \otimes I_{N_2}, A_{N_1} \cup A_{N_2}, cv_{N_1} \cup cv_{N_2}, rf_{N_1} \cup rf_{N_2})$$

7 Hiding

In this section we explain how to formally represent hiding in a denotational semantics with risk. As explained in Section 2.3 we must take care not to hide incidents that affect assets belonging to externally observable interfaces, when we hide internal interactions. An interface is externally observable if it interacts with interfaces in the environment. We define operators for hiding assets and interface names from a component name and from the semantic representation of a component. The operators are defined in such a way that partial hiding of internal interaction is allowed. Thus internal events that affect assets belonging to externally observable interfaces may remain observable after hiding. Note that hiding of assets and interface names is optional. The operators defined below simply makes it possible to hide e.g. all assets belonging to a certain interface n, as well as all events in an execution where n is the active party. We sketch the proof strategies for the lemmas and theorems in this section and refer to Brændeland et al. [2] for the full proofs.

Until now we have identified a component by the set of names of its interfaces. This has been possible because an interface is uniquely determined by its name, and the operator for composition is both associative and commutative. Hence, until now it has not mattered in which order the interfaces and resulting components have been composed. When we in the following introduce two hiding operators this becomes however an issue. For example, consider a component identified by $N \overset{\text{def}}{=} \{c_1, c_2, c_3\}$. Then we need to distinguish the component $\delta c_2 : N$, obtained from N by hiding interface c_2, from the component $\{c_1, c_3\}$. To do that we build the hiding information into the name of a component obtained with the use of hiding operators. A component name is from now one either:

(a) a set of interface names,
(b) of the form $\delta n : N$ where N is a component name and n is an interface name,
(c) of the form $\sigma a : N$ where N is a component name and a is an asset, or
(d) of the form $N_1 + \!\!+ N_2$ where N_1 and N_2 are component names and at least one of N_1 or N_2 contains a hiding operator.

Since we now allow hiding operators in component names we need to take this into consideration when combining them. We define a new operator for combining two component names N_1 and N_2 as follows:

$$(27) \quad N_1 \uplus N_2 \overset{\text{def}}{=} \begin{cases} N_1 \cup N_2 \text{ if neither } N_1 \text{ nor } N_2 \text{ contain hiding operators} \\ N_1 + \!\!+ N_2 \text{ otherwise} \end{cases}$$

By $\mathsf{in}(N)$ we denote the set of all hidden and not hidden interface names occurring in the component name N. We generalise definitions (18) to (21) to component names with hidden assets and interface names as follows:

$$(28) \quad \mathcal{E}_{\sigma a : N} \overset{\text{def}}{=} \mathcal{E}_N \qquad\qquad \mathcal{E}_{\delta n : N} \overset{\text{def}}{=} \mathcal{E}_{\mathsf{in}(N) \setminus \{n\}}$$

$$(29) \quad \mathcal{E}^{\downarrow}_{\sigma a : N} \overset{\text{def}}{=} \mathcal{E}^{\downarrow}_N \qquad\qquad \mathcal{E}^{\downarrow}_{\delta n : N} \overset{\text{def}}{=} \mathcal{E}^{\downarrow}_{\mathsf{in}(N) \setminus \{n\}}$$

$$(30) \quad \mathcal{H}_{\sigma a : N} \overset{\text{def}}{=} \mathcal{H} \cap \mathcal{E}_{\sigma a : N}{}^{\omega} \qquad\qquad \mathcal{H}_{\delta n : N} \overset{\text{def}}{=} \mathcal{H} \cap \mathcal{E}_{\delta n : N}{}^{\omega}$$

$$(31) \quad \mathcal{B}_{\sigma a : N} \overset{\text{def}}{=} \mathcal{B}_N \qquad\qquad \mathcal{B}_{\delta n : N} \overset{\text{def}}{=} ((\mathcal{E}_{\overline{\mathsf{in}(N)}} \setminus \mathcal{E}^{\downarrow}_n) \cup \mathcal{E}_{\mathsf{in}(N)}) \circledS \mathcal{B}_N$$

Definition 12 (Hiding of interface in a probabilistic component execution). *Given an interface name n and a probabilistic component execution I_N we define:*

$$\delta n : I_N(\alpha) \overset{\text{def}}{=} (D_{\delta n \,:\, N}(\alpha), \mathcal{F}_{\delta n \,:\, N}(\alpha), f_{\delta n \,:\, N}(\alpha))$$

$$\text{where} \quad D_{\delta n \,:\, N}(\alpha) \overset{\text{def}}{=} \{\mathcal{E}_{\delta n \,:\, N} \circledS t \mid t \in D_N(\delta n : \alpha)\}$$

$$\mathcal{F}_{\delta n \,:\, N}(\alpha) \overset{\text{def}}{=} \sigma(C_E(D_{\delta n \,:\, N}(\alpha))) \text{ i.e., the cone-}\sigma\text{-field of } D_{\delta n \,:\, N}(\alpha)$$

$$f_{\delta n \,:\, N}(\alpha)(c) \overset{\text{def}}{=} f_N(\delta n : \alpha)(\{t \in D_N(\delta n : \alpha) \mid \mathcal{E}_{\delta n \,:\, N} \circledS t \in c\})$$

$$\delta n : \alpha \overset{\text{def}}{=} \left(\left(\overline{\mathcal{E}_{\mathsf{in}(N)}} \setminus \mathcal{E}_n^{\downarrow}\right) \cup \mathcal{E}_{\mathsf{in}(N)}\right) \circledS \alpha$$

When hiding an interface name n from a queue history α, as defined in the last line of Definition 12, we filter away the external input to n but keep all internal transmissions, including those sent to n. This is because we still need the information about the internal interactions involving the hidden interface to compute the probability of interactions it is involved in, after the interface is hidden from the outside.

Lemma 3. *If I_N is a probabilistic component execution and n is an interface name, then $\delta n : I_N$ is a probabilistic component execution.*

PROOF SKETCH: We must show that: (1) $D_{\delta n \,:\, N}(\alpha)$ is a set of well-formed traces; (2) $\mathcal{F}_{\delta n:N}(\alpha)$ is the cone-σ-field of $D_{\delta n \,:\, N}(\alpha)$; and (3) $f_{\delta n \,:\, N}(\alpha)$ is a conditional probability measure on $\mathcal{F}_{\delta n \,:\, N}(\alpha)$. (1) If a trace is well-formed it remains well-formed after filtering away events with the hiding operator, since hiding interface names in a trace does not affect the ordering of events. The proof of (2) follows straightforwardly from Definition 12.

In order to show (3), we first show that $f_{\delta n \,:\, N}(\alpha)$ is a measure on $\mathcal{F}_{\delta n \,:\, N}(\alpha)$. In order to show this, we first show that the function $f_{\delta n \,:\, N}$ is well defined. I.e., for any $c \in \mathcal{F}_{\delta n \,:\, N}(\alpha)$ we show that $\{t \in D_N(\delta n : \alpha) \mid \mathcal{E}_{\delta n \,:\, N} \circledS t \in c\} \in \mathcal{F}_N(\delta n : \alpha)$. We then show that $f_N(\delta n : \alpha)(\emptyset) = 0$ and that $f_N(\delta n : \alpha)$ is σ-additive. Secondly, we show that $f_{\delta n \,:\, N}(\alpha)(D_{\delta n \,:\, N}(\alpha)) \leq 1$. When $f_{\delta n \,:\, N}(\alpha)$ is a measure on $\mathcal{F}_{\delta n \,:\, N}(\alpha)$ such that $f_{\delta n \,:\, N}(\alpha)(D_{\delta n \,:\, N}(\alpha)) \leq 1$ we can show that $f_{\delta n \,:\, N}(\alpha)$ is a conditional probability measure on $\mathcal{F}_{\delta n \,:\, N}(\alpha)$.

Definition 13 (Hiding of component asset). *Given an asset a and a component (I_N, A_N, cv_N, rf_N) we define:*

$$\sigma a : (I_N, A_N, cv_N, rf_N) \overset{\text{def}}{=} (I_N, \sigma a : A_N, \sigma a : cv_N, \sigma a : rf_N)$$

$$\text{where} \quad \sigma a : A_N \overset{\text{def}}{=} A_N \setminus \{a\}$$

$$\sigma a : cv_N \overset{\text{def}}{=} cv_N \setminus \{(e, a) \mapsto c \mid e \in \mathcal{E} \wedge c \in \mathbb{N}\}$$

$$\sigma a : rf_N \overset{\text{def}}{=} rf_N \setminus \{(c, p, a) \mapsto r \mid c, r \in \mathbb{N} \wedge p \in [0, 1]\}$$

As explained in Section 6 we see a function as a set of maplets. Hence, the consequence and risk function of a component with asset a hidden is the set-difference between the original functions and the set of maplets that has a as one of the parameters of its first element.

Theorem 4. *If N is a component and a is an asset, then $\sigma a : N$ is a component.*

PROOF SKETCH: This can be shown from Definition 13 and Definition 10.

We generalise the operators for hiding interface names and assets to the hiding of sets of interface names and sets of assets in the obvious manner.

Definition 14 (Hiding of component interface). *Given an interface name n and a component (I_N, A_N, cv_N, rf_N) we define:*

$$\delta n : (I_N, A_N, cv_N, rf_N) \overset{\text{def}}{=} (\delta n : I_N, \sigma A_n : A_N, \sigma A_n : cv_N, \sigma A_n : rf_N)$$

Theorem 5. *If N is a component and n is an interface name, then $\delta n : N$ is a component.*

PROOF SKETCH: This can be show from Lemma 3 and Theorem 4.

Since, as we have shown above, components are closed under hiding of assets and interface names, the operators for composition of components, defined in Section 5, are not affected by the introduction of hiding operators. We impose the restriction that two components can only be composed by $\otimes$ if their sets of interface names are disjoint, independent of whether they are hidden or not.

8   Related Work

There are a number of proposals to integrate security requirements into the requirements specification, such as SecureUML and UMLsec. SecureUML [20] is a method for modelling access control policies and their integration into model-driven software development. SecureUML is based on role-based access control and specifies security requirements for well-behaved applications in predictable environments. UMLsec [15] is an extension to UML that enables the modelling of security-related features such as confidentiality and access control. Neither of these two approaches have particular focus on component-oriented specification. Khan and Han [17] characterise security properties of composite systems, based on a security characterisation framework for basic components [16]. They define a *compositional security contract* CsC for two components, which is based on the compatibility between their required and ensured security properties. This approach has been designed to capture security properties, while our focus is on integrating risks into the semantic representation of components.

Our idea to use queue histories to resolve the external nondeterminism of probabilistic components is inspired by the use of schedulers, also known as adversaries, which is a common way to resolve external nondeterminism in reactive systems [7,27,6]. Segala and Lynch [27,26] use a randomised scheduler to model input from an external environment and resolve the nondeterminism of a probabilistic I/O automaton. They define a probability space for each probabilistic execution of an automaton, given a scheduler. Seidel uses a similar approach in an extension of CSP with probabilities [28], where a process is represented by a conditional probability measure that, given a trace produced by the environment, returns a probability distribution over traces. Sere and Troubitsyna [29] handle external nondeterminism by treating the assignment of probabilities of alternative choices as a refinement step. Alfaro et al. [6] present a probabilistic model for variable-based systems with trace semantics similar to that of Segala and Lynch. Unlike the model of Segala and Lynch, theirs allows multiple schedulers to resolve the nondeterminism of each component. This is done to achieve deep compositionality, where the semantics of a composite system can be obtained from the semantics of its constituents.

Our decision to use a cone-based probability space to represent probabilistic systems is inspired by Segala [26] and Refsdal et al. [24,23]. Segala uses probability spaces whose σ-fields are cone-σ-fields to represent fully probabilistic automata, that is, automata with probabilistic choice but without nondeterminism. In pSTAIRS [23] the ideas of Segala is applied to the trace-based semantics of STAIRS [12,25]. A probabilistic system is represented as a probability space where the σ-field is generated from a set of cones of traces describing component interactions. In pSTAIRS all choices are global. The different types of choices may only be specified for closed systems, and there is no nondeterminism stemming from external input. Since we wish to represent the behaviour of a component independently of its environment we cannot use global choice operators of the type used in pSTAIRS.

9   Conclusion

We have presented a component model that integrates component risks as part of the component behaviour. The component model is meant to serve as a formal basis for component-based risk analysis. To ensure modularity of our component model we represent a stakeholder by the component interface, and identify assets on behalf of component interfaces. Thus we avoid referring to concepts that are external to a component in the component model

In order to model the probabilistic aspect of risk, we represent the behaviour of a component by a probability distribution over traces. We use queue histories to resolve both internal and external non-determinism. The semantics of a component is the set of probability spaces given all possible queue histories of the component. We define composition in a fully compositional manner: The semantics of a composite component is completely determined by the semantics of its constituents. Since we integrate the notion of risk into component behaviour, we obtain the risks of a composite component by composing the behavioural representations of its sub-components.

The component model provides a foundation for component-based risk analysis, by conveying how risks manifests themselves in an underlying component implementation. By component-based risk analysis we mean that risks are identified, analysed and documented at the component level, and that risk analysis results are composable. Our semantic model is not tied to any specific syntax or specification technique. At this point we have no compliance operator to check whether a given component implementation complies with a component specification. In order to be able to check that a component implementation fulfils a requirement to protection specification we would like to define a compliance relation between specifications in STAIRS, or another suitable specification language, and components represented in our semantic model.

We believe that a method for component-based risk analysis will facilitate the integration of risk analysis into component-based development, and thereby make it easier to predict the effects on component risks caused by upgrading or substituting sub-parts.

Acknowledgements. The research presented in this paper has been partly funded by the Research Council of Norway through the research projects COMA 160317 (Component-oriented model-based security analysis) and DIGIT 180052/S10 (Digital interoperability with trust), and partly by the EU 7th Research Framework Programme through the Network of Excellence on Engineering Secure Future Internet Software Services and Systems (NESSoS).

We would like to thank Bjarte M. Østvold for creating lpchk:, which is a proof analyser for proofs written in Lamport's style [19], which is used in the full proofs of all the results presented in this paper, to be found in the technical report [2]. The proof analyser lpchk checks consistency of step labelling and performs parentheses matching, and also for proof reading and useful comments.

References

1. Ahrens, F.: Why it's so hard for Toyota to find out what's wrong. The Washington Post (March 2010)
2. Brændeland, G., Refsdal, A., Stølen, K.: A denotational model for component-based risk analysis. Technical Report 363, University of Oslo, Department of Informatics (2011)
3. Brændeland, G., Stølen, K.: Using model-driven risk analysis in component-based development. In: Dependability and Computer Engineering: Concepts for Software-Intensive Systems. IGI Global (2011)
4. Broy, M., Stølen, K.: Specification and development of interactive systems – Focus on streams, interfaces and refinement. Monographs in computer science. Springer (2001)
5. Courant, R., Robbins, H.: What Is Mathematics? An Elementary Approach to Ideas and Methods. Oxford University Press (1996)
6. de Alfaro, L., Henzinger, T.A., Jhala, R.: Compositional Methods for Probabilistic Systems. In: Larsen, K.G., Nielsen, M. (eds.) CONCUR 2001. LNCS, vol. 2154, pp. 351–365. Springer, Heidelberg (2001)
7. Derman, C.: Finite state Markovian decision process. Mathematics in science and engineering, vol. 67. Academic Press (1970)
8. Dudley, R.M.: Real analysis and probability. Cambridge studies in advanced mathematics, Cambridge (2002)
9. Probability theory. Encyclopædia Britannica Online (2009)
10. Folland, G.B.: Real Analysis: Modern Techniques and Their Applications. Pure and Applied Mathematics, 2nd edn. John Wiley and Sons Ltd., USA (1999)
11. Halmos, P.R.: Measure Theory. Springer (1950)
12. Haugen, Ø., Husa, K.E., Runde, R.K., Stølen, K.: STAIRS towards formal design with sequence diagrams. Software and System Modeling 4(4), 355–357 (2005)

13. He, J., Josephs, M., Hoare, C.A.R.: A theory of synchrony and asynchrony. In: IFIP WG 2.2/2.3 Working Conference on Programming Concepts and Methods, pp. 459–478. North Holland (1990)
14. ISO. Risk management – Vocabulary, ISO Guide 73:2009 (2009)
15. Jürjens, J. (ed.): Secure systems development with UML. Springer (2005)
16. Khan, K.M., Han, J.: Composing security-aware software. IEEE Software 19(1), 34–41 (2002)
17. Khan, K.M., Han, J.: Deriving systems level security properties of component based composite systems. In: Australian Software Engineering Conference, pp. 334–343 (2005)
18. Komjáth, P., Totik, V.: Problems and theorems in classical set theory. Problem books in mathematics. Springer (2006)
19. Lamport, L.: How to write a proof. American Mathematical Monthly 102(7), 600–608 (1993)
20. Lodderstedt, T., Basin, D., Doser, J.: SecureUML: A UML-Based Modeling Language for Model-Driven Security. In: Jézéquel, J.-M., Hussmann, H., Cook, S. (eds.) UML 2002. LNCS, vol. 2460, pp. 426–441. Springer, Heidelberg (2002)
21. Meyn, S.: Control Techniques for Complex Networks. Cambridge University Press (2007)
22. OMG. Unified Modeling Language^{TM} (OMG UML), Superstructure, Version 2.3 (2010)
23. Refsdal, A.: Specifying Computer Systems with Probabilistic Sequence Diagrams. PhD thesis, Faculty of Mathematics and Natural Sciences, University of Oslo (2008)
24. Refsdal, A., Runde, R.K., Stølen, K.: Underspecification, Inherent Nondeterminism and Probability in Sequence Diagrams. In: Gorrieri, R., Wehrheim, H. (eds.) FMOODS 2006. LNCS, vol. 4037, pp. 138–155. Springer, Heidelberg (2006)
25. Runde, R.K., Haugen, Ø., Stølen, K.: The Pragmatics of STAIRS. In: de Boer, F.S., Bonsangue, M.M., Graf, S., de Roever, W.-P. (eds.) FMCO 2005. LNCS, vol. 4111, pp. 88–114. Springer, Heidelberg (2006)
26. Segala, R.: Modeling and Verification of Randomized Distributed Real-Time Systems. PhD thesis, Laboratory for Computer Science, Massachusetts Institute of Technology (1995)
27. Segala, R., Lynch, N.A.: Probabilistic simulations for probabilistic processes. Nordic Journal of Computing 2(2), 250–273 (1995)
28. Seidel, K.: Probabilistic communicationg processes. Theoretical Computer Science 152(2), 219–249 (1995)
29. Sere, K., Troubitsyna, E.: Probabilities in action system. In: Proceedings of the 8th Nordic Workshop on Programming Theory (1996)
30. Skorokhod, A.V.: Basic principles and application of probability theory. Springer (2005)
31. Standards Australia, Standards New Zealand. Australian/New Zealand Standard. Risk Management, AS/NZS 4360:2004 (2004)
32. Weisstein, E.W.: CRC Concise Encyclopedia of Mathematics, 2nd edn. Chapman & Hall/CRC (2002)

Synthesis of Hierarchical Systems

Benjamin Aminof[1], Fabio Mogavero[2,*], and Aniello Murano[2,*]

[1] Hebrew University, Jerusalem 91904, Israel
[2] Università degli Studi di Napoli "Federico II", 80126 Napoli, Italy
benj@cs.huji.ac.il, {mogavero,murano}@na.infn.it

Abstract. In automated synthesis, given a specification, we automatically create a system that is guaranteed to satisfy the specification. In the classical temporal synthesis algorithms, one usually creates a "flat" system "from scratch".
However, real-life software and hardware systems are usually created using preexisting libraries of reusable components, and are not "flat" since repeated subsystems are described only once.

In this work we describe an algorithm for the synthesis of a hierarchical system from a library of hierarchical components, which follows the "bottom-up"
approach to system design. Our algorithm works by synthesizing in many rounds,
when at each round the system designer provides the specification of the currently
desired module, which is then automatically synthesized using the initial library
and the previously constructed modules. To ensure that the synthesized module
actually takes advantage of the available high-level modules, we guide the algorithm by enforcing certain modularity criteria.

We show that the synthesis of a hierarchical system from a library of hierarchical components is EXPTIME-complete for μ-calculus, and 2EXPTIME-complete
for LTL, both in the cases of complete and incomplete information. Thus, in all
cases, it is not harder than the classical synthesis problem (of synthesizing flat
systems "from scratch"), even though the synthesized hierarchical system may
be exponentially smaller than a flat one.

1 Introduction

Synthesis is the automated construction of a system from its specification. The basic idea is simple and appealing: instead of developing a system and verifying that it
is correct w.r.t. its specification, we use instead an automated procedure that, given a
specification, constructs a system that is correct by construction. The first formulation
of synthesis goes back to Church [7]; the modern approach to this problem was initiated
by Pnueli and Rosner who introduced linear temporal logic (LTL) synthesis [23], later
extended to handle branching-time specifications, such as μ-calculus [10].

The Pnueli and Rosner idea can be summarized as follows. Given sets Σ_I and Σ_O
of inputs and outputs, respectively (usually, $\Sigma_I = 2^I$ and $\Sigma_O = 2^O$, where I is a set of
input signals and O is a set of output signals), we can view a system as a strategy
$P : \Sigma_I^* \to \Sigma_O$ that maps a finite sequence of sets of input signals into a set of output
signals. When P interacts with an environment that generates infinite input sequences,

* Partially supported by ESF GAMES grant 4112, Vigevani Project Prize 2010-2011, and by
University of Napoli Federico II under the F.A.R.O. project.

F. Arbab and P.C. Ölveczky (Eds.): FACS 2011, LNCS 7253, pp. 42–60, 2012.
© Springer-Verlag Berlin Heidelberg 2012

it associates with each input sequence an infinite computation over $\Sigma_I \cup \Sigma_O$. Though the system P is deterministic, it induces a computation tree. The branches of the tree correspond to external nondeterminism, caused by different possible inputs. Thus, the tree has a fixed branching degree $|\Sigma_I|$, and it embodies all the possible inputs (and hence also computations) of P. When we synthesize P from an LTL specification φ, we require φ to hold in all the paths of P's computation tree. However, in order to impose possibility requirements on P, we have to use a branching-time logic like μ-calculus. Given a branching specification φ over $\Sigma_I \cup \Sigma_O$, realizability of φ is the problem of determining whether there exists a system P whose computation tree satisfies φ. Correct synthesis of φ then amounts to constructing such a P.

In spite of the rich theory developed for system synthesis in the last two decades, little of this theory has been reduced to practice. In fact, the main approaches to tackle synthesis in practice are either to use heuristics (e.g., [13]) or to restrict to simple specifications (e.g., [22]). Some people argue that this is because the synthesis problem is very expensive compared to model-checking [16]. There is, however, something misleading in this perception: while the complexity of synthesis is given with respect to the specification only, the complexity of model-checking is given also with respect to a program, which can be very large. A common thread in almost all of the works concerning synthesis is the assumption that the system is to be built "from scratch". Obviously, real-world systems are rarely constructed this way, but rather by utilizing many preexisting reusable components, i.e., a library. Using standard preexisting components is sometimes unavoidable (for example, access to hardware resources is usually under the control of the operating system, which must be "reused"), and many times has other benefits (apart from saving time and effort, which may seem to be less of a problem in a setting of automatic - as opposed to manual - synthesis), such as maintaining a common code base, and abstracting away low level details that are already handled by the preexisting components. Another reason that may also account, at least partially, for the limited use of synthesis in practice, is the fact that synthesized systems are usually monolithic and look very unnatural from the system designer's point of view. Indeed, in classical temporal synthesis algorithms, one usually creates a "flat" system, i.e., a system in which sub-systems may be repeated many times. On the contrary, real-life software and hardware systems are hierarchical (or even recursive) and repeated sub-systems (such as sub-routines) are described only once. While hierarchical systems may be exponentially more succinct than flat ones, it has been shown that the cost of solving questions about them (like model-checking) are in many cases not exponentially higher [5,6,12]. Hierarchical systems can also be seen as a special case of recursive systems [2,3], where the nesting of calls to sub-systems is bounded. However, having no bound on the nesting of calls gives rise to infinite-state systems, and this results in a higher complexity.

In this work we provide a uniform algorithm, for different temporal logics, for the synthesis of hierarchical systems (or, equivalently, *transducers*) from a library of hierarchical systems, which mimics the "bottom-up" approach to system design, where one builds a system by iteratively constructing new modules based on previously constructed ones[1]. More specifically, we start the synthesis process by providing the algorithm with an initial

---

[1] While for systems built from scratch, a top-down approach may be argued to be more suitable, we find the bottom-up approach to be more natural when synthesizing from a library.

library $\mathcal{L}_0$ of available hierarchical components (as well as atomic ones). We then proceed by synthesizing in rounds. At each round i, the system designer provides a specification formula φ_i of the currently desired hierarchical component, which is then automatically synthesized using the currently available components as possible sub-components. Once a new component is synthesized, it is added to the library to be used by subsequent iterations. We show that while hierarchical systems may be exponentially smaller than flat ones, the problem of synthesizing a hierarchical system from a library of existing hierarchical systems is EXPTIME-complete for μ-calculus, and 2EXPTIME-complete for LTL. Thus, this problem is not harder than the classical synthesis problem of flat systems "from scratch". Furthermore, we show that this is true also in the case where the synthesized system has incomplete information about the environment's input.

Observe that it is easily conceivable that if the initial library $\mathcal{L}_0$ contains enough atomic components then the synthesis algorithm may use them exclusively, essentially producing a flat system. We thus have to direct the single-round synthesis algorithm in such a way that it produces modular and not flat results. The question of what makes a design more or less modular is very difficult to answer, and has received many (and often widely different) answers throughout the years (see [21], for a survey). We claim that some very natural modularity criteria are regular, and show how any criterion that can be checked by a parity tree automaton can be easily incorporated into our automata based synthesis algorithm.

Related Work.   The issues of specification and correctness of modularly designed systems have received a fair attention in the formal verification literature. Examples of important work on this subject are [8,17,26,27]. design" [8]. On the other hand, the problem of automatic synthesis from reusable components, which we study here, has received much less attention. The closest to our work is Lustig and Vardi's work on LTL synthesis from libraries of (flat) transducers [18]. The technically most difficult part of our work is an algorithm for performing the synthesis step of a single round of the multiple-rounds algorithm. To this end, we use an automata-theoretic approach. However, unlike the classical approach of [23], we build an automaton whose input is not a computation tree, but rather a system description in the form of a *connectivity tree* (inspired by the "control-flow" trees of [18]), which describes how to connect library components in a way that satisfies the specification formula. Taken by itself, our single-round algorithm extends the "control-flow" synthesis work from [18] in four directions. **(i)** We consider not only LTL specifications but also the modal μ-calculus. Hence, unlike [18], where co-Büchi tree automata were used, we have to use the more expressive parity tree automata. Unfortunately, this is not simply a matter of changing the acceptance condition. Indeed, in order to obtain an optimal upper bound, a widely different approach, which makes use of the machinery developed in [6] is needed. **(ii)** We need to be able to handle libraries of hierarchical transducers, whereas in [18] only libraries of flat transducers are considered. **(iii)** A synthesized transducer has no top-level exits (since it must be able to run on all possible input words), and thus, its ability to serve as a sub-transducer of another transducer (in future iterations of the multiple-rounds algorithm) is severely limited (it is like a function that never returns to its caller). We therefore need to address the problem of synthesizing exits for such transducers. **(iv)** As discussed above, we incorporate into the algorithm the enforcing of modularity criteria.

Recently, an extension of [18] appeared in [19], where the problem of *Nested-Words Temporal Logic* (NWTL) synthesis from recursive component libraries has been investigated. NWTL extends LTL with special operators that allow one to handle "call and return" computations [1] and it is used in [19] to describe how the components have to be connected in the synthesis problem. We recall that in our framework the logic does not drive (at least not explicitly) the way the components have to be connected. Moreover, the approach used in [19] cannot be applied directly to the branching framework we consider in this paper, as we recall that already the satisfiability problem for μ-calculus with "call and return" is undecidable even for very restricted cases [4].

Due to lack of space some proofs are omitted and reported in a full version found at the authors' web page.

2 Alternating Tree Automata

Let $\mathcal{D}$ be a set. A $\mathcal{D}$-*tree* is a prefix-closed subset $T \subseteq \mathcal{D}^*$ such that if $x \cdot c \in T$, where $x \in \mathcal{D}^*$ and $c \in \mathcal{D}$, then also $x \in T$. The *complete* $\mathcal{D}$-*tree* is the tree $\mathcal{D}^*$. The elements of T are called *nodes*, and the empty word ε is the *root* of T. Given a word $x = y \cdot d$, with $y \in \mathcal{D}^*$ and $d \in \mathcal{D}$, we define $last(x)$ to be d. For $x \in T$, the nodes $x \cdot d \in T$, where $d \in \mathcal{D}$, are the *sons* of x. A *leaf* is a node with no sons. A *path* of T is a set $\pi \subseteq T$ such that $\varepsilon \in T$ and, for every $x \in \pi$, either x is a leaf or there is a unique $d \in \mathcal{D}$ such that $x \cdot d \in \pi$. For an alphabet Σ, a Σ-*labeled* $\mathcal{D}$-*tree* is a pair $\langle T, V \rangle$ where $T \subseteq \mathcal{D}^*$ is a $\mathcal{D}$-tree and $V : T \to \Sigma$ maps each node of T to a letter in Σ.

Alternating tree automata are a generalization of nondeterministic tree automata [20] (see [16], for more details). Intuitively, while a nondeterministic tree automaton that visits a node of the input tree sends exactly one copy of itself to each of the sons of the node, an alternating automaton can send several copies of itself to the same son.

An (asymmetric) *Alternating Parity Tree Automaton* (APT) is a tuple $\mathcal{A} = \langle \Sigma, \mathcal{D}, Q, q_0, \delta, F \rangle$, where Σ, $\mathcal{D}$, and Q are non-empty finite sets of *input letters*, *directions*, and *states*, respectively; $q_0 \in Q$ is an *initial state*, F is a *parity acceptance condition* to be defined later, and $\delta : Q \times \Sigma \mapsto \mathcal{B}^+(\mathcal{D} \times Q)$ is an *alternating transition function*, which maps a state and an input letter to a positive boolean combination of elements in $\mathcal{D} \times Q$. Given a set $S \subseteq \mathcal{D} \times Q$ and a formula $\theta \in \mathcal{B}^+(\mathcal{D} \times Q)$, we say that S satisfies θ (denoted by $S \models \theta$) if assigning **true** to elements in S and **false** to elements in $(\mathcal{D} \times Q) \setminus S$, makes θ true. A *run* of an APT $\mathcal{A}$ on a Σ-labeled $\mathcal{D}$-tree $\mathcal{T} = \langle T, V \rangle$ is a $(T \times Q)$-labeled $\mathbb{N}$-tree $\langle T_r, r \rangle$, where $\mathbb{N}$ is the set of non-negative integers, such that (i) $r(\varepsilon) = (\varepsilon, q_0)$ and (ii) for all $y \in T_r$, with $r(y) = (x, q)$, there exists a set $S \subseteq \mathcal{D} \times Q$, such that $S \models \delta(q, V(x))$, and there is one son y' of y, with $r(y') = (x \cdot d, q')$, for every $(d, q') \in S$. Given a node x of a run $\langle T_r, r \rangle$, with $r(x) = (z, q) \in T \times Q$, we define $last(r(y)) = (last(z), q)$. An alternating parity automaton $\mathcal{A}$ is nondeterministic (denoted NPT), iff when its transition relation is rewritten in disjunctive normal form each disjunct contains at most one element of $\{d\} \times Q$, for every $d \in \mathcal{D}$. An automaton is universal (denoted UPT) if all the formulas that appear in its transition relation are conjunctions of atoms in $\mathcal{D} \times Q$.

A *symmetric* alternating parity tree automaton with ε-moves (SAPT) [14] does not distinguish between the different sons of a node, and can send copies of itself only in a universal or an existential manner. Formally, an SAPT is a tuple $\mathcal{A} = \langle \Sigma, Q, q_0, \delta, F \rangle$, where Σ is a finite input alphabet; Q is a finite set of states, partitioned into universal

$(Q^\wedge)$, existential $(Q^\vee)$, ε-and $(Q^{(\varepsilon,\wedge)})$, and ε-or $(Q^{(\varepsilon,\vee)})$ states (we also write $Q^{\vee,\wedge} = Q^\vee \cup Q^\wedge$, and $Q^\varepsilon = Q^{(\varepsilon,\vee)} \cup Q^{(\varepsilon,\wedge)}$); $q_0 \in Q$ is an initial state; $\delta : Q \times \Sigma \to (Q \cup 2^Q)$ is a transition function such that for all $\sigma \in \Sigma$, we have that $\delta(q,\sigma) \in Q$ for $q \in Q^{\vee,\wedge}$, and $\delta(q,\sigma) \in 2^Q$ for $q \in Q^\varepsilon$; and F is a parity acceptance condition, to be defined later. We assume that Q contains in addition two special states ff and tt, called *rejecting sink* and *accepting sink*, respectively, such that $\forall a \in \Sigma : \delta(tt,a) = tt, \delta(ff,a) = ff$. The classification of ff and tt is arbitrary. Transitions from states in Q^ε launch copies of $\mathcal{A}$ that stay on the same input node as before the transition, while transitions from states in $Q^{\vee,\wedge}$ launch copies that advance to sons of the current node (note that for an SAPT the set $\mathcal{D}$ of directions of the input trees plays no role in the definition of a run). When a symmetric alternating tree automaton $\mathcal{A}$ runs on an input tree it starts with a copy in state q_0 whose reading head points to the root of the tree. It then follows δ in order to send further copies. For example, if a copy of $\mathcal{A}$ that is in state $q \in Q^{(\varepsilon,\vee)}$ is reading a node x labeled σ, and $\delta(q,\sigma) = \{q_1,q_2\}$, then this copy proceeds either to state q_1 or to state q_2, and its reading head stays in x. As another example, if $q \in Q^\wedge$ and $\delta(q,\sigma) = q_1$, then $\mathcal{A}$ sends a copy in state q_1 to every son of x. Note that different copies of $\mathcal{A}$ may have their reading head pointing to the same node of the input tree. Formally, a *run* of $\mathcal{A}$ on a Σ-labeled $\mathcal{D}$-tree $\langle T,V \rangle$ is a $(T \times Q)$-labeled $\mathbb{IN}$-tree $\langle T_r,r \rangle$. A node in T_r labeled by (x,q) describes a copy of $\mathcal{A}$ in state q that reads the node x of T. A run has to satisfy $r(\varepsilon) = (\varepsilon, q_0)$ and, for all $y \in T_r$ with $r(y) = (x,q)$, the following hold:

– If $q \in Q^\wedge$ (resp. $q \in Q^\vee$) and $\delta(q,V(x)) = p$, then for each son (resp. for exactly one son) $x \cdot d$ of x, there is a node $y \cdot i \in T_r$ with $r(y \cdot i) = (x \cdot d, p)$.
– If $q \in Q^{(\varepsilon,\wedge)}$ (resp. $q \in Q^{(\varepsilon,\vee)}$) and $\delta(q,V(x)) = \{p_0,...,p_k\}$, then for all $i \in \{0..k\}$ (resp. for one $i \in \{0..k\}$) the node $y \cdot i \in T_r$, and $r(y \cdot i) = (x, p_i)$;

A *parity condition* is given by means of a coloring function on the set of states. Formally, a *parity condition* is a function $F : Q \to C$, where $C = \{C_{min},...,C_{max}\} \subset \mathbb{IN}$ is a set of colors. The size $|C|$ of C is called the *index* of the automaton. For an SAPT, we also assume that the special state tt is given an even color, and ff is given an odd color. For an infinite path $\pi \subseteq T_r$ of a run $\langle T_r,r \rangle$, let $maxC(\pi)$ be the maximal color that appears infinitely often along π. Similarly, for a finite path π, we define $maxC(\pi)$ to be the maximal color that appears at least once in π. An infinite path $\pi \subseteq T_r$ satisfies the acceptance condition F iff $maxC(\pi)$ is even. A run $\langle T_r,r \rangle$ is accepting iff all its infinite paths satisfy F. The automaton $\mathcal{A}$ accepts an input tree $\langle T,V \rangle$ if there is an accepting run of $\mathcal{A}$ on $\langle T,V \rangle$. The language of $\mathcal{A}$, denoted $L(\mathcal{A})$, is the set of Σ-labeled $\mathcal{D}$-trees accepted by $\mathcal{A}$. We say that an automaton $\mathcal{A}$ is nonempty iff $L(\mathcal{A}) \neq \emptyset$.

A wide range of branching-time temporal logics can be translated to alternating tree automata (details can be found in [16]). In particular:

Theorem 1. *[11,16] Given a temporal-logic formula φ, it is possible to construct a SAPT $\mathcal{A}_\varphi$ such that $L(\mathcal{A}_\varphi)$ is exactly the set of trees satisfying φ. Moreover, (i) if φ is a μ-calculus formula, then $\mathcal{A}_\varphi$ is an alternating parity automaton with $O(|\varphi|)$ states and index $O(|\varphi|)$; and (ii) if φ is an LTL formula, then $\mathcal{A}_\varphi$ is a universal parity automaton with $2^{O(|\varphi|)}$ states, and index 2.*

3   Hierarchical Transducers

In this section, we introduce *hierarchical transducers* (alternatively, *hierarchical Moore machines*), which are a generalization of classical transducers in which repeated sub-structures (technically, *sub-transducers*) are specified only once. Technically, some of the states in a hierarchical transducer are *boxes*, in which inner hierarchical transducers are nested. Formally, a hierarchical transducer is a tuple $\mathcal{K} = \langle \Sigma_I, \Sigma_O, \langle \mathcal{K}_1, ..., \mathcal{K}_n \rangle \rangle$, where Σ_I and Σ_O are respectively non-empty sets of input and output letters, and for every $1 \leq i \leq n$, the sub-transducer $\mathcal{K}_i = \langle W_i, \mathcal{B}_i, in_i, Exit_i, \tau_i, \delta_i, \Lambda_i \rangle$ has the following elements.

- W_i is a finite set of *states*. $in_i \in W_i$ is an *initial state*[2], and $Exit_i \subseteq W_i$ is a set of *exit-states*. States in $W_i \setminus Exit_i$ are called *internal states*.
- A finite set $\mathcal{B}_i$ of *boxes*. We assume that $W_1, ..., W_n, \mathcal{B}_1, ..., \mathcal{B}_n$ are pairwise disjoint.
- An *indexing function* $\tau_i : \mathcal{B}_i \to \{i+1, ..., n\}$ that maps each box of the i-th sub-transducer to a sub-transducer with an index greater than i. If $\tau_i(b) = j$ we say that b *refers* to $\mathcal{K}_j$.
- A *transition function* $\delta_i : (\bigcup_{b \in \mathcal{B}_i}(\{b\} \times Exit_{\tau_i(b)}) \cup (W_i \setminus Exit_i)) \times \Sigma_I \to W_i \cup \mathcal{B}_i$. Thus, when the transducer is at an internal state $u \in (W_i \setminus Exit_i)$, or at an exit e of a box b, and it reads an input letter $\sigma \in \Sigma_I$, it moves either to a state $s \in W_i$, or to a box $b' \in \mathcal{B}_i$. A move to a box b' implicitly leads to the unique initial state of the sub-transducer that b' refers to.
- A *labeling function* $\Lambda_i : W_i \to \Sigma_O$ that maps states to output letters.

The sub-transducer $\mathcal{K}_1$ is called the *top-level* sub-transducer of $\mathcal{K}$. Thus, for example, the top-level boxes of $\mathcal{K}$ are the elements of $\mathcal{B}_1$, etc. We also call in_1 the initial state of $\mathcal{K}$, and $Exit_1$ the *exits* of $\mathcal{K}$. For technical convenience we sometimes refer to functions (like the transitions and labeling functions) as relations, and in particular, we consider $\emptyset$ to be a function with an empty domain. Note that the fact that boxes can refer only to sub-transducers of a greater index implies that the nesting depth of transducers is finite. In contrast, in the *recursive* setting such a restriction does not exist. Also note that moves from an exit $e \in Exit_i$ of a sub-transducer $\mathcal{K}_i$ are not specified by the transition function δ_i of $\mathcal{K}_i$, but rather by the transition functions of the sub-transducers that contain boxes that refer to $\mathcal{K}_i$. The exits of $\mathcal{K}$ allow us to use it as a sub-transducer of another hierarchical transducer. When we say that a hierarchical transducer $\mathcal{K} = \langle \Sigma_I, \Sigma_O, \langle \mathcal{K}_1, ..., \mathcal{K}_n \rangle \rangle$ is a sub-transducer of another hierarchical transducer $\mathcal{K}' = \langle \Sigma_I, \Sigma_O, \langle \mathcal{K}'_1, ..., \mathcal{K}'_{n'} \rangle \rangle$, we mean that $\{\mathcal{K}_1, ..., \mathcal{K}_n\} \subseteq \{\mathcal{K}'_2, ..., \mathcal{K}'_{n'}\}$. The size $|\mathcal{K}_i|$ of a sub-transducer $\mathcal{K}_i$ is the sum $|W_i| + |\mathcal{B}_i| + |\delta_i|$. The size $|\mathcal{K}|$ of $\mathcal{K}$ is the sum of the sizes of its sub-transducers. We sometimes abuse notation and refer to the *hierarchical transducer* $\mathcal{K}_i$ which is formally the hierarchical transducer $\langle \Sigma_I, \Sigma_O, \langle \mathcal{K}_i, \mathcal{K}_{i+1}, ..., \mathcal{K}_n \rangle \rangle$ obtained by taking $\mathcal{K}_i$ to be the top-level sub-transducer.

Flat Transducers.   A sub-transducer without boxes is *flat*. A hierarchical transducer $\mathcal{K} = \langle \Sigma_I, \Sigma_O, \langle W, \emptyset, in, Exit, \emptyset, \delta, \Lambda \rangle \rangle$ with a single (hence flat) sub-transducer is flat, and

---

[2] We assume a single entry for each sub-transducer. Multiple entries can be handled by duplicating sub-transducers.

we denote it using the shorter notation $\mathcal{K} = \langle \Sigma_I, \Sigma_O, \langle W, in, Exit, \delta, \Lambda \rangle \rangle$. Each hierarchical transducer $\mathcal{K}$ can be transformed into an equivalent flat transducer $\mathcal{K}^f = \langle \Sigma_I, \Sigma_O, \langle W^f, in_1, Exit_1, \delta^f, \Lambda^f \rangle \rangle$ (called its *flat expansion*) by recursively substituting each box by a copy of the sub-transducer it refers to. Since different boxes can refer to the same sub-transducer, states may appear in different contexts. In order to obtain unique names for states in the flat expansion, we prefix each copy of a sub-transducer's state by the sequence of boxes through which it is reached. Thus, a state $(b_0, ..., b_k, w)$ of $\mathcal{K}^f$ is a vector whose last component w is a state in $\cup_{i=1}^n W_i$, and the remaining components $(b_0, ..., b_k)$ are boxes that describe its context. The labeling of a state $(b_0, ..., b_k, w)$ is determined by its last component w. For simplicity, we refer to vectors of length one as elements (that is, w, rather than (w)).[3] Formally, given a hierarchical transducer $\mathcal{K} = \langle \Sigma_I, \Sigma_O, \langle \mathcal{K}_1, ..., \mathcal{K}_n \rangle \rangle$, for each sub-transducer $\mathcal{K}_i = \langle W_i, \mathcal{B}_i, in_i, Exit_i, \tau_i, \delta_i, \Lambda_i \rangle$ we inductively define its flat expansion $\mathcal{K}_i^f = \langle W_i^f, in_i, Exit_i, \delta_i^f, \Lambda_i^f \rangle$ as follows.

- The set of states $W_i^f \subseteq W_i \cup (\mathcal{B}_i \times (\bigcup_{j=i+1}^n W_j^f))$ is defined as follows: (i) if w is a state of W_i then w belongs to W_i^f; and (ii) if b is a box of $\mathcal{K}_i$ with $\tau_i(b) = j$, and the tuple $(u_1, ..., u_h)$ is a state in W_j^f, then $(b, u_1, ..., u_h)$ belongs to W_i^f.
- The transition function δ_i^f is defined as follows: (i) If $\delta_i(u, \sigma) = v$, where $u \in W_i$, or $u = (b, e)$ with $b \in \mathcal{B}_i$ and $e \in Exit_{\tau_i(b)}$, then if v is a state, we have that $\delta_i^f(u, \sigma) = v$; and if v is a box, we have that $\delta_i^f(u, \sigma) = (v, in_{\tau_i(v)})$. Note that $(v, in_{\tau_i(v)})$ is indeed a state of W_i^f by the second item in the definition of states above; and (ii) if b is a box of $\mathcal{K}_i$, and $\delta_{\tau_i(b)}^f((u_1, ..., u_h), \sigma) = (v_1, ..., v_{h'})$ is a transition of $\mathcal{K}_{\tau_i(b)}^f$, then $\delta_i^f((b, u_1, ..., u_h), \sigma) = (b, v_1, ..., v_{h'})$ is a transition of $\mathcal{K}_i^f$.
- Finally, if $u \in W_i$ then $\Lambda_i^f(u) = \Lambda_i(u)$; and if $u \in W_i^f$ is of the form $u = (b, u_1, ..., u_h)$, where $b \in \mathcal{B}_i$, then $\Lambda_i(u) = \Lambda_{\tau_i(b)}^f(u_1, ..., u_h)$.

The transducer $\langle \Sigma_I, \Sigma_O, \langle \mathcal{K}_1^f \rangle \rangle$ is the required flat expansion $\mathcal{K}^f$ of $\mathcal{K}$. An *atomic transducer* is a flat transducer made up of a single node that serves as both an entry and an exit. For each letter $\varsigma \in \Sigma_O$ there is an atomic transducer $K_\varsigma = \langle \{p\}, p, \{p\}, \emptyset, \{(p, \varsigma)\} \rangle$ whose single state p is labeled by ς.

Run of a Hierarchical Transducer. Consider a hierarchical transducer $\mathcal{K}$ with $Exit_1 = \emptyset$ that interacts with its environment. At point j in time, the environment provides $\mathcal{K}$ with an input $\sigma_j \in \Sigma_I$, and in response $\mathcal{K}$ moves to a new state, according to its transition relation, and outputs the label of that state. The result of this infinite interaction is a computation of $\mathcal{K}$, called the *trace* of the run of $\mathcal{K}$ on the word $\sigma_1 \cdot \sigma_2 \cdots$. In the case that $Exit_1 \neq \emptyset$, the interaction comes to a halt whenever $\mathcal{K}$ reaches an exit $e \in Exit_1$, since top-level exits have no outgoing transitions. Formally, a *run* of a hierarchical transducer $\mathcal{K}$ is defined by means of its flat expansion $\mathcal{K}^f$. Given a finite input word $v = \sigma_1 \cdots \sigma_m \in \Sigma_I^*$, a *run (computation)* of $\mathcal{K}$ on v is a sequence of states $r = r_0 \cdots r_m \in (W^f)^*$ such that $r_0 = in_1$, and $r_j = \delta^f(r_{j-1}, \sigma_j)$, for all $0 < j \leq m$. Note that since $\mathcal{K}$ is deterministic it has at most one run on every word, and that if $Exit_1 \neq \emptyset$ then $\mathcal{K}$ may not have a run on some words. The *trace* of the run of $\mathcal{K}$ on v is the word of

---

[3] A helpful way to think about this is using a stack — the boxes $b_0, ..., b_k$ are pushed into the stack whenever a sub-transducer is called, and are popped in the corresponding exit.

inputs and outputs $trc(\mathcal{K},v) = (\Lambda^f(r_1),\sigma_1)\cdots(\Lambda^f(r_m),\sigma_m) \in (\Sigma_O \times \Sigma_I)^*$. The notions of traces and runs are extended to infinite words in the natural way.

The computations of $\mathcal{K}$ can be described by a *computation tree* whose branches correspond to the runs of $\mathcal{K}$ on all possible inputs, and whose labeling gives the traces of these runs. Note that the root of the tree corresponds to the empty word ε, and its labeling is not part of any trace. However, if we look at the computation tree of $\mathcal{K}$ as a sub-tree of a computation tree of a transducer $\mathcal{K}'$ of which $\mathcal{K}$ is a sub-transducer, then the labeling of the root of the computation tree of $\mathcal{K}$ is meaningful, and it corresponds to the last element in the trace of the run of $\mathcal{K}'$ leading to the initial state of $\mathcal{K}$. Formally, given $\sigma \in \Sigma_I$, the computation tree $\mathcal{T}_{\mathcal{K},\sigma} = \langle T_{\mathcal{K},\sigma}, V_{\mathcal{K},\sigma} \rangle$, is a $(\Sigma_O \times \Sigma_I)$-labeled $(W^f \times \Sigma_I)$-tree, where: *(i)* the root ε is labeled by $(\Lambda^f(in_1),\sigma)$; *(ii)* a node $y = (r_1,\sigma_1)\cdots(r_m,\sigma_m) \in (W^f \times \Sigma_I)^+$ is in $T_{\mathcal{K},\sigma}$ iff $in_1 \cdot r_1 \cdots r_m$ is the run of $\mathcal{K}$ on $v = \sigma_1 \cdots \sigma_m$, and its label is $V_{\mathcal{K},\sigma}(y) = (\Lambda^f(r_m),\sigma_m)$. Thus, for a node y, the labels of the nodes on the path from the root (excluding the root) to y are exactly $trc(\mathcal{K},v)$. Observe that the leaves of $\mathcal{T}_{\mathcal{K},\sigma}$ correspond to pairs (e,σ'), where $e \in Exit_1$ and $\sigma' \in \Sigma_I$. However, if $Exit_1 = \emptyset$, then the tree has no leaves, and it represents the runs of $\mathcal{K}$ over all words in Σ_I^*. We sometimes consider a leaner computation tree $\mathcal{T}_{\mathcal{K}} = \langle T_{\mathcal{K}}, V_{\mathcal{K}} \rangle$ that is a Σ_O-labeled Σ_I-tree, where a node $y \in \Sigma_I^+$ is in $T_{\mathcal{K}}$ iff there is a run r of $\mathcal{K}$ on y. The label of such a node is $V_{\mathcal{K}}(y) = \Lambda^f(last(r)))$ and the label of the root is $\Lambda^f(in_1)$. Observe that for every $\sigma \in \Sigma_I$, the tree $\mathcal{T}_{\mathcal{K}}$ can be obtained from $\mathcal{T}_{\mathcal{K},\sigma}$ by simply deleting the first component of the directions of $\mathcal{T}_{\mathcal{K},\sigma}$, and the second component of the labels of $\mathcal{T}_{\mathcal{K},\sigma}$.

Recall that the labeling of the root of a computation tree of $\mathcal{K}$ is not part of any trace (when it is not a sub-tree of another tree). Hence, in the definition below, we arbitrarily fix some letter $\rho \in \Sigma_I$. Given a temporal logic formula φ, over the atomic propositions AP where $2^{AP} = \Sigma_O \times \Sigma_I$, we have the following:

Definition 1. *A hierarchical transducer* $\mathcal{K} = \langle \Sigma_I, \Sigma_O, \langle \mathcal{K}_1,...,\mathcal{K}_n \rangle \rangle$, *with* $Exit_1 = \emptyset$, *satisfies a formula* φ *(written* $\mathcal{K} \models \varphi$*), iff the tree* $\mathcal{T}_{\mathcal{K},\rho}$ *satisfies* φ.

Observe that given φ, finding a flat transducer $\mathcal{K}$ such that $\mathcal{K} \models \varphi$ is the classic synthesis problem studied (for LTL formulas) in [23].

A *library* L is a finite set of hierarchical transducers with the same input and output alphabets. Formally, $L = \{\mathcal{K}^1,...,\mathcal{K}^\lambda\}$, and for every $1 \leq i \leq \lambda$, we have that $\mathcal{K}^i = \langle \Sigma_I, \Sigma_O, \langle \mathcal{K}_1^i,...,\mathcal{K}_{n_i}^i \rangle \rangle$. Note that a transducer in the library can be a sub-transducer of another one, or share common sub-transducers with it. The set of transducers in L that have no top-level exits is denoted by $L^{=\emptyset} = \{\mathcal{K}^i \in L : Exit_1^i = \emptyset\}$, and its complement is $L^{\neq\emptyset} = L \setminus L^{=\emptyset}$.

4 Hierarchical Synthesis

In this section, we describe our synthesis algorithm. We start by providing the algorithm with an initial library L_0 of hierarchical transducers. A good starting point is to include in L_0 all the atomic transducers, as well as any other relevant hierarchical transducers, for example from a standard library. We then proceed by synthesizing in rounds. At each round $i \geq 0$, the system designer provides a specification formula φ_i of the currently desired hierarchical transducer $\mathcal{K}^i$, which is then automatically synthesized using the transducers in L_{i-1} as possible sub-transducers. Once a new transducer is synthesized it is added to the library, for use in subsequent rounds. Technically, the hierarchical transducer synthesized in the last round as the output of the algorithm.

Input: An initial library $\mathcal{L}_0$, and a list of specification formulas $\varphi_1, ..., \varphi_m$
Output: A hierarchical transducer satisfying φ_m
for $i = 1$ to m **do**
    synthesize $\mathcal{K}^i$ satisfying φ_i using the transducers in $\mathcal{L}_{i-1}$ as sub-transducers
    $\mathcal{L}_i \leftarrow \mathcal{L}_{i-1} \cup \{\mathcal{K}^i\}$
end
return $\mathcal{K}^m$

Algorithm 1. Hierarchical Synthesis Algorithm

The main challenge in implementing the above hierarchical synthesis algorithm is of course coming up with an algorithm for performing the synthesis step of a single round. As noted in Section 1, a transducer that was synthesized in a previous round has no top-level exits, which severely limits its ability to serve as a sub-transducer of another transducer. Our single-round algorithm must therefore address the problem of synthesizing exits for such transducers. In Section 4.1, we give our core algorithm for single-round synthesis of a hierarchical transducer from a given library of hierarchical transducers. In Section 4.2, we address the problem of enforcing modularity, and add some more information regarding the synthesis of exits. Finally, in Section 4.3, we address the problem of synthesis with imperfect information.

4.1 Hierarchical Synthesis from a Library

We now formally present the problem of hierarchical synthesis from a library (that may have transducers without top-level exits) of a single temporal logic formula. Given a transducer $\mathcal{K} = \langle \Sigma_I, \Sigma_O, \langle \mathcal{K}_1, ..., \mathcal{K}_n \rangle \rangle \in \mathcal{L}^{=0}$, where $\mathcal{K}_1 = \langle W_1, \mathcal{B}_1, in_1, \emptyset, \tau_1, \delta_1, \Lambda_1 \rangle$, and a set $E \subseteq W_1$, the transducer $\mathcal{K}^E$ is obtained from $\mathcal{K}$ by setting E to be the set of top-level exits, and removing all the outgoing edges from states in E. Formally, $\mathcal{K}^E = \langle \Sigma_I, \Sigma_O, \langle \langle W_1, \mathcal{B}_1, in_1, E, \tau_1, \delta'_1, \Lambda_1 \rangle, \mathcal{K}_2, ..., \mathcal{K}_n \rangle \rangle$, where the transition relation δ'_1 is the restriction of δ_1 to sources in $W_1 \setminus E$. For convenience, given a transducer $\mathcal{K} \in \mathcal{L}^{\neq 0}$ we sometimes refer to it as $\mathcal{K}^{Exit_1}$. For every $\mathcal{K} \in \mathcal{L}$, we assume some fixed ordering on the top-level states of $\mathcal{K}$, and given a set $E \subseteq W_1$, and a state $e \in E$, we denote by $idx(e, E)$ the relative position of e in E, according to this ordering. Given a library $\mathcal{L}$, and an upper bound $el \in \mathbb{N}$ on the number of allowed top-level exits, we let $\mathcal{L}^{el} = \mathcal{L}^{\neq 0} \cup \{\mathcal{K}^E : \mathcal{K} \in \mathcal{L}^{=0} \wedge |E| \leq el\}$. The higher the number el, the more exits the synthesis algorithm is allowed to synthesize, and the longer it may take to run. As we show later, el should be at most polynomial[4] in the size of φ. In general, we assume that el is never smaller than the number of exits in any sub-transducer of any hierarchical transducer in $\mathcal{L}$. Hence, for every $\mathcal{K}^E \in \mathcal{L}^{el}$ and every $e \in E$, we have that $1 \leq idx(e, E) \leq el$.

Definition 2. *Given a library $\mathcal{L}$ and a bound $el \in \mathbb{N}$, we say that:*

---

[4] In practical terms, the exits of a sub-module represent its set of possible return values. Since finite state modules are usually not expected to have return values over large domains (such as the set of integers), we believe that our polynomial bound for el is not too restrictive.

- A *hierarchical transducer* $\mathcal{K} = \langle \Sigma_I, \Sigma_O, \langle \mathcal{K}_1, \ldots \mathcal{K}_n \rangle \rangle$ is $\langle L, el \rangle$-*composed if (i) for every* $2 \leq i \leq n$, *we have that* $\mathcal{K}_i \in L^{el}$; *(ii) if* $w \in W_1$ *is a top-level state, then the atomic transducer* $K_{\Lambda_1(w)}$ *is in* L.
- A *formula* φ *is* $\langle L, el \rangle$-*realizable iff there is an* $\langle L, el \rangle$-*composed hierarchical transducer* $\mathcal{K}$ *that satisfies* φ. *The* $\langle L, el \rangle$-*synthesis problem is to find such a* $\mathcal{K}$.

Intuitively, an $\langle L, el \rangle$-composed hierarchical transducer $\mathcal{K}$ is built by synthesizing its top-level sub-transducer $\mathcal{K}_1$, which specifies how to connect boxes that refer to transducers from L^{el}. To eliminate an unnecessary level of indirection, boxes that refer to atomic transducers are replaced by regular states. Note that this also solves the technical problem that, by definition, the initial state in_1 cannot be a box. This is also the reason why we assume from now on that every library has at least one atomic transducer. Note that for each transducer $\mathcal{K}' \in L^{=0}$ we can have as many as $\Omega(|\mathcal{K}'|)^{el}$ copies of $\mathcal{K}'$ in L^{el}, each with a different set of exit states. In Section 4.2 we show how, when we synthesize $\mathcal{K}$, we can limit the number of such copies that $\mathcal{K}$ uses to any desired value (usually one per $\mathcal{K}'$).

Connectivity Trees. In the classical automata-theoretic approach to synthesis [23], synthesis is reduced to finding a regular tree that is a witness to the non-emptiness of a suitable tree automaton. Here, we also reduce synthesis to the non-emptiness problem of a tree automaton. However, unlike the classical approach, we build an automaton whose input is not a computation tree, but rather a system description in the form of a *connectivity tree* (inspired by the "control-flow" trees of [18]), which describes how to connect library components in a way that satisfies the specification formula. Specifically, given a library $L = \{\mathcal{K}^1, \ldots, \mathcal{K}^\lambda\}$ and a bound $el \in \mathbb{N}$, connectivity trees represent hierarchical transducers that are $\langle L, el \rangle$-composed, in the sense that every regular $\langle L, el \rangle$-composed hierarchical transducer induces a connectivity tree, and vice versa. Formally, a *connectivity tree* $\mathcal{T} = \langle T, V \rangle$ for L and el, is an L^{el}-labeled complete $(\{1, \ldots, el\} \times \Sigma_I)$-tree, where the root is labeled by an atomic transducer.

Intuitively, a node x with $V(x) = \mathcal{K}^E$ represents a top-level state q if $\mathcal{K}^E$ is an atomic transducer, and otherwise it represents a top-level box b that refers to $\mathcal{K}^E$. The label of a son $x \cdot (idx(e, E), \sigma)$ specifies the destination of the transition from the exit e of b (or from a state q, if $\mathcal{K}^E$ is atomic — in which case it has a single exit) when reading σ. Sons $x \cdot (i, e)$, for which $i > |E|$, are ignored. Thus, a path $\pi = (i_0, \sigma_0) \cdot (i_1, \sigma_1) \cdots$ in a connectivity tree $\mathcal{T}$ is called *meaningful*, iff for every $j > 0$, we have that i_j is not larger than the number of top-level exits of $V(i_{j-1}, \sigma_{j-1})$.

A connectivity tree $\mathcal{T} = \langle T, V \rangle$ is *regular* if there is a flat transducer $\mathcal{M} = \langle \{1, \ldots, el\} \times \Sigma_I, L^{el}, \langle M, m_0, \emptyset, \delta^T, \Lambda^T \rangle \rangle$, such that $\mathcal{T}$ is equal to the (lean) computation tree $\mathcal{T}_{\mathcal{M}}$. A regular connectivity tree induces an $\langle L, el \rangle$-composed hierarchical transducer $\mathcal{K}$, whose top-level sub-transducer $\mathcal{K}_1$ is basically a replica of $\mathcal{M}$ (see the full version at the authors' web page for the reverse transformation). Every node $m \in M$ becomes a state of $\mathcal{K}_1$ if $\Lambda^T(m)$ is an atomic-transducer and, otherwise, it becomes a box of $\mathcal{K}_1$ which refers to the top-level sub-transducer of $\Lambda^T(m)$. The destination of a transition from an exit e of a box m, with $\Lambda^T(m) = \mathcal{K}^E$, when reading a letter $\sigma \in \Sigma_I$, is given by $\delta^T(m, (idx(e, E), \sigma))$. If m is a state, then $\Lambda^T(m)$ is an atomic transducer with a single exit and thus, the destination of a transition from m when reading a letter $\sigma \in \Sigma_I$, is given by $\delta^T(m, (1, \sigma))$. For a box b of $\mathcal{K}_1$, let $\Lambda^T(b) = \langle \Sigma_I, \Sigma_O, \langle \mathcal{K}_{(b,1)}, \ldots \mathcal{K}_{(b,n_b)} \rangle \rangle$, and denote by $sub(b) = \{\mathcal{K}_{(b,1)}, \dots \mathcal{K}_{(b,n_b)}\}$ the set of sub-transducers of $\Lambda^T(b)$, and by $E(b)$ the set of top-level exits of $\Lambda^T(b)$. Formally, $\mathcal{K} = \langle \Sigma_I, \Sigma_O, \langle \mathcal{K}_1, \dots, \mathcal{K}_a \rangle \rangle$, where $\mathcal{K}_1 = \langle W_1, \mathcal{B}_1, m_0, \tau_1, \delta_1, \Lambda_1 \rangle$, and:

- $W_1 = \{w \in M : \exists \varsigma \in \Sigma_O \text{ s.t. } \Lambda^T(w) = K_\varsigma\}$. Note that since the root of a connectivity tree is labeled by an atomic transducer then $m_0 \in W_1$.
- $\mathcal{B}_1 = M \setminus W_1$.
- The sub-transducers $\{\mathcal{K}_2, \dots, \mathcal{K}_a\} = \bigcup_{\{b \in B_1\}} sub(b)$.
- For $b \in \mathcal{B}_1$, we have that $\tau_1(b) = i$, where i is such that $\mathcal{K}_i = \mathcal{K}_{(b,1)}$.
- For $w \in W_1$, and $\sigma \in \Sigma_I$, we have that $\delta_1(w, \sigma) = \delta^T(w, (1, \sigma))$.
- For $b \in \mathcal{B}_1$, we have that $\delta_1((b, e), \sigma) = \delta^T(b, (idx(e, E(b)), \sigma))$, for every $e \in E(b)$ and $\sigma \in \Sigma_I$.
- Finally, for $w \in W_1$ we have that $\Lambda_1(w) = \varsigma$, where ς is such that $\Lambda^T(w) = K_\varsigma$.

From Synthesis to Automata Emptiness. Given a library $L = \{\mathcal{K}^1, \dots, \mathcal{K}^\lambda\}$, a bound $el \in \mathbb{N}$, and a temporal logic formula φ, our aim is to build an APT $\mathcal{A}_\varphi^T$ such that $\mathcal{A}_\varphi^T$ accepts a regular connectivity tree $T = \langle T, V \rangle$ iff it induces a hierarchical transducer $\mathcal{K}$ such that $\mathcal{K} \models \varphi$. Recall that by Definition 1 and Theorem 1, $\mathcal{K} \models \varphi$ iff $T_{\mathcal{K}, \rho}$ is accepted by the SAPT $\mathcal{A}_\varphi$. The basic idea is thus to have $\mathcal{A}_\varphi^T$ simulate all possible runs of $\mathcal{A}_\varphi$ on $T_{\mathcal{K}, \rho}$. Unfortunately, since $\mathcal{A}_\varphi^T$ has as its input not $T_{\mathcal{K}, \rho}$, but the connectivity tree T, this is not a trivial task. In order to see how we can solve this problem, we first have to make the following observation.

Let $T = \langle T, V \rangle$ be a regular connectivity tree, and let $\mathcal{K}$ be the hierarchical transducer that it induces. Consider a node $u \in T_{\mathcal{K}, \rho}$ with $last(u) = ((b, in_{\tau_1(b)}), \sigma)$, where b is some top-level box, or state[5], of $\mathcal{K}$ that refers to some transducer $\mathcal{K}^E$ (note that the root of $T_{\mathcal{K}, \rho}$ is such a node). Observe that the sub-tree T^u, rooted at u, represents the traces of computations of $\mathcal{K}$ that start from the initial state of $\mathcal{K}^E$, in the context of the box b. The sub-tree $prune(T^u)$, obtained by pruning every path in T^u at the first node $\hat{u}$, with $last(\hat{u}) = ((b, e), \hat{\sigma})$ for some $e \in E$ and $\hat{\sigma} \in \Sigma_I$, represents the portions of these traces that stay inside $\mathcal{K}^E$. Note that $prune(T^u)$ is essentially independent of the context b in which $\mathcal{K}^E$ appears, and is isomorphic to the tree $T_{\mathcal{K}^E, \sigma}$ (the isomorphism being to simply drop the component b from every letter in the name of every node in $prune(T^u)$). Moreover, every son v (in $T_{\mathcal{K}, \rho}$), of such a leaf $\hat{u}$ of $prune(T^u)$, is of the same form as u. I.e., $last(v) = ((b', in_{\tau_1(b')}), \sigma')$, where $b' = \delta_1((b, e), \sigma')$ is a top-level box (or state) of $\mathcal{K}$. It follows that $T_{\mathcal{K}, \rho}$ is isomorphic to a concatenation of sub-trees of the form $T_{\mathcal{K}^E, \sigma}$, where the transition from a leaf of one such sub-tree to the root of another is specified by the transition relation δ_1, and is thus given explicitly by the connectivity tree T.

The last observation is the key to how $\mathcal{A}_\varphi^T$ can simulate, while reading T, all the possible runs of $\mathcal{A}_\varphi$ on $T_{\mathcal{K}, \rho}$. The general idea is as follows. Consider a node u of $T_{\mathcal{K}, \rho}$ such that $prune(T^u)$ is isomorphic to $T_{\mathcal{K}^E, \sigma}$. A copy of $\mathcal{A}_\varphi^T$ that reads a node y of T labeled by $\mathcal{K}^E$ can easily simulate, without consuming any input, all the portions of the runs of any copy of $\mathcal{A}_\varphi$ that start by reading u and remain inside $prune(T^u)$. This simulation can be done by simply constructing $T_{\mathcal{K}^E, \sigma}$ on the fly and running $\mathcal{A}_\varphi$ on it.

---

[5] Here we think of top-level states of $\mathcal{K}$ as boxes that refer to atomic transducers.

For every simulated copy of $\mathcal{A}_\varphi$ that reaches a leaf $\hat{u}$ of $prune(\mathcal{T}^u)$, (recall that $last(\hat{u})$ is of the form $((b,e),\hat{\sigma}))$, the automaton $\mathcal{A}_\varphi^{\mathcal{T}}$ sends copies of itself to the sons of y in the connectivity tree, in order to continue the simulation on the different sub-trees rooted at sons of $\hat{u}$ in $T_{\mathcal{K},\rho}$. The simulation of a copy of $\mathcal{A}_\varphi$ that proceeds to a son $v = \hat{u} \cdot ((b',in_{\tau_1(b')}),\sigma')$, where b' is a top-level box (or state) of $\mathcal{K}$, is handled by a copy of $\mathcal{A}_\varphi^{\mathcal{T}}$ that is sent to the son $z = y \cdot (idx(e,E),\sigma')$.

Our construction of $\mathcal{A}_\varphi^{\mathcal{T}}$ implements the above idea, with one main modification. In order to obtain optimal complexity in successive rounds of Algorithm 1, it is important to keep the size of $\mathcal{A}_\varphi^{\mathcal{T}}$ independent of the size of the transducers in the library. Unfortunately, simulating the runs of $\mathcal{A}_\varphi$ on $\mathcal{T}_{\mathcal{K}^E,\sigma}$ on the fly would require an embedding of $\mathcal{K}^E$ inside $\mathcal{A}_\varphi^{\mathcal{T}}$. Recall, however, that no input is consumed by $\mathcal{A}_\varphi^{\mathcal{T}}$ while running such a simulation. Hence, we can perform these simulations offline instead, in the process of building the transition relation of $\mathcal{A}_\varphi^{\mathcal{T}}$. Obviously, this requires a way of summarizing the possibly infinite number of runs of $\mathcal{A}_\varphi$ on $\mathcal{T}_{\mathcal{K}^E,\sigma}$, which we do by employing the concept of summary functions from [6].

First, we define an ordering $\succeq$ on colors by letting $c \succeq c'$ when c is better, from the point of view of acceptance by $\mathcal{A}_\varphi$, than c'. Formally, $c \succeq c'$ if the following holds: if c' is even then c is even and $c \geq c'$; and if c' is odd then either c is even, or c is also odd and $c \leq c'$. We denote by $\min^{\succeq}$ the operation of taking the minimal color, according to $\succeq$, of a finite set of colors. Let $\mathcal{A}_\varphi = \langle \Sigma_O \times \Sigma_I, Q_\varphi, q_\varphi^0, \delta_\varphi, F_\varphi \rangle$, let $\mathcal{A}_\varphi^q$ be the automaton $\mathcal{A}_\varphi$ using $q \in Q$ as an initial state, and let C be the set of colors used in the acceptance condition F_φ. Consider a run $\langle T_r, r \rangle$ of $\mathcal{A}_\varphi^q$ on $\mathcal{T}_{\mathcal{K}^E,\sigma}$. Note that if $z \in T_r$ is a leaf, then $last(r(z)) = ((e,\sigma'),q)$, where $q \in Q_\varphi^{\vee,\wedge}$ (i.e., q is not an ε-state), and $e \in E$. We define a function $g_r : E \times \Sigma_I \times Q_\varphi^{\vee,\wedge} \to C \cup \{\dashv\}$, called the *summary function* of $\langle T_r, r \rangle$, which summarizes this run. Given $h \in E \times \Sigma_I \times Q_\varphi^{\vee,\wedge}$, if there is no leaf $z \in T_r$, such that $last(r(z)) = h$, then $g_r(h) = \dashv$; otherwise, $g_r(h) = c$, where c is the maximal color encountered by the copy of $\mathcal{A}_\varphi$ which made the least progress towards satisfying the acceptance condition, among all copies that reach a leaf $z \in T_r$ with $last(r(z)) = h$. Formally, let $paths(r,h)$ be the set of all the paths in $\langle T_r, r \rangle$ that end in a leaf $z \in T_r$, with $last(r(z)) = h$. Then, $g_r(h) = \dashv$ if $paths(r,h) = \emptyset$ and, otherwise, $g_r(h) = \min^{\succeq}\{maxC(\pi) : \pi \in paths(r,h)\}$.

Let $Sf(\mathcal{K}^E,\sigma,q)$ be the set of summary functions of the runs of $\mathcal{A}_\varphi^q$ on $\mathcal{T}_{\mathcal{K}^E,\sigma}$. If $\mathcal{T}_{\mathcal{K}^E,\sigma}$ has no leaves, then $Sf(\mathcal{K}^E,\sigma,q)$ contains only the empty summary function ε. For $g \in Sf(\mathcal{K}^E,\sigma,q)$, let $g^{\neq\dashv} = \{h \in E \times \Sigma_I \times Q_\varphi^{\vee,\wedge} : g(h) \neq \dashv\}$. Based on the ordering $\succeq$ we defined for colors, we can define a partial order $\succeq$ on $Sf(\mathcal{K}^E,\sigma,q)$, by letting $g \succeq g'$ if for every $h \in (E \times \Sigma_I \times Q_\varphi^{\vee,\wedge})$ the following holds: $g(h) = \dashv$, or $g(h) \neq \dashv \neq g'(h)$ and $g(h) \succeq g'(h)$. Observe that if r and r' are two non-rejecting runs, and $g_r \succ g_{r'}$, then extending r to an accepting run on a tree that extends $\mathcal{T}_{\mathcal{K}^E,\sigma}$ is always not harder than extending r' - either because $\mathcal{A}_\varphi$ has less copies at the leaves of r, or because these copies encountered better maximal colors. Given a summary function g, we say that a run $\langle T_r, r \rangle$ *achieves* g if $g_r \succeq g$; we say that g is *feasible* if there is a run $\langle T_r, r \rangle$ that achieves it; and we say that g is *relevant* if it can be achieved by a memoryless[6] run

---

[6] A run of an automaton $\mathcal{A}$ is memoryless if two copies of $\mathcal{A}$ that are in the same state, and read the same input node, behave in the same way on the rest of the input.

that is not rejecting (i.e., by a run that has no infinite path that does not satisfy the acceptance condition of $\mathcal{A}_\varphi$). We denote by $Rel(\mathcal{K}^E, \sigma, q) \subseteq Sf(\mathcal{K}^E, \sigma, q)$ the set of relevant summary functions.

We are now ready to give a formal definition of the automaton $\mathcal{A}_\varphi^T$. Given a library $\mathcal{L} = \{\mathcal{K}^1, ..., \mathcal{K}^\lambda\}$, a bound $el \in \mathbb{N}$, and a temporal-logic formula φ, let $\mathcal{A}_\varphi = \langle \Sigma_O \times \Sigma_I, Q_\varphi, q_\varphi^0, \delta_\varphi, F_\varphi \rangle$, let $C = \{C_{min}, ..., C_{max}\}$ be the colors in the acceptance condition of $\mathcal{A}_\varphi$, and for $\mathcal{K}^E \in \mathcal{L}^{el}$, let Λ^E be the labeling function of the top-level sub-transducer of $\mathcal{K}^E$. The automaton $\mathcal{A}_\varphi^T = \langle \mathcal{L}^{el}, (\{1, ..., el\} \times \Sigma_I), (\Sigma_I \times Q_\varphi^{\vee, \wedge} \times C) \cup \{q_0\}, q_0, \delta, \alpha \rangle$, has the following elements:

- For every $\mathcal{K}^E \in \mathcal{L}^{el}$ we have that $\delta(q_0, \mathcal{K}^E) = \delta((\rho, q_\varphi^0, C_{min}), \mathcal{K}^E)$ if $\mathcal{K}^E$ is an atomic transducer and, otherwise, $\delta(q_0, \mathcal{K}^E) = \textbf{false}$.
- For every $(\sigma, q, c) \in \Sigma_I \times Q_\varphi^{\vee, \wedge} \times C$, and every $\mathcal{K}^E \in \mathcal{L}^{el}$, we have $\delta((\sigma, q, c), \mathcal{K}^E) = \bigvee_{g \in Rel(\mathcal{K}^E, \sigma, q)} \bigwedge_{(e, \hat{\sigma}, \hat{q}) \in g^{\neq \dashv}} \bigoplus_{\sigma' \in \Sigma_I} ((idx(e, E), \sigma'), (\sigma', \delta_\varphi(\hat{q}, (\Lambda^E(e), \hat{\sigma})), g(e, \hat{\sigma}, \hat{q})))$, where $\bigoplus = \bigwedge$ if $\hat{q} \in Q_\varphi^\wedge$, and $\bigoplus = \bigvee$ if $\hat{q} \in Q_\varphi^\vee$.
- $\alpha(q_0) = C_{min}$; and $\alpha((\sigma, q, c)) = c$, for every $(\sigma, q, c) \in \Sigma_I \times Q_\varphi^{\vee, \wedge} \times C$.

The construction above implies the following lemma:

Lemma 1. $\mathcal{A}_\varphi^T$ *accepts a regular connectivity tree* $\mathcal{T} = \langle T, V \rangle$ *iff* $\mathcal{T}$ *induces a hierarchical transducer* $\mathcal{K}$, *such that* $\mathcal{T}_{\mathcal{K}, \rho}$ *is accepted by* $\mathcal{A}_\varphi$.

Proof (sketch). Intuitively, $\mathcal{A}_\varphi^T$ first checks that the root of its input tree $\mathcal{T}$ is labeled by an atomic proposition (and is thus a connectivity tree), and then proceeds to simulate all the runs of $\mathcal{A}_\varphi$ on $\mathcal{T}_{\mathcal{K}, \rho}$. A copy of $\mathcal{A}_\varphi^T$ at a state (σ, q, c), that reads a node y of $\mathcal{T}$ labeled by $\mathcal{K}^E$, considers all the non-rejecting runs of $\mathcal{A}_\varphi^q$ on $\mathcal{T}_{\mathcal{K}^E, \sigma}$, by looking at the set $Rel(\mathcal{K}^E, \sigma, q)$ of summary functions for these runs. It then sends copies of $\mathcal{A}_\varphi^T$ to the sons of y to continue the simulation of copies of $\mathcal{A}_\varphi$ that reach the leaves of $\mathcal{T}_{\mathcal{K}^E, \sigma}$.

The logic behind the definition of $\delta((\sigma, q, c), \mathcal{K}^E)$ is as follows. Since every summary function $g \in Rel(\mathcal{K}^E, \sigma, q)$ summarizes at least one non-rejecting run, and it is enough that one such run can be extended to an accepting run of $\mathcal{A}_\varphi$ on the remainder of $\mathcal{T}_{\mathcal{K}, \rho}$, we have a disjunction on all $g \in Rel(\mathcal{K}^E, \sigma, q)$. Every $(e, \hat{\sigma}, \hat{q}) \in g^{\neq \dashv}$ represents one or more copies of $\mathcal{A}_\varphi$ at state $\hat{q}$ that are reading a leaf $\hat{u}$ of $\mathcal{T}_{\mathcal{K}^E, \sigma}$ with $last(\hat{u}) = (e, \hat{\sigma})$, and all these copies must accept their remainders of $\mathcal{T}_{\mathcal{K}, \rho}$. Hence, we have a conjunction over all $(e, \hat{\sigma}, \hat{q}) \in g^{\neq \dashv}$.

A copy of $\mathcal{A}_\varphi$ that starts at the root of $\mathcal{T}_{\mathcal{K}^E, \sigma}$ may give rise to many copies that reach a leaf $\hat{u}$ of $\mathcal{T}_{\mathcal{K}^E, \sigma}$ with $last(\hat{u}) = (e, \hat{\sigma})$, but we only need to consider the copy which made the least progress towards satisfying the acceptance condition, as captured by $g(e, \hat{\sigma}, \hat{q})$. To continue the simulation of such a copy on its remainder of $\mathcal{T}_{\mathcal{K}, \rho}$, we send to a son $y \cdot (idx(e, E), \sigma')$ of y in the connectivity tree, whose label specifies where $\mathcal{K}$ should go to from the exit e when reading σ', a copy of $\mathcal{A}_\varphi^T$ as follows. Recall that the leaf $\hat{u}$ corresponds to a node u of $\mathcal{T}_{\mathcal{K}, \rho}$ such that $last(u) = ((b, e), \hat{\sigma})$ and b is a top-level box of $\mathcal{K}$ that refers to $\mathcal{K}^E$. Also recall that every node in $\mathcal{T}_{\mathcal{K}, \rho}$ has one son for every letter $\sigma' \in \Sigma_I$. Hence, a copy of $\mathcal{A}_\varphi$ that is at state $\hat{q}$ and is reading u, sends one copy in state $q' = \delta_\varphi(\hat{q}, (\Lambda^E(e), \hat{\sigma}))$ to each son of u, if $\hat{q} \in Q_\varphi^\wedge$; and only one such copy, to one of the sons of u, if $\hat{q} \in Q_\varphi^\vee$. This explains why $\bigoplus$ is a conjunction in the first case, and is a disjunction in the second. Finally, a copy of $\mathcal{A}_\varphi^T$ that is sent to direction $(idx(e,E),\sigma')$ carries with it the color $g(e,\hat{\sigma},\hat{q})$, which is needed in order to define the acceptance condition. The color assigned to q_0 is of course arbitrary.

The core of the proof uses a game based approach. Recall that the game-based approach to model checking a flat system S with respect to a branching-time temporal logic specification φ, reduces the model-checking problem to solving a game (called the *membership game* of S and A_φ) obtained by taking the product of S with the alternating tree automaton $\mathcal{A}_\varphi$ [16]. In [6], this approach was extended to hierarchical structures, and it was shown there that given a hierarchical structure S and an SAPT $\mathcal{A}$, one can construct a hierarchical membership game $G_{S,\mathcal{A}}$ such that Player 0 wins $G_{S,\mathcal{A}}$ iff the tree obtained by unwinding S is accepted by $\mathcal{A}$. In particular, when $\mathcal{A}$ accepts exactly all the tree models of a branching-time formula φ, the above holds iff S satisfies φ. Furthermore, it is shown in [6] that one can *simplify* the hierarchical membership game $G_{S,\mathcal{A}}$, by replacing boxes of the top-level arena with gadgets that are built using Player 0 summary functions, and obtain an equivalent flat game $G_{S,\mathcal{A}}^s$.

Given a regular connectivity tree $\mathcal{T} = \langle T, V \rangle$, that induces a hierarchical system $\mathcal{K}$, we prove Lemma 1 by showing that the flat membership game $G_{S,\mathcal{A}_\varphi}^s$, where S is a hierarchical structure whose unwinding is the computation tree $\mathcal{T}_{\mathcal{K},\rho}$, is equivalent to the flat membership game $G_{K^T,\mathcal{A}_\varphi^T}$, of $\mathcal{A}_\varphi^T$ and a Kripke structure K^T whose unwinding is $\mathcal{T}$. Thus, $\mathcal{A}_\varphi$ accepts $\mathcal{T}_{\mathcal{K},\rho}$ iff $\mathcal{A}_\varphi^T$ accepts $\mathcal{T}$. The equivalence of these two games follows from the fact that they have isomorphic arenas and winning conditions. Consequently, our proof of Lemma 1 is mainly syntactic in nature, and amounts to little more then constructing the structures S and K^T, constructing the game $G_{S,\mathcal{A}_\varphi}$, simplifying it to get $G_{S,\mathcal{A}_\varphi}^s$, and constructing the membership game $G_{K^T,\mathcal{A}_\varphi^T}$. The remaining technical details can be found in the full version on the authors' web page   □

We now state our main theorem.

Theorem 2. *The $\langle L, el \rangle$-synthesis problem is* EXPTIME-*complete for a μ-calculus formula φ, and is* 2EXPTIME-*complete for an* LTL *formula (for el that is at most polynomial in $|\varphi|$ for μ-calculus, or at most exponential in $|\varphi|$ for* LTL).*

Proof. The lower bounds follow from the same bounds for the classical synthesis problem of flat systems [15,25], and the fact that it is immediately reducible to our problem if L contains all the atomic transducers. For the upper bounds, since an APT accepts some tree iff it accepts some regular tree (and $\mathcal{A}_\varphi^T$ obviously only accepts trees which are connectivity trees), by Lemma 1 and Theorem 1, we get that an LTL or a μ-calculus formula φ is $\langle L, el \rangle$-realizable iff $L(\mathcal{A}_\varphi^T) \neq \emptyset$. Checking the emptiness of $\mathcal{A}_\varphi^T$ can be done either directly, or by first translating it to an equivalent NPT $\mathcal{A}_\varphi'^T$. For reasons that will become apparent in subsection 4.2, we choose the latter. Note that the known algorithms for checking the emptiness of an NPT are such that if $L(\mathcal{A}_\varphi^T) \neq \emptyset$, then one can extract a regular tree in $L(\mathcal{A}_\varphi^T)$ from the emptiness checking algorithm [24]. The upper bounds follow from the analysis given below of the time required to construct $\mathcal{A}_\varphi^T$ and check for its non-emptiness.

By Theorem 1, the number of states $|Q_\varphi|$ and the index k of $\mathcal{A}_\varphi$ is $|Q_\varphi| = 2^{O(|\varphi|)}$, $k = 2$ for LTL, and $|Q_\varphi| = O(|\varphi|)$, $k = O(|\varphi|)$ for μ-calculus. The most time consuming part in the construction of $\mathcal{A}_\varphi^T$ is calculating for every $(\mathcal{K}^E, \sigma, q) \in (\mathcal{L}^{el} \times \Sigma_I \times Q_\varphi)$, the set $Rel(\mathcal{K}^E, \sigma, q)$. Calculating $Rel(\mathcal{K}^E, \sigma, q)$ can be done by checking for every summary function $g \in Sf(\mathcal{K}^E, \sigma, q)$ if it is relevant. Our proof of Lemma 1 also yields that, by [6], the latter can be done in time $O((|K| \cdot |Q_\varphi|)^k \cdot (k+1)^{|E| \cdot |Q_\varphi| \cdot k})$. Observe that the set $Sf(\mathcal{K}^E, \sigma, q)$ is of size $(k+1)^{|E|}$, and that the number of transducers in $\mathcal{L}^{el}$ is $O(\lambda \cdot m^{el})$, where m is the maximal size of any $\mathcal{K} \in \mathcal{L}$. It follows that for an LTL (resp. μ-calculus) formula φ, the automaton $\mathcal{A}_\varphi^T$ can be built in time at most polynomial in the size of the library, exponential in el, and double exponential (resp. exponential) in $|\varphi|$.

We now analyze the time it takes to check for the non-emptiness of $\mathcal{A}_\varphi^T$. Recall that for every $\eta \in (\mathcal{L}^{el} \times \Sigma_I \times Q_\varphi)$, the set $Rel(\eta)$ is of size at most $(k+1)^{el}$, and thus, the size of the transition relation of $\mathcal{A}_\varphi^T$ is polynomial in $|\mathcal{L}|$ and $|\varphi|$, and exponential in el. Checking the emptiness of $\mathcal{A}_\varphi^T$ is done by first translating it to an equivalent NPT $\mathcal{A}_\varphi'^T$. By [20], given an APT with $|Q|$ states and index k, running on Σ-labeled $\mathcal{D}^*$-trees, one can build (in time polynomial in the descriptions of its input and output automata) an equivalent NPT with $(|Q| \cdot k)^{O(|Q| \cdot k)}$ states, an index $O(|Q| \cdot k)$, and a transition relation of size $|\Sigma| \cdot (|Q| \cdot k)^{O(|D| \cdot |Q| \cdot k)}$. It is worth noting that this blow-up in the size of the automaton is independent from the size of the transition relation of $\mathcal{A}_\varphi^T$. By [16,28], the emptiness of $\mathcal{A}_\varphi'^T$ can be checked in time $|\Sigma| \cdot (|Q| \cdot k)^{O(|D| \cdot |Q|^2 \cdot k^2)}$ (and if it is not empty, a witness is returned). Recall that $|\Sigma| = |\mathcal{L}^{el}| = O(\lambda \cdot m^{el})$, and that $|D| = el \cdot |\Sigma_I|$. By substituting the values calculated above for $|Q|$ and k, the theorem follows. $\square$

Note that in Algorithm 1, it is conceivable that the transducer $\mathcal{K}^i$ synthesized at iteration i will be exponential (or even double-exponential for LTL) in the size of the specification formula φ_i. At this point it is probably best to stop the process, refine the specifications, and try again. However, it is important to note that even if the process is continued, and $\mathcal{K}^i$ is added to the library, the time complexity of the succeeding iterations does not deteriorate since the single-round $\langle \mathcal{L}, el \rangle$-synthesis algorithm is only polynomial in the maximal size m of any transducer in the library.

4.2   Enforcing Modularity

In this section, we address two main issues that may hinder the efforts of our single-round $\langle \mathcal{L}, el \rangle$-synthesis algorithm to synthesize a succinct hierarchical transducer $\mathcal{K}$. The first issue is that of ensuring that, when possible, $\mathcal{K}$ indeed makes use of the more complex transducers in the library (especially transducers synthesized in previous rounds) and does not rely too heavily on the less complex, or atomic, transducers. An obvious and most effective solution to this problem is to simply not have some (or all) of the atomic transducers present in the library. The second issue is making sure that $\mathcal{K}$ does not have too many sub-transducers, which can happen if it uses too many copies of the same transducer $\mathcal{K}' \in \mathcal{L}^{=0}$, each with a different set of exits. We also discuss some other points of interest regarding the synthesis of exits. We address the above issues by constructing, for each constraint we want to enforce on the synthesized transducer $\mathcal{K}$, an APT $\mathcal{A}$, called the constraint monitor, such that $\mathcal{A}$ accepts only connectivity trees that satisfy the constraint. We then synthesize $\mathcal{K}$ by checking the non-emptiness not of $\mathcal{A}_\varphi^T$, but of the product of $\mathcal{A}_\varphi^T$ with all the constraints monitors. Note that a nondeterministic monitor (i.e., an NPT) of exponential size can also be used, without adversely affecting the time-complexity, if the product with it is taken *after* we translate the product of A_φ^T and the other (polynomial) APT monitors, to an equivalent NPT.

A simple and effective way to enforce modularity in Algorithm 1 is that once a transducer $\mathcal{K}^i$ is synthesized in round i, one incorporates in subsequent rounds a monitor that rejects any connectivity tree containing a node labeled by some key sub-transducers of $\mathcal{K}^i$. This effectively enforces any transducer synthesized using a formula that refers to atomic propositions present only in $\mathcal{K}^i$ (and its disallowed sub-transducers) to use $\mathcal{K}^i$, and not try to build its functionality from scratch. As to other ways to enforce modularity, the question of whether one system is more modular than another, or how to construct a modular system, has received many, and often widely different, answers. Here we only discuss how certain simple modularity criteria can be easily implemented on top of our algorithm. For example, some people would argue that a function that has more than, say, 10 consecutive lines of code in which no other function is called, is not modular enough. A monitor that checks that in no path in a connectivity tree there are more than 10 consecutive nodes labeled with an atomic transducer, can easily enforce such a criterion. We can even divide the transducers in the library into groups, based on how "high level" they are, and enforce lower counts on lower level groups. Essentially, every modularity criterion that can be checked by a polynomial APT, or an exponential NPT, can be used. Enforcing one context-free property can also be done, albeit with an increase in the time complexity. Other non-regular criteria may be enforced by directly modifying the non-emptiness checking algorithm instead of by using a monitor, and we reserve this for future work.

As for the issue of synthesized exits, recall that for each transducer $\mathcal{K}' \in \mathcal{L}^{=0}$, we can have as many as $\Omega(|\mathcal{K}'|)^{el}$ copies of $\mathcal{K}'$ in $\mathcal{L}^{el}$, each with a different set of exit states. Obviously, we would not like the synthesized transducer $\mathcal{K}$ to use so many copies as sub-transducers. It is not hard to see that one can, for example, build an NPT of size $O(|\mathcal{L}^{el}|)$ that guesses for every $\mathcal{K}' \in \mathcal{L}^{=0}$ a single set of exits E, and accepts a connectivity tree iff the labels of all the nodes in the tree agree with the guessed exits. Note that after the end of the current round of synthesis, we may choose to add $\mathcal{K}'^E$ to the library (in addition, or instead of $\mathcal{K}'$).

Another point to note about the synthesis of exits is that while a transducer $\mathcal{K}$ surely satisfies the formula φ_i it was synthesized for, $\mathcal{K}^E$ may not. Consider for example a transducer $\mathcal{K}$ which is simply a single state, labeled with p, with a self loop. If we remove the loop and turn this state into an exit, it will no longer satisfy $\varphi_i = p \wedge Xp$ or $\varphi_i = Gp$. Now, depending on one's point of view, this may be either an advantage (more flexibility) or a disadvantage (loss of original intent). We believe that this is mostly an advantage, however, in case it is considered a disadvantage, a few possible solutions come to mind. First, for example if $\varphi_i = Gp$, one may wish for $\mathcal{K}$ to remain without exits and enforce $E = \emptyset$. Another option, for example if $\varphi_i = p \wedge Xp$, is to synthesize in round i a modified formula like $\varphi_i' = p \wedge \neg exit \wedge X(p \wedge exit)$, with the thought of exits in mind. Yet another option is to add, at iterations after i, a monitor that checks that if K^E is the label of a node in the connectivity tree then φ_i is satisfied. The monitor can check that φ_i is satisfied inside K^E, in which case the monitor is a single state automaton, that only accepts if E is such that $K^E \models \varphi_i$ (possibly using semantics over truncated paths [9]); alternatively, the monitor can check that φ_i is satisfied in the currently synthesized connectivity tree, starting from the node labeled by K^E, in which case the monitor is based on $\mathcal{A}_{\varphi_i}^T$.

4.3 Incomplete Information

A natural setting that was considered in the synthesis literature is that of incomplete information [15]. In this setting, in addition to the set of input signals I that the system can read, the environment also has internal signals H that the system cannot read, and one should synthesize a system whose behavior depends only on the readable signals, but satisfies a specification which refers also to the unreadable signals. Thus, the specification is given with respect to the alphabet $\Sigma_I = 2^{I \cup H}$, but the behavior of the system must be the same when reading two letters that differ only in their H components. The main source of difficulty is that a finite automaton cannot decide whether or not a computation tree is of a system that behaves in a way which is consistent with its partial view of the input signals. However, since the automaton at the heart of our algorithm does not run on computation trees, but rather on connectivity trees, handling of incomplete information comes at no cost at all. All we have to do is to define the connectivity trees to be $\mathcal{L}^{el}$-labeled complete $(\{1,...,el\} \times 2^I)$-trees, instead of $(\{1,...,el\} \times 2^{I \cup H})$-trees to ensure that the synthesized transducer behaves in the same way on input letters that differ only in their hidden components (this of course implies that the expression $\bigoplus_{\sigma' \in \Sigma_I}$ in the transition function of $\mathcal{A}_\varphi^T$ becomes $\bigoplus_{\sigma' \in 2^I}$). Thus, our algorithm solves, with the same complexity, also the hierarchical synthesis problem with incomplete information.

5 Discussion

We presented an algorithm for the synthesis of hierarchical systems which takes as input a library of hierarchical transducers and a sequence of specification formulas. Each formula drives the synthesis of a new hierarchical transducer based on the current library, which contains all the transducers synthesized in previous iterations together with the starting library. The main challenge in this approach is to come up with a single-round synthesis algorithm that is able to efficiently synthesize the required transducer at each round. We have provided such an algorithm that works efficiently (i.e., not worst than the corresponding one for flat systems) and uniform (i.e., it can handle different temporal logic specifications, including the modal μ-calculus). In order to ensure that the single-round algorithm makes real use of previously synthesized transducers we have suggested the use of auxiliary automata to enforce modularity criteria. We believe that by decoupling the process of enforcing modularity from the core algorithm for single-round synthesis we gain flexibility that allows one to apply different approaches to enforcing modularity, as well as future optimizations to the core synthesis algorithm.

References

1. Alur, R., Arenas, M., Barceló, P., Etessami, K., Immerman, N., Libkin, L.: First-Order and Temporal Logics for Nested Words. In: Logical Methods in Computer Science, vol. 4 (2008)

2. Alur, R., Benedikt, M., Etessami, K., Godefroid, P., Reps, T.W., Yannakakis, M.: Analysis of recursive state machines. ACM Trans. Program. Lang. Syst. 27(4), 786–818 (2005)
3. Alur, R., Chaudhuri, S., Etessami, K., Madhusudan, P.: On-the-Fly Reachability and Cycle Detection for Recursive State Machines. In: Halbwachs, N., Zuck, L.D. (eds.) TACAS 2005. LNCS, vol. 3440, pp. 61–76. Springer, Heidelberg (2005)
4. Alur, R., Chaudhuri, S., Madhusudan, P.: A fixpoint calculus for local and global program flows. In: POPL 2006, pp. 153–165. ACM (2006)
5. Alur, R., Yannakakis, M.: Model checking of hierarchical state machines. ACM Trans. Program. Lang. Syst. 23(3), 273–303 (2001)
6. Aminof, B., Kupferman, O., Murano, A.: Improved Model Checking of Hierarchical Systems. In: Barthe, G., Hermenegildo, M. (eds.) VMCAI 2010. LNCS, vol. 5944, pp. 61–77. Springer, Heidelberg (2010)
7. Church, A.: Logic, arithmetics, and automata. In: Proc. International Congress of Mathematicians, 1962, pp. 23–35. Institut Mittag-Leffler (1963)
8. de Alfaro, L., Henzinger, T.A.: Interface-based design. In: Engineering Theories of Software-Intensive Systems. NATO Science Series: Mathematics, Physics, and Chemistry, vol. 195, pp. 83–104. Springer (2005)
9. Eisner, C., Fisman, D., Havlicek, J., Lustig, Y., McIsaac, A., Van Campenhout, D.: Reasoning with Temporal Logic on Truncated Paths. In: Hunt Jr., W.A., Somenzi, F. (eds.) CAV 2003. LNCS, vol. 2725, pp. 27–39. Springer, Heidelberg (2003)
10. Emerson, E.A.: Temporal and modal logic. In: Van Leeuwen, J. (ed.) Handbook of Theoretical Computer Science, ch. 16, vol. B, pp. 997–1072. Elsevier, MIT Press (1990)
11. Emerson, E.A., Jutla, C.: Tree automata, μ-calculus and determinacy. In: FOCS 1991, pp. 368–377 (1991)
12. Göller, S., Lohrey, M.: Fixpoint Logics on Hierarchical Structures. In: Sarukkai, S., Sen, S. (eds.) FSTTCS 2005. LNCS, vol. 3821, pp. 483–494. Springer, Heidelberg (2005)
13. Guelev, D.P., Ryan, M.D., Schobbens, P.Y.: Synthesising features by games. Electr. Notes Theor. Comput. Sci. 145, 79–93 (2006)
14. Janin, D., Walukiewicz, I.: Automata for the Modal μ-Calculus and Related Results. In: Hájek, P., Wiedermann, J. (eds.) MFCS 1995. LNCS, vol. 969, pp. 552–562. Springer, Heidelberg (1995)
15. Kupferman, O., Vardi, M.Y.: μ-Calculus Synthesis. In: Nielsen, M., Rovan, B. (eds.) MFCS 2000. LNCS, vol. 1893, pp. 497–507. Springer, Heidelberg (2000)
16. Kupferman, O., Vardi, M.Y., Wolper, P.: An automata-theoretic approach to branching-time model checking. J. of the ACM 47(2), 312–360 (2000)
17. Lanotte, R., Maggiolo-Schettini, A., Peron, A.: Structural Model Checking for Communicating Hierarchical Machines. In: Fiala, J., Koubek, V., Kratochvíl, J. (eds.) MFCS 2004. LNCS, vol. 3153, pp. 525–536. Springer, Heidelberg (2004)
18. Lustig, Y., Vardi, M.Y.: Synthesis from Component Libraries. In: de Alfaro, L. (ed.) FOSSACS 2009. LNCS, vol. 5504, pp. 395–409. Springer, Heidelberg (2009)
19. Lustig, Y., Vardi, M.Y.: Synthesis from Recursive-Components libraries. In: GandALF 2011. EPTCS, vol. 54, pp. 1–16 (2011)
20. Muller, D.E., Schupp, P.E.: Alternating automata on infinite trees. J. of Theor. Comp. Sc. 54, 267–276 (1987)
21. Müller, P.: Modular specification and verification of object-oriented programs. Springer (2002)
22. Piterman, N., Pnueli, A., Sa'ar, Y.: Synthesis of Reactive(1) Designs. In: Emerson, E.A., Namjoshi, K.S. (eds.) VMCAI 2006. LNCS, vol. 3855, pp. 364–380. Springer, Heidelberg (2005)

23. Pnueli, A., Rosner, R.: On the synthesis of a reactive module. In: POPL 1989, pp. 179–190. ACM Press (1989)

24. Rabin, M.O.: Weakly definable relations and special automata. In: Proc. Symp. Math. Logic and Foundations of Set Theory, pp. 1–23. North Holland (1970)

25. Rosner, R.: Modular Synthesis of Reactive Systems. PhD thesis, Weizmann Institute of Science (1992)

26. Sifakis, J.: A framework for component-based construction extended abstract. In: SEFM 2005, pp. 293–300. IEEE Computer Society (2005)

27. Bliudze, S., Sifakis, J.: Synthesizing Glue Operators from Glue Constraints for the Construction of Component-Based Systems. In: Apel, S., Jackson, E. (eds.) SC 2011. LNCS, vol. 6708, pp. 51–67. Springer, Heidelberg (2011)

28. Wilke, T.: Alternating tree automata, parity games, and modal μ-calculus. Bull. Soc. Math. Belg. 8(2) (2001)

A Modal Specification Theory
for Components with Data*

Sebastian S. Bauer[1,2], Kim Guldstrand Larsen[2], Axel Legay[3],
Ulrik Nyman[2], and Andrzej Wąsowski[4]

[1] Institut für Informatik, Ludwig-Maximilians-Universität München, Germany
[2] Department of Computer Science, Aalborg University, Denmark
[3] INRIA/IRISA, Rennes, France
[4] IT University of Copenhagen, Denmark

Abstract. Modal specification is a well-known formalism used as an abstraction theory for transition systems. Modal specifications are transition systems equipped with two types of transitions: *must*-transitions that are mandatory to any implementation, and *may*-transitions that are optional. The duality of transitions allows to develop a unique approach for both logical and structural compositions, and eases the step-wise refinement process for building implementations.

We propose Modal Specifications with Data (MSD), the first *modal* specification theory with explicit representation of data. Our new theory includes all the essential ingredients of a specification theory. As MSD are by nature potentially infinite-state systems, we propose symbolic representations based on effective predicates. Our theory serves as a new abstraction-based formalism for transition systems with data.

1 Introduction

Modern IT systems are often large and consist of complex assemblies of numerous reactive and interacting components. The components are often designed by independent teams, working under a common agreement on what the interface of each component should be. Consequently, the search for mathematical foundations which support *compositional reasoning* on interfaces is a major research goal. A framework should support inferring properties of the global implementation, designing and advisedly reusing components.

Interfaces are specifications and components that implement an interface are understood as models, or implementations. Specification theories should support various features including (1) *refinement*, which allows to compare specifications as well as to replace a specification by another one in a larger design, (2) *structural composition*, which allows to combine specifications of different components, (3) *logical conjunction*, expressing the intersection of the set of requirements expressed by two or more specifications for the same component, and last (4) a *quotient operator* that is dual to structural composition and allows synthesizing a component from a set of assumptions.

* Work supported by the German Academic Exchange Service (DAAD), grant D/10/46169, by an "Action de Recherche Collaborative" ARC (TP)I, by MT-LAB, VKR Centre of Excellence, and by the EU project ASCENS, 257414.

F. Arbab and P.C. Ölveczky (Eds.): FACS 2011, LNCS 7253, pp. 61–78, 2012.
© Springer-Verlag Berlin Heidelberg 2012

Among existing specification theories, one finds modal specifications [1], which are labeled transition systems equipped with two types of transitions: *must*-transitions that are mandatory for any implementation, and *may*-transitions which are optional for an implementation. Modal specifications are known to achieve a more flexible and easy-to-use compositional development methodology for CCS [2], which includes a considerable simplification of the step-wise refinement process proposed by Milner and Larsen. While being very close to logics (conjunction), the formalism takes advantage of a behavioral semantics allowing for easy composition with respect to process construction (structural composition) and synthesis (quotient). However, despite the many advantages, only a few implementations have been considered so far. One major problem is that contrary to other formalisms based on transition systems, there exists no theory of modal specification equipped with rich information such as data variables.

In this paper, we add a new stone to the cathedral of results on modal specifications [3, 4], that is we propose the first such theory equipped with rich data values. Our first contribution is to design a semantical version of modal specifications whose states are split into locations and valuations for possibly infinite-domain variables. For every component, we distinguish between local variables, that are locally controlled by the component, and uncontrolled variables that are controlled by other components and can be accessed, but not modified. Combining variables with sets of actions labeling transitions offers a powerful set of communication primitives that cannot be captured by most existing specification theories. We also propose a symbolic predicate-based representation of our formalism. We consider effective predicates that are closed under conjunction, union, and membership—classical assumptions in existing symbolic theories (e.g. [5]). While the semantic level is possibly infinite-state, the syntactical level permits us to reason on specifications just like one would with the original modal specifications, but with the additional power of rich data.

Continuing our quest, we study modal refinement between specifications. Refinement, which resembles simulation between transition systems, permits to compare sets of implementations in a syntactic manner. Modal refinement is defined at the semantic level, but can also be checked at the symbolic level. We propose a predicate abstraction approach that simplifies the practical complexity of the operation by reducing the number of states and simplifying the predicates. This approach is in line with the work of Godefroid et al. [6], but is applied to specification-based verification rather than to model checking.

We then propose definitions for both logical and structural composition, on the level of symbolic representations of specifications. These definitions are clearly not direct extensions of the ones defined on modal specifications as behaviors of both controlled and uncontrolled variables have to be taken into account. As usual, structural composition offers the property of independent implementability, hence allowing for elegant step-wise refinement. In logical composition, two specifications which disagree on their requirements can be reconciled by synthesizing a new component where conflicts have been removed. This can be done with a symbolic pruning of bad states, which terminates if the system is finite-state, or if the structure of the transition system induced by the specification relies, for instance, on a well-quasi order [7]. Finally, we also propose a quotient operation, that is the dual operation of structural composition, which works for a subclass of systems, and we discuss its limitation. This operator, absent from most existing behavioral and logical specification theories, allows synthesizing a component from a set of assumptions.

In Sect. 2 we introduce modal specifications with data and their finite symbolic representations, refinement, an implementation relation and consistency. In Sect. 3 we define the essential operators of every specification theory, that is parallel composition, conjunction and quotient. For verification of refinement between infinite-state specifications we propose in Sect. 4 an approach based on predicate abstraction techniques. We summarize related works in Sect. 5 and conclude in Sect. 6.

2   Modal Specifications with Data

We will first introduce specifications which are finite symbolic representations of modal specifications with data. We will then propose modal refinement and derive an implementation relation and a consistency notion.

In the following, $\mathscr{P}(M)$ denotes the powerset of M, $\mathscr{P}_{\geq 1}(M) = \mathscr{P}(M) \setminus \{\emptyset\}$, and the union of two disjoint sets is denoted by $M \uplus N$, which is $M \cup N$ with $M \cap N = \emptyset$.

We assume that variables range over a fixed domain $\mathbb{D}$. For a given set V of variables, a *data state* s over V is a mapping $s : V \to \mathbb{D}$. If $V = \{x_1, x_2, \ldots, x_n\}$ and $d_1, d_2, \ldots, d_n \in \mathbb{D}$, we write $[x_1 \mapsto d_1, x_2 \mapsto d_2, \ldots, x_n \mapsto d_n]$ for the data state s which maps every x_i to d_i, for $1 \leq i \leq n$. We write $[\![V]\!]$ for the set of all possible data states over V. For disjoint sets of variables V_1 and V_2 and data states $s_1 \in [\![V_1]\!]$ and $s_2 \in [\![V_2]\!]$, the operation $(s_1 \cdot s_2)$ composes the data states resulting in a new state $s = (s_1 \cdot s_2) \in [\![V_1 \uplus V_2]\!]$, such that $s(x) = s_1(x)$ for all $x \in V_1$ and $s(x) = s_2(x)$ for all $x \in V_2$. This is naturally lifted to sets of states: if $S_1 \subseteq [\![V_1]\!]$ and $S_2 \subseteq [\![V_2]\!]$ then $(S_1 \cdot S_2) = \{(s_1 \cdot s_2) \mid s_1 \in S_1, s_2 \in S_2\} \subseteq [\![V_1 \uplus V_2]\!]$.

Like in the work of de Alfaro et al. [8] we define specifications with respect to an assertion language allowing suitable predicate representation. Given a set V of variables, we denote by $Pred(V)$ the set of first-order predicates with free variables in V; we assume that these predicates are written in some specified first-order language with existential ($\exists$) and universal ($\forall$) quantifiers and with interpreted function symbols and predicates; in our examples, the language contains the usual arithmetic operators and boolean connectives ($\vee, \wedge, \neg, \Rightarrow$). Given a set of variables V we denote by $(V)'$ an isomorphic set of 'primed' variables from V: so if $x \in V$ then $(x)' \in (V)'$. We use this construction to represent pre- and post-values of variables. A variable $(x)' \in (V)'$ represents the next state value of the variable $x \in V$. Given a formula $\varphi \in Pred(V)$ and a data state $s \in [\![V]\!]$, we write $\varphi(s)$ if the predicate formula φ is true when its free variables are interpreted as specified by s. Given a formula $\psi \in Pred(V_1 \uplus (V_2)')$ and states $s_1 \in [\![V_1]\!]$, $s_2 \in [\![V_2]\!]$, we often write $\psi(s_1, s_2)$ for $\psi(s_1 \cdot t_2)$ where $t_2 \in [\![(V_2)']\!]$ such that $t_2((x)') = s_2(x)$ for all $x \in V_2$. Given a predicate $\varphi \in Pred(V)$, we write $(\varphi)' \in Pred((V)')$ for the predicate obtained by substituting x with $(x)'$ in φ, for all $x \in V$; similarly, for $\varphi \in Pred((V)')$ we write $\varphi \downarrow \in Pred(V)$ for the predicate obtained by substituting every $(x)' \in (V)'$ with its unprimed version. We write $[\![\varphi]\!]$ for the set $\{s \in [\![V]\!] \mid \varphi(s)\}$ which consists of all states satisfying $\varphi \in Pred(V)$ (for predicates with primed and unprimed variables), and φ is *consistent* if $[\![\varphi]\!] \neq \emptyset$. We write

$\exists V \varphi$ meaning existential quantification of φ over all variables in the set V, and similar for universal quantification. Finally, for a predicate $\psi \in Pred(V_1 \uplus (V_2)')$, we write $^\circ \psi$ for $\exists (V_2)' \psi$, and ψ° for $\exists V_1 \psi$.

Our theory enriches modal automata with variables. Specifications not only express constraints on the allowed sequences of actions, but also their dependence and effect on the values of variables. Like in the loose approach of modal specifications [1] which allows under-specification using *may* and *must* modalities on transitions, we allow loose specification of the effects of actions on the data state. From a given location and a given data state, a transition to another location is allowed to lead to several next data states. Unlike in modal specifications, variables are observable in our framework, allowing for modeling shared variable communication.

A *signature* $Sig = (\Sigma, V^L, V^G)$ determines the alphabet of actions Σ and the set of variables $V = V^L \uplus V^G$ of an interface. The variables in V^L are *local (controlled) variables*, owned by the interface and visible to any other component. V^G contains the *uncontrolled variables* owned by the environment, which are read-only for the interface.

Specifications are finite modal transition systems where transitions are equipped with predicates. A transition predicate $\psi \in Pred(V \uplus (V^L)')$ relates a previous state, determined by all controlled and uncontrolled data states, with the next possible controlled data state.

Definition 1. *A* specification *is a tuple* $\mathbf{A} = (Sig, Loc, \ell^0, \varphi^0, E_\Diamond, E_\Box)$ *where* $Sig = (\Sigma, V^L, V^G)$ *is a signature, Loc is a finite set of locations,* $\ell^0 \in Loc$ *is the initial location,* $\varphi^0 \in Pred(V^L)$ *is a predicate on the initial local state, and* $E_\Diamond, E_\Box$ *are finite may- and must-transition relations respectively:*

$$E_\Diamond, E_\Box \subseteq Loc \times \Sigma \times Pred(V \uplus (V^L)') \times Loc.$$

Given a specification $\mathbf{A}$, locations $\ell, \ell' \in Loc$, and action $a \in \Sigma$, we refer to the set of transition predicates on may-transitions by $May^a(\ell, \ell') = \{\psi \mid (\ell, a, \psi, \ell') \in E_\Diamond\}$ and on must-transitions by $Must^a(\ell, \ell') = \{\psi \mid (\ell, a, \psi, \ell') \in E_\Box\}$.

Example 1. Consider a specification of a print server, shown in Fig. 1. Must-transitions are drawn with solid arrows and may-transitions with dashed ones. Every solid arrow representing a must-transition has an implicit may-transition shadowing it which is not shown. Every transition is equipped with a transition predicate over unprimed variables, referring to the pre-state, and primed variables, referring to the poststate. The print server receives new print jobs (**newPrintJob**), stores them and assigns them either a low or high priority; the numbers of low and high priority jobs are modeled by controlled variables l and h, respectively; l and h are natural numbers. A job with low priority can also be reclassified to high priority (**incPriority**). The printer server can send (**send**) a job to a printer, and then wait for the acknowledgment (**ack**). In state ℓ_1, if there is a job with high priority and the uncontrolled boolean variable *priorityMode* is true, then there must be a send transition. The specification is loose in the sense that if a second print job is received in state ℓ_1, then the behavior is left unspecified.

We now define the kind of transition systems which will be used for formalizing the semantics of specifications. A specification is interpreted as a variant of modal transition

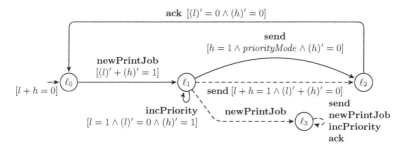

Fig. 1. Abstract specification **P** of a print server.

systems where the *state space* is formed by the cartesian product $Loc \times [\![V^L]\!]$, i.e. a *state* is a pair (ℓ, s) where $\ell \in Loc$ is a location and $s \in [\![V^L]\!]$ is a valuation of the controlled variables. To motivate the choice of the transition relations in the semantics of specifications, we first describe the intended meaning of may- and must-transitions.

A may-transition $(\ell, a, \psi, \ell') \in E_\diamond$ in the specification expresses that in any implementation, in any state (ℓ, s) and for any guard $g \in [\![V^G]\!]$ (that is a valuation of uncontrolled variables V^G) the implementation is *allowed* to have a transition with guard g and action a to a next state (ℓ', s') such that $\psi(s \cdot g, s')$. The interpretation of a must-transition $(\ell, a, \psi, \ell') \in E_\square$ is a bit more involved: Any implementation, in state (ℓ, s), and for any guard $g \in [\![V^G]\!]$, if there is a valuation $s' \in [\![V^L]\!]$ such that $\psi(s \cdot g, s')$, then the implementation is *required* to have a transition from state (ℓ, s) with guard g and action a to *at least some* state t' such that $\psi(s \cdot g, t')$. The requirement expressed by must-transitions cannot be formalized by standard modal transition systems, but fortunately, a generalization called disjunctive modal transition systems introduced in [9] can precisely capture these requirements. May-transitions target (as usual) only one state, but must-transitions branch to several possible next states (thus must-transitions are hypertransitions), with an existential interpretation: there must exist at least one transition with some target state which is an element from the set of target states of the hypertransition.

Definition 2. *A* modal specification with data (MSD) *is a tuple*

$$\mathbf{S} = (Sig, Loc, \ell^0, S^0, \longrightarrow_\diamond, \longrightarrow_\square)$$

where Sig, Loc, ℓ^0 are like in Def. 1, $S^0 \subseteq [\![V^L]\!]$ is a set of initial data states, and $\longrightarrow_\diamond, \longrightarrow_\square \subseteq Loc \times [\![V^L]\!] \times [\![V^G]\!] \times \Sigma \times (Loc \times \mathscr{P}_{\geq 1}([\![V^L]\!]))$ are the may- ($\diamond$) and must- ($\square$) transition relations such that every may-transition targets a single state: if $(\ell, s, g, a, (\ell', S')) \in \longrightarrow_\diamond$ then $|S'| = 1$.

A state $(\ell, s) \in Loc \times [\![V^L]\!]$ is called syntactically consistent *iff targets reachable by must-transitions are also reachable by may-transitions: if $(\ell, s, g, a, (\ell', S')) \in \longrightarrow_\square$ then $(\ell, s, g, a, (\ell', \{s'\})) \in \longrightarrow_\diamond$ for all $s' \in S'$. $\mathbf{S}$ is syntactically consistent iff all states are syntactically consistent, and the set of initial data states is nonempty, i.e. $S^0 \neq \emptyset$.*

May-transitions $(\ell, s, g, a, (\ell', S')) \in \longrightarrow_\diamond$ are often written $(\ell, s) \xrightarrow{g\,a}_\diamond (\ell', S')$, and similarly for must-transitions.

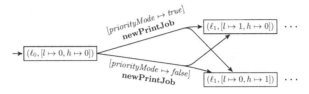

Fig. 2. Excerpt of the semantics of the abstract print server specification

We can now define formally how a specification translates to its semantics in terms of an MSD. As already described above, the semantics of a may-transition of the specification is given by the set of may-transitions pointing to single admissible target states, and a must-transition gives rise to (must-)hypertransitions targeting all the admissible poststates.

Definition 3. *The semantics of a specification* $\mathbf{A} = (Sig, Loc, \ell^0, \varphi^0, E_\diamond, E_\square)$ *is given by the MSD* $\langle \mathbf{A} \rangle_{\text{sem}} = (Sig, Loc, \ell^0, S^0, \longrightarrow_\diamond, \longrightarrow_\square)$ *where* $S^0 = [\![\varphi^0]\!]$ *and the transition relations are defined as follows. For each* $\ell, \ell' \in Loc, \ s, s' \in [\![V^L]\!], \ g \in [\![V^G]\!],$ *and* $a \in \Sigma$:

   i. *If* $(\ell, a, \psi, \ell') \in E_\diamond$ *and* $\psi(s \cdot g, s')$ *then* $(\ell, s) \xrightarrow{g\,a}_\diamond (\ell', \{s'\}),$

   ii. *If* $(\ell, a, \psi, \ell') \in E_\square$ *and* $\psi(s \cdot g, s')$ *then* $(\ell, s) \xrightarrow{g\,a}_\square (\ell', \{t' \in [\![V^L]\!] \mid \psi(s \cdot g, t')\}).$

A specification $\mathbf{A}$ is called *syntactically consistent* iff its semantics $\langle \mathbf{A} \rangle_{\text{sem}}$ is syntactically consistent. In the following we will always assume that specifications and MSD are syntactically consistent.

Example 2. An excerpt of the semantics of our abstract specification of the print server (see Fig. 1) can be seen Fig. 2. As before, we draw must-transitions with a solid arrow, and has an implicit set of may-transitions shadowing it which are not shown, i.e. for each target (ℓ, S') of a must-transition and each $s \in S'$ there is a may-transition with the same source state and with target state $(\ell, \{s\})$.

The first must-transition $(\ell_0, \mathbf{newPrintJob}, (l)' + (h)' = 1, \ell_1) \in E_\square$ of the print server specification gives rise to the transitions shown in Fig. 2. Any new print job must be stored in either l or h but which one is not yet fixed by the specification. Thus in the semantics this is expressed as a disjunctive must-transition to the unique location ℓ_1 and the next possible data states $[l \mapsto 1, h \mapsto 0]$ and $[l \mapsto 0, h \mapsto 1]$.

A *refinement relation* allows to relate a concrete specification with an abstract specification. Refinement should satisfy the following substitutability property: If $\mathbf{A}$ refines $\mathbf{B}$ then replacing $\mathbf{B}$ with $\mathbf{A}$ in a context $\mathcal{C}[\cdot]$ gives a specification $\mathcal{C}[\mathbf{A}]$ refining $\mathcal{C}[\mathbf{B}]$. Refinement will be a precongruence, i.e. it is compatible with the structural and logical operators on specifications in the above sense.

Our definition of refinement is based on modal refinement [10, 9] for (disjunctive) modal transition systems, where the may-transitions determine which actions are permitted in a refinement while the must-transitions specify which actions must be present in a refinement and hence in any implementation. We adapt it with respect to data states.

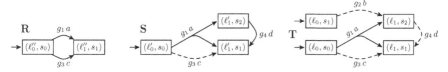

Fig. 3. Successive refinement of an MSD **T**

Example 3. We motivate our adaption of modal refinement to take into account data states with the help of a small example shown in Fig. 3. We draw may-transitions with a dashed arrow, and must-transitions with a solid arrow. Every must-transition has an implicit set of may-transitions shadowing it which are not shown. The MSD **T** (to the right) has two initial states, both having ℓ_0 as the initial location. The must-transition starting from (ℓ_0, s_0) expresses that in any implementation there must be a transition leading to at least one of the states (ℓ_1, s_1) and (ℓ_1, s_2). The MSD **T** can be refined to the MSD **S** (by dropping one may-transition and turning one may-transition to a must-transition), and then **S** is refined by the MSD **R**, by refining the must-transition $(\ell'_0, s_0, g_1, a, (\ell'_1, \{s_1, s_2\}))$ in **S** to the must-transition $(\ell''_0, s_0, g_1, a, (\ell''_1, \{s_1\}))$ in **R**, and by strengthening the transition with guard g_3 and action c to a must-transition.

Definition 4. *Let* $\mathbf{T}_1 = (Sig, Loc_1, \ell_1^0, S_1^0, \longrightarrow_{\diamond,1}, \longrightarrow_{\Box,1})$ *and* $\mathbf{T}_2 = (Sig, Loc_2, \ell_2^0, S_2^0, \longrightarrow_{\diamond,2}, \longrightarrow_{\Box,2})$ *be MSD over the same signature* $Sig = (\Sigma, V^L, V^G)$. *A relation* $R \subseteq Loc_1 \times Loc_2 \times [\![V^L]\!]$ *is a* refinement relation *iff for all* $(\ell_1, \ell_2, s) \in R$:

 i. *Whenever* $(\ell_1, s) \xrightarrow{g\,a}_{\diamond,1} (\ell'_1, \{s'\})$ *then there exists* $(\ell_2, s) \xrightarrow{g\,a}_{\diamond,2} (\ell'_2, \{t'\})$ *such that* $s' = t'$ *and* $(\ell'_1, \ell'_2, s') \in R$.
 ii. *Whenever* $(\ell_2, s) \xrightarrow{g\,a}_{\Box,2} (\ell'_2, S'_2)$ *then there exists* $(\ell_1, s) \xrightarrow{g\,a}_{\Box,1} (\ell'_1, S'_1)$ *such that* $S'_1 \subseteq S'_2$ *and* $(\ell'_1, \ell'_2, s') \in R$ *for all* $s' \in S'_1$.

We say that $\mathbf{T}_1$ refines $\mathbf{T}_2$, *written* $\mathbf{T}_1 \leq_{\text{sem}} \mathbf{T}_2$, *iff* $S_1^0 \subseteq S_2^0$ *and there exists a refinement relation* R *such that for any* $s \in S_1^0$ *also* $(\ell_1^0, \ell_2^0, s) \in R$. *A specification* $\mathbf{A}_1$ *refines another specification* $\mathbf{A}_2$, *written* $\mathbf{A}_1 \leq \mathbf{A}_2$, *iff* $\langle\mathbf{A}_1\rangle_{\text{sem}} \leq_{\text{sem}} \langle\mathbf{A}_2\rangle_{\text{sem}}$.

The refinement relation is a preorder on the class of all specifications. Refinement can be checked in polynomial time in the size of the state space of the MSD (for variables with finite domains). In general the domain may be infinite, or prohibitively large, so in Sect. 4 we revisit the question of refinement checking using abstraction techniques.

Example 4. The semantics of our abstract print server specification, shown in Fig. 2, can be refined as shown in Fig. 4. Now, both must-transitions point to the location ℓ_1 with the data state $[l \mapsto 1, h \mapsto 0]$ which means that any new incoming print job is assigned a low priority, independent of the uncontrolled variable *priorityMode*.

An MSD for which the conditions (1) $\longrightarrow_{\diamond} = \longrightarrow_{\Box}$ and (2) $|S^0| = 1$ are satisfied, can be interpreted as (an abstraction of) an *implementation*: there are no design choices left open as (1) all may-transitions are covered by must-transitions and (2) there is only one initial data state possible. Any MSD for which the conditions (1) and (2) are satisfied, is called *transition system with data (TSD)* in the following. Note that TSD cannot be

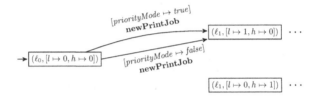

Fig. 4. Refinement of the MSD shown in Fig. 2

strictly refined, i.e. for any TSD **I** and any MSD **S** with the same signature, **S** $\leq_{sem}$ **I** implies **I** $\leq_{sem}$ **S**.

An implementation relation connects specifications to implementations (given as TSD) satisfying them. We can simply use refinement as the implementation relation. Given a specification **A** and some TSD **I**, we write **I** $\models$ **A** for **I** $\leq_{sem} \langle$**A**$\rangle_{sem}$, so our implementation **I** is seen as the model which satisfies the property expressed by the specification **A**. Now the set of implementations of a specification is the set of all its refining TSD: given a specification **A**, we define $Impl(\mathbf{A}) = \{\mathbf{I} \mid \mathbf{I} \models \mathbf{A}\}$.

Our implementation relation $\models$ immediately leads to the classical notion of consistency as existence of models. A specification **A** is *consistent* iff $Impl(\mathbf{A})$ is non-empty. Consequently, as modal refinement is reflexive, any specification **A** for which $\langle$**A**$\rangle_{sem}$ is a TSD, is consistent.

By transitivity, modal refinement entails implementation set inclusion: for specifications **A** and **B**, if **A** $\leq$ **B** then $Impl(\mathbf{A}) \subseteq Impl(\mathbf{B})$. The relation $Impl(\mathbf{A}) \subseteq Impl(\mathbf{B})$ is sometimes called *thorough refinement* [11]. Just like for modal transition systems, thorough refinement does not imply modal refinement in general [12]. To establish equivalence we follow [13] by imposing a restriction on **B**, namely that it is deterministic. An MSD is *deterministic* if it is satisfied that

(1) if $(\ell, s, g, a, (\ell', S')), (\ell, s, g, a, (\ell'', S'')) \in \longrightarrow_\Box$ then $\ell' = \ell''$ and $S' = S''$,
(2) if $(\ell, s, g, a, (\ell', \{s'\})), (\ell, s, g, a, (\ell'', \{s''\})) \in \longrightarrow_\Diamond$ then $\ell' = \ell''$.

A specification **B** is *deterministic*, if the MSD $\langle$**B**$\rangle_{sem}$ is deterministic. Note that for may-transitions, determinism only requires that for the same source state, guard and action, the transition leads to a unique next location. The reason why this is sufficient is that modal refinement explicitly distinguishes states by their data state part: two states (ℓ', s') and (ℓ'', s'') can only be related if their data state parts s', s'' coincide.

Now, turning back to the relationship of modal refinement and inclusion of implementation sets (thorough refinement), we can prove the following theorem. Under the restriction of determinism of the refined (abstract) specification we can prove completeness of refinement. This theorem effectively means that modal refinement, as defined for MSD, is characterized by set inclusion of admitted implementations.

Theorem 1. *Let* **A** *and* **B** *be two specifications with the same signature such that* **B** *is deterministic. Then* **A** $\leq$ **B** *if and only if* $Impl(\mathbf{A}) \subseteq Impl(\mathbf{B})$.

3   Compositional Reasoning

In this section we propose all the essential operators on specifications a good specification theory should provide. We will distinguish between structural and logical composition. Structural composition mimics the classical composition of transition systems at the specification level. Logical composition allows to compute the intersection of sets of models and hence can be used to represent the conjunction of requirements made on an implementation. Furthermore we will introduce a quotient operator which is the dual operator to structural composition.

From now on, we assume that for any two specifications with the signatures $Sig_1 = (\Sigma_1, V_1^L, V_1^G)$ and $Sig_2 = (\Sigma_2, V_2^L, V_2^G)$, respectively, we can assume that $\Sigma_1 = \Sigma_2$ and $V_1^L \uplus V_1^G = V_2^L \uplus V_2^G$. This is not a limitation, as one can apply the constructions of [4] to equalize alphabets of actions and sets of variables.

Parallel composition. Two specifications $\mathbf{A}_1$ and $\mathbf{A}_2$ with $Sig_1 = (\Sigma, V_1^L, V_1^G)$ and $Sig_2 = (\Sigma, V_2^L, V_2^G)$, respectively, are *composable* iff $V_1^L \cap V_2^L = \emptyset$. Then their signatures can be composed in a straightforward manner to the signature

$$Sig_1 \times Sig_2 =_{def} (\Sigma, V_1^L \uplus V_2^L, (V_1^G \cup V_2^G) \setminus (V_1^L \uplus V_2^L))$$

in which the set of controlled variables is the disjoint union of the sets of controlled variables of $\mathbf{A}_1$ and $\mathbf{A}_2$, and the set of uncontrolled variables consists of all those uncontrolled variables of $\mathbf{A}_1$ and $\mathbf{A}_2$ which are controlled neither by $\mathbf{A}_1$ nor by $\mathbf{A}_2$.

Definition 5. *Let $\mathbf{A}_1$ and $\mathbf{A}_2$ be two composable specifications. The* parallel composition *of $\mathbf{A}_1$ and $\mathbf{A}_2$ is defined as the specification*

$$\mathbf{A}_1 \parallel \mathbf{A}_2 = (Sig_1 \times Sig_2, Loc_1 \times Loc_2, (\ell_1^0, \ell_2^0), \varphi_1^0 \wedge \varphi_2^0, E_\Diamond, E_\Box)$$

where the transition relations $E_\Diamond$ and $E_\Box$ are the smallest relations satisfying the rules:

1. *if $(\ell_1, a, \psi_1, \ell_1') \in E_{\Diamond,1}$ and $(\ell_2, a, \psi_2, \ell_2') \in E_{\Diamond,2}$ then $((\ell_1, \ell_2), a, \psi_1 \wedge \psi_2, (\ell_1', \ell_2')) \in E_\Diamond$,*
2. *if $(\ell_1, a, \psi_1, \ell_1') \in E_{\Box,1}$ and $(\ell_2, a, \psi_2, \ell_2') \in E_{\Box,2}$ then $((\ell_1, \ell_2), a, \psi_1 \wedge \psi_2, (\ell_1', \ell_2')) \in E_\Box$.*

Composition of specifications, similar to the classical notion of modal composition for modal transition systems [10], synchronizes on matching shared actions and only yields a must-transition if there exist corresponding matching must-transitions in the original specifications. Composition is commutative (up to isomorphism) and associative. Our theory supports independent implementability of specifications, which is a crucial requirement for any compositional specification framework [14].

Theorem 2. *Let $\mathbf{A}_1, \mathbf{A}_2, \mathbf{B}_1, \mathbf{B}_2$ be specifications such that $\mathbf{A}_2$ and $\mathbf{B}_2$ are composable. If $\mathbf{A}_1 \leq \mathbf{A}_2$ and $\mathbf{B}_1 \leq \mathbf{B}_2$, then $\mathbf{A}_1 \parallel \mathbf{B}_1 \leq \mathbf{A}_2 \parallel \mathbf{B}_2$.*

The analog of parallel composition on the level of specifications is parallel composition $\parallel_{sem}$ on the level of MSD which is a straightforward translation of the above symbolic rules. In fact one can prove that both parallel compositions $\parallel$ and $\parallel_{sem}$ are equivalent, i.e. that $\langle \mathbf{A}_1 \parallel \mathbf{A}_2 \rangle_{sem} = \langle \mathbf{A}_1 \rangle_{sem} \parallel_{sem} \langle \mathbf{A}_2 \rangle_{sem}$ for any two composable specifications $\mathbf{A}_1, \mathbf{A}_2$.

Remark 1. Interface theories based on transition systems labeled with input/output actions usually involve a notion of compatibility, which is a relation between interfaces determining whether two components can work properly together. Since the present theory does not have a notion of input/output it is enough to require that two components are composable, i.e. that their local variables do not overlap. A pessimistic input/output compatibility notion has been proposed in our previous work [15]. Optimistic input/output compatibility based on a game semantics allows computing all the environments in which two components can work together. Following our recent works in [16, 4], one can enrich labels of transitions in the present theory with input and output and apply the same game-based semantics in order to achieve an optimistic composition.

Syntactical consistency. Our next two specification operators, conjunction and quotient, may yield specifications which are *syntactically inconsistent*, i.e. either there is no legal initial data state or there are states with a must-transition but without corresponding may-transition.

In general, given a specification $\mathbf{A}$, syntactic consistency implies consistency, i.e. $Impl(\mathbf{A}) \neq \emptyset$, but in general, the reverse does not hold. However, every consistent specification can be "pruned" to a syntactically consistent one, by pruning backwards from all syntactically inconsistent states, removing states which have to reach some of the "bad" states. Pruning will be shown to preserve the set of implementations.

For a specification $\mathbf{A} = (Sig, Loc, \ell^0, \varphi^0, E_\Diamond, E_\Box)$, the pruning (or reduction) of $\mathbf{A}$, denoted by $\rho(\mathbf{A})$, is done as follows. Let $B : Loc \to Pred(V^L)$ be a mapping of locations to predicates over the local variables. We define a predecessor operation, iteratively computing all states that are forced to reach a "bad" state. Define a weakest precondition predicate, for $\psi \in Pred(V \uplus (V^L)')$, $\varphi \in Pred(V^L)$, by

$$\mathsf{wp}_\psi[\varphi] =_{def} \exists V^G.{}^\circ \psi \wedge (\forall (V^L)'.\psi \Rightarrow (\varphi)')$$

which computes the largest set of local states such that there exists an uncontrolled state $g \in [\![V^G]\!]$ such that ψ maps to at least one next state, and all next states satisfy φ. Then

$$\mathsf{predec}(B)(\ell) =_{def} B(\ell) \vee \bigvee_{a \in \Sigma, \ell' \in Loc, \psi \in Must^a(\ell, \ell')} \mathsf{wp}_\psi[B(\ell')]$$

and $\mathsf{predec}^0(B) =_{def} B$, $\mathsf{predec}^{j+1}(B) =_{def} \mathsf{predec}(\mathsf{predec}^j(B))$ for $j \geq 0$, and $\mathsf{predec}^*(B) =_{def} \bigcup_{j \geq 0} \mathsf{predec}^j(B)$. Define $\mathsf{bad} : Loc \to Pred(V^L)$, for $\ell \in Loc$, by

$$\mathsf{bad}(\ell) =_{def} \bigvee_{a \in \Sigma, \ell' \in Loc, \psi \in Must^a(\ell, \ell')} \exists V^G.{}^\circ \psi \wedge \left(\forall (V^L)'.\psi \Rightarrow \bigwedge_{\psi' \in May^a(\ell, \ell')} \neg \psi' \right)$$

and thus $\mathsf{bad}(\ell)$ is satisfied by a valuation $s \in [\![V^L]\!]$ iff there is a must-transition for which no choice of the next data state is permitted by the may-transitions.

In general, for infinite-domain variables, the computation of $\mathsf{predec}^*(\mathsf{bad})$ may not terminate. In [7], it was shown that reachability and related properties in well-structured transition systems with data values, that are monotonic transition systems with a well-quasi ordering on the set of data values, is decidable. This result can be used for specifications with infinite-domain variables to show that under these assumptions, there is some $j \geq 0$ such that for all $\ell \in Loc$, $[\![\mathrm{predec}^j(\mathrm{bad})(\ell)]\!] = [\![\mathrm{predec}^{j+1}(\mathrm{bad})(\ell)]\!]$. In the following, for the specification operators conjunction and quotient (which may result in a syntactically inconsistent specification and hence need to be pruned) we assume that such a $j \geq 0$ exists.

The *pruning* $\rho(\mathbf{A})$ of $\mathbf{A}$ is defined if $\varphi^0 \wedge \neg \mathrm{predec}^j(\mathrm{bad})(\ell^0)$ is consistent; and in this case, $\rho(\mathbf{A})$ is the specification $(Sig, Loc, \ell^0, \varphi^0 \wedge \neg\mathrm{predec}^j(\mathrm{bad})(\ell^0), E_\Diamond^\rho, E_\Box^\rho)$ where, for $\chi_{bad} = \mathrm{predec}^j(\mathrm{bad})$,

$$E_\Diamond^\rho = \{(\ell_1, a, \neg\chi_{bad}(\ell_1) \wedge \psi \wedge \neg(\chi_{bad}(\ell_2))', \ell_2) \mid (\ell_1, a, \psi, \ell_2) \in E_\Diamond\},$$
$$E_\Box^\rho = \{(\ell_1, a, \neg\chi_{bad}(\ell_1) \wedge \psi \wedge \neg(\chi_{bad}(\ell_2))', \ell_2) \mid (\ell_1, a, \psi, \ell_2) \in E_\Box\}.$$

Crucially the pruning operator has the expected properties:

Theorem 3. *Let $\mathbf{A}$ be a deterministic, possibly syntactically inconsistent specification. Then $\rho(\mathbf{A})$ is defined if and only if $\mathbf{A}$ is consistent. And if $\rho(\mathbf{A})$ is defined, then*

1. *$\rho(\mathbf{A})$ is a syntactically consistent specification,*
2. *$\rho(\mathbf{A}) \leq \mathbf{A}$,*
3. *$Impl(\mathbf{A}) = Impl(\rho(\mathbf{A}))$, and*
4. *for any syntactically consistent specification $\mathbf{B}$, if $\mathbf{B} \leq \mathbf{A}$, then $\mathbf{B} \leq \rho(\mathbf{A})$.*

Logical composition. Conjunction of two specifications yields the greatest lower bound with respect to modal refinement. Syntactic inconsistencies arise if one specification requires a behavior disallowed by the other.

Definition 6. *Let $\mathbf{A}_1$ and $\mathbf{A}_2$ be two specifications with the same signature $Sig = (\Sigma, V^L, V^G)$. The conjunction of $\mathbf{A}_1$ and $\mathbf{A}_2$ is defined as the possibly syntactically inconsistent specification*

$$\mathbf{A}_1 \wedge \mathbf{A}_2 = (Sig, Loc_1 \times Loc_2, (\ell_1^0, \ell_2^0), \varphi_1^0 \wedge \varphi_2^0, E_\Diamond, E_\Box)$$

where the transition relations $E_\Diamond$, $E_\Box$ are the smallest relations satisfying the rules, for any $\ell_1, \ell_1' \in Loc_1$, $\ell_2, \ell_2' \in Loc_2$, $a \in \Sigma$,

1. *If $(\ell_1, a, \psi_1, \ell_1') \in E_{\Diamond,1}$, $(\ell_2, a, \psi_2, \ell_2') \in E_{\Diamond,2}$, then*
   $((\ell_1, \ell_2), a, \psi_1 \wedge \psi_2, (\ell_1', \ell_2')) \in E_\Diamond$,
2. *If $(\ell_1, a, \psi_1, \ell_1') \in E_{\Box,1}$, then*
   $((\ell_1, \ell_2), a, \psi_1 \wedge (\bigvee_{\psi_2 \in May_2^a(\ell_2, \ell_2')} \psi_2), (\ell_1', \ell_2')) \in E_\Box$,
3. *If $(\ell_2, a, \psi_2, \ell_2') \in E_{\Box,2}$, then*
   $((\ell_1, \ell_2), a, \psi_2 \wedge (\bigvee_{\psi_1 \in May_1^a(\ell_1, \ell_1')} \psi_1), (\ell_1', \ell_2')) \in E_\Box$,
4. *If $(\ell_1, a, \psi_1, \ell_1') \in E_{\Box,1}$ then*
   $((\ell_1, \ell_2), a, {}^\circ\psi_1 \wedge (\forall(V^L)'.\psi_1 \Rightarrow \bigwedge_{\psi_2 \in M} \neg\psi_2), (\ell_1, \ell_2)) \in E_\Box$,
   where $M = \bigcup_{\ell_2' \in Loc_2} May_2^a(\ell_2, \ell_2')$,
5. *If $(\ell_2, a, \psi_2, \ell_2') \in E_{\Box,2}$ then*
   $((\ell_1, \ell_2), a, {}^\circ\psi_2 \wedge (\forall(V^L)'.\psi_2 \Rightarrow \bigwedge_{\psi_1 \in M} \neg\psi_1), (\ell_1, \ell_2)) \in E_\Box$,
   where $M = \bigcup_{\ell_1' \in Loc_1} May_1^a(\ell_1, \ell_1')$.

The first rule composes may-transitions (with the same action) by conjoining their predicates. Rule (2) and (3) express that any required behavior of $\mathbf{A}_1$ ($\mathbf{A}_2$ resp.), as long as it is allowed by $\mathbf{A}_2$ ($\mathbf{A}_1$ resp.), is also a required behavior in $\mathbf{A}_1 \wedge \mathbf{A}_2$. Rules (4) and (5) capture the case when a required behavior of $\mathbf{A}_1$ is not allowed by $\mathbf{A}_2$. Conjunction is commutative and associative.

Refinement is a precongruence with respect to conjunction for deterministic specifications. Moreover, under the assumption of determinism, the conjunction construction yields the greatest lower bound with respect to modal refinement:

Theorem 4. *Let* $\mathbf{A}$, $\mathbf{B}$, $\mathbf{C}$ *be specifications with the same signature and let* $\mathbf{A}$ *and* $\mathbf{B}$ *be deterministic. If* $\mathbf{A} \wedge \mathbf{B}$ *is consistent then*

1. $\rho(\mathbf{A} \wedge \mathbf{B}) \leq \mathbf{A}$ *and* $\rho(\mathbf{A} \wedge \mathbf{B}) \leq \mathbf{B}$,
2. $\mathbf{C} \leq \mathbf{A}$ *and* $\mathbf{C} \leq \mathbf{B}$ *implies* $\mathbf{C} \leq \rho(\mathbf{A} \wedge \mathbf{B})$,
3. $Impl(\rho(\mathbf{A} \wedge \mathbf{B})) = Impl(\mathbf{A}) \cap Impl(\mathbf{B})$.

Quotient as the dual operator to structural composition. The quotient operator allows factoring out behaviors from larger specifications. Given two specifications $\mathbf{A}$ and $\mathbf{B}$ the quotient of $\mathbf{B}$ by $\mathbf{A}$, in the following denoted $\mathbf{B} \backslash\!\backslash \mathbf{A}$, is the most general specification that can be composed with $\mathbf{A}$ and still refines $\mathbf{B}$.

In the following, we assume for the signatures $Sig_{\mathbf{A}} = (\Sigma, V_{\mathbf{A}}^L, V_{\mathbf{A}}^G)$ and $Sig_{\mathbf{B}} = (\Sigma, V_{\mathbf{B}}^L, V_{\mathbf{B}}^G)$ that $V_{\mathbf{A}}^L \subseteq V_{\mathbf{B}}^L$. The signature of the quotient $\mathbf{B} \backslash\!\backslash \mathbf{A}$ is then $Sig_{\mathbf{B}\backslash\!\backslash\mathbf{A}} = (\Sigma, V_{\mathbf{B}\backslash\!\backslash\mathbf{A}}^L, V_{\mathbf{B}\backslash\!\backslash\mathbf{A}}^G)$ with $V_{\mathbf{B}\backslash\!\backslash\mathbf{A}}^L = V_{\mathbf{B}}^L \setminus V_{\mathbf{A}}^L$ and $V_{\mathbf{B}\backslash\!\backslash\mathbf{A}}^G = V_{\mathbf{B}}^G \uplus V_{\mathbf{A}}^L$. Note that, as said before, we restrict ourselves to the case where $V_{\mathbf{A}}^L \uplus V_{\mathbf{A}}^G = V_{\mathbf{B}}^L \uplus V_{\mathbf{B}}^G$.

It is unknown if in our general model of specifications a finite quotient exists. For specifications involving variables with finite domains only, a semantic quotient operation can be defined, which works on the (finite) semantics of $\mathbf{A}$ and $\mathbf{B}$. As already noticed in previous works, e.g. [17], non-determinism is problematic for quotienting, and thus specifications are assumed to be deterministic. In our case, even when assuming deterministic specifications, the non-determinism with respect to the next local data state is still there: thus the quotient $\mathbf{B} \backslash\!\backslash \mathbf{A}$, when performing a transition, does not know the next data state of $\mathbf{A}$. However, due to our semantics, in which transitions are guarded by uncontrolled states, the quotient can always observe the current data state of $\mathbf{A}$. This extension of the usual quotient can be shown that it satisfies the following soundness and maximality property: Given MSD $\mathbf{S}$ and $\mathbf{T}$ such that $\mathbf{S}$ is deterministic and $\mathbf{T} \backslash\!\backslash_{\mathrm{sem}} \mathbf{S}$ is consistent, and assume a semantic pruning operator ρ_{sem} which is the straightforward translation of pruning ρ to the semantic level. Then $\mathbf{X} \leq_{\mathrm{sem}} \rho_{\mathrm{sem}}(\mathbf{T} \backslash\!\backslash_{\mathrm{sem}} \mathbf{S})$ if and only if $\mathbf{S} \|_{\mathrm{sem}} \mathbf{X} \leq_{\mathrm{sem}} \mathbf{T}$ for any MSD $\mathbf{X}$.

Now our goal is to compute the quotient at the symbolic level of specifications. We do this for a restricted subclass of specifications in which each occurring transition predicate ψ is *separable*, meaning that ψ is equivalent to $^\circ\psi \wedge \psi^\circ$. Although this might seem as a serious restriction, we can often transform transition systems with transition predicates of the form $(x)' = x + 1$ to transition systems with separable transition predicates while keeping the same set of implementations. For instance, if we know that there are only finitely many possible values $v_1, \ldots, v_n$ for x in the current state, we can "unfold" the specification and replace the transition predicates $(x)' = x + 1$ by $(x)' = v_i$, for $1 \leq i \leq n$.

The symbolic quotient introduces two new locations, the universal state (univ) and an error state ($\bot$). In the universal state the quotient can show arbitrary behavior and is needed to obtain maximality, and the error state is a syntactically inconsistent state used to encode conflicting requirements. The state space of the quotient is given by $Loc_{\mathbf{B}} \times Loc_{\mathbf{A}} \times Pred(V_{\mathbf{A}}^L)$, so every state stores not only the current location of $\mathbf{B}$ and $\mathbf{A}$ (like in [17]) but includes a predicate about the current possible data states of $\mathbf{A}$. For notational convenience, for $\varphi \in Pred(V_1 \uplus V_2)$ and $\varphi_1 \in Pred(V_1)$, we write $\varphi \parallel \varphi_1$ for $(\forall V_1.\varphi_1 \Rightarrow \varphi) \in Pred(V_2)$.

Definition 7. *Let $\mathbf{A}$ and $\mathbf{B}$ be two specifications such that $V_{\mathbf{A}}^L \subseteq V_{\mathbf{B}}^L$. The quotient of $\mathbf{B}$ by $\mathbf{A}$ is defined as the possibly syntactically inconsistent specification $\mathbf{B} \backslash\backslash \mathbf{A} = (Sig_{\mathbf{B}\backslash\mathbf{A}}, (Loc_{\mathbf{B}} \times Loc_{\mathbf{A}} \times Pred(V_{\mathbf{A}}^L)) \cup \{\text{univ}, \bot\}, (\ell_{\mathbf{B}}^0, \ell_{\mathbf{A}}^0, \varphi_{\mathbf{A}}^0), \varphi_{\mathbf{B}}^0 \parallel \varphi_{\mathbf{A}}^0, E_\Diamond, E_\Box)$ where the transition relations are given by, for all $a \in \Sigma$ and all $\xi_{\mathbf{A}} \in Pred(V_{\mathbf{A}}^L)$,*

1. *if $(\ell_{\mathbf{B}}, a, \psi_{\mathbf{B}}, \ell_{\mathbf{B}}') \in E_{\Diamond, \mathbf{B}}$ and $(\ell_{\mathbf{A}}, a, \psi_{\mathbf{A}}, \ell_{\mathbf{A}}') \in E_{\Diamond, \mathbf{A}}$, then*
   $((\ell_{\mathbf{B}}, \ell_{\mathbf{A}}, \xi_{\mathbf{A}}), a, \xi_{\mathbf{A}} \wedge {}^\circ\psi_{\mathbf{B}} \wedge {}^\circ\psi_{\mathbf{A}} \wedge (\psi_{\mathbf{B}}^\circ \parallel \psi_{\mathbf{A}}^\circ), (\ell_{\mathbf{B}}', \ell_{\mathbf{A}}', \psi_{\mathbf{A}}^\circ\!\downarrow)) \in E_\Diamond$,
2. *if $(\ell_{\mathbf{B}}, a, \psi_{\mathbf{B}}, \ell_{\mathbf{B}}') \in E_{\Box, \mathbf{B}}$ and $(\ell_{\mathbf{A}}, a, \psi_{\mathbf{A}}, \ell_{\mathbf{A}}') \in E_{\Box, \mathbf{A}}$, then*
   $((\ell_{\mathbf{B}}, \ell_{\mathbf{A}}, \xi_{\mathbf{A}}), a, \xi_{\mathbf{A}} \wedge {}^\circ\psi_{\mathbf{B}} \wedge {}^\circ\psi_{\mathbf{A}} \wedge (\psi_{\mathbf{B}}^\circ \parallel \psi_{\mathbf{A}}^\circ), (\ell_{\mathbf{B}}', \ell_{\mathbf{A}}', \psi_{\mathbf{A}}^\circ\!\downarrow)) \in E_\Box$,
3. *if $(\ell_{\mathbf{B}}, a, \psi_{\mathbf{B}}, \ell_{\mathbf{B}}') \in E_{\Box, \mathbf{B}}$ and $(\ell_{\mathbf{A}}, a, \psi_{\mathbf{A}}, \ell_{\mathbf{A}}') \in E_{\Box, \mathbf{A}}$, then*
   $((\ell_{\mathbf{B}}, \ell_{\mathbf{A}}, \xi_{\mathbf{A}}), a, \xi_{\mathbf{A}} \wedge {}^\circ\psi_{\mathbf{B}} \wedge {}^\circ\psi_{\mathbf{A}} \wedge \neg(\psi_{\mathbf{B}}^\circ \parallel \psi_{\mathbf{A}}^\circ), \bot) \in E_\Box$,
4. *if $(\ell_{\mathbf{B}}, a, \psi_{\mathbf{B}}, \ell_{\mathbf{B}}') \in E_{\Box, \mathbf{B}}$, then*
   $((\ell_{\mathbf{B}}, \ell_{\mathbf{A}}, \xi_{\mathbf{A}}), a, \xi_{\mathbf{A}} \wedge {}^\circ\psi_{\mathbf{B}} \wedge \bigwedge_{\psi_{\mathbf{A}} \in M} \neg{}^\circ\psi_{\mathbf{A}}, \bot) \in E_\Box$
   where $M = \bigcup_{\ell_{\mathbf{A}}' \in Loc_{\mathbf{A}}} Must_{\mathbf{A}}^a(\ell_{\mathbf{A}}, \ell_{\mathbf{A}}')$,
5. *$((\ell_{\mathbf{B}}, \ell_{\mathbf{A}}, \xi_{\mathbf{A}}), a, \neg\xi_{\mathbf{A}}, \text{univ}) \in E_\Diamond$,*
6. *$((\ell_{\mathbf{B}}, \ell_{\mathbf{A}}, \xi_{\mathbf{A}}), a, \xi_{\mathbf{A}} \wedge \bigwedge_{\psi_{\mathbf{A}} \in M} \neg{}^\circ\psi_{\mathbf{A}}, \text{univ}) \in E_\Diamond$*
   where $M = \bigcup_{\ell_{\mathbf{A}}' \in Loc_{\mathbf{A}}} May_{\mathbf{A}}^a(\ell_{\mathbf{A}}, \ell_{\mathbf{A}}')$,
7. *$(\text{univ}, a, true, \text{univ}) \in E_\Diamond$,*
8. *$(\bot, a, true, \bot) \in E_\Box$.*

Rules (1) and (2) capture the cases when both $\mathbf{A}$ and $\mathbf{B}$ can perform a may- and must-transition, respectively. Rules (3) and (4) capture any inconsistencies which can arise if for a must-transition in $\mathbf{B}$ there is no way to obtain a must-transition by composition of the quotient with $\mathbf{A}$. In order to obtain maximality, we add a universal state univ in which the behavior of the quotient is not restricted (rules (5)–(7)). Finally, the rule (8) makes the error state syntactically inconsistent.

Since we only have finitely many transition predicates $\psi_{\mathbf{A}}$ in $\mathbf{A}$, and they are all separable, the set of locations $(Loc_{\mathbf{B}} \times Loc_{\mathbf{A}} \times (\{\psi_{\mathbf{A}}^\circ\!\downarrow \mid \psi_{\mathbf{A}} \text{ occurring in } \mathbf{A}\} \cup \{\varphi_{\mathbf{A}}^0\})) \cup \{\text{univ}, \bot\}$ of $\mathbf{B} \backslash\backslash \mathbf{A}$ is also finite. Thus we can construct the symbolic quotient in a finite number of steps, starting in the initial state $(\ell_{\mathbf{B}}^0, \ell_{\mathbf{A}}^0, \varphi_{\mathbf{A}}^0)$, and iteratively constructing the transitions. Soundness and maximality of the quotient follows from the following theorem.

Theorem 5. *Let $\mathbf{A}$ and $\mathbf{B}$ be specifications such that $V_{\mathbf{A}}^L \subseteq V_{\mathbf{B}}^L$, all transition predicates of $\mathbf{A}$ and $\mathbf{B}$ are separable, $\mathbf{A}$ is deterministic and $\mathbf{B} \backslash\backslash \mathbf{A}$ is consistent. Then for any specification $\mathbf{C}$ such that $Sig_{\mathbf{C}} = Sig_{\mathbf{B}\backslash\mathbf{A}}$, $\mathbf{C} \leq \rho(\mathbf{B} \backslash\backslash \mathbf{A})$ if and only if $\mathbf{A} \parallel \mathbf{C} \leq \mathbf{B}$.*

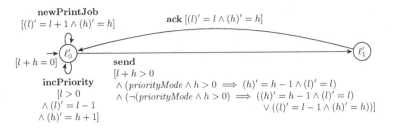

Fig. 5. Refined print server specification **Q**

4 Predicate Abstraction for Verification of Refinement

We now switch our focus to the problem of deciding whether a specification **A** refines another specification **B** (which reduces to checking $\langle \mathbf{A} \rangle_{\text{sem}} \leq_{\text{sem}} \langle \mathbf{B} \rangle_{\text{sem}}$). As soon as domains of variables are infinite, $\langle \mathbf{A} \rangle_{\text{sem}}$ and $\langle \mathbf{B} \rangle_{\text{sem}}$ may be MSD with infinitely many states and transitions. In this case, this problem is known to be undecidable in general. Thus we propose to resort to predicate abstraction techniques [18]. Given two specifications **A** and **B** we derive over- and under-approximations $\mathbf{A}^o$ and $\mathbf{B}^u$ which are guaranteed to be *finite* MSD. Then, we show that $\mathbf{A}^o \leq_{\text{sem}} \mathbf{B}^u$ implies $\mathbf{A} \leq \mathbf{B}$.

Example 5. Fig. 5 shows a print server specification **Q** which we will show is a refinement of the abstract specification **P** in Fig. 1. The behavior of the print server is now fixed for any number of print jobs. Moreover, the send transition has been refined such that depending on the priority mode (provided by the environment of the print server) a job with high priority (in case *priorityMode* is true) or a job with low priority (otherwise) is chosen next.

Given a specification $\mathbf{A} = (Sig, Loc, \ell^0, \varphi^0, \longrightarrow_\diamond, \longrightarrow_\square)$ with $Sig = (\Sigma, V^L, V^G)$, we partition the local state space and the uncontrolled state space using finitely many predicates $\phi_1, \phi_2, \ldots, \phi_N \in Pred(V^L)$ and $\chi_1, \chi_2, \ldots, \chi_M \in Pred(V^G)$. We fix these predicates in the following to simplify the presentation. The signature of the abstraction is then given by $Sig_{abstr} = (\Sigma, V^L_{abstr}, V^G_{abstr})$, where $V^L_{abstr} = \{x_1, x_2, \ldots, x_N\}$ and $V^G_{abstr} = \{y_1, y_2, \ldots, y_M\}$. All variables x_i, y_j have Boolean domain. A variable x_i (y_j) encodes whether the predicate ϕ_i (χ_j) holds or not.

Any abstract state $\nu \in [\![V^L_{abstr}]\!]$ is a conjunction of predicates $\bigwedge_{i=1}^N \phi_i^{\nu(x_i)}$, where $\phi_i^{\nu(x_i)} = \phi_i$ if $\nu(x_i) = 1$, else $\phi_i^{\nu(x_i)} = \neg\phi_i$. Further, a set of abstract states $N \subseteq [\![V^L_{abstr}]\!]$ corresponds to $\bigvee_{\nu \in N} \nu$. Similarly for any $\omega \in [\![V^G_{abstr}]\!]$ and for $M \subseteq [\![V^G_{abstr}]\!]$.

The transition relation of the over-approximation expands the allowed behaviors and limits the required behaviors. Dually, the under-approximation will further restrict the allowed behavior and add more required transitions. In other words, over-approximation is an *existential* abstraction on may-transitions and *universal* abstraction on must-transitions; dually for the under-approximation.

Formally, the *over-approximation* $\mathbf{A}^o$ of $\mathbf{A}$ is defined by the finite MSD $(Sig_{abstr}, Loc, \ell^0, S^0_{abstr}, \longrightarrow_{\diamond, abstr}, \longrightarrow_{\square, abstr})$, where the initial abstract state S^0_{abstr} contains all partitions containing some concrete initial state, i.e. the initial abstract state is defined by $S^0_{abstr} = \{\nu \in [\![V^L_{abstr}]\!] \mid \exists V^L.\nu \wedge \varphi^0\}$, and the abstract transition relations are derived as follows. For all $\ell, \ell' \in Loc$, $a \in Act$, $\nu, \dot{\nu} \in [\![V^L_{abstr}]\!]$, $\omega \in [\![V^G_{abstr}]\!]$,

i. If $\exists V.\exists (V^L)'.\nu \wedge \omega \wedge (\bigvee_{\psi \in May^a(\ell,\ell')} \psi) \wedge (\dot{\nu})'$, then $(\ell, \nu) \xrightarrow{\omega\,a}_{\diamond, abstr} (\ell', \{\dot{\nu}\})$, so there is a may-transition between partitions in the abstraction if there was a may-transition between any states in these partitions in the concrete system.

ii. Whenever, for some $N \subseteq [\![V^L_{abstr}]\!]$, the predicate

$$\forall V.\nu \wedge \omega \Rightarrow \bigvee_{\psi \in Must^a(\ell,\ell')} {}^\circ\psi \wedge (\forall (V^L)'.\psi \Rightarrow (N)')$$

is true and N is minimal with respect to this property, then $(\ell, \nu) \xrightarrow{\omega\,a}_{\square, abstr} (\ell', N)$.

For the *under-approximation* $\mathbf{B}^u$ of $\mathbf{B}$, we assume that every transition predicate ψ on a must-transition must be separable (see page 72). Moreover, in order to soundly capture must-transitions, we must be able to exactly describe the target set of (concrete) local states by a union of abstract states; so for any $(\ell, a, \psi, \ell') \in E_{\square, \mathbf{B}}$, there exists a set $N \subseteq [\![V^L_{abstr}]\!]$ such that $\forall (V^L)'. \psi^\circ \Leftrightarrow (N)'$. The under-approximation $\mathbf{B}^u$ is the finite MSD $(Sig_{abstr}, Loc, \ell^0, S^0_{abstr}, \longrightarrow_{\diamond, abstr}, \longrightarrow_{\square, abstr})$, where $S^0_{abstr} = \{\nu \in [\![V^L_{abstr}]\!] \mid \forall V^L.\nu \Rightarrow \varphi^0\}$, and for all $\ell, \ell' \in Loc$, $a \in Act$, $\nu, \dot{\nu} \in [\![V^L_{abstr}]\!]$, $\omega \in [\![V^G_{abstr}]\!]$,

i. If $\forall V.\forall (V^L)'.\nu \wedge \omega \wedge (\dot{\nu})' \Rightarrow \bigvee_{\psi \in May^a(\ell,\ell')} \psi$ then $(\ell, \nu) \xrightarrow{\omega\,a}_{\diamond, abstr} (\ell', \{\dot{\nu}\})$,

ii. For every $(\ell, a, \psi, \ell') \in E_\square$, if $\exists V.\nu \wedge \omega \wedge {}^\circ\psi$, then $(\ell, \nu) \xrightarrow{\omega\,a}_{\square, abstr} (\ell', N)$ where $N \subseteq [\![V^L_{abstr}]\!]$ such that $\forall (V^L)'. \psi^\circ \Leftrightarrow (N)'$.

Correctness of the abstraction follows from the following theorem.

Theorem 6. $\mathbf{A}^o \leq_{sem} \mathbf{B}^u$ *implies* $\mathbf{A} \leq \mathbf{B}$.

Example 6. Fig. 6 and Fig. 7 are over- and under-approximations of $\mathbf{Q}$ and $\mathbf{P}$, respectively. The MSD represent abstractions w.r.t. the predicates $\phi_{0,0} =_{def} h = l = 0$, $\phi_{0,1} =_{def} l = 0 \wedge h = 1$, $\phi_{1,0} =_{def} l = 1 \wedge h = 0$, and $\phi_{>1} =_{def} h + l > 1$ for the controlled variables l and h, and $\omega_1 =_{def} priorityMode$, $\omega_2 =_{def} \neg priorityMode$ for the uncontrolled variable $priorityMode$. Note that all transition predicates in $\mathbf{P}$ are separable, and all possible (concrete) poststates can be precisely captured by the predicates $\phi_{0,0}, \phi_{0,1}, \phi_{1,0}, \phi_{>1}$. For better readability we have omitted most of the guards ω_1, ω_2, i.e. every transition without guard stands for two transitions with the same action, source and target state(s), and with ω_1 and ω_2 as guard, respectively. Moreover, the state $(\ell_3, \phi_{0,0} \vee \phi_{0,1} \vee \phi_{1,0} \vee \phi_{>1})$ is a simplified notation which represents all the states (ℓ_3, ϕ) with $\phi \in \{\phi_{0,0}, \phi_{0,1}, \phi_{1,0}, \phi_{>1}\}$ and all may-transitions leading to it lead to each of the states, and the may-loop stands for all the transitions between each of the states. Obviously, $\mathbf{Q}^o \leq_{sem} \mathbf{P}^u$, and from Thm. 6 it follows that $\mathbf{Q} \leq \mathbf{P}$.

Even though this abstraction technique requires separability of predicates, it is applicable to a larger set of specifications. Sometimes, as already described in the previous section, transitions with non-separable predicates can be replaced by finite sets of transitions to achieve separability, without changing the semantics of the specification. Automatic procedures for generation of predicates are subject of future work. Finally, our abstraction also supports compositional reasoning about parallel composition in the following sense:

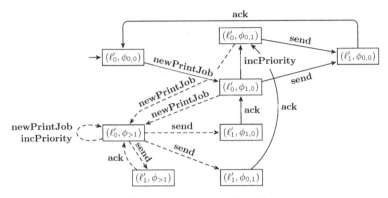

Fig. 6. Over-approximation $\mathbf{Q}^o$

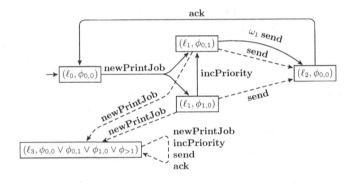

Fig. 7. Under-approximation $\mathbf{P}^u$

Theorem 7. *Let $\mathbf{A}$ and $\mathbf{B}$ be two composable specifications, and $V^G_{\mathbf{A}\|\mathbf{B}} = (V^G_{\mathbf{A}} \cup V^G_{\mathbf{B}}) \setminus (V^L_{\mathbf{A}} \uplus V^L_{\mathbf{B}})$. Let $E_{\mathbf{A}} \subseteq Pred(V^L_{\mathbf{A}})$, $E_{\mathbf{A}} \subseteq Pred(V^L_{\mathbf{B}})$, and $F \subseteq Pred(V^G_{\mathbf{A}\|\mathbf{B}})$ be sets of predicates partitioning the respective data states.*

$\mathbf{A}$ is approximated w.r.t. $E_{\mathbf{A}}$ for $V^L_{\mathbf{A}}$, and $E_{\mathbf{B}} \cup F$ for $V^G_{\mathbf{A}} = V^G_{\mathbf{A}\|\mathbf{B}} \uplus V^L_{\mathbf{B}}$ and similarly, $\mathbf{B}$ is approximated w.r.t. $E_{\mathbf{B}}$ and $E_{\mathbf{A}} \cup F$. Finally, $\mathbf{A} \parallel \mathbf{B}$ is approximated w.r.t. $E_{\mathbf{A}} \cup E_{\mathbf{B}}$ for $V^L_{\mathbf{A}\|\mathbf{B}} = V^L_{\mathbf{A}} \uplus V^L_{\mathbf{B}}$, and F for $V^G_{\mathbf{A}\|\mathbf{B}}$. We assume that each predicate, in any abstraction of $\mathbf{A}$, $\mathbf{B}$, or $\mathbf{A} \parallel \mathbf{B}$, is encoded with the same variable.

Then $(\mathbf{A} \parallel \mathbf{B})^o \leq_{\mathrm{sem}} \mathbf{A}^o \parallel_{\mathrm{sem}} \mathbf{B}^o$, and $\mathbf{A}^u \parallel_{\mathrm{sem}} \mathbf{B}^u \leq_{\mathrm{sem}} (\mathbf{A} \parallel \mathbf{B})^u$.

This result allows reusing abstractions of individual components in a continued development and verification process. For instance, if we want to verify $\mathbf{A} \parallel \mathbf{B} \leq \mathbf{C}$ then we can compute (or reuse) the less complex abstractions $\mathbf{A}^o$ and $\mathbf{B}^o$. Thm. 7 implies then that from $\mathbf{A}^o \parallel_{\mathrm{sem}} \mathbf{B}^o \leq_{\mathrm{sem}} \mathbf{C}^u$ we can infer $\mathbf{A} \parallel \mathbf{B} \leq \mathbf{C}$.

5   Related Work

The main difference to related approaches based on modal process algebra taking data states into account, e.g. [19], is that they cannot naturally express logical and structural composition in the same formalism. A comparison between modal specifications and other theories such as interface automata [20] and process algebra [2] can be found in [3]. In [8], the authors introduced sociable interfaces, that is a model of I/O automata [21] equipped with data and a game-based semantics. While their communication primitives are richer, sociable interfaces do not encompass any notion of logical composition and quotient, and their refinement is based on an alternating simulation.

Transition systems enriched with predicates are used, for instance, in the approach of [22, 23] where they use symbolic transition systems (STS), but STS do not support modalities and loose data specifications as they focus more on model checking than on the (top down) development of concurrent systems by refinement.

In [15] modal I/O automata has been extended by pre- and postconditions viewed as contracts, however, only semantics in terms of sets of implementations have been defined (implementations with only input actions correspond to our TSD). Modal refinement as defined in [15] is coarser than in this paper, and moreover, neither conjunction nor a quotient operation are defined.

6   Conclusion

We have proposed a specification theory for reasoning about components with rich data state. Our formalism, based on modal transition systems, supports: refinement checking, consistency checking with pruning of inconsistent states, structural and logical composition, and a quotient operator. The specification operators are defined on the symbolic representation which allows for automatic analysis of specifications. We have also presented a predicate abstraction technique for the verification of modal refinement. We believe that this work is a significant step towards practical use of specification theories based on modal transition systems. The ability to reason about data domains permits the modeling of industrial case studies.

In the future, we intend to develop larger case studies. Furthermore, we would like to extend the formalism with more complex communication patterns and to investigate in which cases we can still obtain all the operators on specifications, in particular the quotient operator. We are also planning to implement the theory in the MIO Workbench [24, 25], a verification tool for modal input/output interfaces.

Acknowledgment. We would like to thank Rolf Hennicker for valuable comments on a draft of the paper.

References

[1] Larsen, K.G.: Modal Specifications. In: Sifakis, J. (ed.) CAV 1989. LNCS, vol. 407, pp. 232–246. Springer, Heidelberg (1990)

[2] Milner, R.: A Calculus of Communication Systems. LNCS, vol. 92. Springer (1980)

[3] Nyman, U.: Modal Transition Systems as the Basis for Interface Theories and Product Lines. PhD thesis, Department of Computer Science, Aalborg University (October 2008)

[4] Raclet, J.-B., Badouel, E., Benveniste, A., Caillaud, B., Legay, A., Passerone, R.: Modal interfaces: unifying interface automata and modal specifications. In: Chakraborty, S., Halbwachs, N. (eds.) EMSOFT. ACM (2009)

[5] Abdulla, P.A., Bouajjani, A., d'Orso, J.: Monotonic and downward closed games. J. Log. Comput. 18(1), 153–169 (2008)

[6] Godefroid, P., Huth, M., Jagadeesan, R.: Abstraction-Based Model Checking Using Modal Transition Systems. In: Larsen, K.G., Nielsen, M. (eds.) CONCUR 2001. LNCS, vol. 2154, pp. 426–440. Springer, Heidelberg (2001)

[7] Abdulla, P.A., Cerans, K., Jonsson, B., Tsay, Y.-K.: Algorithmic analysis of programs with well quasi-ordered domains. Inf. Comput. 160(1-2), 109–127 (2000)

[8] de Alfaro, L., da Silva, L.D., Faella, M., Legay, A., Roy, P., Sorea, M.: Sociable Interfaces. In: Gramlich, B. (ed.) FroCos 2005. LNCS (LNAI), vol. 3717, pp. 81–105. Springer, Heidelberg (2005)

[9] Larsen, K.G., Xinxin, L.: Equation solving using modal transition systems. In: LICS, pp. 108–117. IEEE Computer Society (1990)

[10] Larsen, K.G., Thomsen, B.: A modal process logic. In: LICS, pp. 203–210. IEEE Computer Society (1988)

[11] Antonik, A., Huth, M., Larsen, K.G., Nyman, U., Wąsowski, A.: Complexity of Decision Problems for Mixed and Modal Specifications. In: Amadio, R.M. (ed.) FOSSACS 2008. LNCS, vol. 4962, pp. 112–126. Springer, Heidelberg (2008)

[12] Larsen, K.G., Nyman, U., Wąsowski, A.: On Modal Refinement and Consistency. In: Caires, L., Vasconcelos, V.T. (eds.) CONCUR 2007. LNCS, vol. 4703, pp. 105–119. Springer, Heidelberg (2007)

[13] Benes, N., Kretínský, J., Larsen, K.G., Srba, J.: On determinism in modal transition systems. Theor. Comput. Sci. 410(41), 4026–4043 (2009)

[14] de Alfaro, L., Henzinger, T.A.: Interface Theories for Component-Based Design. In: Henzinger, T.A., Kirsch, C.M. (eds.) EMSOFT 2001. LNCS, vol. 2211, pp. 148–165. Springer, Heidelberg (2001)

[15] Bauer, S.S., Hennicker, R., Wirsing, M.: Interface theories for concurrency and data. Theor. Comput. Sci. 412(28), 3101–3121 (2011)

[16] Larsen, K.G., Nyman, U., Wąsowski, A.: Modal I/O Automata for Interface and Product Line Theories. In: De Nicola, R. (ed.) ESOP 2007. LNCS, vol. 4421, pp. 64–79. Springer, Heidelberg (2007)

[17] Raclet, J.-B.: Residual for component specifications. Electr. Notes Theor. Comput. Sci. 215, 93–110 (2008)

[18] Graf, S., Saïdi, H.: Construction of Abstract State Graphs with PVS. In: Grumberg, O. (ed.) CAV 1997. LNCS, vol. 1254, pp. 72–83. Springer, Heidelberg (1997)

[19] van de Pol, J., Valero Espada, M.: Modal Abstractions in μCRL. In: Rattray, C., Maharaj, S., Shankland, C. (eds.) AMAST 2004. LNCS, vol. 3116, pp. 409–425. Springer, Heidelberg (2004)

[20] de Alfaro, L., Henzinger, T.A.: Interface automata. SIGSOFT Softw. Eng. Notes 26, 109–120 (2001)

[21] Lynch, N., Tuttle, M.R.: An introduction to Input/Output automata. CWI-quarterly 2(3) (1989)

[22] Fernandes, F., Royer, J.-C.: The STSLib project: Towards a formal component model based on STS. Electr. Notes Theor. Comput. Sci. 215, 131–149 (2008)

[23] Barros, T., Ameur-Boulifa, R., Cansado, A., Henrio, L., Madelaine, E.: Behavioural models for distributed fractal components. Annales des Télécommunications 64(1-2), 25–43 (2009)

[24] Bauer, S.S., Mayer, P., Schroeder, A., Hennicker, R.: On Weak Modal Compatibility, Refinement, and the MIO Workbench. In: Esparza, J., Majumdar, R. (eds.) TACAS 2010. LNCS, vol. 6015, pp. 175–189. Springer, Heidelberg (2010)

[25] Bauer, S.S., Mayer, P., Legay, A.: MIO Workbench: A Tool for Compositional Design with Modal Input/Output Interfaces. In: Bultan, T., Hsiung, P.-A. (eds.) ATVA 2011. LNCS, vol. 6996, pp. 418–421. Springer, Heidelberg (2011)

Evaluating the Performance of Model Transformation Styles in Maude*

Roberto Bruni[1] and Alberto Lluch Lafuente[2]

[1] Department of Computer Science, University of Pisa, Italy
[2] IMT Institute for Advanced Studies Lucca, Italy

Abstract. Rule-based programming has been shown to be very successful in many application areas. Two prominent examples are the specification of model transformations in model driven development approaches
and the definition of structured operational semantics of formal languages. General rewriting frameworks such as Maude are flexible enough
to allow the programmer to adopt and mix various rule styles. The choice
between styles can be biased by the programmer's background. For instance, experts in visual formalisms might prefer graph-rewriting styles,
while experts in semantics might prefer structurally inductive rules. This
paper evaluates the performance of different rule styles on a significant
benchmark taken from the literature on model transformation. Depending on the actual transformation being carried out, our results show that
different rule styles can offer drastically different performances. We point
out the situations from which each rule style benefits to offer a valuable
set of hints for choosing one style over the other.

1 Introduction

Many engineering activities are devoted to manipulate software artifacts to enhance or customize them, or to define their possible ordinary evolutions and
exceptional reconfigurations. The concept of *model* as unifying software artifact
representation has been promoted as a means to facilitate the specification of
such activities in a generic way. Many dynamic aspects can be conceived as
model transformations: e.g. architectural reconfigurations, component adapta-
tions, software refactorings, and language translations. Rule-based specifications
have been widely adopted as a declarative approach to enact model-driven transformations, thanks to the intuitive meaning and solid foundations offered by
rule-based machineries like term [1] and graph rewriting [2].

Recently we have investigated the possibility to exploit the structure of models to enhance software description and to facilitate model transformations [3,4].
Indeed, many domains exhibit an inherently hierarchical structure that can
be exploited conveniently to guarantee scalability. We mention, among others,
nested components in software architectures and reflective object-oriented systems, nested sessions and transactions in business processes, nested membranes

---

* Work supported by the EU Project ASCENS and the Italian MIUR Project IPODS.

F. Arbab and P.C. Ölveczky (Eds.): FACS 2011, LNCS 7253, pp. 79–96, 2012.
© Springer-Verlag Berlin Heidelberg 2012

in computational biology, composition associations in UML-like modeling frameworks, semi-structured data in XML-like formats, and so on. Very often such layering is represented in a plain manner by overlapping the intra- and the inter-layered structure. For instance, models are usually formalised as flat object configurations (e.g. graphs) and their manipulation is studied with tools and techniques based on rewriting theories that do not fully exploit the hierarchical structure. On the other hand, an *explicit* treatment of the hierarchical structure for specifying and transforming model-based software artifacts is possible. As a matter of fact, some layering structures (like composition relations in UML-like languages) can be conveniently represented by an explicit hierarchical structure enabling then hierarchical manipulations of the resulting models.

We have investigated such issues in previous work [3] proposing an approach analogous to the *russian dolls* of [5,6], where objects can be nested within other objects. In this view, *structured* models are represented by terms that can be manipulated by means of term-rewrite techniques like conditional term rewriting [1]. In [3] we compared the flat representation against the nested one, showing that they are essentially equivalent in the sense that one can bijectively pass from one to the other. Each representation naturally calls for different rule styles and the comparison in [3] mainly addressed methodological aspects, leaving one pragmatical issue open: how to decide in advance which approach is more efficient for actually executing a model transformation?

We offer an answer to this question in this paper. We have selected two prominent approaches to model transformation. The first one is archetypal of the graph-transformation based model-driven community and follows the style of [7]. The second one is quite common in process calculi and goes along the tradition of Plotkin's structural operational semantics, as outlined in [3]. Both approaches can be adopted in flexible rule-based languages like Maude [8] (the rewriting logic based language and framework we have chosen). In order to obtain significant results we have implemented three test cases widely used in the literature: the reconfiguration of components that migrate from one location to another one, the transformation of class diagrams into relational schemas, and the refactoring of class diagrams by pulling up attributes. As a byproduct we offer a novel implementation of these three classical transformations based on conditional rules. Indeed, such style of programming model transformations has not been proposed by other authors, as far as we know.

Our experimental results stress the importance of choosing the right transformation style carefully to obtain the best possible performance. We point out some features of the examples that impact on the performance of each rule format, thus providing the programmer with a set of valuable guidelines for programming model transformations in expressive rule-based frameworks like Maude.

Synopsis. § 2 presents a graph-based algebraic representation of models as nested object collections and describes rewrite rule styles for implementing model transformations in Maude. § 3 presents some enhancements that can be applied to the transformation styles. § 4 describes our benchmark. § 5 presents the experimental results. § 6 concludes the paper.

2   Preliminaries

In this section we illustrate the two key model transformation paradigms and the Maude notation we shall exploit in the rest of the paper over a basic example of transformation, namely from trees to list. A classical approach would provide ad-hoc data structures for trees and lists and an ad-hoc algorithm for implementing the transformation. Model driven approaches, instead, consider a common representation formalism for both data structures and a generic transformation procedure that acts on such formalism. In our setting, the representation formalism for models are collections of attributed objects and the transformation procedure is based on rewrite rules.

The Maude language already provides some machinery for this purpose, called object-based configurations [8], which we tend to follow with slight modifications aimed to ease the presentation. More precisely we represent models as *nested object collections* [3] (following an idea originally proposed in [5] and initially sketched in [6]), which can be understood as a particular class of attributed, hierarchical graphs. We then implement transformations as sets of rewrite rules.

Rewriting Logic and Maude.   Maude modules describe theories of rewriting logic [1], which are tuples $\langle \Sigma, E, R \rangle$ where Σ is a signature, specifying the basic syntax (function symbols) and type machinery (sorts, kinds and subsorting) for terms, e.g. model descriptions; E is a set of (possibly conditional) equations, which induce equivalence classes of terms, and (possibly conditional) membership predicates, which refine the typing information; R is a set of (possibly conditional) rules, e.g. model transformations.

The signature Σ and the equations E of a rewrite theory form a *membership equational theory* $\langle \Sigma, E \rangle$, whose initial algebra is denoted by $T_{\Sigma/E}$. Indeed, $T_{\Sigma/E}$ is the state space of a rewrite theory, i.e. states (e.g. models) are equivalence classes of Σ-terms modulo the least congruence induced by the axioms in E (denoted by $[t]_E$ or t for short). Sort declarations takes the form sort S and subsorting (i.e. subtyping) is written subsort S < T. For instance, the sort of objects (sort Obj) is a subsort of configurations (sort Configuration) as declared by subsort Obj < Configuration.

Operators are declared in Maude notation as op f : TL -> T [As] where f is the operator symbol (possibly with mixfix notation where underscores _ stand for argument placeholders), TL is a (possibly empty, blank separated) list of domain sorts, T is the sort of the co-domain, and As is a set of equational attributes (e.g. associativity, commutativity). For example, object configurations (sort Configuration) are constructed with operators for the empty configuration (op none: -> Configuration), single objects (via subsorting) or the union of configurations (juxtaposition op _ _ : Configuration Configuration -> Configuration [assoc comm id:none]), declared to be associative, commutative and to have none as its identity operator (i.e. they are multisets).

Each object represents an entity and its properties. Technically, an object is defined by its identifier (of sort Oid), its class (of sort Cid) and its attributes (of sort AttSet). Objects are built with an operation op < _ : _ | _ >: Oid Cid

`AttSet -> Obj`. Following Maude conventions, we shall use quoted identifiers like `'a` as object identifiers, while class identifiers will be defined by ad-hoc constructors. In our running example we use the constants `Node` and `Item` of sort `Cid` to denote the classes of tree nodes and list items, respectively.

The attributes of an object define its properties and relations to other objects. They are basically of two kinds: datatype attributes and association ends. Datatype attributes take the form `n: v`, where `n` is the attribute name and `v` is the attribute value. For instance, in our running example we shall consider a natural attribute `value` (sort `Nat`), representing the value of a node or item. A node with identifier `'a` and value 5 is denoted by `< 'a : Node | value: 5 >`.

Relations between objects can be represented in different ways. One typical approach is to use a pair of references (called *association ends* in UML terminology) for each relation. So if an object `o1` is in relation `R` with object `o2` then `o1` is equipped with a reference to `o2` and vice versa. In our case this is achieved with attributes of the form `R: O2` and `opp(R): O1` where `R` indicates the relation name and `O1`, `O2` are sets of object identifiers (sort `OidSet`). Association ends of the same relation within one object are grouped together (hence the use of identifier sets as domain of association attributes). In our example we have two relations `left` and `right` between a node and its left and right children, and one relation `next` between an item of the list and the next one. Clearly, the opposite relations of `left`, `right` and `next` are the parent and previous relations. As an example of a pair of references consider a node `< 'a : Node | value: 5 , left: 'b >` and its son `< 'b : Node | value: 3 , opp(left): 'a >`. Of course an object can be equipped with any number of attributes. Actually, the attributes of an object form a set built out of singleton attributes, the empty set (`none`) and union set (denoted with `_ , _`).

The following simple configuration represents a tree with three nodes.

```
< 'a : Node | value: 5 , left: 'b , right: 'c >
< 'b : Node | value: 3 , opp(left): 'a >
< 'c : Node | value: 7 , opp(right): 'a >
```

Operation `<< _ >> : Configuration -> Model` wraps a configuration into a model.

Functions (and equations that cannot be declared as equational attributes) are defined by a set of confluent and terminating conditional equations of the form `ceq t = t' if c`, where where `t, t'` are Σ-terms, and `c` is an application condition. When the application condition is vacuous, the simpler syntax `eq t = t'` can be used. For example, an operator `op size : Configuration -> Nat` for measuring the number of objects in a configuration is inductively defined by equations `eq size(none) = 0` and `eq size(O C) = 1 + size(C)` (with `O, C` being variables of sort `Obj`, `Configuration`, respectively). Roughly, an equational rule can be applied to a term `t''` if we find a match `m` (i.e. a variable substitution) for `t` at some place in `t''` such that `m(c)` holds (i.e. `c` after the application of the substitution `m` evaluates to true). The effect is that of substituting the matched part with `m(t')`. For example, calculating the size of the above tree is done by reducing `size(< 'a : Node | value: 5 ,`

```
left: 'b , right: 'c > < 'b : Node | value: 3 , opp(left): 'a > <
'c : Node | value: 7 , opp(right): 'a >) to 1 + size(< 'b : Node |
value: 3 , opp(left): 'a > < 'c : Node | value: 7 ,opp(right): 'a
>), then to 2 + size(< 'c : Node | value: 7 , opp(right): 'a >) and
```
finally to 3.

Structured models. A *nested object collection* allows objects to have *container attributes*, i.e. configuration domain attributes. While in a plain object collection a containment relation r between two objects o1 and o2 is represented by exploiting a pair of association end attributes r and opp(r), now o2 is embedded into o1 by means of the container attribute r. For instance, the above tree becomes

```
< 'a : Node | value: 5 ,
            left: < 'b : Node | value: 3 > ,
            right: < 'c : Node | value: 7 > > >
```

The hierarchical structure of models forms a tree. The two approaches that we have described differ essentially in the way we represent such a tree. Indeed, flat and nested representations are in bijective correspondence, i.e. for each flat object collection we can obtain a unique nested collection and vice versa as shown in [3], so that we can pass from one to the other as we find more convenient for specific applications or analyses.

Transformations as sets of rewrite rules. Transformations can be defined by means of rewrite rules, which take the form crl t => t' if c, where t, t' are Σ-terms, and c is an application condition (a predicate on the terms involved in the rewrite, further rewrites whose result can be reused, membership predicates, etc.). When the application condition is vacuous, the simpler syntax rl t => t' can be used. Matching and rule application are similar to the case of equations with the main difference being that rules are not required to be confluent and terminating (as they represent possibly non-deterministic concurrent actions rather than functions). Equational simplification has precedence over rule application in order to simulate rule application modulo equational equivalence.

SPO transformations. The need for visual modelling languages and the graph-based nature of models have contributed to the success of graph transformation approaches to model transformations. In such approaches, transformations are programmed in a declarative way by means of a set of graph rewrite rules. The transformation style that we consider here is based on the algebraic graph transformation approach [2]. The main idea is that each rule has a left-hand side and a right-hand side pattern. Each pattern is composed by a set of objects (nodes) possibly interrelated by means of association ends (edges). A rule can be applied to a model whenever the left-hand side can be matched with part of the model, i.e. each object in the left-hand side is (injectively) identified with an object and idem for the association ends. The application of a rule removes the matched part of the model that does not have a counterpart in the right-hand side and, vice versa, adds to the model a fresh copy of the right-hand side part that is not present in the left-hand side. Items in common between the left-hand side and the right-hand side are preserved during the application of the rule. Very often, rules are equipped with additional application conditions, including those typical of graph transformation systems (e.g. to avoid dangling edges) and its extensions like *Negative Application Conditions* (NACs).

In our setting, this means that rules have in general the following format:

```
crl << lhs conf1 >> => << rhs conf1 >> if applicable(lhs conf1) .
```

where `lhs` and `rhs` stand for the rule's left- and right-hand side configurations, `conf1` as the context in which the rule will be applied, and `applicable` is the boolean function implementing the application condition. Simpler forms are possible, e.g. in absence of application conditions the context is not necessary and rules take the form: `rl lhs => rhs` .

In our running example the transformation rules basically take a node x and its children y and z and puts them in some sequence, with x before y and z. This rule might introduce branches in the sequence that are solved by appropriate rules. A couple of rules are needed to handle some special cases, like x being the root or a node that has already been put in the list (in the middle, tail or head). Let us show one of the basic rules (the rest of the rules are very similar):

```
rl [nodeToItem]
    << < x : Node | value: vx , left: y , right: z , next: u , Ax >
       < y : Node | value: vy , op(left): x, Ay >
       < z : Node | value: vz , op(right): x, Az >
       < u : Node | value: vu , op(next): x, Au >
       conf1 >> =>
    << < x : Item | value: vx , next: y , Ax>
       < y : Node | value: vy , op(next): x, next: z , Ay >
       < z : Node | value: vz , op(next): y, next: u , Az >
       < u : Node | value: vu , op(next): z, Au >
       conf1 >> .
```

SOS transformations. We now describe transformation rules in the style of *Structural Operational Semantics* [9] (SOS). The basic idea is to define a model transformation by structural induction, which in our setting basically amounts to exploiting set union and (possibly) nesting.

We recall that SOS rules make use of labels to coordinate rule applications. We first present the implementation style of SOS semantics in rewriting logic as described in [10] and then present our own encoding of SOS which provides a more efficient implementation, though circumscribed to some special cases.

The approach of [10] requires to enrich the signatures with sorts for rule labels (Lab), label-prefixed configurations `LabConfiguration`, and a constructor `{_}_` : `Lab Configuration => LabConfiguration` for label-prefixed configurations. In addition, rule application is allowed at the top-level of terms only (via Maude's `frozen` attribute [11]) so that sub-terms are rewritten only when required in the premise of a rule (as required by the semantics of SOS rules). With this notation a term {lab1}conf1 represents that a configuration conf1 has been obtained after application of a lab1-labelled rule.

One typical rule format in our case allows us to conclude a transformation lab3 for a configuration made of two parts conf1 and conf2 provided that each part can respectively perform some transformation lab1, lab2:

```
crl conf1 conf2 => {lab3} conf3 conf4
 if conf1 => {lab1} conf3
 /\ conf2 => {lab2} conf4 .
```

Typically, the combination of labels will follow some classical form. For instance, with Milner-like synchronisation, lab1, lab2 can be complementary actions, in which case lab3 would be a silent action label. Instead, Hoare-like synchronisation would require lab1, lab2 and lab3 to be equal.

Consider now a hierarchical representation of models based on nested object collections. In this situation we need rules for dealing with nesting. Typically, the needed rule format is the one that defines the transformation lab1 of an object oid1 conditional to some transformation lab2 of one of its contents c:

```
crl < oid1 : cid1 | c: conf1 , attSet1 > =>
    {lab1} < oid1 : cid1 | c: conf2 , f(attSet1) >
 if conf1 => {lab2} conf2 .
```

Such rules might affect the attributes of the container object (denoted with function f) but will typically not change the object's identifier or class. More elaborated versions of the above rule are also possible, for instance involving more than one object or not requiring any rewrite of contained objects.

In our running example we have the following rule that transforms a tree provided that its subtrees can be transformed into lists

```
crl [root] : < x : Node | value: vx , left: leftTree , right: rightTree >
        => {toList}
           list1
           < tail : Item | value: vt , opp(next): y , next: x >
           < x : Item | value: vx , opp(next): tail , next: head >
           < head : Item | value: vh, opp(next): x , next: z >
           list2
 if leftTree => {toList} list1 < tail : Item | value: vt , opp(next): y >
 /\ rightTree => {toList}  < head : Item | value: vh , next: z > list2 .
```

Note that head and tail of the transformed sublists are identified by the lack of next and opp(next) attributes. Rules are also needed to handle leafs:

```
rl [leaf] : < x : Node | value: vx > => {toList} < x : Node | value: vx > .
```

Finally, rules are needed to close the transformations at the level of models. Such rules have the following format:

```
crl << conf1 >> => << conf2 >> if conf1 => {lab1} conf2 .
```

In our example the rule would be

```
crl << conf1 >> => << conf2 >> if conf1 => {toList} conf2 .
```

3   Enhanced SOS Implementation

While performing our preliminary experiments we discovered a more efficient way to encode SOS rules in rewriting logic that we call SOS*.

The most significant improvement applies to those cases in which the labels of the sub-configurations are known in advance. As a matter of fact this was the case of all test cases we consider in the next section. The idea is to put the labels on the left-hand side of rules as a sort of context requiring the firing of transformations with such label. In other words, we pass from post- to pre-rule applicability checks.

As a more general example the above rule scheme becomes now:

```
crl {lab3} conf1 conf2 => conf3 conf4
 if {lab1} conf1 => conf3
 /\ {lab2} conf2 => conf4 .
```

The main difference is that now `lab1` and `lab2` are known in advance and not obtained as a result of the conditional rewrites. A notable example where this alternative encoding cannot be immediately applied are the semantics of process calculi where synchronisation rules do not know in advance which signals are ready to perform their subprocesses.

Another slight improvement is the object-by-object decomposition of object collections instead of the one based on a pair of subsets presented above. For example the above rule scheme becomes:

```
crl {lab3} obj1 conf2 => obj3 conf4
 if {lab1} obj1 => obj3
 /\ {lab2} conf2 => conf4 .
```

A more significant improvement is that in some cases we allow to contextualise rules at any place of a term. We recall that in a SOS derivation this is typically achieved by rules that lift up *silent* (e.g. τ-labelled) actions. Technically this is essentially achieved by declaring as frozen the labelling operator `{_}_` only. This allows to apply rules to transform a sub-configuration at any level of the nesting hierarchy. That is, SOS rules like the ones for lifting silent actions across the nesting hierarchy like

```
crl < oid1 : cid1 | c: conf1 , attSet1 > =>
    {tau} < oid1 : cid1 | c: conf2 , attSet1 >
 if conf1 => {tau} conf2 .
```

or rules to lift silent actions among object configurations at the same level of the hierarchy like

```
crl obj1 conf2 => {tau}  obj3 conf2
 if obj1 => {tau}  obj3 .
```

are not necessary in the SOS* style.

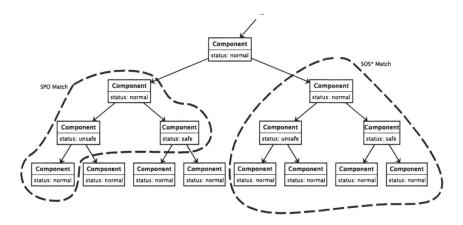

Fig. 1. An instance of the model reconfiguration test case

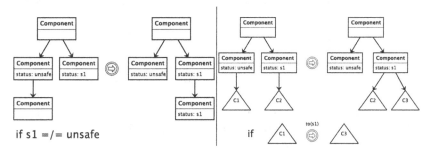

Fig. 2. An SPO rule (left) and a SOS rule (right) for architectural reconfiguration

4   Benchmark

Our benchmark consists of three test cases selected from the literature as archetypal examples of model reconfigurations, transformations and refactorings. In the following we describe the main features of each test case, emphasizing the most relevant details.

Architectural reconfiguration. The first test case we consider is the typical reconfiguration scenario in which some components must be migrated from one compromised location to another one. Many instances of this situation arise in practice (e.g. clients or jobs that must be migrated from one server to another one). Some instances of this scenario can be found e.g. in [7,12]. In what follows we consider a scenario in which components can be nested within each other. Components within an *unsafe* component x must be migrated into an uncle

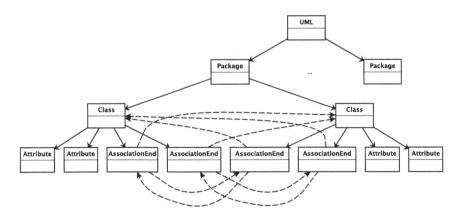

Fig. 3. An instance of the model translation test case

component y with the additional requirement of changing their status according to the status of their new container y. Figure 1 depicts one possible instance of the scenario.[1]

The most significant SPO rule[2] is depicted on the left of Fig. 2. It takes an unsafe component and a safe component that are neighbours (they have a common container) and moves the component inside the compromised component one to the safe one while changing its status. More rules are needed (for instance for considering top-level rooms without containers) and some of them have application conditions. As a consequence, the applicability of those rule requires to check the whole model and there is no predefined order on which rules to apply first. The safe system (the system without components in need of evacuation) is reached when no more transformation rules are applicable. For instance, Fig. 1 shows a possible match for the SPO rule. The effect of applying the SPO rule will be to move the normal component under the unsafe one to its new location (under the safe component) while changing its status into safe.

On the right of Fig. 2 instead we the see the main SOS rule: all the components c1 contained in a unsafe component are evacuated into a safe neighbor component, while changing their status inductively (via to(s1)-labelled rules). Figure 1 shows a possible instance of the SOS rule. The effect of the SOS rule will be to migrate the two normal components contained in the unsafe component to the safe component while changing their status (in addition the unsafe component is removed).

Model translation. Our second test case is the classical translation of class diagrams into relational database schemes (a description can be found in [13]). The

---

[1] The figures in the paper follow an intuitive UML-like notation, with boxes for objects and arrows for references. We prefer to use this intuitive notation to sketch the scenarios.

[2] The big encircled arrow separates the rule's left- and right-hand side. Object identifiers are dropped for the sake of clarity and are to be identified by their spatial location.

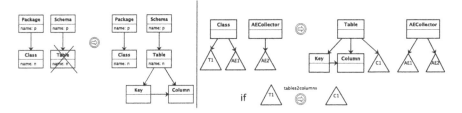

Fig. 4. An SPO rule (left) and a SOS rule (right) for model translation

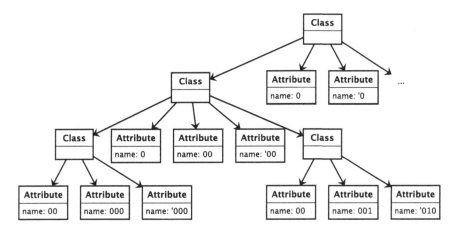

Fig. 5. An instance of the model refactoring test case

main idea is that classes are transformed into tables and their attributes into columns of the tables. Associations between classes are transformed into auxiliary tables with foreign keys from the tables corresponding to the associated classes. Figure 3 depicts one possible instance of the scenario.

Figure 4 sketches two illustrative transformation rules. The SPO rule transforms a class (belonging to a package) into a table (within the corresponding schema). It also creates a primary key and the corresponding column for the table. A negative application condition forbids the application of the rule in case the table already exists. The, let us say, corresponding rule in SOS format transforms a class into a table provided that its attributes are transformed into columns and its association ends are properly collected. An auxiliary object is used as a container where to put association ends of the same relation in the same context so that they can be transformed properly by another rule.

Refactoring. The example of model refactoring we consider is the classical attribute *pull-up* as described in [14]. The main idea is very simple: if all the subclasses of a class c declare the same attribute, then the attribute should be declared at c only. This preserves the semantics of the diagram (as the subclasses will inherit the attribute) while removing redundancies. Figure 5 depicts one possible instance of the scenario.

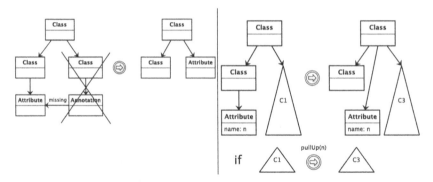

Fig. 6. An SPO rule (left) and a SOS rule (right) for model refactoring

Figure 6 depicts two illustrative transformation rules. The SPO rule pulls an attribute up provided that it is not annotated as *missing* by another class (a set of rules takes care of creating such annotations). The SOS rule instead pulls the attribute up provided that all sibling sub-classes agree to pull it up.

5   Experiments

This section presents our experimental results. Experiments were run on an Ubuntu Linux server equipped with Intel Xeon 2.67GHz processors and 24GB of RAM. Each experiment consists on the transformation of instances of a test case using the discussed representation and transformation styles. Instances are automatically generated with the help of parameterizable instance generators that allow us, for instance, to scale up the instances to check scalability of the various approaches. For each experiment we have recorded the number of rewrites and the running time (not always proportional), put in the y-axis of separate plots. Each experiment is performed for an increased size factor that typically makes the model grow exponentially. The x-axis corresponds to the size of the instance in terms of overall number of objects. The timeout for the experiments is of an hour. We do not present results for instances larger than those where at least one of the techniques already times out (which is denoted by the interruption of the plot).

The goal of the experiments is to collect evidence of performance differences, draw hypotheses about the causes of those differences and validate our hypotheses with further experiments. Our benchmark consists of the three test cases presented in Section 4.

5.1   SOS vs SOS*

1st experiment. We start testing the impact of our improved encoding of SOS (SOS*) with a basic set of instance generators. The generator for the reconfiguration test cases has a single parameter which is the depth of the component

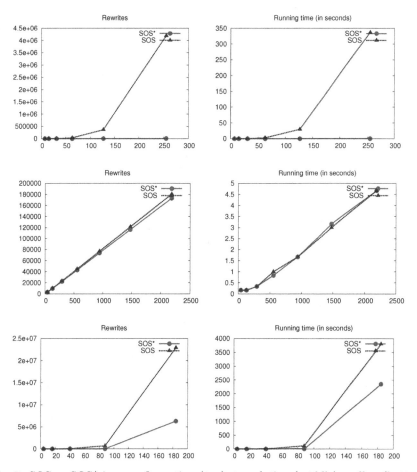

Fig. 7. SOS vs SOS* in reconfiguration (top), translation (middle), pullup (bottom)

containment tree, i.e. for a given natural number n, it generates a binary tree of depth n. The grandfathers of leafs have exactly one unsafe component and one safe component as children. All other components are normal. Figure 1 sketches one such instance. The parameter of the instance generator for the model transformation case is the branching factor of the containment tree, i.e. for a given natural number n, it generates a UML domain with n packages, each containing $2n$ classes, each containing n attributes and n associations. The i-th association of class c with c even (resp. odd) has as opposite the i-th association of class $c+1$ (resp. $c-1$). So-built domains have n packages, $2n^2$ classes and n^3 association pairs (cf. Fig. 3).

The instance generator for the refactoring test case produces binary trees of class hierarchies. Hence, each class has two sub-classes. In addition each sub-class has one local attribute (that will not be pulled up) and one (non-local) attribute inherited from its parent. The topmost class has only one local attribute and one (non-local) attribute (cf. Fig. 5).

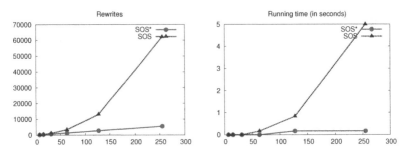

Fig. 8. SOS vs SOS*: effect of disabling new attempts

The results of Fig. 7 show a clear superiority of SOS* in most cases. The only exception is the model translation test case. We argue that there are two reasons. First, SOS* allows to contextualise some reconfigurations at an arbitrary level of the nesting hierarchy while SOS has to derive the reconfiguration at the top level by lifting up silent rewrite steps. The second reason is that SOS* performs less transformation attempts as it does not try rules that have unnecessary labels.

The reconfiguration test case is a perfect example for both issues. First, regarding the free contextualisation of top SOS* rules we observe that in the considered instances the rule can be applied at the bottom of the term, while the SOS rules require in addition to lift the application of such rule up to the root. In addition, determining whether a transformation can be carried out can be determined by the non-applicability of rules in the SOS* case, while in the SOS case requires to perform many unsuccessful transformation attempts. In the model translation both styles are essentially equivalent as the top rule must necessarily apply at the top of the term representing the model and after transformation the rules are deactivated as the necessary patterns disappear.

2nd experiment. In order to validate the first hypothesis we have performed experiments where safe components do not accept reconfigurations. In addition a component whose sub-components are safe becomes safe. This does not only disable reconfigurations after a migration but also prevents reconfiguration attempts. The results are depicted in Fig. 8 where it can be seen that now SOS scales better than in the previous experiment (still SOS* outperforms it) since the number of rewrite attempts for silent transitions is reduced (safe components and their containment are not checked for reconfiguration).

3rd experiment. Another improvement of SOS* regards the top-down imposition of labels in rewrite conditions. In order to validate the effect of top-down enacting of transformations we have conducted further experiments with the model reconfiguration test case with a different instance generator: now the root is a normal component, the two sons of the root are an unsafe and a safe component that contain a fixed number components, each able to change into safe plus any status of a set of size n, the parameter of the generator. So, for $n = 0$, the components to be migrated are able to change into safe, for $n = 1$ they are ready to

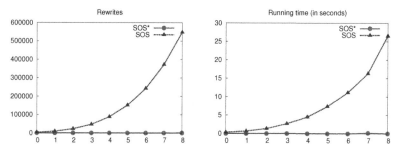

Fig. 9. SOS vs SOS*: effect of increasing the number of enabled actions

change into safe and another status, and so on. The results of such experiment are depicted in Fig. 9.

As expected the SOS* transformation is not affected as n increases. Indeed, the SOS* transformation rules will call for a transformation into safe, while in the SOS transformation all possible status changes will be attempted. As a result the computational effort of SOS transformations blows up with the increase of n.

5.2   SPO vs SOS*

In this set of experiments we compare the SPO approach against the SOS* one.

1st experiment. We start with the first set of instance generators used in §5.1.

The results of Fig. 10 show that SOS* is superior in the reconfiguration test case only. The situation can be roughly explained as follows: matching the migration rule consists on finding a subtree whose root is a component having two subtrees: one having a unsafe component as root and one having a safe one as root. In the SPO case the tree is not parsed: indeed we are given a graph and have to check all possible subsets of nodes to see if they constitute indeed a tree. Instead in the SOS* case the tree is already parsed (the parsing is a term of the hierarchical representation) which enormously facilitates rule matching (recall that matching amounts to subgraph isomorphism which is NP-complete). As a consequence, the SPO transformation involves more unsuccessful rule attempts and this is the main reason of the drastic difference in running time (and not in number of effective rewrites).

In the rest of the test cases SPO performs better. This is particularly evident in the refactoring test case where the performance of SOS* degenerates mainly due to the lack of a smart transformation strategy. Indeed it can happen that a pull up has to be attempted at some class every time one of the terms corresponding to one of the subclasses changes. Clearly applying rules bottom up would result in better results but this would require a cumbersome implementation.

We focus now on the transformation test case were we see that SPO performs only slightly better. There are various reasons. First, the structure of the model is rather flat. Indeed the hierarchy is limited to a fixed depth as packages contain classes, classes contain only attributes and associations. So containment trees are of depth 3. In addition, association pairs have to be lifted to the top level in the

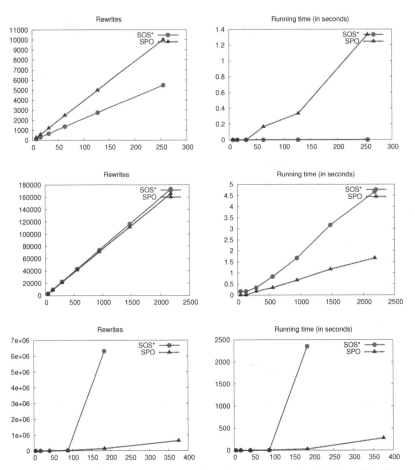

Fig. 10. SPO vs SOS* in reconfiguration (top), translation (middle), pullup (bottom)

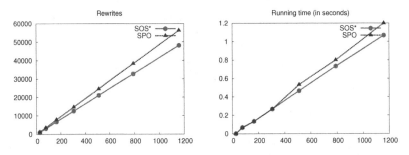

Fig. 11. SPO vs SOS*: effect of removing associations

SOS* transformation since the transformation rule that translates them needs them to be in a common context. This involves an overhead that makes SOS* exhibit a worse performance.

2nd experiment. In order to check the impact of such overhead we have performed an additional experiment in which the instances have no associations at all. Figure 11 shows the results where we see how SOS* offers the best performance this time confirming our hypothesis.

6   Conclusion

We have presented an empirical evaluation of the performance of two transformation styles that are very popular in rule-based programming and specification. For instance, in the process algebra community they essentially correspond to the rule formats used for specifying reduction and transition label semantics.

We have focused on model transformations and as a result of our experience we have obtained a set of hints that could be useful for future development of model transformations (or other kind of rule-based specifications) in Maude or to enhance the existing ones (e.g. [15]). We think that it might be worth to investigate to which extent our experience can be exported to other rule-based frameworks like CafeOBJ [16], Stratego [17] or XSLT [18] with a particular attention to model transformation frameworks such as MOMENT2-MT [15], ATL [19], Stratego/XT [20], and SiTra [21]. To this aim one should also clarify the influence of Maude's matching and rewriting strategies in the obtained performances. The study could also be enlarged to other rule styles or alternative implementations of SOS in Maude (e.g. [22,23,24]). Particularly interesting is [24] which includes a performance evaluation of operational semantics styles. Another interesting aspect to be investigated is to understand if and how strategy languages (c.f. [22]) or heuristics (c.f. [25]) can be exploited to appropriately guide the model transformation process in the most convenient way.

It is worth to remark that the aim of the paper is not to compare the performance of transformation tools as done in various works and competitions [26,27]. Rather we assume the point of view of a transformation programmer, which is given a fixed rule-based tool and can only obtain performance gains by adopting the appropriate programming style.

Even if we have focused fundamentally on deterministic transformations many cases (e.g. reconfigurations) are inherently non-deterministic. This gives rise to a state space of possible configurations, whose complexity and required computational effort is clearly influenced by the chosen rule style (evidenced as well by experiments not presented here).

References

1. Meseguer, J.: Conditional rewriting logic as a unified model of concurrency. Theoretical Computer Science 96, 73–155 (1992)
2. Rozenberg, G. (ed.): Handbook of Graph Grammars. World Scientific (1997)
3. Bruni, R., Lluch Lafuente, A., Montanari, U.: On structured model-driven transformations. International Journal of Software and Informatics (IJSI) 2, 185–206 (2011)

4. Boronat, A., Bruni, R., Lluch Lafuente, A., Montanari, U., Paolillo, G.: Exploiting the Hierarchical Structure of Rule-Based Specifications for Decision Planning. In: Hatcliff, J., Zucca, E. (eds.) FMOODS/FORTE 2010. LNCS, vol. 6117, pp. 2–16. Springer, Heidelberg (2010)

5. Meseguer, J., Talcott, C.: Semantic Models for Distributed Object Reflection. In: Magnusson, B. (ed.) ECOOP 2002. LNCS, vol. 2374, pp. 1–36. Springer, Heidelberg (2002)

6. Meseguer, J.: A logical theory of concurrent objects. In: OOPSLA/ECOOP 1990, pp. 101–115 (1990)

7. Boronat, A., Meseguer, J.: An Algebraic Semantics for MOF. In: Fiadeiro, J.L., Inverardi, P. (eds.) FASE 2008. LNCS, vol. 4961, pp. 377–391. Springer, Heidelberg (2008)

8. Clavel, M., Durán, F., Eker, S., Lincoln, P., Martí-Oliet, N., Meseguer, J., Talcott, C.: All About Maude. LNCS, vol. 4350. Springer, Heidelberg (2007)

9. Plotkin, G.D.: A structural approach to operational semantics. Journal of Logic and Algebraic Programming 60-61, 17–39 (2004)

10. Verdejo, A., Martí-Oliet, N.: Executable structural operational semantics in Maude. Journal of Logic and Algebraic Programming 67, 226–293 (2006)

11. Bruni, R., Meseguer, J.: Semantic foundations for generalized rewrite theories. Theoretical Computer Science 360, 386–414 (2006)

12. Bruni, R., Lluch Lafuente, A., Montanari, U., Tuosto, E.: Style based architectural reconfigurations. Bulletin of the EATCS 94, 161–180 (2008)

13. Boronat, A., Knapp, A., Meseguer, J., Wirsing, M.: What Is a Multi-Modeling Language? In: Corradini, A., Montanari, U. (eds.) WADT 2008. LNCS, vol. 5486, pp. 71–87. Springer, Heidelberg (2009)

14. Biermann, E., Ehrig, K., Köhler, C., Kuhns, G., Taentzer, G., Weiss, E.: EMF model refactoring based on graph transformation concepts. In: 3rd Workshop on Software Evolution through Transformations, vol. 3. ECEASST (2006)

15. MOMENT2: http://www.cs.le.ac.uk/people/aboronat/tools/moment2-gt/

16. CafeObj, http://www.ldl.jaist.ac.jp/cafeobj/

17. Stratego, http://www.program-transformation.org/Stratego/

18. XSLT, http://www.w3.org/TR/xslt20/

19. ATL, http://www.eclipse.org/atl/

20. StrategoXT, http://strategoxt.org/

21. SiTra, http://www.cs.bham.ac.uk/~bxb/SiTra.html

22. Braga, C., Verdejo, A.: Modular structural operational semantics with strategies. ENTCS 175, 3–17 (2007)

23. K Framework, http://fsl.cs.uiuc.edu/index.php/K

24. Şerbănuţă, T.F., Roşu, G., Meseguer, J.: A rewriting logic approach to operational semantics. Information and Computation 207, 305–340 (2009)

25. Kessentini, M., Sahraoui, H., Boukadoum, M., Omar, O.: Search-based model transformation by example. Software and Systems Modeling 11(2), 209–226 (2010)

26. 3rd Rewrite engines competition (REC III), WRLA 2010 (2010), http://www.lcc.uma.es/~duran/rewriting_competition/

27. Graph Transformation Contest, http://fots.ua.ac.be/events/grabats2008/

Interactive Transformations from Object-Oriented Models to Component-Based Models

Dan Li[1,*], Xiaoshan Li[1], Zhiming Liu[2], and Volker Stolz[2,3]

[1] Faculty of Science and Technology, University of Macau, China
[2] UNU-IIST, Macau, China
[3] Dept. of Informatics, University of Oslo, Norway

Abstract. Consider an object-oriented model with a class diagram, and a set of object sequence diagrams, each representing the design of object interactions for a use case. This article discusses how such an OO design model can be automatically transformed into a component-based model for the purpose of reusability, maintenance, and more importantly, distributed and independent deployment. We present the design and implementation of a tool that transforms an object-oriented model to a component-based model, which are both formally defined in the rCOS method of model driven design of component-based software, in an interactive, stepwise manner. The transformation is designed using QVT Relations and implemented as part of the rCOS CASE tool.

Keywords: Model-driven development, OO design model, sequence diagram, component model, model transformation, QVT.

1 Introduction

In the rCOS [3, 12] model-driven design of component-based software, the model of the requirements is represented in a component-based architecture. Each *use case* is modeled as a component in the requirements model. The *interface* of the component provides methods through which the actors of the use case interact with the component. The functionality of each method $m()$ of the interface is specified by pre- and post-conditions $m()\{pre \vdash post\}$, and the order of the interactions (called the use-case *protocol*) between the actors and the component as a set of traces of method invocations, graphically represented by a UML sequence diagram. One component may have a *required interface* through which it uses the provided methods of other components. The linkages (dependency) between components forms a static component-based structure modeled as a *component diagram*. The types of the variables of the components, i.e. its objects and data, are modeled by a UML class diagram, that has a textual counterpart specification in rCOS. Therefore the model of the *component-based architecture of the requirements* consists of a model of the component-based static structure (graphically represented as a UML component diagram), a class model (graphically a class diagram), an interaction protocol (graphically a sequence diagram for each component), and a specification of the data functionality of the interface methods.

---

* On leave from Guizhou Academy of Sciences, Guizhou, China.

F. Arbab and P.C. Ölveczky (Eds.): FACS 2011, LNCS 7253, pp. 97–114, 2012.
© Springer-Verlag Berlin Heidelberg 2012

In the design, the functionality specification of the interface methods of each component is then refined by decomposition and assignment of responsibilities to objects of the component, obtaining an OO model of object interactions represented by an object sequence diagram. This object sequence diagram refines the sequence diagram of the component (use case). For the purpose of reusability, maintenance, and more importantly, distributed and independent deployment (third party composition) [19], the OO model is abstracted to a model of *interactions of components*, that is graphically represented as a *component sequence diagram* defined in the UML profile for rCOS.

This paper presents the design and implementation of a tool for the transformation of a model of object interaction to a model of component interaction. The tool requires user interactions. In each step of interaction, the users decide which objects will be turned into a component, then the tool automatically performs the model transformation. However, we need to define the criteria for the selection of objects to form a component as the validity conditions of the selection. The tool automatically checks the validity, and the transformation of the sequence diagram is carried out if selection passes the check. The transformation also automatically and consistently transform the static structure and reactive behavior (state machine diagram), obtaining a model of component-based design architecture, that correctly refines the component-based architecture of the requirements.

Through a finite number of transformation steps with valid selection on the OO model of each component in the model of requirements, the object sequence diagram is transformed to a component sequence diagram in which the lifelines represent only components. Also, a complete component diagram is generated with the interface protocols as sets of traces and the reactive behavior modeled by state machine diagrams of the components. The transformations of the OO design of all components thus, one by one, obtain a correct refinement of the model of requirements architecture to a component-based design architecture in which each component in the requirements is a composition of a number of components.

The semantic correctness of the transformation and consistency among the different resulting views (diagrams) can be reasoned about within the rCOS framework. The tool is not only applicable in a top-down design process. If object-interaction models can be obtained from packages (modules) of OO programs, the tool can be used to transform OO programs to components, at least on the modeling level. An extension would be required to transform existing source code within a transformation step.

The paper is organized as follows. We start in Section 2 to discuss the concepts of rCOS model to facilitate the definition of the transformation. We present the major principles of the transformation in Section 3, and describe the implementation of the transformation tool. Section 4 shows how the transformation be applied to a case study. Our conclusions and the related work of this paper are discussed in Section 5.

2   UML Profile of rCOS Models

rCOS provides a notation and an integrated semantic theory to support separation of concerns and allows us to factor a system model into models of different viewpoints [3, 12]. The formal semantics and refinement calculus developed based on it are needed for the development and use of tools for model verification and transformations. The aim of the development of rCOS tools is to support a component-based software development process that is driven by automatic model transformations. The model transformations implement semantic correctness preserving refinement relations between models at different level of abstraction. It is often the case that the models before and/or after a transformation need to be verified or analyzed, and in that case verification and analysis tools are invoked. The rCOS project focuses on tool development for model transformations, and this paper in particular is about the transformation from object-oriented design models to component-based design models.

UML Profile [15] is a mechanism to support extending and customizing standard UML. This mechanism is carried out by defining stereotypes, tagged values and additional constraints. Through such a UML profile, rCOS models can be supported by standard UML infrastructure and CASE tools, minimizing the effort to develop a new tool, and meeting the requirements for standardization and interoperability.

The rCOS development process involves the following models:

1. The requirements model includes a *component diagram*, a *conceptual class diagram* in which classes do not have methods, and a set of *sequence diagrams*. They all have their formal rCOS textual counter parts. Also, each method of the provided interface has a *pre-* and *post-condition specification*. The sequence diagrams are *component sequence diagrams* in which the lifelines are components, and interactions are inter-component interactions.

2. Each component in the requirements model go through an OO design phase and its sequence diagram is refined into an *object sequence diagram* in which each lifeline is an object, and interactions are intra-object interactions within the component. The conceptual class diagram in the requirements model is also refined into a *design class diagram* in which methods for the intra-object interactions of the object sequence diagrams are assigned to the classes.

3. Then each OO sequence diagram of a component in the previous stage is abstracted to a component sequence diagram; thus the component is decomposed into a composition of a number of components. After the abstraction transformation is done for all components of the requirements model, the component-diagram of the requirements is refined to another component diagram with more hierarchical components being introduced.

Note that the transformation described here is not limited to rCOS models—rather, rCOS just prescribes the wellformedness of the input models, and the semantics of the communication model that will be preserved through the transformation. We refer to our publications [3, 12] for detailed discussions. The rCOS class model is rather a UML standard class model. In the rest of this section, we define the metamodels of rCOS components and sequence diagrams.

2.1 The Metamodel of rCOS Components

The component model is an essential part of rCOS. Its metamodel is defined by a UML profile diagram shown in Fig. 1, in where an element in the light yellow box represents a stereotype of rCOS, and the ones in the dark yellow boxes are standard UML metamodel elements. In the metamodel, an rCOS component model consists of:

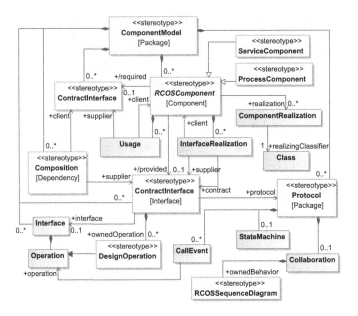

Fig. 1. The metamodel of rCOS component model

- ContractInterface: Extended from UML *Interface*, a contract interface provides an interaction point for a component, and defines the static portion of a rCOS interface contract. DesignOperations specify the static functionality of an operation. It is defined as an rCOS design in the form of *pre ⊢ post*. An rCOS Field, which is not shown in the figure explicitly, is implemented as a UML *Property* of a contract interface. (For ease of layout of the diagram, the same ContractInterface element appears twice in Fig. 1.)
- Protocol: A contract interface has a Protocol that specifies the traces of invocations to the *Operations* of the *Interface* of the contract interface. A protocol contains a *StateMachine*, a *Collaboration* and a set of *CallEvents*. A *call event* is an invocation of an operation of the contract interface, resulting in the execution of the called operation. Especially, here a *Collaboration* owns a UML *Interaction* defined as a RCOSSequenceDiagram, whose metamodel is given in the next subsection.
- RCOSComponent: There are two kinds of components in rCOS, ServiceComponents and ProcessComponents. A service component, for short a component here, provides services to the environments through its *provided* interfaces, and requires services from other components through it required interfaces. rCOS defines separate contracts for the provided interface and required interface of a component. Thus, the metamodel defines one provided contract interface, and optionally a required contract interface.
- We realize the connection between a component and its provided interface using a UML *InterfaceRealization*. A UML *Usage*, a specialized *Dependency* relationship, is used to link a required interface to its owner component. In addition, we

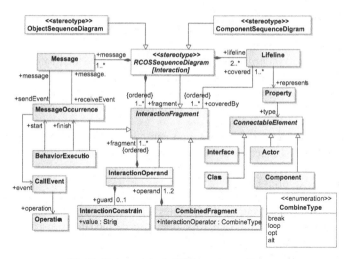

Fig. 2. Metamodel of rCOS sequence diagram

define a stereotype **Composition**, which is also an extension of UML *dependency*, to plug a provided interface of a component to a required interface of another component (here, rCOS component operations do not translate naturally to UML component composition). Furthermore, a component may be realized by a set of classes through *ComponentRealizations*.

2.2   Metamodel of rCOS Sequence Diagrams

Fig. 2 shows the metamodel of rCOS sequence diagrams. It conforms to the interaction metamodel provided by OMG [15]. In the metamodel, a UML *Interaction* contains a number of *Lifelines*, and a set of *Messages*.

A *message* specifies a communication from a sender lifeline to a receiver lifeline. It has a *sendEvent* and *receiveEvent* which express the *MessageOccurrences* along the lifelines, appearing in pairs. A message occurrence represents the synchronous invocation of an *operation*. The *BehaviorExecution* (green segment of a lifeline in the later diagrams) represents the duration of an operation, and plays no role in our models (yet it is an artefact from the graphical editor).

rCOS has two kinds of sequence diagrams, object sequence diagrams and component sequence diagrams. A lifeline may represent an actor, an object (of a particular class), or a component. When a lifeline represents an object or a component, we call it *object lifeline* or *component lifeline*. A *CombinedFragment* represents a nested block that covers lifelines and their messages to express flow of control, such as an alternative block (alt) or an iteration block (loop), with their attached boolean *guard* conditions. Sequence diagrams here do not express recursion.

The two kinds of sequence diagrams are needed to combine both OO design and component-based design in rCOS. The abstract stereotype **RCOSSequenceDiagram** has subtypes of **ObjectSequenceDiagram** and **ComponentSequenceDiagram**, that satisfy the following well-formed conditions, respectively.

1. ObjectSequenceDiagram:
   - There is one lifeline representing an *Actor*, and all other lifelines represent objects or components.
   - Messages are *synchronous calls* to an operation provided by the type of the target lifeline, or a constructor/create messages.
   - A message flow starts with a message from the actor to a single component, from components to components or objects, or from objects to objects, but never from objects to components.

   Therefore, and object-sequence diagram can contain both component and object lifelines, and thus also serves as an intermediate data structure for the transformations, until all objects have been transformed.

2. ComponentSequenceDiagram:
   - One lifeline represents an *Actor*, and all other lifelines represent components.
   - All receive events occur on the lifelines representing components.
   - Each message is a method call to an operation defined in the provided interfaces of the component represented by the target lifeline.
   - There should be a *composition* relation between two component if there is a message between them in a sequence diagram.
   - No create messages exists in the diagram.

The static semantics, i.e. well-formedness of the rCOS sequence diagrams, including the above conditions, is defined by a set of OCL rules in the rCOS CASE tool. These rules are used to automatically check the well-formedness conditions and the structural consistency of the UML model: for example, the object creation event on a lifeline must precede all other events on the lifeline, and a fragment must include both the sender and the receiver of any event occurring in the fragment.

rCOS also has a dynamic model represented by state diagrams. The metamodel of state diagrams is largely the same as the labelled transition systems provided by standard UML state diagrams, where guarded transitions are again linked to interface methods. We leave the metamodel definition out of this paper.

3   Transformation from Object- to Component Sequence Diagrams

We now describe the interactive transformations from an object sequence diagram to a component sequence diagram. The transformations start with an object sequence diagram and a design class diagram. Through a number of steps of interactions between the user and the tool, they generate a component diagram, a component sequence diagram, and the protocols of the provided interface and required interface of each component in the component diagram. In each step, the user selects a set of object lifelines that she intends to make into a component. The tool will check the validity conditions for this set to form a component. If the selection passes the check, the tool combines the selected object lifelines into a component lifeline, adding a component to the component diagram, and generates the protocols for the component. We describe the principles of the selection and the validity of selection, as well as the generation of a component from the selected lifelines below. As the UML metamodel especially for sequence diagrams is quite verbose as shown in the previous section, we use an alternate, more concise representation here (at the cost of not having established the formal correspondence between the two levels).

3.1   Selection of Object Lifelines

First, one object lifeline is designated as the *controller object* of the selection by the user. The principles for picking such a control object not only depend on checkable conditions of the object but also on design considerations of reusability, maintainability, and organization of the system being modeled. The major checkable condition is that this object should be a *permanent object* in the sequence diagram. This means it should have existed before the start of the execution of the sequence diagram (specified by the precondition of the first message), and it will not be destroyed during the execution (rCOS does not have destructor methods). This also includes software objects representing the control of physical devices, such as barcode readers, controllers of printers, lights, and operating system objects, such as the system clock.

Then the selection of further objects should be made by the user with consideration of the following conditions and principles:

1. any object lifeline that is a receive end of a creation event from a lifeline that is already included in the selection must be selected,
2. the objects in the selection must be *strongly connected*, i.e. for any lifeline ℓ in the selection there is at least one message path from the controller object to ℓ,
3. consider low coupling and high cohesion principle that the selected lifelines have more intensive interaction with each other than with lifelines outside the selection.
4. lifelines that represent objects which will be deployed on different nodes of a distributed system should not be included in the same selection.

The first two conditions are must condition and can be easily checked, as discussed in the next sub-section. The third condition is a desirable principle, and the fourth is a platform dependent condition. The latter two can never lead to an inconsistent model, but to a model that does not capture the intentions correctly, and a detailed discussion of them is out the scope of the paper.

3.2   Validating the Lifeline Selection

Given an object sequence diagram D, we define some notations for the describing the validation of a selection. We use $D.lines$ to denote the set of all lifelines of D, $D.messages$ the set of messages, and a message is represented by $m[\ell_i, \ell_j]$ as an invocation of m of ℓ_j from ℓ_i. *Create*-messages indicate constructor invocations.

Let $D.selection \subseteq D.lines$ be a selection, and ℓ_c the designated controller object, and define $D.rest = D.lines - D.selection$. Further, we define

$$IntraM = \{m[\ell_i, \ell_j] \: : \: \ell_i, \ell_j \in D.selection\} \qquad \text{Messages among the selected lifelines}$$

$$InM = \{m[\ell_i, \ell_j] \: : \: \ell_i \in D.rest \wedge \ell_j \in D.selection\} \quad \text{Incoming messages to selected lifelines}$$

$$OutM = \{m[\ell_i, \ell_j] \: : \: \ell_i \in D.selection \wedge \ell_j \in D.rest\} \quad \text{Outgoing messages from selected lifelines}$$

$$OutsideM = \{m[\ell_i, \ell_j] \: : \: \ell_i, \ell_j \in D.rest\} \qquad \text{Messages outside the selected lifelines}$$

A lifeline ℓ in sequence diagram D can be either an object lifeline, denoted by $type(\ell) = Class$, or a component lifeline, denoted by $type(\ell) = Component$. Now we define the conditions below for checking the validity of a selection.

1. All lifelines selected must be object lifelines

$$\forall \ell \in D.selection \cdot type(\ell) = Class$$

2. The controller object ℓ_c must be a permanent object. This is done by checking it is not on the receive end of an object creation message.

$$\forall \ell \in D.lines \cdot (create[\ell, \ell_c] \notin D.messages)$$

3. The transformation starts with those lifelines that directly interact with the actor, then those directly receiving message from the lifelines that have been made into component lifelines. Therefore any incoming message to the current selection should be from either the actor or a component lifeline

$$\forall m[\ell_i, \ell_j] \in InM \cdot (type(\ell_i) = Actor \vee type(\ell_i) = Component)$$

4. Creation messages can only be sent between lifelines inside the selection or between objects outside the selection

$$\forall \ell_i, \ell_j \in D.lines \cdot (create[\ell_i, \ell_j] \in IntraM \vee create[\ell_i, \ell_j] \in OutsideM)$$

5. Any incoming message to the selection is received either by the controller object or by a lifeline which has a direct path of message from the controller object

$$\forall m[\ell_i, \ell_j] \in InM \cdot (\ell_j = \ell_c \vee \exists m[\ell_c, \ell_j] \in IntraM)$$

6. The lifelines of the selection must be strongly connected, meaning that for any selected lifeline ℓ, there must be a path of messages from the controller object

$$m[\ell_c, \ell_1], m_1[\ell_1, \ell_2], \ldots, m_i[\ell_i, \ell]$$

Notice that Conditions 4&6 are closure properties required of the section, and that the initial object-sequence diagram of a use case in rCOS always has a use case controller object that satisfies Conditions 2,3&5. Using induction on the number of lifelines, these conditions all together ensures existence of a valid selection for any well-formed sequence diagram that contains object lifelines. Every OO sequence diagram can be translated into the trivial component sequence diagram which internalises *all* object lifelines into the controller.

3.3 Generating a Component from Selected Lifelines

If the selection passes the validity checking, the transformation will be executed to generate the target models, otherwise an error message is fed back to the tool user. The transformation is specified in the QVT relational notation (see Section 3.4). For the understandability to the formal specification community, we describe the specification in terms of the relation between the source model and the target model, similar to the pre- and postcondition specification of a program.

Given a source sequence diagram D, that is an object sequence diagram, and a valid selection $D.selection$, let D' denote the target sequence diagram after one step of the transformation. For a lifeline ℓ in D (or D'), we use $type(\ell, D)$ to denote the type of the lifeline ℓ in D (respectively $type(\ell, D')$ in D'). For a component lifeline ℓ in D (or D'), pIF denotes the provided interface of the component that ℓ represents, and rIF the required interface. We now describe the relation between D and D' as the conjunction of the following predicates.

1. The controller object ℓ_c in D is changed to a component lifeline in D'

$$\ell_c \in D.selection \wedge type(\ell_c, D) = Class$$
$$\wedge \ell_c \in D'.lines \wedge type(\ell_c, D') = Component$$

2. An incoming message to the selection in D becomes an invocation to the interface methods of ℓ_c in D'

$$\forall m[\ell_i, \ell_j] \in InM \cdot (m[\ell_i, \ell_c] \in D'.messages \wedge m \in pIF(\ell_c))$$

Notice that the order of the messages and fragments are not to be changed.

3. All the intra-object interactions in the selection in D are collapsed, more precisely hidden inside the component ℓ_c

$$\forall m[\ell_i, \ell_j] \in IntraM \cdot (\ell_i, \ell_j \notin D'.lines \wedge m[\ell_i, \ell_j] \notin D'.messages)$$

4. All the outgoing messages from the selection become sending messages from the component that ℓ_c represents in D', with the order and fragments preserved, and they become the required methods of the component

$$\forall m[\ell_i, \ell_j] \in OutM \cdot (m[\ell_c, \ell_j] \in D'.messages \wedge m \in rIF(\ell_c))$$

5. No lifelines and messages outside the selection are changed

$$\forall m[\ell_i, \ell_j] \in OutsideM \cdot (m[\ell_i, \ell_j] \in D'.messages)$$

From the definition of the resulting sequence diagram D', its static counterparts, the components can be defined. The change for the component diagram can be specified in a similar way. The protocols of the provided interface $pIF(\ell_c)$ and the required interface $rIF(\ell_c)$ of the newly constructed component ℓ_c in D' will be generated.

Next, we give an intuition into how the relations defined above can be directly put to use through QVT-Relations.

3.4   Implementation of the Transformation

The object sequence diagram to component sequence diagram transformation is implemented through the QVT Relations language using the QVTR-XSLT tool we recently developed [10]. The MOF 2.0 Query/View/Transformation (QVT) [14] is a model transformation standard proposed by OMG. QVT has a hybrid declarative/imperative nature.

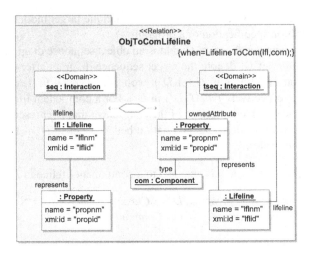

Fig. 3. An example of a QVTR relation

In its declarative language, called QVT Relations (QVT-R), a transformation is defined as a set of *relations* between the elements of source metamodels and target metamodels. QVT-R has both textual and graphical notations, and the graphical notation provides a concise, intuitive way to specify transformations.

The QVTR-XSLT tool supports the graphical notation of QVT-R. It provides a graphical editor in which a transformation can be specified using the graphical syntax, and a code generator that automatically generates executable XSLT [21] programs for the transformation. The tool supports *in-place transformations* so we can focus on defining rules only for the parts of a model we want to change. Multiple input and output models are also supported in the tool.

In the graphical notation, a *relation* defines how two object diagrams, called *domain patterns*, relate to each other. Fig. 3 illustrates an example QVT relation in graphical notation which specifies the generation of a component lifeline from an object lifeline. Starting from the root object *seq* tagged with label ≪*Domain*≫, the source domain pattern (left part) of the relation consists of a *Lifeline lfl* with its representing *Property* under the *seq*. The target domain pattern (right part) has a similar structure. The patterns are used for structural matching in the source- and target model, respectively.

When the relation is executed, the source domain pattern is searched in the source model. If a match is found, the *lifeline* and the *property* are bound to instances of source model elements. The target domain pattern of the relation acts as a template to create objects and links in the target model. In this example, the target domain pattern creates a *lifeline* object and a *property* object. Both objects own a *name* and an *xmi:id* attributes. These two attributes get values from the corresponding model instances bound by the source domain pattern. Moreover, the *property* object of the target model has now the association *type* set to the component *com*, which is bound (and possible created) by invoking relation *LifelineToCom* in the *when* clause. These clauses specify additional matching conditions and can either refer to other relations, or OCL expressions.

At the implementation level, a complete model consists of a UML model and a DI (diagram interchange) [13] model. The former contains the abstract syntax information that is described in Section 2, and it is stored in Eclipse Modeling Framework (EMF) XMI format, which is supported by many UML CASE tools. The latter contains the layout information in the form of UML 2.0 Diagram Interchange standard [13]. In fact, these two models are technically separate models and saved in different XML files. When the UML model is modified by the transformation, the DI model must be synchronously updated in order to correctly display the corresponding diagrams. The changes to the DI model are also specified using QVT-R, and transformed by the QVTR-XSLT tool. The resulting diagrams for the case study are the result of those transformations after minimal visual cleanup. The transformation is specified by three transformation models. In total, they contain 105 relations, and 45 functions and queries. About 6300 lines of XSLT code are generated for the implementation of the transformation.

To support the rCOS methodology, we have developed a CASE tool [4] with graphical interfaces for designing use cases, classes, component-, sequence- and state diagrams, and the syntactic consistency among these views can be checked. The tool is implemented as an Eclipse-plugin on top of the Eclipse Graphical Modelling Framework and TOPCASED [16]. We have integrated the XSLT programs of the transformation into the user interface of the tool. A user can select a group of lifelines from the interface, and then the XSLT transformation programs are invoked by the tool with these lifelines as parameters. If these lifelines are allowed to become a component, the transformation is executed and the user interface will be automatically refreshed to show the transformation results.

4   Case Study

The Common Component Modelling Example (CoCoME) [3, 17] describes a trading system that is typically used in supermarkets. This case study deals with the various business processes, including processing sales at a cash desk, handling payments, and updating the inventory. The system maintains a catalog of product items, as well as the amount of each item available. It also keeps the historical records of sales; each of them consists of a number of line items, determined by the product item and the amount sold.

At the end of the object-oriented design stage, we get a design model which contains a set of design class diagrams and object sequence diagrams. Fig. 4 shows a simplified version of the design class diagram for the CoCoME example, where the class *CashDesk* is the control class. Fig. 5 depicts the object sequence diagram of use case *process sale*, which describes the check out process: a customer takes the products she wants to buy to a cash desk, the cashier records each product item, and finally the customer makes the payment. Applying the transformations discussed in the previous sections, we transform the object sequence diagram into an rCOS component sequence diagram in a stepwise, incremental manner. Meanwhile the object model automatically evolves to a component-based model.

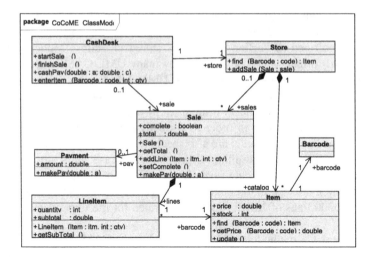

Fig. 4. The design class model of CoCoME

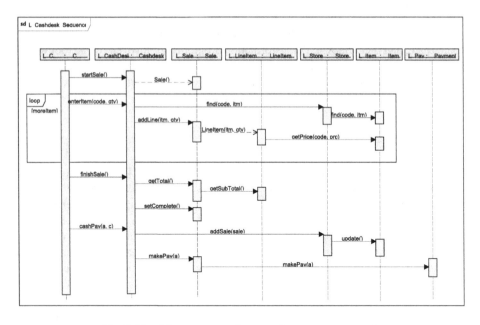

Fig. 5. The object sequence diagram of usecase *process sale*

The object sequence diagram of Fig. 5 consists of seven lifelines. The leftmost life-line is the *Actor*, and followed by lifelines *L_CashDesk*, *L_Sale*, *L_LineItem*, *L_Store*, *L_Item* and *L_Pay*, representing objects of class *CashDesk*, *Sale*, *LineItem*, *Store*, *Item* and *Payment*, respectively. Based on our interpretation of the case study, we decide to apply the transformation three times.

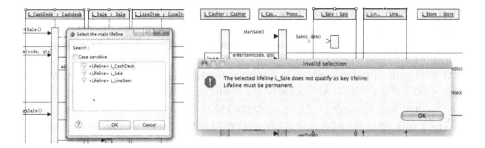

Fig. 6. Select lifelines

Fig. 7. Validation error message

The first step deals with the lifeline *L_CashDesk*, which is directly interacting with the actor. Since lifeline *L_Sale* is created by *L_CashDesk*, and *L_LineItem* is created by *L_Sale*, they have to be in the same component. As shown in Fig. 6, we select these three lifelines from the sequence diagram, set *L_CashDesk* as the controller object (main lifeline in the figure), and transform them into a service component *COM_L_CashDesk*. The component has a provided interface *ConInter_L_CashDesk* and a required interface *RInter_L_CashDesk*. The resulting sequence diagram is shown in Fig. 8, in which lifeline *L_CashDesk* now represents the new component, and lifelines *L_Sale* and *L_LineItem*, along with their internal messages, are removed from the diagram.

As we mentioned before, the tool will check whether the selected lifelines can be transformed to a component, and provides an error message if the selection is not valid. For instance, if we choose lifelines *L_Sale*, *L_Store* and *L_Item* to become a component, the tool will display an error message, as shown in Fig. 7.

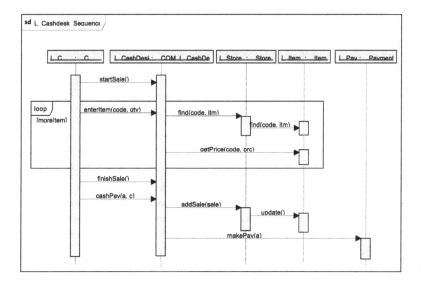

Fig. 8. The sequence diagram after the first transformation

For the second transformation, we select the lifelines *L_Store* and *L_Item* from the sequence diagram of Fig. 8, and indicate *L_Store* as the controller object. Since class *Store* is composed with class *Item*, the transformation is allowed, and the two lifelines are transformed into a service component *COM_L_Store*.

As the result of the second transformation, the lifeline *L_Store* now represents the component *COM_L_Store*. Accordingly, the component diagram is changed, where the provided interface *ConInter_L_Store* is plugged to the required interface *RInter_L_Cash Desk* (we only show the final resulting component diagram later in Fig. 11).

For each generated component, we also generate an rCOS protocol, which consists of a sequence diagram and a state diagram, for its provided interface. The protocol for component *COM_L_Store* is shown in Figs. 9 & 10. The left part of the sequence diagram in Fig. 9 specifies the interactions of the component with its environment (represented by a fresh actor), and the right part defines the interactions between the component and its internal objects. We notice that a message originally sent from a non-selected lifeline and received by another selected lifeline, such as the *getPrice* message in Fig. 5, now becomes two messages. The first *getPrice* message is received by the component *COM_L_Store*, and then delegated to the original receiving lifeline *L_Item* using the second *getPrice* message.

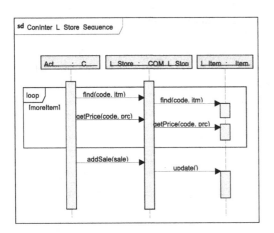

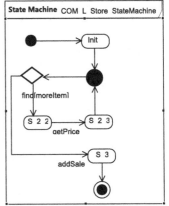

Fig. 9. Sequence diagram of *COM_L_Store*   **Fig. 10.** State diagram of *COM_L_Store*

In the third transformation, we turn *L_Pay*, the only object lifeline left, into component *COM_L_Pay*. Thus we get the final component diagram shown in Fig. 11, which depicts the relationships among the three components of the model. We obtain the final component sequence diagram, in which all lifelines represent components, except the one representing the actor (see Fig. 12), fulfilling the structural well-formedness rules of component sequence models as discussed in Section 2.

Through applying the object sequence diagram to component sequence diagram transformation three times, we have successfully developed the design model of Co-CoME into a component model. The component model includes component sequence

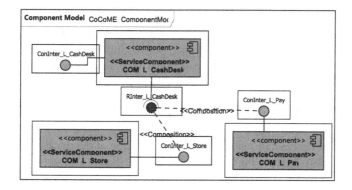

Fig. 11. Final component diagram of the CoCoME example

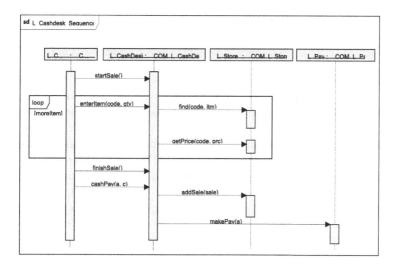

Fig. 12. Final rCOS component sequence diagram for usecase *process sale*

diagrams and component diagrams to define the relationship of components. Each component has its provided/required interfaces, as well as a protocol, that consists of a sequence diagram and a state diagram, to define the behaviors of the component.

5   Conclusion

A major research objective of the rCOS method is to improve the scalability of semantic correctness preserving refinement between models in model-driven software engineering. The rCOS method promotes the idea that component-based software design is driven by model transformations in the front end, and verification and analysis are integrated through model transformations.

As nearly all existing component-based technologies are realized in object-oriented technologies, most design processes start with an OO development process and then at the end of the process an OO design is directly implemented by using a component-based technology, such .COM or .NET. It is often the case that an OO program is developed first and then it is transformed into component software. Our approach improve this practice by allowing a component-based model of the requirements, and a seamless combination of OO design and component-based design for each components in the requirements. The combination is supported by the interactive transformations from OO design to component-based design presented in this paper, in a stepwise and compositional manner. This allows the object-oriented and component-based design patterns to be used in the OO design and captured in the specification of the transformation.

In the tool implementation, the transformation is specified in a subset of the graphical QVT Relations notation. The correct implementation of the interactive transformation requires the definition of a UML profile of the abstract syntax of the rCOS model that is presented in the paper. The QVT specification of the transformation is automatically transformed to an executable XSLT program, that can be run through an Eclipse-plugin. The presented technique and tool can be combined with reverse engineering techniques for transformation of OO programs into component-based programs.

5.1 Related Work

As a natural step of model driven development, object-oriented models are further evolved to component-based models to get the benefits of reusability, maintenance, as well as distributed and independent deployment. Surveys of approaches and techniques for identification reusable components from object-oriented models can be found in [2,20]. Based on the principle of "high cohesion and low coupling", researchers try to cluster classes into components. The basic ideas are: calculate the strength of semantics dependencies between classes and transform them into the form of weighted directional graph, then cluster the graph using graph clustering or matrix analysis techniques [20]. Using clustering analysis, components with high cohesion and low coupling are expected to be obtained in order to reduce composition cost.

Particularly, since use cases are applied to describe the functionality of the system, the work of [18] focuses on applying various clustering methods to cluster use cases into several components. In [6], the static and dynamic relationships between classes are used for clustering related classes in components, where static relationship measures the relationship strength, and dynamic relationship measures the frequency of message exchange at runtime. COMO [9] proposed a method which measures inter-class relationships in terms of *create*, *retrieve*, *update* and *delete* (CRUD) operations of model elements. It uses dynamic coupling metric between objects to measure the potential number of messages exchanged. All above approaches are based on clustering algorithms, which makes them much different from our approach, where transformations are applied at the *design stage* by a human.

Identifying reusable components from object-oriented models was considered to be one of the most difficult tasks in the software development process [6]. Most existing approaches just provide general guidelines for component identification. They lack more precise criteria and methods [5]. Because of the complexity of source information and the component model itself, it is not advisable for component designers to manually develop component-based models from object-oriented models [20]. Alas, there are almost no (semi)-automatic tools to help designers in the development process [18]. The work of the paper makes a useful attempt to address this problem, and provide a tool supporting.

Sequence diagrams have of course already been used informally in UML-based modeling since their conception. Recently, [7] presents a rigorously defined variant called "Life Sequence Charts" with tool support to use them for system design. The focus there is however not on component modeling, but giving a formal semantics to sequence charts for synthesis.

In [3], we have studied this top-down development process, carried out by hand, for the CoCoME case study. Our process is motivated by an industrial CASE tool, MASTERCRAFT [11]. There, the focus is on the design and refinement of the relational method specifications using the rCOS language [8, 22].

5.2   Future Work

There are still many challenges in the automation of model transformations, especially on the level of method specifications, such as applying the expert pattern in the object-oriented design stage. It is not enough to only provide a library of transformations, but more importantly, the tool should provide guiding information on which rule is to be used [12]. Since our methodology (unsurprisingly) coincides with textbook-approaches to design of OO- and component software, we hope that the tool can also become a foundation for education in software engineering. It should guide the user through the different stages with recommendations, e.g. where detail should be added to the model, or where refinement is necessary. Based on metrics, the tool could also propose concrete transformation parameters. It is also difficult to support consistent and correct reuse of existing components when designing a new component. We will continue working in this direction to overcome these challenges.

The rCOS Modeler that implements the transformations discussed here can be downloaded together with examples from http://rcos.iist.unu.edu.

Acknowledgements. Partially supported by the ARV and GAVES grants of the Macau Science and Technology Development Fund, the National Natural Science Foundation of China (Grant No. 60970031 and 61073022), and the Guizhou International Scientific Cooperation Project G[2011] 7023 and GY[2010]3033.

References

1. Arbab, F., Sirjani, M. (eds.): FSEN 2009. LNCS, vol. 5961. Springer, Heidelberg (2010)
2. Birkmeier, D., Overhage, S.: On Component Identification Approaches – Classification, State of the Art, and Comparison. In: Lewis, G.A., Poernomo, I., Hofmeister, C. (eds.) CBSE 2009. LNCS, vol. 5582, pp. 1–18. Springer, Heidelberg (2009)
3. Chen, Z., Liu, Z., Ravn, A.P., Stolz, V., Zhan, N.: Refinement and verification in component-based model driven design. Sci. Comput. Program. 74(4), 168–196 (2009)
4. Chen, Z., Morisset, C., Stolz, V.: Specification and validation of behavioural protocols in the rCOS modeler. In: Arbab and Sirjani [1], pp. 387–401

5. Choi, M., Cho, E.: Component Identification Methods Applying Method Call Types between Classes. J. Inf. Sci. Eng. 22, 247–267 (2006)
6. Fan-Chao, M., Den-Chen, Z., Xiao-Fei, X.: Business Component Identification of Enterprise Information System: A Hierarchical Clustering Method. In: Proc. of the 2005 IEEE Intl. Conf. on e-Business Engineering (2005)
7. Harel, D., Marelly, R.: Come, Let's Play: Scenario-Based Programming Using LSC's and the Play-Engine. Springer (2003)
8. He, J., Liu, Z., Li, X.: rCOS: A refinement calculus of object systems. Theor. Comput. Sci. 365(1-2), 109–142 (2006)
9. Lee, S.D., Yang, Y.J., Cho, F.S., Kim, S.D., Rhew, S.Y.: COMO: A UML-based component development methodology. In: 6th Asia Pacific Softw. Eng. Conf., pp. 54–61. IEEE (1999)
10. Li, D., Li, X., Stolz, V.: QVT-based model transformation using XSLT. SIGSOFT Softw. Eng. Notes 36, 1–8 (2011)
11. Liu, Z., Mencl, V., Ravn, A.P., Yang, L.: Harnessing theories for tool support. In: Proc. of the Second Intl. Symp. on Leveraging Applications of Formal Methods, Verification and Validation, isola 2006, pp. 371–382. IEEE Computer Society Press (August 2006)
12. Liu, Z., Morisset, C., Stolz, V.: rCOS: theory and tools for component-based model driven development. In: Arbab and Sirjani [1], pp. 62–80
13. Object Management Group. UML 2.0 Diagram Interchange Specification (September 2003), `http://www.omg.org/cgi-bin/doc?ptc/2003-09-01`
14. Object Management Group. Meta Object Facility (MOF) 2.0 Query/View/Transformation Specification, Version 1.1 (December 2009)
15. Object Management Group. Unified Modeling Language: Superstructure, version 2.3 (May 2010), `http://www.omg.org/spec/UML/2.3/Superstructure`
16. Pontisso, N., Chemouil, D.: TOPCASED Combining formal methods with model-driven engineering. In: ASE 2006: Proc. of the 21st IEEE/ACM Intl. Conf. on Automated Software Engineering, pp. 359–360. IEEE Computer Society, Washington, DC (2006)
17. Rausch, A., Reussner, R., Mirandola, R., Plášil, F. (eds.): The Common Component Modeling Example. LNCS, vol. 5153. Springer, Heidelberg (2008)
18. Shahmohammadi, G., Jalili, S., Hasheminejad, S.M.H.: Identification of System Software Components Using Clustering Approach. Journal of Object Technology 9(6), 77–98 (2010)
19. Szyperski, C., Gruntz, D., Murer, S.: Component software: beyond object-oriented programming. Addison-Wesley Professional (2002)
20. Wang, Z., Xu, X., Zhan, D.: A survey of business component identification methods and related techniques. International Journal of Information Technology 2(4), 229–238 (2005)
21. WWW Consortium. XSL Transformations (XSLT) Version 2.0, W3C Recommendation (January 2007), `http://www.w3.org/TR/2007/REC-xslt20-20070123/`
22. Zhao, L., Liu, X., Liu, Z., Qiu, Z.: Graph transformations for object-oriented refinement. Formal Aspects of Computing 21(1-2), 103–131 (2009)

Runtime Verification of Temporal Patterns for Dynamic Reconfigurations of Components

Julien Dormoy[1], Olga Kouchnarenko[1], and Arnaud Lanoix[2]

[1] University of Franche-Comté, Besançon, France
{jdormoy,okouchnarenko}@lifc.univ-fcomte.fr
[2] Nantes University, Nantes, France
arnaud.lanoix@univ-nantes.fr

Abstract. Dynamic reconfigurations increase the availability and the reliability of component-based systems by allowing their architectures to evolve at runtime. Recently we have proposed a temporal pattern logic, called FTPL, to characterize the correct reconfigurations of component-based systems under some temporal and architectural constraints.

As component-based architectures evolve at runtime, there is a need to check these FTPL constraints on the fly, even if only a partial information is expected. Firstly, given a generic component-based model, we review FTPL from a runtime verification point of view. To this end we introduce a new four-valued logic, called RV-FTPL (Runtime Verification for FTPL), characterizing the "potential" (un)satisfiability of the architectural constraints in addition to the basic FTPL semantics. Potential true and potential false values are chosen whenever an observed behaviour has not yet lead to a violation or satisfiability of the property under consideration. Secondly, we present a prototype developed to check at runtime the satisfiability of RV-FTPL formulas when reconfiguring a Fractal component-based system. The feasability of a runtime property enforcement is also shown. It consists in supervising on the fly the reconfiguration execution against desired RV-FTPL properties. The main contributions are illustrated on the example of a HTTP server architecture.

1 Introduction

This paper deals with the formal specification and verification of dynamic reconfigurations of component-based systems at runtime. Dynamic reconfigurations increase the availability and the reliability of those systems by allowing their architectures to evolve at runtime.

Dynamic reconfiguration of distributed applications is an active research topic [1,2,21] motivated by practical distributed applications like, e.g., those in Fractal [10] or OSGi[1]. In many recent works, the idea of using temporal logics to manage applications at runtime has been explored [6,18,8,14].

---

[1] http://www.osgi.org

F. Arbab and P.C. Ölveczky (Eds.): FACS 2011, LNCS 7253, pp. 115–132, 2012.
© Springer-Verlag Berlin Heidelberg 2012

In [14], we have proposed a temporal pattern logic, called FTPL, to characterize the correct reconfigurations of component-based systems under some temporal and architectural constraints (**1**). We have also explained in [19], how to reuse a generic formal model to check the component-based model consistency through reconfigurations, and to ensure that dynamic reconfigurations satisfy architectural and integrity constraints, invariants, and also temporal constraints over (re)configuration sequences (**2**).

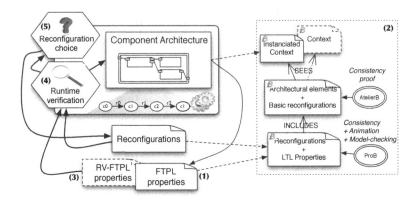

Fig. 1. Principle and contributions

As component-based architectures evolve at runtime, there is a need to evaluate the FTPL constraints on the fly, even if only a partial information can be expected. Indeed, an FTPL property often cannot be evaluated to true or false during the system execution. In addition, the reconfigurations change the validity of FTPL constraints by modifying the component architecture. In this paper, given a generic component-based model, we review FTPL from a runtime verification point of view (**3**). To this end we introduce a new four-valued logic, called RV-FTPL (Runtime Verification for FTPL), characterizing the "potential" (un)satisfiability of the architectural constraints in addition to the basic FTPL semantics. Like in RV-LTL [8], potential true and potential false values are chosen whenever an observed behaviour has not yet lead to a violation or acceptance of the property under consideration.

We then integrate the runtime verification of temporal patterns into the Fractal component model [10]. More precisely, we describe a prototype developed to check at runtime—by reusing the FPath and FScript [12] tool supports—the satisfiability of RV-FTPL formulas. This verification is performed when reconfigurating a component-based system (**4**). More, the feasability of a runtime property enforcement is also shown. It consists in supervising at runtime the reconfiguration execution in order to ensure that the RV-FTPL property of interest is fulfilled (**5**): our 4-valued logic can help in guiding the reconfiguration process, namely in choosing the next reconfiguration operations to be applied. The main contributions are illustrated on the example of a HTTP server architecture.

The remainder of the paper is organised as follows. After introducing a motivating example in Sect. 2, we briefly recall, in Sects. 3 and 4, the considered architectural (re-)configuration model and the FTPL syntax and semantics. We then define in Sect. 5 the runtime verification of FTPL (RV-FTPL) refining FTPL semantics with potential true and potential false values. Section 6 describes a prototype implementing the RV-FTPL verification, and its integration into the Fractal framework. Section 7 explains how to enforce, at runtime, Fractal component system reconfigurations against desired RV-FTPL properties. Finally, Section 8 concludes before discussing related work.

2 Motivating Example

To motivate and to illustrate our approach, let us consider an example of an HTTP server from [11]. The architecture of this server is displayed in Fig. 2.

The **RequestReceiver** component reads HTTP requests from the network and transmits them to the **RequestHandler** component. In order to keep the response time as short as possible, **RequestHandler** can either use a cache (with the component **CacheHandler**) or directly transmit the request to the **RequestDispatcher** component. The number of requests (load) and the percentage of similar requests (deviation) are two parameters defined for the **RequestHandler** component:

- The **CacheHandler** component is used only if the number of similar HTTP requests is high.
- The memorySize for the **CacheHandler** component must depend on the overall load of the server.
- The validityDuration of data in the cache must also depend on the overall load of the server.
- The number of used file servers (like the **FileServer1** and **FileServer2** components) used by **RequestDispatcher** depends on the overall load of the server.

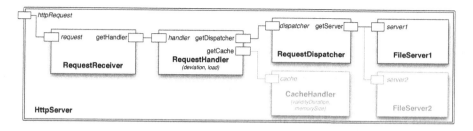

Fig. 2. HTTP Server architecture

We consider that the HTTP server can be reconfigured during the execution by the following reconfiguration operations:

1. AddCacheHandler and RemoveCacheHandler which are respectively used to add and remove the **CacheHandler** component when the deviation value increased/decreased around 50;
2. AddFileServer and removeFileServer which are respectively used to add and remove the **FileServer2** component;
3. MemorySizeUp and MemorySizeDown which are respectively used to increase and to decrease the MemorySize value;
4. DurationValidityUp and DurationValidityDown to respectively increase and decrease the ValidityDuration value.

As an illustration, we specify the AddCacheHandler reconfiguration expressed in the FScript language [12]. When the deviation value exceeds 50, the reconfiguration consists in instantiating a **CacheHandler** component. Then, the component is integrated into the architecture, and the binding with the required interface of **RequestHandler** is established. Finally, the component **CacheHandler** is started.

```
1   action AddCacheHandler(root)
2     newCache = new("CacheHandler");
3     add($root, $newCache);
4     bind($root/child::RequestHandler/interface::getcache, $newCache/
          interface::cache);
5     start($newCache);
```

3   Architectural (Re-)Configuration Model

This section recalls the generic model for component-based architectures given in [14] and inspired by the model in [20,21] for Fractal. Both models are graphs allowing one to represent component-based architectures and reconfiguration operations and to reason about them.

Component-based models must provide mechanisms for systems to be dynamically adapted—through their reconfigurations—to their environments during their lifetime. These dynamic reconfigurations may happen because of architectural modifications specified in primitive operations. Notice that reconfigurations are not the only manner to make an architecture evolve. The normal running of different components also changes the architecture by modifying parameter values or stopping components, for instance.

3.1   Component-Based Architectures

In general, the system configuration is the specific definition of the elements that define or prescribe what a system is composed of. The architectural elements we consider (components, interfaces and parameters) are the core entities of a component-based system and relations over them to express various links between these basic architectural elements. We consider a graph-based representation illustrated by Fig. 3.

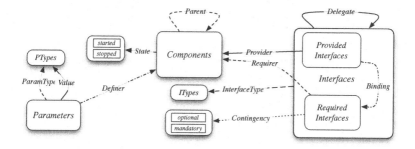

Fig. 3. Architectural elements and relations between them

In our model, a configuration c is a tuple $\langle Elem, Rel \rangle$ where $Elem$ is a set of architectural elements, and $Rel \subseteq Elem \times Elem$ is a relation over architectural elements.

The architectural elements of $Elem$ are the core entities of a component-based system:

- *Components* is a non-empty set of the core entities, i.e components;
- *RequiredInterfaces* and *ProvidedInterfaces* are defined to be subsets of *Interfaces*. Their union is disjunctive;
- *Parameters* is a set of component parameters.

The architectural relation Rel then expresses various links between the previously mentioned architectural elements.

- *InterfaceType* is a total function that associates a type with each required and provided interface;
- *Provider* is a total surjective function which gives the component having at least a provided interface, whereas *Requirer* is only a total function;
- *Contingency* is a total function which indicates for each required interface if it is *mandatory* or *optional*;
- *Definer* is a total function which gives the component of a considered parameter;
- *Parent* is a partial function linking sub-components to the corresponding composite component. Composite components have no parameter, and a sub-component must not be a composite including its parent component, and so on;
- *Binding* is a partial function which connects together a provided interface and a required one: a provided interface can be linked to only one required interface, whereas a required interface can be the target of more than one provided interface. Moreover, two linked interfaces do not belong to the same component, but their corresponding instantiated components are sub-components of the same composite component. The considered interfaces must have the same interface type, and they have not yet been involved in a delegation;

- *Delegate* expresses delegation links. It is a partial bijection which associates a provided (resp. required) interface of a sub-component with a provided (resp. required) interface of its parent. Both interfaces must have the same type, and they have not yet been involved in a binding;
- *State* is a total function which associates a value from {*started, stopped*} with each instantiated component: a component can be *started* only if all its mandatory required interfaces are bound or delegated;
- Last, *Value* is a total function which gives the current value of a considered parameter.

Complete and formal definitions can be found in [19].

Example 1. Figure 4 gives a graph-based representation of the example from Sect. 2. In this figure, the architectural elements are depicted as boxes and circles, whereas architectural relations are represented by arrows.

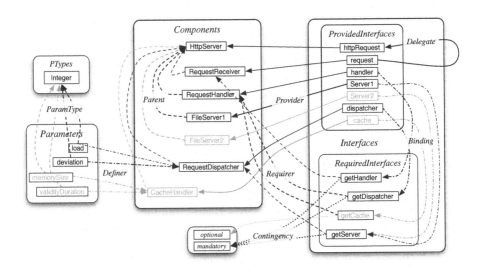

Fig. 4. Graph-based representation of the HTTP Server example

3.2 Dynamicity of Component Architectures

To support system evolution, some component models provide mechanisms to dynamically reconfigure the component-based architecture, during their execution. These dynamic reconfigurations are then based on architectural modifications, among the following primitive operations:

- instantiation/destruction of components;
- addition/removal of components;
- binding/unbinding of component interfaces;

- starting/stopping components;
- setting parameter values of components;

or combinations of them. A component architecture may also evolve by modifying parameter values or stopping components, like in the example.

Considering the component-based architecture model recalled in Sect. 3.1, a reconfiguration action is modelled by a graph transformation operation adding or removing nodes and/or arcs in the graph of the configuration. An evolution operation op transforms a configuration $c = \langle Elem, Rel \rangle$ into another one $c' = \langle Elem', Rel' \rangle$. It is represented by a transition from c to c', noticed $c \xrightarrow{op} c'$. Among the evolution operations (running operations and reconfigurations), we particularly focus on the reconfiguration ones, which are either the above-mentioned primitive architectural operations or their compositions. The remaining running operations are all represented by a generic operation, called the run operation; it is also the case for sequences of running operations.

The evolution of a component architecture is defined by the transition system $\langle \mathcal{C}, \mathcal{R}_{run}, \rightarrow \rangle$ where:

- $\mathcal{C} = \{c, c_1, c_2, \ldots\}$ is a set of configurations;
- $\mathcal{R}_{run} = \mathcal{R} \cup \{run\}$ is a finite set of evolution operations;
- $\rightarrow \subseteq \mathcal{C} \times \mathcal{R}_{run} \times \mathcal{C}$ is the reconfiguration relation.

Given the model $M = \langle \mathcal{C}, \mathcal{R}_{run}, \rightarrow \rangle$, an evolution path (or a path for short) σ of M is a (possibly infinite) sequence of configurations $c_0, c_1, c_2, \ldots$ such that $\forall i \geq 0. \exists r_i \in \mathcal{R}_{run}. c_i \xrightarrow{r_i} c_{i+1} \in \rightarrow)).$

We use $\sigma(i)$ to denote the i-th configuration of a path σ. The notation σ_i denotes the suffix path $\sigma(i), \sigma(i+1), \ldots$, and σ_i^j denotes the segment path $\sigma(i), \sigma(i+1), \sigma(i+2), ..., \sigma(j-1), \sigma(j)$. The segment path is infinite in length when the last state of the segment is repeated infinitely often. We write Σ to denote the set of evolution paths, and Σ^f $(\subseteq \Sigma)$ for the set of finite paths.

Fig. 5. Part of an evolution path of the HTTP server example

Example 2. A possible evolution path of the HTTP server is given in Fig. 5. In this path,

- c_0 is a configuration of the HTTP server without the **CacheHandler** nor **FileServer2** components;
- c_1 is obtained from c_0: the load value was changed following the running of the **RequestHandler** component;
- c_1' is the same configuration as c_1: Without the **CacheHandler** component, the RemoveCacheHandler reconfiguration cannot terminate, it is then roll-backed without any modification;

- c_2 is obtained from the configuration c_1 by adding **CacheHandler**, following the AddCacheHandler reconfiguration operation;
- c_3 is the configuration c_2 in which the memorySize value was increased;
- c_3' is the same configuration as c_3: The result of the running is not observable;
- c_4 is obtained from c_3 by adding the **FileServer2** component;
- c_5 is like the configuration c_6 but the durationValidity value was increased.

4   FTPL

In this section, we recall the syntax of the linear temporal logic for dynamic reconfigurations introduced in [14] and called FTPL. It allows characterizing the correct behaviour of reconfiguration-based systems by using architectural invariants and linear temporal logic patterns. FTPL has been inspired by proposals in [15], and their temporal extensions for JML [24,9,17].

Let us first recall the FTPL syntax as presented in [14]. A *configuration property*, denoted with *conf*, is a first order logic formula over sets and relational operations on the primitive sets and over relations defined in Sect. 3.1. A *trace property*, denoted with *trace*, is a temporal constraint on (a part of) the execution of the dynamic reconfiguration model. Further, for a reconfiguration operation *ope*, its ending is considered as an event.

```
event ::= ope terminates
        |  ope exceptional
        |  ope normal
trace ::= always conf
        |  eventually conf
        |  trace_1 ∧ trace_2
        |  trace_1 ∨ trace_2
temp  ::= after event temp
        |  before event trace
        |  trace until event
```

The *trace properties* specify the constraints to ensure on a sequence of reconfigurations. We mainly specify the **always** and **eventually** constraints which respectively describe that a property has to be satisfied by every configuration of the sequence for the former, or by at least one configuration of the sequence for the latter.

Every *temporal property* concerns a part of the execution trace on which the property should hold: it is specified with special keywords, like e.g., **after**, **before** or **until** a particular event has happened.

The set of FTPL formulae is denoted with $FTPL$. The complete and detailed semantics can be found in [14].

Example 3. Let us now illustrate the FTPL language on the example of the HTTP server from Sect. 2. Notice that the reconfiguration AddCacheHandler (resp. RemoveCacheHandler) adds (resp. removes) **CacheHandler** when the deviation value is greater (resp. less) than 50:

Property 1 :   **after** RemoveCacheHandler **terminates**
(**eventually** *deviation*>50
until AddCacheHandler **terminates**)

The previous property specifies that the deviation value eventually becomes greater than 50 between the two considered reconfigurations.

5   Runtime Verification for FTPL: RV-FTPL

As component-based architectures evolve at runtime, there is a need to check the FTPL constraints on the fly, even if only a partial information is expected. Indeed, an FTPL property often cannot be evaluated to true or false during the system execution, as only the history of the system is available and no specification of its future evolution exists. In addition, as architectural reconfigurations change the component architecture, they also change the values of FTPL constraints.

In this paper we review the FTPL semantics from a runtime verification point of view. To this end we introduce a new four-valued logic, called RV-FTPL (Runtime Verification for FTPL), characterizing the "potential" (un)satisfiability of the architectural constraints in addition to the basic FTPL semantics. Intuitively, potential true and potential false values are chosen whenever an observed behaviour has not yet lead to a violation or acceptance of the property under consideration.

Let S be a set and R a relation over $S \times S$. R is a pre-ordering iff it is reflexive and transitive, and a partial ordering iff it is anti-symmetric in addition. For a partial ordering R, the pair (S, R) is called a partially ordered set; it is sometimes denoted S when the ordering is clear. A lattice is a partially ordered set (S, R) where for each $x, y \in S$, there exists (i) a unique greatest lower bound, and (ii) a unique least upper bound. A lattice is finite iff S is finite. Every finite lattice has a well-defined unique least element, often called the minimum, and a well-defined greatest element, often called the maximum.

More specifically, let $\mathbb{B}_4 = \{\bot, \bot^p, \top^p, \top\}$ be a set where $\bot, \top$ stand resp. for *false* and *true* values where as $\bot^p, \top^p$ stand resp. for *potential false* and *potential true* values. We consider $\mathbb{B}_4$ together with the truth non-strict ordering relation $\sqsubseteq$ satisfying $\bot \sqsubseteq \bot^p \sqsubseteq \top^p \sqsubseteq \top$. On $\mathbb{B}_4$ we define the unary operation $\neg$ as $\neg\bot = \top$, $\neg\top = \bot$, $\neg\bot^p = \top^p$, and $\neg\top^p = \bot^p$, and we define two binary operations $\sqcap$ and $\sqcup$ as the minimum, respectively the maximum, interpreted with respect to $\sqsubseteq$. Thus, $(\mathbb{B}_4, \sqsubseteq)$ is a finite *de Morgan* lattice but not a Boolean lattice.

Before defining the RV-FTPL semantics, let us recall that a configuration property $conf \in FTPL$ is valid on a configuration $c = \langle Elem, Rel \rangle$ when the evaluation of $conf$ on the configuration $c = \langle Elem, Rel \rangle$ is true, written $[c \models conf] = \top$; otherwise, the property $conf$ is not valid on c, written $[c \models conf] = \bot$.

Definition 1 (RV-FTPL Semantics). *Let $\sigma_0^n \in \Sigma^f$ be a finite execution path of the length $n + 1$. Given an FTPL property, its value on σ_0^n is given by the interpretation function $[\_ \models \_]_{rv} : \Sigma^f \times FTPL \rightarrow \mathbb{B}_4$ defined as follows:*

1. For the configuration properties and events:

$$[\sigma_0^n(i) \models conf]_{rv} = \begin{cases} \top & if \ [\sigma_0^n(i) \models conf] = \top \\ \bot & otherwise \end{cases}$$

$$[\sigma_0^n(i) \models ope \ \textbf{normal}]_{rv} = \begin{cases} \top & if \ 0 < i \leqslant n \ \wedge \sigma_0^n(i-1) \neq \sigma_0^n(i) \\ & \wedge \ \sigma_0^n(i-1) \xrightarrow{ope} \sigma_0^n(i) \in \rightarrow \\ \bot & otherwise \end{cases}$$

$$[\sigma_0^n(i) \models ope \ \textbf{exceptional}]_{rv} = \begin{cases} \top & if \ 0 < i \leqslant n \ \wedge \sigma_0^n(i-1) = \sigma_0^n(i) \\ & \wedge \ \sigma_0^n(i-1) \xrightarrow{ope} \sigma_0^n(i) \in \rightarrow \\ \bot & otherwise \end{cases}$$

$$[\sigma_0^n(i) \models ope \ \textbf{terminates}]_{rv} = \begin{cases} \top & if \ ope \ \textbf{normal} \ \vee \ ope \ \textbf{exceptional} \\ \bot & otherwise \end{cases}$$

2. *For the trace properties:*

$$[\sigma_0^n \models \textbf{always} \ conf]_{rv} = \begin{cases} \bot & if \ \exists i.(0 \leqslant i \leqslant n \ \wedge [\sigma_0^n(i) \models conf]_{rv} = \bot) \\ \top^p & otherwise \end{cases}$$

$$[\sigma_0^n \models \textbf{eventually} \ conf]_{rv} = \begin{cases} \top & if \ \exists i.(0 \leqslant i \leqslant n \ \wedge [\sigma_0^n(i) \models conf]_{rv} = \top) \\ \bot^p & otherwise \end{cases}$$

$$[\sigma_0^n \models trace_1 \wedge trace_2]_{rv} = [\sigma_0^n \models trace_1]_{rv} \sqcap [\sigma_0^n \models trace_2]_{rv}$$

$$[\sigma_0^n \models trace_1 \vee trace_2]_{rv} = [\sigma_0^n \models trace_1]_{rv} \sqcup [\sigma_0^n \models trace_2]_{rv}$$

3. *For the temporal properties:*

$$[\sigma_0^n \models \textbf{after} \ event \ temp]_{rv} = \begin{cases} \top^p & if \ \forall i.(0 \leqslant i \leqslant n \ \wedge [\sigma_0^n(i) \models event]_{rv} = \top \\ & \Rightarrow [\sigma_i^n \models temp]_{rv} = \top) \vee \forall i.(0 < i \leqslant n \\ & \Rightarrow [\sigma_0^n(i) \models event]_{rv} = \bot) \\ \bot & if \ \exists i.(0 \leqslant i \leqslant n \ \wedge [\sigma_0^n(i) \models event]_{rv} = \top \\ & \wedge [\sigma_i^n \models temp]_{rv} = \bot) \\ \bot^p & if \ \exists i.(0 \leqslant i \leqslant n \ \wedge [\sigma_0^n(i) \models event]_{rv} = \top \\ & \wedge [\sigma_i^n \models temp]_{rv} = \bot^p) \end{cases}$$

$$[\sigma_0^n \models \textbf{before} \ event \ trace]_{rv} = \begin{cases} \top^p & if \ \forall i.(0 < i \leqslant n \ \wedge [\sigma_0^n(i) \models event]_{rv} = \top \\ & \Rightarrow [\sigma_0^{i-1} \models trace]_{rv} \in \{\top, \top^p\}) \vee \\ & \forall i.(0 < i \leqslant n \Rightarrow [\sigma_0^n(i) \models event]_{rv} = \bot) \\ \bot & if \ \exists i.(0 < i \leqslant n \ \wedge [\sigma_0^n(i) \models event]_{rv} = \top \\ & \wedge [\sigma_0^{i-1} \models trace]_{rv} \in \{\bot, \bot^p\}) \end{cases}$$

$$[\sigma_0^n \models trace \ \textbf{until} \ event]_{rv} = \begin{cases} \top^p & if \ \forall i.(0 < i \leqslant n \ \wedge [\sigma_0^n(i) \models event]_{rv} = \top \\ & \Rightarrow [\sigma_0^{i-1} \models trace]_{rv} \in \{\top, \top^p\}) \\ \bot & if \ ([\sigma_0^n \models trace]_{rv} = \bot) \vee \\ & (\exists i.(0 < i \leqslant n \ \wedge [\sigma_0^n(i) \models event]_{rv} = \top \\ & \wedge [\sigma_0^{i-1} \models trace]_{rv} = \bot^p) \\ \bot^p & if \ \forall i.(0 < i \leqslant n \ \Rightarrow [\sigma_0^n(i) \models event]_{rv} = \bot \end{cases}$$

Let us now comment and illustrate the above definition. The goal of our work is to be able to detect when the FTPL properties become false. So, for configuration properties and events, the interpretation does only depend on the fact that considered configurations actually belong to the path σ_0^n. For events, the basic FTPL semantics is reflected in the interpretation function.

For trace properties the intuition is as follows.

– The **always** *conf* property is not satisfied on σ_0^n if there is a configuration of σ_0^n which does not satisfy *conf*. For the other cases, the property is evaluated to be "potentially true". Indeed, if the execution terminated in σ_0^n, the property would be satisfied.

- The **eventually** $conf$ property is satisfied on σ_0^n if at least one configuration of σ_0^n satisfies $conf$. In the other cases, the property is evaluated to be "potentially false". Indeed, if the execution terminated in σ_0^n, the property would be violated.

Example 4. Figure 6 displays an evolution path of the HTTP example. The next array illustrates the evaluation of two trace properties on each configuration, depending on the chosen either FTPL or RV-FTPL semantics:

Fig. 6. Part of an evolution path of the HTTP server example

		c_0	c_1	c_2	c_3	c_4	c_5	c_6	c_7	...
always $deviation < 50$	FTPL	?	?	?	?	?	$\bot$	$\bot$	$\bot$	$\bot$
	RV-FTPL	$\top^p$	$\top^p$	$\top^p$	$\top^p$	$\top^p$	$\bot$	$\bot$	$\bot$	$\bot$
eventually $deviation > 50$	FTPL	?	?	?	?	?	$\top$	$\top$	$\top$	$\top$
	RV-FTPL	$\bot^p$	$\bot^p$	$\bot^p$	$\bot^p$	$\bot^p$	$\top$	$\top$	$\top$	$\top$

Considering the FTPL semantics, we cannot conclude about the interpretation of the considered properties, until we reach the configuration c_5. On the contrary, in RV-FTPL we say at the beginning that the **always** property is expected to be true in the future, until we reach c_5 where it is false.

The intuition of the definition of temporal properties is as follows:

- The value of the **after** $event\ temp$ property is potentially true either if the $event$ event does not occur in all considered configurations, or if the occurrence of the $event$ event on a configuration implies that the $temp$ temporal property is evaluated to true on the suffix of the path starting at this configuration. The **after** $event\ temp$ property is evaluated to false if there is a configuration $\sigma_0^n(i)$ of σ_0^n where the $event$ event happens and $temp$ is evaluated to false on the suffix σ_i^n. The **after** $event\ temp$ property is evaluated to potentially false if there is a configuration $\sigma_0^n(i)$ of σ_0^n where the $event$ event occurs, and $temp$ is evaluated to potentially false on the suffix σ_i^n.
- The value of the **before** $event\ trace$ property is potentially true if either the $event$ event does not occur in all considered configurations, or if $trace$ is evaluated either to true or to potentially true on the prefix of the path where the $event$ event occurs. The **before** $event\ trace$ property is evaluated to false if there is a configuration $\sigma_0^n(i)$ of σ_0^n where $event$ happens, and $trace$ is evaluated either to false or to potentially false on the path ending at $\sigma_0^n(i)$, non including this configuration.

- The value of the *trace* **until** *event* property is potentially true if the *trace* property is evaluated either to true or to potentially true on the prefix of the path where there is a configuration satisfying *event*, the prefix being without that configuration. The *trace* **until** *event* property is evaluated to false either if there is a configuration $\sigma_0^n(i)$ of σ_0^n where *event* happens, and if *trace* is either false or potentially false on the path ending at $\sigma_0^n(i)$ but non-including it; or if σ_0^n does not satisfy the *trace* property when *event* does not happen on σ_0^n. The property is potentially false if the *event* event does not occur in all considered configurations.

Example 5. Let us again consider the path in Fig. 6 and the FTPL property 1

> after RemoveCacheHandler **terminates**
> (**eventually** *deviation*>50
> **until** AddCacheHandler **terminates**)

explained in Example 3. The following array displays the value of the considered property interpreted respectively in FTPL and in RV-FTPL:

		c_0	c_1	c_2	c_3	c_4	c_5	c_6	c_7	...
Property 1	FTPL	?	?	?	?	?	?	$\top$	$\top$	$\top$
	RV-FTPL	$\top^p$	$\top^p$	$\perp^p$	$\perp^p$	$\perp^p$	$\perp^p$	$\top^p$	$\top^p$	$\top^p$

From the FTPL semantics point of view, we cannot conclude about the validity of the property until we reach the configuration c_6. Using the RV-FTPL semantics, the property interpretation is potential true before the reconfiguration RemoveCacheHandler is executed. Then, the property value becomes potential false until the deviation becomes greater than 50 on c_5; as a consequence the property value becomes potentially true because of partial information.

6   Using RV-FTPL Properties to Check Reconfigurations

The proposals of the paper have been applied to the Fractal component model. Thsi section presents the prototype we have been developing to check at runtime the satisfiability of RV-FTPL formulas on Fractal component-based systems. To this end, it exploits and adapts the FPath and FScript [12] tool supports for Fractal to evaluate the desired RV-FTPL formulas after each reconfiguration operation.

6.1   Overview of Fractal, FPath and FScript

The Fractal model is a hierarchical and reflective component model intended to implement, deploy and manage software systems [10]. A Fractal component is both a design and a runtime entity that consists of a unit of encapsulation, composition and configuration. A component is wrapped in a membrane which can show and control a casually connected representation of its encapsulated content. This content is either directly an implementation in case of a primitive component, or sub-components for composite components.

In order to control the internal structure of a component at runtime, the Fractal model also defines standard interfaces named *controllers*. In addition, the Fractal model can be extended thanks to new controllers which allow the user to integrate new features.

FPath [12] is a domain-specific language inspired by the XPath language that provides a notation and introspection mechanisms to navigate inside Fractal architectures. FPath expressions use the properties of components (e.g. the value of a component attribute or the state of a component) or architectural relations between components (e.g. the subcomponents of a composite component) to express queries about Fractal architectures.

FScript [12] is a language that allows the definition of reconfigurations of Fractal architectures. FScript integrates FPath seamlessly in its syntax, FPath queries being used to select the elements to reconfigure. To ensure the reliability of its reconfigurations, FScript considers them as transactions and integrates a back-end that implements this semantics on top of the Fractal model.

6.2   Integrating RV-FTPL Property Verification into Fractal

To check RV-FTPL properties at runtime, we have implemented two Fractal controllers which observe the Fractal component model: our first controller, called the *reconfiguration controller*, permits capturing reconfiguration invocations, whereas the second controller, called the *RV-FTPL controller*, handles RV-FTPL formulas.

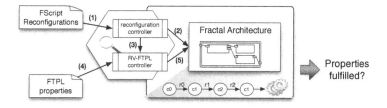

Fig. 7. RV-FTPL runtime verification principle

Figure 7 explains how both controllers are used to evaluate properties of interest. When a reconfiguration is invoked (**1**), the reconfiguration controller executes the reconfiguration (**2**)—specified in a FScript file—on the considered component-based architecture. It then invokes the RV-FTPL controller (**3**) to evaluate the RV-FTPL properties from a file (**4**) where those properties are specified. The RV-FTPL controller uses the instantiated component model (**5**) and executes queries over it: to post up the property evaluation result to the user, the RV-FTPL controller parses the property of interest and uses a visitor to evaluate it on the current configuration using FPath. In the case of the future patterns containing the **after** keyword, the visitor waits for the reconfiguration event before evaluating the temporal part of the property. On the contrary, for the past patterns, i.e., the RV-FTPL properties without the **after** keyword, the trace part of the property is evaluated before the reconfiguration event appears. This avoids us from saving all the previous configurations needed to evaluate the property once the event appears.

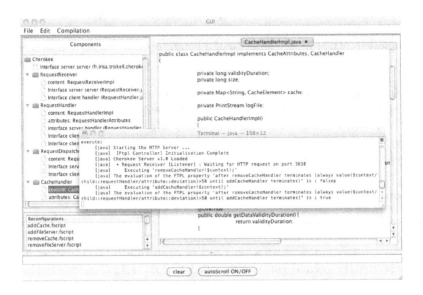

Fig. 8. Running prototype

The above verification procedure has been integrated into the EVA4Fractal tool previously described in [13]. Figure 8 shows our prototype in action: a Fractal implementation of the HTTP server example is running and the FTPL property

> **after** RemoveCacheHandler **terminates**
> (**eventually** *deviation*>50
> **until** AddCacheHandler **terminates**)

is evaluated at runtime after each reconfiguration execution. The reader can notice that after the execution of the reconfiguration RemoveCacheHandler, the value of the property is potential false. If the value of deviation raises above 50, when the reconfiguration AddCacheHandler is applied, the property value becomes true.

7   Using RV-FTPL Properties to Enforce Reconfigurations

As explained in Sect. 1, one of the main motivations of the present work is to use the RV-FTPL property evaluation to control the execution of reconfigurations.

Actually, for some kind of systems like critical systems or embedded systems, the behaviour where the property evaluation becomes false might be not acceptable. To this end, we can use potential true or potential false values to enforce the reconfigurations.

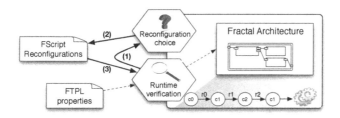

Fig. 9. RV-FTPL runtime enforcement principle

In this section, we show the capability of our monitor to enforce the component-based system reconfigurations by using the interpretation of desired properties. The principle is illustrated in Fig. 9. While interpreting RV-FTPL properties **(1)**, the potential true or potential false values can be used to guide the choice of the next reconfiguration operation **(2)** which will be applied to the component architecture **(3)**. Let us give an intuition about our approach:

1. Let us consider the RV-FTPL property 3 valued $\perp^p$ on the current architectural configuration c_5 from the path given in Fig. 6;
2. We are looking for enabling the reconfiguration operations that make the component-architecture evolve to a new architectural configuration where the RV-FTPL property will be enforced;
3. The reconfiguration manager chooses the reconfiguration AddCacheHandler to be applied;
4. The property will be enforced: it is valued to $\top^p$ on the new configuration c_6.

In Fractal an obvious manner to implement the *reconfiguration choice* procedure is to reuse the transaction mechanism of FScript [12], allowing the system to rollback to a consistent state when a reconfiguration operation failed. We propose to exploit this mechanism to evaluate the RV-FTPL property on the possible target configurations, until a reconfiguration operation where the system benefits enforcement in the best possible way, is found.

We display in Fig. 10 the execution scenario using this mechanism. For each FScript reconfiguration, a transaction is started and the considered reconfiguration operation is executed. Then, the RV-FTPL property is evaluated on the reached configuration. If the interpretation value is true, there is no need to consider remaining reconfiguration operations, so the transaction is committed and the execution goes on. For other interpretation values, the transaction is rollbacked and the results of the reconfiguration valuation are recorded. When all the enable reconfigurations are explored, the recorded results are used to

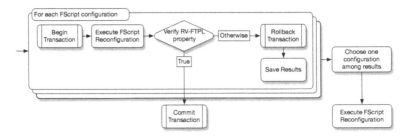

Fig. 10. Enforcement scenario

choose the most appropriate reconfiguration operation which is then applied to the system. To help this choice, adaptation policies [13,11] defined by the user, or distributed controllers [18] for knowledge-based priority properties, or runtime enforcement monitors [16] built automatically for several enforcable properties, can be used.

If for every reconfiguration operation the property of interest is violated, the execution should be either stopped or continued with special recovery operations, and the user should be informed. This reaction clearly depends on the system features (safety critical systems, embedded systems, etc.). Again, adaptation policies can be used to handle events associated with the property violation on the one hand, and to specify special recovery reconfiguration operations, on the other hand.

8   Conclusion

As component-based architectures evolve at runtime, this paper pays particular attention to checking—on the fly—temporal and architectural constraints expressed with a linear time temporal logic over (re)configuration sequences, FTPL [14]. Unfortunately, an FTPL property often cannot be evaluated to true or false during the system execution. Indeed, only a partial information about the system evolution is available: only a (finite) history of the system state is known, and no specification about its future evolutions exists. To remedy this problem, we have reviewed the FTPL semantics from a runtime verification point of view. Inspired by proposals in [8], we have introduced a new four-valued logic, called RV-FTPL, characterizing the "potential" (un)satisfiability of the architectural FTPL constraints in addition to the basic FTPL semantics.

The paper has also reported on the prototype we have been developing to verify and enforce RV-FTPL properties. Given a Fractal component-based system [10] and some desired temporal and archtectural FTPL contraints, to make it possible the system to reconfigure, the prototype interprets RV-FTPL formulas at runtime. The feasability of a runtime property enforcement has also been discussed: the proposed 4-valued logic not only captures information absence, but also helps the monitor in guiding the reconfiguration process, namely in choosing the next reconfiguration operations to be applied.

Related Work.
In the context of dynamic reconfigurations, ArchJava [3] gives means to reconfigure Java architectures, and the ArchJava language guarantees communication integrity at runtime. Barringer and al. give a temporal logic based framework to reason about the evolution of systems [5]. In [4], a temporal logic is proposed to specify and verify properties on graph transformation systems.

In the Fractal-based framework, the work in [21] has defined integrity constraints on a graph-based representation of Fractal, to specify the reliability of component-based systems. Unlike [21], our model lays down only general architectural constraints, thus providing an operational semantics to other component-based systems, to their refinements and property preservation issues. On the integrity constraints side, the FTPL logic allows specifying architectural constraints more complex than architectural invariants in [12]. Let us remark that architectural invariants as presented in [12] can be handled within the FTPL framework by using **always** *cp*, where *cp* represents the considered architectural invariant.

Among other applications, our proposals aim at a monitoring of component-based systems. In [6], Basin and al. have shown the feasibility of monitoring temporal safety properties (and, more recently, security properties) using a runtime monitoring approach for metric First-order temporal logic (MFOTL). In [23,22], monitors are used to check some policies at runtime, and to enforce the program to evolve correctly by applying reconfigurations. A similar approach based on a three-valued variant of LTL has been proposed in [7]. Contrary to those works, we focus on temporal and architectural constraints to make it possible *component-based* systems to reconfigure at runtime.

In [8], a three-valued and a four-valued LTL are studied from a logic point of view. In [16], the authors have studied the class of enforceable properties from the point of view of the well-known temporal property hierarchies. The automatic monitor generation for enforceable properties has also been proposed. In this direction, it would be interesting and important to characterize the FTPL temporal patterns wrt. the class of enforceable properties. For non-enforceable temporal patterns, we intend to exploit event-based adaptation policies to make the system behave and reconfigure according to a given recovery policy when the desired property is violated.

References

1. Aguilar Cornejo, M., Garavel, H., Mateescu, R., De Palma, N.: Specification and Verification of a Dynamic Reconfiguration Protocol for Agent-Based Applications. Research Report RR-4222, INRIA (2001)
2. Aguirre, N., Maibaum, T.: A temporal logic approach to the specification of reconfigurable component-based systems. In: Automated Software Engineering (2002)
3. Aldric, J.: Using types to enforce architectural structure. In: WICSA 2008, pp. 23–34 (2008)
4. Baldan, P., Corradini, A., König, B., Lluch Lafuente, A.: A Temporal Graph Logic for Verification of Graph Transformation Systems. In: Fiadeiro, J.L., Schobbens, P.-Y. (eds.) WADT 2006. LNCS, vol. 4409, pp. 1–20. Springer, Heidelberg (2007)

5. Barringer, H., Gabbay, D.M., Rydeheard, D.E.: From Runtime Verification to Evolvable Systems. In: Sokolsky, O., Taşıran, S. (eds.) RV 2007. LNCS, vol. 4839, pp. 97–110. Springer, Heidelberg (2007)
6. Basin, D.A., Klaedtke, F., Müller, S., Pfitzmann, B.: Runtime monitoring of metric first-order temporal properties. In: IARCS, FSTTCS 2008, India. LIPIcs, vol. 2, pp. 49–60. Schloss Dagstuhl - Leibniz-Zentrum fuer Informatik (2008)
7. Bauer, A., Leucker, M., Schallhart, C.: Model-based runtime analysis of distributed reactive systems. In: ASWEC'iso 2006. IEEE (2006)
8. Bauer, A., Leucker, M., Schallhart, C.: Comparing LTL Semantics for Runtime Verification. Journal of Logic and Computation (JLC) (2010)
9. Bellegarde, F., Groslambert, J., Huisman, M., Julliand, J., Kouchnarenko, O.: Verification of liveness properties with JML. Technical report RR-5331, INRIA (2004)
10. Bruneton, E., Coupaye, T., Leclercq, M., Quéma, V., Stefani, J.-B.: The fractal component model and its support in java. Softw., Pract. Exper. 36(11-12), 1257–1284 (2006)
11. Chauvel, F., Barais, O., Borne, I., Jézéquel, J.-M.: Composition of qualitative adaptation policies. In: ASE 2008, pp. 455–458. IEEE (2008) (short paper)
12. David, P.-C., Ledoux, T., Léger, M., Coupaye, T.: FPath and FScript: Language support for navigation and reliable reconfiguration of Fractal architectures. Annales des Télécommunications 64(1-2), 45–63 (2009)
13. Dormoy, J., Kouchnarenko, O.: Event-based Adaptation Policies for Fractal Components. In: AICCSA 2010, pp. 1–8. IEEE (May 2010)
14. Dormoy, J., Kouchnarenko, O., Lanoix, A.: Using Temporal Logic for Dynamic Reconfigurations of Components. In: Barbosa, L.S., Lumpe, M. (eds.) FACS 2010. LNCS, vol. 6921, pp. 200–217. Springer, Heidelberg (2010)
15. Dwyer, M.B., Avrunin, G.S., Corbett, J.C.: Patterns in property specifications for finite-state verification. In: ICSE, pp. 411–420 (1999)
16. Falcone, Y., Mounier, L., Fernandez, J.-C., Richier, J.-L.: Runtime enforcement monitors: composition, synthesis, and enforcement abilities. Formal Methods in System Design 38(3), 223–262 (2011)
17. Giorgetti, A., Groslambert, J., Julliand, J., Kouchnarenko, O.: Verification of class liveness properties with java modelling language. IET Software (2008)
18. Graf, S., Peled, D., Quinton, S.: Achieving Distributed Control through Model Checking. In: Touili, T., Cook, B., Jackson, P. (eds.) CAV 2010. LNCS, vol. 6174, pp. 396–409. Springer, Heidelberg (2010)
19. Lanoix, A., Dormoy, J., Kouchnarenko, O.: Combining proof and model-checking to validate reconfigurable architectures. In: FESCA 2011. ENTCS (2011)
20. Léger, M.: Fiabilité des Reconfigurations Dynamiques dans les Architectures à Composant. PhD thesis, Ecole Nationale Supérieure des Mines de Paris (2009)
21. Léger, M., Ledoux, T., Coupaye, T.: Reliable Dynamic Reconfigurations in a Reflective Component Model. In: Grunske, L., Reussner, R., Plasil, F. (eds.) CBSE 2010. LNCS, vol. 6092, pp. 74–92. Springer, Heidelberg (2010)
22. Ligatti, J., Bauer, L., Walker, D.: Run-time enforcement of nonsafety policies. ACM TISSEC 12, 19:1–19:41 (2009)
23. Schneider, F.B.: Enforceable security policies. ACM TISSEC 3, 30–50 (2000)
24. Trentelman, K., Huisman, M.: Extending JML Specifications with Temporal Logic. In: Kirchner, H., Ringeissen, C. (eds.) AMAST 2002. LNCS, vol. 2422, pp. 334–348. Springer, Heidelberg (2002)

Timed Conformance Testing for Orchestrated Service Discovery*

Jose Pablo Escobedo[1], Christophe Gaston[1], and Pascale Le Gall[2]

[1] CEA, LIST, Point Courrier 94, 91191, Gif-sur-Yvette, France
{jose-pablo.escobedo,christophe.gaston}@cea.fr
[2] Laboratoire MAS, Grande Voie des Vignes, 92195 Châtenay-Malabry, France
pascale.legall@ecp.fr

Abstract. Orchestrations are systems deployed on the Internet where there is a central component (called orchestrator) coordinating other components (called Web services), pre-existing to the orchestration design phase. Web services are made available through repositories on the Internet to orchestration designers. Service discovery refers to the activity of identifying Web services offered by third parties. We propose an approach to discover Web services by taking into account the intended behaviors of Web services as they can be inferred from the orchestrator specifications. Web services are tested with respect to those behaviors to decide whether or not they can be selected. Specifications of orchestrators are Timed Input/Output Symbolic Transition Systems. Web service intended behaviors are elicited by means of symbolic execution and projection techniques. Those behaviors can be used as test purposes for our timed symbolic conformance testing algorithm.

Keywords: Web service discovery, orchestrations, conformance testing, timed testing, symbolic execution.

1 Introduction

As explained in [18], the World Wide Web has now evolved from a place where we share and find data to a place where we share and find dedicated functionalities. Such functionalities, called *Web services*, can be assembled to build systems whose particularity is that basic functional units (*i.e.* Web services) are developed and offered by different parties and are physically stored in different places on the Internet. The process of building systems by combining Web services is known as *Web service composition*. Composing Web services may be achieved by means of several architectural approaches. Here we focus on *orchestration* architectures [14,19]. An *orchestration* is a Web service system containing a controller component, called an *orchestrator* which serves as an interface for users and is responsible for coordinating Web services invocations accordingly to the user needs. In order to build orchestrations, the first step is to find required Web services: this activity is often referenced as (Web) Service Discovery [20]. Web

---

* Work partially supported by the french TeCoS project funded by DGA.

F. Arbab and P.C. Ölveczky (Eds.): FACS 2011, LNCS 7253, pp. 133–150, 2012.
© Springer-Verlag Berlin Heidelberg 2012

services must be published and accessible on some known repositories, and must be associated with descriptions allowing the designer to select them. Those descriptions contain usually only functional aspects (what are the offered functionalities), and pieces of information may be syntactic (*e.g.* what is the interface of a service in terms of offered methods for example). As discussed in [20], such descriptions ground discovery procedures by matching orchestration requirements with descriptions of candidate Web services.

In this paper we aim at completing those existing matching procedures mainly based on static analysis by techniques exploiting Web service executions. Provided that the system designer produces a behavioral description of the orchestrator before the Web service selection phase, we aim at taking benefits of the knowledge of the orchestrator to select Web services. Since the orchestrator is responsible for Web service invocations, orchestrator executions mainly contain sequences of Web service invocations conditioned by Web service reactions. Therefore an orchestrator greatly constrains the set of acceptable behaviors (*i.e.* sequences of emissions/receptions that are called *traces*) of Web services to be selected. Our proposal is to use that set of acceptable traces to guide a selection procedure based on testing techniques.

Technically, orchestrators are specified by means of *Timed Input/Output Symbolic Transition Systems* (TIOSTS), that we define as an extension of *Input/Output Symbolic Transition Systems* [8, 12] to deal with timing issues. Regardless of symbolic representations of data, TIOSTS can be seen as a sub class of Timed Automata [1] with one clock per transition. Taking time into account in our work is mandatory because defining timers and reasoning about them is very common in orchestrator descriptions. Typically, one of the most well known ways to describe orchestrators is the WS-BPEL specification language [9]. Operations that can be made on clocks in TIOSTS reflect the common usage of timers in WS-BPEL, which are used to guard orchestrator reactions, typically in situations when some Web service does not react to stimuli of the orchestrator. [3] provides a systematic and detailed translation of the WS-BPEL language towards a particular family of TIOSTS. Advantages of using TIOSTS are twofold: first, we can take benefits of the formal testing framework that we previously defined [8, 10, 13] by extending it to timing issues. Secondly, we use symbolic execution techniques to analyze the orchestrator description: from a tree-like structure symbolically representing all possible executions of the orchestrator and by means of projection and mirroring techniques, we transform those behaviors into intended Web service behaviors. From those behaviors we extract test purposes to be used in a testing algorithm. A Web service conforming to the test purpose extracted from the orchestrator becomes a good candidate to be integrated in the orchestration. The testing algorithm is a timed extension of the one we defined in [13] and further adapted to the test of orchestrators in context in [8].

Using formal techniques to evaluate the compatibilty of Web services (in particular relatively to timing aspects) in Web service systems has been addressed several times, but very often ([6, 7, 15, 16]) based on verification techniques applied on (parts of) system models (including Web service models or communication protocol models). On the contrary, we use testing techniques to discover Web services for which no model is supposed to be available (we only have knowledge of their interface to send them inputs and receive their outputs). Our proposal is close to the one given in [2] where the goal is to evaluate conformance of Web services to orchestrators thanks to testing techniques. While they use model-checking algorithms applied to testing without considering timing issues, we use symbolic execution techniques within a timed setting.

2   Timed Input Output Symbolic Transition Systems

2.1   Syntax

TIOSTS are symbolic communicating automata introducing constraints over execution delays of transitions. We represent data by means of classical typed equational logic. A *data type signature* is a couple $\Omega = (S, Op)$ where S is a set of types and Op is a set of operations, each one provided with a profile $s_1 \cdots s_{n-1} \rightarrow s_n$ (for $i \leq n$, $s_i \in S$). A set of *S-typed variables* is a set V of the form $\coprod_{s \in S} V_s$. The set of Ω-*terms* with variables in V is denoted as $T_\Omega(V) = \bigcup_{s \in S} T_\Omega(V)_s$ and is inductively defined as usual over Op and V. $T_\Omega(\emptyset)$ is simply denoted T_Ω. A Ω-*substitution* is a function $\sigma : V \rightarrow T_\Omega(V)$ preserving types. In the following, we note $T_\Omega(V)^V$ the set of all Ω-substitutions of the variables in V. Any substitution σ may be canonically extended to terms. The *identity Ω-substitution* over the variables in V, Id_V, is defined as $Id_V(v) = v$ for all $v \in V$. The set $Sen_\Omega(V)$ of all typed equational Ω-*formulas* contains the truth values *true*, *false* and all formulas built using the equality predicates $t = t'$ for $t, t' \in T_\Omega(V)_s$, and the usual connectives $\neg, \vee, \wedge$. In the sequel, we suppose that a signature $\Omega = (S, Op)$ is given. S necessarily contains a distinguished type name *time*, provided with constant symbols in the so-called *set of delays* $D \subseteq \mathbb{R}_+{}^*$ (the set of strictly positive real numbers) and also provided with: the constant symbols 0 and $\infty :\rightarrow time$ representing the first non countable ordinal, and with the usual arithmetic operators as $+, -, <, \leq \dots$. Moreover D is supposed to be stable under addition, i.e. for any $d, d' \in D$ we have $d + d' \in D$ and under subtraction, i.e. for any $d, d' \in D$ with $d < d'$, then $d' - d \in D$.

TIOSTS are then defined over so-called *TIOSTS signatures*. A TIOSTS signature Σ is a tuple $(\mathcal{V}, C)$, where $\mathcal{V}$ is a set of *data variables*, and C is a set of *communication channels*. A transition of a TIOSTS is a tuple composed of: a source state, a minimal and a maximal delay for the transition firing, a formula called a *guard over variables* defining a constraint on variable interpretations for the transition firing, a *communication action*, an affectation on data variables to update variable assignments, and a target state. Communication actions are receptions (inputs, denoted by ?) or emissions (outputs, denoted by !) through channels of C, or the unobservable communication action (denoted τ). The set of *communication actions* over Σ is defined as $Act(\Sigma) = I(\Sigma) \cup O(\Sigma) \cup \{\tau\}$, where: $I(\Sigma) = \{c?x \mid x \in V, c \in C\}$ and $O(\Sigma) = \{c!t \mid t \in T_\Omega(V), c \in C\}$.

Definition 1 (TIOSTS). *Let* $\Sigma = (V, C)$ *be a TIOSTS signature. A* TIOSTS *over* Σ *is* $\mathcal{G} = (Q, init, Tr)$ *where:* Q *is a set of* state names, $init \in Q$ *is the initial state and* $Tr \subseteq Q \times (D \cup \{0\}) \times (D \cup \{\infty\}) \times Sen_\Omega(V) \times Act(\Sigma) \times T_\Omega(V)^V \times Q$ *is a set of* transitions.

In the sequel, for any TIOSTS $\mathcal{G} = (Q, init, Tr)$ over Σ, we note $Q_\mathcal{G}$, $init_\mathcal{G}$, $Tr_\mathcal{G}$, and $L^\mathcal{G}$ respectively for Q, $init$, Tr, and $Act(\Sigma)$. For any transition $tr \in Tr_\mathcal{G}$ of the form $(q, \delta_{min}, \delta_{max}, \psi, act, \rho, q')$, δ_{min} is intuitively the minimum delay to wait before the transition can be fired, and δ_{max} is the maximum delay beyond which the transition can not be fired anymore. If δ_{max} is ∞, there is no upper delay for the transition firing. The class of constraints that can be expressed concerning time in TIOSTS is a sub class of those that can be expressed in timed automata: constraints characterizing an interval of possible delays before an action occurrence. Reasoning with that simplified class of constraints simplify the rules defining the algorithm given in Section 4. We use the notations $source(tr)$, $\delta_{min}(tr)$, $\delta_{max}(tr)$, $guard(tr)$, $act(tr)$, $sub(tr)$, and $target(tr)$ in order to refer respectively to, q, δ_{min}, δ_{max}, ψ , act, ρ, and q'.

In the sequel, as in [11, 23], we only consider so-called *strongly responsive* TIOSTS that do not contain an infinite sequence of transitions whose actions are in $O(\Sigma) \cup \{\tau\}$.

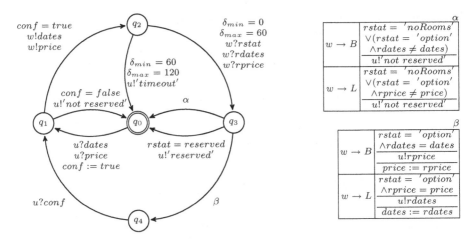

Fig. 1. $\mathcal{O}$: TIOSTS for the *Business* (B) and *Low Cost* (L) Hotel Reservation examples

Example 1. Figure 1 depicts the Business (B) and Low Cost (L) Hotel Reservation examples. They consist of two simplified versions of an orchestration used to reserve a room in a hotel for some given prices and dates, giving priority to dates while varying the price for the Business version, and giving priority to the price while varying the dates for the Low Cost version. Since they are very similar, we abusively represent them in the same figure. The only difference consists in transitions labeled with α and β, for which we provide the guards, communication actions and affectations in the table. Data variables V are $\{dates, price, conf, rstat, rdates, rprice\}$. Communication channels C are $\{u, w\}$ (u to communicate with the user, and w with the Hotel Web service). In both cases, the orchestrator ($\mathcal{O}$) receives the desired dates and price from the user (transition[1] $q_0 \rightarrow q_1$) and tries to find a room by using the Hotel Web service (transition $q_1 \rightarrow q_2$). The answer from the Hotel Web service must arrive before 60 seconds, else a timeout error message is sent to the user (transition $q_2 \rightarrow q_0$). This answer can be: (1) $'reserved'$, if a room was found and reserved for those dates and price, (2) $'option'$, if a room was found with a date and/or price close to the ones given as input, and (3) $'noRooms'$, indicating that there are no available rooms at all. According to the answer from the Hotel Web service, the orchestrator may in turn: (1) confirm the reservation; (2) notify the user that it is not possible to find a room: it may be due to the answer $'noRoom'$ from the Hotel Web service or it is $'option'$ and, (2.1) for the Business version (see α in the figure for $w \rightarrow B$), the dates of the optional reservation are not the ones given by the user; (2.2) for the Low Cost version (see α in the figure for $w \rightarrow L$), the price of the optional reservation is not the one given by the user; (3) if the answer is $'option'$ and: (3.1) for the Business version (see β in the figure for $w \rightarrow B$), the dates are the ones desired by the user but the price is different (usually higher), then the user is asked to confirm the new price before trying again to make the reservation (transitions $q_3 \rightarrow q_4 \rightarrow q_1$); (3.2) for the Low Cost version (see β in the figure for $w \rightarrow L$), the price is the one desired by the user but the dates are different, then the user is asked to confirm the new dates (transitions $q_3 \rightarrow q_4 \rightarrow q_1$).

2.2 Semantics

In order to associate semantics to TIOSTS, we begin by interpreting data occurring in Ω: an Ω-model is a set M whose elements are associated with a type in S, and we note $M_s \subseteq M$ the subset of M whose elements are associated with s. Moreover for each $op : s_1 \cdots s_{n-1} \rightarrow s_n$ in Op, M is associated with a function $\overline{op} : M_{s_1} \times \cdots \times M_{s_{n-1}} \rightarrow M_{s_n}$. We define Ω-interpretations as applications ν from V to M preserving types and extended to terms in $T_\Omega(V)$. M^V is the set of all Ω-interpretations of V in M. A model M satisfies a formula φ, denoted by $M \models \varphi$, if and only if, for all interpretations ν, $M \models_\nu \varphi$, where $M \models_\nu t = t'$ is defined by $\nu(t) = \nu(t')$, and where the truth values and the connectives are handled as usual. Given a model M and a formula φ, φ is said satisfiable in M if there exists an interpretation ν such that $M \models_\nu \varphi$. In the sequel, we suppose that an Ω-model M is given, in which all operations of the time sort are interpreted as expected.

---

[1] For concision purpose, several inputs (resp. outputs) can be grouped together in a single transition. Such a feature is practical to model orchestrators and does not raise technical difficulties in our framework, where they can be seen as inputs or outputs of structured pieces of data.

TIOSTS are associated with automata where messages and delays between them are interpreted in M. Such automata are called *Timed Input Output Labeled Transition Systems* (TIOLTS) [5, 17, 21], and are simply automata whose transitions are labeled either by actions (inputs, outputs, or the internal action τ) or by delays.

Definition 2 (TIOLTS). *Let* $L = (L_i, L_o)$ *such that* $L_i \cap L_o = \emptyset$ *and such that* $(L_i \cup L_o) \cap (\{\tau\} \cup \mathbb{R}_+^*) = \emptyset$. *A TIOLTS over* L *is a tuple* $\mathbb{G} = (Q, init, Tr)$ *where* Q *is a set of* states, $init \in Q$ *is the* initial state *and* $Tr \subseteq Q \times (L \cup \{\tau\} \cup D) \times Q$ *is a set of* transitions.

Elements of L_i and L_o are *actions* that are respectively called inputs and outputs. In the sequel, we will often assimilate L with $L_i \cup L_o$: for example, $l \in L$ will mean $l \in L_i \cup L_o$ and so on. Only transitions carrying elements of D represent delays: other transitions are instantaneously triggered. For any $tr = (q, a, q')$ of Tr, $source(tr)$, $act(tr)$ and $target(tr)$ stand respectively for q, a and q'. As for TIOSTS, for any TIOLTS $\mathbb{G} = (Q, init, Tr)$ over L, we note $Q_{\mathbb{G}}$, $init_{\mathbb{G}}$, $Tr_{\mathbb{G}}$, and $L^{\mathbb{G}}$ respectively for Q, $init$, Tr, and L.

For any TIOSTS signature Σ, elements of $I(\Sigma)$ and $O(\Sigma)$ can be interpreted as actions in the sense of Definition 2: for any $\nu \in M^{\mathcal{V}}$, we note $\nu(c?x)$ for $c?\nu(x)$, and $\nu(c!t)$ for $c!\nu(t)$. We note $L_i^\Sigma = \{\nu(i) | i \in I(\Sigma) \wedge \nu \in M^{\mathcal{V}}\}$, we note $L_o^\Sigma = \{\nu(o) | o \in O(\Sigma) \wedge \nu \in M^{\mathcal{V}}\}$, and we note $L^\Sigma = (L_i^\Sigma, L_o^\Sigma)$.

Any TIOSTS over Σ can then be associated with a TIOLTS over L^Σ, by building TIOLTS-transitions reflecting all possible triggerings of all symbolic transitions: roughly, for any transition tr we identify all the possible couples delay/interpreted action and for each of them, we build two consecutive transitions, the first one labeled by the delay and the second one labeled by the action.

Definition 3 (Runs of transitions). *For any TIOSTS* $\mathcal{G}$, *let* $Q_{\mathcal{G}}^M$ *stands for* $Q_{\mathcal{G}} \times D \times M^{\mathcal{V}}$. *For any transition* $tr \in Tr_{\mathcal{G}}$, *the run of transition* tr *is defined as* $Run(tr) \subseteq (Q_{\mathcal{G}}^M \times D \times Q_{\mathcal{G}}^M).(Q_{\mathcal{G}}^M \times (L^\Sigma \cup \{\tau\}) \times Q_{\mathcal{G}}^M)$, *where* $((q_i, t_i, \nu^i), d, (q_i, t_d, \nu^i)).((q_i, t_d, \nu^i), l, (q_f, t_d, \nu^f)) \in Run(tr)$ *iff* $q_i = source(tr)$, $q_f = target(tr)$, $\nu^i \models guard(tr)$, $t_d = t_i + d$, $\delta_{min}(tr) \leq d \leq \delta_{max}(tr)$ *and:*

- *if* $act(tr)$ *is of the form* $c!t$ *(resp.* τ*), then* $\nu^f = \nu^i \circ sub(tr)$, *and* $l = \nu^i(c!(t))$ *(resp.* τ*);*
- *if* $act(tr)$ *is of the form* $c?x$, *then there exists* ν^a *such that* $\nu^a(z) = \nu^i(z)$ *for every* $z \neq x$, $\nu^f = \nu^a \circ sub(tr)$, *and* $l = \nu^a(c?x)$.

The set of transitions of the TIOLTS associated to a TIOSTS contains all those occurring in all runs of all TIOSTS transitions. Moreover we add initialization transitions and transitions denoting that whenever no reactions (delays or outputs) are specified from a given state the time may elapse. That TIOLTS is defined as follows.

Definition 4 (TIOSTS unfolding). *The* unfolding of the TIOSTS $\mathcal{G}$ *is the* TIOLTS $\mathbb{G} = (\{init\} \cup Q_{\mathcal{G}}^M, init, Tr)$ *over* L^Σ, *where* $init$ *is a(n arbitrary) state satisfying* $init \notin Q_{\mathcal{G}}^M$ *and* $Tr \subseteq (\{init\} \cup Q_{\mathcal{G}}^M) \times (L^\Sigma \cup \{\tau\} \cup D) \times (\{init\} \cup Q_{\mathcal{G}}^M)$ *is defined as follows:*

Initialization transitions: *for any* $\nu \in M^{\mathcal{V}}$, $(init, \tau, (init_{\mathcal{G}}, 0, \nu)) \in Tr$,

Run transitions: *for any* $tr \in Tr_{\mathcal{G}}$, *for any* $(Q_1, d, Q_2).(Q_2, l, Q_3) \in Run(tr)$,
   we have $(Q_1, d, Q_2) \in Tr$ *and* $(Q_2, l, Q_3) \in Tr$,

Time elapsing transitions: *for any* $Q \in \{init\} \cup Q_{\mathcal{G}}^M$ *s.t. for all* $tr \in Tr$ *with*
   $source(tr) = Q$, $act(tr) \in L_i^{\Sigma}$, *then for any* $d \in D$ *we have* $(Q, d, Q) \in Tr$.

The semantics of $\mathcal{G}$ is the set of all sequences of actions and delays that can be associated to $\mathbb{G}$. Such sequences, called *timed traces*, are defined from the set of *paths* of[2] $\mathbb{G}$, denoted $Path(\mathbb{G}) \subseteq Tr_{\mathbb{G}}^*$, containing the empty sequence ε and all sequences of the form $tr_1 \ldots tr_n$ such that $source(tr_1) = init_{\mathbb{G}}$, and such that for all $i < n, target(tr_i) = source(tr_{i+1})$. Let p be a path of $\mathbb{G}$, the *trace of p* is the sequence $tr(p) = \varepsilon$ if $p = \varepsilon$, and $tr(p) = tr(p').act(t)$ (resp. $tr(p) = tr(p')$) if p is of the form $p'.t$ and $act(t) \neq \tau$ (resp. $act(t) = \tau$). $Traces(\mathbb{G})$ is the set of traces of all paths of $Path(\mathbb{G})$. For a trace ϱ of the form $\varrho'.d.\varrho''$ and for a decomposition $d = d_1 + d_2$, the trace $\varrho'.d_1.d_2.\varrho''$ is called a decomposition of ϱ. The decomposition operation can be reiterated for all delays occurring in the trace. Similarly, the reverse operation, called the composition operation, consists in transforming the trace $\varrho'.d_1.d_2.\varrho''$ into the trace $\varrho.d.\varrho'$. The set of all traces that can be obtained by applying both decomposition and composition operations on ϱ as many times as desired is denoted $Timed(\varrho)$, and more generally, for a set $\mathcal{T}$ of traces, we note $Timed(\mathcal{T}) = \bigcup_{\varrho \in \mathcal{T}} Timed(\varrho)$. We note $TTraces(\mathbb{G}) = Timed(Traces(\mathbb{G}))$.

Finally, we define the semantics of $\mathcal{G}$ as $Sem(\mathcal{G}) = TTraces(\mathbb{G})$.

3   Web Service Discovery: Testing Framework

Regarding the question of testing Web services from timed behaviors of orchestrators, we now present our technical results using preferentially TIOLTS than TIOSTS. Indeed it is commonly accepted that implementations are modeled as TIOLTS since black-box testing induces an observational point of view that leads the tester to perceive the implementation directly as a set of traces. Moreover any TIOSTS can be associated with its unfolding (see Definition 4).

3.1   Timed Conformance Relation

Implementations are considered to be TIOLTS which accept any input at any moment [22] and in such a way that time is correctly modeled from an observational point of view (mainly, time is elapsing if no message occurs).

Definition 5 (Implementation). *An* implementation *over L is a strongly responsive TIOLTS* $(Q, init, Tr)$ *over L satisfying the following properties:*

Input enableness: $\forall q \in Q$, $\forall a \in L_i$, $\exists q' \in Q$ *such that* $(q, a, q') \in Tr$

---

[2] A^* denotes the set of words where letters are in A, ε denotes the empty word and $w_1.w_2$ represents the concatenation of the words w_1 and w_2.

Time additivity: $\forall q_1, q_2, q_3 \in Q, \forall d_1, d_2 \in D,$
$$((q_1, d_1, q_2) \in Tr \wedge (q_2, d_2, q_3) \in Tr) \Rightarrow (q_1, d_1 + d_2, q_3) \in Tr$$
Time decomposition: $\forall q_1, q_2 \in Q, \forall d_1, d_2 \in D,$
$$(q_1, d_1 + d_2, q_2) \in Tr \Rightarrow \exists q \in Q, ((q_1, d_1, q) \in Tr \wedge (q, d_2, q_2) \in Tr)$$
τ **closure:** $\forall q_1, q_2, q_3 \in Q, \forall d \in D, ((a_1, a_2) = (\tau, d) \vee (a_1, a_2) = (d, \tau)) \Rightarrow$
$$(((q_1, a_1, q_2) \in Tr \wedge (q_2, a_2, q_3) \in Tr) \Rightarrow (q_1, d, q_3) \in Tr)$$
Time elapsing: $\forall q \in Q, \exists (a, q') \in (L_o \cup \{\tau\} \cup D) \times Q$ such that $(q, a, q') \in Tr$.

Property 1. Let $\mathbb{I}$ be an implementation over L. Then $Traces(\mathbb{I}) = TTraces(\mathbb{I})$.

The well-known so-called **ioco** conformance relation ([22]) defined for IOLTS without time has already been extended to take time into account. Our definition is similar[3] to the ones of [4, 5, 17, 21] which basically include any time delays in the set of observable outputs.

Definition 6 (*tioco*). *Let* $\mathbb{G}$ *be a TIOLTS over* L *and let* $\mathbb{I}$ *be an implementation over* L. $\mathbb{I}$ *conforms to* $\mathbb{G}$, *denoted* $\mathbb{I}$ *tioco* $\mathbb{G}$, *if and only if:*
$$\forall \varrho \in TTraces(\mathbb{G}), \forall a \in D \cup L_o, \varrho.a \in Traces(\mathbb{I}) \Rightarrow \varrho.a \in TTraces(\mathbb{G})$$

Other variants of timed conformance relations have been proposed (see [21] for a detailed presentation).

3.2   Testing Web Service from Orchestrator Behaviours

We first introduce technical operations (projection, mirror and composition) that we will perform on orchestrators to elicit expected behaviors for Web services.

Definition 7 (Projection). *Let* $\mathbb{G} = (Q, init, Tr)$ *be a TIOLTS over* L. *Let* $L' = (L_i', L_o')$, *with* $L_i' \cap L_o' = \emptyset$, $L_i' \subseteq L$, *and* $L_o' \subseteq L$. *The projection of* $\mathbb{G}$ *on* L' *is the TIOLTS over* L' *defined as* $\mathbb{G}_{\downarrow L'} = (Q, init, Tr_{\downarrow L'})$, *such that* $Tr_{\downarrow L'} = \{(q, a, q')_{\downarrow L'} \mid (q, a, q') \in Tr\}$ *with* $(q, a, q')_{\downarrow L'} = (q, a, q')$ *if* $a \in L' \cup D$, *and* $(q, a, q')_{\downarrow L'} = (q, \tau, q')$ *otherwise.*

In particular, by only considering labels of L', we consider that transitions carrying labels of $L \setminus L'$ are performed, but are no more observable: this explains why these labels are simply translated as τ in $\mathbb{G}_{\downarrow L'}$. This operation corresponds to the hiding operation [10, 23] encapsulating some designated pieces of interface. The projection $._{\downarrow L'}$ can canonically be extended to paths and traces. The mirror operation changes the status (input or output) of actions: it simply depends on the construction of $L' = (L_i', L_o')$.

Definition 8 (Mirror). *Let* $\mathbb{G}$ *be a TIOLTS over* L. *The* mirror *of* $\mathbb{G}$, $M(\mathbb{G})$, *is the TIOLTS* $\mathbb{G}$ *over* $L^{M(\mathbb{G})} = M(L)$, *with* $M(L) = (L_o, L_i)$.

---

[3] The slight technical differences are essentially inherited from symbolic executions involved in the test case generation algorithm.

The mirror operation can be applied to all elements (transitions, paths, traces) issued from TIOLTS by simply exchanging the role of input and output actions. The mirror operation is often used to design a system interacting with a targeted system: test cases are typically such reactive systems which may be defined by using the mirror operation on the reference model $\mathbb{G}$. Roughly speaking, as test cases send messages expected by $\mathbb{G}$ and wait for emissions specified in $\mathbb{G}$, inputs and outputs are reversed both in the traces of $\mathbb{G}$ and the test case, until a verdict is computed.

Systems can be composed by taking into account communications between them. As usual, input and output actions will be synchronized when they share the same name. The passing of time will also be synchronized by requiring that any global elapsed time result from the synchronization of subsystem transitions carrying the same delay value. Thus, the global system shares with its components exactly the same perception of time. This means that our system composition corresponds to locally deployed component-based systems. Particularly in the case of an orchestrator communicating with Web services, this means that the modeling of a Web service is composed of a remote Web service and of message transmissions on the Internet: all the sending and receptions of messages will be stamped with the same clock than the orchestrator clock.

Definition 9 (Composition). *Let $\mathbb{G}_1$ and $\mathbb{G}_2$ be two TIOLTS respectively over $L^{\mathbb{G}_1}$ and $L^{\mathbb{G}_2}$ such that $L_i^{\mathbb{G}_1} \cap L_i^{\mathbb{G}_2} = L_o^{\mathbb{G}_1} \cap L_o^{\mathbb{G}_2} = \emptyset$. $\mathbb{G}_1 \otimes \mathbb{G}_2$ is the TIOLTS $(Q, init, Tr)$ over $L^{\mathbb{G}_1 \otimes \mathbb{G}_2}$, such that $L_o^{\mathbb{G}_1 \otimes \mathbb{G}_2} = L_o^{\mathbb{G}_1} \cup L_o^{\mathbb{G}_2}$, and such that $L_i^{\mathbb{G}_1 \otimes \mathbb{G}_2} = (L^{\mathbb{G}_1} \cup L^{\mathbb{G}_2}) \setminus (L_o^{\mathbb{G}_1} \cup L_o^{\mathbb{G}_2})$, $Q = Q_{\mathbb{G}_1} \times Q_{\mathbb{G}_2}$ and $init = (init_{\mathbb{G}_1}, init_{\mathbb{G}_2})$. Tr is defined as follows:*

Handshake: *if $(q_1, a, q_1') \in Tr_{\mathbb{G}_1}$ and $(q_2, a, q_2') \in Tr_{\mathbb{G}_2}$ with $a \in L^{\mathbb{G}_1 \otimes \mathbb{G}_2} \cup D$, then $((q_1, q_2), a, (q_1', q_2')) \in Tr$.*

Asynchronous execution: *for any $(q_1, a, q_1') \in Tr_{\mathbb{G}_1}$ where $a \notin L^{\mathbb{G}_2} \cup D$, then for any $q_2 \in Q_{\mathbb{G}_2}$ we have $((q_1, q_2), a, (q_1', q_2)) \in Tr$ (a similar definition holds by reversing the roles of $\mathbb{G}_1$ and $\mathbb{G}_2$).*

Property 2. For $p \in Path(\mathbb{G}_1 \otimes \mathbb{G}_2)$ with $\varrho = tr(p)$, for $i \in \{1, 2\}$ we define $p_{\mathbb{G}_i}$ and $\varrho_{\mathbb{G}_i}$ as paths and traces over[4] $L^{\mathbb{G}_i}$:

- if $p = \varepsilon$ then $p_{\mathbb{G}_i} = \varepsilon$ and $\varrho_{\mathbb{G}_i} = \varepsilon$,
- if $p = p'.((q_1, q_2), a, (q_1', q_2'))$ with $\varrho' = tr(p')$ where the last transition is an handshake transition, then $p_{\mathbb{G}_i} = p'_{\mathbb{G}_i}.(q_i, a, q_i')$ and $\varrho_{\mathbb{G}_i} = \varrho'_{\mathbb{G}_i}.a$.
- if $p = p'.((q_1, q_2), a, (q_1', q_2))$ with $\varrho' = tr(p')$ where the last transition is an asynchronous execution with $a \notin L^{\mathbb{G}_2} \cup D$, then $p_{\mathbb{G}_1} = p'_{\mathbb{G}_1}.(q_1, a, q_1')$, $\varrho_{\mathbb{G}_1} = \varrho'_{\mathbb{G}_1}.a$, $p_{\mathbb{G}_2} = p'_{\mathbb{G}_2}$ and $\varrho_{\mathbb{G}_2} = \varrho'_{\mathbb{G}_2}$. A symmetric reasoning holds for an asynchronous transition with $a \notin L^{\mathbb{G}_1} \cup D$.

Then by construction, for $i = 1, 2$, $p_{\mathbb{G}_i} \in Path(\mathbb{G}_i)$ and $\varrho_{\mathbb{G}_i} \in Traces(\mathbb{G}_i)$. Moreover, we have $\varrho_{\mathbb{G}_i} = tr(p)_{\mathbb{G}_i} = tr(p_{\mathbb{G}_i}) = tr(p)_{\downarrow L^{\mathbb{G}_i}} = tr(p_{\downarrow L^{\mathbb{G}_i}})$.

---

[4] Let us remark that labels of $L_i^{\mathbb{G}_1} \cap L_o^{\mathbb{G}_2}$ change of status between $\mathbb{G}_1 \otimes \mathbb{G}_2$ and $p_{\mathbb{G}_1}$ and $\varrho_{\mathbb{G}_1}$.

Property 3. Let $L_{1,2} = (L_i^1 \cap L_o^2, L_o^1 \cap L_i^2)$ and $L_{2,1} = M(L_{1,2})$.
   Let $p_1 \in Path(\mathbb{G}_1)$ and $p_2 \in Path(\mathbb{G}_2)$ such that $tr(p_{1 \downarrow L_{1,2}}) = tr(p_{2 \downarrow L_{2,1}})$.
Then there exists a path p of $\mathbb{G}_1 \otimes \mathbb{G}_2$ such that $p_{\mathbb{G}_1} = p_1$ and $p_{\mathbb{G}_2} = p_2$.

An orchestrator interacts on one hand with the end-user and on the other hand with Web services. Orchestrator actions will be split accordingly[5].

Definition 10 (Orchestrator). *An* orchestrator *is defined as a TIOLTS over* L, $\mathbb{O} = (Q, init, Tr)$, *with a distinguished set* $L^W = (L_i^W, L_o^W)$, *with* $L_i^W \subseteq L_i$ *and* $L_o^W \subseteq L_o$ *of so called* Web service actions, *and satisfying the so-called* "consistent Web service invocation" *property:*
   There do not exist $a \in L_i^W \cup D$ *and a trace* ϱ *on* L^W *issued from two distinct paths* p_1, p_2 *of* $\mathbb{O}$, *that is* $tr(p_1)_{\downarrow L^W} = tr(p_2)_{\downarrow L^W} = \varrho$, *such that:*

- *there exists a path of* $\mathbb{O}$ *of the form* $p_1.p_1'$ *with* $tr(p_1.p_1')_{\downarrow L^W} = \varrho.a$
- *for all paths of* $\mathbb{O}$ *of the form* $p_2.p_2'$, *we have* $tr(p_2.p_2')_{\downarrow L^W} \neq \varrho.a$.

In the sequel, we also call *Orchestrator* a TIOSTS $\mathcal{O}$ over $(\mathcal{V}, C)$ with a distinguished set $C^W \subseteq C$ such that if we note $\mathbb{O}$ the unfolding of $\mathcal{O}$ and L^W the set of all numeric actions built on C^W then $\mathbb{O}$ is an orchestrator.
   The "consistent Web service invocation" property simply expresses that if there are two distinct contexts (paths p_1 and p_2) from the orchestrator point of view that are perceived as similar from the Web service (p_1 and p_2 have a common projected trace ϱ on L^W), then the orchestrator should anticipate exactly the same set of reactions from the Web service. It means that designing an orchestrator should take into account that the set of possible Web service reactions depends only on the observational context as perceived by the Web service: only traces projected on L^W are relevant to define observational contexts.

Definition 11 ($Require_{\mathbb{O}}(\mathbb{W})$). *Let* $\mathbb{O}$ *be an orchestrator over* L *with a distinguished subset* L^W. *Let* $\mathbb{W}$ *be an implementation over*[6] $L^W = M(L^W)$. $\mathbb{W}$ *satisfies requirements issued from* $\mathbb{O}$, *noted as* $Require_{\mathbb{O}}(\mathbb{W})$, *if:*
   For all paths p *of the system* $\mathbb{O} \otimes \mathbb{W}$ *such that the set of traces of the form* $\{tr(p_{\mathbb{O}}).a \mid a \in L_i^W \cup D, p_{\mathbb{O}}.(q, a, q') \in Path(\mathbb{O})\}$ *is not empty, there exists at least a path* $p.p'$ *of* $\mathbb{O} \otimes \mathbb{W}$ *such that* $tr(p.p') = tr(p).a'$, *with* $a' \in L_i^W \cup D$.

The property $Require_{\mathbb{O}}(\mathbb{W})$ means that at any reachable state (target state of p) in the resulting system $\mathbb{O} \otimes \mathbb{W}$, $\mathbb{W}$ meets the expectations of $\mathbb{O}$ if $\mathbb{W}$ provides at least one of the behaviors specified by $\mathbb{O}$ at this point: the behaviors are either a possible input coming from $\mathbb{W}$ or a delay synchronizing behaviors of $\mathbb{O}$ and $\mathbb{W}$. In other words, to satisfy the $Require_{\mathbb{O}}(\mathbb{W})$ property, $\mathbb{W}$ cannot cause a deadlock[7] a in the system $\mathbb{O} \otimes \mathbb{W}$: the path $p.p'$ is precisely an extension in $\mathbb{O} \otimes \mathbb{W}$ of the path p according to a reaction ($a' \in L_i^W \cup D$) of $\mathbb{W}$ expected by $\mathbb{O}$.

---

[5] For simplicity purpose, we will consider that orchestrators interact only with one Web service.

[6] In practice, $\mathbb{W}$ can be specified over any set L' containing at least $M(L^W)$.

[7] Another interesting but stronger condition would consist in requiring that the Web service should be able to provide all a in $L_i^W \cup D$ that extend paths in $\mathbb{O}$.

Theorem 1. *Let $\mathbb{O}$ be an orchestrator over L with $L^W \subseteq L$ and let $\mathbb{W}$ be an implementation over $M(L^W)$.*

$$\mathbb{W} \ tioco \ M(\mathbb{O}_{\downarrow L^W}) \Rightarrow Require_{\mathbb{O}}(\mathbb{W})$$

By Theorem 1, in order to know whether or not a Web service implementation $\mathbb{W}$ is suitable to be integrated with a given orchestration (i.e. satisfies the $Require_{\mathbb{O}}(\mathbb{W})$ property), it suffices to test it accordingly to the *tioco* conformance relation and with respect to the behavior deductible from $\mathbb{O}$ model using the mirror and projection operations along L^W.

Proof. Let us suppose that $\mathbb{W}$ *tioco* $M(\mathbb{O}_{\downarrow L^W})$ and let us show that $Require_{\mathbb{O}}(\mathbb{W})$ holds. Let us consider a path p of $\mathbb{O} \otimes \mathbb{W}$ such that there exists a path $p_{\mathbb{O}}.(q, a, q')$ of $\mathbb{O}$ with $tr(p_{\mathbb{O}}.(q, a, q')) = tr(p_{\mathbb{O}}).a$ with $a \in L_i^W \cup D$.

It exists $a' \in L_o^W \cup D$ and p' such that $p_{\mathbb{W}}.p'$ is a path of $\mathbb{W}$ whose trace is $tr(p_{\mathbb{W}}).a'$. Indeed, the time elapsing property allows one to extend paths with transitions carrying actions in $L_o^W \cup \{\tau\} \cup D$. If the considered action would be τ, then we we can reapply the property until getting an action different from τ. $\mathbb{W}$ is strongly responsive: it cannot contain an infinite sequence of τ action.

As $\mathbb{W}$ conforms to $M(\mathbb{O}_{\downarrow L^W})$, since $tr(p_{\mathbb{W}})$ is a trace of both $M(\mathbb{O}_{\downarrow L^W})$ and $\mathbb{W}$, this means that $tr(p_{\mathbb{W}}).a'$ with $a' \in L_o^W \cup D$ is also a trace of $M(\mathbb{O}_{\downarrow L^W})$. Thanks to the "consistent Web service invocation" property, $p_{\mathbb{O}}$ can be extended as a path $p_{\mathbb{O}}.p''$ with $tr(p_{\mathbb{O}}.p'') = tr(p_{\mathbb{O}}).a'$.

Paths p' of $\mathbb{W}$ and p'' of $\mathbb{O}$ share the same projection on L^W, the common part of $L^{\mathbb{O}}$ and L^W. By Prop.3, they can be synchronized in $\mathbb{O} \otimes \mathbb{W}$: there exists a path $p.\rho$ s.t. $\rho_{\mathbb{W}} = p'$, $\rho_{\mathbb{O}} = p''$ and $tr(p.\rho) = tr(p_{\mathbb{O}}).a'$ with $a' \in L_i^W \cup D$.

4 Symbolic Timed Testing

As in our previous works ([8, 13]), our testing algorithm is based on symbolic execution techniques, with the novelty here that timed behaviors are also taken into account.

4.1 Symbolic Execution

Symbolically executing a TIOSTS comes to represent its possible executions as a tree structure. Any path of the tree represents in a symbolic way a set of traces associated to a path of the TIOSTS. In the sequel we consider that a set $F = \bigcup_{s \in S} F_s$ (disjoint of any set of variables introduced in TIOSTS signatures) is given. We also consider a set F_D of time variables (typed on D). We note $Sen(F_D)$ the set of all conjunctions of formulas $x \leq d$ or $d' \leq x$ with $x \in F_D$, $d \in D \cup \{\infty\}$ and $d' \in D \cup \{0\}$. In order to store pieces of information concerning the possible traces of a path we use *symbolic states*. Those pieces of information are: the last state of the path, the symbolic values assigned to variables, and the constraints on those symbolic values as well as on delays between communication actions occurring in the path. So, a *symbolic state* η is a tuple of the form

$(q, \sigma, \pi, \vartheta)$, where $q \in Q$, $\sigma \in T_\Omega(F)^\mathcal{V}$, $\pi \in Sen_\Omega(F)$, and $\vartheta \in Sen(F_D)$. In the sequel we note $\mathcal{S}$ the set of all such symbolic states. For any $\eta \in \mathcal{S}$ of the form $(q, \sigma, \pi, \vartheta)$, we use the notations $state(\eta)$, $sub(\eta)$, $\pi(\eta)$ and $\vartheta(\eta)$ to refer respectively to q, σ, π, and ϑ. η is said *satisfiable* if and only if there exists $\nu \in M^F$ and $\nu' \in D^{F_D}$ such that $\nu \models \pi$ and $\nu' \models \vartheta$. $\mathcal{S}_{sat}$ is the set of all satisfiable symbolic states.

Definition 12 (Symbolic execution of a transition). *Let $\mathcal{G}$ be a TIOSTS over $\Sigma = (\mathcal{V}, C)$. Let Σ_F stand for (F, C). For any $tr \in Tr_\mathcal{G}$ and $\eta \in \mathcal{S}$, such that $source(tr) = state(\eta)$, a symbolic execution of tr from η is a triple of the form $(\eta, sd.sa, \eta') \in \mathcal{S} \times (F_D.Act(\Sigma_F)) \times \mathcal{S}$, such that sd is a fresh variable, $state(\eta') = target(tr)$, $\vartheta(\eta') = \vartheta(\eta) \wedge (\delta_{min}(tr) \leq sd) \wedge (sd \leq \delta_{max}(tr))$, and:*

- *if $act(tr) = c!t$ (resp. τ), then $sa = c!z$ (resp. $sa = \tau$), where z is a variable of F, $sub(\eta') = sub(\eta) \circ sub(tr)$, and the path condition of the target state is $\pi(\eta') = \pi(\eta) \wedge sub(\eta)(guard(tr)) \wedge z = sub(\eta)(t)$,*
- *if $act(tr) = c?x$, then there exists a substitution $\sigma \in T_\Omega(F)^\mathcal{V}$ such that it satisfies $y \neq x \Rightarrow \sigma(y) = sub(\eta)(y)$, and $\sigma(x)$ is a variable of F such that $sa = c?\sigma(x)$, $sub(\eta') = \sigma \circ sub(tr)$, and $\pi(\eta') = \pi(\eta) \wedge sub(\eta)(guard(tr))$.*

In the following, str denotes a triple $(\eta, sd.sa, \eta')$, and notations $source(str)$, $act(str)$, and $target(str)$ refer to, respectively, η, $sd.sa$, and η'.

Definition 13 (Symbolic execution of a TIOSTS). *A symbolic execution of $\mathcal{G}$, denoted $SE(\mathcal{G})$, is a couple $(init, \mathcal{R}_{sat})$, where $init = (init_\mathcal{G}, \sigma_0, true, true)$ is a symbolic state such that $\forall x \in \mathcal{V}$, $\sigma_0(x) \in F$ and σ_0 is injective, and such that $\mathcal{R}_{sat} \subseteq \mathcal{S}_{sat} \times (F_D.Act(\Sigma_F)) \times \mathcal{S}_{sat}$ is the restriction to $\mathcal{S}_{sat}$ of the relation $\mathcal{R} \subseteq \mathcal{S} \times (F_D.Act(\Sigma_F)) \times \mathcal{S}$ where for all $\eta \in \mathcal{S}$ and for any $tr \in Tr$ with $source(tr) = state(\eta)$, there exists exactly one symbolic execution of tr from η in $\mathcal{R}$. Moreover, for any $(\eta_1, sd_1.c\triangle z, \eta_1')$ and $(\eta_2, sd_2.d\triangle w, \eta_2')$ in $\mathcal{R}$ with $\triangle \in \{!, ?\}$, we have $sd_1 \neq sd_2$ and $z \neq w$.*

Note that the symbolic execution is unique, up to the choice of the involved fresh variables. The symbolic execution of a TIOSTS can be associated with a set of traces that is exactly the one associated to the TIOLTS denoting its unfolding. Traces of a path $p = (init, sd_1.sa_1, \eta_1) \cdots (\eta_{n-1}, sd_n.sa_n, \eta_n)$ are the traces of the form $\nu'(sd_1).\nu(sa_1) \cdots \nu'(sd_n).\nu(sa_n)$ with[8] $\nu \in M^F$ and $\nu' \in D^{F_D}$ two interpretations such that $\nu \models \pi(\eta_n)$ and $\nu' \models \vartheta(\eta_n)$.

4.2   Algorithm

In order to assess tioco-conformance of an implementation $\mathbb{I}$, the key point is that delays appearing in $\mathbb{I}$ may be formulated differently than they appear in traces of $SE(\mathcal{G})$: the way they are observed depends on the periodicity of observation in the testing architecture. Therefore our algorithm has to compare traces of $\mathbb{I}$ to timed traces of $SE(\mathcal{G})$ defined up to delay composition and decomposition.

---

[8] We apply the convention that $\nu(\tau)$ is the empty word.

Test Purpose: Our algorithm takes behaviors to be tested as inputs in order to pilot the testing process. Such behaviors are called *test purposes*. Those behaviors are characterized as finite paths of so-called *symbolic execution trees* which are couples $ST = (init, \mathcal{R})$ where $init \in \mathcal{S}_{sat}$ and $\mathcal{R} \subseteq \mathcal{S}_{sat} \times F_d.Act(\Sigma_F) \times \mathcal{S}_{sat}$. Typical examples of symbolic execution trees are symbolic execution trees of TIOSTS but we use other structures in Section 5 for Web service elicitation. Test purposes are finite subtrees of ST whose last transition of each path is not labeled by an input.

Definition 14. *Let $ST = (init, \mathcal{R})$ be a symbolic execution tree. A ST-test purpose is $TP = (init, \mathcal{R}_{TP})$, where $\mathcal{R}_{TP} \subseteq \mathcal{R}$ is a finite set such that for any $str \in \mathcal{R}_{TP}$ then either $source(str) = init$ or there exists $str_1 \cdots str_j$ for some $j \geq 1$ such that:*

- *for all $i \leq j$, $str_i \in \mathcal{R}_{TP}$, $source(str_1) = init$, $target(str_j) = source(str)$,*
- *for all $i \leq j - 1$, $target(str_i) = source(str_{i+1})$,*
- *if there is no transition $str' \in \mathcal{R}_{TP}$ such that $source(str') = target(str)$, then $act(str) \notin F_D.I(\Sigma_F)$.*

We introduce some technical notations related to test purpose:

- $Accept(TP) \subseteq \mathcal{S}_{sat}$ is the set of all η satisfying:
  $(\exists str \in \mathcal{R}_{TP}, \eta = target(str)) \wedge (\forall str \in \mathcal{R}_{TP}, \eta \neq source(str))$.
- The set $Reach(\eta, TP)$ is the set of all symbolic states reachable from η in TP. It contains η and all η' such that there exists a sequence $(\eta, act_1, \eta_1)(\eta_1, act_2, \eta_2) \cdots (\eta_{n-1}, act_n, \eta')$ of transitions of $\mathcal{R}_{TP}$.
- We note $Accept(\eta, TP) = Reach(\eta, TP) \cap Accept(TP)$ the set of all states of $Accept(TP)$ which are reachable from η.
- $targetCond(\eta)$ is the condition $\bigvee_{\eta' \in Accept(\eta, TP)} (\pi(\eta') \wedge \vartheta(\eta'))$

We write $\eta \in TP$ to signify that η occurs in some transition of $\mathcal{R}_{TP}$.

Rule Based Algorithm: Before giving the rules of our algorithm, we introduce the notion of *context* (η, f_d, f_t, θ). While interacting with $\mathbb{I}$, we build testing traces. We have to identify paths of ST that admit them as traces. A context denotes the target state of such a path. Moreover it also contains pieces of information to identify symbolic values with concrete ones (those occurring in the testing trace). It is composed of a symbolic state $\eta \in \mathcal{S}_{sat}$ and of two formulae: f_d expresses constraints induced by the sequence of data exchanged with $\mathbb{I}$ while f_t expresses constraints on delays. Finally, in order to identify when the observation occurred, we introduce a duration $\theta \in D$. The meaning of the context can be intuitively understood as follow:

The trace observed until now can be seen as a trace of the form $\varrho.\theta$, where ϱ is a trace of the path leading to η. Interpretations of variables that occur in communication actions of the path have to satisfy f_d in order to be consistent with values observed in ϱ. In the same way, interpretations of symbolic delays of the path have to satisfy f_t to be consistent with concretely observed delays in ϱ. Thus, η may have been reached θ units of time ago.

As there may be many contexts compatible with a testing trace, we use sets of contexts generically noted SC (for Set of Contexts). Sequences of stimuli and observations built from the interaction between the algorithm and $\mathbb{I}$ are modeled as elements of $Traces(\mathbb{I})$. Practically, an observation, noted $obs(r)$, is given by $r \in D \cup L_o^\Sigma$. A stimulus, noted $stim(i)$, is given by $i \in L_i^\Sigma$.

We define several technical notations to denote evolutions of sets of contexts:

- $NextTrigger(a, SC)$, where $a \in L^\Sigma \cup \{\tau\}$, is the set of all contexts that can be reached by triggering a transition of ST consistently with the action a. $(\eta', f_d', f_t', \theta') \in NextTrigger(a, SC)$ if and only if $\theta' = 0$ and, if a is of the form $\mathbb{C}\triangle Z$ with $\triangle \in \{?, !\}$ (resp. τ) then there exists $(\eta, f_d, f_t, \theta) \in SC$, and $(\eta, sd.\mathbb{C}\triangle U, \eta') \in \mathcal{R}$ (resp. $(\eta, sd.\tau, \eta') \in \mathcal{R}$), s.t. f_d' is $f_d \wedge (T = U)$ (resp. f_d), f_t' is $f_t \wedge \theta = sd$, and both $f_d' \wedge \pi(\eta')$ and $f_t' \wedge \vartheta(\eta')$ are satisfiable.
- $Wait(d, SC)$, where $d \in D$, is the set of contexts obtained by waiting while progressing to a situation where a transition can be triggered. $(\eta', f_d', f_t', \theta') \in Wait(d, SC)$ iff there exists $d' > d$, $a \in L^\Sigma \cup \{\tau\}$ and $C = (\eta, f_d, f_t, \theta) \in SC$ s.t. $NextTrigger(a, \{(\eta, f_d, f_t, \theta + d')\}) \neq \emptyset$, $\eta' = \eta$, $f_d' = f_d$, $f_t' = f_t$ and $\theta' = \theta + d$.
- $\Delta(d, SC)$, where $d \in D$, is the set of contexts obtained by observing a quiescence situation. $(\eta', f_d', f_t', \theta') \in \Delta(d, SC)$ if and only if there exists $(\eta, f_d, f_t, \theta) \in SC$ such that $\eta' = \eta$, $f_t' = f_t$, $\theta' = \theta + d$ and if we note $react(\eta)$ the set of all transitions of $\mathcal{R}$ whose action is not of the form $sd.i$ with $i \in I(\Sigma)$, $\delta(\eta)$ the formula reduced to $true$ if $react(\eta) = \emptyset$ and equal to $\bigwedge_{str \in react(\eta)} \neg \pi(target(str))$ otherwise, then f_d' is $f_d \wedge \delta(\eta)$ and f_d' is satisfiable.
- $TimeElaps(d, SC) = Wait(d, SC) \cup \Delta(d, SC)$ represents the set of contexts reachable from SC after having waited d time units.

For any set of contexts SC, we note:
$Skip(SC) = \{(\eta, f_d, f_t, \theta) | (\eta, f_d, f_t, \theta) \in SC, \eta \in TP,$
$\qquad\qquad\qquad (targetCond(\eta) \wedge f_d \wedge f_t)$ is satisfiable $\}$

$Pass(SC) = \{(\eta, f_d, f_t, \theta) \in Skip(SC), \eta \in Accept(TP)\}$

We use $Skip$ and $Pass$ for shortcuts to $Skip(SC)$ and $Pass(SC)$ when the context is clear. Each verdict is described by means of inference rules holding on sets of contexts. Those rules are of the form: $\frac{SC}{Result} \, cond(ev)$, where SC is a set of contexts, $Result$ is either a set of contexts or a verdict, and $cond(ev)$ is a set of conditions on events including the observation $obs(r)$ or the stimulus $stim(i)$. Such rules express that, given the current set of contexts SC, if $cond(ev)$ is verified then the algorithm may achieve a step with ev as elementary action.

As in [13], our algorithm provides four verdicts: $FAIL$, when the behavior belongs neither to TP nor to ST (**Rule 3**); $INCONC$, (for inconclusive) when the behavior belongs to ST and not to TP (**Rule 2**), $PASS$ when the behavior belongs to a path of TP ending by an accept state and not to any other path of ST (**Rule 5**); and $WeakPASS$, when the behavior belongs to a path of TP ending by an accept state and to at least one other path of ST (**Rule 4**).

Rule 0: Initialization

$$\frac{}{\{(init, true, true, 0)\}}$$

Rule 1: No observed outputs for a delay d, consistently with reaching an accept state.

$$\frac{SC}{TimeElaps(d, SC)} \; obs(d), \; Skip \neq \emptyset, \; Pass = \emptyset$$

Rule 1 (bis): Observation of an output o, consistently with reaching an accept state.

$$\frac{SC}{NextTrigger(o, SC)} \; obs(o), \; Skip \neq \emptyset, \; Pass = \emptyset$$

Rule 2: The set of reached contexts is outside the test purpose.

$$\frac{SC}{INCONC} \; SC \neq \emptyset, \; Skip = \emptyset$$

Rule 3: The set of reached contexts is empty.

$$\frac{SC}{FAIL} \; SC = \emptyset$$

Rule 4: One accept state is reached but not all reached states are accept ones.

$$\frac{SC}{WeakPASS} \; Pass \neq \emptyset, \; SC \neq Pass$$

Rule 5: All reached states are accept ones.

$$\frac{SC}{PASS} \; Pass \neq \emptyset, \; SC = Pass$$

Rule 6: The tester stimulates by sending an input i.

$$\frac{SC}{NextTrigger(i, SC)} \; stim(i), SC \neq \emptyset, \; Skip(NextTrigger(i, SC)) \neq \emptyset$$

Regarding to our contribution in [8, 13], a real novelty here is **Rule 1** which computes the impact of time passing on the set of current contexts with respect to the test purpose. Note that **Rule 6** is the only one that can be applied non deterministically with respect to others. An application strategy defines a test case generation algorithm. The goal of the generic algorithm is similar to the one of the algorithm described in [4]. The two main differences are that we handle data symbolically and our test purposes are defined as symbolic trees instead of properties given as automata. As we will automatically elicit intended behaviors for Web services as symbolic trees from orchestrator specifications, our testing approach is suitable for service discovery.

5   Elicitation of Web Service Test Purposes

For any (TIOSTS) orchestrator $\mathcal{O}$ we identify the interface corresponding to the Web service to be elicited: it is a subset C^W of the set of channels C of $\mathcal{O}$. We note $SE(\mathcal{O}) = (init, \mathcal{R}_{sat})$, and $(init, \mathcal{R}^P)$ the couple reflecting the projection on channels of C^W in $SE(\mathcal{O})$. Formally, for any $str \in \mathcal{R}_{sat}$, if we note $act(str)$ as $\delta.a$ then we have: if a is of the form $c\Delta u$ with $c \in C^W$ and $\Delta \in \{?, !\}$ then

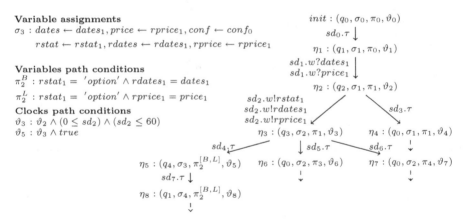

Variable assignments
$\sigma_3 : dates \leftarrow dates_1, price \leftarrow rprice_1, conf \leftarrow conf_0$
$\qquad rstat \leftarrow rstat_1, rdates \leftarrow rdates_1, rprice \leftarrow rprice_1$

Variables path conditions
$\pi_2^B : rstat_1 = {}'option' \wedge rdates_1 = dates_1$
$\pi_2^L : rstat_1 = {}'option' \wedge rprice_1 = price_1$

Clocks path conditions
$\vartheta_3 : \vartheta_2 \wedge (0 \leq sd_2) \wedge (sd_2 \leq 60)$
$\vartheta_5 : \vartheta_3 \wedge true$

Fig. 2. Elicited behaviors for the Hotel Web service

$str \in \mathcal{R}^P$, else $(source(str), \delta.\tau, target(str)) \in \mathcal{R}^P$. We then apply a mirror operation: we consider the couple $(init, \mathcal{R}^W)$ such that for any $str \in \mathcal{R}^P$, if we note $act(str)$ as $\delta.a$ we have: if a is τ then $str \in \mathcal{R}^W$; if a is of the form $c?u$ then $(source(str), \delta.c!u, target(str)) \in \mathcal{R}^W$; if a is of the form $c!u$ then $(source(str), \delta.c?u, target(str)) \in \mathcal{R}^W$. $(init, \mathcal{R}^W)$ forms a symbolic tree that is a symbolic counterpart to the TIOLTS $M(\mathbb{O}_{\downarrow LW})$ (where $\mathbb{O}$ is the unfolding of $\mathcal{O}$), and we use it to extract test purposes for testing some candidate Web service $\mathbb{W}$ in order to evaluate the validity of $Require_{\mathbb{O}}(\mathbb{W})$ thanks to Theorem 1.

Example 2. Figure 2 shows the elicited behaviors for the Hotel Web service participating in both versions of the Hotel Reservation example[9] (Business B and Low Cost L).

The only difference between the elicited behaviors from the Business and Low Cost versions is in the path condition π_2, where for the former version the dates are kept unchanged, while for the other one the price is kept unchanged.

Let us suppose that we want to test an implementation of a Hotel Web service that is to be used in the Business version. Even if a given implementation of the Web service could be used in both versions, we want to find an implementation of the Web service that does not modify the dates. Moreover, we would expect that a room is found in the first iteration or at least in the second one. Thus, we define the symbolic state η_3 as the only accept state, and if we reach it we also check the path condition π_2 (either the answer is $'reserved'$ or it is $'option'$ with the dates kept unchanged) in order to determine if the Web service *behaves* as expected. Then, we can know if it fulfills the expectations of the orchestrator. Even if the Hotel Web service answers with different dates, or if no room is found, no $FAIL$ verdict would be emitted. However, those are not the behaviors that we expect. Thus, this example shows that, in order to use a Web service within an orchestration so that it can precisely provide behaviors expected by the orchestrator, it has to be tested against test purposes covering these tar-

---

[9] In the figure, we only show the information related to η_3 since it is the *accept* state.

geted behaviors. Obviously, the choice of behaviors that should be primarily ensured by Web services to be integrated depends on the subjective analysis of the orchestration designer. This methodological subjectivity is similar to the one guiding the choice of appropriate test purposes in a testing activity.

6 Conclusion

In this paper we have shown how to elicit, from an orchestrator specification, intended behaviors of Web services likely to interact with it, and we have shown how to use them as test purposes at the Web service discovery phase. Orchestrator specifications are given in a symbolic way and include timing constraints. We have identified a property reflecting the absence of deadlock in an orchestration by relating the orchestrator and Web services of the orchestration. This property serves as reference to select candidate Web service. Technically our testing approach comes to test the conformance of Web services to symbolic behaviors obtained by symbolically executing the orchestrator specification and by applying projection and mirroring techniques.

References

1. Alur, R., Dill, D.L.: A theory of timed automata. Theor. Comput. Sci. 126(2), 183–235 (1994)
2. De Angelis, F., Polini, A., De Angelis, G.: A Counter-Example Testing Approach for Orchestrated Services. In: Intl. Conf. Software Testing, Verification and Validation (ICST), pp. 373–382. IEEE Computer Society (2010)
3. Bentakouk, L., Poizat, P., Zaïdi, F.: A Formal Framework for Service Orchestration Testing Based on Symbolic Transition Systems. In: Núñez, M., Baker, P., Merayo, M.G. (eds.) TESTCOM/FATES 2009. LNCS, vol. 5826, pp. 16–32. Springer, Heidelberg (2009)
4. Bertrand, N., Jéron, T., Stainer, A., Krichen, M.: Off-Line Test Selection with Test Purposes for Non-deterministic Timed Automata. In: Abdulla, P.A., Leino, K.R.M. (eds.) TACAS 2011. LNCS, vol. 6605, pp. 96–111. Springer, Heidelberg (2011)
5. Briones, L.B., Brinksma, E.: A Test Generation Framework for *quiescent* Real-Time Systems. In: Grabowski, J., Nielsen, B. (eds.) FATES 2004. LNCS, vol. 3395, pp. 64–78. Springer, Heidelberg (2005)
6. Dong, J.S., Liu, Y., Sun, J., Zhang, X.: Verification of Computation Orchestration Via Timed Automata. In: Liu, Z., Kleinberg, R.D. (eds.) ICFEM 2006. LNCS, vol. 4260, pp. 226–245. Springer, Heidelberg (2006)
7. Dyaz, G., Cambronero, M.E., Pardo, J.J., Valero, V., Cuartero, F.: Automatic generation of correct web services choreographies and orchestrations with model checking techniques. In: Advanced Intl. Conf. on Internet and Web Applications and Services (2006)
8. Escobedo, J.P., Le Gall, P., Gaston, C., Cavalli, A.: Testing web service orchestrators in context: a symbolic approach. In: Proc. of Software Engineering Formal Methods (SEFM). IEEE Computer Society (2010)

9. Alves, A., et al.: Web Services Business Process Execution Language Version 2.0. OASIS (April 2007),
http://docs.oasis-open.org/wsbpel/2.0/OS/wsbpel-v2.0-OS.html

10. Faivre, A., Gaston, C., Le Gall, P.: Symbolic Model Based Testing for Component Oriented Systems. In: Petrenko, A., Veanes, M., Tretmans, J., Grieskamp, W. (eds.) TESTCOM/FATES 2007. LNCS, vol. 4581, pp. 90–106. Springer, Heidelberg (2007)

11. Frantzen, L., Tretmans, J.: Model-Based Testing of Environmental Conformance of Components. In: de Boer, F.S., Bonsangue, M.M., Graf, S., de Roever, W.-P. (eds.) FMCO 2006. LNCS, vol. 4709, pp. 1–25. Springer, Heidelberg (2007)

12. Frantzen, L., Tretmans, J., Willemse, T.A.C.: Test Generation Based on Symbolic Specifications. In: Grabowski, J., Nielsen, B. (eds.) FATES 2004. LNCS, vol. 3395, pp. 1–15. Springer, Heidelberg (2005)

13. Gaston, C., Le Gall, P., Rapin, N., Touil, A.: Symbolic Execution Techniques for Test Purpose Definition. In: Uyar, M.Ü., Duale, A.Y., Fecko, M.A. (eds.) TESTCOM 2006. LNCS, vol. 3964, pp. 1–18. Springer, Heidelberg (2006)

14. Gortmaker, J., Janssen, M., Wagenaar, R.: The advantages of web service orchestration in perspective. In: Intl. Conf. on Electronic Commerce (ICEC), pp. 506–515. ACM (2004)

15. Guermouche, N., Godart, C.: Asynchronous Timed Web Service-Aware Choreography Analysis. In: van Eck, P., Gordijn, J., Wieringa, R. (eds.) CAiSE 2009. LNCS, vol. 5565, pp. 364–378. Springer, Heidelberg (2009)

16. Kazhamiakin, R., Pandy, R., Pistore, M.: Timed modelling and analysis in web service compositions. In: Intl. Conf. on Availability, Reliability and Security, ARES (2006)

17. Krichen, M., Tripakis, S.: Black-Box Conformance Testing for Real-Time Systems. In: Graf, S., Mounier, L. (eds.) SPIN 2004. LNCS, vol. 2989, pp. 109–126. Springer, Heidelberg (2004)

18. Krummenacher, R., Hepp, M., Polleres, A., Bussler, C., Fensel, D.: WWW or What Is Wrong with Web services. In: IEEE European Conf. on Web Services (ECOWS), pp. 235–243 (2005)

19. Peltz, C.: Web services orchestration and choreography. Computer, 46–52 (2003)

20. Pilioura, T., Tsalgatidou, A., Batsakis, R.: Using wsdl/uddi and daml-s in web service discovery. In: WWW 2003 Workshop on E-Services and the Semantic Web (2003)

21. Schmaltz, J., Tretmans, J.: On Conformance Testing for Timed Systems. In: Cassez, F., Jard, C. (eds.) FORMATS 2008. LNCS, vol. 5215, pp. 250–264. Springer, Heidelberg (2008)

22. Tretmans, J.: Test generation with inputs, outputs and repetitive quiescence. Software - Concepts and Tools 17(3), 103–120 (1996)

23. van der Bijl, M., Rensink, A., Tretmans, J.: Compositional Testing with ioco. In: Petrenko, A., Ulrich, A. (eds.) FATES 2003. LNCS, vol. 2931, pp. 86–100. Springer, Heidelberg (2004)

Realizability of Choreographies for Services Interacting Asynchronously

Gregor Gössler[1] and Gwen Salaün[2]

[1] INRIA Grenoble – Rhône-Alpes, France
[2] Grenoble INP, INRIA, France

Abstract. Choreography specification languages describe from a global point of view interactions among a set of services in a system to be designed. Given a choreography specification, the goal is to obtain a distributed implementation of the choreography as a system of communicating peers. These peers can be given as input (*e.g.*, obtained using discovery techniques) or automatically generated by projection from the choreography. Checking whether some set of peers implements a choreography specification is called *realizability*. This check is in general undecidable if asynchronous communication is considered, that is, services interact through message buffers. In this paper, we consider conversation protocols as a choreography specification language, and leverage a recent decidability result to check automatically the realizability of these specifications by a set of peers under an asynchronous communication model with a priori unbounded buffers.

1 Introduction

Specification and analysis of interactions among distributed components play an important role in service-oriented applications. A *choreography* is a specification of interactions, from a global point of view, among a set of services participating in a composite service to be designed. One important problem in choreography analysis is figuring out whether a choreography specification can be implemented by a set of distributed peers which communicate using message passing. Even if these peers are obtained by projection [17,22] from the choreography specification, this does not ensure that they precisely implement the corresponding choreography. This problem is known as *realizability*.

Most of the work dedicated to realizability assumes a synchronous communication model, see for instance [22,7,6,20]. Only a few works focused on the study of this problem considering an *asynchronous communication* model, that is communication using message queues or buffers. Fu *et al.* [11] proposed three conditions that guarantee a realizable conversation protocol. Bultan and Fu [5] also recently defined some sufficient conditions to test realizability of choreographies specified with collaboration diagrams. But defining such conditions is quite restrictive because if they are not satisfied, nothing can be concluded about the system (choreography and peers) being analysed. In [23], the authors refine and extend this former work with an automatic check for bounded asynchronous

F. Arbab and P.C. Ölveczky (Eds.): FACS 2011, LNCS 7253, pp. 151–167, 2012.
© Springer-Verlag Berlin Heidelberg 2012

communication. The realizability of bounded MSC graphs has also been studied and some decidability results presented in [3]. Su *et al.* state in [24] that "*it remains an open problem whether the realizability problem is decidable*".

More recently, [9] proved the *quasi-static scheduling* problem of scheduling a set of non-deterministic communicating processes so as to ensure boundedness of buffers, to be undecidable in general, and identified a decidable subclass.

In this paper, we consider conversation protocols [11,12] (CPs) as choreography specification language, and propose an approach to check automatically the realizability of these specifications by a set of peers interacting over an asynchronous communication model (Fig. 1). We do not require the model to be existentially bounded, that is, the proposed approach decides realizability even if it is not known a priori whether the specification can be realized with finite buffers, and if it can, for what buffer sizes. We present here a solution that makes this check decidable if the system is *well-formed*, *i.e.*, (1) in each state a peer can either send one message to a buffer (which we will call a *channel*), read a message from one channel, or non-deterministically choose between one or more internal actions; and (2) the system is activated by a request from the environment, and a new request is not emitted unless the previous action is completed. Both conditions allow for a class of realistic systems, *e.g.*, peers including a choice among several emissions or receptions, while excluding the class of undecidable systems. We will show how to model such behaviours in Section 3. Condition (1) means that non-deterministic choice is made explicit and excludes race conditions. Condition (2) typically corresponds to service-based systems in which a client (the environment) submits a request and a set of services interact together until returning a response to this request.

Our approach consists of two main steps. First, we explore a sub-behavior — called the *canonical schedule* — of the possibly infinite state space of the peers interacting via channels. As the canonical schedule may be infinite, only a finite part of it is explored to decide whether in spite of (uncontrollable) internal choices there exists a bounded execution. This check relies on [9], and verifies whether the canonical schedule computed from the set of peers given as input is finite. If such a finite execution does not exist, the choreography is not realizable. Otherwise, in a second step, we check realizability by comparing the behaviors of the choreography specification with the previously constructed finite sub-behavior of the peers.

The rest of this paper is organized as follows: Section 2 introduces peers, conversation protocols and our running example. Section 3 presents our approach to checking realizability. Section 4 compares our proposal to related work, and Section 5 ends the paper with some concluding remarks.

2   Peers and Conversation Protocols

In this section, we present the notations we use in the rest of this paper to specify choreographies and peers.

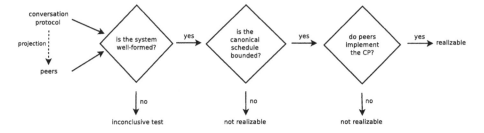

Fig. 1. Overview of the realizability check

Peers are described using Labelled Transition Systems (LTSs). Peers interact by message passing through point-to-point channels. In this paper, we consider asynchronous communication where each peer is equipped with one *channel* for each type of message the peer can receive from a given sending peer. In the peer transition systems, write and read actions to and from a channel *ch* are written *ch*! and *ch*?, respectively.

Definition 1 (Peer). *A peer is a Labelled Transition System (LTS) $P = (S, s^0, \Sigma, T)$ where S is a finite set of states, $s^0 \in S$ is the initial state, $\Sigma = \Sigma^! \uplus \Sigma^? \uplus \Sigma^{int}$ is a finite alphabet partitioned into a set of sending, receiving, and choice actions (internal actions), and $T \subseteq S \times \Sigma \times S$ is a transition relation.*

A peer can either send on a channel *ch* with action $ch! \in \Sigma^!$, read from a channel *ch* with $ch? \in \Sigma^?$, or choose among one or more internal actions $a \in \Sigma^{int}$. Final states are not made explicit and correspond to states without outgoing transitions.

A conversation protocol is an LTS specifying the desired set of conversations from a global point of view. Each transition specifies an interaction between two peers P_s, P_r on a specific channel *ch*. A conversation protocol makes explicit the application order of interactions. Sequence, choice, and loop are modeled using a sequence of transitions, several transitions going out from a same state, and a cycle in the LTS, respectively.

Definition 2 (Conversation protocol). *A conversation protocol CP for a set of peers P_i, $i \in \{1, .., n\}$ is an LTS $CP = (S, s^0, L, T)$ where a label $l \in L$ is a tuple (j, k, ch) where P_j and P_k are the sending peer and receiving peer, respectively, $P_j \neq P_k$, and ch is a channel on which those peers interact. We require that each channel has a unique sender and receiver: $\forall (i, j, ch), (i', j', ch') \in L : ch = ch' \implies i = i' \wedge j = j'$.*

Running Example. In this paper, for illustration purposes, we use a bug report repository involving four peers: a client or environment (env), a bug report repository interface (int), a database (db), and a counter (c). We give successively a conversation protocol (Fig. 2) describing the requirements, that is what the designer expects from the composition-to-be, and four candidate peers (Fig. 3). The conversation protocol starts with a login interaction between environment and interface, followed by the submission of a bug. Then, interface sends the bug to database to store it, and interacts with counter which stores the number of submitted bugs. Finally, database sends a bug identifier which is forwarded by interface to environment. Interactions in Figure 2 are written using exponent notation, *e.g.*, submit^{env,int} stands for (env, int, submit).

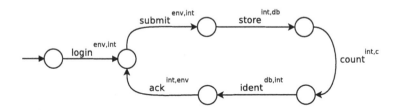

Fig. 2. Running example: conversation protocol

Figure 3 shows four peers that are candidate to a distributed implementation of our conversation protocol example. For instance, interface receives login information (login?) and a bug (submit?) from environment, sends the bug to database (store!), interacts with counter (count!), receives the identifier from database (ident?), and finally sends the acknowledgement to environment (ack!).

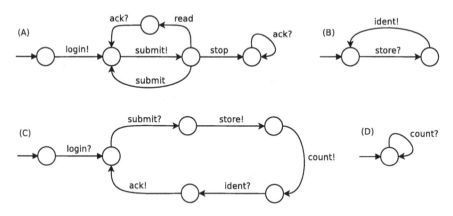

Fig. 3. Running example: peers (A) environment, (B) database, (C) interface, (D) counter

Although these peers seem to implement the conversation protocol, it is hard by visual analysis only to claim whether this is the case or not, even for such a simple example. Moreover, since we assume an asynchronous communication model, deciding whether the conversation protocol can be implemented by the peers communicating through bounded buffers, is in general non-trivial. In the rest of this paper we propose an automated technique to check whether a conversation protocol is bounded-realizable by a system of interacting peers.

3   Checking Bounded Realizability

In this section, we present the different steps of our method to check whether a set of peers interacting asynchronously implements a (centralized) conversation protocol. It works in two successive steps. First, we analyse the canonical schedule generated from the peer composition using results presented in [9]. If the schedule is finite, we check realizability by comparing the behaviors of the conversation protocol with the schedule. Otherwise, the conversation protocol is not bounded-realizable by the system of communicating peers.

Definition 3 (Asynchronous product). *The asynchronous product of a set of peers* $P_i = (S_i, s_i^0, \Sigma_i, T_i)$ *is the peer* $P_1 \| ... \| P_n = (S, s^0, \Sigma, T)$ *where* $S = S_1 \times ... \times S_n$, $s^0 = (s_1^0, ..., s_n^0)$, $\Sigma = \bigcup_i \Sigma_i$, *and*

$$T = \left\{ \left((s_1, ..., s_n), a, (s_1', ..., s_n')\right) \mid \exists i : (s_i, a, s_i') \in T_i \land \forall j \neq i : s_j' = s_j \right\}$$

A *composite* is a set of peers communicating through emissions and receptions over a set of point-to-point channels.

Definition 4 (Composite). *A composite is a tuple* (P, Ch) *of a set* $P = \{P_i \mid i = 1, ..., n\}$ *of peers* $P_i = (S_i, s_i^0, \Sigma_i, T_i)$ *equipped with a set of channels* $Ch = \{ch_i\}$. *We require that* $\Sigma_i^! \cap \Sigma_j^! \neq \emptyset \implies i = j$ *and* $\Sigma_i^? \cap \Sigma_j^? \neq \emptyset \implies i = j$, *that is, each channel has a unique reader and writer. Furthermore, we assume that* $\Sigma_i^! \cap \Sigma_i^? = \emptyset$ *for all* i, *that is, each channel links two different peers.*

From a conversation protocol CP we can compute a composite where each peer is obtained by making abstraction from all other peers in CP, and keeping the same channels as in CP:

Definition 5 (Projection). *The composite obtained by translation of a conversation protocol* $CP = (S, s^0, L, T)$ *over channels* Ch *is a tuple* $\pi(CP) = (\{P_i\}, Ch)$ *where* $P_i = (S_i, s_i^0, \Sigma_i, T_i)$ *is the LTS obtained by replacing in* CP *each action label* $(p, q, ch) \in L$ *with* $ch!$ *if* $p = i$; *with* $ch?$ *if* $q = i$; *and with* τ *(internal action) otherwise, and finally removing the* τ-*transitions by applying the standard determinization algorithms [15].*

By Definition 2 it can be shown that $\pi(CP)$ satisfies the requirements of Definition 4 that each channel has a unique reader and writer, and both are different.

Example 1. We show in Figure 4 the peer **database** obtained by projection from the conversation protocol presented in Section 2. The final peer (right-hand side) is obtained by determinization and minimization of the left-hand side peer.

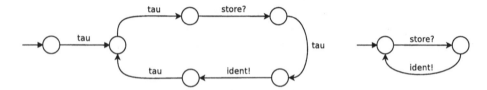

Fig. 4. Peer database generated by projection: (left) before and (right) after determinization and minimization

A configuration of a set of channels $Ch = \{ch_1, ..., ch_n\}$ is a vector in $\mathbb{N}_{\geq 0}^n$ of non-negative integers associating with each channel the number of buffered messages. Let $\mathbf{0}$ denote the tuple of n empty channels.

Definition 6 (Semantics of a composite). *The semantics of a composite* $C = (\{P_i\}, Ch)$ *with* $\| P_i = (S, s^0, \Sigma, T)$ *is the LTS* $sem(C) = (Q, q^0, \Sigma, \rightarrow)$ *where* $Q = S \times \mathbb{N}_{\geq 0}^{|Ch|}$, $q^0 = (s^0, \mathbf{0})$, *and* $\rightarrow \subseteq Q \times \Sigma \times Q$ *is the least transition relation satisfying the following rules:*

$$\frac{(s, ch_k!, s') \in T}{\big(s, (c_1, ..., c_k, ..., c_n)\big) \overset{ch_k!}{\rightarrow} \big(s', (c_1, ..., c_k + 1, ..., c_n)\big)} \quad (SND)$$

$$\frac{(s, ch_k?, s') \in T \quad c_k \geq 1}{\big(s, (c_1, ..., c_k, ..., c_n)\big) \overset{ch_k?}{\rightarrow} \big(s', (c_1, ..., c_k - 1, ..., c_n)\big)} \quad (RCV)$$

$$\frac{(s, a, s') \in T \quad a \in \Sigma^{int}}{(s, c) \overset{a}{\rightarrow} (s', c)} \quad (INT)$$

For a tuple $\mathbf{b} = (b_i)_{ch_i \in Ch}$ *of channel bounds, let* $sem(C)/\mathbf{b} = (Q', q^0, \Sigma, \rightarrow')$ *with*

$$Q' = \{\big(s, (c_1, ..., c_n)\big) \in Q \mid \forall i = 1, ..., n : c_i \leq b_i\}$$

and $\rightarrow' = \{(q, a, q') \in \rightarrow \mid q, q' \in Q'\}$ *be the sub-graph of* $sem(C)$ *restricted to the states satisfying the buffer bounds.*

For a state $q \in Q$, *let* $enabled(q)$ *be the set of actions* $a \in \Sigma$ *such that* $q \overset{a}{\rightarrow} q'$ *for some* q'.

We now define when a composite implements a conversation protocol. The composite can be obtained by projection of the conversation protocol, or by assembling existing (off-the-shelf) peers.

Definition 7 (Implements, $\models_\mathbf{b}$). *Given a conversation protocol* $CP = (S, s^0, L, T)$ *over peers* $1, ..., n$ *and a set of channels* Ch, *a composite* $C = (\{P_i \mid i = 1, ..., m\}, Ch')$ *with* $m \geq n$ *and* $P = \|\{P_i \mid i = 1, ..., m\}$ *over alphabets* Σ_i, *and* $G = (Q, q^0, \Sigma, \rightarrow)$ *a sub-graph of* $sem(C)$, *let* $\preceq \subseteq Q \times S$ *be the greatest relation* $\prec$ *such that if* $q \prec s$ *then:*

1. If $(s, (i, j, ch), s') \in T$ then $\exists k \geq 0\ \exists q_1, ..., q_k \in Q\ \exists a_1, ..., a_k \in \Sigma^{C \backslash CP}$:

$$q \xrightarrow{a_1} q_1 \xrightarrow{a_2} ... \xrightarrow{a_k} q_k \xrightarrow{ch!} q'$$

with $ch! \in \Sigma_i$ and $\forall i = 1, ..., k : q_i \prec s$ and $q' \prec s'$ (communication in CP);
2. If $q \xrightarrow{ch!} q'$ with $ch! \in \Sigma_i$ and $ch \in Ch$ then $\exists s' : (s, (i, j, ch), s') \in T$ and $q' \prec s'$ (send in C);
3. If $q \xrightarrow{a} q'$ with $a \in \Sigma^{C \backslash CP}$ then $q' \prec s$ (unobservable transition of C)

where $\Sigma^{C \backslash CP} = \{ch! \in \Sigma \mid ch \notin Ch\} \cup \Sigma^? \cup \Sigma^{int}$.
    G refines CP, written $G \preceq CP$, if $q^0 \preceq s^0$.
    Given a tuple $\mathbf{b} = (b_i)_{ch_i \in Ch}$ of channel bounds, C implements CP under $\mathbf{b}$, written $C \models_{\mathbf{b}} CP$, if $sem(C)/\mathbf{b} \preceq CP$.

Intuitively, the conversation protocol and the composite must be bisimilar with respect to the communication over channels in Ch. The composite may encompass additional peers and use auxiliary channels that are not part of the conversation protocol, and execute internal actions. Other notions of implementation could have been chosen such as weaker notions [17] or notions taken receptions into account as well [21].

Remark 1. $\pi(CP) \not\models CP$, in general, as $\pi(CP)$ may have more behaviors than CP. Some solutions exist that either propose well-formedness rules to enforce the choreography specification to be realizable [7], or extend the choreography language with new constructs (named dominated choice and loop) that make the peers obtained by projection respect the choreography specification [22]. However, these approaches focus on synchronous communication and do not provide any solution to the boundedness issue inherent to asynchronous communication.

Example 2. If we compare, using Definition 7, the execution traces that can be produced from the conversation protocol given in Figure 2 with those executed by the composite consisting of the peers presented in Figure 3, this check says that the composite does not implement the conversation protocol because the trace login!, login?, submit!, submit?, store!, store?, ident! belongs to the composite but is not a valid trace for the conversation protocol. Indeed, the latter specifies that the interaction between interface and counter ($count^{int,c}$ in Figure 2) must occur before database sends its response to interface. However, this cannot be imposed according to the different peers we reuse for implementation purposes. To work this out, the designer has two possible choices: (i) to relax the choreography specification constraints by making explicit that $count^{int,c}$ and $ident^{db,int}$ can be executed in any order (this would be specified using a diamond of interleaved transitions in the conversation protocol), or (ii) to use extra synchronizations such as those proposed in [23] to enforce peers to respect the ordering constraints specified in the conversation protocol.

Definition 8 (Bounded-realizable). A conversation protocol CP is bounded-realizable by a composite $C = (\{P_i\}, Ch)$ if there exists a tuple of bounds $\mathbf{b} = (b_i)_{ch_i \in Ch}$ on the channels such that $C \models_{\mathbf{b}} CP$.

For a given composite, the existence of a non-blocking *quasi-static scheduler* that ensures boundedness of the channels in spite of uncontrollable non-determinism of the peers, has shown to be undecidable in general [9]. The goal of the remainder of this section is to define a decidable subclass of composites and effectively decide, for a system of this class, whether a conversation protocol is bounded-realizable by a set of peers. In order to tackle this question we need some more definitions.

Definition 9 (Data-branching [9]). *A peer* $P = (S, s^0, \Sigma, T)$ *is data-branching if for any* $s \in S$, *one of the following is true:*

- *All outgoing transitions are choice transitions, and there is at least one such transition (and s is called* choice state*).*
- *s has exactly one outgoing transition* (s, a, s') *and* $a \in \Sigma^!$ *(and s is a* sending state*).*
- *s has at most one outgoing transition* (s, a, s') *and* $a \in \Sigma^?$ *(and s is a* polling state*).*

In particular, a state without any outgoing transition is a polling state.

Intuitively, the data-branching assumption ensures that non-determinism in the global behavior only comes from internal choice and not from race conditions caused by simultaneous listening on several channels, or non-deterministic emission to several channels. The transitions issued from choice states can be seen as the non-deterministic choice obtained from conditional branching after making abstraction from data. Ruling out concurrently enabled emissions is not a restriction, due to the asynchronous model of communication. Figure 5 shows how a choice state can be used to encode non-deterministic emissions: each emission is preceded by a choice transition (this pattern corresponds to an internal choice in process algebra, see CSP [14] for instance).

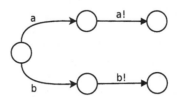

Fig. 5. Modeling non-deterministic emissions

Next we define *round-separation* of a composite, ensuring that a new request is not emitted unless the previous execution of the composite is completed.

Definition 10 (Round-separated). *A composite* $C = (\{P_i\}, Ch)$ *of peers* $P_i = (S_i, s_i^0, \Sigma_i, T_i)$ *with* $sem(C) = (Q, q^0, \Sigma, \rightarrow)$ *is round-separated if*

1. *there exists some peer* P_k *and action* $init \in \Sigma_k^!$ *such that* $enabled(q^0) = \{init\}$;

2. $\forall q = ((s_1, ..., s_n), c) \in Q : init \in enabled(q) \implies \forall j \neq k : s_j$ is a polling state and $c = \mathbf{0}$; and

3. from any reachable state of C, $final(C) = \{q = (s, c) \mid enabled(q) \subseteq \{init\} \wedge c = \mathbf{0}\}$ is reachable.

In a round-separated composite the only action enabled in q^0 — call it $init$ — is enabled only in states $q = (s, c) \in Q$ where all other peers are polling in states and all channels are empty. The set $final(C)$ is the set of $final$ states where at most $init$ is enabled, all other peers are in polling states, and all channels are empty.

Example 3. The composite consisting of the peers presented in Figure 3 is round-separated: there is some $init$ action (login!) initiating the interaction process (condition 1 in Definition 10), this action is never reached again (therefore condition 2 does not need to be verified), and from any reachable state in the composite state, a $final$ state with empty channels is reachable where all peers are in polling states (condition 3 in Definition 10), see the shaded states in Figure 6.

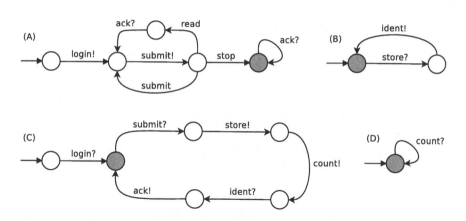

Fig. 6. Running example: final state of the composite

As the requirement of Definition 10 is expressed on the semantics of C, we have two ways to effectively check it: by using some syntactic check that is a sufficient but not necessary condition, or on-the-fly during the state-space exploration. In the approach presented here we choose the second option.

Definition 11 (Well-formed). *A composite is well-formed if it is round-separated and its peers are data-branching.*

The condition of well-formedness allows us to leverage the results of [9] to effectively decide whether a conversation protocol is bounded-realizable. For the sake of a self-contained presentation we cite the following definitions, slightly adapted from [9] to match our framework.

Definition 12 (P_{poll}^q, P_{choice}^q, $P_{send-min}^q$). *Given a composite $C = (\{P_i\}, Ch)$ of data-branching peers and a state $q = (s, c)$ with $s = (s_1, ..., s_n)$ and $c = (c_1, ..., c_n)$ of $sem(C)$, let P_{poll}^q, P_{choice}^q, and P_{send}^q be the sets of indices of the peers that are in a polling state, a choice state, and a sending state, respectively. Let $P_{send-min}^q \subseteq P_{send}^q$ be the set of indices i such that $ch_k! \in \Sigma_i^! \cap enabled(q)$ with $c_k = \min\{c_j\}$ be the subset of peers ready to send a message to a channel holding a minimal number of messages.*

The basic idea of a canonical schedule is to constrain the execution of a composite by giving priority to read and choice actions over write actions. In the case where only write actions are enabled, one of those writing to a channel containing a minimal number of messages is chosen.

Definition 13 (Canonical schedule). *Given a composite $C = (\{P_i\}, Ch)$ with $P_i = (S_i, s_i^0, \Sigma_i, T_i)$ and $\|P_i = (S, s^0, \Sigma, T)$, the canonical schedule of C is the least sub-graph $CS(C) = (Q_{ca}, q^0, \Sigma, \rightarrow_{ca})$ of $sem(C) = (Q, q^0, \Sigma, \rightarrow)$ such that $q^0 \in Q_{ca}$ and for any $q = (s, c) \in Q_{ca}$ with $s = (s_1, ..., s_n)$:*

- *If $P_{poll}^q \cup P_{choice}^q \neq \emptyset$ and $q \xrightarrow{a} q'$ with $q' = (s', c')$, $s' = (s_1', ..., s_n')$, and $a \in \Sigma_k^? \cup \Sigma_k^{int}$ where $k = \min P_{poll}^q \cup P_{choice}^q$, then $q \xrightarrow{a}_{ca} q'$.*
- *Otherwise, if $q \xrightarrow{a} q'$ with $a \in \Sigma_k^!$ where $k = \min P_{send-min}^q$, $q' = (s', c')$, $s' = (s_1', ..., s_n')$, and $(s_k, a, s_k') \in T_k$, then $q \xrightarrow{a}_{ca} q'$.*

As the canonical schedule may be infinite, an order between prefixes is defined next that will be used to explore only a finite part.

Given an LTS $(S, s^0, \Sigma, \rightarrow)$, states $q, q' \in S$, and a sequence $\sigma = a_1 a_2 \cdots a_n \in \Sigma^*$, we write $q_1 \xrightarrow{\sigma} q_n$ if there are states $q_1, ..., q_{n-1} \in S$ such that $q \xrightarrow{a_1} q_1 \xrightarrow{a_2} ... \xrightarrow{a_n} q'$.

Definition 14 ($\prec_{ca}$). *Let $\sigma, \sigma' \in \Sigma^*$ with $q^0 \xrightarrow{\sigma} (s, c)$ and $q^0 \xrightarrow{\sigma'} (s', c')$. Define $\prec_{ca}$ such that $\sigma \prec_{ca} \sigma'$ if all of the following conditions hold:*

1. *σ is a prefix of σ'*
2. *$s = s'$ and $\forall ch \in Ch, c(ch) \leq c'(ch)$*
3. *there exists some $ch \in Ch$ such that*
    - *$\sigma = \sigma_1 ch!$ for some $\sigma_1 \in \Sigma^*$ with $max(\sigma_1) < max(\sigma)$; and*
    - *$\sigma' = \sigma_2 ch!$ for some $\sigma_2 \in \Sigma^*$ with $max(\sigma_2) < max(\sigma')$*

where

$$max(\sigma) = \max \left\{ \max\{c_1, ..., c_n \mid q^0 \xrightarrow{\sigma'} (s, (c_1, ..., c_n))\} \mid \sigma' \text{ is a prefix of } \sigma \right\}$$

Algorithm 1 (Decision procedure). *Given a composite $C = (\{P_i\}, Ch)$ with $\|P_i = (S, s^0, \Sigma, T)$ and $sem(C) = (Q, q^0, \Sigma, \rightarrow)$, we construct a finite coverability tree [9] $Tr(C) \subseteq \Sigma^*$ as follows. First, $\varepsilon \in Tr(C)$. For any $\sigma \in Tr(C)$ and $a \in \Sigma$ with $q^0 \xrightarrow{\sigma} q_\sigma$ and $q_\sigma \xrightarrow{a}_{ca} q' = (s, c)$:*

- *If* $init \in enabled(q')$ *and either* $|enabled(q')| \geq 2$ *or* $c \neq 0$ *then* C *is not round-separated; stop.*
- *Otherwise, if there exists* $\sigma' \in Tr(C)$ *such that* $\sigma' \prec_{ca} \sigma a$ *then* C *is unbounded or* $final(C)$ *is unreachable; stop.*
- *Otherwise, if there is no* $\sigma' \in Tr(C)$ *such that* $q^0 \xrightarrow{\sigma'} q_\sigma$ *then add* σa *to* $Tr(C)$.

It can be shown that Algorithm 1 terminates, since either the canonical schedule is finite and all states have been explored, or there are two prefixes σ, σ' such that $\sigma \prec_{ca} \sigma'$ [9].

Example 4. We give in Figure 7, the canonical schedule generated from the composite given in Figure 3 by application of Definition 13 (peers are ordered *wrt.* their alphabetical identifiers A, B, C, D). One can see that the choice made by the environment is present in the canonical schedule and three possible behaviours are derived.

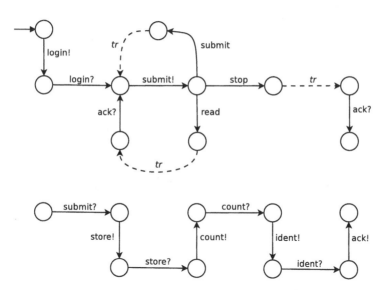

Fig. 7. Running example: behavior of the canonical schedule (top) where *tr* is the transition sequence shown on bottom; the (infinite) state space of the buffers is not shown

The canonical schedule is unbounded: if the environment decides to submit several bugs without consuming acknowledgements (submit branch in the peer environment), then by applying Algorithm 1, we can generate traces from the canonical schedule where the channel size increases (in particular, the size of the channel in the peer environment storing acknowledgements), and case 2 of this algorithm detects this unboundedness case. A solution to this issue is to use a peer environment' which systematically consumes acknowledgements sent by the peer interface, as in Figure 8. If we use this new peer environment' and the other peers presented in Figure 3, the corresponding canonical schedule (given in Figure 9) is bounded because each channel is read immediately after being written.

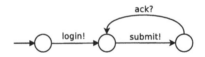

Fig. 8. A candidate peer environment' avoiding the unboundedness issue

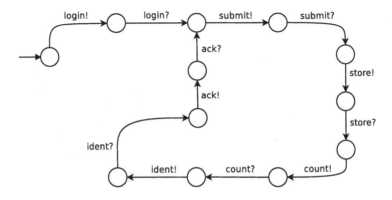

Fig. 9. Example: behavior of the canonical schedule (buffer states are omitted) obtained with the peer environment' given in Figure 8

Theorem 1 (Bounded schedule). *Consider a conversation protocol CP and a composite C composed of data-branching peers.*

1. *If C is round-separated then Algorithm 1 does not terminate with a negative round-separation result.*
2. *Otherwise, if Algorithm 1 terminates with a negative boundedness or reachability result, then CP is not bounded-realizable by C.*
3. *If Algorithm 1 terminates without a negative result (round-separation, boundedness, or reachability), then C is well-formed and CS(C) is finite.*

Proof. 1. The claim follows directly from Definition 10.
2. If Algorithm 1 terminates with a negative boundedness or reachability result, then the non-boundedness of C or unreachability of $final(C)$ follows from Proposition 8 of [9]. The only difference in our setting is that we explicitly model resets in the form of *init* transitions. As by hypothesis of this item, C is round-separated, $final(C)$ is reachable by Definition 10. Therefore, C is unbounded, and the claim follows.

3. Round-separation under the canonical schedule is ensured by the normal termination of the algorithm. Round-separation on arbitrary runs is obtained by a reordering argument similar to that used in [9]. Well-formedness then follows directly from the hypothesis of data-branching peers and round-separation.

Example 5. If we consider the peer environment' given in Figure 8 and the three other peers presented in Figure 3, Algorithm 1 terminates with a positive result, meaning that the composite is well-formed and the canonical schedule is finite (see Figure 9).

Notice that even if the canonical schedule $CS(C)$ of a composite C is finite, the semantic graph $sem(C)$ may still be infinite. However, if C is well-formed and $CS(C)$ is finite, then bounded-realizability of a conversation protocol CP by C can be effectively verified.

Theorem 2 (Bounded-realizability). *Given a conversation protocol CP and a well-formed composite C, CP is bounded-realizable by C if and only if the canonical schedule $CS(C) = (Q, q^0, \Sigma, \rightarrow)$ is finite and $C \models_\mathbf{b} CP$, where $\mathbf{b} = (b_i)_{ch_i \in Ch}$ with $\forall i$, $b_i = \max \{c_i \mid \exists s \, \exists c = (c_1, ..., c_n) : q^0 \rightarrow^* (s, c)\}$, and $\rightarrow^*$ denotes the reflexive and transitive closure of $\rightarrow$.*

That is, CP is bounded-realizable by C if and only if it is bounded-realizable for channel bounds used by the canonical schedule.

Proof. (sketch) "If": if $C \models_\mathbf{b} CP$ then clearly, CP is bounded-realizable by C.
    "Only if": suppose that CP is bounded-realizable by C, say $C \models_{\mathbf{b}'} CP$ for some tuple $\mathbf{b}'$ of buffer bounds. Then $\mathbf{b}' \geq \mathbf{b}$ by construction of the canonical schedule. In particular, $CS(C)$ is finite. Moreover, $sem(C)/\mathbf{b}$ is a sub-graph of $sem(C)/\mathbf{b}'$. Therefore, it can be shown by structural induction that items 2. and 3. of Definition 7 still hold for $sem(C)/\mathbf{b}$. Moreover, as C is well-formed and thus round-separated, $final(C)$ is reachable from any reachable state of $sem(C)$. This ensures that all pending write actions will eventually be executed, such that item 1. of Definition 7 is still satisfied. It follows that $C \models_\mathbf{b} CP$.

Example 6. Although the canonical schedule generated from the peer environment' given in Figure 8 and the peers database, interface, and counter presented in Figure 3 is finite, the corresponding semantic graph is infinite because the counter has no obligation to read. To check bounded-realizability, the required channel size is one for all channels since each channel can be read immediately after being written. If we consider an extension of the conversation protocol given in Figure 2 where count^{int,c} and return^{db,int} can be interleaved — as discussed in Example 2 —, then this conversation protocol is bounded-realizable by the composite.

4   Related Work

The realizability results we present in this paper rely on [9] where the authors identify a decidable class of systems consisting of non-deterministic communicating processes that can be scheduled while ensuring boundedness of buffers. There has been quite some work on the analysis of infinite communication buffers in concurrent systems. Abdulla *et al.* [1] proposed some verification methods for Communicating Finite State Machines. They showed the decidability and provided algorithms for verification (safety and some forms of liveness properties) of *lossy* channel systems. A sufficient condition for the unboundedness of communication channel was proposed in [16]. In [18,19], the authors present an incomplete boundedness test for communication channels in Promela and UML RT models. They also provide a method to derive *upper bound* estimates for the maximal occupancy of each individual message buffer. More recently, [10] proposed a causal chain analysis to determine upper bounds on buffer sizes for multi-party sessions with asynchronous communication. Our goal here is to compute the *minimal* buffer sizes which make the interacting peers realize the choreography, but this does not mean that a bound exists for each buffer. Therefore, the results presented in [18,19,10] would not help to solve the problem we tackle here.

Most of the work dedicated to the realizability issue assumes a synchronous communication model, see for instance [6,20,7,22]. In [6,20], the authors define models for choreography and orchestration, and formalise a conformance relation between both models. The results presented in [7,22] formalise some well-formedness rules to enforce the specification to be realizable. More precisely, in [7], the authors identify three principles for global description under which they define a sound and complete end-point projection, that is the generation of distributed processes from the choreography description. In [22], the authors propose a choreography language with new constructs (named dominated choice and loop) in order to implement unrealizable choreographies. During the projection of these new operators, some communications are added in order to make peers respect the choreography specification. However, these solutions prevent the designer from specifying what (s)he wants to, and it also complicates the design by obliging the designer to make explicit extra-constraints in the choreography specification, *e.g.*, by associating *dominant roles* to certain peers.

Only a few works focused on the realizability problem assuming an asynchronous communication model, that is communication using message buffers. Fu *et al.* [11] proposed three sufficient conditions (lossless join, synchronous compatible, autonomous) that guarantee a realizable conversation protocol. More recently, Sasu and Bultan proposed to check conformance using *synchronizability* [4]: A set of peers is synchronizable if systems produced on one hand with synchronous communication, and on the other with 1-bounded asynchronous communication, are equivalent. If a set of peers is synchronizable, one can check whether it is conformant to a choreography using existing finite state verification tools. However, if one of the conditions in [11] or synchronizability is not satisfied, nothing can be concluded. Our approach works for systems that are not synchronizable.

Bultan and Fu [5] defined some sufficient conditions to test realizability of choreographies specified with collaboration diagrams (CDs). In [23], the authors refine and extend this former work with some techniques to enforce realizability (by adding additional synchronization messages among peers), and a tool-supported approach to automatically check the realizability of CDs for bounded asynchronous communication. Branching and cyclic behaviours are not well supported by CDs (*e.g.*, only loops on a same message), and this is a restriction to specify more expressive choreographies. The realizability problem for Message Sequence Charts (MSCs) has also been studied (see for instance [2,26,3]). For example, [3] presents some decidability results on bounded MSC graphs, that are basically graphs obtained from MSCs using bounded buffers.

Lohmann and Wolf [21] show how realizability of choreography automaton can be verified by using existing techniques for the *controllability* problem, which checks whether a service has compatible partner processes. Their approach works for peers interacting via arbitrary bounded buffers, and only consider finite conversations, whereas we can handle infinite state space systems.

Genest *et al.* [13] establish equivalence of existentially bounded communicating automata with globally cooperative compositional message sequence graphs and monadic second-order logic.

In [8] on quasi-static scheduling of free-choice Petri nets, a coverability criterion is defined whose function, similar to the relation $\prec_{ca}$, is to explore only a finite part of a potentially infinite state space. The authors conjecture completeness of the criterion. Based on [8], [25] uses discrete controller synthesis to automatically construct converters between peers so as to ensure bounded buffering and deadlock freedom.

Compared to all these works, our approach provides a check for realizability under asynchronous communication, and goes beyond most results which assume arbitrary bounded buffers, this check being undecidable for unbounded buffers. Here, we rely on a boundedness analysis of the peer composition, and provide a decidable technique for well-formed systems of communicating peers. We also extend existing results for conversation protocol realizability by considering peer composition (*e.g.*, those which are not synchronizable) for which existing solutions [11,4] cannot conclude anything.

5   Concluding Remarks

In this paper, we have presented an approach for checking whether a conversation protocol can be implemented by a set of distributed peers interacting asynchronously. The realizability check relies on the boundedness of the canonical schedule computed from the candidate peers. If this schedule is infinite, the conversation protocol cannot be realized with bounded buffers by the peers. If this schedule is finite, we compare the LTS obtained from the conversation protocol with the LTS generated from the peer composition to check whether these peers implement the choreography specification.

An interesting direction of future work we intend to study is the generalization of our framework to multi-session protocols. This will require several generalizations to our results, in particular extending the modeling formalism and refinement relation, and relaxing the round-separation requirement.

References

1. Abdulla, P.A., Bouajjani, A., Jonsson, B.: On-the-Fly Analysis of Systems with Un-bounded, Lossy FIFO Channels. In: Vardi, M.Y. (ed.) CAV 1998. LNCS, vol. 1427, pp. 305–318. Springer, Heidelberg (1998)
2. Alur, R., Etessami, K., Yannakakis, M.: Inference of Message Sequence Charts. IEEE Transactions on Software Engineering 29(7), 623–633 (2003)
3. Alur, R., Etessami, K., Yannakakis, M.: Realizability and Verification of MSC Graphs. Theoretical Computer Science 331(1), 97–114 (2005)
4. Basu, S., Bultan, T.: Choreography Conformance via Synchronizability. In: Proc. WWW 2011. ACM Press (2011)
5. Bultan, T., Fu, X.: Specification of Realizable Service Conversations using Col-laboration Diagrams. Service Oriented Computing and Applications 2(1), 27–39 (2008)
6. Busi, N., Gorrieri, R., Guidi, C., Lucchi, R., Zavattaro, G.: Choreography and Orchestration Conformance for System Design. In: Ciancarini, P., Wiklicky, H. (eds.) COORDINATION 2006. LNCS, vol. 4038, pp. 63–81. Springer, Heidelberg (2006)
7. Carbone, M., Honda, K., Yoshida, N.: Structured Communication-Centred Pro-gramming for Web Services. In: De Nicola, R. (ed.) ESOP 2007. LNCS, vol. 4421, pp. 2–17. Springer, Heidelberg (2007)
8. Cortadella, J., Kondratyev, A., Lavagno, L., Passerone, C., Watanabe, Y.: Quasi-Static Scheduling of Independent Tasks for Reactive Systems. IEEE Trans. on CAD of Integrated Circuits and Systems 24(10), 1492–1514 (2005)
9. Darondeau, P., Genest, B., Thiagarajan, P.S., Yang, S.: Quasi-Static Scheduling of Communicating Tasks. In: van Breugel, F., Chechik, M. (eds.) CONCUR 2008. LNCS, vol. 5201, pp. 310–324. Springer, Heidelberg (2008)
10. Deniélou, P.-M., Yoshida, N.: Buffered Communication Analysis in Distributed Multiparty Sessions. In: Gastin, P., Laroussinie, F. (eds.) CONCUR 2010. LNCS, vol. 6269, pp. 343–357. Springer, Heidelberg (2010)
11. Fu, X., Bultan, T., Su, J.: Conversation Protocols: A Formalism for Specification and Verification of Reactive Electronic Services. Theor. Comput. Sci. 328(1-2), 19–37 (2004)
12. Fu, X., Bultan, T., Su, J.: Synchronizability of Conversations among Web Services. IEEE Transactions on Software Engineering 31(12), 1042–1055 (2005)
13. Genest, B., Kuske, D., Muscholl, A.: A kleene theorem and model checking algo-rithms for existentially bounded communicating automata. Inf. Comput. 204(6), 920–956 (2006)
14. Hoare, C.A.R.: Communicating Sequential Processes. Prentice-Hall (1984)
15. Hopcroft, J.E., Ullman, J.D.: Introduction to Automata Theory, Languages and Computation. Addison Wesley (1979)
16. Jéron, T., Jard, C.: Testing for Unboundedness of FIFO Channels. Theor. Comput. Sci. 113(1), 93–117 (1993)
17. Kazhamiakin, R., Pistore, M.: Analysis of Realizability Conditions for Web Service Choreographies. In: Najm, E., Pradat-Peyre, J.-F., Donzeau-Gouge, V.V. (eds.) FORTE 2006. LNCS, vol. 4229, pp. 61–76. Springer, Heidelberg (2006)
18. Leue, S., Mayr, R., Wei, W.: A Scalable Incomplete Test for Message Buffer Overflow in Promela Models. In: Graf, S., Mounier, L. (eds.) SPIN 2004. LNCS, vol. 2989, pp. 216–233. Springer, Heidelberg (2004)

19. Leue, S., Mayr, R., Wei, W.: A Scalable Incomplete Test for the Boundedness of UML RT Models. In: Jensen, K., Podelski, A. (eds.) TACAS 2004. LNCS, vol. 2988, pp. 327–341. Springer, Heidelberg (2004)

20. Li, J., Zhu, H., Pu, G.: Conformance Validation between Choreography and Orchestration. In: Proc. TASE 2007, pp. 473–482. IEEE Computer Society (2007)

21. Lohmann, N., Wolf, K.: Realizability Is Controllability. In: Laneve, C., Su, J. (eds.) WS-FM 2009. LNCS, vol. 6194, pp. 110–127. Springer, Heidelberg (2010)

22. Qiu, Z., Zhao, X., Cai, C., Yang, H.: Towards the Theoretical Foundation of Choreography. In: Proc. WWW 2007, pp. 973–982. ACM Press (2007)

23. Salaün, G., Bultan, T.: Realizability of Choreographies Using Process Algebra Encodings. In: Leuschel, M., Wehrheim, H. (eds.) IFM 2009. LNCS, vol. 5423, pp. 167–182. Springer, Heidelberg (2009)

24. Su, J., Bultan, T., Fu, X., Zhao, X.: Towards a Theory of Web Service Choreographies. In: Dumas, M., Heckel, R. (eds.) WS-FM 2007. LNCS, vol. 4937, pp. 1–16. Springer, Heidelberg (2008)

25. Tivoli, M., Fradet, P., Girault, A., Gössler, G.: Adaptor Synthesis for Real-Time Components. In: Grumberg, O., Huth, M. (eds.) TACAS 2007. LNCS, vol. 4424, pp. 185–200. Springer, Heidelberg (2007)

26. Uchitel, S., Kramer, J., Magee, J.: Incremental Elaboration of Scenario-based Specifications and Behavior Models using Implied Scenarios. ACM Transactions on Software Engineering and Methodology 1(13), 37–85 (2004)

Networks of Real-Time Actors
Schedulability Analysis and Coordination

Mohammad Mahdi Jaghoori[1,*], Ólafur Hlynsson[2], and Marjan Sirjani[2,3]

[1] CWI, Amsterdam, The Netherlands
[2] Reykjavik University, Iceland
[3] University of Tehran, Iran
jaghoori@cwi.nl,{olafurh05,marjan}@ru.is

Abstract. We present an automata theoretic framework for modular schedulability analysis of networks of real-time asynchronous actors. In this paper, we use the coordination language Reo to structure the network of actors and as such provide an exogenous form of scheduling between actors to complement their internal scheduling. We explain how to avoid extra communication buffers during analysis in some common Reo connectors. We then consider communication delays between actors and analyze its effect on schedulability of the system. Furthermore, in order to have a uniform analysis platform, we show how to use UPPAAL to combine Constraint Automata, the semantic model of Reo, with Timed Automata models of the actors. We can derive end-to-end deadlines, i.e., the deadline on a message from when it is sent until a reply is received.

1   Introduction

Schedulability analysis in a real-time system amounts to checking whether all tasks can be accomplished within the required deadlines. In a client-server perspective on distributed systems, tasks are created on a client, sent to the server (e.g., as a message), and then finally performed on the server. A deadline given by the client for a task covers three parts: the network delay until the message reaches the server, the queuing time until the task starts executing, and the execution time. In case a reply is sent back to the client, an end-to-end deadline also includes the network delay until the reply reaches the client and is processed.

In previous work [10,15–17], we employed automata theory to provide a modular approach to the schedulability analysis of real-time actor models, assuming direct and immediate communication between actors, i.e., zero communication delays. An actor [1,13] (à la Rebeca [26]) is an autonomous entity with a single thread of execution. Actors communicate by asynchronous message passing, i.e., incoming messages are buffered and the code for handling each message is defined in a corresponding method. We model each method as a timed automaton [3] where a method can send messages while computation is abstracted in passage of time. In our framework, an actor can define a local scheduler and thus reduce

---

* The work by this author is supported by the HATS project (EU FP7-231620).

F. Arbab and P.C. Ölveczky (Eds.): FACS 2011, LNCS 7253, pp. 168–186, 2012.
© Springer-Verlag Berlin Heidelberg 2012

the nondeterminism; a proper choice of a scheduling strategy is indeed necessary to make the actor schedulable.

Section 2 explains a modular way to analyze a system of actors. To be able to do so, the expected usage of each actor is specified in a separate timed automaton, called its *behavioral interface*; this is a contract between the actor and its environment [23], which among other things, includes the schedulability requirements for the actor in terms of deadlines. Every actor is checked individually for schedulability with regard to its behavioral interface. We showed in [16] that schedulable actors need finite buffers; the upper-bound on buffer size can be computed statically. When composing a number of individually schedulable actors, the global schedulability of the system can be concluded from the *compatibility* of the actors [17]. Being subject to state-space explosion, we gave a technique in [17] to test compatibility.

The contribution of this paper is twofold. First in Section 3, we extend the above framework with Reo [4] to enable exogenous coordination of the actors. This provides a separation of concerns between computation and coordination. Reo can be used as a "glue code" language for compositionally building connectors that orchestrate the cooperation between components or services in a component-based system or a service-oriented application. An important feature of Reo is that it allows for anonymous communication, i.e., the sender of a message does not need to know the recipient; instead the Reo connector will forward the message to the proper receiver.

With Reo, individually schedulable actors can be used as off-the-shelf modules in a wider variety of network structures. This requires a new compatibility check for our analysis that incorporates the Reo connectors. Our extension preserves the asynchronous nature of the actors, therefore the Reo connectors must have a buffer at every input/output node, which may lead to state-space explosion. To avoid this problem, we provide techniques to optimize the analysis by reusing internal actor buffers in the Reo connectors that are single-input and/or single-output. We show that in this approach the upper-bound on the size of the buffers of the schedulable actors need not be increased. In Section 5, we give examples of other Reo connectors that can take advantage of the same optimization technique. In any case, we assume coordination and data flow by Reo happens in zero time.

As our second contribution, we analyze in Section 4 the effect of communication delays on the schedulability of a distributed system. For simplicity in presentation, we assume no coordination with Reo in this section. The communication medium between every pair of actors is modeled abstractly by a fixed delay value, called their *distance*. We first describe how to implement the effect of delay on messages in an efficient manner with respect to schedulability analysis. Secondly we extend the compatibility check to take message delays into account. The latter is non-trivial because sending and receiving messages do not happen at the same time any more. Nevertheless, this complication can be hidden from the end user by implementing it in an automatic test-case generation algorithm.

We argue in Section 5 that coordination with Reo and communication delays are orthogonal and can be combined.

As a running example, we consider a client/server composition of two actors. Assuming that the client is faster, the overall system would not be schedulable because the server would not be able to respond in time. This situation can be remedied by using Reo to connect the client to multiple server instances in order to compensate for their slowness. Nonetheless, the client still thinks it is communicating with one server, i.e., coordination is transparent to the client and the server actors. In other words, modularity of the analysis is preserved.

1.1 Related Work

Schedulability has usually been analyzed for a whole system running on a single processor, whether at modeling [2, 11] or programming level [7, 19]. We address distributed systems modeled as a network of actors (connected by Reo circuits) where each actor has a dedicated processor and scheduling policy.

The work in [12] is also applicable to distributed systems but is limited to rate monotonic analysis. Our analysis being based on automata can handle non-uniformly recurring tasks as in Task Automata [11]. In Task automata, however, a task is purely specified as computation times and cannot create sub-tasks.

In our approach, behavioral interfaces are key to modularity. A behavioral interface models the most general message arrival pattern for an actor. The behavioral interface can be viewed as a contract, as in 'design by contract' [23], or as a most general assumption in modular model checking [21] (based on assume-guarantee reasoning). Schedulability is guaranteed if the real use of the actor satisfies this assumption.

RT-Synchronizers [24] also provide some sort of coordination among actors, however, they are designed for declarative specification of timing constraints over groups of untimed actors. Therefore, they do not speak of schedulability of the actors themselves; in fact, a deadline associated to a message is for the time before it is executed and therefore cannot deal with the execution time of the task itself or sub-task generation.

In [9, 15], our approach is extended to accommodate synchronization statements and *replies* of the Creol language [18]. Asynchronous message passing in Creol is augmented with explicit return values and message synchronization. Therefore, Creol has the natural means to model end-to-end deadlines, however the work in [9, 15] does not support network delays. In present work, an end-to-end deadline including network delays can be computed manually by adding up the deadlines of the message and its corresponding reply message.

There are several coordination languages that can be used to coordinate actors, two of which are worth mentioning. First there is the ARC model [25], which aims at coordinating resource usage and QoS goals, and is based on state transition systems. Secondly there is the PBRD model [22], which aims at logical communication behavior, and is based on rewriting logic. Apart from modeling capabilities, unlike the two above, Reo has automata based semantics which allows us to connect naturally to our automata-theoretic framework in [16].

Fig. 1. The behavioral interfaces of Client (left) and Server (right) are symmetric

Several semantic models have been suggested for Reo in order to handle data-transfer delays, e.g. [20]. None of these models are yet able to consider the delay in setting up a connection in a distributed way. Therefore in this work, we restrict to centralized Reo connectors and we assume that coordination happens in negligible time. This assumption is reasonable when Reo connectors are deployed local to actors. In this paper, we provide no real-time extensions of Reo; although we propose an algorithm to translate some Reo connectors into Timed Automata.

2 Preliminaries: Real-Time Actors

We use automata theory for modular schedulability analysis of actor-based systems [16,17]. An actor consists of a set of methods which are specified in Timed Automata (TA) [3]. This enables us to use existing tools, for example UPPAAL [6], to perform analysis. Each actor should provide a behavioral interface that specifies at a high level, and in the most general terms, how this actor may be used. As explained later in this section, behavioral interfaces are key to modular analysis of actors. Actors specify local scheduling strategies, e.g., based on fixed priorities, earliest deadline first, or a combination of such policies. Real-time actors may need certain customized scheduling strategies in order to meet their QoS requirements. We describe in this section how to model and analyze actors.

Modeling behavioral interfaces. A behavioral interface consists of the messages an actor may receive and send; thus it provides an abstract overview of the actor behavior in a single automaton. A behavioral interface abstracts from specific method implementations, the message buffer in the actor and the scheduling strategy.

To formally define a behavioral interface, we assume a finite global set $\mathcal{M}$ for method names. A behavioral interface B providing a set of method names $M_B \subseteq \mathcal{M}$ is a deterministic timed automaton over alphabet Act^B such that Act^B is partitioned into two sets of actions:

- outputs: $Act_O^B = \{m?|m \in \mathcal{M} \wedge m \notin M_B\}$
- inputs: $Act_I^B = \{m(d)!|m \in M_B \wedge d \in \mathbb{N}\}$

Notice the unusual use of ! and ? signs; this is to simplify the analysis as will be explained later. The integer d associated to input actions represents a deadline. A correct implementation of the actor should be able to finish method m before d time units.

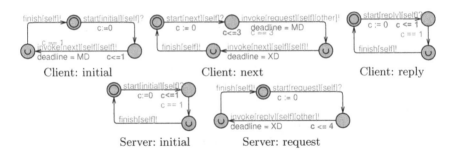

Client: initial   Client: next   Client: reply

Server: initial   Server: request

Fig. 2. Method implementations for client and server actors

Example. Fig. 1 depicts the UPPAAL models for behavioral interfaces of two actors that can communicate in a client-server fashion by sending request and reply messages. In UPPAAL, messages are sent along the *invoke* channel and deadlines are passed using the global variable *deadline*. To uniquely identify messages between different actors, every message in $\mathcal{M}$ is represented in UPPAAL with three parameters of invoke[msg][snd][rcv] showing the message name, sender and receiver, respectively.

Modeling classes. One can define a class as a set of methods implementing a specific behavioral interface. A class R implementing the behavioral interface B is a set $\{(m_1, A_1), \ldots, (m_n, A_n)\}$ of methods, where

- $M_R = \{m_1, \ldots, m_n\} \subseteq \mathcal{M}$ is a set of method names such that $M_B \subseteq M_R$;
- for all i, $1 \leq i \leq n$, A_i is a timed automaton representing method m_i with the alphabet $Act_i = \{m! | m \in M_R\} \cup \{m(d)! \mid m \in \mathcal{M} \land d \in \mathbb{N}\}$;

Method automata only send messages while computations are abstracted into time delays by using a clock c. Receiving and buffering messages is handled by the scheduler automata (explained below). Sending a message $m \in M_R$ is called a self call. A self call with no explicit deadline inherits the (remaining) deadline of the task that triggers it (called delegation); in this case the *delegate* channel must be used.

Classes have an *initial* method which is implicitly called upon initialization and is used for the system startup. Execution of a method begins after receiving a signal on the start channel and terminates by sending a signal on the finish channel; this way the scheduler can control execution of the methods. Fig. 2 shows an implementation of the methods of our example.

Modeling schedulers. The scheduler for each actor, containing also its message buffer, is modeled separately as a timed automaton (see Fig. 3). The *buffer* is modeled using arrays in UPPAAL and thus it can be modeled compactly, i.e., without different locations for different buffer states. The scheduler automaton begins with putting an *initial* message in the buffer via the *initialize* function.

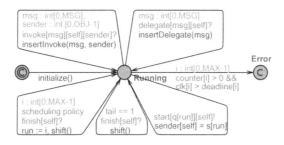

Fig. 3. A general scheduler automaton

The scheduler is input-enabled, i.e., it allows receiving any message from any sender on the *invoke* channel. The buffer stores along each message its sender and deadline. A free clock is assigned to each message and reset to zero upon insertion in the buffer. These are in the *insertInvoke* function. By reusing this clock, a new message may inherit the remaining deadline of another message; this is captured in the *insertDelegate* function. If a clock assigned to a message ($counter[i] > 0$) passes its deadline, the scheduler moves to an Error location.

When there are multiple messages in the buffer, the scheduler decides the order of their execution. The next method to be executed (via a signal on the start channel) should be chosen based on a specific *scheduling strategy*. If the index 0 of the buffer is always selected during context switch, the automaton serves as a First Come First Served (FCFS) scheduler. The remaining deadline of each message i can be used in the scheduling policy (e.g., Earliest Deadline First) as $deadline[i] - clk[i]$. When a method is finished (via synchronization on the finish channel), it is taken out of the buffer by shifting.

For more details on modeling actors and schedulers, please refer to our previous work [14].

2.1 Modular Schedulability Analysis

An actor is an instance of a class together with a scheduler. A closed system of actors is schedulable if and only if all tasks finish within their deadlines. We have shown in [16] that schedulable actors do not put more than $\lceil d_{max}/b_{min} \rceil$ messages in the buffer, where d_{max} is the longest deadline for the messages and b_{min} is the shortest termination time of its method automata. One can calculate the best case runtime for timed automata as shown by Courcoubetis and Yannakakis [8]. Formally, schedulability is defined as follows.

Definition 1 (System Schedulability). *A closed system of actors is schedulable if and only if none of the scheduler automata can reach the Error location or exceeds the buffer limit of $\lceil d_{max}/b_{min} \rceil$.*

Thus, schedulability analysis can be reduced to reachability analysis in a tool like UPPAAL. The intrinsic asynchrony of actors and their message buffers practically lead to state-space explosion. Our approach to modular analysis of the actors (as in [16]) combines model checking and testing techniques to overcome this problem. This is done in the two steps described below.

Individual Actor Analysis. The methods of an actor can in theory be called in infinitely many ways, which makes their analysis impossible. However, it is reasonable to restrict only to the incoming method calls specified in its behavioral interface. Input actions in the behavioral interface correspond to incoming messages. Incoming messages are buffered in the actor; this can be interpreted as creating a new task for handling that message. The behavioral interface doesn't capture internal tasks triggered by self calls. Therefore, one needs to consider both the internal tasks and the tasks triggered by the behavioral interface, which abstractly models the acceptable environments. We can analyze all possible behaviors of an actor in UPPAAL by model checking the network of timed automata consisting of its method automata, behavioral interface automaton B and a scheduler automaton. Inputs of B written $m!$ match inputs in the scheduler written $m?$, and outputs of B written $m?$ match outputs of method automata written $m!$. An actor is schedulable w.r.t. its behavioral interface iff the scheduler cannot reach the Error location and does not exceed its buffer limit.

Compatibility Check. Once an actor is verified to be schedulable with respect to its behavioral interface, it can be used as an off-the-shelf component. In this section, we assume that actors communicate directly with no communication delays. As in modular verification [21], which is based on assume-guarantee reasoning, individually schedulable actors can be used in systems *compatible* with their behavioral interfaces. Schedulability of such systems is then guaranteed. Intuitively, the product of the behavioral interfaces, called B, shows the acceptable sequences of messages that may be communicated between actors.

Definition 2 (Compatibility). *Compatibility is defined as the inclusion of the visible traces of the system in the traces of B [17], where visible actions correspond to messages communicated between actors.*

Checking compatibility is prone to state-space explosion due to the size of the system; we avoid this by means of testing techniques. A naive approach could take a trace from the system S as a test case and check whether it exists also in B. This test case generation method is not efficient due to the great deal of nondeterminism in S. As proposed in [17], we generate test-cases from B. A test-case, first of all, *drives* the system along a trace taken from B and thus restricts system behavior. Secondly, it *monitors* the system along this trace checking for any action that is forbidden in B (as a possible witness for incompatibility). To do the monitoring, every communication between different actors has to be intervened by the test-case automaton. Receiving and forwarding these messages in the test-case are separated by a 'committed' location so that UPPAAL executes them with no interruption.

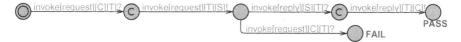

Fig. 4. In this test case, C, S and T represent Client, Server and Test-case, respectively

Example. Fig. 4 shows a test-case that proves the Server and Client implementations in Fig. 2 to be incompatible. This test-case considers one round of *expected* request-reply scenario. This scenario is captured in the main line of the test-case (leading to PASS verdict). For the sake of simplicity, we only monitor for one *forbidden* behavior in this test-case which leads to the FAIL verdict: a lack of a timely reply is captured as sending two requests without an intermediate reply. When executing this test-case, the FAIL location is indeed reachable because the client in Fig. 2 (i.e., its 'next' method) is faster than the server (i.e., its 'request' method). We show in Section 3 how Reo can bring flexibility in composing actors such that we can remedy this problem; specifically by allowing us to use two servers with one client.

3   Using Reo for Coordination

Reo can help us coordinate the actors to avoid unexpected message-passing scenarios. That is, we can impose a strict communication pattern on the components, e.g., replicating requests and merging replies or ordering the messages. This can be seen as an exogenous scheduler that might be crucial in schedulability of a composed system. An advantage of Reo for us is its automata-theoretic semantic model, namely Constraint Automata (CA). The idea is that CA models of Reo networks have a high potential to be used in combination with Timed Automata models of actors and thus allow us to analyze our models in UPPAAL.

Complex Reo connectors can be composed out of a basic set of channels. Each channel has exactly two ends that have their own unique identities. A channel end can be a source or a sink. Data enters at the source end and leaves the channel through the sink. To build complex connectors, channels are connected by means of nodes (also called ports). A node is like a pumping station that takes the data on one of the incoming 'sink' ends and replicates the data onto all of its outgoing 'source' ends. Therefore, channels can be connected by: sequential composition where the data flows from one channel to the next one; a non-deterministic choice of data from multiple channels merging to one; or, replication of data from one channel to many. All this happens in one synchronous step.

Table 1 illustrates a set of primitive channels. The synchronous channel accepts data at the source and dispenses data through the sink as soon as both source and sink are ready. The lossy synchronous channel can always accept data at the source. The data flows from the source to the sink if the sink can accept data at that instance; otherwise, it is lost. The synchronous drain has two source ends; it takes the data on its sources if and only if they are both ready. It acts like a channel synchronizer and does not transfer any data. The FIFO1 channel

Table 1. Basic Channels and their constraint automata

A ○———→○ B $\{A, B\}$ $data(A) = data(B)$	A ○—▭—→○ B $\{A\}$ $d = data(A)$ $\{B\}$ $data(B) = d$
Synchronous channel	FIFO1 channel with variable d
A ○·······→○ B $\{A, B\}$ $\{A\}$ $data(A) = data(B)$	A ○→———←○ B $\{A, B\}$
Lossy synchronous channel	Synchronous drain

transfers data from the source to the sink in two transitions, thereby acting like a one-place data storage. A FIFO channel can also be unbounded.

Transitions of constraint automata are labeled with a set of port names and a data constraint. A transition is taken when all of the ports on its label are ready. In that case, the data constraint determines the data flow in a declarative fashion, e.g., when a synchronous channel fires the data at both ends will be the same. Direction of data flow is understood from the types of channel ends. As in FIFO1, a CA can have variables to temporarily store data values. The initial state of the CA for FIFO1 depends on whether it is initially full or empty.

When channels are composed into a connector, the behavior of the connector is derived compositionally as the product of the CA of its constituent channels. Furthermore, the hiding operator can be applied to create a simple and intuitive CA that accurately describes how the connector works, without exposing the internal ports. Please refer to [5] for a formal definition of product and hiding.

3.1 Integrating Real-Time Actors with Reo

Integrating actors with Reo is complicated by the asynchronous nature of actors: Actors can send messages whenever they have to; therefore, a Reo connector may not block them exogenously. A natural way of solving this issue is to add a FIFO channel as a message buffer at every input port of a Reo connector. The problem is that for model checking, a suitable bound for these FIFOs is necessary. Furthermore, the number of buffers needed quickly blows up the state-space. As a workaround, we suggest using the buffers that already exist in the actors for this purpose. Nevertheless, the upper bound for these buffers need not be increased as discussed below. This approach can be thought of as a low-level optimization of the schedulability check, where we produce a behavior which at a high-level is indistinguishable from adding buffers to the input ports of the connectors. Before explaining the details, we need to restrict the allowable Reo connectors.

A Reo connector may not lose a message. In fact when a message is lost, it can never meet its deadline, and the system will not be schedulable. If we were to allow lossy connectors, one may argue that lost messages can be seen as having met their deadlines; this can be justified by assuming that the Reo connector is in charge and has rightfully decided to lose the message. But this causes a problem if the connector has a buffer to store messages before they are lost (which is the case as explained above). Since we assume that a Reo connector operates in zero time, it may lose any arbitrary number of messages in zero time and therefore, we cannot statically compute a bound on the size of this buffer for a schedulable system. This restriction, however, does not greatly reduce the expressiveness of Reo as witnessed by the examples provided in this section and in Section 5. Notice that drain and lossy synchronous channels can still be used.

Another restriction is that only bounded FIFO channels may be used. Therefore, the CA for these connectors is finite-state. Now we explain how to optimize analysis for two patterns of Reo connectors:

- **Single-input, multiple-output (e.g. Fig. 5.a):** Since the output ports are directly connected to a message buffer in an actor, they are always enabled. Therefore, as soon as there is a message on the input port of this connector, it can decide the destination of the message. Since the connector does not lose the message, it may directly go to an actor or it is stored in a FIFO channel. In either case, we do not need an extra buffer at the input port.
- **Multiple-input, single-output (e.g. Fig. 5.b):** In this case, the destination of all messages is the same, namely the actor connected to the output node. Therefore, we can reuse the buffer of this actor to hold also the messages pending at the input ports. To distinguish these messages from the ones actually in the actor's buffer, these pending messages are flagged so that the actor scheduler cannot select them. This flag will be removed from a message whenever the Reo connector decides that this message can actually be delivered to the recipient actor.

As a consequence, the Reo models do not need to include extra buffers at the input, and rather focus on the coordination logic (cf. Fig. 5). Compared to a normal buffer (as in Section 2, disabling a message only delays its execution, whereas its deadline counts since it is generated. Therefore, as before, a queue with more than $\lceil d_{max}/b_{min} \rceil$ messages is not schedulable. Subsection 3.2 describes how we can implement the above solutions in UPPAAL. Section 5 introduces more patterns in which such optimizations are possible.

Client-Server connectors. In our example of client-server we have one client and two servers. The requests and replies between the client and the servers are routed through the connectors shown in Fig. 5. The request sequencer accepts messages from the client through the input port I and routes them to the servers through the output ports O_1 and O_2 in a strict sequence. The reply sequencer accepts messages through input ports I_1 and I_2 and routes them back to the client through output port O, in the order in which they were sent. In both connectors we have a circular configuration of FIFO1 channels, this is to produce an alternating behavior of port selection. For the request sequencing we see that

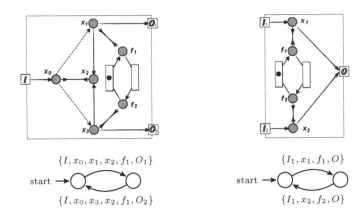

Fig. 5. Request and Reply sequencing

one FIFO1$_1$ channel is initially full, this causes ports $\{I, x_0, x_1, x_2, f_1, O_1\}$ to become enabled when a message is put on input port I and the request flows through output port 1 O_1. Now the FIFO1$_2$ channel is full, so for the next request the ports $\{I, x_0, x_3, x_2, f_1, O_2\}$ are enabled for the next message, causing the data to flow through output port O_2. Similarly, for the request sequencing we have that FIFO1$_1$ channel is initially full, which forces a strict sequencing on the order in which the replies are put into the buffer of the client. To avoid blocking the input ports I_1 or I_2, in principle we need to add extra buffers on the input ports; this extra buffer is avoided by reusing the buffer of Client as we explained above. In the next section, we show how to implement this in UPPAAL. In the sequel, we hide internal ports $\{x_0, x_1, x_2, x_3, f_1, f_2\}$ in the CA models.

3.2   Analysis in UPPAAL

To be able to perform analysis in UPPAAL, we need to give a representation of CA in terms of UPPAAL timed automata. We work with the CA representing each connector, i.e., after the product of the CA of the constituent channels has been computed. Furthermore, all internal ports should be hidden. Therefore, we are not concerned with composing two translated CA.

The idea is that synchronization on port names can be translated to channel synchronization in UPPAAL. We can reuse the *invoke* channel for this purpose. Recall from Section 2 that *invoke* is used for sending messages. An action on an input (resp. output) port is translated to a 'receive' (resp. 'emit') on the channel. Variables in CA can be directly translated to variables in UPPAAL, therefore, data constraints can be simply translated to assignments in UPPAAL.

The main challenge is that transitions in CA may require synchronization on multiple ports, whereas in UPPAAL channels provide binary synchronization. To solve this, whenever multiple ports should synchronize, they are put on consecutive transitions separated by committed locations. This produces an

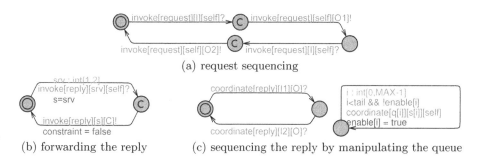

(a) request sequencing

(b) forwarding the reply   (c) sequencing the reply by manipulating the queue

Fig. 6. Integrating Constraint Auomata into UPPAAL

equivalent behavior as these transitions are all taken in zero time and without being interleaved with other automata instances. In the following, we show how to implement the optimizations for the two Reo patterns mentioned previously.

- **Single-input, multiple-output:** In this case (e.g., the request sequencer), the message can immediately be processed and the sender will never be blocked. Therefore, the above translation from CA to timed automata is enough and the CA can directly intermediate between the sender and receiver actors. For example in Fig. 6.(a), the synchronous step on I and O_1 is modeled by first reading a request message on I and then writing the message on O_1. Similarly, I and O_2 are synchronized at the next step.
- **Multiple-input, single output:** As explained in previous subsection, actor buffers need to be extended such that every message has a boolean flag called 'enabled'. As long as this flag is false, the message will be not be selected by the scheduler. The extended *insertInvoke* function (cf. Section 2) assigns variable 'constraint' to the 'enabled' field corresponding to every incoming message. The variable 'constraint' is always set to true, except when a message is sent via a "multiple-input, single-output" connector (cf. Fig. 6.(b)). Via this connector, all messages are directly passed on to the buffer of the single receiver with their 'enabled' flag set to false.

  Another automaton, shown in Fig. 6.(c), captures the coordination logic, i.e., it has the exact form of the constraint automata for the Reo connector. The second automaton in Fig. 6.(c) is an extension to the scheduler automata which follows the coordination logic to enable messages in the queue. Therefore, these messages are enabled at the moment that is allowed by the CA. In this figure q[i] shows a message at index i of the queue which was sent by s[i]. Note that this automaton selects only disabled messages, i.e., it does not consider a message twice. However, as shown in this figure, it does not distinguish between different instances of the same message. Since every message already has a clock assigned to it which keeps track of how long it has been in the queue, we can use that clock to select the oldest message instance. To do so, we need to extend the guard like this:

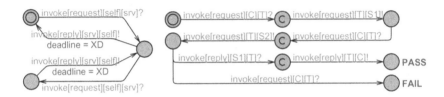

Fig. 7. A client that can send two requests in a row and a corresponding test-case

```
i < tail && ! enable[i] &&
forall (m : int[0,MAX-1]) (
    enable[m] || m>=tail ||
    q[i] != q[m] || s[i] != s[m] ||
    clk[ca[i]]-clk[ca[m]]>=0
)
```

where $\text{clk}[\text{ca}[i]]$ shows the clock assigned to the message at $q[i]$.

Compatibility Check. To check the compatibility of actors coordinated using Reo connectors, we need to compose the behavioral interfaces of the actors with the Constraint Automata models of the Reo connectors. This composed automaton will serve as the basis for test case generation. In this composition, we will use the transformed version of the constraint automata into UPPAAL format. However, the coordinate channels need to be converted back to invoke channel so that the behavioral interfaces can communicate with them. Note that converting Constraint Automata to Timed Automata can ideally be automated such that these conversions would be safe from human error.

Fig. 7 shows a new behavioral interface for the client that accommodates a late reply by incorporating the possibility of sending two requests in a row. On the right side, a (simplified) test case is shown that is generated from the composition of behavioral interfaces of one client and two servers connected with the sequencer Reo connectors. Compared to the test case in Section 2, this test case can identify two servers S1 and S2. This test case cannot reach the FAIL verdict. This is because before the client wants to send a third request, the servers will provide the replies.

4 Actors with Communication Delays

In this section, we show how to extend the modeling framework of Section 2 and the corresponding schedulability analysis to take account of communication delays between actors. We assume here that actors communicate directly, i.e., there is no Reo connector.

We assume a fixed delay for communications between every pair of actors, called their *distance*. This is a reasonable assumption if the communication medium between the actors is fixed for all messages. Therefore, the delays in the whole network can be modeled as a matrix; this matrix will be symmetric if we assume the uplink and downlink connections have the same properties. For example, for the client-server example, we assume the distance 1 between the client and the server (see Fig. 8). The distance of an actor to itself is then zero.

Extension of the actor framework with network delays must properly address the following concerns:

1. The time difference since a message is sent and is executed (at receiver) cannot be smaller than the distance between the sender and the receiver.
2. The deadline associated to each message (specified by the sender) should also include the network delay.
3. The modularity of the analysis techniques should be preserved.

$$
\begin{array}{cc}
 & C \quad S \\
\begin{array}{c} C \\ S \end{array} &
\begin{pmatrix} 0 & 1 \\ 1 & 0 \end{pmatrix}
\end{array}
$$

Fig. 8. The distance matrix

A naive solution to handle network delays is to introduce network buffers, e.g., by adding an extra actor. This actor should delay each message exactly as intended and reduce its remaining deadline correspondingly. This, however, introduces a great overhead in the size of the model: there will be at least a buffer (and its corresponding clocks) between every pair of actors in each direction, i.e., an exponential number of buffers and clocks. Additionally, finding a reasonable upper bound on the size of these buffers is not trivial.

To avoid introducing this overhead, we place the messages directly into the buffer of the receiving actors. To model the distances, the messages in the buffer should be *disabled* as long as the network delay has not passed (concern 1). As explained in Section 2, $clk[msg]$ is reset to zero when msg is added to the buffer. With the distance matrix available, we can use this guard:

$$distance[sender][receiver] < clk[msg]$$

as the enabling condition for each message. Recall that scheduling policies are implemented as guards in the scheduler automata in UPPAAL, which model the selection condition of every message. The above enabling condition can therefore be hard coded into this guard. Thus we avoid extra variables in the buffer representation to capture the enabling conditions of messages, which leads to a very efficient implementation. Additionally, using $clk[msg]$ together with the original deadline of the message satisfies the second concern in a straightforward way.

This approach brings about two new concerns:

4. In this approach, the order of messages in a buffer are based on their sending time rather than their arrival time, i.e., when they become enabled.
5. While preserving schedulability, the buffer of every actor needs to be big enough to contain all messages, including disabled messages.

Since messages may arrive from different actors with different distances, multiplexing them into the same buffer should preserve their order of arrival rather than their order of sending. This is important in scheduling strategies that depend on the arrival order of the messages, e.g., FIFO. To address this issue, we

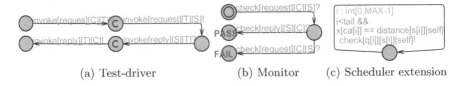

(a) Test-driver   (b) Monitor   (c) Scheduler extension

Fig. 9. Checking compatibility while considering network delays

need to re-implement such schedulers based on the waiting time of messages after they become enabled, which is equal to $clk[msg] - distance[sender][receiver]$; this value should be used when it is not negative.

Finally, we show that the size of buffer for schedulable actors does not need to be increased in presence of network delays. As argued in previous section, disabling a message may only delay its execution, whereas the deadline associated to all messages (disabled or enabled) is still in effect and approaching. Therefore, if there are $n > \lceil d_{max}/b_{min} \rceil$ messages in the buffer, one of them inevitably misses its deadline. This means that individually schedulable actors can still be used provided that the compatibility check is adapted, i.e., modularity is preserved.

4.1 Compatibility Check

Definition 2 defines compatibility as the inclusion of visible traces of the system S in the traces of B, where B is the composition of the behavioral interfaces. The actions in these traces are instantaneous communication of messages; however, in presence of network delays, communication is not instantaneous any more. The main challenge here is to bridge the time gap between the traces in S which capture the sending times and the traces in B which reflect the arrival times.

Definition 3 (Compatibility with delay). *For every trace from S, say $\sigma = (m_1, t_1) \ldots (m_i, t_i) \ldots$, which captures the sending time of each message, there should exist a corresponding trace $\sigma' = (m_1, t_1 + x_1) \ldots (m_i, t_i + x_i) \ldots$ in B, where x_i is the distance between the sender and receiver of m_i (cf. Fig. 8).*

Furthermore, a deadline on the server side (in the behavioral interface) only includes the buffer time and the execution time, whereas a deadline on the client side (in a method) includes also the network delay. In other words, the compatibility check must ensure that the client side deadline is not smaller than the deadline on the server side plus the distance between the actors.

To check compatibility, as explained in Section 2, we generate test cases from the more abstract side, i.e., the composition of the behavioral interfaces B. A test-case in the original framework [17] both drives the system under test and monitors it for unexpected behavior. These tasks must be separated now: a *test-driver* automaton communicates with the system based on the send times (cf. Fig. 9.(a)); a *monitor* automaton checks whether the arrival time of messages

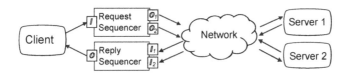

Fig. 10. Graphical illustration of the client-server example

matches the expectations in B (cf. Fig. 9.(b)). The latter is not trivial as the arrival time of a message is when it become enabled. Therefore, the scheduler automata must send a signal on a new channel, *check*, at the actual arrival time of the message, i.e., $clk[msg]$ reaches $distance[sender][receiver]$ (cf. Fig. 9.(c)).

A test-driver is a linear timed automaton generated from a trace taken from B. To be able to drive the system under test, the arrival times must be changed to sending times. As a result, we may need to reorder the transitions of the original trace so that the messages are sent in the correct chronological order.

The monitor automaton is obtained in the same way as in Section 2 when no delays are present. However, it does not drive the system behavior any more. Instead it uses the check channel to see if an actor in the system could receive a message outside the expected time as specified in its behavioral interface. Fig. 9.(b) considers the client/server model in Section 2 where two consecutive request messages are disallowed.

5   Discussion and Future Work

We extended our previous work on schedulability analysis of real-time actors to consider complex networks of actors. On one hand, the coordination language Reo is applied. Reo can be used to take better advantage of off-the-shelf components, where in our case components are modeled as actors. We showed with our simple example that with the help of Reo we can combine actors in such a way that their combination becomes schedulable; in addition, more complicated systems can be built. On the other hand, we showed how to consider communication delays between actors. This is especially important when actors are to be deployed on remote machines.

In an ideal situation, Reo connectors can carry timing information and as such also include the network delays. However, as already mentioned, there is currently no fully satisfactory real-time extension of Reo. As a result, we continue with the assumption that the coordination in Reo connectors happens in negligible time (as in Section 3). Furthermore, we assume that Reo connectors are local to actors. Therefore, the use of a distance matrix as introduced in Section 4 is orthogonal to using Reo. This means that one can directly combine the techniques in the previous two sections to analyze coordinated networks of actors in presence of delays.

In Fig. 10 we illustrate this implementation graphically for our running example. The request and reply sequencing connectors are local to the Client actor.

The real delay happens in the network cloud (formally modeled in the distance matrix). By assuming a fixed delay between every pair of actors, we can essentially look at the network as a black-box, i.e. we don't need to know any details about the network, only how long it takes to send messages through the network.

For checking compatibility, we need to generate the separate test-driver and monitor automata because of the delay in the network. Nevertheless, the test cases should be generated from the composition of the behavioral interfaces and the constraint automata models of the Reo connectors, as depicted in Section 3.

Reo Patterns. In this paper, we considered only two patterns of Reo connectors, i.e., single input or single output. Although this may seem a strict restriction on use of Reo, many useful connectors can still be used. Another example of such connectors is shown in Fig. 11.(a). In this example, the client actor requires two services $m1$ and $m2$ (say 'BookFlight' and 'BookHotel') but there is no server actor that can provide both. The connectors in this figure can be used to connect such a client to two servers each providing one of these services. In this connector filter channels are used which may pass the incoming data only if it matches the pattern provided and thus e.g. distinguishing $m1$ and $m2$. The replies from the two servers can be simply merged using a merger as shown in Fig. 11.(b).

Although applying a multiple input multiple output connector may in general require an extra buffer at its input, this can be avoided again in several kinds of connectors, which need to be considered individually. Another example where we can optimize the implementation is a barrier synchronizer, shown in Fig. 11.(c).

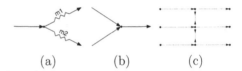

(a)   (b)   (c)

Fig. 11. More Reo connectors

A barrier synchronizer delays the messages from the fast client actors until all inputs are ready and only then forwards them to their destinations. In this connector, the destination actor for each input port is statically known; therefore, the buffer of that actor can be used to store messages on the respective input port.

References

1. Agha, G.: The Structure and Semantics of Actor Languages. In: de Bakker, J.W., Rozenberg, G., de Roever, W.-P. (eds.) REX 1990. LNCS, vol. 489, pp. 1–59. Springer, Heidelberg (1991)
2. Altisen, K., Gößler, G., Sifakis, J.: Scheduler modeling based on the controller synthesis paradigm. Real-Time Systems 23(1-2), 55–84 (2002)
3. Alur, R., Dill, D.L.: A theory of timed automata. Theoretical Computer Science 126(2), 183–235 (1994)
4. Arbab, F.: Reo: A channel-based coordination model for component composition. Mathematical Structures in Computer Science 14, 329–366 (2004)
5. Arbab, F., Baier, C., Rutten, J.J., Sirjani, M.: Modeling component connectors in Reo by constraint automata. In: Proceedings of FOCLASA 2003. ENTCS, vol. 97, pp. 25–46. Elsevier (2004)

6. Behrmann, G., David, A., Larsen, K.G.: A Tutorial on UPPAAL. In: Bernardo, M., Corradini, F. (eds.) SFM-RT 2004. LNCS, vol. 3185, pp. 200–236. Springer, Heidelberg (2004)
7. Closse, E., Poize, M., Pulou, J., Sifakis, J., Venter, P., Weil, D., Yovine, S.: TAXYS: A Tool for the Development and Verification of Real-Time Embedded Systems. In: Berry, G., Comon, H., Finkel, A. (eds.) CAV 2001. LNCS, vol. 2102, pp. 391–395. Springer, Heidelberg (2001)
8. Courcoubetis, C., Yannakakis, M.: Minimum and maximum delay problems in real-time systems. Formal Methods in System Design 1(4), 385–415 (1992)
9. de Boer, F., Chothia, T., Jaghoori, M.M.: Modular Schedulability Analysis of Concurrent Objects in Creol. In: Arbab, F., Sirjani, M. (eds.) FSEN 2009. LNCS, vol. 5961, pp. 212–227. Springer, Heidelberg (2010)
10. de Boer, F.S., Grabe, I., Jaghoori, M.M., Stam, A., Yi, W.: Modeling and Analysis of Thread-Pools in an Industrial Communication Platform. In: Breitman, K., Cavalcanti, A. (eds.) ICFEM 2009. LNCS, vol. 5885, pp. 367–386. Springer, Heidelberg (2009)
11. Fersman, E., Krcal, P., Pettersson, P., Yi, W.: Task automata: Schedulability, decidability and undecidability. Information and Computation 205(8), 1149–1172 (2007)
12. Garcia, J.J.G., Gutierrez, J.C.P., Harbour, M.G.: Schedulability analysis of distributed hard real-time systems with multiple-event synchronization. In: Proc. 12th Euromicro Conference on Real-Time Systems, pp. 15–24. IEEE (2000)
13. Hewitt, C.: Procedural embedding of knowledge in planner. In: Proc. the 2nd International Joint Conference on Artificial Intelligence, pp. 167–184 (1971)
14. Jaghoori, M.M.: Time at your service. Ph.D. dissertation. LIACS, Leiden University (2010)
15. Jaghoori, M.M., Chothia, T.: Timed automata semantics for analyzing Creol. In: Proc. 9th International Workshop on the Foundations of Coordination Languages and Software Architectures (FOCLASA 2010). EPTCS, vol. 30, pp. 108–122 (2010)
16. Jaghoori, M.M., de Boer, F.S., Chothia, T., Sirjani, M.: Schedulability of asynchronous real-time concurrent objects. J. Logic and Alg. Prog. 78(5), 402–416 (2009)
17. Jaghoori, M.M., Longuet, D., de Boer, F.S., Chothia, T.: Schedulability and compatibility of real time asynchronous objects. In: Proc. RTSS 2008, pp. 70–79. IEEE CS (2008)
18. Johnsen, E.B., Owe, O.: An asynchronous communication model for distributed concurrent objects. Software and Systems Modeling 6(1), 35–58 (2007)
19. Kloukinas, C., Yovine, S.: Synthesis of safe, QoS extendible, application specific schedulers for heterogeneous real-time systems. In: Proc. ECRTS 2003, pp. 287–294. IEEE CS (2003)
20. Kokash, N., Changizi, B., Arbab, F.: A Semantic Model for Service Composition with Coordination Time Delays. In: Dong, J.S., Zhu, H. (eds.) ICFEM 2010. LNCS, vol. 6447, pp. 106–121. Springer, Heidelberg (2010)
21. Kupferman, O., Vardi, M.Y., Wolper, P.: Module checking. Information and Computation 164(2), 322–344 (2001)
22. Meseguer, J., Talcott, C.: Semantic Models for Distributed Object Reflection. In: Magnusson, B. (ed.) ECOOP 2002. LNCS, vol. 2374, pp. 1–36. Springer, Heidelberg (2002)
23. Meyer, B.: Eiffel: The language. Prentice-Hall (1992)
24. Ren, S., Agha, G.: RTsynchronizer: language support for real-time specifications in distributed systems. ACM SIGPLAN Notices 30(11), 50–59 (1995)

25. Ren, S., Yu, Y., Chen, N., Marth, K., Poirot, P.-E., Shen, L.: Actors, Roles and Coordinators — A Coordination Model for Open Distributed and Embedded Systems. In: Ciancarini, P., Wiklicky, H. (eds.) COORDINATION 2006. LNCS, vol. 4038, pp. 247–265. Springer, Heidelberg (2006)
26. Sirjani, M., Movaghar, A., Shali, A., de Boer, F.S.: Modeling and verification of reactive systems using Rebeca. Fundamamenta Informaticae 63(4), 385–410 (2004)

A Formal Model of Object Mobility
in Resource-Restricted Deployment Scenarios*

Einar Broch Johnsen, Rudolf Schlatte, and Silvia Lizeth Tapia Tarifa

Department of Informatics, University of Oslo, Norway
{einarj,rudi,sltarifa}@ifi.uio.no

Abstract. Software today is often developed for deployment on different architectures, ranging from sequential machines via multicore and distributed architectures to the cloud. In order to apply formal methods, models of such systems must be able to capture different deployment scenarios. For this purpose, it is desirable to express aspects of low-level deployment at the abstraction level of the modeling language. This paper considers formal executable models of concurrent objects executing with user-defined cost models. Their execution is restricted by deployment components which reflect the execution capacity of groups of objects between observable points in time. We model strategies for object relocation between components. A running example demonstrates how activity on deployment components causes congestion and how object relocation can alleviate this congestion. We analyze the average behavior of models which vary in the execution capacity of deployment components and in object relocation strategies by means of Monte Carlo simulations.

1   Introduction

Software is increasingly often developed as a range of systems. Different versions of a software may provide different functionality and advanced features, depending on target users. In addition to such functional variability, software systems need to adapt to different *deployment scenarios*. For example, *operating systems* adapt to specific hardware and even to different numbers of available cores; *virtualized applications* are deployed on a varying number of (virtual) servers; and *services on the cloud* may need to adapt dynamically to the underlying cloud infrastructure. This kind of adaptability raises new challenges for the modeling and analysis of component-based applications [33]. To apply formal methods to such applications, it is interesting to lift aspects of low-level deployment concerns to the abstraction level of the modeling language. In this paper we propose abstract performance analysis for formal object-oriented models, in which objects may migrate between deployment components that are parametric in the amount of concurrent processing resources they provide to their objects.

The work presented in this paper is based on ABS [20], a modeling language for distributed concurrent objects which communicate by asynchronous method

---

* Partly funded by the EU project FP7-231620 HATS: Highly Adaptable and Trustworthy Software using Formal Models (http://www.hats-project.eu).

F. Arbab and P.C. Ölveczky (Eds.): FACS 2011, LNCS 7253, pp. 187–204, 2012.
© Springer-Verlag Berlin Heidelberg 2012

calls. ABS is an executable language, but still allows abstractions (i.e., functions and abstract data types can be used to specify internal, sequential computations). ABS is a successor of Creol [21], simplifying that language by removing some features such as class inheritance and internal non-deterministic choice, but retaining a concurrent object model similar to Actors [1] and Erlang processes [5]: objects are inherently concurrent, with at most one process active per object. Concurrent objects and actors have attracted attention as an alternative to multi-thread concurrency in object-orientation (e.g., [9]), and been integrated with, e.g., Java [30, 32] and Scala [15]. ABS uses Creol's *cooperative scheduling* of processes inside concurrent objects, which eliminates some common programming errors (specifically, race conditions are much harder to introduce inadvertently) and enables *compositional* verification of models [2, 12].

In order to capture deployment scenarios for ABS models, previous work by the authors proposes an extension of the ABS language with *deployment components* which are parametric in the amount of concurrent activity they allow within a time interval [23]. This allows us to analyze how the amount of concurrent execution resources allocated to a deployment component influences the performance of objects deployed on the component. For this purpose, we work with a notion of timed concurrent objects [8], extended to capture parametric concurrent activities between observable points in time. To validate and compare the concurrent behavior of models under restricted concurrency assumptions, the timed operational semantics of our ABS extension, defined in an SOS style [29], is expressed in rewriting logic [26], which enables the use of Maude [11] as a simulation and analysis tool for ABS models.

The contribution of this paper goes in three directions, compared to our previous work. First, we propose a formalization of *object mobility* in resource-restricted deployment scenarios. This allows models to capture dynamic object deployment, which was not expressible in our previous work. We show how object mobility naturally integrates in ABS in an elegant and simple way, and how it allows dynamic deployment scenarios such as load balancing strategies to be expressed and executed in parallel with the functional parts of the model. This technical contribution complements the work presented in [22], which formalizes load balancing by resource reallocation. Second, user-defined cost models for resource usage are introduced. Where our previous work used fixed cost models for processing capacity, user-defined cost models are given by functional expressions at the abstraction level of the modeling language and introduced in the models in the form of annotations, providing a separation of concerns between the functional aspect of the model and its resource consumption. Third, we extend our simulation tool to support Monte Carlo simulations; i.e., non-determinism in the semantics is resolved in the simulation tool by means of a sequence of pseudo-random numbers which is controlled by a seed when starting a simulation. In principle, this allows the possible execution paths of a model to be systematically inspected up to a given time, and allows us to analyze *average behavior* for models with user-defined cost. We demonstrate the use of Monte Carlo simulations to analyze the resource usage of distributed system models

```
type Pixels = Int;

interface Agent {Session getsession(); Unit free(Session session);}
interface Session {Bool thumbnailImage(Pixels size);}

class SessionImp(Agent agent) implements Session {
  Time start = now;

  Bool thumbnailImage(Pixels size) {
      Int cost = size / 150;
      Int deadline = size / 2400;
      start = now;
      while (cost > 0){[Cost: 1] cost = cost - 1; }
      agent.free(this);
      return (now-start) ≤ deadline);
  }
}

class AgentImp implements Agent {
  Set<Session> sessions = EmptySet;
  Unit free(Session session) {sessions = Insert(sessions, session);}
  Session getsession() {Session session;
    if (emptySet(sessions)) {session = new SessionImp(this);}
    else {session = select(sessions);
          sessions = remove(sessions,session);}
    return session;
  }
}
{// Main block
 DC server = new DeploymentComponent(30);
 Agent a    = new AgentImp() in server;}
```

Fig. 1. A web application model in ABS

in ABS in order to compare the behavior of models ranging over resources and load-balancing strategies. This enables designers to anticipate the behavior of distributed systems at an early stage in the design process.

Paper Overview. Section 2 introduces the load balancing problem developed in the running example of the paper. Section 3 presents timed resource-restricted ABS and our associated simulation tool. Section 4 shows how we can use our interpreter to simulate the behavior of our example ranging over deployment scenarios. Section 5 talks about load balancing strategies, Section 6 discusses related work, and Section 7 concludes the paper.

2   Motivating Example

Let us consider a service which produces *thumbnail images* for images of different *sizes* by scaling the images to a unique reduced-size; e.g., *150 pixels*. The ABS model of such a service is given in Fig. 1 (Sec. 3 contains a detailed explanation of the language syntax). In our example, clients use the *thumbnail* service by first calling the getSession method of an Agent object. An Agent hands out Session objects from a dynamically growing pool. Clients then call the thumbnailImage method of their Session instance, which has as an actual parameter the size of the image. After completing the service, the session object is returned to the agent's pool. Our model defines a user-datatype Pixels as the unit to measure the size of an image.

Let the thumbnailImage method of a session have a certain computation cost and deadline calculated in terms of the parameter size; a service request is successful if it can be handled within the deadline. Let us assume that our service reduces the size of any given image to *150 pixels*, and that we are expecting to process an average of *2400 pixels* per time interval; then we calculated the cost as size/150 and the deadline as size/2400. For simplicity, we abstract from the specific functionality of our service. The *cost annotation* in the while-loop expresses the granularity of resource consumption. In our model, the actual cost cost is decomposed into a number of cumulative steps. In contrast, an annotation with the full cost would express that the computation must happen within one time interval; e.g., [Cost: cost] **skip**.

In the Agent class, the attribute sessions stores a set of Session objects. (ABS has a datatype for sets, with operations emptySet to check for the empty set, denoted EmptySet, select to select an element of a non-empty set, and the usual remove and Insert operators). When a client requests a Session, the Agent takes a session from the available sessions if possible, otherwise it creates a new session. The method free inserts the session in the available sessions of the Agent, and is called by the session itself upon completion of a *thumbnail* service request. This model captures the architecture and control flow of a service oriented application, while abstracting from many functionality and implementation details (such as thread pools, data models, sessions spanning multiple requests, etc.) which can be added to the model if needed.

The main block of the model specifies the initial state for model execution as a *deployment scenario* in which an Agent object is deployed on a deployment component server (of the predefined type DC), which will also contain the Session objects. The parameter to the server specifies its execution capacity in terms of abstract *concurrent resources*, which reflect the amount of potential abstract execution cycles available to the objects deployed on the server between observable points in time. The agent creates concurrently executing Session objects on the same server as needed. It is easy to see that heavy client traffic may lead to congestion on the server, which may in turn cause a lot of unsuccessful requests to the service.

3   Models of Deployed Concurrent Objects in ABS

ABS is an abstract behavioral specification language for distributed concurrent objects [20]. Concurrent objects are, like Actors [1] and Erlang [5] processes, dynamically created and inherently concurrent. ABS is an object-oriented language, so objects are dynamically created instances of classes, with attributes initialized to default type-correct values. An optional *init* method may be used to redefine attributes. Objects are typed by interface and communicate by asynchronous method calls, spawning concurrent activities in the called object. Active

behavior, specified by an optional *run* method, is interleaved with passive behavior, triggered by such asynchronous method calls. Thus, an object has a set
of processes to be executed, which stem from method activations. Among these,
at most one process is *active*. The others are *suspended* on a queue. Process
scheduling is by default non-deterministic, but controlled by *processor release
points* in a cooperative way. ABS is strongly typed: for well-typed programs,
invoked methods are supported by the called object (when not *null*), and formal
and actual parameters match. We assume that programs are well-typed.

Deployment components were proposed in [23] to restrict the inherent concurrency of objects in ABS by mapping the logical concurrency to a model of
physical computing resources. Deployment components abstract from the number and speed of the available physical processors by a notion of concurrent
processing resource, reflecting the processing capacity of a component. Concurrent processing resources can be consumed in parallel or in sequential order,
which reflects the number of processors and their speeds relative to the intervals
between observable points in time. A simple time model suffices to define the
points in time when the executing system is observable. How an object consumes
resources depends on a *cost model*, which reflects the processing costs of different
activities in the objects. In [23], we worked with a simplistic cost model which
assigned a fixed cost to **skip** and to statements with write-access to memory.
In [22], we introduced reflection into this component model, such that an object
could inspect the *load* of its deployment component, and reallocate resources
between deployment components. However, objects were statically deployed on
a deployment component when they were created, and the same simplistic cost
model was used.

In ABS, objects are deployed on deployment components with given amounts
of resources. Objects deployed on a component may consume resources within a
time interval until the component runs out of resources or the objects are otherwise blocked. This way, the logical concurrency model of a group of concurrent
objects is controlled by their associated deployment component. A deployment
component is parametric in the computational resources it offers to a group
of dynamically created objects, which makes it easy to configure deployment
scenarios varying in their concurrent resources.

In this paper, we generalize our previous approach by allowing a user-defined
cost model in which the processing costs of a statement are given in terms of
a cost expression e which depends on the current state of the object and the
local variables of the active process. The expression is introduced into the ABS
syntax as an optional annotation [Cost: e] s to statements s; thus, we obtain
a separation of concerns between the cost and functional behavior of models.
Statements without annotations are given a default cost and models without
annotations are valid models in the resource-restricted extension to ABS. Furthermore, the statement **goto**(e) is introduced to the language. This statement
expresses object mobility such that an object may relocate to a target deployment component e. This way, deployment scenarios may be modeled in which

Syntactic categories.   *Definitions.*
C, I, m in Names $IF ::= $ **interface** $I \{ \overline{[Sg]} \}$
g in Guard $CL ::= $ **class** $C [(\overline{I\ x})]$ [**implements** $\overline{I}$] $\{ [\overline{I\ x};] \overline{M} \}$
s in Stmt $Sg ::= I\ m\ ([\overline{I\ x}])$
x in Var $M ::= Sg \{ [\overline{I\ x};]\ s \}$
e in Expr $g ::= b \mid x? \mid g \wedge g$
b in BoolExpr $s ::= s; s \mid [Cost : e]\, s \mid$ **skip** $\mid x = rhs$
r in Resource $\mid$ **suspend** $\mid$ **await** $g \mid$ **while** $b \{ s \} \mid$ **goto**(e)
                      $\mid$ **if** b **then** $\{ s \}$ [**else** $\{ s \}$] $\mid$ **return** e
               $e ::= x \mid b \mid r \mid$ **this** $\mid$ **thiscomp** $\mid$ **now** $\mid$ **total**
                      $\mid$ **load**$(e) \mid$ **random**(e)
          $rhs ::= e \mid cm \mid$ **new** $C(\overline{e})$ [**in** e] $\mid$ **component** (e)
            $cm ::= [e]!m(\overline{e}) \mid [e].m(\overline{e}) \mid x.$**get**

Fig. 2. ABS syntax. Terms such as $\overline{e}$ and $\overline{x}$ denote lists over the corresponding syntactic categories, square brackets [] denote optional elements.

objects dynamically change deployment components. For readability, we present the syntax of the full language with the proposed extensions below.

Figure 2 gives the syntax of timed ABS with deployment components. A *program* consists of interface and class definitions and a *main block* to configure the initial state. *IF* defines an interface with name *I* and method signatures *Sg*. A class implements a set $\overline{I}$ of interfaces, which specify types for its instances. *CL* defines a class with name *C*, interfaces $\overline{I}$, class parameters and state variables *x* (of type *I*), and methods *M*. (The *attributes* of the class are both its parameters and declared fields.) A method signature *Sg* declares the return type *I* of a method with name *m* and formal parameters $\overline{x}$ of types $\overline{I}$. *M* defines a method with signature *Sg*, a list of local variable declarations $\overline{x}$ of types $\overline{I}$, and a statement *s*.

Statements. Assignment $x = rhs$, sequential composition $s_1; s_2$, **skip**, **if**, **while**, and **return** *e* are standard. The statement **goto**(e) moves the object to deployment component *e*. The statement **suspend** unconditionally releases the processor by suspending the active process. The guard *g* controls processor release in statements **await** *g*, and consists of Boolean expressions *b* over attributes and return tests *x*? (see below). If *g* evaluates to false, the current process is *suspended*. In this case, any enabled process from the pool of suspended processes may be activated. The scheduling of processes is *cooperative* in the sense that processes explicitly yield control and execution in one process may enable the further execution in another. The annotated statement [Cost:*e*] *s* expresses that the cost of executing *s* will be *e* resources, where *e* is evaluated in the current state of the object.

Expressions rhs include pure expressions *e*, communications *cm*, and the creation of deployment components and objects. The expression **component** (e) creates a component with *e* concurrent resources. Resources are modeled by a type `Resource` which extends the natural numbers with an "unlimited resource" ω. The set of concurrent objects deployed on a component, representing

$$cn ::= \epsilon \mid obj \mid msg \mid fut \mid cn\ cn$$
$$obj ::= o(\sigma, p, q)$$
$$p ::= \{\sigma|s\} \mid idle$$

Fig. 3. The syntax for timed runtime configurations

the logically concurrent activities, may grow dynamically. Object creation **new** $C(\bar{e})$ has an optional clause **in** e to specify the targeted deployment component: here the C object is to be deployed on component e. (If the target component is omitted, the new object will be deployed on the same component as its parent. The behavior of ABS models without deployment restrictions on their functional behavior is captured by a main deployment component with ω resources.)

Pure expressions e are variables x, Boolean expressions b, resources r, **this** (the object's identifier) and **thiscomp** (the object's current deployment component), and **now**, which returns the current time. Timed ABS uses an implicit time model [8], comparable to a system clock which updates every n milliseconds (representing a time interval). Time values are totally ordered by the less-than operator; comparing two time values results in a Boolean value suitable for guards in **await** statements. From an object's local perspective, the passage of time is indirectly observable via **await** statements. Time advances when no other activity may occur. This model of time is used to handle the amount of concurrent activity allowed within a time interval in order to model resource constraints for different deployment scenarios. The total number of resources allocated to objects on the current deployment component are given by **total**, and the average load on the component for the last e time intervals by **load**(e). The expression **random**(e) returns some integer value between 0 and the value of e. (The full language includes a functional expression language with standard operators for data types such as strings, integers, lists, sets, maps, and tuples. These are omitted here, and explained when used in the examples.)

Communications cm are based on asynchronous method calls. After making an asynchronous call $x = e!m(\bar{e})$, the caller may proceed without waiting for the method reply. Here x is a *future variable*, which refers to a return value which may still need to be computed. Two operations on future variables control synchronization in ABS [20]. First, the guard **await** x? *suspends* the active process until a return to the call associated with x has arrived. This suspends execution of the process, but allows other processes to run. Second, the return value is retrieved by the expression x.**get**, which *blocks* all execution in the object until the return value is available. Two commonly used communication patterns are now explained; the statement sequence $x = e!m(\bar{e});\ y = x$.**get** encodes a *blocking call*, conveniently abbreviated $y = e.m(\bar{e})$ (often referred to as a synchronous call), whereas the statement sequence $x = e!m(\bar{e});$ **await** x?; $y = x$.**get** encodes a non-blocking, *preemptable call.*

(RESTRICTEDEXEC)
$$\frac{thiscomp(o) = dc \quad [\![e]\!]^t_{\sigma ol} = c \quad c \leq n}{o(\sigma, \{l|s\}, q) \; cl(t) \; cn \rightarrow o(\sigma', p', q') \; cl(t) \; cn'}$$
$$o(\sigma, \{l|[\text{cost}:e]s\}, q) \; dc(n, u, \overline{h}) \; cl(t) \; cn$$
$$\rightarrow o(\sigma', p', q') \; dc(n - c, u + c, \overline{h}) \; cl(t) \; cn'$$

(RUNTOCOMPLETION)
$$\frac{cn \; cl(t) \xrightarrow{!} cn' \; cl(t) \quad cn' \xrightarrow{!}_\tau cn''}{\{cn \; cl(t)\} \rightarrow_\tau \{cn'' \; cl(t+1)\}}$$

(RESET)
$$\frac{u > 0}{dc(n, u, \overline{h}) \rightarrow_\tau dc(n + u, 0, (\overline{h}; u))}$$

Fig. 4. A reduction semantics for timed resource-restricted execution

3.1   Operational Semantics

The operational semantics of ABS is given as an SOS [29] style reduction system. We briefly outline the semantics here in order to explain the extension with user-defined cost annotations (the full details may be found in[20]). The runtime syntax is given in Fig. 3. A configuration cn consists of objects obj, messages msg, and futures fut. An object $o(\sigma, p, q)$ has an identity o, a state σ, and active process p, and a queue of pending processes q. The active process consists of a list of statements s to be executed in the context of local variable bindings σ, unless the active process is $idle$ (in which case a pending process from q is scheduled for execution). Messages represent method calls and futures represent method returns.

Given a reduction relation $\rightarrow$, a *run* is in general a possibly non-terminating sequence of terms $t_0, t_1, \ldots$ such that $t_i \rightarrow t_{i+1}$. Let $t \xrightarrow{!} t'$ denote that t' is the final term of a terminating run from the initial term t; i.e., there is no term t'' such that $t' \rightarrow t''$. We shall denote by $\rightarrow$ the reduction relation of ABS, which is defined inductively over the legal configurations cn. For an object $o(\sigma, \{l|s\}, q)$, there are in particular rules which reduce the head of the statement list s, defined by cases for the statements of ABS. In addition, there is a rule for binding a message msg to a method activation p, which is put into the object queue q, and for scheduling a suspended process from q when the active process is idle. (Observe that many processes may be schedulable at the same time, which leads to non-determinism in the semantics.) ABS objects are asynchronous in the sense that no reduction rules have two objects on the left hand side.

The runtime syntax of *timed* runtime configurations with deployment components is given by the following extension of the syntax of Figure 3:

$$tcn ::= \{ \; cl(t) \; cn \; \} \qquad\qquad cn ::= dc(n, u, \overline{h}) \; | \; \ldots$$

A *timed configuration* consists of a configuration cn and a clock $cl(t)$ (where t is the current global time). Extended configurations cn may contain deployment components $dc(n, u, \overline{h})$, where dc is the identity of the component, n is the number of available processing resources, u the used resources, and $\overline{h}$ the (possibly empty) sequence of resource usage over time. Observe that the standard ABS reduction relation $\rightarrow$ is not defined for active processes in which the head of the statement list is annotated. Figure 4 defines the extension to $\rightarrow$ for such annotated statement lists, a reduction relation $\rightarrow_\tau$ which expresses the effect of advancing time, and the timed resource-restricted reduction relation $\rightarrow_r$.

The rule RESTRICTEDEXEC extends the relation $\rightarrow$ to capture the reduction of an object o in which the head of the statement list in the active process has an annotation of cost e. This can be done according to the standard rules for $\rightarrow$ if the current deployment component of o has enough resources to do a reduction step. In this rule, we use thiscomp(o) to denote the current deployment component of o, $[\![e]\!]_\sigma^t$ to denote the evaluation of an expression e in the substitution σ at time t. Observe that the resources required to do the reduction are subtracted from the available resources of the deployment component and added to its used resources. Rule RESET expresses the effect of time advance on a deployment component; the available resources n are reset to amount of resources allocated to the component, and the history of resource consumption is extended with the the used resources u of the previous time interval.

The rule RUNTOCOMPLETION captures the timed resource-restricted reduction relation $\rightarrow_r$ between timed configurations. Time advances from a timed configuration $\{cn\ cl(t)\}$ by the reduction relation $\rightarrow_r$ if cn can be reduced to a normal form cn' by application of $\rightarrow$, after which all deployment components in cn' have been reset by rule $\rightarrow_\tau$. A *run* of a timed, resource-restricted ABS model is a (possibly non-terminating) sequence of configurations $tcn_0, tcn_1, tcn_2, \ldots$ such that $tcn_i \rightarrow_r tcn_{i+1}$, which represent the configurations at the *observable points in time* during the execution of the timed resource-restricted ABS model. Observe that a non-terminating run by the ABS reduction relation $\rightarrow$ corresponds to an infinitely fast execution in timed, resource-restricted ABS; there is no observable successor state.

3.2   ABS Analysis Tool

The SOS semantics of timed, resource-restricted ABS has previously been translated to rewriting logic [26] and implemented in Maude [11], to provide an interpreter for ABS models for the fixed cost model of our previous work. The details of this rewriting logic semantics for ABS are reported in [22]. As a technical contribution of this paper, we have extended this interpreter to accomodate user-defined cost models, as defined above, and the **goto**-statement and **random**-expression proposed in this paper. Whereas the implementation of the **goto**-statement translates into an assignment of the **thiscomp** field of an object, the **random**-expression is implemented such that it depends on a sequence of pseudo-random numbers, controlled by a *seed* provided as an argument to the execution of the model. The sequence of pseudo-random numbers is also used to make *scheduling decisions* in the simulator of the ABS semantics; i.e., if an object has a list of n schedulable processes in its queue, the interpreter will select for execution the **random**(n)'th process from this list. This interpreter for the semantics of timed resource-restricted ABS is used as a basis for Monte Carlo simulations. Whereas our previous work on deployment components could only

```
...
interface Client { }

class AsyncClientImp (Int cycles, Int frequency, Pixels size, Agent a)
implements Client {
 Unit run() {
    Time t = now;
    Fut<Session> f = a!getsession(); await f?; Session s = f.get;
    s!thumbnailImage(size*(random(3)+1));
    cycles = cycles-1;
    if (cycles > 0) {
      Int jitter = 3-(random(4)+1);
      await duration(frequency+jitter, frequency+jitter);
      this!run(); }
    }
}
{// Main block
  ...
  new AsyncClientImp(15,4,5000,a);
  new AsyncClientImp(15,3,4000,a);
  new AsyncClientImp(15,3,3000,a);
  new AsyncClientImp(15,4,2000,a); }
```

Fig. 5. A configurable asynchronous client which provides the workload scenario

simulate one arbitrary run of the model, this extension allows us to simulate n runs with different sequences of pseudo-random numbers, which in principle allows us to exhaust the full state space of executions. The individual runs of the Monte Carlo simulations use the ABS interpreter, a query language allows us to extract information from the runtime states of these simulations, and to combine this information from the different runs of a deployment scenario. The use of this analysis tool is shown in the following sections.

4   Comparing Resource-Restricted Behaviors

In order to investigate the effects of specific deployment scenarios on the timing behavior of timed software models, we use the analysis tool to simulate and test ABS models. The *test purpose* for these scenarios using *Monte Carlo simulations* is to reach a conclusion on whether redeployment on a different configuration leads to an observable difference in timing behavior. We compare the behavior of ABS models with the same functional behavior and workload when the models are deployed on components with different amounts of resources.

We extend the example given in Section 2 with a workload scenario. Figure 5 shows the implementation of a *configurable asynchronous client*. The run method of an AsyncClientImp object has as actual parameters the *number of images* to process represented by the parameter cycles; the frequency of requests to the *thumbnail* service, represented by the parameter frequency and a *random jitter* value in the interval *[-2, +2]*; and a *varying image size* given by the parameter size which varies the sizes of the images in the interval *[size, 4·size]*.

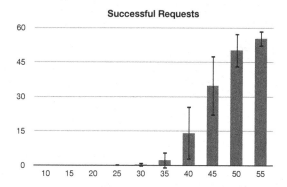

Fig. 6. Single-server simulation results: number of successful, i.e., non-timeout responses for 60 requests, with server capacity varying between 10 and 55. The numbers show mean and standard deviation of 100 runs for each server capacity.

Objects of the `AsyncClientImp` class are used to model the expected usage scenario and run with unlimited resources.

Figure 6 shows simulations results using four asynchronous clients running concurrently and making a total of 60 thumbnail request with a frequency ranging between [1,6] and image's size ranging over [2 000, 20 000] pixels. As we can see from Fig. 6, the server is basically unresponsive up to 35 resources, at 45 resources it can successfully handle approximately 50% of the requests, and above 50 resources it can successfully handle more than 75% of the requests.

5   Load Balancing Strategies

ABS models may be augmented with *load balancing strategies* with the aim of decreasing congestion and thus improving the overall quality of service compared to models with static deployment scenarios. Load balancing strategies may be expressed in ABS using the resource-related language constructs **total**, **load**, and **goto**.

We illustrate how ABS models may be augmented with load balancing strategies using the running example of the thumbnail image service, and compare the results of load balancing to the results for basic deployment scenarios presented in Section 4. In this section we model and explore two different load balancing strategies; (1) a *load-balancing agent* which moves sessions to a backup server when the load on the main server is above a given threshold, and (2) *self-monitoring sessions* which move themselves to the backup server if the processing of their requests takes more than a given time limit. Both of these dynamic deployment scenarios are analyzed using the same workload scenario as in Section 4. Other, more elaborate load-balancing strategies may be modeled in the same style.

```
interface Agent {Session getsession(); Unit free(Session session);}
interface Session {Bool thumbnailImage(Pixels size);
                   Unit moveto(DC server);}

class SessionImp(Agent agent) implements Session {
 Time start = now;
 Bool thumbnailImage(Pixels size){ ... } // As before
 Unit moveto(DC server){if (thiscomp != server){
                        [Cost: 1] goto(server);[Cost: 1] skip;}}}

class AgentImp(DC origserver, DC backupserver) implements Agent {
 Set<Session> sessions = EmptySet;
 Unit free(Session session){ ... // As before
   session!moveTo(origserver);}

 Session getsession() { Session session;
  if (emptySet(sessions)){session = new SessionImp(this);}
  else {session = select(sessions);
   sessions = remove(session,sessions);}
  if ((total - load(4)) < total/3){ // Move session to backup server
   session!moveto(backupserver);}
  return session;}}
```

Fig. 7. An agent which performs load-balancing for the thumbnail image service

Figure 7 shows the ABS model of a load-balancing agent which moves sessions to a backup server when the load on the main server increases beyond $2/3$ of the total resources allocated to the main server. This is a simple load balancing strategy which tries to minimize the amount of work done on the backup server, while maintaining an acceptable quality of service. The cost annotation of the **goto** statement expresses the cost of moving the object; i.e., the marshaling of the object. The cost annotation of the succeeding **skip** statement expresses the corresponding cost of demarshaling, which take place on server. For simplicity, we have here set both cost values to 1. Figure 8 shows an ABS model of self-monitoring session objects which move themselves to the backup server if the execution of the current request takes more than a given amount of time (the limit). Here, the active method run serves as a monitor. Once the session has moved, the monitor sets timeToMove to infinite time ∞ to ensure that it will not be applied again to the same request. The next request resets timeToMove to the limit again, which reenables the monitor.

Simulations of Load-Balancing Deployment Scenarios. For the simulations of the running example augmented with load balancing strategies, we added a second deployment component to the initial configurations of Section 4, and let both deployment components have the same capacity. Figure 9 summarizes all three scenarios (single server, smart agent, and self-balancing sessions) with deployment component capacities ranging from 10 to 55. It can be seen that the load balancing strategies outperform the single server in all cases (as they should, since these scenarios have twice the total number of resources). The simulations show that under constrained scenarios, the monitor strategy outperforms the smart agent for our example model and usage scenario.

```
interface Agent { Session getsession(); Unit free(Session session);}
interface Session { Bool thumbnailImage(Pixel size); }

class SessionImp(Agent agent,  Time limit, DC backupserver)
implements Session {
 Time start = now; Bool active = False;
 Time timeToMove = limit; DC origserver = thiscomp;

 Bool thumbnailImage(Pixels size) { // With monitor
  Int cost = size/150; Int deadline = size/2400;
  start = now; active = True; timeToMove= now+limit;
  while (cost > 0)  {[Cost: 1] cost = cost - 1; suspend;}
  active = False;  agent!free(this);
  Bool success = (now-start) <= deadline;
  if (thiscomp != origserver){[Cost: 1] goto(server);[Cost: 1] skip;}
  return  (success);}

Unit run() { // The monitor
 await (active ∧ now > timeToMove);
 [Cost: 1] goto(backupserver); [Cost: 1] skip;
 timeToMove = ∞;
 this!run();}
}

class AgentImp(Time limit, DC backupserver) implements Agent {
 // Same as in Fig. 1 but creating Session objects
 // with a parameter backupserver
}
```

Fig. 8. Self-monitoring session objects for a thumbnail image service

Our simulation tool can also record behavior of models over time. Figure 10 shows the time progression of the average load (of 100 simulation runs) on the two deployment components under both balancing strategies, with main and backup deployment component both running with 35 resources. The simulation runs vary quite a bit, with standard deviation around 15 for all servers, except for the main server under the monitor strategy, which exhibits a standard deviation of approximately 10 throughout the run. It can also be seen that the server utilization under the monitor strategy is more stable, with the main server load around 30 (of 35) on average, and less work being transferred to the backup server. In summary, our simulation tools can be used both for quantitative insights into aggregated model behavior, and for understanding of timed behavior of models.

6   Related Work

Asynchronously communicating software units, known from Actors and Erlang, are interesting due to their inherent compositionality. Concurrent objects with asynchronous method calls and futures combine asynchronous communication with object orientation [2, 9, 30, 32]. In these models, each software unit is also a unit of concurrency. There is a vast literature on formal models of mobility, based on, e.g., agents, ambient calculi, and process algebras, which is

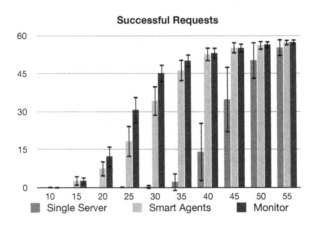

Fig. 9. Simulation results of single server, smart agent and monitoring load balancing strategies: number of successful, i.e., non-timeout responses for 60 requests, with server capacity varying between 10 and 55. The numbers show mean and standard deviation of 100 runs for each server capacity for each scenario.

typically concerned with maintaining correct interactions between the moving entities with respect to, e.g., security, link failure, or location failure. For non-functional properties, access to shared resources have been studied through type and effect systems (e.g., [17, 18]), QoS-aware processes proposed for negotiating contracts [27], and space control achieved by typing for space-aware processes [7]. Closer to our work, timed synchronous CCS-style processes can be compared for speed using faster-than bisimulation [25], albeit without notions of mobility or location. We are not aware of other formal models connecting execution capacities to locations as in the deployment components studied in our paper.

This paper is part of ongoing work on resource-restricted execution contexts for concurrent objects [4, 22, 23]. Whereas [4] considers memory usage, deployment components with parametric concurrent resources were introduced in [23], extending work on a timed rewriting logic semantics for Creol [8]. A follow-up paper considers resources as first-class citizens of the language, formalizing the semantics of ABS with resource reallocation in rewriting logic [22]. In contrast, the present paper considers object mobility using a **goto** statement to allow an object to move to another deployment component, formalized in a more abstract SOS semantics. Relocation is possible due to the inherent compositionality of concurrent objects [12]: processes are encapsulated inside objects and the state of other objects can only be accessed through asynchronous method calls. This way the object is in control of its own location, which fits with the encapsulation of both state and control in the concurrent object model. Resource reallocation and object mobility are in a sense complementary means to achieve load balancing: both have applications where they seem most natural.

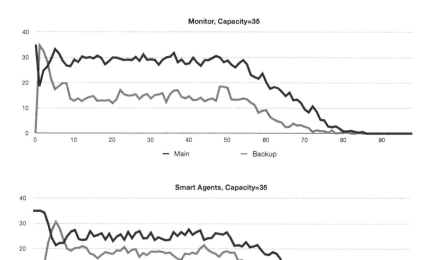

Fig. 10. Main and backup server with 35 resources, using the monitoring (top) and smart agent (bottom) load-balancing strategies. Mean value of 100 runs plotted, standard deviation was around 15 resources (not plotted) throughout, with different runs exhibiting load spikes at different points in time.

Techniques and methodologies for predictions or analysis of non-functional properties are based on either *measurement* or *modeling*. Measurement-based approaches apply to existing implementations, using dedicated profiling or tracing tools like, e.g., JMeter or LoadRunner. Model-based approaches allow abstraction from specific system details, but depend on parameters provided by domain experts [13]. A survey of model-based performance analysis techniques is given in [6]. Formal approaches using Petri Nets, game theory, and timed automata (e.g., [10, 14, 24]) have been applied in the embedded software domain, but also to the schedulability of tasks in concurrent objects [19]. That work complements ours as it does not consider resource restrictions on the concurrency model, but associates deadlines with method calls.

Work on object-oriented models with resource constraints is more scarce. Based on a UML profile for schedulability, performance and time, the informally defined Core Scenario Model (CSM) [28] targets questions in performance model building. CSM has a notion of resource context, which reflects the set of resources used by an operation. CSM aims to bridge the gap between UML specifications and techniques to generate performance models [6]. UML models with stochastic annotations for performance prediction have been proposed for components [16]. Closer to our work is a VDM++ extension to simulate embedded real-time systems [31], in which architectures are explicitly modeled using CPUs and buses, and resources statically bound to the CPUs. However, their work does not address relocation and load balancing strategies.

7 Discussion and Future Work

As software is increasingly developed to be deployed on a variety of architectures, it is important to be able to analyze the behavior of a model under different resource assumptions. ABS uses deployment components with parametric resources to express deployment scenarios for high-level executable models. This paper proposes a primitive for relocating concurrent objects between deployment components, expressed at the abstraction level of ABS, which integrates with the formal framework of deployment components in an elegant and simple way. Furthermore, we consider the problem of modeling systems with different load balancing strategies by allowing objects to move between deployment components, depending on the work load of their component. We demonstrate how a simple language extension is sufficient to naturally express dynamic object relocation strategies in this setting; our example shows how traffic on deployment components may cause congestion in the model, resulting in performance degradation for given deployment scenarios, and how load balancing strategies can be used to dynamically alleviate the congestion and thus to improve the overall performance of the model in a given deployment scenario. For the analysis of the deployment scenarios, we have extended ABS with a random expression and our simulation tool to do Monte Carlo simulations, which allows us to observe average behavior for the deployment scenarios.

As a technical contribution of this paper, we have extended ABS with support for user-defined cost models in terms of annotations, which provide a much more flexible framework for expressing processing cost than in our previous work. For example, the cost of an assignment may depend on the cost of evaluating a function on the right hand side of the assignment, which again may depend on the size of the input to the function. While this is expressible by user annotations as proposed in this paper, it leaves significant responsibility with the modeler. In future work, we will consider how the modeler may be assisted in this task by means of tools. In particular, static analysis techniques may in many cases be applicable to approximate the actual cost of a statement in terms of worst-case upper bounds (e.g., following [3]). In a recent paper [4], we have shown how static analysis may be combined with simulation for the memory analysis of untimed ABS models. However, it remains to combine this approach with user-defined cost models and time, and to integrate the tools. In a more long term perspective, we are interested in how to combine different user-defined resources in the same model.

References

1. Agha, G.A.: ACTORS: A Model of Concurrent Computations in Distributed Systems. The MIT Press, Cambridge (1986)

2. Ahrendt, W., Dylla, M.: A system for compositional verification of asynchronous objects. Science of Computer Programming,
   `http://dx.doi.org/10.1016/j.scico.2010.08.003`
   (available online August 2010)

3. Albert, E., Arenas, P., Genaim, S., Puebla, G.: Closed-form upper bounds in static cost analysis. Journal of Automated Reasoning 46, 161–203 (2011)

4. Albert, E., Genaim, S., Gómez-Zamalloa, M., Johnsen, E.B., Schlatte, R., Tapia Tarifa, S.L.: Simulating Concurrent Behaviors with Worst-Case Cost Bounds. In: Butler, M., Schulte, W. (eds.) FM 2011. LNCS, vol. 6664, pp. 353–368. Springer, Heidelberg (2011)

5. Armstrong, J.: Programming Erlang: Software for a Concurrent World. Pragmatic Bookshelf (2007)

6. Balsamo, S., Marco, A.D., Inverardi, P., Simeoni, M.: Model-based performance prediction in software development: A survey. IEEE Transactions on Software Engineering 30(5), 295–310 (2004)

7. Barbanera, F., Bugliesi, M., Dezani-Ciancaglini, M., Sassone, V.: Space-aware ambients and processes. Theoretical Computer Science 373(1-2), 41–69 (2007)

8. Bjørk, J., Johnsen, E.B., Owe, O., Schlatte, R.: Lightweight time modeling in Timed Creol. Electronic Proceedings in Theoretical Computer Science 36, 67–81 (2010); Proceedings of 1st Intl. Workshop on Rewriting Techniques for Real-Time Systems (RTRTS 2010)

9. Caromel, D., Henrio, L.: A Theory of Distributed Object. Springer (2005)

10. Chakrabarti, A., de Alfaro, L., Henzinger, T.A., Stoelinga, M.: Resource Interfaces. In: Alur, R., Lee, I. (eds.) EMSOFT 2003. LNCS, vol. 2855, pp. 117–133. Springer, Heidelberg (2003)

11. Clavel, M., Durán, F., Eker, S., Lincoln, P., Martí-Oliet, N., Meseguer, J., Talcott, C.: All About Maude - A High-Performance Logical Framework. LNCS, vol. 4350. Springer, Heidelberg (2007)

12. de Boer, F.S., Clarke, D., Johnsen, E.B.: A Complete Guide to the Future. In: De Nicola, R. (ed.) ESOP 2007. LNCS, vol. 4421, pp. 316–330. Springer, Heidelberg (2007)

13. Epifani, I., Ghezzi, C., Mirandola, R., Tamburrelli, G.: Model evolution by run-time parameter adaptation. In: Proc. 31st Intl. Conf. on Software Engineering (ICSE 2009), pp. 111–121. IEEE (2009)

14. Fersman, E., Krcál, P., Pettersson, P., Yi, W.: Task automata: Schedulability, decidability and undecidability. Information and Computation 205(8), 1149–1172 (2007)

15. Haller, P., Odersky, M.: Scala actors: Unifying thread-based and event-based programming. Theoretical Computer Science 410(2-3), 202–220 (2009)

16. Happe, J., Koziolek, H., Reussner, R.: Parametric performance contracts for software components with concurrent behaviour. In: Proc. Third Intl. Workshop on Formal Aspects of Component Software (FACS 2006). Electronic Notes in Theoretical Computer Science, vol. 182, pp. 91–106 (2007)

17. Hennessy, M.: A Distributed Pi-Calculus. Cambridge University Press (2007)

18. Igarashi, A., Kobayashi, N.: Resource usage analysis. ACM Transactions on Programming Languages and Systems 27(2), 264–313 (2005)

19. Jaghoori, M.M., de Boer, F.S., Chothia, T., Sirjani, M.: Schedulability of asynchronous real-time concurrent objects. Journal of Logic and Algebraic Programming 78(5), 402–416 (2009)

20. Johnsen, E.B., Hähnle, R., Schäfer, J., Schlatte, R., Steffen, M.: ABS: A Core Language for Abstract Behavioral Specification. In: Aichernig, B.K., de Boer, F.S., Bonsangue, M.M. (eds.) FMCO 2010. LNCS, vol. 6957, pp. 142–164. Springer, Heidelberg (2011)

21. Johnsen, E.B., Owe, O.: An asynchronous communication model for distributed concurrent objects. Software and Systems Modeling 6(1), 35–58 (2007)

22. Johnsen, E.B., Owe, O., Schlatte, R., Tapia Tarifa, S.L.: Dynamic Resource Reallocation Between Deployment Components. In: Dong, J.S., Zhu, H. (eds.) ICFEM 2010. LNCS, vol. 6447, pp. 646–661. Springer, Heidelberg (2010)

23. Johnsen, E.B., Owe, O., Schlatte, R., Tapia Tarifa, S.L.: Validating Timed Models of Deployment Components with Parametric Concurrency. In: Beckert, B., Marché, C. (eds.) FoVeOOS 2010. LNCS, vol. 6528, pp. 46–60. Springer, Heidelberg (2011)

24. Katelman, M., Meseguer, J., Hou, J.: Redesign of the LMST Wireless Sensor Protocol Through Formal Modeling and Statistical Model Checking. In: Barthe, G., de Boer, F.S. (eds.) FMOODS 2008. LNCS, vol. 5051, pp. 150–169. Springer, Heidelberg (2008)

25. Lüttgen, G., Vogler, W.: Bisimulation on speed: A unified approach. Theoretical Computer Science 360(1-3), 209–227 (2006)

26. Meseguer, J.: Conditional rewriting logic as a unified model of concurrency. Theoretical Computer Science 96, 73–155 (1992)

27. De Nicola, R., Ferrari, G.-L., Montanari, U., Pugliese, R., Tuosto, E.: A Process Calculus for QoS-Aware Applications. In: Jacquet, J.-M., Picco, G.P. (eds.) COORDINATION 2005. LNCS, vol. 3454, pp. 33–48. Springer, Heidelberg (2005)

28. Petriu, D.B., Woodside, C.M.: An intermediate metamodel with scenarios and resources for generating performance models from UML designs. Software and System Modeling 6(2), 163–184 (2007)

29. Plotkin, G.D.: A structural approach to operational semantics. Journal of Logic and Algebraic Programming 60-61, 17–139 (2004)

30. Schäfer, J., Poetzsch-Heffter, A.: JCoBox: Generalizing Active Objects to Concurrent Components. In: D'Hondt, T. (ed.) ECOOP 2010. LNCS, vol. 6183, pp. 275–299. Springer, Heidelberg (2010)

31. Verhoef, M., Larsen, P.G., Hooman, J.: Modeling and Validating Distributed Embedded Real-Time Systems with VDM++. In: Misra, J., Nipkow, T., Sekerinski, E. (eds.) FM 2006. LNCS, vol. 4085, pp. 147–162. Springer, Heidelberg (2006)

32. Welc, A., Jagannathan, S., Hosking, A.: Safe futures for Java. In: Proc. Object Oriented Programming, Systems, Languages, and Applications (OOPSLA 2005), pp. 439–453. ACM Press, New York (2005)

33. Yacoub, S.M.: Performance Analysis of Component-Based Applications. In: Chastek, G.J. (ed.) SPLC 2002. LNCS, vol. 2379, pp. 299–315. Springer, Heidelberg (2002)

The Logic of XACML

Carroline Dewi Puspa Kencana Ramli, Hanne Riis Nielson, and Flemming Nielson

Department of Informatics and Mathematical Modelling
Danmarks Tekniske Universitet Lyngby, Denmark
{cdpu,riis,nielson}@imm.dtu.dk

Abstract. We study the international standard XACML 3.0 for describing security access control policy in a compositional way. Our main contribution is to
derive a logic that precisely captures the idea behind the standard and to formally
define the semantics of the policy combining algorithms of XACML. To guard
against modelling artefacts we provide an alternative way of characterizing the
policy combining algorithms and we formally prove the equivalence of these approaches. This allows us to pinpoint the shortcoming of previous approaches to
formalization based either on Belnap logic or on $\mathcal{D}$-algebra.

1 Introduction

XACML (eXtensible Access Control Markup Language) is an approved OASIS [1] Standard access control language [1,14]. XACML describes both an access control policy language and a request/response language. The policy language is used to express access
control policies (*who can do what when*) while the request/response language expresses
queries about whether a particular access should be allowed (*requests*) and describes
answers to those queries (*responses*).

In order to manage modularity in access control, XACML constructs policies into
several components, namely *PolicySet*, *Policy* and *Rule*. A PolicySet is a collection of
other PolicySets or Policies whereas a Policy consists of one or more Rules. A Rule is
the smallest component of XACML policy and each Rule only either grants or denies
an access. As an illustration, suppose we have access control policies used within a
National Health Care System. The system is composed of several access control policies
of local hospitals. Each local hospital has its own policies such as patient policy, doctor
policy, administration policy, etc. Each policy contains one or more particular rules, for
example, in the patient policy there is a rule that only the designated patient can read
his or her record. In this illustration, both the National Health Care System and local
hospital policies are PolicySets. However the patient policy is a Policy and one of its
rules is the patient record policy. Every policy is only applicable to a certain target and a
policy is applicable when a request matches to its target, otherwise, it is not applicable.
The evaluation of composing policies is based on a particular combining algorithm –
the procedure for combining decisions from multiple policies. There are four standard

---

[1] OASIS (Organization for the Advancement of Structured Information Standard) is a non-for-
profit, global consortium that drives the development, convergence, and adoption of e-business
standards. Information about OASIS can be found at http://www.oasis-open.org.

F. Arbab and P.C. Ölveczky (Eds.): FACS 2011, LNCS 7253, pp. 205–222, 2012.
© Springer-Verlag Berlin Heidelberg 2012

combining algorithms in XACML i.e., (i) permit-overrides, (ii) deny-overrides, (iii) first-applicable and (iv) only-one-applicable.

The syntax of XACML is based on XML format [2], while its standard semantics is described normatively using natural language in [12,14]. Using English paragraphs in standardization leads to misinterpretation and ambiguity. In order to avoid this drawback, we define an abstract syntax of XACML 3.0 and a formal XACML components evaluation based on XACML 3.0 specification in Section 2. Furthermore, the evaluation of the XACML combining algorithms is explained in Section 3.

Recently there are some approaches to formalizing the semantics of XACML. In [8], Halpern and Weissman show XACML formalization using First Order Logic (FOL). However, their formalization does not capture whole XACML specification. It is too expensive to express XACML combining algorithms in FOL. Kolovski *et al.* in [10,11] maps a large fragment of XACML to Description Logic (DL) – a subset of FOL – but they leave out the formalization of only-one-applicable combining algorithm. Another approach is to represent XACML policies in term of Answer Set Programming (ASP). Although Ahn *et al.* in [3] show a complete XACML formalization in ASP, their formalization is based on XACML 2.0 (see [12]), which is out-of-date nowadays. More particular, the combining algorithms evaluation in XACML 2.0 is simpler than XACML 3.0. Our XACML 3.0 formalization is closer to multi-valued logic approach such as Belnap logic [4] and $\mathcal{D}$-algebra [13]. Bruns *et al.* in [5,6] and Ni *et al.* in [13] define a logic for XACML using Belnap logic and $\mathcal{D}$-algebra, respectively. In some cases, both works show different results from the XACML standard specification. We discuss the shortcoming of formalization based either on Belnap logic or on $\mathcal{D}$-algebra in Section 4 and we conclude in Section 5.

2   XACML Components

The syntax of XACML is described verbosely in XACML format (see XACML 3.0 specification in [14]). For our analysis purpose, first of all we do abstracting XACML components. From the XACML abstraction, we show how XACML evaluates policies. For illustration we give an example at the end of this section.

2.1   Abstracting XACML Components

There are three main policy components in XACML, namely PolicySet, Policy and Rule[2]. PolicySet is the root of all XACML policies. A PolicySet contains of a sequence of other PolicySets or Policies. The sequence of PolicySets (or Policies) is combined with a combining algorithm function that has been defined already in XACML. A PolicySet is applicable if its Target matches with the Request.

A Policy contains a sequence of Rules. It is the same case like PolicySet, the sequence of Rules is combined with a combining algorithm function. A Policy is applicable if its Target matches with the Request.

---

[2] We use uppercase for Rule, Policy and PolicySet to denote XACML entities. Lowercase "rule" and "policy" are used as common English terminologies

Rule is the smallest policy entity in XACML that defines an individual rule in the policy. A Rule only has one effect, i.e., either *deny* or *permit* an access. When Rule's Target matches with the Request, the applicability of the Rule is refined by Rule's Condition.

A Request contains a set of attributes information about access request. There are four attributes categories used in XACML, namely *subject* attributes, *action* attributes, *resource* attributes and *environment* attributes. A Request also contains additional information about external state, e.g. the current time, the temperature, etc. A Request contains error message when there is an error during attribute evaluation.

We present in Table 1 a succinct syntax of XACML 3.0 that is faithful to the more verbose syntax used in the standard [14].

Table 1. Abstraction of XACML 3.0 Components

XACML Policy Components		
PolicySet ::= $\langle$Target, $\langle$PolicySet$_1$,..., PolicySet$_m\rangle$, CombID$\rangle$		
	$\langle$Target, $\langle$Policy$_1$,..., Policy$_m\rangle$, CombID$\rangle$	where $m \geq 0$
Policy ::= $\langle$Target, $\langle$Rule$_1$,..., Rule$_m\rangle$, CombID$\rangle$		where $m \geq 1$
Rule ::= $\langle$Effect, Target, Condition$\rangle$		
Condition ::= *propositional formulae*		
Target ::= Null		
	AnyOf$_1 \wedge ... \wedge$ AnyOf$_m$	where $m \geq 1$
AnyOf ::= AllOf$_1 \vee ... \wedge$ AllOf$_m$		where $m \geq 1$
AllOf ::= Match$_1 \wedge ... \wedge$ Match$_m$		where $m \geq 1$
Match ::= $att(val)$		
CombID ::= po	do	fa	ooa		
Effect ::= **d**	**p**		
att ::= subject	action	resource	enviroment		
val ::= *attribute value*		
XACML Request Component		
Request ::= $\{ A_1,..., A_m \}$		where $m \geq 1$
A ::= $att(val)$	error	*external state*		

2.2   XACML Evaluation

The evaluation of XACML components starts from Match evaluation and it is continued iteratively until PolicySet evaluation. The Match, AllOf, AnyOf, and Target values are either *match*, *not match* or *indeterminate*. Indeterminate value takes place if there is an error during the evaluation so that the decision cannot be made at that moment. The Rule evaluation depends on Target evaluation and Condition evaluation. The Condition component is a set of propositional formulae which each formula is evaluated to either *true*, *false* or *indeterminate*. An empty Condition is always evaluated to *true*. The result of Rule is either *applicable*, *not applicable* or *indeterminate*. An applicable Rule has effect either *deny* or *permit*. Finally, the evaluation of Policy and PolicySet are based on a combining algorithm of which the result can be either *applicable* (with its effect either *deny* or *permit*), *not applicable* or *indeterminate*.

2.2.1   Three-Valued Lattice

We modelling the XACML evaluation using lattice theory. We define $\mathcal{L}_3 = \langle V_3, \leq \rangle$ be *three-valued lattice* where V_3 is the set $\{\top, I, \bot\}$ and $\bot \leq I \leq \top$. Given a subset S of V_3, we denote the greatest lower bound (glb) and the least upper bound (lub) at S (w.r.t. $\mathcal{L}_3$) by $\bigsqcap S$ and $\bigsqcup S$, respectively. Recall that $\bigsqcap \emptyset = \top$ and $\bigsqcup \emptyset = \bot$.

We use $[\![.]\!]$ notation to map XACML elements into their evaluation values. The evaluation of XACML components to values in V_3 is summarized in Table 2.

Table 2. Mapping V_3 into XACML Evaluation Values

V_3	Match and Target value	Condition value	Rule, Policy and PolicySet value
$\top$	match	true	applicable (either deny or permit)
$\bot$	not match	false	not applicable
I	indeterminate	indeterminate	indeterminate

2.2.2   Match Evaluation

A Match element $\mathcal{M}$ is an attribute value that a request should fulfil. Given a Request component $\mathcal{Q}$, the evaluation of Match element is as follows:

$$[\![\mathcal{M}]\!](\mathcal{Q}) = \begin{cases} \top & \mathcal{M} \in \mathcal{Q} \text{ and } \texttt{error} \notin \mathcal{Q} \\ \bot & \mathcal{M} \notin \mathcal{Q} \text{ and } \texttt{error} \notin \mathcal{Q} \\ I & \texttt{error} \in \mathcal{Q} \end{cases} \qquad (1)$$

2.2.3   Target Evaluation

Let $\mathcal{M}$ be a Match, $\mathcal{A} = \mathcal{M}_1 \wedge \ldots \wedge \mathcal{M}_m$ be an AllOf, $\mathcal{E} = \mathcal{A}_1 \vee \ldots \vee \mathcal{A}_n$ be an AnyOf, $\mathcal{T} = \mathcal{E}_1 \wedge \ldots \wedge \mathcal{E}_o$ be a Target and $\mathcal{Q}$ be a Request. Then, the evaluations of AllOf, AnyOf, and Target are as follows:

$$[\![\mathcal{A}]\!](\mathcal{Q}) = \bigsqcap_{i=1}^{m} [\![\mathcal{M}_i]\!](\mathcal{Q}) \qquad (2)$$

$$[\![\mathcal{E}]\!](\mathcal{Q}) = \bigsqcup_{i=1}^{n} [\![\mathcal{A}_i]\!](\mathcal{Q}) \qquad (3)$$

$$[\![\mathcal{T}]\!](\mathcal{Q}) = \bigsqcap_{i=1}^{o} [\![\mathcal{E}_i]\!](\mathcal{Q}) \qquad (4)$$

In summary, we can simplify the Target evaluation as follows:

$$[\![\mathcal{T}]\!](\mathcal{Q}) = \bigsqcap \bigsqcup \bigsqcap [\![\mathcal{M}]\!](\mathcal{Q}) \qquad (5)$$

An empty Target – indicated by $\texttt{Null}$ – is always evaluated to $\top$.

2.2.4 Condition Evaluation

We define the conditional evaluation function *eval* as an arbitrary function to evaluate Condition to value in V_3 given a Request component Q. The evaluation of Condition is defined as follows:

$$[\![\mathcal{C}]\!](Q) = eval(\mathcal{C}, Q) \tag{6}$$

2.2.5 Extended Values

In order to distinguish an applicable policy that deny an access (i.e., has value **d**) from applicable policy that permit an access (i.e., has value **p**), we extend $\top$ in V_3 to $\top_{\mathbf{d}}$ and $\top_{\mathbf{p}}$, respectively. The same case also applies to indeterminate value. The extended indeterminate value contains potential effect value(s) that could have been returned had there been no error during evaluation. The possible extended indeterminate values are [14]:

- Indeterminate Deny ($I_{\mathbf{d}}$): an indeterminate from a policy which could have evaluated to deny but not permit, e.g., a Rule which evaluates to indeterminate and its effect is deny.
- Indeterminate Permit ($I_{\mathbf{p}}$): an indeterminate from a policy which could have evaluated to permit but not deny, e.g., a Rule which evaluates to indeterminate and its effect is permit.
- Indeterminate Deny Permit ($I_{\mathbf{dp}}$): an indeterminate from a policy which could have effect either deny or permit.

We extend the set V_3 to $V_6 = \{\top_{\mathbf{d}}, \top_{\mathbf{p}}, I_{\mathbf{d}}, I_{\mathbf{p}}, I_{\mathbf{dp}}, \bot\}$ and we use V_6 for XACML policies evaluations.

2.2.6 Rule Evaluation

Let $\mathcal{R} = \langle *, \mathcal{T}, \mathcal{C}\rangle$ be a Rule and Q be a Request. Then, the evaluation of Rule is determined as follows:

$$[\![\mathcal{R}]\!](Q) = \begin{cases} \top_* & [\![\mathcal{T}]\!](Q) = \top \text{ and } [\![\mathcal{C}]\!](Q) = \top \\ \bot & ([\![\mathcal{T}]\!](Q) = \top \text{ and } [\![\mathcal{C}]\!](Q) = \bot) \text{ or } [\![\mathcal{T}]\!](Q) = \bot \\ I_* & \text{otherwise} \end{cases} \tag{7}$$

Let F and G be two values in V_3. We define a new operator $\rightsquigarrow: V_3 \times V_3 \to V_3$ as follows:

$$F \rightsquigarrow G = \begin{cases} G & F = \top \\ F & \text{otherwise} \end{cases} \tag{8}$$

We define a function $\sigma: V_3 \times \{\mathbf{d}, \mathbf{p}\} \to V_6$ that maps a value in V_3 into a value in V_6 given a particular Rule's grant as follows:

$$\sigma(X, *) = \begin{cases} X & X = \bot \\ X_* & \text{otherwise} \end{cases} \tag{9}$$

Proposition 1. *Let $\mathcal{R} = \langle *, \mathcal{T}, \mathcal{C} \rangle$ be a Rule and $\mathcal{Q}$ be a Request. Then, the following equation holds*

$$[\![\mathcal{R}]\!](\mathcal{Q}) = \sigma\left([\![\mathcal{T}]\!](\mathcal{Q}) \rightsquigarrow [\![\mathcal{C}]\!](\mathcal{Q}), *\right) \tag{10}$$

2.2.7 Policy Evaluation

The standard evaluation of Policy element taken from [14] is as follows

Target value	Rule value	Policy Value
match	At least one Rule value is applicable	Specified by the combining algorithm
match	All Rule values are not applicable	not applicable
match	At least one Rule value is indeterminate	Specified by the combining algorithm
not match	Don't care	not applicable
indeterminate	Don't care	indeterminate

Let $\mathcal{P} = \langle \mathcal{T}, \mathbb{R}, \text{CombID} \rangle$ be a Policy where $\mathbb{R} = \langle \mathcal{R}_1, \ldots, \mathcal{R}_n \rangle$ is a sequence of Rules. Let $\mathcal{Q}$ be a Request and $\mathbb{R}' = \langle [\![\mathcal{R}_1]\!](\mathcal{Q}), \ldots, [\![\mathcal{R}_n]\!](\mathcal{Q}) \rangle$. The evaluation of Policy is defined as follows:

$$[\![\mathcal{P}]\!](\mathcal{Q}) = \begin{cases} I_* & [\![\mathcal{T}]\!](\mathcal{Q}) = I \text{ and } \bigoplus_{\text{CombID}}(\mathbb{R}') \in \{\top_*, I_*\} \\ \bot & [\![\mathcal{T}]\!](\mathcal{Q}) = \bot \text{ or} \\ & [\![\mathcal{T}]\!](\mathcal{Q}) = \top \text{ and } \forall \mathcal{R}_i : [\![\mathcal{R}_i]\!](\mathcal{Q}) = \bot \\ \bigoplus_{\text{CombID}}(\mathbb{R}') & \text{otherwise} \end{cases} \tag{11}$$

Note 1. The combining algorithms denoted by $\bigoplus$ is explained in Section 3.

2.2.8 PolicySet Evaluation

The evaluation of PolicySet is similar to Policy evaluation. However, the input of the combining algorithm is a sequence of either PolicySets or Policies.

Let $\mathcal{PS} = \langle \mathcal{T}, \mathbb{P}, \text{CombID} \rangle$ be a PolicySet where $\mathbb{P} = \langle \mathcal{P}_1, \ldots, \mathcal{P}_n \rangle$ is a sequence of PolicySets (or Policies). Let $\mathcal{Q}$ be a Request and $\mathbb{P}' = \langle [\![\mathcal{P}_1]\!](\mathcal{Q}), \ldots, [\![\mathcal{P}_n]\!](\mathcal{Q}) \rangle$. The evaluation of PolicySet is defined as follows:

$$[\![\mathcal{PS}]\!](\mathcal{Q}) = \begin{cases} I_* & [\![\mathcal{T}]\!](\mathcal{Q}) = I \text{ and } \bigoplus_{\text{CombID}}(\mathbb{P}') \in \{\top_*, I_*\} \\ \bot & [\![\mathcal{T}]\!](\mathcal{Q}) = \bot \text{ or} \\ & [\![\mathcal{T}]\!](\mathcal{Q}) = \top \text{ and } \forall \mathcal{P}_i : [\![\mathcal{P}_i]\!](\mathcal{Q}) = \bot \\ \bigoplus_{\text{CombID}}(\mathbb{P}') & \text{otherwise} \end{cases} \tag{12}$$

2.3 Example

The following example simulates briefly how a policy is built using the abstraction. The example is motivated by [7,9] which presents a health information system for a small nursing home in New South Wales, Australia.

Example 1 (Patient Policy). The general policy in the hospital in particular:

1. Patient Record Policy

   RP1: only designated patient **can** read his or her patient record except that if the patient is less than 18 years old, the patient's guardian is **permitted** also read the patient's record,

   RP2: patients **may** only write patient surveys into their own records

   RP3: both doctors and nurses are **permitted** to read any patient records,

2. Medical Record Policy

   RM1: doctors **may** only write medical records for their own patients and

   RM2: **may not** write any other patient records,

The encoding of this example using our abstraction is shown below. The topmost policy in this example is the Patient PolicySet that contains two policies, namely the Patient Record Policy and the Medical Record Policy. The access is granted if either one of the Patient Record Policy or the Medical Record Policy gives a permit access. Thus in this case, we use permit-overrides combining algorithm to combine those two policies. In order to restrict the access, each policy denies an access if there is a rule denies it. Thus, we use deny-overrides combining algorithms to combine the rules.

```
PS_patient = <Null, <P_patient_record, P_medical_record>, po>
P_patient_record = <Null, <RP1, RP2, RP3>, do>
P_medical_record = <Null, <RM1, RM2>, do>

RP1a =
< p,
   subject(patient) ∧ action(read) ∧ resource(patient_record),
   patient(id,X) ∧ patient_record(id,X) >

RP1b =
< p,
   subject(guardian) ∧ action(read) ∧ resource(patient_record),
   guardian(id, X) ∧ patient_record(id,Y) ∧ guardian_patient(X,Y) ∧ (age(Y) > 18) >

RP2 =
< p,
   subject(patient) ∧ action(write) ∧ resource(patient_survey),
   patient(id,X) ∧ patient_survey(id, X)>

RP3=
< p,
   (subject(doctor) ∨ subject(nurse)) ∧ action(read) ∧ resource(patient_record),
   true>

RM1 =
< p,
   subject(doctor) ∧ action(write) ∧ resource(medical_record),
   doctor(id,X) ∧ patient(id,Y) ∧ medical_record(id, Y) ∧ doctor_patient(X,Y)>

RM2 =
< d,
   subject(doctor) ∧ action(write) ∧ resource(medical_record),
   doctor(id,X), patient(id,Y), medical_record(id, Y), not doctor_patient(X,Y)>
```

The XACML Policy for Patient Policy

Suppose now there is an emergency situation and a doctor D asks permission to read patient record P. The Request is as follows:

```
{ subject(doctor), action(read), resource(patient_record),
  doctor(id,D), patient(id,P), patient_record(id,P)}
```

Only Target RP3 matches for this request and the effect of RP3 is permit. Thus, the final result is doctor D is allowed to read patient record P. Now, suppose that after doing some treatment, the doctor wants to update the medical record. A request is sent

```
{ subject(doctor), action(write), resource(medical_record),
  doctor(id,D), patient(id,P), medical_record(id,P)}
```

The Target RM1 and the Target RM2 match for this request, however because doctor D is not registered as patient P's doctor thus Condition RM1 is evaluated to *false* while Condition RM2 is evaluated to *true*. In consequence, Rule RM1 is not applicable while Rule RM2 is applicable with effect deny.

3   Combining Algorithms

Currently, there are four basic combining algorithms in XACML, namely (i) *permit-overrides* (po), (ii) *deny-overrides* (do), (iii) *first-applicable* (fa), and (iv) *only-one-applicable* (ooa). The input of a combining algorithm is a sequence of Rule, Policy or PolicySet values. In this section we give formalizations of the XACML 3.0 combining algorithms based on [14]. To guard against modelling artefacts we provide an alternative way of characterizing the policy combining algorithms and we formally prove the equivalence of these approaches.[3]

3.1   Pairwise Policy Values

In V_6 we define the truth values of XACML components by extending $\top$ to $\top_p$ and $\top_d$ and I to I_d, I_p and I_{dp}. This approach shows straightforwardly the status of XACML component. However, in general, numerical encoding is more helpful for computing policy compositions. Thus, we encode all the values returned by algorithms as pairs of natural numbers.

In this numerical encoding, the value **1** represents an applicable value (either deny or permit), $\frac{1}{2}$ represents indeterminate value and **0** means there is no applicable value. In each tuple, the first element represents the deny value ($\top_d$) and the later represents permit value ($\top_p$). We can say $[0, 0]$ for not applicable ($\bot$) because neither deny nor permit is applicable, $[1, 0]$ for applicable with deny effect ($\top_d$) because only deny value is applicable, $[\frac{1}{2}, 0]$ for I_d because the deny part is indeterminate, $[\frac{1}{2}, \frac{1}{2}]$ for I_{dp} because both deny and permit have indeterminate values. The conversion applies also for permit.

A set of *pairwise policy values* is $\mathbf{P} = \{ [0,0], [\frac{1}{2},0], [0,\frac{1}{2}], [1,0], [\frac{1}{2},\frac{1}{2}], [0,1] \}$. Let $[D, P]$ be an element on $\mathbf{P}$. We denote $d([D, P]) = D$ and $p([D, P]) = P$ for the function that returns the deny value and permit value, respectively.

---

[3] An extended version of this paper with all the proofs is available at
http://www2.imm.dtu.dk/~cdpu/Papers/
the_logic_of_XACML-extended.pdf

We define $\delta : V_6 \to \mathbf{P}$ as a mapping function that maps V_6 into $\mathbf{P}$ as follows:

$$\delta(X) = \begin{cases} [0,0] & X = \bot \\ [1,0] & X = \top_\mathbf{d} \\ [0,1] & X = \top_\mathbf{p} \\ [\frac{1}{2},0] & X = I_\mathbf{d} \\ [0,\frac{1}{2}] & X = I_\mathbf{p} \\ [\frac{1}{2},\frac{1}{2}] & X = I_\mathbf{dp} \end{cases} \tag{13}$$

We define δ over a sequence S as $\delta(S) = \langle \delta(s) | s \in S \rangle$.

We use pairwise comparison for the order of $\mathbf{P}$. We define an order $\sqsubseteq_\mathbf{P}$ for $\mathbf{P}$ as follows $[D_1, P_1] \sqsubseteq_\mathbf{P} [D_2, P_2]$ iff $D_1 \le D_2$ and $P_1 \le P_2$ with $0 \le \frac{1}{2} \le 1$. We write $\boldsymbol{P}_\mathbf{P}$ for the partial ordered set (poset) $(\mathbf{P}, \sqsubseteq_\mathbf{P})$ illustrated in Figure 1.

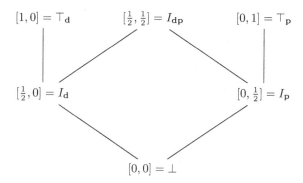

Fig. 1. The Partial Ordered Set $\boldsymbol{P}_\mathbf{P}$ for Pairwise Policy Values

Let $max : 2^\Re \to \Re$ be a function that returns the maximum value of a set of rational numbers and let $min : 2^\Re \to \Re$ be a function that returns the minimum value of a set of rational numbers. We define $Max_{\sqsubseteq_\mathbf{P}} : 2^\mathbf{P} \to \mathbf{P}$ as a function that returns the maximum pairwise policy value which is defined as follows:

$$Max_{\sqsubseteq_\mathbf{P}}(S) = [max(\{\, d(X) \mid X \in S \,\}), max(\{\, p(X) \mid X \in S \,\})] \tag{14}$$

and $Min_{\sqsubseteq_\mathbf{P}} : 2^\mathbf{P} \to \mathbf{P}$ as a function that return the minimum pairwise policy value which is defined as follows:

$$Min_{\sqsubseteq_\mathbf{P}}(S) = [min(\{\, d(X) \mid X \in S \,\}), min(\{\, p(X) \mid X \in S \,\})] \tag{15}$$

3.2 Permit-Overrides Combining Algorithm

The permit-overrides combining algorithm is intended for those cases where a permit decision should have priority over a deny decision. This algorithm (taken from [14]) has the following behaviour:

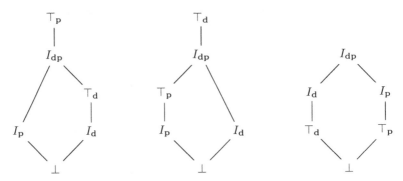

Fig. 2. The Lattice $\mathcal{L}_{po}$ for The Permit-Overrides Combining Algorithm (left), The Lattice $\mathcal{L}_{do}$ for The Deny-Overrides Combining Algorithm (middle) and The Lattice $\mathcal{L}_{ooa}$ for The Only-One-Applicable Combining Algorithm (right)

1. If any decision is $\top_{\mathbf{p}}$ then the result is $\top_{\mathbf{p}}$,
2. otherwise, if any decision is $I_{\mathbf{dp}}$ then the result is $I_{\mathbf{dp}}$,
3. otherwise, if any decision is $I_{\mathbf{p}}$ and another decision is $I_{\mathbf{d}}$ or $\top_{\mathbf{d}}$, then the result is $I_{\mathbf{dp}}$,
4. otherwise, if any decision is $I_{\mathbf{p}}$ then the result is $I_{\mathbf{p}}$,
5. otherwise, if decision is $\top_{\mathbf{d}}$ then the result is $\top_{\mathbf{d}}$,
6. otherwise, if any decision is $I_{\mathbf{d}}$ then the result is $I_{\mathbf{d}}$,
7. otherwise, the result is $\bot$.

We call $\mathcal{L}_{po} = (V_6, \sqsubseteq_{po})$ for the lattice using the permit-overrides combining algorithm where $\sqsubseteq_{po}$ is the ordering depicted in Figure 2. The least upper bound operator for $\mathcal{L}_{po}$ is denoted by $\bigsqcup_{po}$.

Definition 1. *The permit-overrides combining algorithm $\bigoplus_{po}^{V_6}$ is a mapping function from a sequence of V_6 elements into an element in V_6 as the result of composing policies. Let $S = \langle s_1, \ldots, s_n \rangle$ be a sequence of policy values in V_6 and $S' = \{ s_1, \ldots, s_n \}$. We define the permit-overrides combining algorithm under V_6 as follows:*

$$\bigoplus_{po}^{V_6}(S) = \bigsqcup_{po} S' \tag{16}$$

We are going to show how to express the permit-overrides combining algorithm under **P**. The idea is that we inspect the maximum value of deny and permit in the set of pairwise policy values. We conclude that the decision is permit if the permit is applicable (i.e. it has value 1). If the permit is indeterminate (i.e. it has value $\frac{1}{2}$) then the decision is $I_{\mathbf{dp}}$ when the deny is either indeterminate (i.e. it has value $\frac{1}{2}$) or applicable (i.e. it has value 1). Otherwise we take the maximum value of deny and permit from the set of pairwise policy values as the result of permit-overrides combining algorithm.

Definition 2. *The permit-overrides combining algorithm $\bigoplus_{po}^{\mathbf{P}}$ is a mapping function from a sequence of **P** elements into an element in **P** as the result of composing policies.*

Let $S = \langle s_1, \ldots, s_n \rangle$ be a sequence of pairwise policy values and $S' = \{ s_1, \ldots, s_n \}$.
We define the permit-overrides combining algorithm under $\mathbf{P}$ as follows:

$$\overset{\mathbf{P}}{\underset{po}{\bigoplus}}(S) = \begin{cases} [0,1] & Max_{\sqsubseteq_{\mathbf{P}}}(S') = [\_,1] \\ [\frac{1}{2},\frac{1}{2}] & Max_{\sqsubseteq_{\mathbf{P}}}(S') = [D,\frac{1}{2}], D \geq \frac{1}{2} \\ Max_{\sqsubseteq_{\mathbf{P}}}(S') & otherwise \end{cases} \tag{17}$$

Proposition 2. *Let S be a sequence of policy values in V_6. Then*

$$\delta(\overset{V_6}{\underset{po}{\bigoplus}}(S)) = \overset{\mathbf{P}}{\underset{po}{\bigoplus}}(\delta(S))$$

3.3   Deny-Overrides Combining Algorithm

The deny-overrides combining algorithm is intended for those cases where a deny decision should have priority over a permit decision. This algorithm (taken from [14]) has the following behaviour:

1. If any decision is $\top_\mathbf{d}$ then the result is $\top_\mathbf{d}$,
2. otherwise, if any decision is $I_{\mathbf{dp}}$ then the result is $I_{\mathbf{dp}}$,
3. otherwise, if any decision is $I_\mathbf{d}$ and another decision is $I_\mathbf{p}$ or $\top_\mathbf{p}$, then the result is $I_{\mathbf{dp}}$,
4. otherwise, if any decision is $I_\mathbf{d}$ then the result is $I_\mathbf{d}$,
5. otherwise, if decision is $\top_\mathbf{p}$ then the result is $\top_\mathbf{p}$,
6. otherwise, if any decision is $I_\mathbf{p}$ then the result is $I_\mathbf{p}$,
7. otherwise, the result is $\bot$.

We call $\mathcal{L}_{do} = (V_6, \sqsubseteq_{do})$ for the lattice using the deny-overrides combining algorithm where $\sqsubseteq_{do}$ is the ordering depicted in Figure 2. The least upper bound operator for $\mathcal{L}_{do}$ is denoted by $\bigsqcup_{do}$.

Definition 3. *The deny-overrides combining algorithm $\bigoplus_{do}^{V_6}$ is a mapping function from a sequence of V_6 elements into an element in V_6 as the result of composing policies. Let $S = \langle s_1, \ldots, s_n \rangle$ be a sequence of policy values in V_6 and $S' = \{ s_1, \ldots, s_n \}$. We define the deny-overrides combining algorithm under V_6 as follows:*

$$\overset{V_6}{\underset{do}{\bigoplus}}(S) = \underset{do}{\bigsqcup} S' \tag{18}$$

The deny-overrides combining algorithm can be expressed under $\mathbf{P}$ using the same idea as permit-overrides combining algorithm by symmetry.

Definition 4. *The deny-overrides combining algorithm $\bigoplus_{do}^{\mathbf{P}}$ is a mapping function from a sequence of $\mathbf{P}$ elements into an element in $\mathbf{P}$ as the result of composing policies. Let $S = \langle s_1, \ldots, s_n \rangle$ be a sequence of policy values in $\mathbf{P}$ and $S' = \{ s_1, \ldots, s_n \}$. We define the deny-overrides combining algorithm under $\mathbf{P}$ as follows:*

$$\overset{\mathbf{P}}{\underset{do}{\bigoplus}}(S) = \begin{cases} [1,0] & Max_{\sqsubseteq_{\mathbf{P}}}(S') = [1,\_] \\ [\frac{1}{2},\frac{1}{2}] & Max_{\sqsubseteq_{\mathbf{P}}}(S') = [\frac{1}{2},P], P \geq \frac{1}{2} \\ Max_{\sqsubseteq_{\mathbf{P}}}(S') & otherwise \end{cases} \tag{19}$$

Proposition 3. *Let S be a sequence of policy values in V_6. Then*

$$\delta(\overset{V_6}{\underset{do}{\bigoplus}}(S)) = \overset{\mathbf{P}}{\underset{do}{\bigoplus}}(\delta(S))$$

3.4 First-Applicable Combining Algorithm

The result of first-applicable algorithm is the first Rule, Policy or PolicySet element in the sequence whose Target and Condition is applicable. The pseudo-code of the first-applicable combining algorithm in XACML 3.0 [14] shows that the result of this algorithm is the first Rule, Policy or PolicySet that is not "not applicable". The idea is that there is a possibility an indeterminate policy could return to be an applicable policy. The first-applicable combining algorithm under V_6 and $\mathbf{P}$ are defined below.

Definition 5 (First-Applicable Combining Algorithm). *The first-applicable combining algorithm $\bigoplus_{fa}^{V_6}$ is a mapping function from a sequence of V_6 elements into an element in V_6 as the result of composing policies. Let $S = \langle s_1, \ldots, s_n \rangle$ be a sequence of policy values in V_6. We define the first-applicable combining algorithm under V_6 as follows:*

$$\overset{V_6}{\underset{fa}{\bigoplus}}(S) = \begin{cases} s_i & \exists i : s_i \neq \bot \text{ and } \forall j < i : s_j = \bot \\ \bot & \text{otherwise} \end{cases} \tag{20}$$

Definition 6. *The first-applicable combining algorithm $\bigoplus_{fa}^{\mathbf{P}}$ is a mapping function from a sequence of $\mathbf{P}$ elements into an element in $\mathbf{P}$ as the result of composing policies. Let $S = \langle s_1, \ldots, s_n \rangle$ be a sequence of policy values in $\mathbf{P}$. We define the first applicable combining algorithm under $\mathbf{P}$ as follows:*

$$\overset{\mathbf{P}}{\underset{fa}{\bigoplus}}(S) = \begin{cases} s_i & \exists i : s_i \neq [0,0] \text{ and } \forall j < i : s_j = [0,0] \\ [0,0] & \text{otherwise} \end{cases} \tag{21}$$

Proposition 4. *Let S be a sequence of policy values in V_6. Then*

$$\delta(\overset{V_6}{\underset{fa}{\bigoplus}}(S)) = \overset{\mathbf{P}}{\underset{fa}{\bigoplus}}(\delta(S))$$

3.5 Only-One-Applicable Combining Algorithm

The result of the only-one-applicable combining algorithm ensures that one and only one policy is applicable by virtue of their Target. If no policy applies, then the result is not applicable, but if more than one policy is applicable, then the result is indeterminate. When exactly one policy is applicable, the result of the combining algorithm is the result of evaluating the single applicable policy.

We call $\mathcal{L}_{ooa} = (V_6, \sqsubseteq_{ooa})$ for the lattice using the only-one-applicable combining algorithm where $\sqsubseteq_{ooa}$ is the ordering depicted in Figure 2. The least upper bound operator for $\mathcal{L}_{ooa}$ is denoted by $\bigsqcup_{ooa}$.

Definition 7. *The only-one-applicable combining algorithm $\bigoplus_{ooa}^{V_6}$ is a mapping function from a sequence of V_6 elements into an element in V_6 as the result of composing policies. Let $S = \langle s_1, \ldots, s_n \rangle$ be a sequence of policy values in V_6 and $S' = \{ s_1, \ldots, s_n \}$. We define only-one-applicable combining algorithm under V_6 as follows*

$$\bigoplus_{ooa}^{V_6}(S) = \begin{cases} I_{\mathbf{d}} & \exists i, j : i \neq j, s_i = s_j = \top_{\mathbf{d}} \text{ and} \\ & \forall k : s_k \neq \top_{\mathbf{d}} \rightarrow s_k = \bot \\ I_{\mathbf{p}} & \exists i, j : i \neq j, s_i = s_j = \top_{\mathbf{p}} \text{ and} \\ & \forall k : s_k \neq \top_{\mathbf{p}} \rightarrow s_k = \bot \\ \bigsqcup_{ooa} S' & \text{otherwise} \end{cases} \tag{22}$$

We are going to show how to express the only-one-applicable combining algorithm under **P**. The idea is that we inspect the maximum value of deny and permit returned from the given set of pairwise policy values. By inspecting the maximum value for each element, we know exactly the combination of pairwise policy values i.e., if we find that both deny and permit are not 0, it means that the deny value and the permit value are either applicable (i.e. it has value 1) or indeterminate (i.e. it has value $\frac{1}{2}$). Thus, the result of this algorithm is $I_{\mathbf{dp}}$ (based on the XACML 3.0 Specification [14]). However if only one element is not 0 then there is a possibility that many policies have the same applicable (or indeterminate) values. If there are at least two policies with the deny (or permit) are either applicable or indeterminate value, then the result is $I_{\mathbf{d}}$ (or $I_{\mathbf{p}}$). Otherwise we take the maximum value of deny and permit from the given set of pairwise policy values as the result of only-one-applicable combining algorithm.

Definition 8. *The only-one-applicable combining algorithm $\bigoplus_{ooa}^{\mathbf{P}}$ is a mapping function from a sequence of **P** elements into an element in **P** as the result of composing policies. Let $S = \langle s_1, \ldots, s_n \rangle$ be a sequence of policy values in **P** and $S' = \{ s_1, \ldots, s_n \}$. We define only-one-applicable combining algorithm under **P** as follows*

$$\bigoplus_{ooa}^{\mathbf{P}}(S) = \begin{cases} [\frac{1}{2}, \frac{1}{2}] & Max_{\sqsubseteq_{\mathbf{P}}}(S') = [D, P], D, P \geq \frac{1}{2} \\ [\frac{1}{2}, 0] & Max_{\sqsubseteq_{\mathbf{P}}}(S') = [D, 0], D \geq \frac{1}{2} \text{ and} \\ & \exists i, j : i \neq j, d(s_i), d(s_j) \geq \frac{1}{2} \\ [0, \frac{1}{2}] & Max_{\sqsubseteq_{\mathbf{P}}}(S') = [0, P], P \geq \frac{1}{2} \text{ and} \\ & \exists i, j : i \neq j, p(s_i), p(s_j) \geq \frac{1}{2} \\ Max_{\sqsubseteq_{\mathbf{P}}}(S') & \text{otherwise} \end{cases} \tag{23}$$

Proposition 5. *Let S be a sequence of policy values in V_6. Then*

$$\delta(\bigoplus_{ooa}^{V_6}(S)) = \bigoplus_{ooa}^{\mathbf{P}}(\delta(S))$$

4 Related Work

We will focus the discussion on the formalization of XACML using Belnap logic [4] and $\mathcal{D}$-Algebra [13] – those two have a similar approach to the pairwise policy values approach explained in Section 3. We show the shortcoming of the formalization on Bruns *et al.* work in [6] and Ni *et al.* work in [13].

4.1 XACML Semantics under Belnap Four-Valued Logic

Belnap in his paper [4] defines a four-valued logic over $\mathbf{four} = \{\ \top\top, \mathbf{tt}, \mathbf{ff}, \bot\bot\ \}$. There are two orderings in Belnap logic, i.e., the knowledge ordering ($\leq_k$) and the truth ordering ($\leq_t$) (see Figure 3).

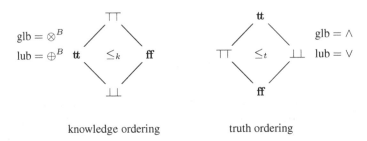

knowledge ordering   truth ordering

Fig. 3. Bi-lattice of Belnap Four-Valued Logic

Bruns *et al.* in PBel [5,6] and also Hankin *et al.* in AspectKB [9] use Belnap four-valued logic to represent the composition of access control policies. The responses of an access control system are $\mathbf{tt}$ when the policy is granted or access permitted, $\mathbf{ff}$ when the policy is not granted or access is denied, $\bot\bot$ when there is no applicable policy and $\top\top$ when conflict arises, i.e., an access is both permitted and denied. Additional operators are added as follows [6]:

- overwriting operator $[y \mapsto z]$ with $y, z \in \mathbf{four}$. Expression $x[y \mapsto z]$ yields x if $x \neq y$, and z otherwise.
- priority operator $x > y$; it is a syntactic sugar of $x[\bot\bot \mapsto y]$.

Bruns *et al.* defined XACML combining algorithms using Belnap four-valued logic as follows [6]:

- **permit-overrides**: $(p \oplus^B q)[\top\top \mapsto \mathbf{ff}]$
- **first-applicable**: $p > q$
- **only-one-applicable**: $(p \oplus^B q) \oplus^B ((p \oplus^B \neg p) \otimes^B (q \oplus^B \neg q))$

Bruns *et al.* suggested that the indeterminate value is treated as $\top\top$. However, with indeterminate as $\top\top$, the permit-overrides combining algorithm is not defined correctly. Suppose we have two policies: p and q where p is permit and q is indeterminate. The result of the permit-overrides combining algorithm is as follows $(p \oplus^B q)[\top\top \mapsto \mathbf{ff}] = (\mathbf{tt} \oplus^B \top\top)[\top\top \mapsto \mathbf{ff}] = \top\top[\top\top \mapsto \mathbf{ff}] = \mathbf{ff}$. Based on the XACML 2.0 [12] and the XACML 3.0 [14], the result of permit-overrides combining algorithm should be permit ($\mathbf{tt}$). However, based on Belnap four-valued logic, the result is deny ($\mathbf{ff}$).

Bruns *et al.* tried to define indeterminate value as a conflict by formalizing it as $\top\top$. However, their formulation of permit-overrides combining algorithm is inconsistent based on the standard XACML specification. Moreover, they said that sometimes indeterminate should be treated as $\bot\bot$ and sometimes as $\top\top$ [5], but there is no explanation about under which circumstances that indeterminate is treated as $\top\top$ or as

$\bot\bot$. The treatment of indeterminate as $\top\top$ is too strong because indeterminate does not always contains information about deny and permit in the same time. Only I_{dp} contains information both deny and permit. However, I_d and I_p only contain information only about deny and permit, respectively. Even so, the value $\bot\bot$ for indeterminate is too weak because indeterminate is treated as not applicable despite that there is information contained inside indeterminate value. The Belnap four-valued logic has no explicit definition of indeterminate. In contrast, the Belnap four-valued has a *conflict* value (i.e. $\top\top$).

4.2 XACML Semantics under $\mathcal{D}$-Algebra

Ni *et al.* in [13] define $\mathcal{D}$-algebra as a decision set together with some operations on it.

Definition 9 ($\mathcal{D}$-**algebra [13]**). *Let D be a nonempty set of elements, 0 be a constant element of D, $\neg$ be a unary operation on elements in $\mathcal{D}$, and $\oplus^{\mathcal{D}}, \otimes^{\mathcal{D}}$ be binary operations on elements in D. A $\mathcal{D}$-algebra is an algebraic structure $\langle D, \neg, \oplus^{\mathcal{D}}, \otimes^{\mathcal{D}}, 0 \rangle$ closed on $\neg, \oplus^{\mathcal{D}}, \otimes^{\mathcal{D}}$ and satisfying the following axioms:*

1. $x \oplus^{\mathcal{D}} y = y \oplus^{\mathcal{D}} x$
2. $(x \oplus^{\mathcal{D}} y) \oplus^{\mathcal{D}} z = x \oplus^{\mathcal{D}} (y \oplus^{\mathcal{D}} z)$
3. $x \oplus^{\mathcal{D}} 0 = x$
4. $\neg\neg x = x$
5. $x \oplus^{\mathcal{D}} \neg 0 = \neg 0$
6. $\neg(\neg x \oplus^{\mathcal{D}} y) \oplus^{\mathcal{D}} y = \neg(\neg y \oplus^{\mathcal{D}} x) \oplus^{\mathcal{D}} x$
7. $x \otimes^{\mathcal{D}} y = \begin{cases} \neg 0 & : x = y \\ 0 & : x \neq y \end{cases}$

In order to write formulae in a compact form, for $x, y \in \mathcal{D}$, $x \odot^{\mathcal{D}} y = \neg(\neg x \oplus^{\mathcal{D}} \neg y)$ and $x \ominus^{\mathcal{D}} y = x \odot^{\mathcal{D}} \neg y$.

Ni *et al.* [13] show that XACML decisions contain three different value, i.e. permit ($\{p\}$), deny ($\{d\}$) and not applicable ($\{\frac{n}{a}\}$). Those decision are *deterministic decisions*. The *non-deterministic decisions* such as I_d, I_p and I_{dp} are denoted by $\{d, \frac{n}{a}\}$, $\{p, \frac{n}{a}\}$, and $\{d, p, \frac{n}{a}\}$, respectively. The interpretation of a $\mathcal{D}$-algebra on XACML decisions is as follows [13]:

- D is represented by $\mathcal{P}(\{p, d, \frac{n}{a}\})$
- 0 is represented by $\emptyset$
- $\neg x$ is represented by $\{p, d, \frac{n}{a}\} - x$ where $x \in D$
- $x \oplus^{\mathcal{D}} y$ is represented by $x \cup y$ where $x, y \in D$
- $\otimes^{\mathcal{D}}$ is defined by axiom 7

There are two values which are not in XACML, i.e. $\emptyset$ and $\{p, d\}$. Simply we say $\emptyset$ for empty policy (or there is no policy) and $\{p, d\}$ for a conflict.

The composition function of permit-overrides using $\mathcal{D}$-Algebra is as follows:

$$f_{po}(x, y) = (x \oplus^{\mathcal{D}} y)$$
$$\ominus^{\mathcal{D}}(((x \otimes^{\mathcal{D}} \{p\}) \oplus^{\mathcal{D}} (y \otimes^{\mathcal{D}} \{p\})) \odot^{\mathcal{D}} \{d, \tfrac{n}{a}\})$$
$$\ominus^{\mathcal{D}}(\neg((x \odot^{\mathcal{D}} y) \otimes^{\mathcal{D}} \{\tfrac{n}{a}\}) \odot^{\mathcal{D}} \{\tfrac{n}{a}\} \odot^{\mathcal{D}} \neg((x \otimes^{\mathcal{D}} \emptyset) \oplus^{\mathcal{D}} (y \otimes^{\mathcal{D}} \emptyset)))$$

The composition function that Ni *et al.* proposed is inconsistent with neither the XACML 3.0 [14] nor the XACML 2.0 [12] as they claimed in [13]. Below we show an example that compares all of the results of permit-overrides combining algorithm under the logics discussed in this paper.

Example 2. Given two policies P_1 and P_2 where P_1 is Indeterminate Permit and P_2 is Deny. Let us use the permit-overrides combining algorithm to compose those two policies. Table 3 shows the result of combining polices under Belnap logic, $\mathcal{D}$-algebra, V_6 and **P**.

Table 3. Result of Permit-Overrides Combining Algorithm for Composing Two Policies P_1 (Indeterminate Permit) and P_2 (Deny) Under Various Approaches

Logic	P_1	P_2	Permit-Overrides Function	Result
Belnap logic	$\top\top$	$\mathbf{ff}$	$(\top\top \oplus^B \mathbf{ff})[\top\top \mapsto \mathbf{ff}]$	$\mathbf{ff}$
$\mathcal{D}$-algebra	$\{\mathbf{p}, \frac{n}{a}\}$	$\{\mathbf{d}\}$	$f_{po}(\{\mathbf{p}, \frac{n}{a}\}, \{\mathbf{d}\})$	$\{\mathbf{p},\mathbf{d}\}$
V_6	$I_{\mathbf{p}}$	$\top_{\mathbf{d}}$	$\bigoplus_{\mathrm{po}}^{V_6}(\langle I_{\mathbf{p}}, \top_{\mathbf{d}}\rangle)$	$I_{\mathbf{dp}}$
P	$[0, \frac{1}{2}]$	$[1, 0]$	$\bigoplus_{\mathrm{po}}^{\mathbf{P}}(\langle [0, \frac{1}{2}], [1, 0]\rangle)$	$[\frac{1}{2}, \frac{1}{2}]$

The result of permit-overrides combining algorithm under Belnap logic is $\mathbf{ff}$ and under $\mathcal{D}$-algebra is $\{\mathbf{p}, \mathbf{d}\}$. Under Bruns *et al.* approach using Belnap logic, the access is denied while under Ni *et al.* approach using $\mathcal{D}$-algebra, a conflict occurs. Both Bruns *et al.* and Ni *et al.* claim that their approaches fit with XACML 2.0 [12]. Moreover $\mathcal{D}$-algebra claims that it fits with XACML 3.0 [14]. However based on XACML 2.0 the result should be Indeterminate and based on XACML 3.0 the result should be Indeterminate Deny Permit and neither Belnap logic nor $\mathcal{D}$-algebra fits the specifications. We have illustrated that Belnap logic and $\mathcal{D}$-algebra in some cases give different result with the XACML specification. Conversely, our approach gives consistent result based on the XACML 3.0 [14] and on the XACML 2.0 [12].

5   Conclusion

We have shown the formalization of XACML 3.0 step by step. We believe that with our approach, the reader can understand better about how XACML works especially in the behaviour of combining algorithms. We show two approaches to formalizing standard XACML combining algorithms, i.e., using V_6 and **P**. To guard against modelling artifacts, we formally prove the equivalence of these approaches.

The pairwise policy values approach is useful in defining new combining algorithms. For example, suppose we have a new combining algorithm "all permit", i.e., the result of composing policies is permit if all policies give permit values, otherwise it is deny. Using pairwise policy values approach the result of composing a set of policies values S is permit ($[0,1]$) if $Min_{\sqsubseteq_\mathbf{P}}(S) = [0, 1] = Max_{\sqsubseteq_\mathbf{P}}(S)$, otherwise, it is deny ($[1,0]$).

Ni *et al.* proposes a $\mathcal{D}$-algebra over a set of decisions for XACML combining algorithms in [13]. However, there are some mismatches between their results and the

XACML specifications. Their formulations are inconsistent based both on the XACML 2.0 [12] and on the XACML 3.0 [14].[4]

Both Belnap four-valued logic and $\mathcal{D}$-Algebra have a conflict value. In XACML, the conflict will never occur because the combining algorithms do not allow that. Conflict value might be a good indication that the policies are not well design. We propose an extended **P** which captures a conflict value in Appendix A.

References

1. eXtensible Access Control Markup Language (XACML),
   http://xml.coverpages.org/xacml.html
2. XML 1.0 specification. w3.org, http://www.w3.org/TR/xml/; (retrieved August 22, 2010)
3. Ahn, G.-J., Hu, H., Lee, J., Meng, Y.: Reasoning about xacml policy descriptions in answer set programming (preliminary report). In: 13th International Workshop on Nonmonotonic Reasoning, NMR 2010 (2010)
4. Belnap, N.D.: A useful four-valued logic. In: Epstein, G., Dunn, J.M. (eds.) Modern Uses of Multiple-Valued Logic, pp. 8–37. D. Reidel, Dordrecht (1977)
5. Bruns, G., Dantas, D.S., Huth, M.: A simple and expressive semantic framework for policy composition in access control. In: Proceedings of the 2007 ACM Workshop on Formal Methods in Security Engineering, FMSE 2007, pp. 12–21. ACM, New York (2007)
6. Bruns, G., Huth, M.: Access-control via belnap logic: Effective and efficient composition and analysis. In: 21st IEEE Computer Security Foundations Symposium (June 2008)
7. Evered, M., Bögeholz, S.: A case study in access control requirements for a health information systems. In: Proceedings of the Second Workshop on Australasian Information Security, Data Mining and Web Intelligence, and Software Internationalisation, ACSW Frontiers 2004, vol. 32, pp. 53–61. Australian Computer Society, Inc., Darlinghurst (2004)
8. Halpern, J.Y., Weissman, V.: Using first-order logic to reason about policies. ACM Transaction on Information and System Security (TISSEC) 11(4), 1–41 (2008)
9. Hankin, C., Nielson, F., Nielson, H.R.: Advice from belnap policies. In: Computer Security Foundations Symposium, pp. 234–247. IEEE (2009)
10. Kolovski, V., Hendler, J.: Xacml policy analysis using description logics. In: Proceedings of the 15th International World Wide Web Conference, WWW (2007)
11. Kolovski, V., Hendler, J., Parsia, B.: Formalizing xacml using defeasible description logics. In: Proceedings of the 15th International World Wide Web Conference, WWW (2007)
12. Moses, T.: eXtensible Access Control Markup Language (XACML) version 2.0. Technical report. OASIS (August 2010), http://docs.oasis-open.org/xacml/2.0/access_control-xacml-2.0-core-spec-os.pdf
13. Ni, Q., Bertino, E., Lobo, J.: D-algebra for composing access control policy decisions. In: ASIACCS 2009: Proceedings of the 4th International Symposium on Information, Computer, and Communications Security, pp. 298–309. ACM, New York (2009)
14. Rissanen, E.: eXtensible Access Control Markup Language (XACML) version 3.0 (committe specification 01). Technical report. OASIS (August 2010), http://docs.oasis-open.org/xacml/3.0/xacml-3.0-core-spec-cd-03-en.pdf

---

[4] The detail of all of XACML decisions under $\mathcal{D}$-algebra can be seen in extended paper at http://www2.imm.dtu.dk/~cdpu/Papers/the_logic_of_XACML-extended.pdf

A   Extended Pairwise Policy Values

We add three values into $\mathbf{P}$, i.e. deny with indeterminate permit ($[1, \frac{1}{2}]$), permit with indeterminate deny ($[\frac{1}{2}, 1]$) and conflict ($[1, 1]$) and we call the *extended pairwise policy values* $\mathbf{P}_9 = \mathbf{P} \cup \{ [1, \frac{1}{2}], [\frac{1}{2}, 1], [1, 1] \}$. The extended pairwise policy values shows all possible combination of pairwise policy values. The ordering of $\mathbf{P}_9$ is illustrated in Figure 4.

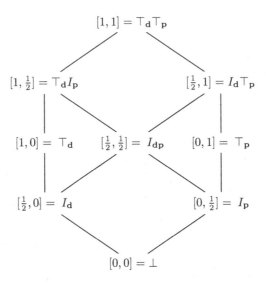

Fig. 4. Nine-Valued Lattice

We can see that $\mathbf{P}_9$ forms a lattice (we call this $\mathcal{L}_9$) where the top element is $[1, 1]$ and the bottom element is $[0, 0]$. The ordering of this lattice is the same as $\sqsubseteq_{\mathbf{P}}$ where the greatest lower bound and the least upper bound for $S \subseteq \mathbf{P}_9$ are defined as follows:

$$\underset{\mathcal{L}_9}{\bigsqcap} S = Max_{\sqsubseteq_{\mathbf{P}}}(S) \text{ and } \underset{\mathcal{L}_9}{\bigsqcup} S = Min_{\sqsubseteq_{\mathbf{P}}}(S)$$

A Proof Assistant Based Formalization
of MDE Components

Mounira Kezadri[1], Benoît Combemale[2], Marc Pantel[1], and Xavier Thirioux[1]

[1] Université de Toulouse, IRIT - France
{Firstname.Lastname}@enseeiht.fr
[2] Université de Rennes 1, IRISA, France
{Firstname.Lastname}@irisa.fr

Abstract. Model driven engineering (MDE) now plays a key role in the development of safety critical systems through the use of early validation and verification of models, and the automatic generation of software and hardware artifacts from the validated and verified models. In order to ease the integration of formal specification and verification technologies, various formalizations of the MDE technologies were proposed by different authors using term or graph rewriting, proof assistants, logical frameworks, etc.

The use of components is also mandatory to improve the efficiency of system development. Invasive Software Composition (ISC) has been proposed by Aßman in [1] to add a generic component structure to existing Domain Specific Modeling Languages in MDE. This approach is the basis of the ReuseWare toolset.

We present in this paper an extension of a formal embedding of some key aspects of MDE in set theory in order to formalize ISC and prove the correctness of the proposed approach with respect to the conformance relation with the base metamodel. The formal embedding we rely on was developed by some of the authors, presented in [25] and then implemented using the Calculus of Inductive Construction and the Coq proof-assistant. This work[1] is a first step in the formalization of composable verification technologies in order to ease its integration for DSML extended with component features using ISC.

1 Introduction

Model driven engineering now plays a key role in the development of safety critical systems through the use of model early validation and verification, and the automatic generation of software or hardware artefacts from the validated and verified models. This approach usually relies on many different Domain Specific Modeling Languages (DSML) either explicitly or through UML and its extensions that provides many different cooperating languages through diagrams (in fact, OMG is currently studying the possibility for the future next major

---

[1] This work was funded by the European Union and the french DGCIS through the ARTEMIS Joint Undertaking inside the CESAR project.

F. Arbab and P.C. Ölveczky (Eds.): FACS 2011, LNCS 7253, pp. 223–240, 2012.
© Springer-Verlag Berlin Heidelberg 2012

version of UML to define it as a collection of cooperating DSML) and profiles. Each DSML is defined as a specific metamodel or as an extension through profiles of a part of a huge metamodel in UML.

The use of components is also mandatory to improve the efficiency of system development. Common DSML do not usually integrate components natively, either because it was not an initial requirement, or to avoid a too complex definition of the language. Invasive Software Composition (ISC) was proposed by Aßman [1] in order to add a generic component structure to any existing DSML. This approach is the basis of REUSEWARE[2] that provides ISC based tools inside the Eclipse Modeling Framework[3]. It allows to define the composition concern relying on elements in the metamodel and then to extract components from existing models with defined composition interface (called fragment boxes), and to compose fragments to produce new fragments or models. All the provided tools are generic and parametrized by the composition concern. The framework allows to adapt and extend an existing language by adding composition facilities at some points called Hook. This extension relies on a metamodel level transformation applied on the language definition based on the specification of the composition concern. The Hook are the variation points introduced in the models whose value can change and thus allows to build components. The main advantage of the ISC technology is that it is generic and can be applied to any language defined by a metamodel. This framework ensures that the result of the composition of fragments extracted from models conforming to a given metamodel is also conforming to the same metamodel. This common conformance is the kind of standard structural properties available in all the MDE frameworks that is verified in this paper. The long term purpose of our work is also to handle behavioral properties and thus tackle the formalization of all kind of compositional verification technologies.

In order to ease the integration of formal specification and verification technologies, some of the authors proposed in [25] a formal embedding of some key aspects of Model Driven Engineering in Set Theory. This embedding was then implemented using the Calculus of Inductive Construction and the CoQ[4] proof-assistant. This first version focused on the notions of models, metamodels, conformance and promotion. It was later extended to express constraints on metamodels using the Object Constraint Language (OCL). The purpose of this framework called CoQ4MDE is to provide sound mathematical foundations for the study and the validation of MDE technologies. The choice of constructive logic and type theory as formal specification language allows to extract prototype tools from the executable specification that can be used to validate the specification itself with respect to external tools implementing the model driven engineering (for example, in the Eclipse Modeling Project).

This paper contributions are the specification of the composition operators provided by the ISC method [1] using an extension of CoQ4MDE and the proof

---

[2] http://www.reuseware.org
[3] http://www.eclipse.org/modeling/emf
[4] http://coq.inria.fr

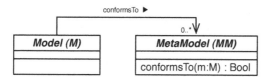

Fig. 1. Model & MetaModel Definition using the UML Class Diagram Notation

of the well-foundedness and termination of these operators. This specification allows to express the models expected properties and the verification technologies for composite models and then provide support for compositional verification. This first contribution focuses on the metamodel structural conformance relation. It relies on the `Model` and `MetaModel` concepts from CoQ4MDE that is extended to represent fragments as proposed by ISC. The various concepts provided by REUSEWARE are formalized leading to the proof that composition preserves metamodel conformity.

First, Section 2 introduces from CoQ4MDE the *Model* and *MetaModel* notions. Then, the REUSEWARE approach for extending DSML with components is presented in Section 3. The CoQ4MDE framework is then extended to support the definition of component interface and the composition operators in Section 4. After that, the validation of a composition function is presented in Section 5. Also, a background of related work is given in Section 6. Finally, conclusion and perspectives are presented in Section 7.

2   Model and MetaModel

This section gives the main insight of our MDE framework CoQ4MDE, derived from [25]. We first define the notions of *model* and *metamodel*. Then, we describe conformity using the *conformsTo* predicate.

Our approach separates the type level from the instance level, and describes them with different structures hence different types. A *Model* (*M*) is the instance level and a *MetaModel* (*MM*) is a modeling language used to define models (Figure 1). A *MM* also specifies the semantic properties of its models. For instance, in UML, a multiplicity is defined on relations to specify the allowed number of objects that have to be linked. Moreover, OCL is used to define more complex structural constraints which may not have any specific graphical notation.

Into our framework, the concept of *MetaModel* is not a specialization of *Model*. They are formally defined in the following way. Let us consider two sets: `Classes`, respectively `References`, represents the set of all possible class, respectively reference, labels. We also consider instances of such classes, the set `Objects` of object labels. `References` includes a specific *inh* label used to specify the inheritance relation. In the following text, we will withdraw the word label and directly talk about classes, references and objects.

Definition 1 (Model). *Let $\mathscr{C} \subseteq$ Classes be a set of classes. Let $\mathscr{R} \subseteq \{\langle c_1, r, c_2 \rangle \mid c_1, c_2 \in \mathscr{C}, r \in$ References$\}$ be the set of references among classes such that $\forall c_1 \in \mathscr{C}, \forall r \in$ References, $card\{c_2 \mid \langle c_1, r, c_2 \rangle \in \mathscr{R}\} \leq 1$.*

A model over $\mathscr{C}$ and $\mathscr{R}$, written $\langle MV, ME \rangle \in$ Model$(\mathscr{C}, \mathscr{R})$ is a multigraph built over a finite set MV of typed object nodes and a finite set ME of reference edges such that:

$$MV \subseteq \{\langle o, c \rangle \mid o \in \text{Objects}, c \in \mathscr{C}\}$$
$$ME \subseteq \{\langle \langle o_1, c_1 \rangle, r, \langle o_2, c_2 \rangle \rangle \mid \langle o_1, c_1 \rangle, \langle o_2, c_2 \rangle \in MV, \langle c_1, r, c_2 \rangle \in \mathscr{R}\}$$

Note that, in case of inheritance, the same object label will be used several time in the same model graph, associated to different classes to build different nodes. This label reuse is related to inheritance polymorphism a key aspect of most OO languages. Inheritance is represented with a special reference called *inh* [5] (usually defined in the metamodeling languages such as MOF [19]).

Accordingly, we first define an auxiliary predicate stating that an object o of type c_1 has a downcast duplicate of type c_2.

$$hasSub(o \in \text{Objects}, c_1, c_2 \in \text{Classes}, \langle MV, ME \rangle) \triangleq$$
$$c_1 = c_2 \vee \exists c_3 \in \text{Classes}, \langle \langle o, c_2 \rangle, inh, \langle o, c_3 \rangle \rangle \in ME$$
$$\wedge hasSub(o, c_1, c_3, \langle MV, ME \rangle)$$

Then, we define the notion of standard inheritance. The first part of the conjunction states that the inheritance relation only conveys duplicate objects. The second part states that every set of duplicates has a common base element (a common inherited class).

$$standardInheritance(\langle MV, ME \rangle) \triangleq$$
$$\forall \langle \langle o_1, c_1 \rangle, inh, \langle o_2, c_2 \rangle \rangle \in ME, o_1 = o_2$$
$$\wedge \forall \langle o_1, c_1 \rangle, \langle o_2, c_2 \rangle \in MV, o_1 = o_2 \Rightarrow \exists c \in \text{Classes},$$
$$hasSub(o_1, c_1, c, \langle MV, ME \rangle)$$
$$\wedge hasSub(o_2, c_2, c, \langle MV, ME \rangle)$$

Finally, the following property states that c_2 is a direct subclass of c_1.

$$subClass(c_1, c_2 \in \text{Classes}, \langle MV, ME \rangle) \triangleq$$
$$\forall \langle o, c \rangle \in MV, c = c_2 \Rightarrow \langle \langle o, c_2 \rangle, inh, \langle o, c_1 \rangle \rangle \in ME$$

Consequently, *Abstract Classes*, that are specified in the metamodel using the *isAbstract* attribute, serve as parent classes and child classes are derived from them. They are not themselves suitable for instantiation. Abstract classes are often used to represent abstract concepts or entities. Features of an abstract class are then shared by a group of sibling sub-classes which may add new properties.

Therefore, a model does not conform to a metamodel if it contains objects that are instances of abstract classes without having instances of concrete derived classes as duplicates.

$$isAsbstract(c_1 \in \text{Classes}, \langle MV, ME \rangle) \triangleq$$
$$\forall \langle o, c \rangle \in MV, c = c_1 \Rightarrow \exists c_2 \in \text{Classes}, \langle \langle o, c_2 \rangle, inh, \langle o, c_1 \rangle \rangle \in ME$$

---

[5] *inh* must not be used in a model or metamodel as a simple reference.

Definition 2 (MetaModel). *A MetaModel is a multigraph representing classes and references as well as semantic properties over instantiation of classes and references. It is represented as a pair composed of a multigraph* (MMV, MME) *built over a finite set* MMV *of class nodes and a finite set* MME *of edges tagged with references, and of a predicate over models representing the semantic properties.*

A metamodel as a pair $\langle (MMV, MME), conformsTo \rangle \in \mathtt{MetaModel}$ *such that:*

$$MMV \subseteq \mathtt{Classes}$$
$$MME \subseteq \{\langle c_1, r, c_2 \rangle \mid c_1, c_2 \in MMV, r \in \mathtt{References}\}$$
$$conformsTo : \mathtt{Model}(MMV, MME) \rightarrow Bool$$

such that $\forall c_1 \in MMV, \forall r \in \mathtt{References}, card\{c_2 \mid \langle c_1, r, c_2 \rangle \in MME\} \leq 1$

Given one model M and one metamodel MM, we can check conformance. The $conformsTo$ predicate embedded in MM achieves this goal. It identifies the set of valid models with respect to a metamodel.

In our framework, the conformance checks on the model M that:

1. every object o in M is the instance of a class C in MM.
2. every link between two objects is such that there exists, in MM, a reference between the two classes typing the two elements. In the following we will say that these links are instances of the reference between classes in MM.
3. finally, every semantic property defined in MM is satisfied in M. For instance, the multiplicity defined on references between concepts denotes a range of possible links between objects of these classes (i.e. concepts). Moreover, structural properties expressed on the metamodel as OCL constraints and behavioural properties will be taken into account in future work as $conformsTo$ predicates.

This notion of conformity can be found in the framework depicted in Figure 1 by a dependency between a M and a MM it conforms to. In fact, the semantic properties associated to the metamodel are encoded into the $conformsTo$ predicate. These semantic properties are not to be given a syntax. Instead, in order to express our properties, we assume an underlying logic that should encompass OCL in terms of expressive power.

In the rest of this paper, we extend the previous MDE framework to formalize compositional technologies. Our final target outside the scope of this paper is to formalize compositional verification activities. CoQ4MDE is extended to support the introduction of components in DSML defined by their metamodels. This extension allows to express fragment boxes (models with defined interface) composition based on concepts from the ISC method.

In the scope of this paper, we take into account a simplified version of the $conformsTo$ predicate (cf. Section 5) called *instanceOf* which is restricted to 1 and 2. We demonstrate that the verification of this *instanceOf* property is compositional relying on the ISC operators (the property of components is preserved in case of composition using the ISC basic operators).

3   ISC and ReuseWare approach

ISC [1] is a generic technology for extending a DSML with model composition facilities. Its first version was defined to compose Java programs and was implemented in the COMPOST system[6]. A universal extension called U-ISC was proposed in [13], this technique deals with textual components that can be described using context-free grammars and then the fragments are represented as trees. The method as presented considers tree merging for the composition. Recently, in order to deal with graphical languages the method was extended to support typed graphs in [15], this method was implemented in the REUSEWARE framework. This last implementation is consistent with the description of models as graphs in our CoQ4MDE framework.

ISC introduces the fragment box structure to group model or source code fragments. The fragment box defines its composition interface and then provides tools and concepts allowing the composition. The composition interface for a fragment box consists of a set of addressable points. Two types of addressable points are defined, the variation points which are elements inside the fragment box that can be used as a receptor for other elements and reference points which are used to address some parts inside a fragment box so they can be used in composition. We formalize thereafter one type of correspondence (variation/reference) points which is the pair (hook/prototype). As described in [12] a hook is a variation point that constitutes a place-holder to contain a fragment referenced by a prototype reference point.

We propose in the following section to extend the CoQ4MDE framework to support ISC concepts and then to define a sound basis to ensure the correctness by construction for this composition style. This enables to describe and to verify structural properties. We plan in future work to extend the formalization to support other kind of properties and especially behavioural properties.

4   Formalizing Model Component Extraction and Composition

4.1   Extended MetaModel with Model Component

We must be able to extend any metamodel to support the definition of fragment boxes. This extension adds the definition of a fragment interface constituted from a set of addressable points. We note the extended metamodel for some metamodel MM as MM^{Ext}. We note ROV the abstract class representing the addressable points, the *Hook* variation point and the *Prototype* reference points are subclasses of ROV. In MM^{Ext}, every node in the graph representing MM can be referenced by an addressable point. For this purpose, an abstract class called *AbsC* is added as a super class for all the classes of MM. This class is linked by the reference *bind* with ROV. The three classes ROV, *Hook* and

---

[6] http://www.the-compost-system.org

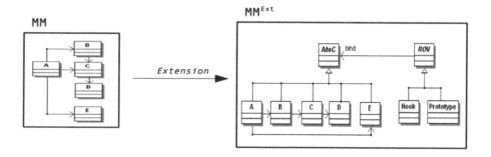

Fig. 2. MetaModel extension

Prototype are also automatically imported to the metamodel with appropriate inheritance relations between them [7].

The following definition represents the extension function implemented in COQ as a graph transformation which is not in the scope of this paper.

Definition 3. *Let* $MM = \langle\langle MMV, MME\rangle, conformsTo\rangle$ *be a metamodel. Let* $ROV, Hook, Prototype, AbsC \in Classes, bind \in References.$ MM^{Ext} *is defined as* $\langle\langle MMV^{Ext}, MME^{Ext}\rangle, conformsTo^{Ext}\rangle$ *such that:*

$$MMV^{Ext} = MMV \cup \{ROV, Hook, Prototype, AbsC\}$$
$$MME^{Ext} = MME \cup \{\langle ROV, bind, AbsC\rangle\}$$
$$conformsTo^{Ext}(\langle MV, ME\rangle) \triangleq conformsTo(\langle MV, ME\rangle)$$
$$\wedge\ isAbstract(ROV)$$
$$\wedge\ subClass(Hook, ROV)$$
$$\wedge\ subClass(Prototype, ROV)$$
$$\wedge\ isAbstract(AbsC)$$
$$\wedge\ \forall c \in MMV, subClass(c, AbsC)$$

The figure 2 shows the example of the extension of the MetaModel MM.

4.2 Component Interface Extraction

The goal of the function `FragmentExtraction` is to construct a fragment box from a model by defining its composition interface. This function takes as parameters: a model, the object referenced in that model and the kind of the addressable point associated to this object.

---

[7] The metamodel extension used in [15] is defined at the third modeling level (metametamodel level) which may use the promotion notion to be defined in the COQ4MDE framework. The extension defined thereafter uses only the second modeling level (metamodel level) which seems to be sufficient.

$FragmentExtraction : Model \times \texttt{Objects} \times \texttt{Classes} \rightarrow Model$ is defined as[8]:

$FragmentExtraction(\langle MV, ME \rangle, o, HP) = \langle MV^{Ext}, ME^{Ext} \rangle$
$where\ HP \in \{Hook, Prototype\}\ and\ \exists c \in \texttt{Classes}, \langle o, c \rangle \in MV$
$such\ that :$
$MV^{Ext} = MV \cup \{\langle h, HP \rangle, \langle h, ROV \rangle, \langle o, AbsC \rangle\}$
$ME^{Ext} = ME \cup \{\langle \langle o, c \rangle, inh, \langle o, AbsC \rangle \rangle,$
$\langle \langle h, ROV \rangle, bind, \langle o, AbsC \rangle \rangle,$
$\langle \langle h, HP \rangle, inh, \langle h, ROV \rangle \rangle\}$

`ElimInterface` eliminates the fragment box interface (all variation and reference points) of a fragment box, it is the inverse function of `FragmentExtraction` in case of only one addressable point in the fragment box. This is implemented in [15] using the *remove* operator which is automatically applied after composition execution to make the component understandable by tools where addressable points semantics is not defined.
$ElimInterface : Model \rightarrow Model$, such as:

$ElimInterface\ \langle MV^{Ext}, ME^{Ext} \rangle = \langle MV, ME \rangle$
$such\ that :$
$MV = \{\langle o, c \rangle \in MV^{Ext} | c \notin \{Hook, Prototype, VOR, AbsC\}\}$
$ME = \{\langle \langle o, c \rangle, r, \langle o', c' \rangle \rangle \in ME^{Ext} | c, c' \notin \{Hook, Prototype, ROV, AbsC\}\}$

The definition of these two functions requires some proofs on multigraphs. First, the proof that the extension of the multigraph representing the model is also a multigraph [9], this is done by proving that adding vertexes to a multigraph generates a multigraph and also adding edges in some conditions to a multigraph is also a multigraph. Second, the proof that deleting some elements from a multigraph representing the fragment box is also a multigraph [10], this is done using a filter function defined on multigraphs. So, Coq4MDE can now support the definition of components with composition interface in any DSML. We describe in the following section the formalization of ISC basics composition operators in Coq4MDE.

4.3   Components Composition

In this section, we present the implementation in our framework of the two basic operators of ISC (*bind* and *extend*) presented in [1] [15] . The difference between these operators is that "the *bind* applied to the hook replaces the hook (i.e., it removes the hook from its containing fragment) while *extend* applied on a hook does not modify the hook itself but uses it as a position for extension (i.e., the hook remains in its containing fragment) ".

---

[8] Another version can be implemented by specifying a set of pairs (o, HP) to add several points at the same time.

[9] http://www.irit.fr/~Mounira.Kezadri/FISC/MMext.html

[10] http://www.irit.fr/~Mounira.Kezadri/FISC/IntElim.html#elimInterface

Bind The bind operator replaces an object $o1$ referenced by a hook variation point by an object $o2$ referenced by a prototype reference point. The links to (resp. from) the object $o1$ are replaced with links to (resp. from) the object $o2$. The composed model is obtained by substituting the object $o1$ by $o2$ in both objects and links sets. $bind : Model \times Model \times (Objects \times Classes) \times (Objects \times Classes) \rightarrow Model$ is defined as:

$$bind(\langle MV1, ME1 \rangle, \langle MV2, ME2 \rangle, \langle b, B \rangle, \langle b', B' \rangle) = \langle MV3, ME3 \rangle$$
$$where \ \langle b, B \rangle \in MV1 \ and \ \langle b', B' \rangle \in MV2, \ we \ have :$$
$$\exists h, p \in Objects, \langle \langle h, Hook \rangle, inh, \langle h, ROV \rangle \rangle \in ME1$$
$$\wedge \langle \langle h, ROV \rangle, bind, \langle b, AbsC \rangle \rangle \in ME1$$
$$\wedge \langle \langle b, B \rangle, inh, \langle b, AbsC \rangle \rangle \in ME1$$
$$\wedge \langle \langle p, Prototype \rangle, inh, \langle p, ROV \rangle \rangle \in ME2$$
$$\wedge \langle \langle p, ROV \rangle, bind, \langle b', AbsC \rangle \rangle \in ME2$$
$$\wedge \langle \langle b', B' \rangle, inh, \langle b', AbsC \rangle \rangle \in ME2$$
$$and \ finally :$$
$$MV3 = substV(\langle b, B \rangle, \langle b', B' \rangle, MV1)$$
$$ME3 = substE(\langle b, B \rangle, \langle b', B' \rangle, ME1)$$

such that $substV(\langle b, B \rangle, \langle b', B' \rangle, MV)$ (resp. $substE(\langle b, B \rangle, \langle b', B' \rangle, ME)$) is the function that replaces $\langle b, B \rangle$ by $\langle b', B' \rangle$ in every element in MV (resp. relation in ME). The condition of the composition is: $B = B'$.

The construction of this function in CoQ requires the proof that substituting an object by another in some multigraph is also a multigraph [11]. The proof is done by induction, it is automatic for the empty graph. In case of a graph built from adding an edge (a reference) to the graph, one reference is presented as $\langle src, dst, a \rangle$, suppose that the substitution replaces $o1$ by $o2$, we must consider all cases of equality between src, dst, $o1$ and $o2$. Last, in case of a graph built by adding a vertex to a graph which considers also cases of equality between the added vertex, $o1$ and $o2$. The current implementation can be largely improved by the definition of some graph operations like the map function, which is currently partially done and will be presented in future work. A recursive call for the previous function using a list of correspondence (Variation/Reference) points allows to replaces several objects at the same time.

Extend. This operator allows to extend a model $\langle MV1, ME1 \rangle$ (the extension point is an object $o1$ addressed as a hook variation point inside the model) by a model $\langle MV2, ME2 \rangle$ at an object $o2$ addressed as a prototype reference point.

This function is parametrized by a metamodel (to insure the type safety) and a name for the added link between $o1$ and $o2$. The composed model consists of a multigraph built over the union of all objects of $\langle MV1, ME1 \rangle$ and $\langle MV2, ME2 \rangle$, all links of the two models in addition to a link between the objects $o1$ and $o2$.

$extend : Model \times Model \times (Objects \times Classes) \times (Objects \times Classes) \times MetaModel \times References \rightarrow Model$ is defined as:

---

[11] http://www.irit.fr/~Mounira.Kezadri/FISC/CompBind.html#GraphSubst

$$extend(\langle MV1, ME1\rangle, \langle MV2, ME2\rangle, \langle b, B\rangle, \langle b', B'\rangle,$$
$$(\langle MMV, MME\rangle, conformsTo), LinkName) = \langle MV3, ME3\rangle$$
$$where \; \exists \; \langle b, B\rangle \in MV1 \; and \; \langle b', B'\rangle \in MV2, \; we \; have:$$
$$extensible(\langle MV1, ME1\rangle, \langle MV2, ME2\rangle, \langle b, B\rangle, \langle b', B'\rangle,$$
$$(\langle MMV, MME\rangle, conformsTo), LinkName) \; such \; that:$$
$$MV3 = MV1 \cup MV2$$
$$ME3 = ME1 \cup ME2 \cup \{\langle\langle b, B\rangle, LinkName, \langle b', B'\rangle\rangle\}$$

The predicate *extensible* checks that a model $\langle MV1, ME1\rangle$ whose interface is $\langle b, B\rangle$ regarding some metamodel $(\langle MMV, MME\rangle, conformsTo)$ can be extended by another model $\langle MV2, ME2\rangle$ whose interface is $\langle b', B'\rangle$.

$$extensible(\langle MV1, ME1\rangle, \langle MV2, ME2\rangle, \langle b, B\rangle, \langle b', B'\rangle,$$
$$(\langle MMV, MME\rangle, conformsTo), LinkName) \triangleq$$
$$isExtendedH(\langle MV1, ME1\rangle, \langle b, B\rangle)$$
$$\wedge isExtendedP(\langle MV1, ME1\rangle), \langle b', B'\rangle)$$
$$\wedge (B, LinkName, B') \in MME$$

The predicate *isExtendedH* verifies that $\langle b, B\rangle$ is a hook in $\langle MV1, ME1\rangle$.

$$isExtendedH\langle MV1, ME1\rangle\langle b, B\rangle \triangleq$$
$$\exists h \in Objects, \langle\langle h, Hook\rangle, inh, \langle h, ROV\rangle\rangle \in ME1$$
$$\wedge \langle\langle h, ROV\rangle, bind, \langle b, AbsC\rangle\rangle \in ME1$$
$$\wedge \langle\langle b, B\rangle, inh, \langle b, AbsC\rangle\rangle \in ME1$$

The predicate *isExtendedP* verifies that $\langle b, B\rangle$ is a prototype in the model.

$$isExtendedP\langle MV2, ME2\rangle\langle b, B\rangle \triangleq$$
$$\exists p, \langle\langle p, Prototype\rangle, inh, \langle p, ROV\rangle\rangle \in ME2$$
$$\wedge \langle\langle p, ROV\rangle, bind, \langle b, AbsC\rangle\rangle \in ME2$$
$$\wedge \langle\langle b, B\rangle, inh, \langle b, AbsC\rangle\rangle \in ME2$$

The construction of this function in CoQ requires the proof that the multigraph built by extending another multigraph as described in the function *extend* is also a multigraph [12].

Here we defined only one type of correspondence variation and reference point (hook/prototype), the method as presented in [15] considers also another type of correspondence (slot/anchor). The second type requires to consider the containment property of an edge. The difference as explained in [15] is that contrarily to hook and prototype the slot variation point and the anchor reference point keeps their containments in case of composition. The first type of correspondence allows to express quite complicated composition functions like described in the following example and is consistent with the current models graph representation. The second type of correspondence can be considered in future work. The operators like described here are applied to the two models, a generalization to

---

[12] http://www.irit.fr/~Mounira.Kezadri/FISC/CompBind.html#compositionExtend

an application on several models at the same time is allowed in REUSEWARE and can be implemented in our framework as an iterative application of the operators by composing the models one by one or by defining more general operators that can be applied on several models.

4.4 Detailed Example

We describe in this section the use of the previously defined basic operators to elaborate a model composition. M_1 is a state machine modeling a door with a lock. The door provides the operations: open, close, pass, lock and unlock. We would like to add the possibility of simple and double locking the door, these two states are described in the model M_2. M_1 and M_2 are described in Fig. 3.

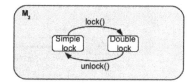

Fig. 3. M_1 and M_2 models

The first step is to define the interface for each model. This is done with the *FragmentExtraction* function, the function applied to the model M_1 defines *Locked* as a hook and applied to M_2 defines *Simple lock* as a prototype like described in Fig. 4.

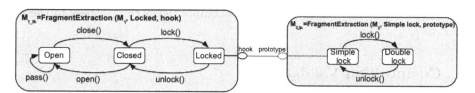

Fig. 4. Variation and reference point for the models M_1 and M_2

The application of the function *bind* on the two fragments as described in Fig. 4 followed by the elimination of the interface produces the model M_{bind} shown in Fig. 5.

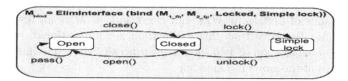

Fig. 5. Model after execution of the *bind* function

Then, *Simple lock* is defined in M_{bind} as a prototype reference point and *Double lock* is defined in $M_{2\_fp\_elim}$ as a hook variation point as shown in Fig. 6.

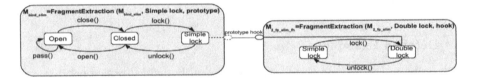

Fig. 6. Fragment boxes extraction

The execution of the function *extend* on the two models in Fig. 6 after the interface elimination generates the model presented in Fig. 7. The model is the state machine for a door with a double lock option.

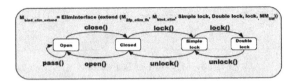

Fig. 7. Model after execution of the *extend* and *ElimInterface* functions

The original contribution of this paper is not the definition of composition operators which is inspired from ISC but their implementation in the CoQ proof assistant, their integration in the CoQ4MDE framework and the proof that the verification of the *instanceOf* property is compositional with respect to these operators.

5   Composition Validation

The **bind** and **extend** operators are defined in order to enforce the well typedness properties. These two operators like all the concepts presented in this paper are encoded in the CoQ proof assistant. The aim of this formalization is to check some properties on the composite models and then provide the basis for the specification and proof of correctness of compositional verification technologies. The first property considered is the well typedness property. This property is related to the conformance defined in Section2. It checks that every object in M is the instance of a class in MM and every link in M is an instance of a relation in MM. To prove that this verification is compositional, we need to prove that the composition of two models instances of the same metamodel is also an instance of the same metamodel.

We define the first validity criteria for any composition function. This criteria is defined as a higher order predicate that checks the well typedness for some function. The function **InstanceOf** is used in that purpose, it checks that all objects and links of a *Model* are instances of classes and references in a meta-model.

$$InstanceOf(\langle\langle MV, ME\rangle, \langle\langle MMV, MME, conformsTo\rangle\rangle\rangle) \triangleq$$
$$\forall \langle o, c\rangle \in MV, c \in MMV \wedge$$
$$\forall \langle\langle o, c\rangle, r, \langle o', c'\rangle\rangle \in ME \wedge \langle c, r, c'\rangle \in MME$$

Then, the predicate `ValidCompositionFunction`$_{MM}$ reflects this criteria. It verifies that using two components instance of MM, the component resulting from the application of a composition function `f` is also instance of MM.

$$ValidCompositionFunction(MM \in MetaModel, f) \triangleq$$
$$\forall M1\ M2 \in Model,$$
$$InstanceOf\ (M1, MM)\ \wedge InstanceOf\ (M2, MM)$$
$$\rightarrow InstanceOf\ ((f\ M1\ M2), MM)$$

We use this predicate to verify the type safety for the composition operator *bind* described in Section 4.3. This is described in the theorem `ValidBind`.

$$\textbf{Theorem}\ ValidBind : \forall\ MM \in MetaModel,$$
$$ValidCompositionFunction(MM, bind)$$

The COQ proof is done for this theorem. It uses intermediate lemmas that prove the preservation of the well typedness by the elementary operations implied in the composition. Among these lemmas, `conformsAddO` ensures that the result of adding an object instance of a class in the metamodel to a component instance of this metamodel is a component instance of the same metamodel.

$$\textbf{Theorem}\ conformsAddO :$$
$$\forall \langle MV, ME\rangle \in Model, \langle\langle MMV, MME\rangle, conformsTo\rangle \in MetaModel.$$
$$\forall o \in \texttt{Objects}, c \in \texttt{Classes}.$$
$$InstanceOf(\langle MV, ME\rangle, \langle\langle MMV, MME\rangle, conformsTo\rangle) \wedge c \in MMV$$
$$\rightarrow InstanceOf(\langle MV \cup \{\langle o, c\rangle\}, ME\rangle, \langle\langle MMV, MME\rangle, conformsTo\rangle)$$

Another COQ proof was done to demonstrate the type safety for the composition operator *extend* described also in Section 4.3. This is encoded in the theorem `ValidExtend`.

$$\textbf{Theorem}\ ValidExtend : \forall\ MM \in MetaModel,$$
$$ValidCompositionFunction(MM, extend)$$

Also, similar correction properties should hold for the fragment extraction function and the elimination function.

$$\textbf{Theorem}\ ValidFragmentExtraction :$$
$$\forall \langle MV, ME\rangle \in Model, \langle\langle MMV, MME\rangle, conformsTo\rangle \in MetaModel.$$
$$\forall o \in \texttt{Objects}, HP \in \{Hook, Prototype\}.$$
$$InstanceOf(\langle MV, ME\rangle, \langle\langle MMV, MME\rangle, conformsTo\rangle)$$
$$\rightarrow InstanceOf(FragmentExtraction(\langle MV, ME\rangle, o, HP),$$
$$\langle\langle MMV^{Ext}, MME^{Ext}\rangle, conformsTo^{Ext}\rangle)$$

Theorem $ValidInterfaceElimination$:
$\forall \langle MV, ME \rangle \in Model, \langle (MMV, MME), conformsTo \rangle \in MetaModel.$
$InstanceOf(\langle MV, ME \rangle, \langle (MMV^{Ext}, MME^{Ext}), conformsTo^{Ext} \rangle)$
$\rightarrow InstanceOf(InterfaceElimination(\langle MV, ME \rangle),$
$\langle (MMV, MME), conformsTo \rangle)$

So, starting from the COQ4MDE framework and from the ISC composition method, we defined a framework for model composition. The definitions of model and metamodel were extended to support the definition of model composition interface, the constituted fragment box is also a model conforms to an extended metamodel. The basic composition operators was described like all elements in this paper using the COQ proof assistant. The source code is about 6400 lines, it is accessible at `http://www.irit.fr/~Mounira.Kezadri/FISC/index.html`. The formalization in COQ ensures the termination[13] of the composition operators, elaborates a compositional verification property and also will enable to describe and prove more richer properties in future work.

6   Related Work

6.1   Composition Approaches

Models are aspects of the system that must be composed to build the final system, similarly to aspects in AOP [16]. Tools and approaches have been proposed aiming to automate the composition task. This problem concerns a wide variety of modeling domains and includes several techniques. We are looking for an approach that supports component extraction from models and model composition from components. The ISC approach supports these two characteristics, it enables to extend arbitrary language to provide reusable components using the fragment box concept. In this method components can be invasively composed, this can be done by adapting or extending the component at some variation points (fragments or positions, which are subject to change) by transformation. Several composition methods were collected in[14]. most of these methods are interested in implementing the merge operator by using some mappings between the models like Rational Software Architect[14] , Bernstein et al. data model [5], Atlas Model Weaver [15] [10], Epsilon [16], Theme/UML [7] and EMF Facet[17]. Merge operators as presented in these works can be implemented in our framework and constitute one of the directions for future work.

---

[13] We can't write any function in COQ if the proof of termination is not given or deduced by COQ.

[14] http://www-306.ibm.com/software/awdtools/architect/swarchitect/

[15] http://www.eclipse.org/gmt/amw/

[16] http://www.eclipse.org/gmt/epsilon/

[17] www.eclipse.org/proposals/emf-facet/

6.2   Formalization of Model Driven Engineering

MoMENT (MOdel manageMENT) [6] is a model management framework based on experiments in formal model transformation and data migration, it provides a set of generic operators to manipulate models. MoMENT relies on algebraic formalisms using the Maude language [8]. In this framework, the metamodels are represented as algebraic specifications and the operators are defined independently of the metamodel. To be used, the operators must be specified in a module called signature that specify the constructs of the metamodel. The approach was implemented in a tool [18] that gives also an automatic translation from an EMF metamodel to a signature model.

A. Vallecillo et al. have designed and implemented previously a different embedding of metamodels, models ([24]) and model transformations ([26]) using MAUDE. This embedding is shallow, it relies strongly on the object structure proposed by MAUDE in order to define model elements as objects, and relies on the object rewriting semantics in order to implement model transformations.

I. Poernomo has proposed an encoding of metamodels and models using type theory ([21]) in order to allow correct by construction development of model transformation using proof assistant like CoQ ([22]). Some simple experiments have been conducted using CoQ mainly on tree-shaped models ([23]) using inductive types. General graph model structure can be encoded using co-inductive types. However, as shown in [20] by C. Picard and R. Matthes, the encoding is quite complex as CoQ enforces structural constraints when combining inductive and co-inductive types that forbid the use of the most natural encodings proposed by Poernomo et al. M. Giorgino et al. rely in [11] on a spanning tree of the graph combined with additional links to overcome that constraint using the ISABELLE proof assistant. This allows to develop a model transformation relying on slightly adapted inductive proofs and then extract classical imperative implementations. These embeddings are all shallow: they rely on sophisticated similar data structure to represent model elements and metamodels (e.g. CoQ (co-)inductive data types for model elements and object and (co-)inductive types for metamodel elements).

The work described in this paper is a deep embedding, each concept from models and metamodels are encoded using elementary constructs instead of relying on similar elements in MAUDE, CoQ or ISABELLE. The purpose of this contribution is not to implement model transformation using correct-by-construction tools but to give a kind of denotational semantics for model driven engineering concepts that should provide a deeper understanding and allow the formal validation of the various implemented technologies.

6.3   Formalization of Models Composition

We have presented a formalization of the ISC concepts that is expressed using the CoQ proof assistant. This formalization focuses on structural properties of the

---

[18] http://moment.dsic.upv.es/

components and extends a previous formalization of MOF MDE metamodeling framework. The composition semantics of ISC is a simple substitution mechanism and do not relies on middleware services providing a sophisticated Model of Computation. Thus, our work is neither based on the previous formalization of ISC that uses Frame Logic (F-Logic [17]) [2] nor on Turing-complete calculus that can formally describe the execution of components such as the form-based composition [18] and the compositional aggregation for the behaviour graph of parallel processes [9]. The advantages of this formalization are the proof of termination for the composition functions and the possibility of extracting the validated executable code after some modifications on functions that are written now for validation purpose.

6.4   Compositional Verification

In order to develop safety critical systems, methods are now needed that allows not only the reuse of components but also of their properties for inferring the global properties of the composite system from properties of its constituent components. Nguyen, T.H. proposes in [4] a compositional verification approach to check safety properties of component-based systems. The systems are described in the BIP (Behavior - Interaction - Priority) language [3]. Another approach allowing to verify systems by composition from verified components was proposed in [27], this approach reduces the complexity of verifying component-based systems by utilizing their compositional structures. In this approach, temporal properties of a software component are specified, verified, and packaged with the component. The selection of a component for reuse considers also its temporal properties. The Ptolemy[19] project proposes a compositional theory for concurrent, real-time, embedded systems. It uses well defined models of computation and defines an unified mathematical framework to relate heterogeneous models of computation. In this paper, regarding the previous cited methods, we adopted a generic composition technology where the interactions and temporal properties are not yet integrated. This is planned for future work.

7   Conclusion

Starting from COQ4MDE our formal framework for model and metamodel definition, we have tackled the problem of model composition. Taking inspiration from the ISC generic method for model composition and also from the REUSE-WARE toolbox, we proposed first a metamodel extension, and associated model operators for expressing component extraction and composition. This yielded a formalization of model components, model extraction and model composition. All these notions are also currently being reflected in the COQ proof assistant, following the line of thought of our previous work around model and metamodel formalization. This embedding provides us correct-by-construction pieces of executable code for the different model operations related to composition. For

---

[19] http://ptolemy.eecs.berkeley.edu/

instance model extraction and model composition are both proved to be terminating, the latter operation being in addition correct, as advocated by the main theorem. As we target a general purpose MDE-oriented framework, our work applies to any model, modeling language, application and is not restricted to some more-or-less implicit language context.

Yet, for the ease of experimentation, we have in a first step somehow restricted the possibilities of our composition framework. For instance, the notion of conformity, a notion at the heart of our formal description, has been temporarily weakened to take into account only instantiation constraints, disregarding any other model property (multiplicity, etc).

As future work, all these constraints should be enforced to achieve a fully-fledged formal model composition framework.

Furthermore, the interplay between model composition (where objects are replaced by others, assuming they have the same type) and sub-typing (where a single object may exhibit many types, due to duplication) needs to be clearly worked out in our framework.

This proposal is a preliminary mandatory step in the formalization of compositional formal verification technologies. We have tackled the formal composition of models from model fragments independently of the properties satisfied by the model fragments and the expected properties for the composite model. The next step in our work is to formalize the notion of model verification relying on several use case from simple static constraints such as typing or verification of OCL constraints satisfaction, to more dynamic properties such as deadlock freedom as proposed in the BIP framework. The expected result of our work is a framework to define compositional verification technologies and to prove the correctness of the associated verification tools.

References

1. Aßmann, U.: Invasive software composition. Springer-Verlag New York Inc. (2003)
2. Azurat, A.: Mechanization of invasive software composition in F-logic. In: Proceedings of the 2007 Annual Conference on International Conference on Computer Engineering and Applications, pp. 89–94. World Scientific and Engineering Academy and Society, WSEAS (2007)
3. Basu, A., Bozga, M., Sifakis, J.: Modeling heterogeneous real-time components in BIP. In: Fourth IEEE International Conference on Software Engineering and Formal Methods, SEFM 2006, pp. 3–12. IEEE (2006)
4. Bensalem, S., Bozga, M., Nguyen, T., Sifakis, J.: Compositional verification for component-based systems and application. IET Software 4(3), 181–193 (2010)
5. Bernstein, P., Halevy, A., Pottinger, R.: A vision for management of complex models. ACM Sigmod Record 29(4), 55–63 (2000)
6. Boronat, A., Meseguer, J.: An algebraic semantics for mof. Formal Asp. Comput. 22(3-4), 269–296 (2010)
7. Clarke, S.: Extending standard UML with model composition semantics. Science of Computer Programming 44(1), 71–100 (2002)
8. Clavel, M., Durán, F., Eker, S., Lincoln, P., Martí-Oliet, N., Meseguer, J., Quesada, J.: Maude: specification and programming in rewriting logic. Theoretical Computer Science 285(2), 187–243 (2002)

9. Crouzen, P., Lang, F.: Smart Reduction. In: Giannakopoulou, D., Orejas, F. (eds.) FASE 2011. LNCS, vol. 6603, pp. 111–126. Springer, Heidelberg (2011)
10. Fabro, M.D.D., Valduriez, P.: Towards the efficient development of model transformations using model weaving and matching transformations. Software and System Modeling 8(3), 305–324 (2009)
11. Giorgino, M., Strecker, M., Matthes, R., Pantel, M.: Verification of the Schorr-Waite Algorithm – From Trees to Graphs. In: Alpuente, M. (ed.) LOPSTR 2010. LNCS, vol. 6564, pp. 67–83. Springer, Heidelberg (2011)
12. Heidenreich, F., Henriksson, J., Johannes, J., Zschaler, S.: On Language-Independent Model Modularisation. In: Katz, S., Ossher, H., France, R., Jézéquel, J.-M. (eds.) Transactions on Aspect-Oriented Software Development VI. LNCS, vol. 5560, pp. 39–82. Springer, Heidelberg (2009)
13. Henriksson, J.: A Lightweight Framework for Universal Fragment Composition with an application in the Semantic Web, PhD thesis. TU Dresden (January 2009)
14. Jeanneret, C.: An Analysis of Model Composition Approaches. Master's thesis. Ecole Polytechnique Fédérale de Lausanne (2007-2008)
15. Johannes, J.: Component-Based Model-Driven Software Development. Ph.D. thesis, vorgelegt an der Technischen Universität Dresden Fakultät Informatik (2011)
16. Kiczales, G., Lamping, J., Menhdhekar, A., Maeda, C., Lopes, C., Loingtier, J.M., Irwin, J.: Aspect-Oriented Programming. In: Aksit, M., Auletta, V. (eds.) ECOOP 1997. LNCS, vol. 1241, pp. 220–242. Springer, Heidelberg (1997)
17. Kifer, M., Lausen, G., Wu, J.: Logical foundations of object-oriented and frame-based languages. Journal of the ACM 42(4), 741–843 (1995)
18. Lumpe, M., Schneider, J.: A form-based meta-model for software composition. Science of Computer Programming 56(1-2), 59–78 (2005)
19. Object Management Group, Inc.: Meta Object Facility (MOF) 2.0 Core Specification (January 2006), http://www.omg.org/docs/formal/06-01-01.pdf (final Adopted Specification)
20. Picard, C., Matthes, R.: Coinductive graph representation: the problem of embedded lists. In: Electronic Communications of the EASST, Special Issue Graph Computation Models, GCM 2010 (2011)
21. Poernomo, I.: The meta-object facility typed. In: Haddad, H. (ed.) SAC, pp. 1845–1849. ACM (2006)
22. Poernomo, I.: Proofs-as-Model-Transformations. In: Vallecillo, A., Gray, J., Pierantonio, A. (eds.) ICMT 2008. LNCS, vol. 5063, pp. 214–228. Springer, Heidelberg (2008)
23. Poernomo, I., Terrell, J.: Correct-by-Construction Model Transformations from Partially Ordered Specifications in Coq. In: Dong, J.S., Zhu, H. (eds.) ICFEM 2010. LNCS, vol. 6447, pp. 56–73. Springer, Heidelberg (2010)
24. Romero, J.R., Rivera, J.E., Durán, F., Vallecillo, A.: Formal and tool support for model driven engineering with maude. Journal of Object Technology 6(9), 187–207 (2007)
25. Thirioux, X., Combemale, B., Crégut, X., Garoche, P.L.: A Framework to Formalise the MDE Foundations. In: Paige, R., Bézivin, J. (eds.) International Workshop on Towers of Models (TOWERS), Zurich, pp. 14–30 (June 2007)
26. Troya, J., Vallecillo, A.: Towards a Rewriting Logic Semantics for ATL. In: Tratt, L., Gogolla, M. (eds.) ICMT 2010. LNCS, vol. 6142, pp. 230–244. Springer, Heidelberg (2010)
27. Xie, F., Browne, J.: Verified systems by composition from verified components. ACM SIGSOFT Software Engineering Notes 28(5), 277–286 (2003)

Controlling an Iteration-Wise Coherence in Dataflow*

Sébastien Limet, Sophie Robert, and Ahmed Turki

Laboratoire d'Informatique Fondamentale d'Orléans, Université d'Orléans, France

Abstract. This paper formalizes a data-flow component model specifically designed for building real-time interactive scientific visualization applications. The advantages sought in this model are performance, coherence and application design assistance. The core of the article deals with the interpretation of a property and constraint based user specification to generate a concrete assembly based on our component model. To fulfill one or many coherence constraints simultaneously, the application graph is processed, particularly to find the optimal locations of filtering objects called regulators. The automatic selection and inter-connection of connectors in order to maintain the requested coherences and the highest performance possible is also part of the process.

Keywords: Composition, Coherence, Coordination, Synchronization.

1 Introduction

Assisted or semi-automated composition is a recurrent feature in component-based frameworks [6], particularly when the end users are not computer scientists. The aim is to provide an abstraction layer that makes composition more intuitive, descriptive and, ideally, close to the natural language. Research in this area addresses the underlying reasoning approaches that would map the user's specification to the concrete assembly of the model's elements. Apart from hiding the technicalities of the model, the purpose of allowing a coarse grained specification is to alleviate the complexity of tuning a whole system, a complexity that grows exponentially with the size of this system.

Automation can take place in two aspects of dataflow composition: consistency and coordination. The former consists in ensuring the compatibility of the data exchanged by the components and is an inescapable feature for scientific workflow designers [2, 13]. The latter deals with the execution order of the components. In models where connection patterns are mainly blocking, i.e. synchronous, the execution of the components is sequential. Solutions have then to be provided to allow users to put loops or branching in their workflows so that they can accurately set up their processing scenarios. While some approaches [4, 7, 11, 14] propose ready-to use control constructs, others [3] suggest composition languages to build advanced coordination patterns out of simpler ones.

---

* This work is supported by the french ANR project FvNano.

F. Arbab and P.C. Ölveczky (Eds.): FACS 2011, LNCS 7253, pp. 241–258, 2012.
© Springer-Verlag Berlin Heidelberg 2012

The level of abstraction of the application's specification that the different approaches propose closely depends on the targeted audience and application areas. The component approach has, for example, been widely used in scientific computing. A variety of Scientific Workflow Management Systems (SWMSs) [18] exist to design, generate, deploy and execute scientific applications. The targeted applications usually consist in carrying out an overall process over a dataset through a sequence of finite steps. Despite the name "workflow", the current state of the art of SWMS is divided into frameworks adopting either a workflow paradigm [5] or a dataflow paradigm [7, 11, 14]. Because they are less dependent on the components' implementations -no function calls between components, only data is exchanged-, dataflow-oriented frameworks promote code reuse better. In SWMSs, the trend is to bring the specification to an always higher level. In [12], the authors suggest to refine the results of a workflow execution with intents and goals expressed at specification. In SWMSs also, the processing pipeline that produced a result is referred to as the *provenance* of this result [15] and is a crucial information for scientists. Provenance is usually recorded and displayed at the end of an execution for analysis [1, 11] or for failure diagnosis [17]. However, because it is itself seen as part of the result set, the SWMSs do not provide any interface for a priori controlling or parameterizing provenance. This would though help ensure the accuracy of a result depending on the coherence of its different sources.

In [10], we introduced a component model specifically designed for high performance interactive scientific applications. In that model, components can encapsulate different kinds of tasks: computing, display, user control management, data conversion, etc. They, by definition, run iteratively and their composition is the loosest possible to promote performance. It was presented along with a coarse grained coordination specification system. Coupling is usually loose in such applications so branching control is not necessary and coordination rather defines the degree of synchronicity between components. Nevertheless, spatial and temporal provenance remain important. That is why, in our model's specification system, we introduced the possibility of imposing tight coherence constraints which consisted in allowing the user to request an exact synchronicity between message flows reaching the same component. This property is, to scientists, among the relevant information [16] when evaluating their results. Our contribution was then to automatically adapt the user's initial graph to fulfill this type of constraints. In the current paper, we intend to enrich the definition of coherence and the component model to allow looser user provenance constraints.

This paper is organized as follows: Section 2 introduces our component model. Section 3 details our methodology to automatically build a coherent dataflow out of a user specification. In Section 4, we evaluate our method and give the axes of our future work.

2   Component Model

In [10], we have defined a component model for Real-time interactive (RTI) applications including a component of iterative nature and five inter-component connection patterns. We also described how this model and our connection patterns can be used to construct an application guaranteeing a tight coherence of the data consumed by a component. In this section, we briefly give a reminder of our model and add to it a new object called the *regulator*.

2.1 Components

A component works iteratively. It is defined as a quadruple $C = (n, I, O, f)$ where n is the name of the component and I and O two sets of user defined input and output ports. I and O respectively include s (for *start*) and e (for *end*), two default triggering input and output ports. f is a boolean to indicate that the component must run *freely* and that its iteration cycle can not be blocked by other components. The iteration cycle of the component consists in

1. receiving new messages on all its connected input ports, including s,
2. when all its input ports are fed, beginning a new iteration,
3. at the end of the iteration, producing new data on all its output ports and an ending signal on e that can be connected to the s port of another object to trigger it.

Each component numbers its iterations. *input* and *output ports* are identified by a *name* and data circulating between ports are called *messages*. Along with the data it transports, a message m also contains *stamps*. A stamp is a small information associated to a message and generated by the sender. Each message contains at least one stamp, denoted $it(m)$, that is the iteration number of the component that produced it. The components of our model can also handle empty messages, i.e. containing no data, allowing it to go out of the waiting state as soon as all of its input ports are supplied. For a component C, $name(C)$ denotes its name and $I(C)$ and $O(C)$ respectively its sets of input and output ports. A port of a component C is denoted $C.i$ with $i \in I(C)$ or $C.o$ with $o \in O(C)$.

2.2 Connectors

Connectors must be set between two components to determine the communication policy between them, i.e. the type of synchronization and the possibility to lose messages or not. A connector c is a quadruple $c = (n, \{s, i\}, \{o\}, t)$ where t is its type and i is an input port and o an output port. n and s are similar to their homonyms in the component. We use the same notations $name(c)$ and $type(c)$ as for components. c can store several messages. When the sender writes a message on an output port, it simply adds this message to the connector and when the receiver reads its input ports, the connector delivers one of its messages.

Because the components might run at different rates, the connectors need to avoid the overflow of messages when the receiver is slower than the sender. On the other hand, the sender might also slow the receiver down if its iteration rate is lower. To tackle these problems, we propose five connection patterns besides the plain *FIFO*, summarized in Figure 1. These connectors needed to be carefully designed in order to express fine inter-components synchronization policies.

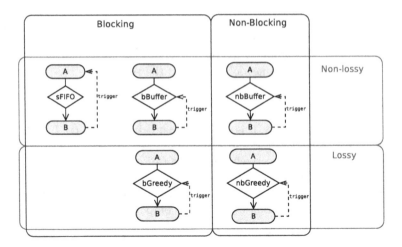

Fig. 1. The five connectors of our framework

- The **sFIFO** connector is a plain FIFO connection where, to prevent overflows, the sender waits for a triggering signal on its s port usually sent by
  the receiver.
- The **bBuffer** and **nbBuffer** keep their incoming messages until the reception
  of a triggering signal and then dispatches the oldest message. These buffered
  FIFO connections can be useful to absorb overflows when one of the two
  components has an irregular iteration rate. The **n(on)b(locking)Buffer**
  connector dispatches empty messages when its buffer is empty whereas the
  b(locking)Buffer blocks the receiver until fresh messages arrive.
- A greedy connector keeps only the last message provided by the sender and
  sends it upon the receiver's request. It is usually used to avoid overflows when
  it is not required that all the messages are processed. The **bGreedy** and the
  nbGreedy are, respectively, the blocking and the non-blocking variants of
  this pattern.

2.3   Regulators

Regulators are special multi-channel connectors that coordinate the message
flows of several communication channels. Their policy is expressed by user-
defined coherence rules to filter the message flows on the different channels.
These rules are linear formulae over message iteration numbers. Formally, a *regulator*, illustrated in Figure 2, is a quintuple $r = (n, I, O, F, b)$ where n is its
name, I and O its sets of input and output ports. I contains a triggering port s.
F is a set of formula, also denoted $F(r)$. A formulae has the form $in_i \circ \alpha \times in_j + \delta$
with $in_i, in_j \in I \setminus \{s\}, \circ \in \{\leq, =, \approx\}$ and $\alpha, \delta \in \mathbf{N}$. The operator $\approx$, used with
$\delta > 0$, denotes an absolute gap tolerance of δ between the two operands in_i
and in_j. b is a boolean that denotes the blocking behaviour of the regulator.

Moreover there is a one to one correspondence between the ports of $I \setminus \{s\}$ and those of O. These two sets thus contain the same number of ports.

Let $M = \{m_1, \ldots, m_n\}$ be a set of messages contained in each buffer of messages received by r on its n input ports. We say that M *validates* $f = in_i \circ \alpha \times in_j + \delta$ of $F(r)$ if $it(m_i) \circ \alpha \times it(m_j) + \delta$. M validates $F(r)$ if it validates all the formulae of $F(r)$.

The behaviour of a regulator is the following:

1. it buffers the messages received on its input ports,
2. each time it receives a signal on its port s, it analyzes the iteration numbers of the messages available in its input buffers,
3. (a) if a set of messages that validates $F(r)$ can be found in the buffers, the regulator moves them to the corresponding output ports and flushes the older messages in the buffers. Besides, if, in an input buffer, more than one messages fulfills the rules, the oldest one is selected.
   (b) otherwise, the regulator dispatches empty messages from all of its output ports if b is set to false and does nothing if not.

Thanks to blocking connectors or to the synchronization mechanisms described in Section 3, the coherence established by a regulator can be maintained throughout the application.

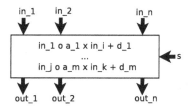

Fig. 2. Schema of the regulator

2.4   Links

Links connect components, connectors and regulators together via their ports. They are denoted by $(x.p, y.q)$ with x, y components, connectors or regulators, $p \in O(x)$ and $q \in I(y)$. There are two types of links:

- **A data link** transmits data messages. For a data link $(x.p, y.q)$, we impose that $p \neq e$, $q \neq s$ and at least x or y is a connector or a regulator. Indeed, as a connector or a regulator is always required to define a communication policy, a data link cannot be directly set between two components.
- A **triggering link** transmits *triggering signals*. For such a link $(x.p, y.q)$, we impose that x is a component, $p = e$ and $q = s$. Please note that, to avoid deadlocks, neither components nor connectors nor regulators wait for a triggering signal before their very first iteration.

2.5   Application Graph

With these elements, an application is represented by a graph called the *application graph*. The vertices of this graph are the components, the connectors and the regulators. The edges represent the links.

Definition 1. *Let $\mathcal{C}$ be a set of components, $\mathcal{L}$ a set of connectors, $\mathcal{R}$ a set of regulators, $\mathcal{D}$ a set of data links, $\mathcal{T}$ a set of triggering links. The graph $\mathcal{G} = (\mathcal{C} \cup \mathcal{L} \cup \mathcal{R}, \mathcal{D} \cup \mathcal{T})$ defines an application graph. In the remainder of this article, we call a data path of $\mathcal{G}$ an acyclic path in the graph $(\mathcal{C} \cup \mathcal{L} \cup \mathcal{R}, \mathcal{D})$.*

With $\mathcal{G}$ an application graph, let us also consider the following additional definitions:

- We call the *source* $src(p)$ the starting vertex of a data path p of $\mathcal{G}$ and *destination* $dest(p)$ its ending vertex,
- A message m arriving at $dest(p)$ is called a *result* of p and the message from the source that originates this result is denoted by $ori(m)$,
- A data path whose source and destination are components is called a *pipeline*,
- $rank_p(x)$ denotes the rank of element x along pipeline p. $rank_p(src(p)) = 1, rank_p(dest(p)) = length(p)$ with $length(p)$ the number of elements of p.

Figure 3 illustrates a sample application graph.

3   Provenance-Based Coherence

This section describes a composition method to build an application that can be deployed on a distributed architecture. We aim to propose an automatic process in a few steps to transform a specification graph defined by a scientist into an application graph respecting all the coherence constraints and allowing the best performance possible.

3.1   Specification Graph

Application specification helps the user focus on the expected properties of the communications in the application, sparing him technicalities. It is done through a directed graph called the *specification graph*. The vertices of this graph are the components of the application and its edges indicate which component ports are connected together. Its vertices are the components defined in Section 2.1. The edges, directed from the sender to the receiver, are labelled with the output and input ports and with constraints on the communications. These constraints are of two types

- the *message policy*, i.e. can this communication drop messages or not,
- the *synchronization policy*, i.e. should the receiver of the message be blocked when no new messages are available.

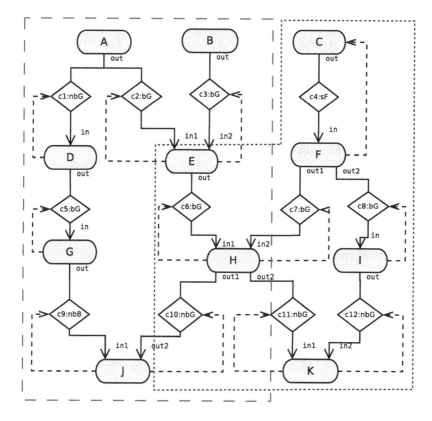

Fig. 3. An application graph

These communication constraints are used to construct a *preliminary application graph* where connectors are automatically chosen to implement the synchronization policy with the best performance possible but without any guarantee on coherence. Besides the graph itself, a set of constraints $\mathcal{K}$ defines the coherence constraints on the input ports of the components. Provenance-based coherence is a fine type of coherence based on the tolerated -positive, null or negative- iteration gap between two messages m_1 and m_2 issued by two output ports, and originating the messages that arrive simultaneously to two input ports of a component at each iteration of it. While in [10] we introduced a tight coherence imposing equalities between message iterations and a common component as message source, this new coherence type aims at allowing more flexible synchronization policies when the application needs not to manipulate data generated exactly at the same iteration by the same component. More formally provenance-based coherence is defined as follows:

Definition 2. *Let C_1, C_2 and D be three components such that $C_1 \neq D, C_2 \neq D, o_i \in O(C_1), o_j \in O(C_2)$ and $\{i_k, i_l\} \subset I(D)$. The coherence constraint κ defined by $D_{i_k, i_l} : C_1.o_i \circ \alpha \times C_2.o_j + \delta$ with $\circ \in \{\leq, =, \approx\}$ and $\{\alpha, \delta\} \in \mathbf{N}$ is* satisfied if, for each pair of pipelines p_1 and p_2 starting respectively at $C_1.o_i$ and $C_2.o_j$ and reaching respectively $D.i_k$ and $D.i_l$, we ensure that $it(ori(m_1)) \circ \alpha \times it(ori(m_2)) + \delta$ where m_1 and m_2 are results of respectively p_1 and p_2 read at the same iteration of D. Such a pair of pipelines p_1 and p_2 are called sibling pipelines with respect to coherence κ. $sib_\kappa(p)$ denotes the set of sibling pipelines of pipeline p with respect to coherence κ.

Figure 4 gives an example of specification graph to which we add the following provenance coherence constraints:

- $\kappa_1 = J_{in_1,in_2} : A.out \approx B.out + 10$, which means that, at each iteration of component J, we do not allow the pair of messages read on in_1 and in_2 of J to reflect an absolute iteration difference between A and B that is greater than 10 iterations.
- $\kappa_2 = K_{in_1,in_2} : E.out \approx C.out + 5$, which has the same meaning as the previous constraint.

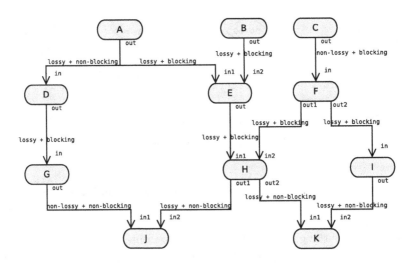

Fig. 4. A specification graph

3.2   Preliminary Application Graph

The first step of the process consists in building a preliminary application graph by replacing each edge of the specification graph with a connector following the rules of Table 1. As in many cases several connectors fit the same combination, this table was created following the rule: *The generated application has to be, first of all, as overflow-safe as possible and then, as fast as possible.*

The application graph of Figure 3 derives from the specification graph of Figure 4. Of course, if no provenance coherence is requested, the application graph can be finalized just after this step.

Table 1. The communication pattern selection

	Blocking policy		Non-blocking or Free receiver
Msg loss	bGreedy		nbGreedy
	Free sender	Sender not free	
No msg loss	bBuffer	sFIFO	nbBuffer

3.3 Coherence Subgraphs

The next steps of the process deal with the solving of the coherence constraints. The first step of the transformation consists in looking, in the application graph, for pipelines that must be coherent. They are collected into coherence subgraphs.

Definition 3. *Given an application graph $\mathcal{G}$ and C_1, C_2 and D three distinct components of $\mathcal{G}$ such that $o_i \in O(C_1), o_j \in O(C_2)$ and $\{i_k, i_l\} \subset I(D)$ and given a coherence constraint $\kappa = D_{i_k, i_l} : C_1.o_i \circ \alpha \times C_2.o_j + \delta$, the coherence subgraph g_κ of κ is the subgraph of $\mathcal{G}$ that contains all the sibling pipelines between the source ports $C_1.o_i$ and $C_2.o_j$ and the destination ports respectively $D.i_k$ and $D.i_l$.*

The coherence subgraphs of κ_1 and κ_2 are in respectively a dashed and a dotted frame in Figure 3. As they intersect, they are merged into one single subgraph to avoid backtrackings in the remaining of the process.

In a subgraph, we can decompose each path into a set of independent synchronous segments according to the following definition.

Definition 4. *A pipeline $(C_1, c_1, \ldots, C_{n-1}, c_{n-1}, C_n)$ where C_i $(1 \leq i \leq n)$ is a component and c_i $(1 \leq i \leq n-1)$ is either a sFIFO or bBuffer connector is called a* synchronous segment.

The message flow is preserved inside a synchronous segment i.e. no messages are lost and no empty messages are produced by the connectors. As a consequence, all the components of the segment perform the same number of iterations.

Property 1. *Let $s = (C_1, c_1, \ldots, C_{n-1}, c_{n-1}, C_n)$ be a synchronous segment and m_n a message produced by C_n, $it(m_n) = it(ori_s(m_n))$.*

The property is obvious since no message is lost inside a synchronous segment. C_n generates as many messages as C_1.

Definition 5. *The connector between two successive synchronous segments is called a* junction *and is either a bGreedy, an nbGreedy or an nbBuffer connector. A junction makes two successive synchronous segments independent as they can run at different iteration rates. Predicate $lossy(j)$ is true if junction j is lossy.*

The next step of our automatic construction consists in the equalization of the number of junctions between all the sibling pipelines of a coherence subgraph.

This is needed to fulfill the coherence constraints. Indeed, controlling the messages entering a synchronous segment allows to control the messages at the end of the segment. To summarize, our method tends to preserve as many junctions as possible in order to preserve as many independent segments as possible from the initial graph. It also ensures that the number of independent segments is the same in all the pipelines from a source port to a destination port of the coherence. Coherence control can then be operated piecewise along them. After path segmentation, junctions of the same level will be grouped inside *plateaus*.

Definition 6. *Let $\mathcal{G}$ be an application graph, p_1 and p_2 two sibling pipelines of a constraint κ in $\mathcal{G}$ starting at components C_1 and C_2 respectively and reaching component D. Due to the segmentation step, $p_1 = (S_1^1, j_1^1, \ldots, j_1^n, D)$ and $p_2 = (S_2^1, j_2^1, \ldots, j_2^n, D)$ are composed of the same number n of synchronous segments where S_1^1 (respectively S_2^1) starts at C_1 (respectively C_2) and are separated by $n-1$ junctions $(j_1^i)_{1 \leq i \leq n-1}$ for p_1 and $(j_2^i)_{1 \leq i \leq n-1}$ for p_2. We say that the junctions j_1^i and j_2^i are of the same level, which is denoted $j_1^i \leftrightarrow j_2^i$. The reflexive-transitive closure of $\leftrightarrow$ is denoted $\leftrightarrow^*$. A plateau is the set of the junctions of the same equivalence class of $\leftrightarrow^*$.*

A plateau is the entry point of several synchronous segments involved in the same constraint -or in interdependent constraints. They are the points where messages circulating in different pipelines will be controlled by regulators and by input or output synchronizations as explained further in Section 3.5. Further in the process, a plateau will either :

1. be replaced by the *primary* regulator of the coherence, the role of which is to establish the coherence as expressed in the formulae of the constraint,
2. or be a synchronization point, maintaining the coherence of the pipelines thanks to input and output synchronization mechanisms.

The equalization of the number of junctions -and thus, of synchronous segments-between multiple pipelines is obtained by allowing the system to switch some connectors from {sFIFO or bBuffer} to nbBuffer, or from {bGreedy or nbGreedy} to {sFIFO, bBuffer or nbBuffer}. It is allowed, for the sake of coherence, to relax blocking, non-blocking or lossy constraints of the connection specification. However, non-lossy constraints are never relaxed. In addition, no blocking connectors can be put before a *free* component either. The path segmentation is solved on the whole application graph. We use a linear system where each variable is associated to a connector. The domain of the variables is $\{0, 1\}$. 0 means that the connector is either a sFIFO or a bBuffer, and 1 any of the three other patterns -and a potential regulator location. Since these three other patterns define junctions, it is sufficient to impose that the sums of the variables of each sibling pipeline be equal to ensure that they have the same number of segments. Additional constraints are also added to the problem to avoid misleading solutions. For each connector c of $\mathcal{G}$, according to the properties of the corresponding connection in the specification graph and those of the sender and the receiver, we determine the set of compatible patterns. If this set contains only elements of {nbBuffer, bGreedy, nbGreedy}, we add $v_c = 1$ to the linear system $Eq_{\mathcal{G}}$.

In this process, it is also crucial to anticipate the placing of the regulators as they will replace plateaus. One regulator is sufficient for a coherence constraint and it will be crossed by all the sibling pipelines so that it can compare their message iterations and adjust their flows. This regulator is called the *primary regulator* of the coherence in contrast with other regulators the pipelines might come across and that may be set to control another coherence.

Definition 7. *Let κ be a coherence constraint, $g_\kappa = \{p_1 \ldots p_z\}$ its subgraph and $\Pi = \{J^1 \ldots J^n\}$ the set of plateaus of g_κ such that $J^i = \{j_1^i \ldots j_z^i\}$. $i \in [1, n]$ denotes the level of the plateau J^i along the pipelines of g_κ. J^i is a location candidate for the primary regulator of κ if $\exists j_k^i \in J^i$ and $\exists p_k \in g_\kappa$ such that $lossy(j_k^i) = true$ and $j_k^i \in p_k$ and $\forall p_l \in sib_\kappa(p_k), \nexists C \in p_l \cap p_k$ such that C is a component and $rank_{p_k}(C) < rank_{p_k}(j_k^i)$. Then, $J^i \in \Pi$ is the primary regulator location for κ if $\nexists J^j \in \Pi$ a primary regulator candidate for κ such that $j < i$.*

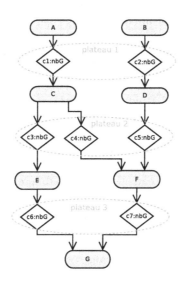

Fig. 5. Simple illutration of the regulator setup policy

The definition of the regulator given in Section 2.3 requires the junctions the primary regulator replaces to be lossy. Consequently, the highest junctions in a coherence subgraph before setting the regulator have to be lossy. In addition, to respect a coherence constraint, data must not be lost before the primary regulator. Otherwise $it(m_1) \neq it(ori(m_1))$ for a message m_1 reaching the regulator and it would not be possible to express a constraint on $it(ori(m_1))$ in the primary regulator anymore. Thus, there must not be other junctions above the first lossy ones on the pipelines. For that, the system forces all the connectors preceding the highest lossy junctions to form a synchronous segment by enforcing $v_c = 0$ for each of them. The primary regulator has also to be set before any intersection between two sibling pipelines. Otherwise, the iteration number of the messages produced by the common component would not allow to distinct the message iterations from the two sources of the sibling pipelines anymore. Figure 5 shows a sample application in which we consider coherence between the two input ports of component G is requested with respect to the outputs of A and B. The regulator has three possible locations represented by plateaus 1, 2 and 3. Obviously, plateau 3 is not convenient as part of the flows from A and B merge at F and become indistinguishable. To guarantee performance, the primary regulator has also to be set as close as possible to the sources of the involved pipelines in order to release the synchronicity as soon as possible. For example, if the primary regulator is set at plateau 2 in Figure 5, the junctions of plateau 1 will necessarily be removed and replaced by synchronous connections. Consequently, the primary regulator will rather be set by the system at plateau 1 so that the desynchronization plateau 2 can be kept.

At this step, if a pipeline appears not to have any lossy connector at all, it will prevent the establishment of the provenance coherence. A warning that a tight coherence [10] can be ensured instead is then raised. The set of additional equations in the linear system is denoted Fix_G. Most of the time, the system has many solutions that are not equivalent from a performance point of view. We then give priority to those that maximize the application's performance, i.e. that preserve at best the initial junctions. This is expressed by the objective function $Maximize(Sum(\mathcal{J}_G))$ where $\mathcal{J}_G$ is the set of junctions initially set in $\mathcal{G}$ and $Sum(\mathcal{J}_G) = \Sigma_{c \in \mathcal{J}_G}(v_c)$. So the linear problem we want to solve is $Eq_G \cup Fix_G \cup Maximize(Sum(\mathcal{J}_G))$.

After the numbers of junctions in the pipelines were made the same, it becomes possible to definitively set the type of each junction. First, plateaus are formed according to Definition 6. Plateaus belonging to different coherences are grouped if they have at least one connector in common. Then, as demonstrated in [10], the connectors of a given plateau must be of the same type to effectively maintain the coherences all the way down to the destination input ports. When a plateau contains connectors of different types, we set all its connectors to nbBuffer if it contains at least one nbBuffer pattern and, otherwise, to nbGreedy if it contains at least one connector of this type.

3.4   Regulator Setup

This step sets the necessary regulators to cover all the coherence constraints. The system iterates over the provenance coherence constraints, setting their primary regulators one by one. If the selected plateau is of type nbGreedy, the regulator will adopt a non-blocking policy on all its output ports, and that for a matter of coherence between them. Otherwise, it will be blocking on all its output ports.

The filtering rules inscribed inside a regulator are adapted to the location of the regulator along the pipelines. Therefore, for each input port of the regulator, the source output port of the pipeline is sought and a rule with respect to sibling pipelines is added. Here, because of merged plateaus, a regulator of a coherence may intersect pipelines of other coherences but without being their primary regulator. It then automatically adds equality rules between all the pipelines which are siblings with respect to other coherences in order to maintain them. In Figure 7, not only does regulator R_2 ensure κ_1 but it also maintains κ_2 established by R_1. More formally, let r be the primary regulator of a coherence constraint $\kappa = D_{i_1,i_2} : C_1.o_i \circ \alpha \times C_2.o_j + \delta$. $F(r)$ consists in the set of filtering rules f_{p_k,p_l} where $p_k \subset P_k$ and $p_l \subset P_l$ such that P_k and P_l are two sibling pipelines and p_k, p_l reach respectively ports in_k and in_l of r. $f_{p_k,p_l} = in_k \circ_f \alpha_f \times in_l + \delta_f$, where $\circ_f = \circ$, $\alpha_f = \alpha$ and $\delta_f = \delta$ if P_k and P_l are sibling with respect to κ and $\circ_f = $ " $= $ ", $\alpha_f = 1$, $\delta_f = 0$ otherwise.

3.5   Coherence Preservation

The coherence between sibling pipelines established by the regulators has to be maintained until the final input ports. This is achieved by setting up, in the remaining plateaus, the tight coherence mechanisms introduced in [10].

Definition 8. *We denote by M a series of messages, by $|M|$ its length and m^i denotes its ith message. A set of series of messages $\{M_1, \ldots, M_n\}$ is called synchronized if $|M_1| = \cdots = |M_n|$ and $\forall i \in [1, |M_1|]$, $it(m_1^i) = \cdots = it(m_n^i)$.*

The synchronicity mechanisms consist in input and output synchronization patterns. While the ouput synchronization mechanism remains as defined in [10], we slightly enrich the input synchronization pattern so that it can also begin with a regulator instead of two junctions.

Definition 9. *In an application graph, an* input synchronization *is a composition pattern that consists of two synchronous segments p_1, p_2 of respectively k and l components and ended by respectively the components C_1^k and C_2^l not necessarily distinct and*

- *either two junctions j_1, j_2 of the same type and not necessarily distinct, triggered by their receivers C_1^1 and C_2^1 and a backward cross-triggering consisting of $(C_1^1.e, j_2.s)$ and $(C_2^1.e, j_1.s)$.*
- *or a regulator r triggered by C_1^1 and C_2^1 and a backward cross-triggering consisting of $(C_1^1.e, r.s)$ and $(C_2^1.e, r.s)$.*

This pattern is denoted $J * (p_1, p_2)$.

The input synchronization ensures that the junctions j_1, j_2 belonging to a plateau P of junctions select their messages at the same time and that no new messages are accepted by the first components before all the components of the segments are ready for a new iteration. If P is a regulator, it may alter the message flows such that the messages entering p_1 and p_2 are coherent with respect to the rules inscribed in it. The simultaneous triggering preserves the synchronicity of the pipelines and of the dispatched messages. If P is non-blocking and does not contain a pair of messages for p_1 and p_2 when it is triggered, it issues a couple of empty messages instead. Figure 6 shows the different input synchronization cases that can be met according to the degree of merging of p_1 and p_2.

In Figure 6(a), p_1 and p_2 begin with the same component so only two triggering links are needed. In Figure 6(b), p_1 and p_2 have two distinct sources. In case there is a regulator instead of the junctions as in Figure 6(c), it is triggered by the components that are its direct receivers. In Figure 6(d), the pipelines are merged before they reach the junction. Their synchronization is then implicit.

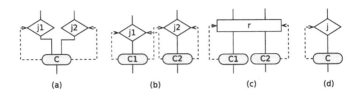

Fig. 6. There are five different input synchronization cases

Definition 10. *In an application graph, an* output synchronization *is a composition pattern involving*

- *two synchronous segments p_1 and p_2 not necessarily distinct of respectively k and l components and ended by respectively components C_1^k and C_2^l,*
- *two bBuffer connectors bB_1 and bB_2 following respectively p_1 and p_2,*
- *a forward cross-triggering consisting of $(C_1^k.e, bB_2.s)$ and $(C_2^l.e, bB_1.s)$.*

This pattern is denoted $(p_1, p_2) * bB$.

This composition pattern ensures that the delay between the synchronous segments to produce messages is absorbed. As the bBuffer connectors select their messages at the same time when all the last components of the synchronous segments are done, the messages are also delivered at the same time. Note that this property is maintained when the two bBuffer connectors are triggered by a same additional set of signals. If $C_1^k = C_2^l$, no additional bBuffers or forward cross-triggering is needed as p_1 and p_2 are naturally synchronized by this common destination component. Moreover, no output synchronization is needed if p_1 and p_2 precede a regulator as the regulator itself buffers incoming messages and outputs and guarantees the simultaneity of these outputs.

In what follows we demonstrate that the different steps of our construction generate an application graph which respects the coherence constraints.

Definition 11. *In an application graph $\mathcal{G}$, the composition $J*(s_1, s_2)*bB$ where s_1 and s_2 are two synchronous segments is called a pair of coherent segments. $[J * (s_1, s_2) * bB]^q$ denotes the composition of q coherent segments $J^1 * (s_1^1, s_2^1) * bB^1 * \cdots * J^q * (s_1^q, s_2^q) * bB^q$.*

Theorem 1. *Let $\mathcal{G}$ be an application graph and $(S_1, S_2) = [J * (s_1, s_2) * bB]^q$ two segments in $\mathcal{G}$. If the series of messages M_1 and M_2 stored in the junctions j_1^1 and j_2^1 of the first coherent segments are synchronized, then the set of messages m_1 and m_2 stored respectively in the bBuffer connectors bB_1^q and bB_2^q of the last coherent segments are such that $it(m_1) = it(m_2)$ and $it(ori_{S_1}(m_1)) = it(ori_{S_2}(m_2))$ when the bBuffers are triggered.*

This theorem comes from [10] where no regulators existed. This result can be easily extended to the case where some junctions (j_1^k, j_2^k) $(1 \leq k \leq q)$ are replaced by a regulator with two input ports in_1^k and in_2^k and that imposes $in_1^k = in_2^k$. Such a constraint plays, indeed, the same role as an input synchronization.

Theorem 2. *Let P_1 and P_2 be two sibling pipelines of a coherence constraint $\kappa = D_{i_1, i_2} : C_1.o_i \circ \alpha \times C_2.o_j + \delta$. Let m_1 and m_2 two messages read by D at the same iteration on respectively i_1 and i_2 ports. Then m_1 and m_2 verify that $it(ori_{P_1}(m_1)) \circ \alpha \times it(ori_{P_2}(m_2)) + \delta$.*

Proof. Since P_1 and P_2 are two sibling pipelines of the constraint κ, we can decompose them into $n + 1$ pairs of coherent segments as follows. $(P_1, P_2) = (p_1, p_2) * J * (C_1' P_1', C_2' P_2')$ with

- (p_1, p_2) two synchronous segments such that the first edge of p_1 is connected to $C_1.o_i$ and the first edge of p_2 is connected to $C_2.o_j$,
- J is in the plateau that is the primary regulator r of κ where p_1 is connected to port in_1 and p_2 to port in_2 of r,
- $C_1' P_1'$ and $C_2' P_2'$ are composed of synchronous segments, begin with components C_1' and C_2' respectively and end at respectively i_1 and i_2 of D.

Let m_1 and m_2 be two messages read at the same iteration of D on respectively ports i_1 and i_2. Since J is the primary regulator of κ, all the other regulators crossed by P_1' and P_2' impose equality on the ports that concerns P_1' and P_2'. Therefore, from Theorem 1, $it(ori_{P_1'}(m_1)) = it(ori_{P_2'}(m_2))$.

Since r is the primary regulator of κ, the rule $f_{P_1, P_2} = in_1 \circ \alpha \times in_2 + \delta$ is in $F(r)$. Therefore, the messages $ori_{P_1'}(m_1)$ and $ori_{P_2'}(m_2)$ belong to a set of messages that validates $F(r)$. This means that we have $it(ori_{C_1' P_1'}(m_1)) \circ \alpha \times it(ori_{C_2' P_2'}(m_2)) + \delta$.

Since p_1 and p_2 are two synchronous segments, we know that for any messages m_1' and m_2' reaching ports in_1 and in_2 of J, we have $it(ori_{p_1}(m_1')) = it(m_1')$ and $it(ori_{p_2}(m_2')) = it(m_2')$. From that, we can conclude that $it(ori_{P_1}(m_1)) \circ \alpha \times it(ori_{P_2}(m_2)) + \delta$.

This theorem proves that the coherence κ is respected in the application graph automatically constructed.

Figure 7 gives the final application graph under two coherence constraints κ_1 and κ_2 of the application specified in Figure 4. To put coherence preservation in practice, the system first adds the backward cross-triggerings to the junctions. Since a plateau may involve more than two segments, our construction generalizes Definition 9. For a plateau $j_1 \ldots j_n$ and the segments $p_1 \ldots p_n$ ending with components $C_1 \ldots C_n$, we add the set of edges $\{(C_i.e, J_j.s) | i \neq j\}$. On the example, regulator R_1 is synchronized by D and E and regulator R_2 is synchronized by G, H and I. Then, to implement the output synchronization, we add one bBuffer connector just after each C_i $(i \in [1, n])$ and add the edges for the forward cross-triggerings. Output synchronization mechanisms can be noticed before plateaus $\{c_9, c_{10}\}$ and $\{c_{11}, c_{12}\}$. These plateaus are also subjected to input synchronization from respectively components J and K.

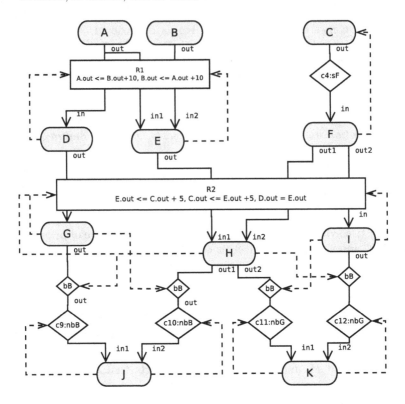

Fig. 7. The final application graph of our example

4   Discussion and Future Work

The great emphasis on performance in the communication between the components of our model targets the building of real-time interactive scientific visualization applications, a particular type of scientific applications to which, to our knowledge, no specific component model is dedicated yet. The intended interactivity in these applications is not limited to a passive manipulation of the graphical output. It is rather active and its effects are propagated throughout the whole running application.

In our approach, we associated to the commonly known spatial provenance its temporal dimension and used it to ensure coherence in a loosely connected system. Provenance-based coherence expands the definition of the tight coherence introduced in [10] allowing the specifications of finer rules. We presented a method to automatically set regulators and connectors to fulfill coherence constraints. As explained, our method sets the regulators as high as possible in the graph to allow the greatest number of desynchronized segments in the pipelines and thus, promote performance. This can however cause one regulator to be primary for multiple coherence constraints having the same sources. The potential drawback of this situation is having conflicting coherence rules inside the same regulator.

Fortunately, unless the conflicting rules are equality+offset rules, the regulator will always output messages, reflecting their lowest common denominator. It is also assumed that a buffer, whether inside a connector or a regulator, has an infinite capacity. At implementation, we are considering the use of a performance model to obtain runtime adaptive buffer sizes. This would, in addition, make non-lossy channels possible in regulators. To prevent overflows, it can also be noticed that our construction method sets, as a priority, sFIFOs and Greedies before Buffers.

The implementation of the complete application generator is ongoing. Meanwhile, representing components, connectors, regulators and small applications as Petri nets [19] serves as a temporary and light model checking means. Our objective is to provide a SWMS specifically designed for real-time interactivity. The current paper addresses the application composition phase and not component programming. Solutions for the latter, focused on code reuse, were presented in [9]. The main solution consists in a high level API to transform C, C++ or Fortran code into FlowVR [8] iterative components. FlowVR is a middleware to develop and run high-performance interactive applications.

In the future, we plan to extend our coherence constraints to data properties other than the iteration number. For example, a module may use the results of two different simulations that generate messages at different rates but stamped with simulation time. In this case the user may impose constraints on these time stamps to get coherent results. Another extension consists in expanding our component definition to supporting not only, regular message streaming but also event-based message emission.

References

1. Callahan, S.P., Freire, J., Santos, E., Scheidegger, C.E., Silva, C.T., Vo, H.T.: VisTrails: visualization meets data management. In: Proceedings of the 2006 ACM SIGMOD International Conference on Management of Data, p. 747. ACM (2006)
2. Chinthaka, E., Ekanayake, J., Leake, D., Plale, B.: CBR Based Workflow Composition Assistant. In: 2009 Congress on Services - I, pp. 352–355 (July 2009)
3. Clarke, D., Proença, J., Lazovik, A., Arbab, F.: Channel-based coordination via constraint satisfaction. Science of Computer Programming 76(8), 681–710 (2011)
4. Velasco Elizondo, P., Lau, K.-K.: A catalogue of component connectors to support development with reuse. Journal of Systems and Software 83(7), 1165–1178 (2010)
5. Goodale, T., Allen, G., Lanfermann, G., Masso, J., Radke, T., Seidel, E., Shalf, J.: The cactus framework and toolkit: Design and applications. In: Vector and Parallel Processing, pp. 1–31 (2002)
6. Groth, P., Gil, Y.: Analyzing the Gap between Workflows and their Natural Language Descriptions. In: 2009 Congress on Services - I, pp. 299–305 (July 2009)
7. Hull, D., Wolstencroft, K., Stevens, R., Goble, C., Pocock, M., Li, P., Oinn, T.: Taverna: a tool for building and running workflows of services. Nucleic Acids Research 34(Web Server issue), W729–W732 (2006)
8. Lesage, J.-D., Raffin, B.: High Performance Interactive Computing with FlowVR. In: IEEE VR 2008 SEARIS Workshop, Reno, USA, pp. 13–16. Shaker Verlag (2008)

9. Limet, S., Robert, S., Turki, A.: FlowVR-SciViz: A component-based framework for interactive scientific visualization. In: Component-Based High Performance Computing (CBHPC 2009), Portland, OR, USA. ACM (November 2009)

10. Limet, S., Robert, S., Turki, A.: Coherence and Performance for Interactive Scientific Visualization Applications. In: Apel, S., Jackson, E. (eds.) SC 2011. LNCS, vol. 6708, pp. 149–164. Springer, Heidelberg (2011)

11. Ludascher, B., Altintas, I., Berkley, C., Higgins, D., Jaeger, E., Jones, M., Lee, E.A., Tao, J., Zhao, Y.: Scientific workflow management and the Kepler system. Concurrency and Computation: Practice and Experience 18(10), 1039–1065 (2006)

12. Pignotti, E., Edwards, P., Preece, A.D., Gotts, N., Polhill, G.: Enhancing Workflow with a Semantic Description of Scientific Intent. In: Bechhofer, S., Hauswirth, M., Hoffmann, J., Koubarakis, M. (eds.) ESWC 2008. LNCS, vol. 5021, pp. 644–658. Springer, Heidelberg (2008)

13. Qin, J., Fahringer, T.: A novel domain oriented approach for scientific Grid workflow composition. In: 2008 SC - International Conference for High Performance Computing, Networking, Storage and Analysis (November 2008)

14. Taylor, I., Shields, M., Wang, I., Harrison, A.: Visual Grid Workflow in Triana. Journal of Grid Computing 3(3-4), 153–169 (2006)

15. Wang, L., Lu, S., Fei, X., Chebotko, A., Victoria Bryant, H., Ram, J.L.: Atomicity and provenance support for pipelined scientific workflows. Future Generation Computer Systems 25(5), 568–576 (2009)

16. Yildiz, U., Guabtni, A., Ngu, A.H.H.: Towards scientific workflow patterns. In: Proceedings of the 4th Workshop on Workflows in Support of Large-Scale Science, pp. 1–10. ACM (2009)

17. Yildiz, U., Mouallem, P., Vouk, M., Crawl, D., Altintas, I.: Fault-Tolerance in Dataflow-Based Scientific Workflow Management. In: 6th World Congress on Services (2010)

18. Zhao, Z., Belloum, A., Wibisono, A., Terpstra, F., de Boer, P.T., Sloot, P., Hertzberger, B.: Scientific workflow management: between generality and applicability. In: Quality Software (QSIC 2005), pp. 357–364. IEEE (2006)

19. Zimmermann, A., Knoke, M., Huck, A., Hommel, G.: Towards version 4.0 of TimeNET. In: 13th GI/ITG Conference Measuring, Modelling and Evaluation of Computer and Communication Systems (2006)

Learning from Failures: A Lightweight Approach to Run-Time Behavioural Adaptation*

José Antonio Martín[1], Antonio Brogi[2], and Ernesto Pimentel[1]

[1] Department of Computer Science, University of Málaga, Málaga, Spain
{jamartin,ernesto}@lcc.uma.es
[2] Department of Computer Science, University of Pisa, Pisa, Italy
brogi@di.unipi.it

Abstract. Software integration needs to face signature and behaviour incompatibilities that unavoidably arise when composing services developed by different parties. While many of such incompatibilities can be solved by applying existing software adaptation techniques, these are computationally expensive and require to know beforehand the behaviour of the services to be integrated. In this paper we present a lightweight approach to dynamic service adaptation which does not require any previous knowledge on the behaviour of the services to be integrated. The approach itself is adaptive in the sense that an initial (possibly the most liberal) adaptor behaviour is progressively refined by learning from failures that possibly occur during service interaction.

1 Introduction

The wide adoption of Web service standards has considerably contributed to simplifying the integration of heterogeneous applications both within and across enterprise boundaries. The languages to describe messaging (SOAP), functionalities (WSDL) and orchestration of services (WS-BPEL) have been standardised, but the actual signatures and interaction protocols of services have not. For this very reason, service adaptation [2,13,17] remains one of the core issues for application integration in a variety of situations. Overcoming various types of mismatches among services developed by different parties, customising existing services to different types of clients, adapting legacy systems to meet new business demands, or ensuring backward compatibility of new service versions are typical examples of such situations.

Various approaches have been proposed to adapt service signatures [6], process behaviour [3], quality of service [7], security [12] or service level agreements [15]. In this paper we focus on signature and behaviour incompatibilities, whose occurrence can impede the very interoperability of services. Many signature and

---

* This work has been partially supported by the project TIN2008-05932 funded by the Spanish Ministry of Education and Science (MEC), FEDER, by project P07-TIC-03131 funded by the Andalusian local Government and by EU-funded project FP7-256980 NESSOS.

F. Arbab and P.C. Ölveczky (Eds.): FACS 2011, LNCS 7253, pp. 259–277, 2012.
© Springer-Verlag Berlin Heidelberg 2012

behaviour incompatibilities can be solved by applying existing (semi-)automated adaptation techniques. However such techniques present two limitations: i) they require signature and behaviour of both parties to be known before service interaction starts, and ii) they are computationally expensive since they explore the whole interaction space in order to devise adaptors capable of solving any possible behaviour mismatch.

In this paper we focus on the problem of dynamic adaptation in applications running on limited capacity devices, as in typical pervasive computing scenarios where (unanticipated) connections and disconnections of peers continuously occur. Unfortunately, the limited computing, storage, and energy resources of such devices inhibit the applicability of most existing adaptation approaches.

We present a lightweight adaptive approach to the adaptation of services that is capable of overcoming signature and behaviour mismatches that would otherwise impede service interoperation. The approach is lightweight in the sense that it requires low computing and storage capabilities to run.

The adaptation is governed by *adaptation contracts* that specify in a declarative way the set of interaction traces to be allowed. While adaptation contracts specify how signature incompatibilities may be solved, they do not require behavioural information (e.g., the partial order with which service operations are offered or requested) to be known a priori. Actually, as we will see, the behaviour of the services to be adapted can even change during the lifespan of an adaptor.

The adaptation process is itself adaptive in the sense that an initial (possibly the most liberal) adaptor behaviour is progressively refined at run-time by learning the behaviour of the services from failures that may occur during service interactions. Roughly speaking, the adaptor initially allows all the interactions that satisfy the current adaptation contract. If an interaction session between the services fails w.r.t. the contract, the adaptor memorises the interaction trace that led to the failure in order to inhibit it in following sessions. Intuitively speaking, the adaptor refines its behaviour based on previous failures so as to converge to allow only *deadlock-free interactions* among the services.

Learning and inhibiting erroneous traces tackle permanent failures such as a behavioural incompatibility which leads the system to a deadlock situation or a hardware malfunction (e.g., due to low battery) which disables part of the functionality. In addition, communications in pervasive computing can be unstable due to changes in the environment. For instance, *shadow fading* [10], where messages might be lost due to the presence of possibly moving obstacles, has deep impact on the reliability of communication channels. We propose several *learning policies* which tackle these sporadic errors. Inhibited traces learned by the adaptor are eventually forgotten so that the adaptor can re-adapt itself to drastic changes in service functionality, temporal changes in the environment or sporadic communication failures.

As one may expect, the results of the refinement performed by this adaptive adaptation approach are particularly interesting when the process starts with a non-empty adaptation contract. However, the approach can overcome message ordering mismatches [11] also in the extreme situation in which no such adaptation contract is available. When compared with the few other existing proposals of lightweight behaviour adaptation of services, such as [5] for instance, our approach features the important advantage of requiring just an adaptation contract based on the services signatures, it does not require to know the interaction behaviour of the services that need adaptation. In other words, the adaptor is not synthesised at design time, instead, it is directly deployed with no other information than an adaptation contract and it will successively learn the behaviour of the services and how to solve their behavioural incompatibilities.

As regards the complexity in time and space of learning adaptors, these only depend on the size and structure of the adaptation contract.

The structure of the paper is the following. We introduce behavioural adaptation in Sect. 2. The lightweight adaptive approach to dynamic service adaptation is formally presented in Sect. 3 and we describe several learning policies in Sect. 4. Then we proceed to evaluate the implementation with an example based on two real-world data-diffusion protocols for sensor networks (Sect. 5). Some related work is discussed in Sect. 6 and we finally conclude with Sect. 7.

2   Behavioural Adaptation

The deployment of suitable "adaptors-in-the-middle" has proven to be an effective way to overcome signature and behaviour incompatibilities between services [3]. Intuitively speaking, such adaptors intercept, collect, and modify the messages exchanged by two parties so as to overcome their incompatibilities. The adaptor behaviour is specified by an adaptation contract defining a set of correspondence rules between actions and (optionally) some constraints on the use of such rules.

Definition 1. *An* adaptation contract *c is a finite state machine (FSM, for short)* $\langle \Sigma^c, S^c, s_0^c, F^c, T^c \rangle$ *where Σ^c is a set of correspondence rules, S^c is a set of states, $s_0^c \in S^c$ is the initial state, $F^c \subseteq S^c$ is the set of final states, and $T^c \subseteq (S^c \times \Sigma^c \times S^c)$ is a set of labelled transitions. Correspondence rules in Σ^c have the form $a \lozenge b$ where:*

- *a and b are input or output communication actions,*
- *one side of the rule can be empty (viz., $a \lozenge$ or $\lozenge b$),*
- *if both a and b are present, then one is an input action and the other is an output action.*

Adaptors act as mediators between two sides. Any communication between those sides must be intercepted and handled by the adaptor. An action on a side of a correspondence rule denotes the complementary action that the adaptor will perform towards the service on that side. For instance, a correspondence rule such as $!msg \lozenge ?msg'$ (where msg and msg' are operation names followed by symbolic parameters) states that if the adaptor receives message msg from the service on the left-hand side then it will have to (eventually) send message msg' to the service on the right-hand side. Every message received by the adaptor is matched against a correspondence rule, and such matching possibly updates the state of stored parameters maintained by the adaptor. Once correspondence rule $!msg \lozenge ?msg'$ is triggered, message msg' is instantiated and inserted in a queue of messages to be eventually sent. If the target service is ready to receive, then the first matching message in the queue can be delivered.

The transition relation T^c can impose restrictions on the order in which correspondence rules can be triggered. In this way, T^c permits to enforce high level policies on the communication such as "do not perform more than three requests" or "after every request there must be an acknowledgment".

Example 1. Our running example is based on a simplified meteorology system. We have three incompatible services with complementary functionality: a) a temperature sensor service, this service could be deployed in a sink of a temperature sensor network; b) a monitoring service which registers the information, this could be located in a laptop; and c) a humidity service which might be deployed in the same infrastructure as the temperature sensor network or otherwise.

The signatures of the services (i.e., their operation names and arguments) are known. The temperature service (service a) has output operations $!user(usr)$ and $!pass(psw)$ to authenticate with its user name (argument usr) and password (psw); an operation to notify of the current temperature, i.e., $!upload(temp)$; two input operations for the upload to be either $?denied()$ or answered with a new interval of time prior the next notification ($?delay(time)$); and finally, an output operation to notify that it finishes it current session, $!end()$. Intuitively speaking, input actions (e.g., $?denied()$) represent the availability of service operations while output actions represent service requests (e.g., $!upload(temp)$), both with the types of their arguments between parentheses.

The monitoring service (service b) might be a new version or come from a different vendor so that it has operations with similar functionalities but incompatible signature. Instead of operations $?user(usr)$ and $?pass(psw)$ expected by service a, it has a single authentication operation $?login(usr, psw)$. The authentication can be $!rejected()$ or $!connected()$. It receives the temperature notifications with an operation $?register(temp)$ and it sends the answer always through $!answer(time)$. This service can receive a $?quit()$ request and it notifies of the finished session with $!end()$. The monitoring service requires humidity information (typed $humid$) before deciding how long to wait for the next temperature update. For this reason, it requests the humidity information to the humidity service (service c) through the request and response $!getHumid()$ and $?getHumid(humid)$. The latter is understood by service c but, instead of the former, service c needs the temperature information to do some calibration via $?getHumid(temp)$ and it finally ends its session with $!finish()$.

Figure 1 illustrates a possible adaptation contract for these services. Rule v_u enables the adaptor to receive action *user* and refers to its argument as U. Rule v_l first receives the password (in P) with action *pass* and, as a consequence, it eventually sends a *login* message with both the user U and password P previously received. The rest of the correspondence rules behave accordingly. The automaton of the contract states that the goal of the system is that, if service

$$\Sigma^c = \{ \ !\underline{u}ser(U) \ \Diamond \qquad (v_u), \qquad !pa\underline{ss}(P) \ \Diamond \ ?\underline{l}ogin(U,P) \qquad (v_l),$$

$$\Diamond \ !\underline{c}onnected() \quad (v_c), \qquad !\underline{u}pload(D) \ \Diamond \qquad (v_p),$$

$$\Diamond \ ?\underline{r}egister(D) \quad (v_r), \quad ?getHumid(D) \ \Diamond \ !g\underline{e}tHumid() \quad (v_g),$$

$$?\underline{d}elay(T) \ \Diamond \ !\underline{a}nswer(T) \quad (v_a), \quad !getHumid(H) \ \Diamond \ ?ge\underline{t}Humid(H) \quad (v_t),$$

$$?\underline{d}enied() \ \Diamond \ !\underline{r}ejected() \quad (v_d), \qquad \Diamond \ ?\underline{q}uit() \qquad (v_q),$$

$$!\underline{e}nd() \ \Diamond \qquad (v_e), \qquad !\underline{f}inish() \ \Diamond \qquad (v_{e'}),$$

$$\Diamond \ !e\underline{n}d() \qquad (v_{e''}) \}$$

(a) Correspondence rules

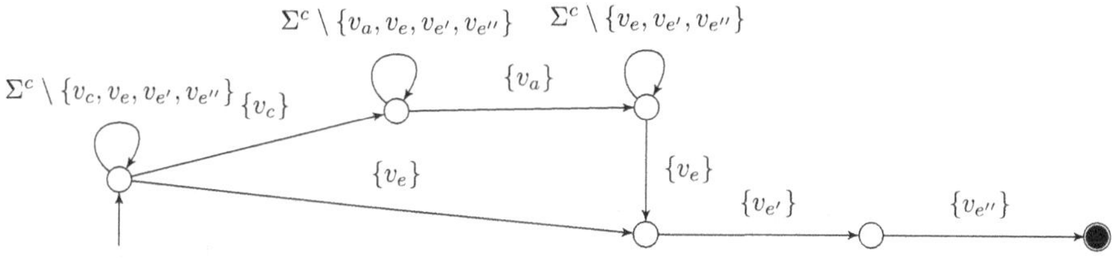

(b) Contract FSM

Fig. 1. An adaptation contract. Underlined letters will serve to abbreviate operation names

c sends *connected* (v_c), then the temperature update must be eventually replied with an *answer* and sent as a *delay* message to service a through correspondence rule v_a. In addition, the automaton states that the session should finish (through $v_e, v_{e'}$ and $v_{e''}$) either at this point or before connecting (i.e., before v_c).

As we have seen in the example, services can employ different alphabets of actions (different names of actions as well as different names, number or order of parameters). The synchronisation rules of the contract (Σ^c) specifies how to solve these signature incompatibilities. In addition, services might also lock due to behavioural incompatibilities between them. These incompatibilities arise because one service offers and requests operations in a different order than the one expected by another.

The intentional semantics of the contract specifies the desired interactions between the services to be adapted, without assuming that their behaviour is known. In order to adapt behavioural incompatibilities without knowing the actual behaviour of the services (which might even change drastically due hardware problems or low battery, for instance) the runtime adaptors presented in this paper must learn to be compliant with the given adaptation contract (i.e., to respect the intentional semantics of its contract) and to avoid the deadlocks that might occur due to incompatibilities between the unknown behaviour of the services.

2.1   Intensional Semantics of Adaptation Contracts

The intensional semantics of an adaptation contract provides the interactions between the services and the adaptor allowed by the contract. Formally, the intentional semantics of an adaptation contract c is defined by a labelled transition system $\xrightarrow{x}_c$ over configurations of the form $\langle s, \Delta \rangle$ where s is the current state of the contract and Δ is a multiset of pending actions that the adaptor will have to eventually perform. A transition $\langle s, \Delta \rangle \xrightarrow{x}_c \langle s', \Delta' \rangle$ indicates that an adaptor could, by contract c, execute action x in state s with pending actions Δ. The transition system $\xrightarrow{x}_c$ is defined by the following inference rules:

$$(\text{I1}) \frac{(s, a \lozenge b, s') \in T^c}{\langle s, \Delta \rangle \xrightarrow{|\bar{a}}_c \langle s', \Delta \cup \{\bar{b}|\} \rangle} \qquad (\text{I2}) \frac{(s, a \lozenge b, s') \in T^c}{\langle s, \Delta \rangle \xrightarrow{\bar{b}|}_c \langle s', \Delta \cup \{|\bar{a}\} \rangle} \qquad (\text{I3}) \frac{}{\langle s, \Delta \cup \{x\} \rangle \xrightarrow{x}_c \langle s, \Delta \rangle}$$

where the complementary action of a non-internal action a is denoted by $\bar{a}$ (e.g., if $a = !do()$ then $\bar{a} = ?do()$, and vice-versa).

Note that the labels denoting the actions of the adaptor are annotated with a left-hand or right-hand bar to explicitly represent whether they are communication actions performed by the adaptor towards the service on the left-hand side ($|\bar{a}$) or towards the service on the right-hand side ($\bar{b}|$), respectively. Note also that an ordered semantics of pending actions is assumed, that is, in rule I3 we assume that if there is more than one x in the multiset Δ, then the emitted x is the oldest in Δ. Finally, since in a correspondence rule $a \lozenge b$ of an adaptation contract either a or b may be absent, the definition of $\xrightarrow{x}_c$ includes also the following rules:

$$(\text{I4}) \frac{(s, a \lozenge \ , s') \in T^c}{\langle s, \Delta \rangle \xrightarrow{|\bar{a}}_c \langle s', \Delta \rangle} \qquad (\text{I5}) \frac{(s, \ \lozenge b, s') \in T^c}{\langle s, \Delta \rangle \xrightarrow{\bar{b}|}_c \langle s', \Delta \rangle}$$

It is worth noting that the intensional semantics defined by rules I1 to I5 may force *eager choices*. Such eager choices may occur, for instance, when an adaptation contract contains more than one correspondence rule for an action a. Consider the simple contract $c = \langle \Sigma^c, S^c, s_0^c, F^c, T^c \rangle$ where $\Sigma^c = \{a \lozenge b, a \lozenge c\}$, $S^c = \{s_0, s_1\}$, $s_0^c = s_0$, $F^c = \{s_1\}$, and $T^c = \{(s_0, a \lozenge b, s_1), (s_0, a \lozenge c, s_1)\}$. Then, two of the transitions that may fire in the initial state, namely $\langle s_0, \emptyset \rangle \xrightarrow{|\bar{a}}_c \langle s_1, \{\bar{b}|\} \rangle$ and $\langle s_0, \emptyset \rangle \xrightarrow{|\bar{a}}_c \langle s_1, \{\bar{c}|\} \rangle$, would force an eager choice of the adaptor, which should pick one of them when executing $\bar{a}$. Intuitively, such an unnecessary eager choice may lead the adaptor to fail adapting some interactions. We could enforce contracts to be deterministic but, instead, we allow such flexibility by providing a lazy choice alternative which results in deterministic adaptors. Lazy choice is modelled by lifting transition system $\xrightarrow{x}_c$ so as to deal with sets of pairs $\langle s, \Delta \rangle$:

$$(\text{L}) \frac{A' = \{\langle s', \Delta' \rangle \mid \exists \langle s, \Delta \rangle \in A \ . \ \langle s, \Delta \rangle \xrightarrow{x}_c \langle s', \Delta' \rangle\} \neq \emptyset}{A \xrightarrow{x}_c A'}$$

Not every execution order among the correspondence rules in the contract avoids deadlocks since deadlocks depend on the actual behaviour of the services, which is unknown. For instance, consider the actual behaviour of the services of our running example were the FSMs depicted in Fig. 2. Internal choices (e.g., `if-then-else` or `switch` conditionals) are modelled by τ actions as usual, while external choices (e.g., WS-BPEL `pick`) are modelled by input-action-labelled transitions leaving from the same state. Now, assuming that service b internally decides to connect (right-hand side τ), then the intensional semantics of the contract in Fig. 1 allows the sequence of rules $v_u : v_l : v_c : v_p : v_q$ (which, among others, corresponds to trace $|?u : |?s : !l| : ?c| : |?p : ?q|$ where actions are represented by their underlined characters and ':' is the append operator). This sequence would lead the system to a deadlock because, in that point, service b cannot participate in the rules needed for service a to reach a final state (i.e., v_d and v_a, at least). Because of these deadlock situations, the intensional semantics of adaptation contracts is refined into a concrete adaptor behaviour capable of controlling the services and leading them to successful states while avoiding locks. This refinement is the key concept of traditional adaptor synthesis proposals [1,3,11,13]. These related works, however, are focused on design time and they require to know in advance the behaviour of the services. Unlike those related works, the goal of the learning process presented in this paper is to do this adaptation at run time without knowing the behaviour of the services.

Example 2. Assuming that the unknown behaviour of the services were the FSMs shown in Fig. 2, the most general adaptor compliant with the contract in Fig. 1 would be the one depicted in Fig. 3. Because of space limitations, actions in Fig. 3 have been reduced to their underlined letters in the contract and have been prefixed with the identification of the communicating service. Such an adaptor could be generated using traditional approaches, being given the contract and the behaviour of the services. The learning adaptors presented in this work do not need to know the behaviour of the services. A learning adaptor for our running example dynamically learns to synchronise with the services in the same way that the adaptor in Fig. 3 does. When the learning adaptor converges, each of its transitions is either one in Fig. 3 or it is offered but never used by the services. In addition, the behaviour of the adaptor does not need to be stored since every transition is generated on-demand.

3   Learning Adaptors

Our proposal is to directly deploy an adaptor with no other information than the adaptation contract, and then the adaptor will dynamically learn the behaviour and incompatibilities of the services. The approach is to initially support every communication allowed by the adaptation contract without any guarantee about the successful termination of the current session. The adaptor learns which sessions ended correctly and, on failures, it will forbid the last communication which led to the failure. The goal is to make this process converge to the most general adaptor which complies with the adaptation contract and the given services. However, depending on the contract and the services (they might not be controllable due to their internal choices) it is possible that no such an adaptor

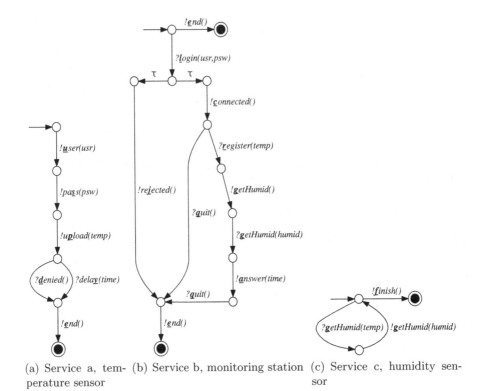

(a) Service a, tem- (b) Service b, monitoring station (c) Service c, humidity sen-
perature sensor   sor

Fig. 2. The (unknown) behaviour of the services of our running example. Underlined letters will serve to abbreviate the operations, hence $a?u$ represents the reception from service a of action $!user(usr)$.

exists. In this case, the process will converge to an empty adaptor (single initial state with no transitions) where no communication is allowed.

The following transition system $\overset{x}{\longmapsto}$ models the way in which an adaptor wraps the service it adapts and interacts with the rest of the environment. An adaptor wrapping a service according to an adaptation contract c is denoted in the transition system $\overset{x}{\longmapsto}$ by a term of the form: $\langle A, I, t \rangle_c [P]$ where A is a set of pairs $\langle s, \Delta \rangle$ (s is a state of the contract and Δ the multiset of pending actions that it should eventually perform), I is a sequence of inhibited traces that have previously led to unsuccessful interactions according to what the adaptor has learned so far, t is the trace of actions executed so far by the adaptor during the current interaction session, c is the adaptation contract and P is the current state of the service being adapted (which is not known by the adaptor). An adaptor at the beginning of a session is denoted by $\langle A_0, I, \lambda \rangle_c [P]$ where $A_0 = \{\langle s_0^c, \emptyset \rangle\}$ and λ is the empty trace. If the adaptor has not learned anything yet, then I is empty.

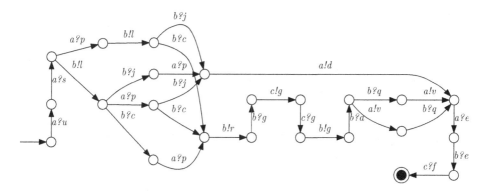

Fig. 3. Static most-general adaptor compliant with the contract and services shown in Fig. 1 and Fig. 2, respectively

In general, I can be modelled as a set, a sequence or a tree. Independently of its implementation, we will write $I \vdash t$ to denote that trace t is inhibited by I. For the sake of simplicity, in this article we will consider I as a sequence of inhibited traces. Each of these traces is a sequence of communication actions ranging over $\mathcal{A}^*$ (where $\mathcal{A}$ represents a global set of communicating actions).

We will denote by $t : a$ the sequence obtained by appending element a to sequence t, by $a.t$ the sequence obtained by prefixing element a to sequence t, and by $t::t'$ the sequence obtained by concatenating sequences t and t'. We will also say that sequence t is a prefix of $t::t'$, where both t and t' can be empty, λ being the empty sequence. A natural way to define the inhibition of traces is given by $I \vdash t$ iff $\exists I_1, I_2 . I = (I_1 : t)::I_2$.

Rules EXT and INT describe the steps that the adaptor can make by offering a communication to the external environment and by interacting with the service it wraps, respectively.

$$(\text{EXT}) \frac{A \xrightarrow{|a|}_c A' \wedge I \nvdash t:|a}{\langle A, I, t \rangle_c [P] \xrightarrow{a} \langle A', I, t:|a \rangle_c [P]} \quad (\text{INT}) \frac{A \xrightarrow{b|}_c A' \wedge P \xrightarrow{\bar{b}} P' \wedge I \nvdash t:b|}{\langle A, I, t \rangle_c [P] \xrightarrow{\tau} \langle A', I, t:b| \rangle_c [P']}$$

Note that the communications offered by the adaptor only depend on the current state of the adaptor, not on the other services. Rule INT models synchronisations between the adaptor and the service to be adapted as silent actions τ as such interactions are not visible by the external environment. Also the internal steps independently made by the wrapped service are modelled as silent actions (TAU). Rules SYN and PAR model (commutative) parallel composition between services and adaptors with synchronous communications in the standard way:

$$(\text{TAU}) \frac{P \xrightarrow{\tau} P'}{A[P] \xrightarrow{\tau} A[P']} \quad (\text{SYN}) \frac{P \xrightarrow{a} P' \wedge Q \xrightarrow{\bar{a}} Q'}{P|Q \xrightarrow{\tau} P'|Q'} \quad (\text{PAR}) \frac{P \xrightarrow{a} P'}{P|Q \xrightarrow{a} P'|Q}$$

By rule OK, an adaptor can consider an interaction session successfully terminated when it is in a final state of the adaptation contract and there are no more
pending communications to perform. Let $OK_c = \{\langle s, \emptyset \rangle \mid s \in F^c\}$.

$$(\text{OK}) \quad \frac{A \cap OK_c \neq \emptyset \ \wedge \ A_0 = \{\langle s_0^c, \emptyset \rangle\}}{\langle A, I, t \rangle_c \, [P] \xmapsto{\ ok(t)\ } \langle A_0, I, \lambda \rangle_c \, [P]}$$

Rule LEARN describes how an adaptor can autonomously decide, after a timed
wait, to inhibit the trace corresponding to an interaction session that has not
(yet) successfully terminated.

$$(\text{LEARN}) \quad \frac{A \cap OK_c = \emptyset \ \wedge \ A_0 = \{\langle s_0^c, \emptyset \rangle\}}{\langle A, I, t \rangle_c \, [P] \xmapsto{\ add(t,I)\ } \langle A_0, add(t, I), \lambda \rangle_c \, [P]}$$

Note that rule LEARN does not constrain the way in which timed waits will
be actually realised in the underlying implementation. From the viewpoint of
the external environment, a learning step made by the adaptor is an internal
action of the latter which may take place at virtually any moment. In Sect. 4
we will show different definitions of $add(t, I)$ that can be employed to define
different learning policies for rule LEARN. The simplest definition of add consists
of appending the new trace to the sequence of previously learned traces, i.e.,
$add_0(t, I) = I : t$.

Note also that rules OK and LEARN specify that the adaptor will be restarted
(to its initial state A_0) when it detects the successful termination of an interaction
session or when it performs a learning step[1].

A natural assumption on the services deployed in limited capacity devices is
that they their behaviour is bounded in length. This does not necessarily mean
that the services will expire but, instead, it means that interactions consist of
finite *sessions* that can be run over and over again. In the sequel we assume
bounded services whose behaviour consists of a finite set of finite length traces.

Due to the fact that the operational semantics of adaptors are trees and the
executed traces are incrementally built by rules EXT and INT, the adaptor will
never allow traces prefixed by any of the inhibited traces. Therefore, if we have
two traces t and $t' = t :: t_s$ and $I \vdash t$ we know that the adaptor will never reach t'
even though, formally, $I \nvdash t'$. In other words, the adaptor will forbid both traces
t explicitly inhibited by I ($I \vdash t$) and all the traces t' prefixed by inhibited traces
($t' = t :: t_s \wedge I \vdash t$). We will formalise how I can change to forbid more traces
using monotonic learning functions.

Informally, we say that a learning function add is monotonic if $add(t, I)$ forbids
(when used in rules EXT and INT) all the traces forbidden by I. In order to

---

[1] Rules OK and LEARN do not enforce an immediate restart of the wrapped service
P and of the service Q interacting with P through the adaptor in a configuration
$Q | \langle A, I, t \rangle_c \, [P]$. The restart of P and Q can be autonomously performed by P and
Q (with a timeout, for instance). Alternatively, it can be triggered by the adaptation
contract itself, which can include explicit restart messages.

formalize this monotonicity notion, we introduce the set of traces prefixed by a sequence I as follows:

$$prefixed(I) = \{u \in \mathcal{A}^* \mid \exists t, t' \in \mathcal{A}^* . I \vdash t \text{ and } u = t::t'\}$$

Function $prefixed(I)$ is equal to all the possible traces forbidden by an adaptor using I.

Definition 2. *A learning function add is* monotonic *if $add(t, I)$ is a monotonic extension of I and $t \in prefixed(add(t, I))$, for each t and I. We say that $add(t, I)$ is a* monotonic extension *of I ($I \sqsubseteq add(t, I)$) if*
$prefixed(I) \subseteq prefixed(add(t, I))$.
We say that $add(t, I)$ is a proper *monotonic extension of I ($I \sqsubset add(t, I)$) if*
$prefixed(I) \subset prefixed(add(t, I))$.

Obviously, the $\sqsubseteq$ relationship defined on sequences of traces is a pre-order.

We now establish that the adaptation process converges if a monotonic learning function add is employed in rule LEARN to adapt bounded services.

Proposition 1 (Convergence). *Let S and P be two bounded services, A_0 be an adaptor for contract c in its initial state $A_0 = \{\langle s_0^c, \emptyset \rangle\}$, and I_0 be a (possibly empty) sequence of inhibited traces. If the adaptor employs a monotonic learning function, then there exists a sequence $I_0, I_1, \ldots, I_n$, with a finite $n \geq 0$, such that:*

1. $\forall j \in [0, n) \; \exists S', P' . \quad S | \langle A_0, I_j, \lambda \rangle_c [P] \overset{\tau}{\longmapsto}^* \overset{I_{j+1}}{\longmapsto} S' | \langle A_0, I_{j+1}, \lambda \rangle_c [P']$
   with $I_j \sqsubseteq I_{j+1}$, and

2. $\nexists S', P', I_{n+1} . \quad S | \langle A_0, I_n, \lambda \rangle_c [P] \overset{\tau}{\longmapsto}^* \overset{I_{n+1}}{\longmapsto} S' | \langle A_0, I_{n+1}, \lambda \rangle_c [P']$
   with $I_n \sqsubset I_{n+1}$.

Proof. The proof immediately descends from the boundedness of S and P and from the monotonicity of the add function.

The previous proposition shows that the training process with bounded services is finite and it always converges to a sequence of inhibited traces I_n. We call such a sequence a *complete* sequence of inhibited traces for S and P.

Now, to establish the correctness of our proposal, we prove that an adaptor with a complete sequence of inhibited traces I_n always leads the interacting services to successful states of the contract (OK_c) while avoiding locks.

Proposition 2 (Correctness). *Let S and P be two bounded services, A_0 be an adaptor for contract c in its initial state $A_0 = \{\langle s_0^c, \emptyset \rangle\}$. If the adaptor employs a monotonic learning function, and I is a complete sequence of inhibited traces, then for every S', A', t' and P' such that*

$$S \mid \langle A_0, I, \lambda \rangle_c [P] \overset{\tau}{\longmapsto}^* S' \mid \langle A', I, t' \rangle_c [P']$$

where $A' \neq A_0$, there exists a sequence of τ transitions

$$S' \mid \langle A', I, t' \rangle_c [P'] \overset{\tau}{\longmapsto}^* S'' \mid \langle A'', I, t'' \rangle_c [P'']$$

such that $A'' \cap OK_c \neq \emptyset$.

Proof sketch. This result is proved by *reductio ad absurdum*. For any sequence of τ transitions as in the proposition it must happen that $t' \neq \lambda$. Therefore, at least one of the rules EXT or INT have been applied. For any continuing sequence of τ transitions which ends in a non-final state in the adaptor (i.e., $A'' \cap OK_c = \emptyset$) we could apply rule LEARN combined with PAR, and therefore the adaptor should proceed with a new $I' = add(t'', I)$. However, since I was already a complete sequence of inhibited traces, one of the prefixes of t'' is inhibited by I, and therefore it is not possible to reach trace t'' because the conditions of rules EXT and INT forbid further synchronisations, which is a contradiction.

Notice that Prop. 2 excludes the particular case of the empty adaptor (since $A' \neq A_0$) for two reasons: i) the adaptor cannot guide the system if it does not participate in its communications; and ii) if it does not exist a correct adaptor for the current services then the learning adaptor converges to the empty adaptor.

Proposition 2 is particularly interesting in those cases where the adaptation contract guarantees that the services have successfully terminated, i.e., those in which S'' and P'' are also final states of their respective services. This happens in our running example because the contract automaton (Fig. 1(b)) is aware of the ending of the services due to correspondence rules v_e, $v_{e'}$ and $v_{e''}$.

It is worth noting that the sequence $\{I_i\}_{i \in \{0,\ldots,n\}}$ of inhibited traces derived from Prop. 1 could be different for each run-time session. In this way, different learning iterations may lead to different complete sequence of inhibited traces. Thus, we need to establish that the learning process is well defined, in the sense that the learning process does not depend on the execution. The following proposition illustrates this result.

Proposition 3 (Well-definedness). *Let S and P be the initial states of two bounded services. Let us consider an adaptation contract c which corresponds to an adaptor with an initial state A_0 and a monotonic learning function. If I and I' are complete sequence of inhibited traces resulting from a learning process starting in $S \mid \langle A_0, I_0, \lambda \rangle_c [P]$, then $I \sqsubseteq I'$ and $I' \sqsubseteq I$.*

Proof sketch. Because of the symmetry of the proposition, it is enough to prove that for every t satisfying $I \vdash t$, there exists t', prefix of t, satisfying $I' \vdash t'$. If we suppose that this prefix t' does not exist, we could reproduce trace t in an adaptor using I' and then, by rule LEARN, that adaptor would include t in I', which is not possible because I' is a complete sequence of inhibited traces.

4   Learning Policies

We now show how different definitions of $add(t, I)$ can be employed to define different learning policies for rule LEARN.

Bounded Learning. An upper bound to the number of traces that are inhibited by an adaptor at any given time may be set for different reasons. The most common is memory capacity, which may limit the size of learned information that can be kept in memory. To respect such a limit, adaptors may need to forget some previously inhibited traces when learning a new trace to be inhibited. A simple bounded learning policy is to forget (if needed) the oldest learned trace when learning a new one:

$$add_1(t, I) = \begin{cases} J : t & \text{if } outOfBound(I : t, \beta) \text{ and } I = u.J \\ I : t & \text{otherwise} \end{cases}$$

where $outOfBound(I : t, \beta)$ holds if the size of $I : t$ exceeds the maximum allowed size β^2. Other types of bounded learning policies can be implemented by defining different $outOfBound$ boundedness conditions (e.g., on the number of traces — rather than on their size) and/or by choosing differently which trace(s) to forget (e.g., one of the longest traces —rather than the oldest one). For instance:

$$add_1'(t, I) = \begin{cases} del(\{u\}, I) : t & \text{if } outOfBound(I : t, \beta) \text{ and } u \in longest(I) \\ I : t & \text{otherwise} \end{cases}$$

where $longest(I) = \{u \in \mathcal{A}^* \mid I \vdash u \text{ and } \not\exists t \in \mathcal{A}^* \;.\; I \vdash t \text{ and } |t| > |u|\}$ and del is recursively defined as follows:

$$del(D, I) = \begin{cases} del(D, J) & \text{if } I = u.J \text{ and } u \in D \\ u.del(D, J) & \text{if } I = u.J \text{ and } u \notin D \\ \lambda & \text{if } I = \lambda \end{cases}$$

Prefix-Driven Absorption. The way in which adaptors forget inhibited traces affects the overall performance of learning adaptors as much as the way in which they learn them. While bounded learning policies indirectly define a (boundedness determined) forget policy, trace prefixing can be exploited to intentionally define a forget policy to shrink the size of learned information. Intuitively speaking, the inhibition of a trace t which is a prefix of a previously inhibited trace $t :: u$ subsumes (by rules EXT and INT) the inhibition of the latter, which hence does not need to be explicitly stored among the inhibited traces anymore. A learning policy based on prefix-driven absorption can be easily specified by defining the add function as:

$$add_2(t, I) = del(prefixedBy(t, I), I) : t$$

where $prefixedBy(t, I) = \{u \in \mathcal{A}^* \mid I \vdash u \text{ and } \exists v \in \mathcal{A}^* \;.\; u = t :: v\}$ is the set of traces in I that are prefixed by t. It is worth observing that different learning policies can be combined together. For instance, prefix-driven absorption and bounded learning policies can be naturally combined into a single policy as follows.

$$add_{2+1}(t, I) = \begin{cases} J & \text{if } outOfBound(I', \beta) \text{ and } I' = u.J \\ I' & \text{otherwise} \end{cases}$$

where $I' = add_2(t, I)$.

---

^{2} Since boundedness conditions are often application- and device-dependent, bounded learning policies are parameterised w.r.t the maximum allowed size β.

It is also worth observing that prefix-driven absorption can also be exploited to identify temporary failures not due to service protocol incompatibilities. To do that we must distinguish "simple" prefixes from "non-simple" prefixes. We say that t is a simple prefix of $t :: u$ if u contains only one element. The normal learning process of an adaptor may inhibit a simple prefix t of a previously inhibited trace $t : a$ whenever the adaptor realises that there is no alternative extension of t. On the other hand, the inhibition of a trace t which is a non-simple prefix of a previously inhibited trace $t :: u$ might be caused by some temporary failure that intervened (e.g., physical communication problems —such as shadow fading or increased physical distance). The detection of temporary failures can be exploited to define refined prefix-driven absorption policies that maintain the set I_T of traces learned from temporary failures separate from the set I_P of traces learned from (supposedly) permanent failures[3], such as the following definition of add. Let $oneprefixedBy(t, I) = \{t{:}\alpha \mid I \vdash t{:}\alpha\}$ be the set of traces $t{:}\alpha$ in I which are prefixed by t and which are only one element longer than t. Then:

$$add_3(t, \langle I_P, I_T \rangle) = \begin{cases} \langle del(J, I_P) : t, del(J, I_T) \rangle & \text{if } onePrefixedBy(t, I_P) \neq \emptyset \text{ and} \\ & J = prefixedBy(t, I_P :: I_T) \\ \langle del(K, I_P), del(K, I_T) : t \rangle & \text{if } onePrefixedBy(t, I_P) = \emptyset \text{ and} \\ & prefixedBy(t, I_P :: I_T) = K \text{ and} \\ & K \neq \emptyset \\ \langle I_P : t, I_T \rangle & \text{otherwise} \end{cases}$$

Combined policies whose bounded learning and/or time-to-forget components prioritarily forget traces corresponding to temporary failures can be easily defined. For instance, let $\langle I'_P, I'_T \rangle = add_3(t, \langle I_P, I_T \rangle)$, then:

$$add_{3+1}(t, \langle I_P, I_T \rangle) = \begin{cases} \langle I'_P, J_T \rangle & \text{if } outOfBound(I'_P{::}I'_T, \beta) \text{ and } I'_T = u.J_T \\ \langle J_P, \emptyset \rangle & \text{if } outOfBound(I'_P{::}I'_T, \beta) \text{ and } I'_T = \emptyset \text{ and } I'_P = u.J_P \\ \langle I'_P, I'_T \rangle & \text{otherwise} \end{cases}$$

Reset on Empty Adaptors. The aforementioned learning policies aim at reducing the memory requirements (add_1 and add_2) and mitigate sporadic errors (add_3). In particular, the main problem of the basic learning policy (add_0) with *sporadic errors* (unforeseen failures in the synchronisations due to instabilities in the communication channels) is that it tends to converge to the empty adaptor. This happens because add_0 does not forget the inhibited traces due to this sporadic errors and, as a result, the adaptor behaviour is constantly reduced every time one of these errors occurs. A straightforward solution to this issue, is to recognise when the process has converged to the empty adaptor and then reset the inhibited traces so that the adaptor can converge to better solutions. This is formalised with the following function.

$$add_4(t, I) = \begin{cases} \lambda & \text{if } t = \lambda \\ I : t & \text{otherwise} \end{cases}$$

---

[3] Rules EXT and INT trivially extend to the case in which I is modelled as a pair $\langle I_P, I_T \rangle$, viz., by turning $I \nvdash t$ into $(I_P :: I_T) \nvdash t$.

Intuitively, add_4 behaves as add_0 when the adaptor is not empty. If it becomes empty, and this is not considered valid by the given contract, then the only rule that can be triggered is the rule LEARN inhibiting the empty trace ($t = \lambda$) as far as no synchronisation is possible with the empty adaptor. When this happens, function add_4 clears the inhibited traces so that the adaptor can synchronise again. As usual, add_4 can be combined with other learning policies, e.g.:

$$add_{4+2+1}(t, I) = \begin{cases} \lambda & \text{if } t = \lambda \\ add_{2+1}(t, I) & \text{otherwise} \end{cases}$$

It is easy to prove that $add_i, i \in \{0, 2, 3\}$ (and their combinations) are monotonic by Definition 2 whereas add_1, add_4 are not (deliberately). We will see in Sect. 5 that, although non-monotonic learning policies do not necessarily converge, they have the advantage of overcoming *sporadic errors* with high success rates.

5   Evaluation and Tool Support: ITACA

Learning adaptors have been implemented and included in the Integrated Toolbox for Automatic Composition and Adaptation (ITACA[4] [4]). We have evaluated our approach with two real-world data-diffusion protocols for sensor networks: TinyDiffusion [14] and SPIN [8]. In this experiment, a TinyDiffusion node was adapted to participate in the communication between two SPIN nodes. We gathered various statistics simulating this real-world example. In these simulations, random traces are simulated one by one, the traces which are stuck in non-final adaptor states (those not in OK_c) trigger rule LEARN and the gathered data is analysed after a certain interval of traces. These simulations are repeated 10 times in order to plot their arithmetic mean and the sample standard deviation.

Different learning policies are compared in Fig. 4, where the number of simulated traces is shown on the horizontal axis. Line reg corresponds to a regular adaptor using add_2. Line dthr represents an adaptor using add_{4+2+1} with a dynamic threshold $\beta \in \mathbb{N}$, initially set to 0, which is incremented each time rule OK is applied, and decremented whenever rule LEARN is used. The adaptive adaptor, athr, also uses add_{4+2+1} with a dynamic threshold $\beta' \in \mathbb{N}$ but, in this case, β' is always set to be equal to the number of transitions in the adaptor. Finally, noi represents an adaptor which does not learn, i.e., I is always empty. The latter is used as a comparative baseline for the other approaches.

The vertical axis of Fig. 4(a) represents the cardinality of the list of inhibited traces. The running example can be solved with 55 inhibited traces (corresponding to 7123 adaptor transitions which do not need to be stored in memory) and it allows a maximum of 5466 successful traces. Other solutions are possible with lower and higher number of inhibited traces, however, these imply a lower variety of successful traces. We can see in Fig. 4(a) that both reg and athr approximate that amount of inhibited traces (55) before 4000 simulated traces. The dthr adaptor, due to the high success rate in spite of behavioural incompatibilities ($\sim 55\%$), it always maintains the list of inhibited traces close to empty.

---

[4] http://itaca.gisum.uma.es/

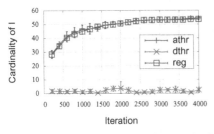

(a) Size of I in adaptors reg, dthr and athr when learning without sporadic errors

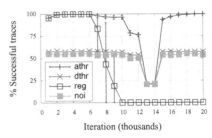

(b) Comparative between adaptors noi, reg, dthr and athr using various *TER* values

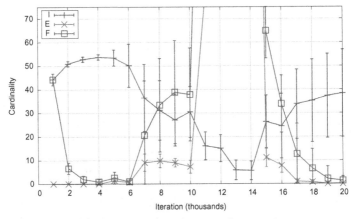

(c) Details of the adaptive adaptor athr

Fig. 4. Statistics gathered from the simulation with different adaptors. Figure 4(b) and Fig. 4(c) have a *TER* equal to 0 between $(0, 4000]$; 10^{-4} between $(4000, 6000]$; 10^{-3} in $(6000, 10000]$; 0.01 in $(10000, 12000]$; 0.1 in $(12000, 14000]$; then, it decreases to 10^{-3} in $(14000, 16000]$; 10^{-4} in $(16000, 18000]$; and it finally becomes 0 in $(18000, 20000]$

Figure 4(b) shows the success rate, i.e., the percentage of simulated traces which were successful in the current interval. In Fig. 4(b) and Fig. 4(c), we use a *transition error rate* parameter ($TER \in [0, 1]$) which represents the probability of a synchronisation to forcibly fail due to sporadic errors. It can be seen that noi remains close to a success rate of 55%, which is reduced proportionally to the *TER*. Adaptor dthr performs slightly better, but not significantly due to its low threshold β. The other adaptors take advantage of the learning process and achieve success rates close to 100%. However, when sporadic errors start to occur (iteration 4000), adaptor reg, which is not able to forget inhibited traces, quickly converges to the empty adaptor and remains so for the rest of the simulation. Finally, athr is also affected by high values of *TER* but it is able to recover when sporadic errors cease to occur, achieving success rates close to 100%.

A detail of the athr adaptor is depicted in Fig. 4(c). It shows the amount of: inhibited traces (I), sporadic errors (E) and the total number of failed traces $(F \geq E)$. The number of inhibited traces initially approximates the desired value of 55. However, when sporadic errors appear (4000), new inhibited traces reduce the size of the adaptor (i.e., number of transitions), this reduces threshold β' which finally reduces the number of inhibited traces. Intuitively, this means that the adaptor reduces its knowledge because it cannot trust it. This phenomenon reappears when TER is increased in subsequent iterations (6000, 8000, 10000 and 12000). The final range $(14000, 20000]$ is more interesting. We can see that, although athr succeeds in recovering from sporadic errors, achieving success rates close to 100%, it does so at the cost of obtaining a suboptimal, but correct, solution. In other words, depending on where the sporadic errors occurred, adaptor athr might prune bigger parts of the behaviour than needed.

Interestingly, adaptor reg enhanced with reset capabilities as dthr (i.e., reg+reset using add_{4+2}) was able to match athr[5]. This means that it is not the dynamic threshold what matters but to be able to notice the convergence to empty adaptor, and thus reset the inhibited traces. Therefore, the most promising adaptor is reg+reset (add_{4+2}) thanks to its simplicity and effectiveness.

Regarding the *computational complexity*, every synchronisation with the adaptor requires a transition in the adaptor behaviour and the possible inclusion of a new inhibited trace. Assuming hash sets and hash maps with constant complexity for membership queries and insertions, the time complexity is $O(|S^c||\Sigma^c|^l)$ where $|S^c|$ is the number of states in the contract automaton, $|\Sigma^c|$ is the number of correspondence rules in the contract and l is the maximum length of a trace. The *spatial complexity* of our approach with $add_i, i \in \{0, 2, 3, 4\}$ is given by the combined size of: the inhibited traces, the adaptor state and the adaptation contract. The space required by inhibited traces can be reduced either by storing them as a tree or using any learning policy based on add_1 (where the size of the inhibited traces is bounded by β). Both approaches result in a spatial complexity of $O(|S^c||\Sigma^c|^l)$. Let us remember that l is bounded and it can be further restricted using acyclic adaptation contracts. In this case, the time and spatial complexity are exponential with regard to the size of the contract but they do not depend on the number or size of the services to adapt. In addition, both complexities are greatly reduced if the adaptation contract is deterministic in the sense that it does not require the lazy-choice represented by rule L. In this case, at any given adaptor state $\langle A, I, t \rangle_c$ it happens that A contains a single element $\langle s, \Delta \rangle$. This simplification results in a time complexity of $O(max(|\Sigma^c|, l))$ and a spatial complexity of $O(|S^c||\Sigma^c| + |\Sigma^c|^l)$.

6   Related Work

The behaviour of an adaptor can be synthesised at design time following other approaches covered in related work [1,4,11,13]. However, adaptor synthesis is exponential with regard to the number and size of the services involved and it

---

[5] The statistics characterising reg+reset are indistiguishable from those of athr.

requires to know in advance the behaviour of these services. This is not feasible in the current setting of nodes with restricted capabilities where the actual behaviour of the services is unknown. For instance, the correspondence rules presented in this work are similar to the adaptation operators presented in [6] and to the mismatch patterns introduced in [11], but their approaches are focussed on design-time. There are few related work which aim at addressing both runtime *and* lightweight behavioural adaptation at the same time.

One of them is [5], where an ontology is required to generate a mapping between the operation of the services. Some properties (expressed in a temporal logic) are dynamically verified by performing forward-search analyses on the behaviour of services. While similar properties can be encoded with our adaptation contract automata, differently from us, [5] requires the behaviour of services to be known and it has to bear with the cost of the forward-search analysis.

Wang et al. [16] propose the dynamic application of adaptation rules. These rules are triggered by the input actions received by the adaptor and then an output action is generated. Our approach is similar to theirs in the sense that we also apply the adaptation contract dynamically without generating the whole adaptor. However, their rules must specify how to solve both signature and behavioural incompatibilities, hence requiring to know the behaviour of the services beforehand. Our contracts, instead, only specify how to solve signature incompatibilities and an optional description of the adaptation goal. Behavioural incompatibilities are dynamically learned and avoided by our adaptors.

Another related work, [9], discussed the problem of controlling services with unknown behaviour. Our approach shares the idea of progressively refining an over-approximated controller when failures occur. The authors of [9] perform such refinement by exploiting (bounded) model checking, whose overhead is not bearable in applications running on limited capacity devices.

7   Conclusion

We have presented a new lightweight approach to behavioural runtime adaptation. Our approach requires an adaptation contract based on the signatures of the services (the collection of operations they require and offer), but no previous knowledge on the behaviour of the services is needed since it will be dynamically learned. We have shown how adaptors can incrementally learn from interaction failures at run time so as to eventually converge to the same behaviour that could be a priori synthesised by means of (computationally expensive) design-time analyses on the behaviour of the services.

Learning adaptors can be applied to perform *zero-knowledge adaptation*, i.e., adaptors without adaptation contract. In this case, there is an implicit contract which assumes that every source and destination service share the same alphabet of actions, therefore presenting a trivial set of one-to-one correspondence rules. Having such a *zero-knowledge contract*, which is dynamically inferred, the adaptor does not perform any adaptation at signature level (it simply forwards messages), but it does learn from possible behavioural incompatibilities between the services (such as messages expected in different order). Therefore, zero-knowledge contracts avoid deadlocks that would be present without adaptation.

References

1. Autili, M., Inverardi, P., Navarra, A., Tivoli, M.: SYNTHESIS: A Tool for Automatically Assembling Correct and Distributed Component-Based Systems. In: Proc. of ICSE 2007, pp. 784–787. IEEE (2007)
2. Bracciali, A., Brogi, A., Canal, C.: A Formal Approach to Component Adaptation. Journal of Systems and Software 74(1), 45–54 (2005)
3. Brogi, A., Popescu, R.: Automated Generation of BPEL Adapters. In: Dan, A., Lamersdorf, W. (eds.) ICSOC 2006. LNCS, vol. 4294, pp. 27–39. Springer, Heidelberg (2006)
4. Cámara, J., Martín, J.A., Salaün, G., Cubo, J., Ouederni, M., Canal, C., Pimentel, E.: ITACA: An Integrated Toolbox for the Automatic Composition and Adaptation of Web Services. In: Proc. of ICSE 2009, pp. 627–630. IEEE (2009)
5. Cámara, J., Canal, C., Salaün, G.: Behavioural Self-Adaptation of Services in Ubiquitous Computing Environments. In: Proc. of SEAMS 2009, pp. 28–37. IEEE (2009)
6. Dumas, M., Spork, M., Wang, K.: Adapt or Perish: Algebra and Visual Notation for Service Interface Adaptation. In: Dustdar, S., Fiadeiro, J.L., Sheth, A.P. (eds.) BPM 2006. LNCS, vol. 4102, pp. 65–80. Springer, Heidelberg (2006)
7. Harney, J., Doshi, P.: Speeding up Adaptation of Web Service Compositions Using Expiration Times. In: Proc. of WWW 2007, pp. 1023–1032. ACM (2007)
8. Heinzelman, W.R., Kulik, J., Balakrishnan, H.: Adaptive protocols for information dissemination in wireless sensor networks. In: Proc. of MobiCom 1999, pp. 174–185. ACM (1999)
9. Holotescu, C.: Controlling the Unknown. In: Proc. of FoVeOOS 2010, Tech. Rep. 13, KIT, June 28-30 (2010)
10. Kim, Y.Y., Li, S.-Q.: Capturing important statistics of a fading/shadowing channel for network performance analysis. Selected Areas in Communications 17(5), 888–901 (1999)
11. Kongdenfha, W., Nezhad, H.R.M., Benatallah, B., Casati, F., Saint-Paul, R.: Mismatch Patterns and Adaptation Aspects: A Foundation for Rapid Development of Web Service Adapters. IEEE Transactions of Services Computing 2(2), 94–107 (2009)
12. Martín, J.A., Pimentel, E.: Contracts for Security Adaptation. Journal of Logic and Algebraic Programming 80(3-5), 154–179 (2011)
13. Mateescu, R., Poizat, P., Salaün, G.: Adaptation of Service Protocols Using Process Algebra and On-the-Fly Reduction Techniques. In: Bouguettaya, A., Krueger, I., Margaria, T. (eds.) ICSOC 2008. LNCS, vol. 5364, pp. 84–99. Springer, Heidelberg (2008)
14. Mysore, M., Golan, M., Osterweil, E., Estrin, D., Rahimi, M.: TinyDiffusion in the extensible sensing system (August 12, 2003),
    http://www.cens.ucla.edu/~mmysore/Design/OPP/
15. Narendra, N.C., Ponnalagu, K., Krishnamurthy, J., Ramkumar, R.: Run-Time Adaptation of Non-Functional Properties of Composite Web Services Using Aspect-Oriented Programming. In: Krämer, B.J., Lin, K.-J., Narasimhan, P. (eds.) ICSOC 2007. LNCS, vol. 4749, pp. 546–557. Springer, Heidelberg (2007)
16. Wang, K.W., Dumas, M., Ouyang, C., Vayssiere, J.: The service adaptation machine. In: Proc. of ECOWS 2008. IEEE (2008)
17. Yellin, D.M., Strom, R.E.: Protocol Specifications and Components Adaptors. ACM Transactions on Programming Languages and Systems 19(2), 292–333 (1997)

Verifying Safety of Fault-Tolerant Distributed Components*

Rabéa Ameur-Boulifa[1], Raluca Halalai[2], Ludovic Henrio[3], and Eric Madelaine[3]

[1] Institut Telecom, Telecom ParisTech, LTCI CNRS, Sophia-Antipolis, France
[2] Technical University of Cluj-Napoca, Cluj, Romania
[3] INRIA-I3S-CNRS, University of Nice Sophia Antipolis, France

Abstract. We show how to ensure correctness and fault-tolerance of distributed components by behavioural specification. We specify a system combining a simple distributed component application and a fault-tolerance mechanism. We choose to encode the most general and the most demanding kind of faults, byzantine failures, but only for some of the components of our system. With Byzantine failures a faulty process can have any behaviour, thus replication is the only convenient classical solution; this greatly increases the size of the system, and makes model-checking a challenge. Despite the simplicity of our application, full study of the overall behaviour of the combined system requires us putting together the specification for many features required by either the distributed application or the fault-tolerant protocol: our system encodes hierarchical component structure, asynchronous communication with futures, replication, group communication, an agreement protocol, and faulty components. The system we obtain is huge and we have proved its correctness by using at the same time data abstraction, compositional minimization, and distributed model-checking.

1 Introduction

Safety in distributed systems is a wide research area which needs to be tackled at several levels: from the safety of the execution platform, to the correctness of the communication protocols and to correctness of the distributed applications. This article aims at evaluating the adequacy of formal method techniques for the verification of real-size distributed applications. The objective tackled by this article is really challenging because the application we consider features several non-functional concerns which contribute to the explosion of the number of states that can be reached by the application. Indeed we choose to provide a model and prove properties for a distributed application featuring fault-tolerance similar to Byzantine fault tolerance (BFT).

Our work is placed in the context of component oriented programming. Indeed from a programming model point of view, components provide well-defined

---

* This work was partialy funded by the ANR international project ANR09-BLAN-0375-01 between INRIA and Un. of Tsinghua, Beijing, China.

F. Arbab and P.C. Ölveczky (Eds.): FACS 2011, LNCS 7253, pp. 278–295, 2012.
© Springer-Verlag Berlin Heidelberg 2012

modularity, and easiness to compose large applications from the composition of basic blocks. Also components require the precise definition of interfaces through which the basic blocks cooperate, which is crucial for a precise design of an application, but also strongly helps the formal specification of the application. Our components also allow a hierarchical and modular design, better specifying the structure of the application. We choose GCM[2] as our component model because it is naturally adapted to distribution, hierarchy, and one-to-many communication, but also it provides reconfiguration capabilities which we want to consider in future works. GCM is an extension of the Fractal component models with support for deployment, scalability, autonomic behaviour, and asynchronous communication; it also shares a lot of similarities with SCA [3]. In the VerCors [8] platform, we provide tools for verifying the behaviour of such distributed component applications.

This paper shows how to specify the behaviour and to verify properties of distributed component applications with request queues, future proxies and group proxies, and one-to-many interfaces. To illustrate our approach, we choose a simple distributed application featuring fault-tolerance by replication. Though the fault-tolerance properties we address are not outstanding, we think this application is a good opportunity to investigate on the use of model-checking to ensure safety of fault-tolerant applications. This article has the following objectives:

- Promote the use of formal methods to ensure safety of distributed systems.
- Provide a model for one-to-many communication.
- Study the modelling of faulty processes, and investigate the use of model-checking for verifying fault-tolerance from an application point of view. Indeed, most of the existing studies on this domain focus on the proof of correctness of the protocols only, not on the whole distributed application [14].
- Investigate the adequacy of distributed model-checking for verifying a distributed and asynchronous application that generates a huge state-space.

We do not model reconfiguration and adaptation, but we design our specification in such a way that those aspects can be added to the model in the future.

In the following, Section 2 presents the related works, with a particular focus on BFT and GCM components. Then, we describe our fault-tolerant application and its modelling in Section 3. Finally, Section 4 describes the distributed model checking phase and the properties we verify.

2   Background and Related Works

2.1   Formal Methods for Component Models

As the formal methods matured, they have been integrated into environments that support the development of component-based systems. They ensure the correct behaviour of the assembly of complex applications in all the stages of the development lifecycle (from specification to execution). However, although those frameworks share the same basic concepts, they substantially differ in the range of application domains and supported features. For instance, some of them are dedicated to embedded systems verification [10,4] while the others are dedicated to software engineering. We focus below on related works for behavioural specification and verification of distributed components.

Creol [19] is a programming model featuring active objects, requests and futures, similarly to our approach. A framework provides component modelling for Creol; it provides a formal language [13] that supports compositional reasoning and makes automatic testing and verification possible. This language is defined over communication labels, and specifies components in terms of traces of observable behaviour at the interfaces.

Cadena [16] is an environment for modelling and verifying CCM component-based systems. The framework offers a rigorous type-based language [20] for describing component connectors, and the interaction between them. The compositional analysis is based on the assume-guarantee reasoning. However, the component model does not support hierarchical structure.

SOFA [24] is a framework for developing distributed systems. It supports component-based development as well as formal verification. The SOFA 2 component model is hierarchical and supports reconfiguration, making it quite close to ProActive/GCM even though one-to-many communication and asynchrony with futures are not offered by default in SOFA. SOFA uses "behaviour protocols" for specifying possible interactions between components and checking the correctness of the assembly, making the verification process in SOFA quite different from ours, but our approach could also be applied to SOFA components.

This article relies on the pNets [1] formalism for describing the behaviour of parametrized networks of LTSs. We showed in [1] how to build models for GCM components, asynchronous communication, and futures. [7] describes how to specify group communication in pNets. Additionally to faulty components, this article extends the preceding semantics by specifying one-to-many communication at the GCM level, and the management of proxy instances.

The CADP toolset [11] is one of the prominent platforms for the specification, verification, and testing of distributed systems in the academic landscape. It handles several input formalisms, and provides an extensible API. The toolset includes engines for building hierarchically the state-space of systems, building and manipulating LTSs on distributed infrastructures, minimizing LTSs along several behavioural equivalences, model-checking properties, checking equivalences between systems, building test suites, evaluating performances, etc.

2.2 Verifying Byzantine Fault-Tolerant Systems

Byzantine fault tolerance (BFT) has a long history [22,26]; results in this research area are very difficult to obtain and to prove. Indeed, BFT supposes that a faulty process can have any behaviour. The name BFT comes from the original problem raised by Lamport relying on Byzantine generals that must all take the same decision (attack or retreat), knowing that some of the generals are traitors. Traitors can say anything to the others, but the others must all act identically. In computer science, this situation represents either a faulty process behaving "randomly" or a malicious entity. BFT has gain new interests since the apparition of a new form of large scale distributed computations relying on entities that, by nature, cannot be trusted. Typically a P2P storage application cannot make any assumption on the kind of misbehaviour the peers can have.

The purpose of this paper is not to prove that a BFT protocol is correct but to understand whether it is possible to represent all the aspects of a complete component application communicating by request-replies, and at the same time reason about the fault-tolerance of this entire application. We focus on a specific application similar to [21] but simplify it: our application consists of a Master component replicating data to be stored on several workers. The master updates the worker value, and gathers replies from workers to retrieve the stored value. If enough non-faulty workers are instantiated, and enough identical replies are returned to the master, the stored value can be retrieved. The objective of this paper is not to study the implementation of the component model, this is why we make the assumption that communications are performed safely. More precisely, we suppose that the middleware ensures that messages systematically follow the bindings, and that a component can only reply to the requests it received. For example, a faulty component cannot communicate to any component of the application, and a faulty components cannot reply instead of a non-faulty one.

Note that the master is supposed to be non-faulty; Protocols for dealing with a faulty master exist and have been heavily studied and implemented. For example, recently [21] implemented a BFT storage in the same settings as our application. Here we simplify the problem and focus on the correct handling of faulty workers, similarly to the case studied in Section 4.2 in [26]. If f is the number of tolerated faults, $2f + 1$ slaves are sufficient for reaching a consensus. However, as it is generally required in BFT, i.e. when the master can be faulty, we instantiate $3f + 1$ slaves. Section 4 will show that specifying a whole application with those simplifying hypotheses already requires the full power of distributed model-checking over a cloud-like architecture.

Our approach for encoding Byzantine faults is the following: faulty slaves can feature any behaviour, upon verification the model-checker will then explore all the possible behaviours, including the malicious ones. We then specify a simple agreement procedure where the Master component waits until enough slaves answered correctly. In order to count them, our architecture description is aware of which slave is faulty, but the business code does not use this information.

2.3   Distributed Components and Their Semantics

This section recalls the component structure and semantics of GCM, a complete definition can be found in [17].

Component Structure. The structure of GCM components is inherited from Fractal: A GCM component can be either *composite* (i.e. composed of subcomponents), or *primitive* (a basic element encapsulating the business code). A component comprises a content (providing the functional code) and a membrane (a container managing non-functional operations). The interfaces are the only access points to components. Each interface is either *client* (emitting invocations)

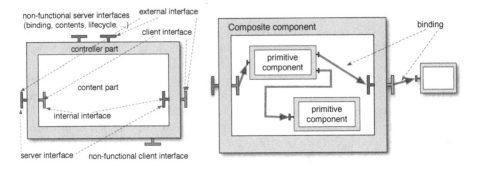

Fig. 1. A GCM component   **Fig. 2.** A component system

or *server* (receiving invocations). We distinguish *functional* interfaces addressing the business of the application from *non-functional* ones invoked to manage, monitor, and introspect the application. A *binding* connects a client interface to a server interface (Fig. 2); a message emitted by a client interface is transmitted to the server interface bound to it. In composite components, interfaces are either *internal* – exposed to the subcomponents – or *external* – exposed to other components. The interface cardinality indicates how many bindings can be made from or to this interface. In this paper, we only use two interface cardinalities: singleton (one-to-one binding) and multicast (one-to-many binding). The different parts of a GCM component are shown in Fig. 1, whereas Fig. 2 shows an assembly of components bound together, on the left there is a composite composed of two primitives; the figure also illustrates different bindings.

Communication. The basic communication paradigm in GCM is asynchronous message sending: communication consists in synchronously dropping a message in a *request queue* at the receiver side, and creating a future to represent the result of the invocation. A future is an empty object representing the result of a computation performed in parallel. Once the future is created, the execution continues immediately on the sender side. When the request treatment is finished, the result is automatically returned to replace all the references to the corresponding future. When a component accesses a future, it is blocked until the result is returned. However, future references can safely be passed between components, inside invocation parameters, or inside a request result. To prevent shared memory between components, parameters and results are copied; no object is passed by reference.

A *multicast* interface is a client interface that transforms a single invocation into a list of invocations, sent in parallel to a set of connected interfaces. The result of an invocation on a multicast interface is a list of results. Invocation parameters can be distributed according to a distribution policy that can be customized. Typical distribution policies include *broadcast* that sends the same parameter to each connected component, and *scatter* that splits the parameter.

Component Behaviour. Primitive components encapsulate the business code, their behaviour is highly dependent on the application; it is provided by the

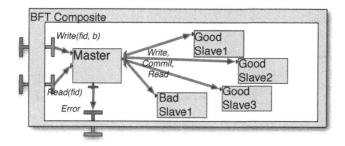

Fig. 3. Component Structure of our application

application programmer. The only constraints they must respect are: they serve requests of the request queue, they emit new requests on their client interfaces, and can receive a result for the futures they hold. We consider here only mono-threaded primitive components: a single request is served at a time.

By contrast, composite components have a predefined behaviour: they serve requests in the reception order, and delegate the requests to sub-components, according to the bindings. For example, when a composite component receives a request from the outside, it delegates its service to one of the sub-components.

3 Our Fault-Tolerant Application and Its Specification

This section describes informally our application, and then presents its behavioural model. We present the architecture using the pNets model [1], a formalism to encode labeled transition systems with value passing, parametrized topologies of processes, and different types of communication. We describe then the primitive component internal behaviour, and the semantic-level process generated from the GCM architecture. We focus on the parts of the specification that are directly related to one-to-many communications and fault-tolerance, details of the other processes are given in [6].

3.1 Distributed Component for Fault-Tolerant Storage

Fig. 3 shows the architecture of our application. It consists of a main composite component BFT-Composite. The white part of the composite is the functional content made of a Master component and several slaves. Some of those slaves are called good slaves, i.e. non-faulty, the bad ones are faulty and behave randomly. In practice one never knows which of the slaves is good or bad but it is necessary that the verification process knows this information to be able to count the number of good and bad slaves.

Properties of Interest. From a high-level point of view, we are interested in the storage properties of our application: *the stored value can be retrieved unchanged, even if some of the slaves are faulty.* Of course, some additional properties are crucial like: the master always finally answers to the requests it

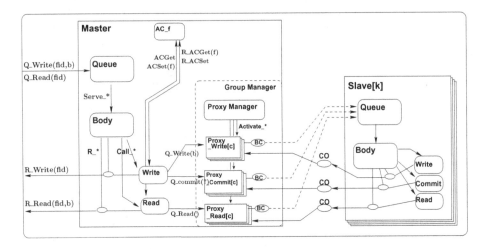

Fig. 4. pNet Architecture for the whole system

receives. Also, the master must rely on the slaves for storing the value, and does not distinguish good slaves from bad slaves, for example, for writing data the master must broadcast a write request to all the slaves.

3.2 Architecture

We describe here the architecture of the semantic model of our use-case. The overall architecture of the system is shown in Fig. 4. It is composed of:

- An indexed family of slaves receiving invocations from the master. Each of them has a queue[1] storing the requests not treated yet, a body part describing how to treat the incoming requests and delegate them to the behavioural specification of methods Write, Commit, and Read. Each requests can reply to the master by updating a future (represented by the arrows between the Write box and the CO element). The system is instantiated with 3 good slaves and 1 bad slave.
- A Master component receiving requests from a client and forwarding them to the slaves (that are bound to it). It also has a request queue and a body delegating the treatment of requests to sub-parts of the master. Treatment of read and write methods will be detailed below.
- The connections that are one-to-one bindings, except for BC (broadcast) that dispatches a request from the master to all the slaves it is bound to, and CO (collect) that carries a reply from one of the slaves to the appropriate proxy. Those 2 bindings will be detailed in Section 3.3.

To optimize the size of the model, the composite has no request queue and calls are directly issued to the *Master* component. This has no consequence because

---

[1] We generate the behaviour of each request queue as an individual process able to store a finite number of requests with their parameters

the requests are directly delegated to the Master component, and the request queue of the Master is sufficient for dealing with asynchrony.

3.3   The Master Body and Its Methods

Let us first describe the communication patterns and name conventions that we use in this paper. All local methods are triggered by a first outgoing communication of the form !Method, then the response is received as parameter of a ?R_Method incoming communication. For example, in Fig. 6 !Get_Write_Proxy requires a new group proxy for invoking the Write method on the slaves. The proxy is returned and stored into p1 by the reply: ?R_Get_Write_Proxy(p1). On the other side, method invocation towards remote components are of the form !Call_Method, those method invocations enqueue a request in the remote request queue, and pass a proxy reference as one of the parameters of the invocation. The remote method will, upon termination, fill the proxy with the calculated value; for this, the !R_Method transition synchronizes at the same time with the invoker that receives the value and with the body of the component containing the method, so that next request can be served.

The Master Body. The body is encoded in generic way: it serves sequentially functional and non-functional requests. In this work, we only use the service of each functional request (on method Read, Write, or SetF). This service calls the adequate method (e.g., !Call_Read), and waits until the method terminates, signaled by R_ events (e.g., ?R_Read); R_Read synchronizes both with the component that triggered the request and with the body. As requests are served one after the other, this encodes a mono-threaded behaviour for the master.

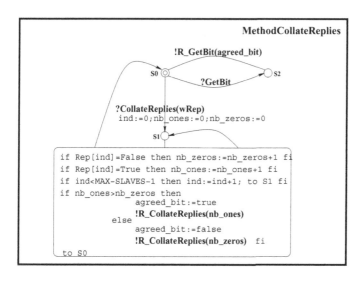

Fig. 5. Behaviour of the method: MasterCollateReplies

The Attribute Controller. In Fractal, the attribute controller provides read and write access to the attributes of the components; the only attribute of the Master component is f – the number of faults that can be handled. The behaviour of the attribute controller is very simple: it simply provides a setter (ACSet) and a getter (ACGet) method for storing and retrieving the value of f.

The Collate Method. Based on the vector of replies received by the proxy, this method computes a consensus in order to know whether enough slaves returned a correct answer. It is used by the methods Read and Write described below. Fig. 5 represents the behaviour of Collate in a format similar to Statecharts [15]: starting from initial state S0, Collate is always used by first triggering a ?CollateReplies sending it a vector of replies currently known; then from state S1, a complex transition counts the number of True and False in the vector. It stores in agreed_bit the reply the most frequent and returns (by !R_CollateReplies) the number of replies that agreed on this value. Then, the agreed value can be retrieved by a ?GetBit, that returns the agreed_bit value.

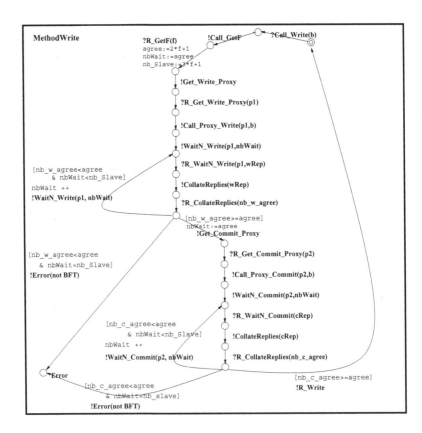

Fig. 6. Behaviour of the Write method

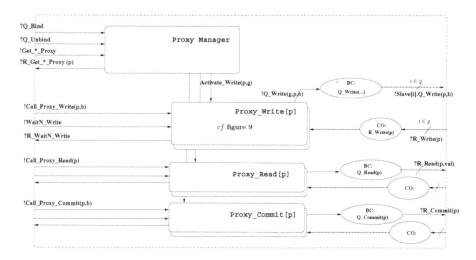

Fig. 7. Focus on the elements for managing the group

The Write Method. The write method is the most complex method of our example, it is shown in Fig. 6. It first gets the current value of f, read from the attribute controller, and initializes the variables agree, awaited, and nb_Slave. It consists of two phases; first, a write request is sent to all the slaves, then the master waits until enough slaves agree on the reply, agree is the number of necessary identical replies, and awaited is the number of awaited replies. If necessary, additional replies are awaited, and awaited is incremented. It is not possible to wait for more replies than the number of slaves; if such a situation occurs, it means that the BFT hypothesis is not verified, more exactly, more than f slaves are faulty and an error is raised. When enough identical replies have been received, the write method enters a commit phase that behaves similarly to the write phase. At the end the method returns to the initial phase, emitting a !R_Write that also indicates the end of the method.

The Read Method. The behaviour of the Read method is very similar to the Write method above. The main difference is that, after triggering remote invocations and waiting for enough identical replies, it inputs the agreed bit found by the collate method and returns this value to the client.

The Master Proxies

Managing Groups of Slaves. We first focus on the management of groups of slaves, i.e. groups to which the write, read and commit requests will be addressed. The part of the pNets that deal with this aspect is shown in Fig. 7. It includes a proxy manager (Fig. 8) that returns an available proxy through its Get_*_Proxy invocations. If reconfiguration was enabled, it would receive bind and unbind requests for adding or removing slaves. When a new proxy is requested, one proxy is activated (among the families of Proxy_write, Proxy_Read, or Proxy_Commit

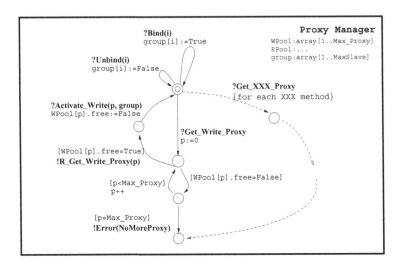

Fig. 8. Behaviour of the Proxy Manager

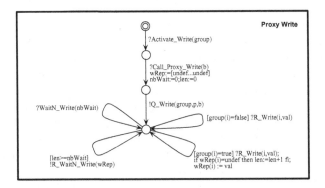

Fig. 9. Behaviour of the Write request proxy (Proxy for Read and Commit are similar)

proxies), and given the group g on which next invocation will be performed. A reference to this proxy is returned, and can be used to remotely invoke Write, Read, or Commit on the slaves. The group g passed upon activation is used later inside the broadcast communication: the circle BC: Q_Write(...) performs a synchronization involving the proxy and all the slaves of g sending them the same invocation, !Slave[i].Q_Write(p,b), where p is the proxy identifier. The symmetric communication is performed by the CO: R_Write(p) that collects replies from all the slaves of g and returns them to the Proxy_Write pNet: each member of g can send a reply to the master. Note that g can be modified inside the manager and a copy of the group is passed upon activation of a proxy. This guarantees that the CO operation will be performed on the same group as the invocation, even if, in the manager, the group is changed in the meantime.

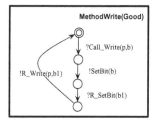
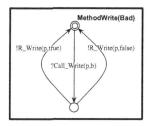

Fig. 10. The Write method of the (Good and Bad) slaves

The Write Proxy. (see Fig. 9) Upon activation, the write proxy waits for an invocation from the master write method. It then initializes the WRep array of received replies as well as len – the number of replies currently received. Its two main behaviours are then (1) to receive a reply from an element of the group, which updates the Wrep array, and the len value; and (2) to fulfill a WaitN_Write invocation from the master write, which returns the current array of received replies once the number of awaited replies is reached. Proxies for read and commit method are similar to the write request proxy.

3.4   The Slave Components and Their Methods

The behaviour of the slaves is much simpler than the one of the master. We encode two kinds of slaves: good slaves behave as expected, whether bad slaves behave randomly and encode the byzantine faulty processes. We instantiate as many faulty processes as the number of faults we can tolerate. The fact that the system description distinguishes between faulty and non-faulty processes has no influence here because the functional parts of the components never use this knowledge: the code of the Master component never distinguishes between the communications towards the faulty slaves, and towards the non-faulty ones.

The slave body serves successively the requests (Commit, Read and Write) arriving at the slave queue much similarly to the master body. The bad slaves and the good slaves have the same body, they all serve the request in a FIFO order, and no two requests are served at the same time: the slaves are mono-threaded. The slaves have three methods: Write, Read and Commit; we show the method Write for the good and bad slaves in Fig. 10, the behaviour of a good slave consists in storing the bit value b received thanks to a call to !SetBit that sets a local attribute of the slave. There is a method !GetBit for reading this value, it is called by the Read request. The bad slave as shown in Fig. 10 replies randomly to each individual request. The commit phase is here to show how a commit phase would be implemented, but it is not used by our slaves: it would be useful if the master could also have a faulty behaviour.

According to the BFT hypothesis, a bad slave can behave arbitrarily. However, we have to restrict a little this behaviour so that it can be encoded and verified by finite model-checking techniques. Here are the hypotheses we make and the reasons why it is safe to make them:

- Bad slaves do not steal the identity of another entity: we suppose here that the underlying middleware guarantees the identity of the components sending requests or replies. It is the classical "oral messages" assumption of [22].
- Bad slaves only reply to required requests. We suppose again that the middleware verifies this to guarantee the integrity of the program execution.
- Bad slaves only reply to requests in the order required. This assumption is stronger but we can show that it has no influence on the final result. First, the master is single threaded, waits for enough replies before requiring another computation, and does not access the future afterward; thus late replies would have no influence on the computation. In principle, a bad slave could serve the request in the wrong order and use this information to behave in a malicious manner; but the exhaustive exploration of all the possible replies is even more general than the scenarios using out of order service of requests.

4   Building the Model, and Running the Verification Tools

In this section we describe the methods and tools used to build the behavioural model of our application and to check its properties, and we discuss the combination of advanced techniques we have used to master the model complexity.

We build the behavioural model of our case-study in three steps (Fig. 11). From the specification of the component architecture and behaviour, our tool ADL2N [8] builds a hierarchical and parametrized pNets model, including the data types, the behaviour, and the architecture of the system. Then abstractions are applied on the data domains, yielding a finitary model. Finally the model is encoded using a combination of several input formalisms from the CADP toolset [11]: the Fiacre language [5] provides syntax for data types and expressions, definition of LTS, and a form of composition of processes by synchronization on channels; the EXP and SVL languages [11] support the hierarchical encoding of our pNets, and the scripting of the various verification tasks.

Then we run a combination of CADP tools, the most important ones are: ceasar.open for generating transition systems from Fiacre programs, either on a single machine, or on parallel infrastructures when used in combination with distributor; exp.open to build product of transition systems described in EXP format; and Evaluator4, the new version of the model-checker that deals with the MCL (Model Checking Language) logics [23], which is an extension of the alternation-free regular μ-calculus with facilities for manipulating data.

The Vercors[2] tool platform should assist the programmer in the encoding and verification of his application. It includes the Vercors editors, the ADL2N, ABS and N2F tools; it is currently under development. For this paper, we already have been able to generate approximately 50% of the Fiacre and EXP code.

One goal of this work is to experiment with various methods for mastering the state explosion inherent to large models, such methods consist of:

---

[2] http://www-sop.inria.fr/oasis/index.php?page=vercors

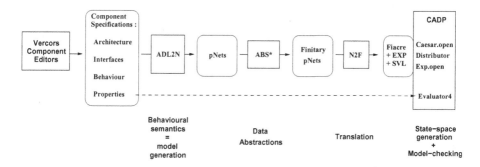

Fig. 11. Tool chain and corresponding processing steps

1. data abstraction
2. hierarchical hiding and minimization
3. use of contextual environment information
4. distributed state-space generation

We have used 1) in several ways. First, all data variables have been given abstract types with (very small) finite domains, in fact we choose the smallest abstract domain that preserves the formulas to be proven. Secondly, the topology parameters of the system (the number of slaves and number of proxy instances) have been reduced to a minimum number, though significant for our scenario; proving properties that would be valid for any values of such parameters is out of the scope of model-checking. Finally, the request queues raises another issue: their explicit representation has a size exponential in the number of values that the queue cells admit. Our approach is to encode a (small) finite model of the queue, including events denoting an error when this finite queue is out-of-bounds. Then we check by model-checking whether this event is reachable, or the chosen size is sufficient. The soundness of these approaches is worth discussing; for the domains of value-passing parameters, we can define finite abstractions that preserve safety and liveness properties [9]; for the length of queues, we are building an under-approximation, and we check explicitly its validity. But for topology parameters, we have no such general result and we only prove properties for a given instantiation, that is already very helpful as a "debugging tool". Proving more general properties is not in the scope of this paper.

Method 2) is now quite classical when using bisimulation-based tools. Let us remark that to be optimal, we have to generate models specifically for each formula to prove. Method 3) has been proposed and advocated by the CADP developers, and is indeed very important when combined with 2). The problem arises when you build subsystems hierarchically without taking into account the specific way in which other pieces of the system interact with a given subsystem. The context information can be built automatically by the CADP tools from the behaviour of the other subsystems (in which case it is guaranteed to be sound), or can be specified manually (that may lead to under-approximations). We chose the second option, and we used the context behaviour to reduce further the possible values of input data of some methods, by symmetry arguments.

Method 4) is a hot research topic. We are using a local Cloud platform, providing large computing resources (>1300 cores and 3 Tbytes of RAM), where we can submit jobs in the form of task workflows. In our case, tasks consist of compilation of input formalisms, generation of transition systems for subsystems, minimization and product of systems, and model-checking. Tasks can be parallel, but for the current version of CADP, only LTS generation can run in a distributed way [12]. We were able to build systems with more than 10^9 states explicitly stored in distributed memory [18], but then the bottleneck is the merging of this structure before minimization or model-checking on a single machine. In practice, the good strategy is to decompose the system in such a way that subsystems are of reasonable size, or can be strongly constrained by contextual information, and to run concurrently the tasks computing the behaviour of each subsystem. Then minimization, product, and model-checking tasks are run as soon as their inputs are available, in a coarse-grain concurrent workflow.

Parameter Domains and System Sizes. We ran the use-case with 3 good slaves and 1 bad slave, allowing for 1 failure. We also generated the model in two different configurations, with the length Q of the Master Queue respectively 2 (for OutOfBounds detection) and 1 (for optimization).

As we do not have yet enough tool support at the level of the formalism compilers, we had to do a significant part of the Fiacre/Exp/SVL programming by hand, so we chose to build one single model with enough events visible to prove our formulas of interest. The intermediate code consists in 43 Fiacre processes for a total of 2900 lines of code, and of 330 lines of synchronization vectors in EXP format encoding 240 pNet structures.

Then the system is divided in 12 subsystems (9 for the Master itself); each part is encoded in a Fiacre source file, and its state space computed using distributor. So we have at this level 12 independent tasks in our workflow, running on 2 to 10 cloud nodes each. Each resulting automaton is reduced by branching bisimulation (with as much local actions hidden as possible), before being composed in a hierarchical way, using 4 synchronization products. The final product is minimized again, before running Evaluator4 for checking our properties. Decomposing the system in an efficiently manner currently requires human operation: the choice of subsystems is a compromise between: identifying processes that may be reused easily (through relabeling); defining subsystems that are big enough to take advantage of a distributed generation; choosing pieces which environment behaviour is well-specified.

The system sizes (states/transitions, after minimization) and computation times are summarized in the following table:

Q. size	Queue	Intermediate	Master	GoodSlave	Global	Total time
Q=1	21/229	542/3107	2M/45M	744/6550	22K/110K	10'
Q=2	237/3189	542/3107	5.8M/103M	5936/61K	34K/164K	59'

The middle columns in the table give reduced sizes for the most interesting subsystems: the Master queue, the biggest intermediate subsystem in our decomposition of the Master, the whole Master component, the (good) Slave component, and finally the global system, comprising the Master, 4 Slaves, and a Client. The last column gives the global computation time.

Correctness Properties. Once the behavioural model generated, we verified several properties, written using the MCL logics; they express various facets of the system correctness. Some properties express global correctness of the application, seen from the (external) client point of view. Others require the visibility of some internal events of the system, and reveal the feasibility of several scenarios, or the impossibility of some errors.

Let us start with simple reachability properties: all requests (Write or Read) sent to the system can terminate and return successfully. The first formula means that for each possible value of fid (the identifier of a client request), the action R_Read denoting the return of the corresponding Read request is reachable with some returned value val. This property is **True**, meaning that the Read request can terminate (this holds also for Write requests).

```
forall fid:nat among {0...2}. exists b:bool.
        <true* . {R_Read !fid !b}> true
```

Next formula checks the reachability of the BFT Error events. This property is **False**, meaning that we instantiated enough good slaves.

```
< true* . 'Error (NotBFT)'> true
```

We then ensure that the Master's queue cannot receive too many requests. Its validity depends on the system client(s). Here we have proved that a queue depth of 1 is sufficient to prove all of our correctness properties, if we have a single client, and if this client waits for replies before sending the next request.

```
< true* . 'Error (Master-OutOfBounds)'> true
```

Also, we have proved *Inevitability* properties like the following one. It ensures that it is (fairly) inevitable that after a Write request, either the system sends the corresponding Write response or raises an error. Here fairness means "fair reachability of predicates" in the sense of Queille and Sifakis [25]:

```
[ true* . ({Q_Write ?fid:nat ?bit:bool})
        . (not ('Error.*' or {R_Write !fid}))* ]
< (not ('Error.*' or {R_Write !fid}))*
    . ('Error.*' or {R_Write !fid}) > true
```

Similarily, we have shown that it is fairly inevitable that Read requests are replied, and also that the system is functionally correct: after a Write request (and before the next one), a Read request will answer with the correct value.

To summarise, we proved by model-checking that our application consisting of 1 master and 4 slaves (3 good ones and bad one) behaves correctly: 1) it answers to Read and Write requests, 2) the answers are correct in the sense that the read value is the value that has been written, 3) for this it relies on the slaves for storing the data (the master only performs a consensus), and 4) enough good slaves have been instantiated and the NotBFT error cannot be raised.

5   Conclusion

This paper shows the modelisation and verification by model-checking of a system that features: one-to-many communication, asynchronous communication with futures, byzantine faults, replication, and consensus. We showed here the possibility to encode and verify the correct behaviour of a whole distributed application that tolerates some faulty processes. Handling byzantine faults is a difficult task, because no assumption can be made on the behaviour of the faulty processes. Such a random behaviour makes automatic verification of the correction of a whole application even more difficult because a lot of possible states must be considered.

A next step could be to integrate the generation of faulty process, replication management, and consensus methods to our specification environment: the user would identify the possibly faulty components and the environment would generate BFT-like behaviour and replication for those components, but also broadcast and consensus operations. The new system could then be model-checked to decide whether the whole application is fault-tolerant.

Another lesson drawn here is that the behaviour of the whole application is huge, we used all the power of the distributed version of CADP on a cloud-like environment to verify the application. This shows that application-level fault-tolerance can be verified by a model-checker, but also that adding any other feature to the system (e.g. reconfiguration for changing the number of replicates at runtime) may be very difficult. To master such complexity we should use semantic properties of the programming model and of the middleware to get better and smaller abstractions at the level of the generated behaviour.

References

1. Barros, T., Ameur-Boulifa, R., Cansado, A., Henrio, L., Madelaine, E.: Behavioural models for distributed Fractal components. Annals of Télécommunications 64(1-2), 25–43 (2009)
2. Baude, F., Caromel, D., Dalmasso, C., Danelutto, M., Getov, V., Henrio, L., Pérez, C.: GCM: a grid extension to Fractal for autonomous distributed components. Annals of Télécommunications (2009)
3. Beisiegel, M., Blohm, H., Booz, D., Edwards, M., Hurley, O.: SCA service component architecture, assembly model specification. Technical report (March 2007)
4. Bensalem, S., Bozga, M., Nguyen, T.-H., Sifakis, J.: Compositional verification for component-based systems and application. IET Software 4(3) (2010)
5. Berthomieu, B., Bodeveix, J.P., Filali, M., Garavel, H., Lang, F., Peres, F., Saad, R., Stoecker, J., Vernadat, F.: The syntax and semantics of Fiacre. In: Rapport LAAS #07264 Rapport de Contrat Projet OpenEmbeDD (Mai 2007)
6. Ameur Boulifa, R., Halalai, R., Henrio, L., Madelaine, E.: Verifying safety of fault-tolerant distributed components (extended version). Research Report RR-7717, INRIA (August 2011)
7. Ameur Boulifa, R., Henrio, L., Madelaine, E.: Behavioural models for group communications. In: WCSI 2010: International Workshop on Component and Service Interoperability, Malaga, Spain (2010)
8. Cansado, A., Madelaine, E.: Specification and Verification for Grid Component-Based Applications: From Models to Tools. In: de Boer, F.S., Bonsangue, M.M., Madelaine, E. (eds.) FMCO 2008. LNCS, vol. 5751, pp. 180–203. Springer, Heidelberg (2009)

9. Cleaveland, R., Riely, J.: Testing-Based Abstractions for Value-Passing Systems. In: Jonsson, B., Parrow, J. (eds.) CONCUR 1994. LNCS, vol. 836, pp. 417–432. Springer, Heidelberg (1994)
10. Eker, J., Janneck, J., Lee, E.A., Liu, J., Liu, X., Ludvig, J., Sachs, S., Xiong, Y.: Taming heterogeneity - the ptolemy approach. Proceedings of the IEEE 91(1), 127–144 (2003)
11. Garavel, H., Lang, F., Mateescu, R., Serwe, W.: CADP 2010: A Toolbox for the Construction and Analysis of Distributed Processes. In: Abdulla, P.A., Leino, K.R.M. (eds.) TACAS 2011. LNCS, vol. 6605, pp. 372–387. Springer, Heidelberg (2011)
12. Garavel, H., Mateescu, R., Bergamini, D., Curic, A., Descoubes, N., Joubert, C., Smarandache-Sturm, I., Stragier, G.: DISTRIBUTOR and BCG_MERGE: Tools for Distributed Explicit State Space Generation. In: Hermanns, H., Palsberg, J. (eds.) TACAS 2006. LNCS, vol. 3920, pp. 445–449. Springer, Heidelberg (2006)
13. Grabe, I., Steffen, M., Torjusen, A.B.: Executable Interface Specifications for Testing Asynchronous Creol Components. Research Report 375. University of Oslo, Dept. of Computer Science (July 2008)
14. Guerraoui, R., Knežević, N., Quéma, V., Vukolić, M.: The next 700 BFT protocols. In: Proceedings of the 5th European Conference on Computer Systems, EuroSys 2010, pp. 363–376. ACM, New York (2010)
15. Harel, D.: Statecharts: A visual formalism for complex systems (1987)
16. Hatcliff, J., Deng, W., Dwyer, M.B., Jung, G., Ranganath, V.: Cadena: An integrated development, analysis, and verification environment for component-based systems. In: Proc. of the 25th Int. Conf. on Software Engineering (2003)
17. Henrio, L., Kammüller, F., Rivera, M.: An Asynchronous Distributed Component Model and its Semantics. In: de Boer, F.S., Bonsangue, M.M., Madelaine, E. (eds.) FMCO 2008. LNCS, vol. 5751, pp. 159–179. Springer, Heidelberg (2009)
18. Henrio, L., Madelaine, E.: Experiments with distributed model-checking of group-based applications. In: Sophia-Antipolis Formal Analysis Workshop, France Sophia-Antipolis, p. 3 (October 2010)
19. Johnsen, E.B., Owe, O., Yu, I.C.: Creol: a types-safe object-oriented model for distributed concurrent systems. Journal of Theoretical Computer Science 365(1-2), 23–66 (2006)
20. Jung, G., Hatcliff, J.: A type-centric framework for specifying heterogeneous, large-scale, component-oriented, architectures. Science of Computer Programming 75(7), 615–637 (2010)
21. Kotla, R., Alvisi, L., Dahlin, M., Clement, A., Wong, E.: Zyzzyva: speculative byzantine fault tolerance. In: Proceedings of Twenty-First ACM SIGOPS Symposium on Operating Systems Principles, SOSP 2007, pp. 45–58. ACM, New York (2007)
22. Lamport, L., Shostak, R., Pease, M.: The byzantine generals problem. ACM Trans. Program. Lang. Syst. 4, 382–401 (1982)
23. Mateescu, R., Thivolle, D.: A Model Checking Language for Concurrent Value-Passing Systems. In: Sere, K., Cuellar, J., Maibaum, T.S.E. (eds.) FM 2008. LNCS, vol. 5014, pp. 148–164. Springer, Heidelberg (2008)
24. Parizek, P., Plasil, F.: Assume-guarantee verification of software components in sofa 2 framework. IET Software 4(3), 210–211 (2010)
25. Queille, J.-P., Sifakis, J.: Fairness and Related Properties in Transition Systems — A Temporal Logic to Deal with Fairness. Acta Informatica 19, 195–220 (1983)
26. Schneider, F.B.: Implementing fault-tolerant services using the state machine approach: a tutorial. ACM Comput. Surv. 22, 299–319 (1990)

Reducing the Model Checking Cost of Product Lines Using Static Analysis Techniques[*]

Hamideh Sabouri[1] and Ramtin Khosravi[1,2]

[1] School of Electrical and Computer Engineering University of Tehran
Karegar Ave., Tehran, Iran
[2] School of Computer Science, Institute for Research in Fundamental
Sciences (IPM), Tehran, Iran

Abstract. Software product line engineering is a paradigm to develop software applications using platforms and mass customization. Component based approaches play an important role in development of product lines: Components represent features, and different component combinations lead to different products. The number of combinations is exponential in the number of features, which makes the cost of product line model checking high. In this paper, we propose two techniques to reduce the number of component combinations that have to be verified. The first technique is using the static slicing approach to eliminate the features that do not affect the property. The second technique is analyzing the property and extracting sufficient conditions of property satisfaction/violation, to identify products that satisfy or violate the property without model checking. We apply these techniques on a vending machine case study to show the applicability and effectiveness of our approach. The results show that the number of generated states and time of model checking is reduced significantly using the proposed reduction techniques.

1 Introduction

Software product line engineering is a paradigm to develop software applications using platforms and mass customization. To this end, the commonalities and differences of the applications should be modeled explicitly [1]. Feature models are widely used to model the variability of software product lines. A feature model is a tree of features, containing mandatory and optional features as well as a number of constraints among them. A product is then defined by a combination of features, and product family is the set containing all of the valid feature combinations [2]. A configuration vector can be used to keep track of inclusion or exclusion of features.

The Vending Machine Example: Feature Model. Throughout this paper, we use a product family of vending machines as a running example. A vending machine may serve coffee and/or tea. It also may add milk to the coffee. Figure 1 shows the feature model of the family of vending machines.

[*] This research was in part supported by a grant form IPM. (No. CS1390-4-02).

F. Arbab and P.C. Ölveczky (Eds.): FACS 2011, LNCS 7253, pp. 296–312, 2012.
© Springer-Verlag Berlin Heidelberg 2012

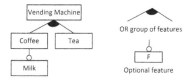

Fig. 1. The feature model of the vending machine example

Software product line engineering enables proactive reuse by developing a family of related products. One of the main approaches to develop software product lines is the compositional approach, in which features are implemented as distinct code units [3]. These code units are reused when the corresponding units are composed to generate each product. Component technology [4] is suitable in this approach as reusability is an important characteristic of software components. In component-based development of product lines, each feature is implemented using a component. Some of the features can be implemented within the components in a fine-grained manner as well, using annotative techniques [5]. Consequently, the behavior of a component may change according to inclusion or exclusion of the features. Software product line engineering is used in the development of embedded and critical systems [6]. Therefore formal modeling and verification of software product lines is essential.

Model checking [7] is a promising technique for developing more reliable systems. Recently, several approaches have been developed for formal modeling of product lines [8,9,10,11,12,13]. These approaches capture the behavior of the entire product family in a single model by including the variability information in it. In other words, it is specified in the model how the behavior changes when a feature is included or excluded. Model checking of product lines is discussed in [10,12,13]. In these approaches, the model checker investigates all of the possible feature combinations when verifying the model of a product family against a property, and the result of model checking is the set of products that satisfy the given property. The focus of these works is on adapting model checking algorithms to verify product families, and they do not address the state space explosion issue. However, the main problem of model checking is its high computational and memory costs which may lead to state space explosion. This problem limits the applicability of model checking technique to verify product lines, as in product families the number of products can be exponential in the number of features. In [14,15], two incremental approaches are proposed for product line verification. In [14], only sequential composition of features is discussed which is a considerable limitation as the approach is not applicable to concurrent systems. The focus of [15] is on reducing the effort of applying deductive verification techniques (not model checking) on product lines. The main idea of our approach is to use static slicing and static analysis techniques to tackle the state space explosion problem in model checking of component-based software product lines.

We use Rebeca to model product families in a component-based manner, as a basis to explain our approach. However, the approach is not limited to Rebeca models, and it is applicable to any modeling language with slicing analysis support. In our approach, each feature is modeled using one component that captures its corresponding behavior, or using an alternative behavior within a component that changes the behavior of the component based on the presence or absence of the feature accordingly. Each product contains the components associated to the features that are included in the product, and the behavior of each of its components is determined according to the features that are included/excluded in that product. The model checker considers all of the possible combinations of components and alternative behaviors, to verify the product family. The focus of this paper is on reducing the number of combinations that should be investigated in model checking. We propose two techniques for this purpose.

The first technique uses the static slicing approach. Static slicing [16] is an analysis technique that extracts the statements from a program that are relevant to a particular computation. This technique has been used as a reduction technique in model checking of Promela [17], CSP [18], Petri-nets [19], and Rebeca [20,21] models. In [22], an evaluation of applying static slicing for model reduction is presented. The result shows significant reductions that are orthogonal to a number of other reduction techniques, and applying slicing is always recommended because of its automation and low computational costs. One of the main approaches for slicing is using reachability analysis on program dependence graph. The nodes of a program dependence graph are the statements of the program, and its edges represent data and control dependencies among the statements. In this paper, we adapt the program dependence graph and the reachability algorithm, to use static slicing to identify the features that do not affect the correctness of the property. By discarding these features, the model checker investigates fewer feature combinations when model checking the product family.

In the second technique, we analyze the property statically to extract sufficient conditions of its satisfaction or violation. These conditions are used along with reachability conditions for variables to conclude satisfaction or violation of the given property for certain products, without verification. The model checker does not verify these products, therefore the number of feature combinations that should be verified is reduced. It should be noted that the proposed techniques (slicing, extracting conditions from property, and investigating reachability of variables) can be applied automatically.

This paper is structured as follows. Section 2 explains how product families are modeled and model checked. In Section 3 we describe the slicing technique that is used to identify the features that do not affect a property. Section 4 describes our approach for extracting sufficient conditions of property satisfaction/violation, and identifying products that satisfy or violate the property, without model checking. In Section 5 we present the results of using the two proposed techniques for reducing the feature combinations of a vending machine case study. Finally, we conclude our work in Section 6.

2 Modeling and Model Checking Product Families

This section introduces the Rebeca modeling language [23], and explains how a product family can be modeled and model checked using Rebeca. We select Rebeca as a basis to describe our approach, because it is suitable for modeling concurrent systems, it is supported by the Modere model checking tool [24], it supports components [25], and the slicing technique is adapted to be applicable on Rebeca models [20,21]. However, our proposed approach is not limited to Rebeca models, and can be applied to other modeling languages with similar facilities as well.

2.1 Rebeca

Rebeca is an actor-based language for modeling concurrent and distributed systems as a set of reactive objects which communicate via asynchronous message passing. A Rebeca model consists of a set of *reactive classes*. Each reactive class contains a set of *state variables* and a set of *message servers*. Message servers execute atomically, and process the receiving messages. The *initial* message server is used for initialization of state variables. A Rebeca model has a *main* part, where a fixed number of objects are instantiated from the reactive classes and execute concurrently. We refer to these objects as *rebecs*. The rebecs have no shared variable, and each rebec has a single thread of execution that is triggered by reading messages from an unbounded message queue. When a message is taken from the queue, its corresponding message server is invoked. In [25], components are added to the Rebeca language to encapsulate tightly coupled reactive objects. In other words, a component is a set of one or more reactive objects.

2.2 Product Family Model

To model product families, we should model optional components (which may be included in some of the products, and excluded in other products), and alternative behaviors of components. Different combinations of optional components and alternative behaviors lead to different products. To this end, we use a special tag $@AC$ before a statement to specify the *application condition* of the statement. An application condition is a propositional logic formula in terms of features. This tag indicates that the statement will be executed only in those products that AC holds. When a feature F corresponds to a component, we use $@F$ tag before all the message server calls to that component. Subsequently, message servers of a component are invoked only if its associated feature is included in a product. If the feature is excluded in a product, no message is sent to its corresponding component, and the component will be excluded. Moreover, these tags can be used to indicate the change of the behavior within components according to presence and absence of features.

The Vending Machine Example: Rebeca Model. Figure 2 shows the Rebeca code for the product family of vending machines. In this model, there is a controller component that manages coffee and tea requests and sends messages to the coffee maker and tea maker components accordingly. The *nextRequest* message server (line 12") is responsible for handling the requests. When there is request for coffee (*req* = 1), the *serveCoffee* message is put in the queue of *coffeeMaker*, if the machine is capable of serving coffee (line 15"). If the machine does not have the coffee option, the coffee request is ignored and the machine processes the next request (line 17"). The tea request (*req* = 2) is handled in a similar way. Consequently, if the coffee or tea feature is excluded in a product, no message is sent to the corresponding component, and the component will be also excluded. In the coffee maker component, the behavior changes according to the existence of the milk feature. If the milk feature is included in a product, milk is added to coffee (line 15). One of the linear temporal logic (LTL) [26] properties that can be considered for this model is $P : \Box(\neg(addingCoffee \wedge addingTea))$, where $\Box$ stands for globally. This property describes that the machine should not add both coffee and tea to a drink at the same time.

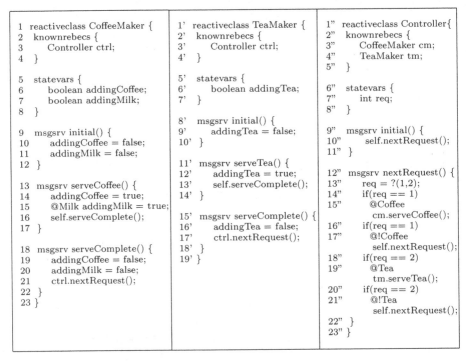

```
1  reactiveclass CoffeeMaker {        1'  reactiveclass TeaMaker {          1"  reactiveclass Controller{
2    knownrebecs {                     2'    knownrebecs {                    2"    knownrebecs {
3       Controller ctrl;               3'       Controller ctrl;             3"       CoffeeMaker cm;
4    }                                 4'    }                                4"       TeaMaker tm;
                                                                             5"    }
5    statevars {                       5'    statevars {
6       boolean addingCoffee;          6'       boolean addingTea;           6"    statevars {
7       boolean addingMilk;            7'    }                               7"       int req;
8    }                                                                       8"    }
                                       8'    msgsrv initial() {
9    msgsrv initial() {                9'       addingTea = false;           9"    msgsrv initial() {
10      addingCoffee = false;          10'   }                               10"      self.nextRequest();
11      addingMilk = false;                                                  11"   }
12   }                                 11'   msgsrv serveTea() {
                                       12'      addingTea = true;            12"   msgsrv nextRequest() {
13   msgsrv serveCoffee() {            13'      self.serveComplete();        13"      req = ?(1,2);
14      addingCoffee = true;           14'   }                               14"      if(req == 1)
15      @Milk addingMilk = true;                                            15"         @Coffee
16      self.serveComplete();          15'   msgsrv serveComplete() {                   cm.serveCoffee();
17   }                                 16'      addingTea = false;           16"      if(req == 1)
                                       17'      ctrl.nextRequest();          17"         @!Coffee
18   msgsrv serveComplete() {          18'   }                                          self.nextRequest();
19      addingCoffee = false;          19' }                                 18"      if(req == 2)
20      addingMilk = false;                                                  19"         @Tea
21      ctrl.nextRequest();                                                            tm.serveTea();
22   }                                                                       20"      if(req == 2)
23 }                                                                         21"         @!Tea
                                                                                       self.nextRequest();
                                                                            22"   }
                                                                            23" }
```

Fig. 2. The Rebeca code of the product family of vending machines

2.3   Model Checking the Product Family

For a product line with n features (where each feature corresponds to a component or an alternative behavior of a component), potentially there exist 2^n products in its corresponding product family. To model check the product family, a configuration vector $C \in \langle I, E, ?\rangle^n$ (I: Included, E: Excluded, ?: not decided) is used to keep track of inclusion and exclusion decisions that are made for each feature [10]. The validity of configuration vector with respect to the feature model can be checked during model checking by transforming the feature model to a propositional logic formula [27] and using a SAT-solver (like [28]) to investigate its satisfiability. The result of model checking a product family against a property is the set of products (represented through configuration vectors) that satisfy the given property.

The Vending Machine Example: Model Checking. We assume the first, second, and third elements of configuration vector correspond to Coffee, Tea, and Milk features, respectively. The result of model checking the product family of vending machines against the property P is:

$$R = \{\langle E, I, E\rangle, \langle I, E, E\rangle, \langle I, I, E\rangle, \langle I, E, I\rangle, \langle I, I, I\rangle\}$$

Note that the configurations $\langle E, E, E\rangle$, $\langle E, E, I\rangle$, and $\langle E, I, I\rangle$ do not appear in R as they do not represent valid products, according to the feature model.

3   Slicing the Model of a Product Family

The main purpose of slicing is to extract the statements of a program that are relevant to a particular computation. A backward program slice consists of the statements that potentially affect the values computed by some statement of interest (referred to as a slicing criterion). A common approach for program slicing is applying a graph reachability algorithm on the program dependence graph. In this section, we first describe the program dependence graph of Rebeca models that capture the behavior of a product family, and then present the slicing algorithm that computes the slice of the product family model, followed by a short discussion on model checking the computed slice.

3.1   Program Dependence Graph

A program dependence graph models the data and control dependencies that exist among the statements of a program. In such a graph, the nodes represent the statements of a program, and the edges are dependencies among them. A *data dependence* edge exists between two statements if one statement assigns a value to a variable and the other statement may read the value of that variable before it is changed by another statement. A *control dependence* edge exists between two statements if one statement determines whether the other statement is executed.

A special dependence graph named *Rebeca Dependence Graph* (RDG), is introduced for Rebeca in [20]. In this graph, there is a *class* node for each reactive class, and *member dependence* edges connect the class nodes to their message servers. Each message server is modeled by an *entry* node, a set of nodes representing its statements, and data dependence and control dependence edges modeling dependencies within the body of the message server. Sending a message is represented through an *activation* node. In addition, an *activation* edge is used to connect the activation node to the entry node of the corresponding message server. Finally, *intra-rebec dependence* edge represents the dependency between a statement that writes on a state variable in a message server, and a statement which reads the value of that variable in another message server. To adapt the dependence graph for product families, we add a tag to the nodes to specify their application conditions.

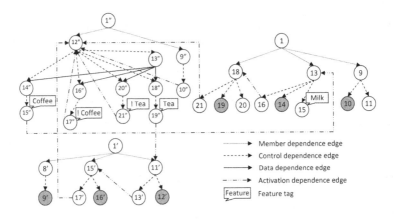

Fig. 3. The RDG of the vending machine example

The Vending Machine Example: RDG. Figure 3 shows the RDG of the vending machine. In this graph the nodes 15, 15", 17", 19", and 21", are tagged with a feature as their corresponding statements in the Rebeca model are tagged with these features.

3.2   Slicing Algorithm

After constructing the program dependence graph, the slice with respect to a property can be computed using a graph reachability algorithm. The slicing criterion consists of the statements that assign values to the variables that appear in the given property. Figure 4 shows the static slicing algorithm that is adapted to extract the features affecting the property as well. To this end, the algorithm traverses the graph backwards (starting from the slicing criterion nodes), and adds the traversed nodes to the slice, and their corresponding features to the relevant features set. In this algorithm, we assume that *Features(v)* gives the set of features that appear in the application condition of node v. The features in the set F are the components and the alternative behaviors that their presence

```
Input: The set of slicing criterions (C) and RDG (Rebeca Dependence Graph)
Output: Slice S, Relevant features set F

S={};                              /*initialize the slice*/
F={};                              /*initialize the relevant features set*/
for each(c_i∈C){                   /*for each slicing criterion*/
    W={c_i};                       /*add the slicing criterion node to the work list*/
    S=S∪{c_i};                     /*add the slicing criterion node to the slice*/
    while(W≠∅){                    /*while the work list is not empty*/
        W=W\{w};                   /*remove one element (w) from the work list*/
        for each(v→w){             /*for each node v on which w depends*/
            if(v∉S){               /*if the node is not included in the slice*/
                W=W∪{v};           /*add it to the work list and the slice*/
                S=S∪{v};
                F=F∪Features(v); /*add the corresponding features to the relevant feature set*/
            }
        }
    }
}
```

Fig. 4. Static slicing algorithm adapted to extract relevant features

or absence affects the correctness of the property. Therefore, the model checker should investigate their different combinations.

The Vending Machine Example: Slicing. The slicing criterion nodes for the property $P : \Box(\neg(addingCoffee \wedge addingTea))$, are indicated by gray nodes in Figure 3. The slice computed by the slicing algorithm contains all of the nodes except 11, 15, 20, and the feature set is $F = \{Coffee, Tea\}$.

3.3   Model Checking the Slice

The features that do not exist in the set F represent the components and alternative behaviors that do not affect the property. Therefore, the combinations of these features can be ignored when model checking the slice of a product family. Having a feature model with n features, there will be at most 2^n feature combinations (products), in the product family. By excluding m features that do not affect the property, the number of products to verify is reduced to $2^{(n-m)}$. The configuration vector is $C \in \langle I, E, ? \rangle^{(n-m)}$, as practically, the value of an element that its associated feature is removed always remains as "?".

The result of model checking the slice of product family against a property is the set R containing the configurations that satisfy the given property. However, these configurations are based on the combinations of $n - m$ features and do not describe identifiable products. As the other m features do not affect the property, we can combine the configurations in R with inclusion and exclusion of each of these features, taking constraints of the feature model into account, to achieve the final result. If we have r configurations such as $C \in \langle I, E \rangle^{(n-m)}$ in R, The ultimate result R' would contain $(r \times 2^m) - u$ configurations in the form $C \in \langle I, E \rangle^n$, where u is the number of feature combinations that are not valid according the feature model.

The Vending Machine Example: Model Checking the Slice. The Milk feature does not affect the property P, and does not appear in the slice. This reduces the number of products in the product family from 2^3 to 2^2. The result of model checking the slice against P is:

$$R = \{\langle E, I \rangle, \langle I, E \rangle, \langle I, I \rangle\}$$

In the next step, the milk feature should be combined with each of the above configurations. So it should be included and be excluded in these configurations (that leads to two new configurations per each configuration). The final result is R' that consists of $(3 \times 2^1) - 1$ configurations ($\langle E, I, I \rangle$ is invalid):

$$R' = \{\langle E, I, E \rangle, \langle I, E, E \rangle, \langle I, E, I \rangle, \langle I, I, E \rangle, \langle I, I, I \rangle\}$$

4 Static Analysis of Property Satisfaction/Violation in Products

In this section, we describe how satisfaction/violation of a property can be inferred for some of the products without model checking. For this purpose, we extract sufficient conditions for property satisfaction/violation in terms of initial values of atomic propositions and the possibility of their change in the model. We assume that a property is described using boolean variables where each variable corresponds to an atomic proposition. Therefore, we can evaluate sufficient conditions using the initial values of the variables and the possibility of their change in different products. The latter is achieved by analyzing the reachability of statements to obtain a condition in terms of presence and absence of features, which describes in which products the value of a variable may change. Using the result of evaluating sufficient conditions, we determine a subset of products that satisfy/violate the property without model checking. In other words, we indicate in which components and in which of their alternative behaviors the value of a variable does not change, and consequently the property is satisfied/violated.

It should be mentioned that this analysis only makes sense for models of product families that capture the behavior of all products. In traditional model checking, the value of a variable changes when the model is executed, and almost always it is not possible to infer satisfaction/violation of a property without model checking.

4.1 Condition Extraction from the Property

In this work, we consider properties expressed in linear temporal logic (LTL) [26]. An LTL formula over the set of AP of atomic propositions is formed according the following grammar:

$$\varphi ::= true \mid false \mid p \mid \neg\varphi \mid \varphi_1 \wedge \varphi_2 \mid \varphi_1 \vee \varphi_2 \mid \Box\varphi \mid \Diamond\varphi \mid \varphi_1 U \varphi_2$$

In the above grammar, $p \in AP$, and $\Box, \Diamond$, and U stand for globally, finally, and until operators respectively.

A transition system TS is a tuple $(S, Act, \rightarrow, I, AP, L)$ where S is a set of states, Act is a set of actions, $\rightarrow \subseteq S \times Act \times S$ is a transition relation, $I \subseteq S$ is a set of initial states, AP is a set of atomic propositions, and $L : S \rightarrow 2^{AP}$ is a labeling function. For simplicity, in this paper we assume a single initial state s_0 for a transition system. A state s is reachable from the initial state, $s_0 \rightarrow^* s$, if there exists a set of actions $\alpha_i \in Act$ such that $s_0 \xrightarrow{\alpha_1} s_1 \xrightarrow{\alpha_2} ... \xrightarrow{\alpha_n} s$.

Figure 5 shows the proposed rules for extracting sufficient conditions of property satisfaction/violation. These conditions are statically inferable from the initial values of atomic propositions, and also the atomic propositions that do not vary in TS. The notation $\overline{V}_{TS}(\varphi)$ means that the LTL formula φ does not vary in TS, because some of the atomic propositions in φ do not change in TS.

Rules 1-8 are trivial. We can infer $TS \vDash \Box\varphi$ from $TS \vDash \varphi$ (Rule 9) if φ does not vary in TS ($\overline{V}_{TS}(\varphi)$). From $TS \nvDash \varphi$ we can conclude that $TS \nvDash \Box\varphi$, as φ should hold in all states and otherwise $\Box\varphi$ is violated (Rule 10). Similar justifications can be made for the other rules.

Using these rules, we extract sufficient conditions for property satisfaction or violation. These conditions are propositional logic formulas in terms of initial values of atomic propositions ($p \in L(s_0)$) and their variability ($\overline{V}_{TS}(p)$).

The Vending Machine Example: Extracting Satisfaction/Violation Conditions. For the property $P : \Box(\neg(addingCoffee \wedge addingTea))$ we can extract sufficient conditions for satisfaction/violation by applying the rules in Figure 5 in the following order (it is assumed that p is ($addingCoffee = true$), and q is ($addingTea = true$)):

$$TS \vDash (\Box(\neg(p \wedge q))) \;\textbf{if}\; (TS \vDash (\neg(p \wedge q))) \wedge \overline{V}_{TS}(\neg(p \wedge q)) \qquad Rule(9)$$
$$TS \vDash (\neg(p \wedge q)) \;\textbf{if}\; TS \nvDash (p \wedge q) \qquad Rule(3)$$
$$TS \nvDash (p \wedge q) \;\textbf{if}\; (TS \nvDash p) \vee (TS \nvDash q) \qquad Rule(8)$$
$$TS \nvDash p \;\textbf{if}\; p \notin L(s_0) \qquad Rule(2)$$
$$TS \nvDash q \;\textbf{if}\; q \notin L(s_0) \qquad Rule(2)$$
$$\overline{V}_{TS}(\neg(p \wedge q)) \;\textbf{if}\; \overline{V}_{TS}(p \wedge q) \qquad Rule(18)$$
$$\overline{V}_{TS}(p \wedge q) \;\textbf{if}\; \overline{V}_{TS}(p) \wedge \overline{V}_{TS}(q) \qquad Rule(22)$$
$$\overline{V}_{TS}(p \wedge q) \;\textbf{if}\; (TS \nvDash p) \wedge \overline{V}_{TS}(p) \qquad Rule(23)$$
$$\overline{V}_{TS}(p \wedge q) \;\textbf{if}\; (TS \nvDash q) \wedge \overline{V}_{TS}(q) \qquad Rule(24)$$

This way, the three extracted sufficient conditions of property satisfaction would be:

$$TS \vDash P \;\textbf{if}\; (p \notin L(s_0) \vee q \notin L(s_0)) \wedge (\overline{V}_{TS}(p) \wedge \overline{V}_{TS}(q))$$
$$TS \vDash P \;\textbf{if}\; (p \notin L(s_0) \vee q \notin L(s_0)) \wedge (p \notin L(s_0) \wedge \overline{V}_{TS}(p))$$
$$TS \vDash P \;\textbf{if}\; (p \notin L(s_0) \vee q \notin L(s_0)) \wedge (q \notin L(s_0) \wedge \overline{V}_{TS}(q))$$

$$TS \vDash p \quad \textbf{if} \quad p \in L(s_0) \qquad\qquad\qquad\qquad \text{Rule(1)}$$
$$TS \nvDash p \quad \textbf{if} \quad p \notin L(s_0) \qquad\qquad\qquad\qquad \text{Rule(2)}$$
$$TS \vDash \neg\varphi \quad \textbf{if} \quad TS \nvDash \varphi \qquad\qquad\qquad\qquad \text{Rule(3)}$$
$$TS \nvDash \neg\varphi \quad \textbf{if} \quad TS \vDash \varphi \qquad\qquad\qquad\qquad \text{Rule(4)}$$
$$TS \vDash (\varphi_1 \vee \varphi_2) \quad \textbf{if} \quad (TS \vDash \varphi_1) \vee (TS \vDash \varphi_2) \qquad \text{Rule(5)}$$
$$TS \nvDash (\varphi_1 \vee \varphi_2) \quad \textbf{if} \quad (TS \nvDash \varphi_1) \wedge (TS \nvDash \varphi_2) \qquad \text{Rule(6)}$$
$$TS \vDash (\varphi_1 \wedge \varphi_2) \quad \textbf{if} \quad (TS \vDash \varphi_1) \wedge (TS \vDash \varphi_2) \qquad \text{Rule(7)}$$
$$TS \nvDash (\varphi_1 \wedge \varphi_2) \quad \textbf{if} \quad (TS \nvDash \varphi_1) \vee (TS \nvDash \varphi_2) \qquad \text{Rule(8)}$$
$$TS \vDash \Box\varphi \quad \textbf{if} \quad (TS \vDash \varphi) \wedge \overline{\mathcal{V}}_{TS}(\varphi) \qquad\qquad \text{Rule(9)}$$
$$TS \nvDash \Box\varphi \quad \textbf{if} \quad TS \nvDash \varphi \qquad\qquad\qquad\qquad \text{Rule(10)}$$
$$TS \vDash \Diamond\varphi \quad \textbf{if} \quad TS \vDash \varphi \qquad\qquad\qquad\qquad \text{Rule(11)}$$
$$TS \nvDash \Diamond\varphi \quad \textbf{if} \quad (TS \nvDash \varphi) \wedge \overline{\mathcal{V}}_{TS}(\varphi) \qquad\qquad \text{Rule(12)}$$
$$TS \vDash (\varphi_1 U \varphi_2) \quad \textbf{if} \quad TS \vDash \varphi_2 \qquad\qquad\qquad \text{Rule(13)}$$
$$TS \nvDash (\varphi_1 U \varphi_2) \quad \textbf{if} \quad (TS \nvDash \varphi_1) \wedge (TS \nvDash \varphi_2) \qquad \text{Rule(14)}$$
$$TS \nvDash (\varphi_1 U \varphi_2) \quad \textbf{if} \quad (TS \nvDash \varphi_2) \wedge \overline{\mathcal{V}}_{TS}(\varphi_2) \qquad \text{Rule(15)}$$

$$\overline{\mathcal{V}}_{TS}(p) \quad \textbf{if} \quad \nexists s \mid (s_0 \rightarrow^* s) \wedge [(p \in L(s_0)) \wedge (p \notin L(s))] \qquad \text{Rule(16)}$$
$$\overline{\mathcal{V}}_{TS}(p) \quad \textbf{if} \quad \nexists s \mid (s_0 \rightarrow^* s) \wedge [(p \notin L(s_0)) \wedge (p \in L(s))] \qquad \text{Rule(17)}$$
$$\overline{\mathcal{V}}_{TS}(\neg\varphi) \quad \textbf{if} \quad \overline{\mathcal{V}}_{TS}(\varphi) \qquad\qquad\qquad\qquad \text{Rule(18)}$$
$$\overline{\mathcal{V}}_{TS}(\varphi_1 \vee \varphi_2) \quad \textbf{if} \quad \overline{\mathcal{V}}_{TS}(\varphi_1) \wedge \overline{\mathcal{V}}_{TS}(\varphi_2) \qquad \text{Rule(19)}$$
$$\overline{\mathcal{V}}_{TS}(\varphi_1 \vee \varphi_2) \quad \textbf{if} \quad (TS \vDash \varphi_1) \wedge \overline{\mathcal{V}}_{TS}(\varphi_1) \qquad \text{Rule(20)}$$
$$\overline{\mathcal{V}}_{TS}(\varphi_1 \vee \varphi_2) \quad \textbf{if} \quad (TS \vDash \varphi_2) \wedge \overline{\mathcal{V}}_{TS}(\varphi_2) \qquad \text{Rule(21)}$$
$$\overline{\mathcal{V}}_{TS}(\varphi_1 \wedge \varphi_2) \quad \textbf{if} \quad \overline{\mathcal{V}}_{TS}(\varphi_1) \wedge \overline{\mathcal{V}}_{TS}(\varphi_2) \qquad \text{Rule(22)}$$
$$\overline{\mathcal{V}}_{TS}(\varphi_1 \wedge \varphi_2) \quad \textbf{if} \quad (TS \nvDash \varphi_1) \wedge \overline{\mathcal{V}}_{TS}(\varphi_1) \qquad \text{Rule(23)}$$
$$\overline{\mathcal{V}}_{TS}(\varphi_1 \wedge \varphi_2) \quad \textbf{if} \quad (TS \nvDash \varphi_2) \wedge \overline{\mathcal{V}}_{TS}(\varphi_2) \qquad \text{Rule(24)}$$
$$\overline{\mathcal{V}}_{TS}(\Box\varphi) \quad \textbf{if} \quad \overline{\mathcal{V}}_{TS}(\varphi) \qquad\qquad\qquad\qquad \text{Rule(25)}$$
$$\overline{\mathcal{V}}_{TS}(\Diamond\varphi) \quad \textbf{if} \quad \overline{\mathcal{V}}_{TS}(\varphi) \qquad\qquad\qquad\qquad \text{Rule(26)}$$
$$\overline{\mathcal{V}}_{TS}(\varphi_1 U \varphi_2) \quad \textbf{if} \quad \overline{\mathcal{V}}_{TS}(\varphi_1) \wedge \overline{\mathcal{V}}_{TS}(\varphi_2) \qquad \text{Rule(27)}$$
$$\overline{\mathcal{V}}_{TS}(\varphi_1 U \varphi_2) \quad \textbf{if} \quad (TS \vDash \varphi_2) \wedge \overline{\mathcal{V}}_{TS}(\varphi_2) \qquad \text{Rule(28)}$$
$$\overline{\mathcal{V}}_{TS}(\varphi_1 U \varphi_2) \quad \textbf{if} \quad (TS \nvDash \varphi_2) \wedge \overline{\mathcal{V}}_{TS}(\varphi_2) \qquad \text{Rule(29)}$$

Fig. 5. Rules for extracting sufficient conditions of property satisfaction/violation, based on initial values of atomic propositions, and the atomic propositions that do not vary in TS

A sufficient condition of property violation for P can be extracted in a similar way:

$$TS \nvDash P \quad \textbf{if} \quad p \in L(s_0) \wedge q \in L(s_0)$$

4.2   Evaluation of the Extracted Conditions

The initial values of atomic propositions ($p \in L(s_0)$ or $p \notin L(s_0)$) are computed based on initialization statements. For simplicity, we assume that the property is described using boolean variables only. It should be mentioned that we can always rewrite a property such as $\Box(x = y + z)$ in the form $\Box(v = true)$, where v is boolean variable representing $x = y + z$. This assumption implies that each atomic proposition is a boolean variable in the Rebeca model, and the value that is assigned to the variable in the initialize message server, determines if $p \in L(s_0)$ or $p \notin L(s_0)$.

The next step is to investigate if the value of the atomic proposition p may vary ($\mathcal{V}_{TS}(p)$). The value of variable v (where v corresponds to p) changes in a product if the product has a reachable statement s that assigns a value to v. According to our model for product families, a tagged statement is executed when its application condition holds in a product. Other statements are executed normally. We assume that $\mathcal{F}(s)$ gives the application condition that is associated to a tagged statement s, and for other ones returns $true$. A statement s is reachable in a product if its associated application condition holds in the product, as well as at least one of the application conditions assigned to those statements on which s is control/activation dependent (possibly indirectly). We compute the reachability condition of the statement s recursively as:

$$RC(s) = \bigvee_{r \xrightarrow{}_{c,a} s} (\mathcal{F}(s) \wedge RC(r))$$

In the above computation, $r \xrightarrow{}_{c,a} s$ is the set of statements on which s is control or activation dependent. To avoid recursion, we mark each statement r when its condition is extracted, and in $r \xrightarrow{}_{c,a} s$ we only consider the unmarked statements. Note that when a behavioral model is inconsistent (e.g. $RC(s)$ contains the conjunction of a feature and its negation), the statement s is not reachable in any of the products.

We assume $Def(v)$ is the set of statements that assign value to the variable v, except the initialization statement which is the one assigning value to v in the initial message server of the Rebeca model. The value of v may change in a product, if at least one of the statements $s \in Def(v)$ are reachable in that product. The atomic proposition p which corresponds to v may vary in transition system TS if:

$$\mathcal{V}_{TS}(p) = \bigvee_{s \in Def(v)} RC(s)$$

Consequently:

$$\overline{V}_{TS}(p) = \neg(\bigvee_{s \in Def(v)} RC(s))$$

The possibility of variation for p is thus described using application conditions, where each application condition is a propositional logic formula in terms of features itself. Substituting the initial values of atomic propositions and their possibility of variation ($\overline{V}_{TS}(p)$) in sufficient conditions of property satisfaction/violation, leads to a number of propositional logic formulas. These formulas describe products that we can conclude satisfaction/violation of the given property in them statically. A product satisfies or violates a property if at least one of the sufficient conditions of property satisfaction or violation holds for it, because of the components and alternative behaviors that it includes. The model checker only verifies the products that their satisfaction or violation cannot be concluded from sufficient conditions.

The Vending Machine Example: Evaluation of the Extracted Conditions. We assume that atomic propositions p and q correspond to *addingCoffee* and *addingTea* variables, respectively. According to the initializations in the Rebeca model, we can conclude that $p \notin L(s_0)$ and $q \notin L(s_0)$. The statements 10 and 14 assign value to *addingCoffee* which means that $Def(addingCoffee) = \{s_{14}, s_{19}\}$. Therefore:

$$\overline{V}_{TS}(p) = \neg(RC(s_{14}) \vee RC(s_{19})) = \neg Coffee$$

Because:

$RC(s_{14}) = RC(s_{13}) = RC(s_{15"}) = Coffee \wedge RC(s_{14"}) = Coffee \wedge RC(s_{12"}) = $
$Coffee \wedge [RC(s_{17'}) \vee RC(s_{17"}) \vee RC(s_{21"}) \vee \underbrace{RC(s_{10"})} \vee RC(s_{21})] = $
$Coffee \wedge [RC(s_{17'}) \vee RC(s_{17"}) \vee RC(s_{21"}) \vee \underbrace{RC(s_{9"})} \vee RC(s_{21})] = $
$Coffee \wedge [RC(s_{17'}) \vee RC(s_{17"}) \vee RC(s_{21"}) \vee \quad true \quad \vee RC(s_{21})] = Coffee$

and:

$$RC(s_{19}) = RC(s_{18}) = RC(s_{16}) = RC(s_{13}) = Coffee$$

Similarly, we can compute $\overline{V}_{TS}(q) = \neg Tea$. By substitution of $\overline{V}_{TS}(p)$ and $\overline{V}_{TS}(q)$ with $\neg Coffee$ and $\neg Tea$ respectively, the following conditions are achieved which describe the products for which satisfaction/violation of P is inferable without model checking:

$$TS \vDash P \ \textit{if} \ (\neg Coffee \wedge \neg Tea)$$
$$TS \vDash P \ \textit{if} \ \neg Coffee$$
$$TS \vDash P \ \textit{if} \ \neg Tea$$

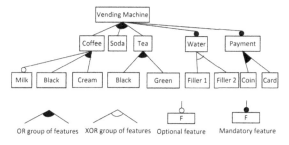

Fig. 6. The feature model of the vending machine case study

According to the above conditions, the products that do not have the Coffee feature, and the products that do not have the Tea feature, satisfy P, and there is no need to verify them. This way, the number of the products that should be model check is reduced to $2^2 - 3$, as we can tell that the products $\langle I, E\rangle$, $\langle E, I\rangle$, and $\langle E, E\rangle$ satisfy P (although $\langle E, E\rangle$ is not a valid product).

5   Results

We applied our proposed approach to a vending machine case study that is much more complex than the running example [1]. The machine includes a controller that handles the requests. Figure 6 shows the feature model of the vending machine. The coffee maker, tea maker, and soda server components are responsible for serving the associated drinks. There is also a milk adder component which adds milk to coffee. There are two coffee container components and two tea container components, containing black coffee, coffee with cream, black tea, and green tea, respectively. The coffee maker and the tea maker components use the proper container to serve the requested drink. They add water through the water component. The water component can be filled using two different mechanisms which are handled by the filler 1 and filler 2 components. Finally, there are two different payment methods for a vending machine: paying by coin, or paying by card. We defined the following six LTL properties to be verified.

- $P_1 = \Box[\neg(ServingCoffee \land ServingTea \land ServingSoda)]$
- $P_2 = \Box(\neg empty)$
- $P_3 = \Box(\neg overFlow)$
- $P_4 = \Box[\neg(addingBlackCoffee \land addingCreamCoffee)]$
- $P_5 = \Box[\neg(addingBlackTea \land addingGreenTea)]$
- $P_6 = \Box\Diamond(ServingSoda)$

The first property describes that the vending machine should not be serving three drinks at the same time. The second and third properties check that the water container should not get empty, or overflow. The forth property describes

---

[1] The source code is available at http://ece.ut.ac.ir/rkhosravi/sourcecode

Table 1. Number of states and time of verification (in seconds) before applying the techniques (first column), after applying the slicing technique (second column), and after identifying products that satisfy/violate the property without model checking (third column), for the vending machine case study

	Complete Model		Static Slicing		Slicing and Static Analysis	
	states	time(sec)	states	time(sec)	states	time(sec)
P_1	-	-	49,307,358	24,574	25,590,940	13,849
P_2	-	-	39,169,329	17,156	39,126,321	17,138
P_3	-	-	39,182,632	18,019	19,571,384	9,119
P_4	-	-	43,484,712	19,623	16,037,384	7,517
P_5	-	-	47,317,992	24,084	14,696,264	6,951
P_6	-	-	114,547,805	142,081	63,357,123	75,356

that the machine should not add black coffee together with coffee and cream to a drink. This fact should be also checked for the tea drink (the fifth property). The last property states that the machine should serve soda infinitely often.

Table 1 shows the number of states and the time of verification (in seconds) for model checking the product family of vending machine case study. The time of applying slicing technique and computing sufficient conditions are negligible comparing to model checking time and are ignored. The complete model can not be model checked against the properties because of state space explosion (first column). After applying the slicing technique and eliminating irrelevant features, the sliced model can be checked against the properties (second column). However, the number of states and time of verification can be reduced even more by extracting sufficient conditions of property satisfaction/violation, and identifying products that satisfy/violate the property without model checking.

6   Conclusion

In this paper we presented two techniques to reduce the number of products of a product line that are model checked against a property. This way, the number of generated states and the required time for verifying product families are reduced. The first technique was to apply static slicing to eliminate the features that do not affect the property. The second technique was to analyze the property and reachability of its variables in different products statically to identify products that satisfy/violate the property without model checking. The results of using these techniques in model checking the vending machine case study show the effectiveness of our approach as the number of generated states and time of verification reduced significantly after applying these techniques. The slicing and static analysis technique are completely automatic, and their cost is negligible comparing to the verification cost which makes using our approach for model checking product families practical.

References

1. Pohl, K., Böckle, G., van der Linden, F.J.: Software Product Line Engineering: Foundations, Principles and Techniques. Springer-Verlag New York, Inc., Secaucus (2005)
2. Kang, K.C., Cohen, S.G., Hess, J.A., Novak, W.E., Peterson, A.S.: Feature-oriented domain analysis (FODA) feasibility study. Technical report. Carnegie-Mellon University Software Engineering Institute (November 1990)
3. Kästner, C., Apel, S., Kuhlemann, M.: Granularity in software product lines. In: Proceedings of the 30th International Conference on Software Engineering, ICSE 2008, pp. 311–320. ACM (2008)
4. Szyperski, C.: Component Software: Beyond Object-Oriented Programming. Addison-Wesley Longman Publishing Co., Inc., Boston (2002)
5. Kästner, C., Apel, S.: Integrating compositional and annotative approaches for product line engineering. In: Proceedings of the GPCE Workshop on Modularization, Composition and Generative Techniques for Product Line Engineering (McGPLE). University of Passau (October 2008)
6. Ebert, C., Jones, C.: Embedded software: Facts, figures, and future. Computer 42, 42–52 (2009)
7. Clarke, E.M., Grumberg, O., Peled, D.A.: Model Checking. The MIT Press (2000)
8. Larsen, K.G., Nyman, U., Wąsowski, A.: Modal I/O Automata for Interface and Product Line Theories. In: De Nicola, R. (ed.) ESOP 2007. LNCS, vol. 4421, pp. 64–79. Springer, Heidelberg (2007)
9. Larsen, K.G., Nyman, U., Wasowski, A.: Modeling software product lines using color-blind transition systems. Int. J. Softw. Tools Technol. Transf. 9(5), 471–487 (2007)
10. Gruler, A., Leucker, M., Scheidemann, K.: Modeling and Model Checking Software Product Lines. In: Barthe, G., de Boer, F.S. (eds.) FMOODS 2008. LNCS, vol. 5051, pp. 113–131. Springer, Heidelberg (2008)
11. Muschevici, R., Clarke, D., Proenca, J.: Feature Petri nets. In: Second Proceedings of the 14th International Conference on Software Product Lines, pp. 99–106 (2010)
12. Classen, A., Heymans, P., Schobbens, P.Y., Legay, A., Raskin, J.F.: Model checking lots of systems: efficient verification of temporal properties in software product lines. In: Proceedings of the 32nd ACM/IEEE International Conference on Software Engineering, ICSE 2010, pp. 335–344. ACM (2010)
13. Sabouri, H., Khosravi, R.: An effective approach for verifying product lines in presence of variability models. In: Second Proceedings of the 14th International Conference on Software Product Lines, pp. 113–120 (2010)
14. Liu, J., Basu, S., Lutz, R.R.: Compositional model checking of software product lines using variation point obligations. Automated Software Engg. 18, 39–76 (2011)
15. Bruns, D., Klebanov, V., Schaefer, I.: Verification of Software Product Lines with Delta-Oriented Slicing. In: Beckert, B., Marché, C. (eds.) FoVeOOS 2010. LNCS, vol. 6528, pp. 61–75. Springer, Heidelberg (2011)
16. Weiser, M.: Program slicing. In: Proceedings of the 5th International Conference on Software Engineering, pp. 439–449 (1981)
17. Millett, L., Teitelbaum, T.: Issues in slicing Promela and its applications to model checking, protocol understanding, and simulation. Software Tools for Technology Transfer, 343–349 (2000)
18. Brückner, I., Wehrheim, H.: Slicing an Integrated Formal Method for Verification. In: Lau, K.-K., Banach, R. (eds.) ICFEM 2005. LNCS, vol. 3785, pp. 360–374. Springer, Heidelberg (2005)

19. Rakow, A.: Slicing Petri Nets with an Application to Workflow Verification. In: Geffert, V., Karhumäki, J., Bertoni, A., Preneel, B., Návrat, P., Bieliková, M. (eds.) SOFSEM 2008. LNCS, vol. 4910, pp. 436–447. Springer, Heidelberg (2008)
20. Sabouri, H., Sirjani, M.: Actor-based slicing techniques for efficient reduction of Rebeca models. Sci. Comput. Program. 75(10), 811–827 (2010)
21. Sabouri, H., Sirjani, M.: Slicing-based reductions for Rebeca. Electron. Notes Theor. Comput. Sci. 260, 209–224 (2010)
22. Dwyer, M.B., Hatcliff, J., Hoosier, M., Ranganath, V., Wallentine, T.: Evaluating the Effectiveness of Slicing for Model Reduction of Concurrent Object-Oriented Programs. In: Hermanns, H., Wallentine, T., Palsberg, J. (eds.) TACAS 2006. LNCS, vol. 3920, pp. 73–89. Springer, Heidelberg (2006)
23. Sirjani, M., Movaghar, A., Shali, A., de Boer, F.: Modeling and verification of reactive systems using Rebeca. Fundamenta Informaticae 63(4), 385–410 (2004)
24. Jaghoori, M., Movaghar, A., Sirjani, M.: Modere: The model-checking engine of Rebeca. In: ACM Symposium on Applied Computing - Software Verification Track, pp. 1810–1815 (2006)
25. Sirjani, M., de Boer, F., Movaghar, A.: Modular verification of a component-based actor language. Journal of Universal Computer Science 11(10), 1695–1717 (2005)
26. Emerson, E.A.: Temporal and modal logic. In: Handbook of Theoretical Computer Science, pp. 995–1072 (1990)
27. Batory, D.S.: Feature Models, Grammars, and Propositional Formulas. In: Obbink, H., Pohl, K. (eds.) SPLC 2005. LNCS, vol. 3714, pp. 7–20. Springer, Heidelberg (2005)
28. Moskewicz, M.W., Madigan, C.F., Zhao, Y., Zhang, L., Malik, S.: Chaff: engineering an efficient SAT solver. In: Proceedings of the 38th Annual Design Automation Conference, DAC 2001, pp. 530–535. ACM (2001)

Bigraphical Modelling of Architectural Patterns

Alejandro Sanchez[1,2], Luís Soares. Barbosa[2], and Daniel Riesco[1]

[1] Departamento de Informática, Universidad Nacional de San Luis,
Ejército de los Andes 950, D5700HHW San Luis, Argentina
{asanchez,driesco}@unsl.edu.ar
[2] HASLab INESC TEC & Universidade do Minho,
Campus de Gualtar, 4710-057 Braga, Portugal
lsb@di.uminho.pt

Abstract. Archery is a language for behavioural modelling of architectural patterns, supporting hierarchical composition and a type discipline. This paper extends Archery to cope with the patterns' structural dimension through a set of (re-)configuration combinators and constraints that all instances of a pattern must obey. Both types and instances of architectural patterns are semantically represented as bigraphical reactive systems and operations upon them as reaction rules. Such a bigraphical semantics provides a rigorous model for Archery patterns and reduces constraint verification in architectures to a type-checking problem.

1 Introduction

In a number of contexts the term architectural pattern is used as an architectural abstraction. The expression is taken in the usual sense – a known solution to a recurring design problem. In [4] it is characterised as a description of element and configuration types, and a set of constraints on how to use them. Available catalogs such as [8] provide a vocabulary for their use at a high abstraction level. However, the lack of formality in their pattern documentation prevents their usage for developing precise architectural specifications on top of them, and in consequence, any tool-supported analysis and verification.

Such is the motivation behind Archery, a language to describe the behaviour of pattern elements, a subset of which was recently presented in [13]. Its semantics is given by translation to mCRL2 [10]. A pattern specification in Archery comprises a set of architectural elements (connectors and components) and their associated behaviours. An architecture describes a particular configuration that instances of a pattern's elements assume. This configuration has an emergent behaviour and constitutes an instance of the pattern. Then, both patterns and elements define the types of behaviour expected from instances. The language supports hierarchical composition of architectures.

This paper, extends Archery to the so-called *structural* dimension of architectural patterns. This comprises the usage of typed variables to contain and identify instances, a set of scripting operations to build architectural configurations, and a set of primitives to specify constrains over such configurations.

F. Arbab and P.C. Ölveczky (Eds.): FACS 2011, LNCS 7253, pp. 313–330, 2012.
© Springer-Verlag Berlin Heidelberg 2012

Constraints restrict the class of valid configurations that architectures, instances of a particular pattern, may adopt. Therefore, reconfigurations are only enabled when respecting the pattern constraints. For instance, a reconfiguration script that connects two clients in a Client-Server architecture violates the intended use of the pattern and should be prevented.

A second contribution of this paper is a semantics for the structural dimension of **Archery** on top of Bigraphical Reactive Systems (BRS) [11]. The theory of BRSs was developed to study systems in which locality and linking of computational agents varies independently, and to provide a general unifying theory in which existing calculi for concurrency and mobility can be represented. The two main constituents of a BRS are a bigraph and a set of parametric reaction rules. The former specifies the BRS structure as two orthogonal graphs upon the same set of nodes, one modelling locality, and another the linking scheme. Rules model its dynamics, *i.e.*, how the structure is reconfigured through reaction.

The theory of BRSs has a precise definition. A bigraph, expressed as a tuple of functions, is an arrow in a category. A more restrictive category can be defined for bigraphs by including in their definition a mechanism, called sorting, that constrains the configurations they can adopt. This setting allows the formal treatment of the encoded system. In particular, if some conditions are met [11], it allows to automatically derive a labelled transition system (LTS) from a BRS, in which behavioural equivalence is a congruence.

The choice of BRS as a semantical framework for **Archery** was motivated by the need to cope with the independent modification of both placing and linking of pattern instances. At a more fundamental level, the structural dimension of patterns and architectures is encoded as arrows in a suitable category[1]. Finally, the use of bigraphs reduces the problem of verifying whether an architectural constraint holds, to a certain kind of type-checking. Actually, once a structural constraint is encoded as a sorting, to check if it is verified by an architecture amounts to translating the latter to a bigraph and prove that such a bigraph belongs to the category defined by the sorting.

The bigraphical encoding presented here is also the basis for, following the approach in [5], exploring the automatic derivation of LTS whose states stand for the different configurations the corresponding architecture can adopt [12] . This makes possible to resort to behavioural equivalence to compare the application of different patterns in reconfiguring systems.

The following sections illustrate how **Archery** can be endowed with a bigraphical semantics. For such purposes we limit ourselves to a subset of the scripting operations. Constraints are just illustrated by an example. The full version of the language can be found in [12]. The rest of the paper is organised as follows: section 2 introduces **Archery**. Section 3 briefly recalls the basic theory of BRS and section 4 develops a formal semantics for the structural dimension of this language. Finally, section 5 concludes and discusses future work.

---

[1] Archery designation comes from a comment in Steve Awodey's book [3] in category theory: " *...the subject might better have been called abstract function theory, or perhaps even better: archery.*"

2 The Archery Language

Archery is structured as a core language and two extensions, referred to as
Archery-Core, Archery-Script, and Archery-Structural-Constraint, respectively. the
basic language, Archery-Core, was originally introduced in [13]. Archery-Script
adds operations to build configurations, whereas Archery-Structural-Constraint
offers primitives for defining structural constraints. While both behavioural and
structural semantics are defined for Archery-Core, only structural semantics is
given to Archery-Script and Archery-Structural-Constraint. Both Archery-Core and
its extensions are endowed with a structural semantics by translation to BRS.
However, the codomain of each translation differs. In particular, the Archery-
Structural-Constraint extension requires a careful consideration.

2.1 Archery-Core

A specification in Archery-Core comprises one or more patterns and a main architecture. The first rule of the grammar, shown in Figure 1, indicates this by
equating the *Spec* non-terminal to one or more *Pat* and a *Var* non-terminals.
Note that several non-terminal are undefined; the grammar leaves out the definition of whatever is not relevant to the structural dimension.

Spec	::=	*Pat*+ *Var*
Pat	::=	**pattern** TYPEID (*PatPars?*) **elements** *Elem*+ **end**
Elem	::=	**element** TYPEID (*ElemPars?*) *Behaviour ElemInterface*
ElemInterface	::=	**interface** *Port*+
Port	::=	(**in**|**out**) ID ;
Var	::=	ID : TYPEID = *Inst* ;
Inst	::=	(*ElemInst*|*PatInst*)
ElemInst	::=	TYPEID (*ElemInstPars?*)
PatInst	::=	**architecture** TYPEID (*PatInstPars?*) *ArchBody* **end**
ArchBody	::=	*Instances Attachments? ArchInterface?*
Instances	::=	**instances** *Var*+
Attachments	::=	**attachments** *Att*+
Att	::=	**from** *PortRef* **to** *PortRef* ;
ArchInterface	::=	**interface** *Ren*+
Ren	::=	*PortRef* **as** ID ;
PortRef	::=	ID.ID

Fig. 1. A grammar fragment for Archery-Core

A pattern is specified according to the rule expanding the *Pat* non-terminal.
Its definition contains a TYPEID token that represents its identifier, an optional
list of formal parameters, and one or more architectural elements specified according to the *Elem* non-terminal. For instance, the specification in Listing 1
includes two patterns: ClientServer and PipeFilter.

Each architectural element in a pattern is specified by a TYPEID token as its identifier, an optional list of formal parameters, a description *Behaviour* of its behaviour, and a description *ElemInterface* of its interface. Behaviour is defined in a dialect of mCRL2 restricted to sequential processes. Its description must contain one ore more process expressions, as the one shown in line 5 of Listing 1, and a list of action definitions, as in line 4. The first process characterises the initial behaviour of the instance and may call other processes defined within the element. The interface contains one or more ports *Port*. A port is defined by a direction indicator, either in or out, and an ID token that has to match an action name in the list of action definitions. For instance, the interface of Server defines two ports in line 6. We adopt a water flow metaphor inspired in [2] for ports: an in port receives input from *any* port connected to it, and an out port sends output to *all* ports connected to it. Communication in a port is assumed to be synchronous; if needed a suitable process algebra expression can be used to emulate any other port behaviour.

Listing 1. Example patterns and architectures

```
1   pattern ClientServer()
2   elements
3     element Server()
4       act rreq, sres, cres;
5       proc Server() = rreq.cres.sres.Server();
6       interface in rreq; out sres;
7     element Client()
8       act prcs, sreq, rres;
9       proc Client() = prcs.sreq.rres.Client();
10      interface in rres; out sreq;
11  end
12  pattern PipeFilter()
13  elements
14  element Pipe()
15    act accept, forward;
16    proc Pipe() = accept.forward.Pipe();
17    interface in accept; out forward;
18  element Filter()
19    act rec, trans, send;
20    proc Filter() = rec.trans.send.Filter();
21    interface in rec; out send;
22  end
23  cs : ClientServer = architecture ClientServer()
24  instances
25      s1 : Server = architecture PipeFilter()
26      instances
27        f1:Filter=Filter(); f2:Filter=Filter();
28        p1:Pipe=Pipe();
29      attachments
30        from f1.send to p1.accept;
```

```
31        from p1.forward to f2.rec;
32        interface
33          f1.rec as rreq;
34          f2.send as sres;
35        end
36      c1 : Client = Client();   c2 : Client = Client();
37    attachments
38      from c1.sreq to s1.rreq;   from c2.sreq to s1.rreq;
39      from s1.sres to c1.rres;   from s1.sres to c2.rres;
40    end
```

A variable and its value is defined according to *Var*. The variable has an ID token as its identifier, followed by a TYPEID token that must match an element or pattern name. The value can be either a pattern *PatInst* or an element *ElemInst* instance. Note that the variable that follows the pattern definitions, as indicated in the first grammar rule, and as shown in line 23 of the example, must refer to an architecture (the main one).

An architecture defines a set of variables and describes the configuration adopted by their instances. It contains: a TYPEID token that must match a pattern name, an optional list of actual arguments, a set of variables *Var*, an optional set of attachments *Att*, and an optional interface *ArchInterface*. Each variable in the set must have as type an element defined in the pattern the architecture is instance of. If the variable refers to an element instance *ElemInst*, it is defined by a TYPEID and a list of actual parameters. If it refers to a pattern instance instead, as in lines 25 to 35 of the example, a nested architecture is defined. Each attachment *Att* includes a port reference *PortRef* to an out port, and another one to an in port. A port reference is an ordered pair of ID tokens, with the first one matching a variable identifier, and the second a port of the variable's instance. Then, an attachment indicates that the out port communicates with the in port. Such is the case of f1.send with p1.accept in line 30. The architecture interface is a set of one or more port renamings *Ren*. Each port renaming contains a port reference and an ID token referring to the external name for the port. Ports not included in this set are not visible from the outside. Including the same port in an attachment and in the interface is incorrect. An example interface with two renamings is shown in lines 33 and 34.

2.2   Archery-Script

Archery-Script is used to specify scripts for creating architectures or for reconfiguring existing ones. It assumes the existence of a process that triggers a script under some conditions. Its combinators are informally described in Table 1 and their use illustrated through the example in Listing 2. An essential feature is that their definition is independent of any pattern. The design principles of patterns are enforced through constraints, as shown in Section 2.3. This independence, and the fact that a variable may contain an instance whose type may not necessarily match the variable's type, allows the reuse of a script in an open family of patterns (related by some refinement relation).

Table 1. Combinators for Archery-Script

Name	Format	Description
Import	import(s)	Receives as a parameter a reference s to an Archery specification and imports it to the environment of the executing script (*e.g.*, line 2 in Listing 2)
Create Variable	v:type	Creates a variable with name v and type type (line 3)
Create Instance	v=type()	Creates a new instance of type type and assigns it to a variable v (line 4)
Add Instance	addInst(a,v)	Adds a variable v and the instance it refers to to the architecture in variable a (line 5)
Attach	attach(f.o, t.i)	Attaches the port o of the instance in variable f to the port i of the instance in variable t (line 8)
Deattach	deattach(f.o, t.i)	Removes the attachment between the port o of the instance in variable f and the port i of the instance in variable t (line 6)
Add Rename	addRen(v.p,q)	Renames port p in variable v to q (line 15)
Remove Rename	remRen(v.q)	Removes rename q in the architecture in variable v (line 14)
Move	move(s,t)	Whatever is referred by variable s becomes referred by variable t (line 16); the reference to the contents of t is lost, but its attachments and renamings remain

The example in Listing 2 is divided in three parts and assumes the existence of an initial configuration denoted by $cs_{initial}$. The configuration is similar to the one in Listing 1, but for the fact that the nested architecture (between lines 25 and 35) is now replaced by a Server instance (in a single line s1:Server=Server();). The first part of the example reconfigures $cs_{initial}$ by adding and connecting a second server. It starts with an import operation that leaves the configuration in variable cs. Operations in lines 3 and 4 create a new variable s2 and assign a fresh instance of Server to it. Upon that s2 is included in the architecture in cs. Then the operations in the next two lines remove the attachments of instances referred to by variables cs.c2 and cs.s1. Subsequently, new attachments are created between the instance in variable cs.c2 with the instance in variable cs.s2. The resulting configuration is referred in the sequel as cs_{first}.

Listing 2. Example script

```
1  script
2     import("initial");  // first part
3     s2 : Server;
4     s2 = Server();
```

```
 5    addInst(cs, s2);
 6    deattach(cs.c2.sreq, cs.s1.rreq);
 7    deattach(cs.s1.sres, cs.c2.rres);
 8    attach(cs.c2.sreq, cs.s2.rreq);
 9    attach(cs.s2.sres, cs.c2.rres);
10    import("pf");   // second part
11    f3 : Filter = new Filter();
12    addInst(pf, f3);
13    attach(pf.p1.forward, pf.f3.rec);
14    remRen(pf.sres);
15    addRen(pf.f3.send, sres);
16    move(pf, cs.s2);
17    c3 : Client =  Client();  // third part
18    addInst(cs, c3);
19    deattach(cs.c2.sreq, cs.s2.rreq);
20    deattach(cs.s2.sres, cs.c2.rres);
21    attach(cs.c2.sreq, cs.c3.rres);
22    attach(cs.c3.sreq, cs.c2.rres);
23  end
```

The second part of the example starts in line 10 and shows how the interface of an architecture is modified and a server is replaced. It assumes the existence of a configuration pf, similar to the one described between lines 25 and 35 in Listing 1, stored in a variable pf of type PipeFilter. The script imports such a configuration, creates a new instance of Filter in variable f3 and includes it in pf. Line 14 removes renaming sres from pf. This has a similar effect to deleting line 34 from Listing 1. Then, a new renaming is included in the interface, but now for port send in variable pf.f3. Subsequently, the instance in pf is moved to variable cs.s2. The instance referred to by variable cs.s2 is now the architecture of type PipeFilter, but the attachments and renamings of the previous instance remain.

The third part begins in line 17. It creates a new client and connects it in an incorrect way. A new variable c3 is created and a new instance of the type Client is assigned to it. Next, the fresh variable is included in the architecture in cs. Subsequently, the attachments between the instances in variables cs.c2 and cs.s2 are removed. Then, the script creates two attachments between instances in variables cs.c3 and cs.c2. The resulting configuration violates the design principle underlying a Client-Server architecture by connecting two clients. It will be referred to as cs_{wrong} in the sequel.

2.3   Archery-Structural-Constraint

Ruling out incorrect configurations, such as cs_{wrong} above, entails the need for mechanisms to constrain what may count as valid instances of a pattern. Since the variable cs in the script of Listing 2 is of type *ClientServer*, we could add to the pattern specification a constraint φ to express that clients can only connect to servers and vice versa. We define φ for all attachments att in an architecture of type $ClientServer$ as follows:

$$client(from(att)) \Leftrightarrow server(to(att)) \land client(to(att)) \Leftrightarrow server(from(att))$$

where $from$ (respectively, to) is a function that returns the variable with out (respectively, in) port in att, and where $client$ (respectively, $server$) is a predicate valid whenever its argument is of type $Client$ (respectively, $Server$).

By constraining patterns in this way, one can prevent the inclusion in a script of operations which may generate an invalid configuration. Clearly, cs_{wrong} does not satisfy the constraint above. In contrast, configuration cs_{first} does. Given a configuration c and a constraint φ, the satisfaction problem can be formulated as $c \models \varphi$, which boils down to a type checking assertion in the bigraphical semantics for Archery. Such is the topic of the following sections.

3   Bigraphical Reactive Systems

A Bigraphical Reactive System (BRS) is an inhabitant of a particular category upon which an algebra of bigraphs is defined. In the next sections we briefly describe bigraphs, the corresponding algebra, and the (parametric) reaction rules that make them dynamic. The reader is referred to [11] for a detailed account.

3.1   Bigraphs

A bigraph contains a set of nodes related vertically, through a parent-child relationship, and horizontally through a linking relationship graphically represented by edges. The former gives rise to a forest structure called the *place graph*, in which the roots of the trees are the nodes without parents. The latter defines a hypergraph, called the *link graph*, where nodes are related by an edge, if each of them has a *port* linked to an end of the edge. A bigraph is said to be *concrete* if its nodes and edges have an identity, and *abstract* if they do not. Figure 2 shows the structure of bigraphs following the anatomy style used in [11]. The abstract bigraph depicted there has a forest with two trees and a hypergraph with two edges.

Every node has an associated *control* (from a set $\mathcal{K}$) which characterises the kind of contribution it makes to the system's encoding. The control also establishes the number of ports the node has through an arity function $ar : \mathcal{K} \to \mathbb{N}$. The tuple $(\mathcal{K}, ar)$ forms the bigraph basic signature. For the example depicted in Figure 2 one has $\mathcal{K} = \{L : 2, M : 3\}$.

New bigraphs can be built from existing ones by plugging. The interface of a bigraph defines both which sort of bigraphs it may contain – the *inner face* — and its own form that any potential containers must accept – the *outer face*. Suppose we divide a bigraph into two parts. A division in a tree leaves a *site* in one part, and a new *root* on the other. A division in an edge generates two open links: one called the *inner name* and another called the *outer name*. Roots

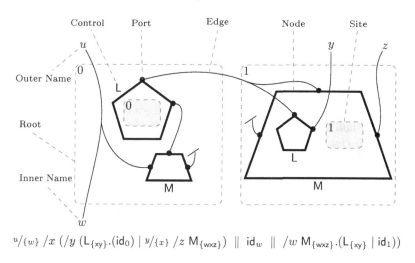

$$^u/_{\{w\}} /x \; (/y \; (\mathsf{L}_{\{xy\}}.(\mathsf{id}_0) \mid {}^y/_{\{x\}} /z \; \mathsf{M}_{\{wxz\}}) \parallel \mathsf{id}_w \parallel /w \; \mathsf{M}_{\{wxz\}}.(\mathsf{L}_{\{xy\}} \mid \mathsf{id}_1))$$

Fig. 2. Anatomy of bigraphs

and outer names form the outer face, while sites and inner names constitute the bigraph inner face. Figure 2 shows the graphic conventions used to depict them.

The category in which a bigraph lives depends on whether it is abstract or concrete as well as on the signature $\mathcal{K}$ over which it is defined. An abstract bigraph becomes an arrow $F : I \to J$ in a category $\mathrm{BG}(\mathcal{K})$. Its domain is a tuple $I = \langle n, X \rangle$, in which n is a set of ordinals $\{0, 1, ..., n-1\}$ acting as indexes for its sites, and X is the set of inner names. Similarly, the codomain is a tuple $J = \langle m, Y \rangle$ with m to index its roots, and Y the set of outer names. If the bigraph is concrete, the space is only a precategory $`\mathrm{BG}(\mathcal{K})$, because composition is not always defined when nodes and edges have an explicit identity.

Undesired arrangements of controls can be ruled out by defining a *sorting* $\Sigma = (\Theta, \mathcal{K}, \Phi)$. Controls in $\mathcal{K}$ are classified with respect to a set of sorts $\Theta = \{\theta_0, ..., \theta_n\}$. Valid combinations of sorts are distinguished through rule Φ. Sorts can be assigned to controls – *place sorting*, or to links according to the ports in controls – *link sorting*. Abstract (respectively, concrete) bigraphs over a sorting Σ inhabit a category $\mathrm{BG}(\Sigma)$ (respectively, precategory $`\mathrm{BG}(\Sigma)$).

3.2 An Algebra of Bigraphs

All bigraphs can be built from elementary ones by applying three basic operations: composition, product and identities. The *composition* $G \circ F : I \to K$, of two bigraphs $F : I \to J$ and $G : J \to K$, yields a new bigraph by plugging F into G. This operation is only defined when the inner face of G matches the outer face of F. The set $|F|$ of node and edge identifiers in F needs to be disjoint to $|G|$ if bigraphs are concrete. When $G \circ F$ is defined, we say that G is a context for F. The *product* of two bigraphs $F_i : \langle m_i, X_i \rangle \to \langle n_i, Y_i \rangle$ $(i = 0, 1)$, is a new bigraph $F_0 \otimes F_1 : \langle m_0 + m_1, X_0 \uplus X_1 \rangle \to \langle n_0 + n_1, Y_0 \uplus Y_1 \rangle$, (with $\uplus$ standing for the union of disjoint sets) in which F_0 and F_1 are placed side by side. $|F_0| \cap |F_1| = \emptyset$ also needs to hold for concrete bigraphs. The *identity* bigraph (arrow) of an interface (object) $I = \langle m, X \rangle$ is the tuple $\langle id_m, id_X \rangle$.

Elementary bigraphs are divided into those which have only roots and sites – *placings* (ϕ), and those which have only (outer and inner) names – *linkings* (λ). Placings can be generated from three elementary forms: a root with no sites $1 : 0 \to 1$; a symmetry $\gamma_{1,1} : 2 \to 2$ that exchanges the indexes of roots with those of sites; and a join combinator $join : 2 \to 1$ of two sites into one root. A merge bigraph can be derived as $merge_{n+1} = join \circ (id_1 \otimes merge_n)$. Similarly, linkings can be generated from two elementary forms: the substitution y/x of a set of names X with one name y; and the closure $/x$ of a link x. The only elementary bigraph that introduces nodes is $\mathsf{K}_{\vec{x}} : 1 \to \langle 1, \{\vec{x}\} \rangle$. Defined for each control $\mathsf{K} : n$ (with n ports), it gives rise to a bigraph with a single node whose n ports are bijectively linked to n names in $\vec{x}$.

It is usual to resort to the following abbreviations: $F \circ G$ standing for $(F \otimes id_I) \circ G$ when there is no ambiguity; $\lambda \circ G$ standing for $(id_m \otimes \lambda) \circ (G \otimes X')$ when m and X are clear from the context, and assuming a linking $\lambda : Y \to Z$ and a bigraph $G : I \to \langle m, X \rangle$ with $Y = X \uplus X'$.

In practice, three derived operations defined on top of the basic ones and elementary bigraphs, are actually used: parallel product, nesting and merge product. The *parallel product* of two bigraphs $F_i : \langle m_i, X_i \rangle \to \langle n_i, Y_i \rangle$ $(i = 0, 1)$ is defined as $F_0 \parallel F_1 : \langle m_0 + m_1, X_0 \cup X_1 \rangle \to \langle n_0 + n_1, Y_0 \cup Y_1 \rangle$, a tensor product with the peculiarity that that the link map may allow name sharing. The result of *nesting* two bigraphs $F : I \to \langle m, X \rangle$ and $G : m \to \langle n, Y \rangle$ that may share names is a bigraph $G.F : I \to \langle n, X \cup Y \rangle$ defined by $(id_X \parallel G) \circ F$. The *merge product* of two bigraphs G_i $(i = 0, 1)$, on the other hand, is $merge \circ (G_0 \parallel G_1)$, i.e., the merge of their parallel product. Common abbreviations are as follows: using $y/x \circ G$ instead of $(y/x \parallel id_I) \circ G$ with $I = \langle n, Z \rangle$, when G has outer face $\langle n, X \uplus Z \rangle$; A for the bigraph A.1 when the control A has no children. In Figure 2 the bigraph depicted is also described by an expression in this algebra.

3.3   Reaction Rules

A parametric reaction rule is a tuple $\langle R : m \to J, R' : m' \to J', \eta \rangle$, where R and R' are bigraphs, called *redex* and *reactum*, respectively, and η is an instantiation map. Map η assigns to each ordinal in $m' = \{0, 1, .., i, .., m' - 1\}$ an ordinal $m = \{0, 1, .., j, .., m - 1\}$. When the *redex* of a rule is matched by a bigraph F this is replaced by the corresponding *reactum*. Sites in F are placed in the sites of the *reactum* according to η. If bigraphs in F are named according to the sites m in the *redex* in which they are placed, we obtain a sequence $d_0, d_1, .., d_j, .., d_m$. Then, expression $\eta(i) = j$ specifies that d_j will be placed in the ith site of the *reactum*.

Bigraphs with an associated set of reaction rules are defined over a *dynamic signature*. This differs from the basic one in that to each control is assigned one of the following values: *atomic* – for controls of nodes without children (barren), *active* – for non-atomic controls that allow reactions to occur among their internal nodes, *passive* – for non-atomic and non-active controls. A reaction only takes place if the bigraph matching the *redex* is in an active context, *i.e.*, in a root, or in an active node with all ancestors active as well.

The abstract (respectively, concrete) BRS with sorting Σ and parametric reaction rules $\mathcal{R}$ ($`\mathcal{R}$) lives in a category (pre-category) $\text{BG}(\Sigma, \mathcal{R})$ ($`\text{BG}(\Sigma, `\mathcal{R})$).

4   Bigraphical Modelling of Archery Specifications

This section introduces a bigraphical semantics for Archery through a translation of Archery-Core and Archery-Script specifications into bigraphs in the categories $\text{BG}(\Sigma_{Arch-Core}, \mathcal{R}_{Arch-Core})$ and $\text{BG}(\Sigma_{Arch-Script}, \mathcal{R}_{Arch-Script})$, respectively. Since each constraint in Archery-Structural-Constraint generates a different category, we limit ourselves to define $\text{BG}(\Sigma_\varphi, \mathcal{R}_{Arch-Core})$ for the example constraint φ given in Section 2.3. The general method is discussed in [12].

4.1   Archery-Core

Function $\mathcal{T}$ below translates an Archery-Core specification into a bigraph in $\text{BG}(\Sigma_{Arch-Core}, \mathcal{R}_{Arch-Core})$. Its output is the parallel product of all bigraphs corresponding to the translation of each pattern Pat, and the variable Var containing the main architecture. Table 2 lists the controls in $\Sigma_{Arch-Core}$ and the sort assignment to their ports; table 3 enumerates the rules in $\mathcal{R}_{Arch-Core}$.

$$\mathcal{T}(Spec) = \underset{Pat+}{\|} \mathcal{T}(Pat) \parallel \mathcal{T}(Var) \tag{1}$$

$$\mathcal{T}(Pat) = \text{Pat}_{TYPEID}.(\underset{Elem+}{\Big|} \mathcal{T}(Elem)) \tag{2}$$

$$\mathcal{T}(Elem) = \text{Elem}_{TYPEID}.(\underset{Port+}{\Big|} \mathcal{T}(Port)) \tag{3}$$

$$\mathcal{T}(\text{in } ID) = \text{NewIn}_{ID}, \quad \mathcal{T}(\text{out } ID) = \text{NewOut}_{ID} \tag{4}$$

$$\mathcal{T}(Var) = \mathcal{T}(Var, 1) \tag{5}$$

$$\mathcal{T}(Var, B) = \text{NewVar}_{ID,TYPEID}.(\mathcal{T}(Inst, ID, B))$$

$$\mathcal{T}(ElemInst, idVar, B) = \text{NewInst}_{TYPEID,idVar}.(B) \tag{6}$$

$$\mathcal{T}(PatInst, idVar, B) = \text{NewInst}_{TYPEID,idVar}.($$
$$\quad \mathcal{T}(idVar, Var+, Att*, Ren*, B))$$

$$\mathcal{T}(idVar, Var\ Var*, Att*, Ren*, B) = \tag{7}$$
$$\quad \mathcal{T}(Var, \text{AddVar}_{idVar,ID}.(\mathcal{T}(idVar, Var*, Att*, Ren*, B)))$$

$$\mathcal{T}(idVar, [\,], Att*, Ren*, B) = \mathcal{T}(Att*, Ren*, B)$$

$$\mathcal{T}(idIF\ idPF\ idIT\ idPT\ Att*, Ren*, B) = \tag{8}$$
$$\quad \text{NewAtt}_{idIF, idPF, idIT, idPT, uniqueId()}.(\mathcal{T}(Att*, Ren*, B))$$

$$\mathcal{T}([\,], Ren*, B) = \mathcal{T}(Ren*, B)$$

$$\mathcal{T}(idInst\ idPrt\ idNew\ Ren*, B) = \qquad (9)$$

$$\text{NewRen}_{idInst,\ idPrt,\ idNew,\ uniqueid()} \cdot (\mathcal{T}(Ren*, B))$$

$$\mathcal{T}([\,], B) = B$$

Table 2. Sorting for Archery-Core

Ctrl	Arity	Activeness	Sorts	Represented Item
Pat	1	passive	u	pattern
Elem	1	passive	u	element
NewIn	1	passive	u	in port within an element definition
In	1	atomic	i	in port within an instance
NewOut	1	passive	u	out port within an element definition
Out	1	atomic	o	out port within an instance
NewInst	2	passive	uu	instance creation and assignment
Inst	1	active	u	instance
NewVar	2	passive	uu	variable creation
Var	2	active	uu	variable
AddVar	2	passive	uu	transference of one variable into another
NewAtt	5	passive	uuuuu	attachment creation
From	2	atomic	fu	attachment end for out port
To	2	atomic	tu	attachment end for in port
NewRen	4	passive	uuuu	renaming creation
Int	2	passive	rr	renaming end for internal variable
Ext	2	passive	rr	renaming end for external instance

The result of applying function $\mathcal{T}$ to the `ClientServer` pattern in Listing 1 is captured in expression (10) and depicted in Figure 3a. A **Pat** node with *ClientServer* as outer name together with the nesting of the merge product of what results from applying clause (3) to each element. In the case of element `Client`, clause (3) creates an **Elem** node with the element identifier as outer name and the nesting of the merge product of respectively calling first and second functions in clause (4) with both the in and out port of the element. The former creates a **NewIn** node with *rres* as outer name, and the latter a node **NewOut** with *sreq* as outer name.

$$\text{Pat}_{ClientServer} \cdot (\ \text{Elem}_{Client} \cdot (\ \text{NewIn}_{rres}\ |\ \text{NewOut}_{sreq}\ )\ |$$
$$\text{Elem}_{Server} \cdot (\ \text{NewIn}_{rreq}\ |\ \text{NewOut}_{sres}\ )) \qquad (10)$$

The result of applying function $\mathcal{T}$ to the architecture between lines 25 and 35 is shown in Figure 3b and expression (11). The translation involves the rules in Table 3 triggered by intermediate bigraphs generated by applying clauses (5) to (9) of function $\mathcal{T}$. The architecture is translated by clause (5) which, in combination with (6) and Rules 1 and 3, creates a **Var** node with a nested **Inst**. The former has *s1*, *Server* and the later *PipeFilter*, as outer names. This

Table 3. Parametric reaction rules for Archery-Core

1	New variable	$NewVar_{yx}.d_0 \rightarrow Var_{yx}.1 \parallel d_0$
2	Create element instance	$Elem_x.d_0 \parallel Var_{y-}.1 \parallel NewInst_{yx}.d_1 \rightarrow$ $Elem_x.d_0 \parallel Var_{y-}.(Inst_x.d_0) \parallel d_1$
3	Create pattern instance	$Pat_x.d_0 \parallel Var_{y-}.1 \parallel NewInst_{yx}.d_1 \rightarrow$ $Pat_x.d_0 \parallel Var_{y-}.Inst_x.1 \parallel d_1$
4	Create in port	$Var_{--}.(Inst_-.(NewIn_y \mid d_0) \mid d_1) \rightarrow$ $/y\, Var_{--}.(Inst_-.(In_y \mid d_0) \mid d_1)$
5	Create out port	$Var_{--}.(Inst_-.(NewOut_y \mid d_0) \mid d_1) \rightarrow$ $/y\, Var_{--}.(Inst_-.(Out_y \mid d_0) \mid d_1)$
6	Add instance	$Var_{x-}.(Inst_-.d_0 \mid d_1) \parallel Var_{y-}.d_2 \parallel AddVar_{xy}.d_3 \rightarrow$ $Var_{x-}.(Inst_-.(Var_{y-}.d_2 \mid d_0) \mid d_1) \parallel d_3$
7	Add attachment	$Var_{f-}.(Inst_-.(Out_o \mid d_0) \mid d_1) \parallel$ $Var_{t-}.(Inst_-.(In_i \mid d_2) \mid d_3) \parallel NewAtt_{fotia}.d_4 \rightarrow$ $Var_{f-}.(Inst_-.(Out_o \mid d_0) \mid From_{oa} \mid d_1) \parallel$ $Var_t.(Inst_-.(In_i \mid d_2) \mid To_{ia} \mid d_3) \parallel d_4$
8	Add renaming out	$Var_{--}.(Inst_-.(/p\, Var_{v-}.(Inst_-.(Out_p \mid d_0) \mid d_1) \mid d_2) \mid d_3) \parallel$ $NewRen_{vpqr}.d_4 \rightarrow$ $/q\, Var_{--}.(Inst_-.(/p\, Var_{v-}.(Inst_-.(Out_p \mid d_0) \mid Int_{pr} \mid d_1) \mid$ $Ext_{qr} \mid Out_q \mid d_2) \mid d_3 \parallel d_4$
9	Add renaming in	$Var_{--}.(Inst_-.(/p\, Var_{v-}.(Inst_-.(In_p \mid d_0) \mid d_1) \mid d_2) \mid d_3) \parallel$ $NewRen_{vpqr}.d_4 \rightarrow$ $/q\, Var_{--}.(Inst_-.(/p\, Var_{v-}.(Inst_-.(In_p \mid d_0) \mid Int_{pr} \mid d_1) \mid$ $Ext_{qr} \mid Out_q \mid d_2) \mid d_3 \parallel d_4$

node nesting is used to represent variable-instance pairs in general. In this case it corresponds to variable s1 of type Server containing a pattern instance of type PipeFilter. In turn, the latter nests the merge product of the encoding of each of the three variable-instance pairs of the architecture, obtained after successive applications of clauses (5), (6) and (7) and rules 1, 2, and 6.

$$
\begin{aligned}
&/rreq\ /sres\ Var_{s1,Server}.(\ Inst_{PipeFilter}.(\\
&\quad /rec\ /send\ Var_{f1,Filter}.(\ Inst_{Filter}.(\ In_{rec} \mid Out_{send}\ )\mid \\
&\qquad From_{send,att1} \mid Int_{rec,ren1})\mid \\
&\quad /accept\ /forward\ Var_{p1,Pipe}.(\ Inst_{Pipe}.(\ In_{accept} \mid Out_{forward}\ )\mid \\
&\qquad To_{accept,att1} \mid From_{forward,att2})\mid \\
&\quad /rec\ /send\ Var_{f2,Filter}.(\ Inst_{Filter}.(\ In_{rec} \mid Out_{send}\ )\mid \\
&\qquad To_{rec,att2} \mid Int_{send,ren2})\mid \\
&\quad In_{rreq} \mid Ext_{rreq,ren1} \mid Out_{sres} \mid Ext_{sres,ren2}\ )\ )
\end{aligned}
\tag{11}
$$

For instance, the encoding of f1 has closures for outer names *rec* and *send*, and a Var with a nested Inst, that in turn nests one In and one Out node, with, respectively, *rec* and *send* names. The encoding of attachments is generated by clause (8) and rule 7. In the case of the one between f1.send and p1.accept,

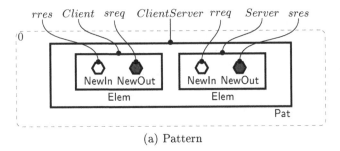

(a) Pattern

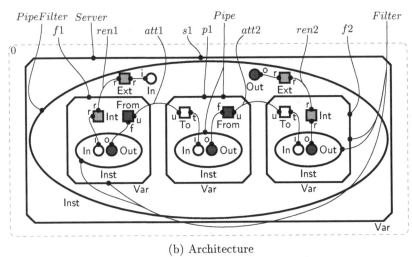

(b) Architecture

Fig. 3. Bigraphs for the Client-Server example

it respectively includes in each Var, a From and a To node. The created nodes share as outer name a unique identifier *att1* that establishes a link between them. Renamings are translated by clause (9) and rules 8 and 9. The encoding for the renaming of f1.rec as rreq of s1 respectively includes an Int and an Ext nodes inside their Var nodes representing f1 and s1. An In node is also created inside the latter. These three nodes share outer names: Int and Ext have a unique identifier *ren1*. Similarly, *rec* is the identifier of Int and (internal) In; *rreq* plays the same role for Ext and (external) In.

The link sorts $\Theta = \{o, f, t, i, r, u\}$ and the formation rule Φ ensure valid configurations representing attachments: they can only connect ports with opposite polarity. Rule Φ restricts the structure as follows: a link with a point o (port or inner name with sort o) can only have other points f or r; a link with a point i can only have other points t or r; a link with a point u has sort u and no constraints. The sorting assignment in Table 2 combined with Φ excludes the possibility of a bigraph representing attachments between two ports with the same direction. Figure 3b shows two edges (with respective sort assignments) satisfying Φ.

4.2   Archery-Script

Let us consider now the translation of a script into a bigraph in $\text{BG}(\Sigma_{Arch-Script}$, $\mathcal{R}_{Arch-Script})$. Both the sorting and the parametric reaction rules extend the ones defined for Archery-Core. $\Sigma_{Arch-Script}$ includes three more controls and $\mathcal{R}_{Arch-Script}$ adds the parametric reaction rules in Table 4.

Table 4. Parametric reaction rules for Archery-Script

10	Remove attachment	$\mathsf{Var_{f\_}}.(\mathsf{Inst\_}.(\mathsf{Out_o} \mid d_0) \mid \mathsf{From_{oa}} \mid d_1) \parallel$ $\mathsf{Var_{t,\_}}.(\mathsf{Inst\_}.(\mathsf{In_i} \mid d_2) \mid \mathsf{To_{ia}} \mid d_3) \parallel \mathsf{RemAtt_a}.d_4 \rightharpoonup$ $\mathsf{Var_{f\_}}.(\mathsf{Inst\_}.(\mathsf{Out_o} \mid d_0) \mid d_1) \parallel$ $\mathsf{Var_{t\_}}.(\mathsf{Inst\_}.(\mathsf{In_i} \mid d_2) \mid d_3) \parallel d_4$
11	Remove renaming out	$/q\ \mathsf{Var_{\_\_\_}}.(\mathsf{Inst\_}.(/p\ \mathsf{Var_{v\_}}.(\mathsf{Inst\_}.(\mathsf{Out_p} \mid d_0) \mid \mathsf{Int_{pr}} \mid d_1) \mid$ $\mathsf{Ext_{qr}} \mid \mathsf{Out_q} \mid d_2) \mid d_3) \parallel \mathsf{RemRen_r}.d_4 \rightharpoonup$ $\mathsf{Var_{\_\_}}.(\mathsf{Inst\_}.(/p\ \mathsf{Var_{v\_}}.(\mathsf{Inst\_}.(\mathsf{Out_p} \mid d_0) \mid d_1) \mid d_2) \mid d_3) \parallel d_4$
12	Remove renaming in	$/q\ \mathsf{Var_{\_\_\_}}.(\mathsf{Inst\_}.(/p\ \mathsf{Var_{v\_}}.(\mathsf{Inst\_}.(\mathsf{In_p} \mid d_0) \mid \mathsf{Int_{pr}} \mid d_1) \mid$ $\mathsf{Ext_{qr}} \mid \mathsf{In_q} \mid d_2) \mid d_3) \parallel \mathsf{RemRen_r}.d_4 \rightharpoonup$ $\mathsf{Var_{\_\_}}.(\mathsf{Inst\_}.(/p\ \mathsf{Var_{v\_}}.(\mathsf{Inst\_}.(\mathsf{In_p} \mid d_0) \mid d_1) \mid d_2) \mid d_3) \parallel d_4$
13	Move instance	$\mathsf{Var_{d\_}}.d_0 \parallel \mathsf{Var_o}.(\mathsf{Inst\_}.(d_1) \mid d_2) \parallel \mathsf{MoveInst_{od}}.d_3 \rightharpoonup$ $\mathsf{Var_{d\_}}.\mathsf{Inst\_}.(d_1) \parallel \mathsf{Var_{o\_}}.(d_2) \parallel d_3$

Function $\mathcal{TS}$ below carries out the translation of a script $t = [t_1\ t_2\ ...\ t_n]$ by processing the first operation and returning a combination of the result and a recursive call applied to the remaining of the script sequence. Each operation t_i has as type one of the listed in Table 1. Clause (12) in $\mathcal{TS}$ definition translates an import operation into the parallel product of the application of $\mathcal{T}$ to the imported specification and then recurs over the rest of the script. Clauses (13) to (19) translate t by nesting the translation of the tail of t in a node that results from translating t_1. The created node partially triggers one of the reaction rules in $\mathcal{R}_{Arch-Script}$.

We introduce now the (passive) controls and rules related to clauses (17), (18) and (19) since they are not present in $\Sigma_{Arch-Core}$ and $\mathcal{R}_{Arch-Core}$. The first clause creates a RemAtt node that represents a remove attachment operation and has one port of sort u. The outer name of the port is a unique identifier that matches the nodes involved in the encoding of the attachment. RemAtt partially triggers rule 10, that removes such nodes, making the edge representing the attachment to disappear. It also places the contents of RemAtt, matching parameter d_4, in a parallel root. Clause (18) creates a RemRen node that represents a remove renaming operation and has one port of sort u. In a similar way, the outer name is a unique id that matches the nodes involved in the representation of the renaming. RemRen triggers either rule 11 or 12, depending on whether the renaming is respectively over a out or a in port. Both rules have the same effect: to remove all nodes encoding the renaming and to place the contents of RemRen in a parallel root. Finally, clause (19) creates a node MoveInst which represents an instance transference operation. The control has two ports with sort u: one identifier vo representing the original container for the instance, and another vd for the container to where it is moved. The node partially matches the *redex* of rule 11. The reaction nests the contents of $\mathsf{Var}_{vo,\,-}$, matching $\mathsf{Inst}_-.(d_1)$, into $\mathsf{Var}_{vd,\,-}$. The former contents of the destination is lost. The original variable keeps the contents matching d_2 (outside the instance), and the contents matching d_3 is placed in a parallel root.

$$\mathcal{TS}([\mathtt{import}(Spec);\ t]) = \mathcal{T}(Spec) \parallel \mathcal{TS}(t) \tag{12}$$

$$\mathcal{TS}([\mathtt{v : type};\ t]) = \mathsf{NewVar}_{v,\ type}.\mathcal{TS}(t) \tag{13}$$

$$\mathcal{TS}([\mathtt{v = type()};\ t]) = \mathsf{NewInst}_{v,\ type}.\mathcal{TS}(t) \tag{14}$$

$$\mathcal{TS}([\mathtt{addInst}(a, v);\ t]) = \mathsf{AddVar}_{a,\ v}.\mathcal{TS}(t) \tag{15}$$

$$\mathcal{TS}([\mathtt{attach}(\mathtt{vf.pf}, \mathtt{vt.pt});\ t]) = \mathsf{NewAtt}_{vf,\ pf,\ vt,\ pt,\ uniqueId()}.\mathcal{TS}(t) \tag{16}$$

$$\mathcal{TS}([\mathtt{deattach}(\mathtt{vf.pf}, \mathtt{vt.pt});\ t]) = \mathsf{RemAtt}_{id(vf,\ pf,\ vt,\ pt)}.\mathcal{TS}(t) \tag{17}$$

$$\mathcal{TS}([\mathtt{remRen}(\mathtt{v.q});\ t]) = \mathsf{RemRen}_{id(v,\ q)}.\mathcal{TS}(t) \tag{18}$$

$$\mathcal{TS}([\mathtt{move}(\mathtt{vo}, \mathtt{vd});\ t]) = \mathsf{MoveInst}_{vo,vd}.\mathcal{TS}(t) \tag{19}$$

$$\mathcal{TS}([\,]) = 1 \tag{20}$$

4.3   Archery-Structural-Constraint

The way constraints are dealt within the bigraphical framework discussed in this paper is now illustrated through an example. Let us consider constraint φ formulated in Section 2.3 to derive from it a place sorting Σ_φ. Note that, in general, this derivation can be automated [12]. Then, a specification that fulfils φ is translated into a bigraph in $\mathrm{BG}(\Sigma_\varphi, \mathcal{R}_{Arch-Core})$. For this example, we define Θ as $\{\mathsf{cli}, \mathsf{ser}, \mathsf{att}, \mathsf{oth}\}$ and Φ. The sort of a $\mathsf{Var}_{-,\ type}$ node depends on *type*: cli if it is Client, and ser if it is Server. From and To nodes have sort att, and other nodes have sort oth. Φ is as follows: a node att immediately *in* a node cli can only have an edge to an att immediately in a node ser. Given two nodes w and w', w is in w' if the former has w' as ancestor in the parent-child relationship.

It can now be verified whether a specification Var of a ClientServer instance preserves constraint φ, by checking if the type of bigraph $\mathcal{T}(Var)$ is $\mathrm{BG}(\Sigma_\varphi, \mathcal{R}_{Arch-Core})$. In Section 2.2 we described cs_{first} and cs_{wrong} as two configurations. Figure 4 partially depicts the bigraphs which encode them, showing only sorts att, cli and ser, as well as the nodes which participate in attachments. Figure 4a contains a bigraph that partially encodes cs_{first}. It can be observed that all four nodes att in cli (respectively, ser) have only edges to nodes att in nodes ser (respectively, cli). Then, the bigraph is $\mathrm{BG}(\Sigma_\varphi, \mathcal{R}_{Arch-Core})$ and configuration cs_{first} satisfies φ. In contrast, the encoding of cs_{wrong} shown in Figure 4b, does not fulfil formation rule Φ: the nodes att in node cli with outer name $c1$, have edges with nodes att in another node cli. Therefore, the bigraph is not an inhabitant of $\mathrm{BG}(\Sigma_\varphi, \mathcal{R}_{Arch-Core})$.

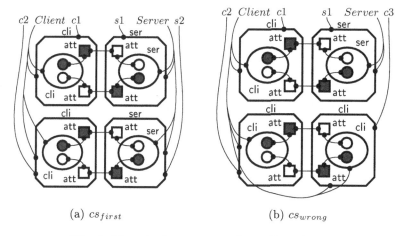

(a) cs_{first} (b) cs_{wrong}

Fig. 4. Bigraphs for two example configurations

5   Conclusions

This paper introduced Archery, a modelling language for software architectural patterns rooted in the process algebra [10]. The language allows for the specification of both the structural and behavioural dimensions of architectures, scripts to (re)configure them, and constraints to ensure that concrete architectures conform to the design principles of the pattern they are instance of.

A second contribution of the paper was the development of a bigraphical semantics for Archery. Due to space limitations, this was fully presented only for Archery-Core, partially so for the scripting component and illustrated through an example for constraints. Note that the biographical semantics makes possible to reduce the verification of constraint satisfaction to a type checking problem.

We can distinguish two approaches in the design of languages that provide support for both behavioural and structural dimensions in architectural design. One is to extend a structure-based language with a behavioural model [6], and the other is to build the architectural language on top of the behavioural model [1], upgrading it with architectural constructs. Our work follows the latter approach but resorting to BRS as a foundation for the structural dimension. Benefits of using the bigraphical theory include its solid categorical framework, its independent treatment of locality and linking of computational agents, and its role as a unifying theory for concurrency and mobile calculi. The work in [9] also provides a bigraphical semantics to an architectural description language. While our encoding uses a single signature to encode any pattern, theirs requires different signatures for different patterns. There are also two main approaches to the reconfiguration of pattern instances: one is to define a generic set of operations and encode patterns' design principles in constraints that prevent illegal configurations. Another one is to design a pattern-specific set of operations that allows the correct (re)configuration of its instances [7]. Our work is aligned with the former. Future work includes the derivation process for sortings that encode constraints. The process must ensure that the resulting sorting does not prevent the automatic derivation of a LTS for a BRS. Research on decidability and complexity of this sort of type-checking will also be pursued.

Acknowledgements. This research was partially supported by projects EVOLVE (Evolutionary Verification, Validation and Certification) under contract QREN 1621, and MONDRIAN supported by FCT under contract PTDC/EIA--CCO/108302/2008.

References

1. Aldini, A., Bernardo, M., Corradini, F.: A Process Algebraic Approach to Software Architecture Design, vol. 54. Springer, London (2010)
2. Arbab, F.: Reo: a channel-based coordination model for component composition. Mathematical Structures in Computer Science 14(3), 329–366 (2004)
3. Awodey, S.: Category Theory (Oxford Logic Guides), 2nd edn. Oxford University Press, USA (2010)
4. Bass, L., Clements, P., Kazman, R.: Software architecture in practice, 2nd edn. Addison-Wesley Longman Publishing Co., Inc. (2003)
5. Birkedal, L., Debois, S., Hildebrandt, T.: On the Construction of Sorted Reactive Systems. In: van Breugel, F., Chechik, M. (eds.) CONCUR 2008. LNCS, vol. 5201, pp. 218–232. Springer, Heidelberg (2008)
6. Bodeveix, J.P., Filali, M., Gaufillet, P., Vernadat, F.: The AADL real-time model A behavioural annex for the AADL. In: Proceedings of the DASIA 2006 - DATA Systems In Aerospace - Conference (2006)
7. Bruni, R., Bucchiarone, A., Gnesi, S., Hirsch, D., Lluch Lafuente, A.: Graph-Based Design and Analysis of Dynamic Software Architectures. In: Degano, P., De Nicola, R., Meseguer, J. (eds.) Concurrency, Graphs and Models. LNCS, vol. 5065, pp. 37–56. Springer, Heidelberg (2008)
8. Buschmann, F., Meunier, R., Rohnert, H., Sommerlad, P., Stal, M.: Pattern-Oriented Software Architecture. A System of Patterns, vol. 1. Wiley (1996)
9. Chang, Z., Mao, X., Qi, Z.: An Approach based on Bigraphical Reactive Systems to Check Architectural Instance Conforming to its Style. In: First Joint IEEE/IFIP Symposium on Theoretical Aspects of Software Engineering, TASE 2007, pp. 57–66. IEEE Computer Society (2007)
10. Groote, J.F., Mathijssen, A., Reniers, M., Usenko, Y., van Weerdenburg, M.: The formal specification language mCRL2. In: Methods for Modelling Software Systems: Dagstuhl Seminar 06351 (2007)
11. Milner, R.: The space and motion of communicating agents, vol. 54. Cambridge University Press (2009)
12. Sanchez, A.: A Calculus of Architectural Patterns. Ph.D. thesis. Universidad Nacional de San Luis (to appear, 2012)
13. Sanchez, A., Barbosa, L.S., Riesco, D.: A Language for Behavioural Modelling of Architectural Patterns. In: Proceedings of the 3rd Workshop on Behavioural Modelling - Foundations and Applications (BM-FA 2011). ACM DL (2011)

Coordinated Execution of Heterogeneous Service-Oriented Components by Abstract State Machines*

Davide Brugali[2], Luca Gherardi[2], Elvinia Riccobene[1], and Patrizia Scandurra[2]

[1] Università degli Studi di Milano, DTI, Crema (CR), Italy
elvinia.riccobene@unimi.it
[2] Università degli Studi di Bergamo, DIIMM, Dalmine (BG), Italy
{brugali,luca.gherardi,patrizia.scandurra}@unibg.it

Abstract. Early design and validation of service-oriented applications is hardly feasible due to their distributed, dynamic, and heterogeneous nature. In order to support the engineering of such applications and discover faults early, foundational theories, modeling notations and analysis techniques for component-based development should be revisited. This paper presents a formal framework for coordinated execution of service-oriented applications based on the OSOA open standard *Service Component Architecture* (SCA) for heterogeneous service assembly and on the formal method *Abstract State Machines* (ASMs) for modeling notions of service behavior, interactions, and orchestration in an abstract but executable way. The proposed framework is exemplified through a Robotics Task Coordination case study of the EU project BRICS.

1 Introduction

Service-oriented applications are playing so far an important role in several application domains (e.g., information technology, health care, robotics, defense and aerospace, to name a few) since they offer complex and flexible functionalities in widely distributed environments by composing, possibly dynamically "on demand", different types of services. Web Services is the most notable example of technology for implementing such components. On top of these service-oriented components, business processes and workflows can be (re-)implemented as composition of services – *service orchestration* or *service coordination*[1]. Examples of composition languages are WS-BPEL[2] and XLANG[3].

This emerging paradigm raises a bundle of problems, which did not exist in traditional component-based design, where abstraction, encapsulation, and modularity were the main concerns. Early designing, prototyping, and testing of the

---

* The research leading to these results has received funding from the European Community's Seventh Framework Programme (FP7/2007-2013) under grant agreement no. FP7-ICT-231940-BRICS (Best Practice in Robotics).
[1] Throughout the paper, the terms coordination and orchestration are interchangeable.
[2] www.oasis-open.org
[3] www.ebpml.org/xlang.htm

F. Arbab and P.C. Ölveczky (Eds.): FACS 2011, LNCS 7253, pp. 331–349, 2012.
© Springer-Verlag Berlin Heidelberg 2012

functionality of such assembled service-oriented applications is hardly feasible since services are discoverable, loosely-coupled, and heterogeneous (i.e. they differ in their implementation/middleware technology) components that can only interact with others on compatible interfaces. Concurrency and coordination aspects [4] that are already difficult to address in component-based system design (though extensively studied), are even more exacerbated in service-oriented system design. Components encapsulate and hide to the rest of the system how computations are ordered in sequential threads and how and when computations alter the system state. The consequence of improper management of the order and containment relationships or the total absence of an explicit coordination model in a complex, concurrent system leads to deadlock and starvation [17].

In order to support the engineering of service-oriented applications, to discover faults early, and to improve the service quality (such as efficiency and reliability), foundational theories and high-level formal notations and analysis techniques traditionally used for component-based systems should be revisited and integrated with emerging service development technologies. In the Robotics context, in particular, as the Internet is leveraged to connect humans to robots and robots to the physical world, there is a strong requirement to investigate service-oriented engineering approaches and knowledge representations to effectively distribute the capabilities offered by robots: *service-oriented robots* [9].

This paper proposes a formal framework for coordinated execution of heterogeneous service-oriented applications. It relies on the *SCA-ASM* language [30] that combines the OSOA open standard model *Service Component Architecture* (SCA) [28] for heterogeneous service assembly in a technology agnostic way, with the formal method *Abstract State Machines* (ASMs) [12] able to model notions of service behavior, interactions, and orchestration [11,7,10] in an abstract but executable way. A designer may use the proposed framework to provide abstract implementations in SCA-ASM of (i) *mock components* (possibly not yet implemented in code or available as off-the-shelf) or of (ii) *core components* containing the main service composition or process that coordinates the execution of other components (possibly implemented using different technologies) providing the real computation. He/she can then validate the behavior of the overall assembled application, by configuring these SCA-ASM models *in place* within an SCA-compliant runtime platform as implementation of (mock or core) components, and then execute them together with the other (local or remote) components implementations according to the chosen SCA assembly.

We, in particular, show the usage of our framework through a Robotics Task Coordination scenario from a case study [26] of the EU project BRICS [13]. In Robotics, service-oriented components embed the control logic of the application. They cooperate with each other locally or remotely through a communication network to achieve a common goal and compete for the use of shared resources, such as a robot sensors and actuators, the robot functionality, and the processing and communication resources. Cooperation and competition are forms of interactions among concurrent activities. So, in this domain, applications are very workflow-oriented and require developing coordination models explicitly [15].

ASMs provide a general method to combine specifications on any desired level of abstraction, ground modeling (requirements capture) techniques and stepwise refinement to executable code providing the basis for experimental validation and mathematical verification [12]. ASM rigorousness, expressiveness, and executability allow for the definition and analysis of complex structured services interaction protocols in a formal way but without overkill. Moreover, the ASM design method is supported by several tools [21,5], useful for validation and verification of ASM-based models of services.

This paper is organized as follows. Section 2 provides background on SCA and ASMs. Section 3 presents the Robotics Task Coordination case study that will be used throughout the paper. Section 4 describes the proposed framework for coordinated execution of service-oriented applications. Section 5 describes some related works, while Section 6 reports our lesson learned in developing the case study. Finally, Section 7 concludes the paper and sketches some future work.

2   Background on SCA and ASMs

Service Component Architecture. SCA is an XML-based metadata model that describes the relationships and the deployment of services independently from SOA platforms and middleware programming APIs (as Java, C++, Spring, PHP, BPEL, Web services, etc.). SCA is supported by a graphical notation (a metamodel-based language developed with the Eclipse-EMF) and runtime environments (like Apache Tuscany and FRAscaTI) that enable to create service components, assemble them into a composite application, provide an implementation for them, and then run/debug the resulting composite application.

Fig. 1 shows an *SCA composite* (or *SCA assembly*) as a collection of SCA components. Following the principles of SOA, loosely coupled service components are used as atomic units or building blocks to build an application.

An *SCA component* is a piece of software that has been configured to provide its business functions (operations) for interaction with the outside world. This interaction is accomplished through: *services* that are externally visible functions provided by the component; *references* (functions required by the component)

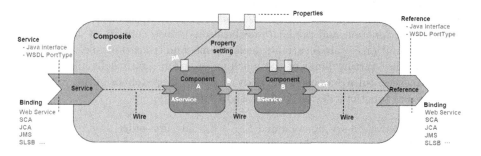

Fig. 1. An SCA composite (adapted from the SCA Assembly Model V1.00 spec)

wired to services provided by other components; *properties* allowing for the configuration of a component implementation with externally set data values; and *bindings* that specify access mechanisms used by services and references according to some technology/protocol (e.g. WSDL binding to consume/expose web services, JMS binding to receive/send Java Message Service, etc.). Services and references are typed by *interfaces*. An interface describes a set of related operations (or business functions) which as a whole make up the service offered or required by a component. The provider may respond to the requester client of an operation invocation with zero or more messages. These messages may be returned synchronously or asynchronously.

Assemblies of service components deployed together are *composite* components consisting of: properties, services, sub-components, required services as references, and wires connecting sub-components.

Abstract State Machines. ASMs are an extension of FSMs [12] where unstructured control states are replaced by states comprising arbitrary complex data. The *states* of an ASM are multi-sorted first-order structures, i.e. domains of objects with functions and predicates (boolean functions) defined on them. The *transition relation* is specified by rules describing how functions change from one state to the next. There is a limited but powerful set of ASM *rule constructors*, but the basic transition rule has the form of *guarded update* "**if** *Condition* **then** *Updates*" where *Updates* is a set of function updates of the form $f(t_1, \ldots, t_n) := t$ which are simultaneously executed[4] when *Condition* is true.

Dynamic functions are those changing as a consequence of agent actions (or *updates*). They are classified as: *monitored* (only read, as events provided by the environment), *controlled* (read and write), *shared* (read and write by an agent and by the environment or by another agent) and *out* (only write) functions.

Distributed computation can be modeled by means of *multi-agent ASMs*: multiple agents interact in parallel in a synchronous/asynchronous way. Each agent's behavior is specified by a basic ASM. The predefined variable (or 0-ary function) *self* can occur in the model and is interpreted by each agent as itself.

Besides ASMs comes with a rigorous mathematical foundation [12], ASMs can be read as pseudocode on arbitrary data structures, and can be defined as the tuple (*header, body, main rule, initialization*): *header* contains the *signature*[5] (i.e. domain, function and predicate declarations); *body* consists of domain and function definitions, state invariants declarations, and transition rules; *main rule* represents the starting point of the machine program (i.e. it calls all the other ASM transition rules defined in the body); *initialization* defines initial values for domains and functions declared in the signature.

---

[4] f is an arbitrary n-ary function and $t_1, \ldots, t_n, t$ are first-order terms. To fire this rule in a state S_i, $i \geq 0$, evaluate all terms $t_1, \ldots, t_n, t$ at S_i and update the function f to t on parameters $t_1, \ldots, t_n$. This produces another state S_{i+1} which differs from S_i only in the new interpretation of the function f.

[5] *Import* and *export* clauses can be also specified for modularization.

Executing an ASM M means executing its main rule starting from a specified initial state. A computation M is a finite or infinite sequence $S_0, S_1, \ldots, S_n, \ldots$ of states of M, where S_0 is an initial state and each S_{n+1} is obtained from S_n by firing simultaneously all of the transition rules which are enabled in S_n.

A lightweight notion of module is also supported. An *ASM module* is an ASM (*header*, *body*) without a main rule, without a characterization of the set of initial states, and the body may have no rule declarations.

An open framework, the *ASMETA tool set* [5], based on the Eclipse/EMF platform and developed around the *ASM Metamodel*, is also available for editing, exchanging, simulating, testing, and model checking models. *AsmetaL* is the textual notation to write ASM models within the ASMETA tool-set.

The SCA-ASM modeling language. By adopting a suitable subset of the SCA standard for modeling service-oriented components assemblies and exploiting the notion of *distributed multi-agent ASMs*, the SCA-ASM modeling language [30] complements the SCA component model with the ASM model of computation to provide ASM-based formal and executable description of the services internal behavior, services orchestration and interactions. According to this implementation type, a service-oriented component is an ASM endowed with (at least) one agent (a business partner or role instance) able to be engaged in conversational interactions with other agents by providing and requiring services to/from other service-oriented components' agents. The service behaviors encapsulated in an SCA-ASM component are captured by ASM transition rules.

The ASM rule constructors and predefined ASM rules (i.e. named ASM rules made available as model library) used as basic SCA-ASM behavioral primitives are recalled in Table 1 by separating them according to the separation of concerns *computation, communication* and *coordination*. In particular, communication primitives provide both synchronous and asynchronous interaction styles (corresponding, respectively, to the *request-response* and *one-way* interaction patterns of the SCA standard). Communication relies on a dynamic domain *Message* that represents message instances managed by an *abstract message-passing* mechanism: components communicate over wires according to the semantics of the communication commands reported above and a message encapsulates information about the partner link and the referenced service name and data transferred. We abstract, therefore, from the SCA notion of *binding*[6].

Fault/compensation handling is also supported (see [30]), but their SCA-ASM constructs are not reported here since they are not used in the case study.

3 Running Case Study: A Robotics Tasks Coordination

We propose a simple scenario where a laser scanner offers its scan service to different clients, which compete for the use of this shared resource. The scenario is defined by three participants:

---

[6] Indeed, we adopt the default SCA binding (`binding.sca`) for message delivering, i.e. the SOAP/HTTP or the Java method invocations (via a Java proxy) depending if the invoked services are remote or local, respectively.

Table 1. SCA-ASM rule constructors for computation, coordination, communication

COMPUTATION AND COORDINATION		
Skip rule	**skip**	do nothing
Update rule	$f(t_1,\ldots,t_n) := t$	update the value of f at $t_1,\ldots,t_n$ to t
Call rule	$R[x_1,\ldots,x_n]$	call rule R with parameters $x_1,\ldots,x_n$
Let rule	**let** $x = t$ **in** R	assign the value of t to x and then execute R
Conditional rule	**it** ϕ **then** R_1 **else** R_2 **endif**	if ϕ is true, then execute rule R_1, otherwise R_2
Iterate rule	**while** ϕ **do** R	execute rule R until ϕ is true
Seq rule	**seq** $R_1 \ldots R_n$ **endseq**	rules $R_1 \ldots R_n$ are executed in sequence without exposing intermediate updates
Parallel rule	**par** $R_1 \ldots R_n$ **endpar**	rules $R_1 \ldots R_n$ are executed in parallel
Forall rule	**forall** x **with** ϕ **do** $R(x)$	forall x satisfying ϕ execute R
Choose rule	**choose** x **with** ϕ **do** $R(x)$	choose an x satisfying ϕ and then execute R
Split rule	**forall** $n \in N$ **do** $R(n)$	split N times the execution of R
Spawn rule	**spawn** child **with** R	create a child agent with program R
COMMUNICATION		
Send rule	**wsend**$[lnk, R, snd]$	send data snd to lnk in reference to rule R (no blocking, no acknowledgment)
Receive rule	**wreceive**$[lnk, R, rcv]$	receive data rcv from lnk in reference to R (blocks until data are received, no ack)
SendReceive rule	**wsendreceive** $[lnk, R, snd, rcv]$	send data snd to lnk in reference to R waits for data rcv to be sent back (no ack)
Reply rule	**wreplay**$[lnk, R, snd]$	returns data snd to lnk, as response of R request received from lnk (no ack)

– A *Laser Scanner*, which executes scans of the environment on demand and writes the acquired values on a data buffer. A scan is a sequence of measures executed in a single task (for example 360 values, one for each degree). The Laser Scanner allows its client to request a scan from an initial angle (start) to a finale one (end) defined as the number of steps between start and end.

– A *3D Perception application*, which requests the measures to the Laser Scanner in order to generate a set of meshes that describe the surface of the objects present in the environment.

– An *Obstacle Avoidance application*, which requests the measures to the Laser Scanner in order to detect the obstacles along the robot path.

The proposed scenario is subjected to the following requirements:

1. The laser scan activity requires a certain amount of time to be completed. This time is not fixed, and depends on the number of measures requested by the client. During this time the client could have the need of executing other activities and so it does not have to wait for the scan termination.

2. A client could request a single scan or multiple scans (for example 4 scans composed each one by 20 measures).

3. While the Laser Scanner is executing a scan requested by a client A, a client B could require another scan. These requests have to be managed according to one of the following policies:

- Policy 1: Discard the scan request.
- Policy 2: Queue the scan request.

Moreover, it is assumed that different clients could simultaneously access to the services offered by the Laser Scanner and that client requests are asynchronous, i.e. a client requests a scan to the Laser Scanner and then it continues to execute its work. In this case the interactions between the clients and the Laser Scanner have to be managed by a third entity: a coordinator. This coordinator, *Sensor Coordinator*, is in charge of forwarding the clients requests to the Laser Scanner and so it has to manage the concurrent access of the clients.

High-level Solution. In order to keep the example simple to expose, we assume in this paper[7] to address only the request management policy 1, i.e. if a request is received while the laser is already scanning the new request will be discarded. With this assumption, the Sensor Coordinator behavior can be captured, as first high-level model, by the finite state machine shown in Fig. 2.

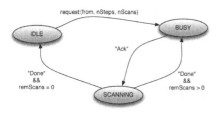

Fig. 2. Sensor Coordinator FSM

Essentially, the Sensor Coordinator receives a request of one or n scans from a client. According to the followed policy (see above) the new request could be discarded, or queued or forwarded (the normal case) to the Laser Scanner. When the request is forwarded, the Laser Scanner starts the scanning work and sends a notification (Ack) to the Sensor Coordinator in order to inform it that the scan has started. Depending on the number of scan requested, the Sensor Coordinator will forward to the Laser Scanner one or more single scans. In case of multiple scans, the Sensor Coordinator will forward n single scan requests to the Laser Scanner (to this purpose, the count variable *remScans*, initially set to n, is used and decremented at each forward). The Laser Scanner then writes each measure on the Measures Buffer until the final angle is reached, and it finally sends a notification ($Done$) to the Sensor Coordinator in order to inform it that the scan is finished. At this point, if there are not remaining scans to execute (*remScans* is equal to 0) it sends a notification to the client in order to inform it that the new measures are available on the Buffer. The client then can access the Measures Buffer to read the measures.

SCA Modeling. The application is heterogeneous: by the icons attached to components, the Sensor Coordinator is implemented in ASM, while the other two components in Java. The clients are considered external entities interacting

---

[7] Details on different variants of this scenario can be found in [26].

with the Sensor Coordinator and with the Measures Buffer through the services offered (promoted) by the composite. More precisely, a client could request a scan by means of the service *SensorCoordinating* and could access the Measures Buffer by means of the service *MeasuresBufferReading*.

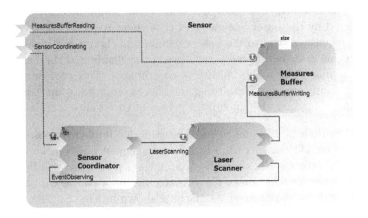

Fig. 3. The Sensor Composite

The definition of the service interfaces is reported in the listing 1.1 using the Java interface construct as IDL (Interface Definition Language). Note that, the interface *EventObserving* is implemented by the Sensor Coordinator to manage the notification received from the Laser Scanner[8].

The ASM (abstract) implementation of the SCA Sensor coordinator's behavior will be provided later in Sect. 4.1. For the sake of space, the Java implementation code of the other components is not reported.

Listing 1.1. Service interfaces definition in Java

```
public interface MeasuresBufferReading { public LaserScan getScan(); }
public interface MeasuresBufferWriting { public void writeMeasure(LaserMeasure measure); }
public interface LaserScanning {
    /**@param from: point from which the laser starts the scan
     * @param numOfSteps: number of steps of the scan */
    @OneWay public void scan(int from, int numOfSteps); }
public interface SensorCoordinating {
    /**@param from: point from which the laser starts the scan
     * @param numOfSteps: number of steps of the scan
     * @param numOfScans: number of scans required */
    @OneWay public void request(int from, int numOfSteps, int numOfScans); }
public interface EventObserving {
    /**@param event: it describe the type of event.
     * For the laser scanner valid values are Ack and Done */
    public void update(String event); }
```

---

[8] So far it is used as a service to resemble a callback (not yet supported in SCA-ASM).

4   Coordinated Execution Framework

The proposed framework relies on the SCA-ASM language originally presented in [30] as a formal and abstract *component implementation type* to cover *computation, communication,* and *coordination* aspects during early execution (or simulation) of an SCA assembly of an heterogeneous service-oriented application. ASMs can be adopted to provide abstract implementations (or prototypes) of *mock* components, or to implement "core" components that contain the main service composition or coordination process that guides the application's execution. The framework relies also on other SCA component implementation types (such as Java, Spring, C++, etc., see [28]) to include components providing the real computation services used by the core component(s) and these components can themselves require services provided by other local or remote components.

The framework was developed by integrating the Eclipse-based SCA Composite Designer, the SCA runtime platform Tuscany [33], and the simulator AsmetaS of the ASM toolset ASMETA [5]. This environment[9] allows us to graphically model, compose, analyze, deploy, and execute heterogeneous service-oriented applications in a technologically agnostic way. As described and exemplified below, an heterogeneous SCA assembly (or composition) of service-oriented components (implemented in ASM or in another implementation language) can be graphically produced using the SCA Composite Designer and also stored or exchanged in terms of an XML-based configuration file. This last file is then used by the SCA runtime to instantiate and execute the system by instrumenting AsmetaS and other execution infrastructures in an unique environment (see Fig. 5).

4.1   Service Component Implementation and Configuration

Through the considered case study, we here show the use of the *ASM implementation type* (i.e. of the SCA-ASM language) for SCA components.

Service Component Implementation. The following listings report the ASM (abstract) implementation of the Sensor Coordinator component (request management policy 1). To this purpose, the AsmetaL textual notation to write ASM models within the ASMETA tool-set is used. Two grammatical conventions must be recalled: a variable identifier starts with $; a rule identifier begins with "r_".

Listing 1.2 shows the header of the ASM. The import clauses include the ASM modules of the provided service interfaces (SensorCoordinating and EventObserving) and required interfaces (the LaserScanning interface) of the component, annotated, respectively, with @Provided and @Required. The @MainService annotation on the import clause for the SensorCoordinating interface denotes the main service (read: main component's agent) that is responsible for initializing the component's state (in the predefined r_init rule). The signature of the machine contains declarations for: references (shared functions annotated with @Reference) as abstract access endpoints to services, back references to requester

---

[9]   https://asmeta.svn.sourceforge.net/svnroot/asmeta/code/experimental/SCAASM

agents (shared functions annotated with *@Backref*), and declarations of ASM domains and functions used by the component for internal computation only. In particular, the variable (a controlled 0-ary function) ctl_state stores the current control state of the ASM.

Listing 1.2. ASM header of the Sensor Coordinator component

```
module SensorCoordinator
import STDL/StandardLibrary
import STDL/CommonBehavior
//@MainService
import SensorCoordinating
//@Provided
import EventObserving
//@Required
import LaserScanning
export *
signature:
//@Reference
shared laserScanning : Agent -> LaserScanning
//@Backref
shared clientSensorCoordinating : Agent -> Agent
//@Backref
shared clientEventObserving : Agent -> Agent
enum domain State = {IDLE | BUSY | SCANNING}
//Internal properties
controlled ctl_state : Agent -> State //stores the current control state
controlled paramScan : Agent -> Prod(Integer,Integer,Integer) //arguments of an scan request
controlled from : Agent -> Integer //stores the start position of an scan request
controlled steps : Agent -> Integer //stores the number of measures of an scan request
controlled remScans : Agent -> Integer //stores the number of scans requested by a client
controlled event : Agent -> String //stores the argument of an update request.
```

The body of the ASM (see Listing 1.3) includes definitions of the services (transition rules annotated with @Service) r_request and r_update, the main transition rule r_SensorCoordinator (that takes by convention the same name of the component), the transition rule with the predefined name r_init that is invoked to initially set up the internal component state (i.e. values of controlled functions), and another utility rule named r_acceptRequest.

The service r_request is in charge of requesting a scan to the laser scanner. When the rule is called, it executes in parallel the following actions: sets the state of the ASM to *BUSY*, stores the arguments of the requested scan, invokes (by a send action) the service *scan* provided by the service Laser Scanning.

The service r_update is in charge of receiving the notification from the laser scanner and updating the control state by resembling the FSM shown in Fig. 2.

The rule r_acceptRequest advances the control state of the machine properly according to the incoming service request (the input parameter $r). In case of a new scan request (*r_request*), this is removed from the requests queue (by invoking r_wreceive) and the input is stored in the variable paramScan. A direct invocation of the service r_request then follows if the input is defined. In case, instead, of a notification (r_update) from the laser scanner, the request is removed from the requests queue (by r_wreceive) and in case the input (stored in the variable event) is defined the service r_update is invoked. Note that all the scan requests received while the scanner is already scanning are discarded (what the policy 1 defines).

The rule r_SensorCoordinator is the program of the main component's agent and is invoked when a client requests a service offered by the Sensor Coordinator. The rule r_acceptRequest is then invoked to handle the request depending on the specific service required.

Listing 1.3. ASM body of the Sensor Coordinator component

```
definitions:
//State invariant: Number of scans required by a client must be non negative
invariant inv_neverNeg over remScans(): not(remScans < 0)
//@Service
rule r_request($a in Agent,$from in Integer,$steps in Integer, $nScans in Integer)=
  par
    ctl_state($a) := BUSY
    from($a) := $from
    steps($a) := $steps
    remScans($a) := $nScans − 1
    r_wsend[laserScanning($a),"r_scan(Agent,Integer,Integer)",($from,$steps)]
  endpar

//@Service
rule r_update($a in Agent, $event in String) =
  if (ctl_state($a)=BUSY and $event="Ack") then ctl_state($a) := SCANNING
  else if (ctl_state($a)=SCANNING and $event="Done" and remScans($a)>0)
        then par //continue with next scan
          ctl_state($a) := BUSY
          remScans($a) := remScans($a)−1
          r_wsend[laserScanning($a),"r_scan(Agent,Integer,Integer)",(from($a),steps($a))] endpar
        else if (ctl_state($a)=SCANNING and $event="Done" and remScans($a)=0)
              then ctl_state($a) := IDLE endif endif endif

rule r_acceptRequest ($a in Agent, $r in String) =
  if (ctl_state($a)=IDLE and $r="r_request(Agent,Integer,Integer,Integer)")
  then seq //first scan
    r_wreceive[clientSensorCoordinating($a),"r_request(Agent,Integer,Integer,Integer)",paramScan
      ($a)]
    if (isDef(paramScan($a))) then
      r_request[$a,first(paramScan($a)),second(paramScan($a)),third(paramScan($a))] endif
  endseq
  else if (not ctl_state($a)=IDLE and $r="r_update(Agent,String)")
        then seq
          r_wreceive[clientEventObserving($a),"r_update(Agent,String)",event($a)]
          if (isDef(event($a))) then r_update[self,event($a)] endif
        endseq endif endif

//Main agent's program
rule r_SensorCoordinator =
  let($r = nextRequest(self)) //Select the next request(if any)
  in if isDef($r) then r_acceptRequest[self,$r] endif endlet //Handle the request $r

rule r_init($a in SensorCoordinating) = //for the startup of the component
  par
    status($a) := READY
    ctl_state($a) := IDLE
    from($a) := 0
    steps($a) := 0
    remScans($a) := 0
  endpar
```

Finally, the rule `r_init` is called during initialization of the component's state. This rule simply sets the status of the agent to *READY*, the control state to *IDLE* and the scan parameters to 0.

The ASM definitions of the sensor coordinator's provided interfaces are reported in the listing 1.4 using the AsmetaL notation. They are ASM modules containing only declarations of business agent types (subdomains of the predefined ASM domain `Agent`), and of business functions (ASM out functions).

Service Component Configuration. Component metadata, describing which services are required and provided by a component, and information that allow the SCA runtime to locate (locally or remotely) the component implementation, must be provided in the SCA XML composite file. Listing 1.5 shows a fragment of the SCA XML composite file regarding the metadata of the component Sensor Coordinator that is implemented (by the tag `implementation.asm`) in ASM.

Listing 1.4. ASM definition of the Sensor Coordinating interface

```
//@Remotable
module SensorCoordinating
import STDL/StandardLibrary
import STDL/CommonBehavior
export *
signature:
// the domain defines the type of this agent
domain SensorCoordinating subsetof Agent
// out is a function that implements the provided service
out request: Prod(Agent,Integer,Integer,Integer) −> Rule
definitions:
//@Remotable
module EventObserving
import STDL/StandardLibrary
import STDL/CommonBehavior
export *
signature:
domain EventObserving subsetof Agent
out update: Prod(Agent,String) −> Rule
definitions:
```

Listing 1.5. XML configuration file

```
<?xml version="1.0" encoding="UTF−8" standalone="no"?>
<sca:composite xmlns:sca="http://www.osoa.org/xmlns/sca/1.0" xmlns:asm="http://asm"
name="Sensor" targetNamespace="http://eclipse.org/CaseStudy/src/Sensor">
  ...
  <sca:component name="SensorCoordinator">
    <asm:implementation.asm location="SensorCoordinator.asm"/>
    <sca:reference name="laserScanning"/>
    <sca:service name="SensorCoordinating">
      <asm:interface.asm location="SensorCoordinating.asm"/>
    </sca:service>
  </sca:component>
  ...
</sca:composite>
```

4.2   In-place Simulation of SCA-ASM Models

SCA-ASM components use annotations to denote services, references, properties, etc. With this information, as better described below, an SCA runtime platform (Tuscany in our case) can create a composition (an application) by tracking service references (i.e. required services) at runtime and injecting required services into a component when they become available.

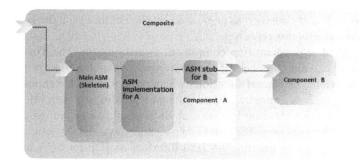

Fig. 4. Instantiating and invoking ASM implementation instances within Tuscany

In-place ASM Simulation Mechanism. Fig. 4 illustrates how the *ASM implementation provider*[10] sets up the environment (the container) within Tuscany for instantiating and handle incoming/outgoing service requests to/from an ASM component implementation instance (like component A in the figure) by instrumenting the ASM simulator AsmetaS. Currently, the implementation scope of an SCA-ASM component is *composite*, i.e. a single component instance – a single *main ASM* instance (see the main ASM for component A in Fig. 4) – is created within AsmetaS for all service calls of the component[11]. This main ASM is automatically created during the setting up of the connections and it is responsible for instantiating the component agent and related resources, and for listening for service requests incoming from the protocol layer and forward them to the component'agent instance (see component A in Fig. 4). Executing an ASM component implementation means executing its main ASM. For each reference, another entity (i.e. another ASM module) is automatically created (and instantiated as ASM agent within the main ASM of the component) as "proxy" for a remote component (see the ASM proxy for component B in Fig. 4) for making an outbound service call from the component. Using a terminology adopted in the Java Remote Method Invocation (RMI) API, this proxy ASM plays the role

---

[10] The Tuscany core delegates the start/stop of component implementation instances and related resources, and the service/reference invocations, to specific *implementation providers* that typically respond to these life-cycle events.

[11] We postpone as future work the implementation of the other two SCA implementation scopes, *stateless* (to create a new component instance on each service call) and *conversation* (to create a component instance for each conversation).

of *stub* to forward a service invocation (and their associated arguments) to an external component's agent, and to send back (through the ASM rule r_replay) the result (if any) to the invoker component's agent (the agent of the component A in Fig. 4). The main ASM, instead, plays the role of *skeleton*, i.e. a proxy for a remote entity that runs on the provider and forwards (through the ASM rule r_sendreceive) client's remote service requests (and their associated arguments) to the appropriate component's agent (usually the main agent of the component), and then the result (if any) of the invoked service is returned to the client component'agent (via stubs). For the sake of space, the ASM implementation of the stub and skeleton (as generated by the runtime) for the component Sensor Coordinator is not reported.

When an ASM implementation component is instantiated, the Tuscany runtime also creates a value for each (if any) externally settable property (i.e. ASM monitored functions, or shared functions when promoted as a composite property, annotated with @Property). Such values or proxies are then injected into the component implementation instance. A data binding mechanism also guarantees a matching between ASM data types and Java data types, including structured data, since we assume the Java interface as IDL for SCA interfaces.

Fig. 5 shows a simulation snapshot of the considered case study where the Sensor Coordinator changes state from IDLE to BUSY (see also the rule r_request in the Listing 1.3) after receiving a first scan request from a client.

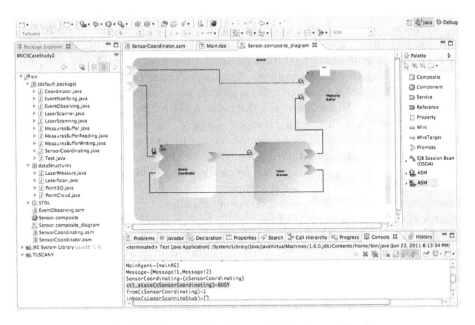

Fig. 5. Simulation of the Sensor Composite application

Other ASM Execution Features. Useful features are currently supported by the AsmetaS simulator when running within the SCA Tuscany platform.

State invariant checker: AsmetaS implements an invariant checker, which at the end of each transition execution checks if the invariants (if any) expressed over the state of the currently executed SCA-ASM component are satisfied or not. If an invariant is not satisfied, AsmetaS throws an `InvalidInvariant-Exception`, which keeps track of the violated invariant. Listing 1.3 shows an example of state invariant (`inv_neverNeg`) for the Sensor Coordinator. It states that the number of scans required by a client must be non negative.

Consistent Updates checking: The simulator also includes a checker for revealing inconsistent updates. In case of inconsistent updates an `UpdateClashException` is thrown by reporting the location which is being inconsistently updated and the two different values which are assigned to that location. The user, analyzing this error, can detect the fault in the ASM component implementation.

Logging: The user can inspect how AsmetaS performs some tasks (e.g. terms evaluation, building of updates set, variables substitution) by a log4j[12] file.

Other ASM Functional Analysis Features. In addition to simulation, the ASMETA toolset [5] supports other *model validation* techniques useful for SCA-ASM models. These validation techniques include: *scenario-based validation* by the ASM validator *AsmetaV*, when the user builds scenarios describing the behavior of a system by looking at the observable interactions between the system and its environment in specific situations; *model-based testing* by the ASMETA ATGT tool, when the specification is used as oracle to compute test cases for a given critical behavior of the system at the same level of the specification. Executable test cases must be then derived from the abstract ones and executed at code level to guarantee conformance between model and code. Another technique for model validation is *model inspection and review* by the *AsmetaMA tool*, which is able to identify defects early in the system development, by determining if a model satisfies some quality properties (called *meta-properties*). *Property verification* is also supported by the *AsmetaSMV* tool, a model checker for ASM. Formal verification should be performed later, once one has a sufficient confidence about model correctness, and it has to be intended as the mathematical proof of system properties, which can be performed by hand or by the aid of *model checkers* (which are usable when the variable ranges are finite) or of *theorem provers* (which require strong user skills to drive the proof).

5 Related Work

Some works devoted to provide software developers with formal methods and techniques tailored to the service domain exist (see, e.g., the survey in [8] for the service composition problem), mostly developed within the EU projects SENSORIA [31] and S-Cube [27]. Several process calculi for the specification of SOA systems have been designed (see, e.g., [22,24,16]). They provide linguistic primitives supported by mathematical semantics, and verification techniques for qualitative and quantitative properties [31]. Still within the SENSORIA project, a declarative modeling language for service-oriented systems, named SRML [32],

---

[12] http://logging.apache.org/

has been developed. SRML supports qualitative and quantitative analysis techniques using the UMC model checker[1] and the PEPA stochastic analyzer[13].

Compared to the formal notations mentioned above, the ASM method has the advantage of being executable. On the formalization of the SCA assembly model, some previous works, like [18,19] to name a few, exist. However, they do not rely on a practical and executable formal method like ASMs. In [25], an analysis tool, *Wombat*, for SCA applications is presented; this approach is similar to our as the tool is used for simulation and verification tasks by transforming SCA modules into composed Petri nets. There is not proven evidence, however, that this methodology scales effectively to large systems.

An abstract service-oriented component model, named *Kmelia*, is formally defined in [6,3] and is supported by a prototype tool (COSTO). In the Kmelia model, services are used as composition units and service behavior is modeled by a labeled transition system. Our proposal is similar to the Kmelia approach; however, we have the advantage of having integrated our SCA-ASM component model and the ASM-related tools with an SCA runtime platform for a more practical use and an easier adoption by developers.

Within the ASM community, the ASM method has been used for the purpose of formalizing business process notations and middleware technologies related to web services, such as [10,11,20,2] to name a few. Some of these previous formalization efforts, as explained in [30], are at the basis of our work.

Concerning the Robotics domain, in [23] a new approach for coordinating the behavior of Orocos RTT (Open Robot Control Software Real Time Toolkit) [29] components is proposed. Orocos RTT is a C++ framework that allows the design and the deployment of component-based robotics control systems. The proposed approach defines the behavior of single components and of entire systems by means of a variant of the UML hierarchical state-charts, which is called *reduced FSM* (rFSM). The main advantages of the rFSM are their hierarchical composability and their applicability in hard-real time applications. Furthermore, despite they are currently used only with Orocos, rFSM are totally framework independent. The main differences between ASMs and rFSMs are that rFSMs do not allow the execution of parallel agent actions and parallel states; moreover, they do not have the universality and broad application of ASMs, and do not offer the same flexibility and tools provided by ASMs.

6   Lesson Learned

We have shown how formal high-level ASM models of service-oriented components can be assembled together with real components through the SCA framework and how we manage the coordination of the overall resulting application by means of the ASM formalism for prototyping and simulation purposes. We experienced that the use of two different frameworks for modeling two different concerns (SCA and its various implementation types for computation, and ASM for coordination) improves the level of flexibility and reusability.

---

[13] http://www.dcs.ed.ac.uk/pepa/

We have shown this by means of a use case in the Robotics field, where flexibility and reusability are very challenging issues [13,14,15]. In general, robotic software applications require and provide a number of different functionalities, which are typically encapsulated in components that cooperate and compete in order to control the behavior of a robot. Cooperation and competition are forms of interaction among concurrent activities and so they have to be coordinated. In order to achieve a good level of reusability and flexibility the coordination and the computation (how the component provides the service) need to be managed separately. So by our experience, the service paradigm seems promising also in the Robotics domain. In particular, we appreciated the possibility to change the coordination policies (see [26]) without modifying the implementation of the services provided by components merely dedicated to computation (such as sophisticated algorithms), thus improving the level of flexibility and reusability.

7   Conclusion and Future Directions

We presented a practical framework for early service design and prototyping that combines the standard SCA and the ASM formal support to assemble service-oriented components as well as intra- and inter- service behavior. The framework is supported by a tool based on the SCA runtime Tuscany and the toolset ASMETA for model execution and functional analysis. The effectiveness of our framework was experimented through various case studies of different complexity and heterogeneity. These include examples taken from the SCA Tuscany distribution, the case study of the EU project BRICS [13] presented here, and also a scenario of the *Finance* case study of the EU project SENSORIA [31].

We plan to support more useful SCA concepts, such as the SCA *callback interface* for bidirectional services and an *event-based style of interaction*. We want also to enrich the SCA-ASM language with interaction and workflow patterns based on the BPMN specification. We also plan to support pre/post-conditions defined on services for contract correctness checking in component assemblies.

On the functional analysis side, we want to integrate further ASMETA analysis techniques with the SCA runtime Tuscany.

References

1. Abreu, J., Mazzanti, F., Fiadeiro, J.L., Gnesi, S.: A Model-Checking Approach for Service Component Architectures. In: Lee, D., Lopes, A., Poetzsch-Heffter, A. (eds.) FMOODS/FORTE 2009. LNCS, vol. 5522, pp. 219–224. Springer, Heidelberg (2009)
2. Altenhofen, M., Friesen, A., Lemcke, J.: ASMs in Service Oriented Architectures. Journal of Universal Computer Science 14(12), 2034–2058 (2008)
3. André, P., Ardourel, G., Attiogbé, C.: Composing Components with Shared Services in the Kmelia Model. In: Pautasso, C., Tanter, É. (eds.) SC 2008. LNCS, vol. 4954, pp. 125–140. Springer, Heidelberg (2008)
4. Arbab, F.: What do you mean, coordination? Bulletin of the Dutch Association for Theoretical Computer Science, 11–22 (March 1998)

5. The ASMETA toolset website (2006), http://asmeta.sf.net/
6. Attiogbé, C., André, P., Ardourel, G.: Checking Component Composability. In: Löwe, W., Südholt, M. (eds.) SC 2006. LNCS, vol. 4089, pp. 18–33. Springer, Heidelberg (2006)
7. Barros, A.P., Börger, E.: A Compositional Framework for Service Interaction Patterns and Interaction Flows. In: Lau, K.-K., Banach, R. (eds.) ICFEM 2005. LNCS, vol. 3785, pp. 5–35. Springer, Heidelberg (2005)
8. Beek, M.T., Bucchiarone, A., Gnesi, S.: Formal Methods for Service Composition. Annals of Mathematics, Computing & Teleinformatics 1(5), 1–10 (2007)
9. Blake, M.B., Remy, S.L., Wei, Y., Howard, A.M.: Robots on the Web: Service-Oriented Computing and Web Interfaces. IEEE Robotics & Automation Magazine (June 2011)
10. Börger Sörensen, O., Thalheim, B.: On Defining the Behavior of OR-joins in Business Process Models. J. UCS 15(1), 3–32 (2009)
11. Börger, E.: Modeling Workflow Patterns from First Principles. In: Parent, C., Schewe, K.-D., Storey, V.C., Thalheim, B. (eds.) ER 2007. LNCS, vol. 4801, pp. 1–20. Springer, Heidelberg (2007)
12. Börger, E., Stärk, R.: Abstract State Machines: A Method for High-Level System Design and Analysis. Springer (2003)
13. EU project BRICS (Best Practice in Robotics), www.best-of-robotics.org/
14. Brugali, D., Scandurra, P.: Component-based robotic engineering (Part I) [Tutorial]. IEEE Robotics & Automation Magazine 16(4), 84–96 (2009)
15. Brugali, D., Shakhimardanov, A.: Component-based Robotic Engineering (Part II): Systems and Models. Robotics XX(1), 1–12 (2010)
16. Bruni, R.: Calculi for Service-Oriented Computing. In: Bernardo, M., Padovani, L., Zavattaro, G. (eds.) SFM 2009. LNCS, vol. 5569, pp. 1–41. Springer, Heidelberg (2009)
17. Davis, J.S.: Order and containment in concurrent system design. PhD thesis. Univ. of California, Berkeley (2000)
18. Ding, Z., Chen, Z., Liu, J.: A rigorous model of service component architecture. Electr. Notes Theor. Comput. Sci. 207, 33–48 (2008)
19. Du, D., Liu, J., Cao, H.: A rigorous model of contract-based service component architecture. In: CSSE (2), pp. 409–412. IEEE Computer Society (2008)
20. Farahbod, R., Glässer, U., Vajihollahi, M.: A formal semantics for the business process execution language for web services. In: Bevinakoppa, S., Pires, L.F., Hammoudi, S. (eds.) WSMDEIS, pp. 122–133. INSTICC Press (2005)
21. ASMs web site (2008), http://www.eecs.umich.edu/gasm/
22. Guidi, C., Lucchi, R., Gorrieri, R., Busi, N., Zavattaro, G.: SOCK: A Calculus for Service Oriented Computing. In: Dan, A., Lamersdorf, W. (eds.) ICSOC 2006. LNCS, vol. 4294, pp. 327–338. Springer, Heidelberg (2006)
23. Klotzbuecher, M., Soetens, P., Bruyninckx, H.: OROCOS RTT-Lua: an Execution Environment for building Real-time Robotic Domain Specific Languages. In: Int. Workshop on Dynamic Languages for RObotic and Sensors (2010)
24. Lanese, I., Martins, F., Vasconcelos, V.T., Ravara, A.: Disciplining orchestration and conversation in service-oriented computing. In: SEFM 2007, pp. 305–314. IEEE (2007)
25. Martens, A., Moser, S.: Diagnosing SCA Components Using WOMBAT. In: Dustdar, S., Fiadeiro, J.L., Sheth, A.P. (eds.) BPM 2006. LNCS, vol. 4102, pp. 378–388. Springer, Heidelberg (2006)

26. EU project BRICS, Tech. Rep. A Coordination Use Case (March 24, 2011),
    www.best-of-robotics.org/wiki/images/e/e0/
    coordinationusecaseubergamo.pdf
27. EU project S-Cube, http://www.s-cube-network.eu/
28. Service Component Architecture (SCA), www.osoa.org
29. The Orocos Project, http://www.orocos.org
30. Riccobene, E., Scandurra, P.: A modeling and executable language for designing
    and prototyping service-oriented applications. In: EUROMICRO Conf. on Software
    Engineering and Advanced Applications, SEAA 2011 (2011)
31. EU project SENSORIA, www.sensoria-ist.eu/
32. SRML: A Service Modeling Language (2009), http://www.cs.le.ac.uk/srml/
33. Apache Tuscany, http://tuscany.apache.org/

Verifying Temporal Properties of Use-Cases in Natural Language

Viliam Simko[1], David Hauzar[1], Tomas Bures[1,2],
Petr Hnetynka[1], and Frantisek Plasil[1,2]

[1] Charles University, Faculty of Mathematics and Physics,
Department of Distributed and Dependable Systems, Malostranské náměstí 25,
Prague 1, 118 00, Czech Republic
{simko,hauzar,bures,hnetynka,plasil}@d3s.mff.cuni.cz
[2] Institute of Computer Science,
Academy of Sciences of the Czech Republic
Pod Vodárenskou věží 2, Prague 8, 182 07, Czech Republic

Abstract. This paper presents a semi-automated method that helps iteratively write use-cases in natural language and verify consistency of behavior encoded within them. In particular, this is beneficial when the use-cases are created simultaneously by multiple developers. The proposed method allows verifying the consistency of textual use-case specification by employing annotations in use-case steps that are transformed into temporal logic formulae and verified within a formal behavior model. A supporting tool for plain English use-case analysis is currently being enhanced by integrating the verification algorithm proposed in the paper.

Keywords: Use-Cases, Behavior Modeling, Verification, Natural Language, Label Transition System, Model-Checking, Requirements Engineering, Temporal Logic .

1 Introduction

In typical software development practice, majority of the requirement documents created in the early phase of a project, are written in natural language [10]. Such a specification is therefore inherently imprecise, ambiguous, and a potential source of contradictions. An important issue is that in a large software project, the specification phase involves collaboration among a number of team members[1] who express their personal views in natural language. In such an environment, there is a high chance of conflicts among individual parts of the specification.

Use-cases are traditionally used in requirement specification because they can easily capture the behavior of a system under discussion (SuD) from the perspective of different actors. Usually, SuD may be equalled to a component where a use-case describes a part of the interaction between the component and its environment.

---

[1] For example, the Agile software development methodology proposes teams of 5-9 people.

F. Arbab and P.C. Ölveczky (Eds.): FACS 2011, LNCS 7253, pp. 350–367, 2012.
© Springer-Verlag Berlin Heidelberg 2012

Since the inclusion of use-cases into the UML standard [14], their use has been greatly extended, making them a mandatory requirement for any object-oriented software development project. As stressed by Cockburn [3] and Larman [9], the main asset of use-cases is that behavior is encoded in natural language and thus accessible to a wide range of stakeholders of a project.

Although an isolated use-case can clearly describe a simple scenario, the overall behavior of combined use-cases may become quite blurry. In particular, the problem can easily appear in specifications where use-cases are composed using *include* and *precede* relationships [3].

The intended behavior expressed by use-cases contains implicit temporal dependencies that are likely violated during the iterative development. Because late detection of such errors leads to significantly higher costs of a project [2], writers of the specification greatly benefit from tools that help them keep the textual specification consistent and that warn them about potential violations immediately during writing.

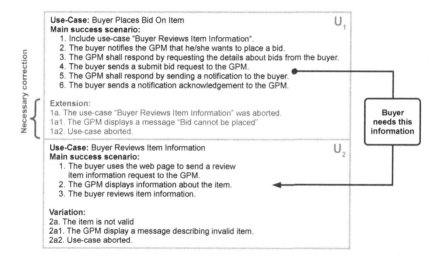

Fig. 1. Example use-cases with aborts (textual form)

Motivation example: Figure 1 shows a pair of the dependent use-cases U_1 and U_2 specified as a sequence of English sentences (U_1 includes U_2). The final text of these use-cases was created in 3 iterations. In the first iteration, an initial version was created with just a simple success scenario. In the second iteration, the use-case U_2 was refined by introducing an optional branch (variation) aborting U_2. However, such specification is not consistent: U_1 does not consider a possible abort in U_2. In more detail, there is a possible trace leading to usage of an unavailable item when U_2 has been aborted.

Problem statement. Such an inconsistency may be detected only when both use-cases are put into context of one another using the *include* relationship. This makes such inconsistencies difficult to notice, especially when specification is large with many use-cases and *include* relationships.

So it would be desirable to propose a method that, in an automatized way, detects such an inconsistency and issues a warning. In the example, as a reaction to such a warning, U_1 could be manually extended by adding an abort-handling branch to affect the set of traces that involve branching transitions. Verification would now succeed because the traces involving the abort step in U_2 would be limited to the abort-handling branch.

Goal. Thus, the goal of this paper is to present a method that allows an early detection of violation of temporal dependencies of use-case steps. The proposed method (Use-Case Temporal Verification – UCTV) allows automated derivation of a formal behavior model (LTS) from use-cases in plain English. Moreover, by adding annotations to use-case steps, it is possible to verify temporal properties in an automatized way in order to identify inconsistencies within the original specification. The detected errors are presented to the user as erroneous traces. For automated transformation of the use-cases into the formal model and verification of temporal dependencies, we designed a software tool (REPROTOOL), which stems from the PROCASOR tool [12,4,15] designed earlier in our group.

Other approaches exist that aim at extracting behavior models from text, for example authors of [18] describe how to generate UML Activity Diagrams from use-cases. The method uses restriction rules [19] imposed on the use-case step sentences. In [7], a method for deriving message sequence charts from textual scenarios is described.

Several languages and formalisms for behavior modeling of software systems have been proposed. They range from very generic ones (e.g., process algebras [6,13]), to those specific to components (e.g., Darwin [11], Interface automata [1], or Threaded Behavior Protocols [8]).

To achieve the goal, the paper is structured as follows: In Section 2 we overview the main concepts in UML use-cases as the terminology base used further in the paper. Section 3 describes how users interact with an application that implements our method. In Section 4 we explain the algorithm in detail, while Section 6 concludes the paper.

2   Use-Cases in Natural Language and UML

The prevalent practice of capturing use-cases is to use textual notation and natural language. Futher, UML Use-Case Diagrams provide means for establishing relations among use-cases.

Although there are different styles of writing use-cases, for our purposes we consider the format depicted in Figure 1 and 4. This format is taken from the book [3] as it is widely accepted.

With regard to the structure of a use-case, the *main success scenario* of a use-case consists of several steps that contribute to achieving the use-case goal. Alternative scenarios can be expressed using *variations* and *extensions*. The difference between extensions and variations is that a variation *replaces* the step to which it is attached, while an extension provides *optional branching* from its parent step. For illustration, consider the use-case U_1 in Figure 4. There is a variation $2a$ attached to the step 2 which means that 2 and $2a$ are mutually exclusive branches. On the other hand, the use-case U_2 contains an extension $1b$ which means that the step 1 is always executed before the optional $1b$ branch.

2.1 Actions in Use-Case Steps

It has been advised by practitioners, e.g. in [3], to use simple sentences when writing use-cases. A sentence should encode a single action, which is either (a) interaction between an actor and SuD, (b) internal action within SuD, or (c) special action (see below). As to the structure of a sentence, in English it should conform to the SVDPI pattern (Subject, Verb, Direct-Object, Preposition, and Indirect-Object); this is very important for an automated processing. The following special actions are introduced in the UCTV method:

Goto action: The trace advances by another step (indicated by this action) within the same use-case. This action is typically used to express looping. Example: *Goto step 1.* (See Figure 4 use-case U_2 step 2a2).

Include action: Similar to calling a procedure, the trace advances in the included use-case, when it is finished, the include action is concluded. Example: *Include use-case "Generate city"* (e.g. use-case U_2, step 1 in Figure 4).

Abort action: The use-case execution is aborted. However, if the aborted use-case U_3 was included into another use-case U_2, the trace immediately advances in U_2. Example: *Use-case aborts* (e.g. use-case U_3, step 2a1 in Figure 4).

2.2 Relations in the UML Use-Case Diagrams

UML provides means for expressing dependencies among use-cases using stereotyped relations in the UML Use-Case Diagrams. The UCTV method takes into account the **«includes»** (via the include special action) and **«precedes»** UML relationships:

U_1 **«includes»** U_2: The *include* relationship allows inserting the behavior from one use-case into another. It minimizes duplication and improves comprehension of the whole specification when used carefully. The use of *include* means that at the given point in use-case A, the trace advances over the steps in B and when B is finished, it returns back to A [9].

U_1 **«precedes»** U_2: Rosenberg and Stephens in the book [16] define the *precedence* relationship as: The use-case U_1 must take place in its entirety before another use-case U_2 even begins, i.e. there is temporal precedence in which U_1 must occur before U_2. For example a *Login* use-case must be completed before *Checkout* is begun.

We use the *Prec* precedence relation formed by the pairs of use-cases, in which first use-case precedes the second one.

3 User's Perspective

Before we present UCTV in a formal way, let us describe use-case design from the user's perspective. Figure 2 contains a screenshot from our application REPROTOOL that the user employs when writing a use-case specification[2].

---

[2] REPROTOOL is based on Eclipse and uses Eclipse Modeling Framework (EMF) as a tool for data representation. The application is still under development and not yet completely finished, see http://code.google.com/a/eclipselabs.org/p/reprotool/

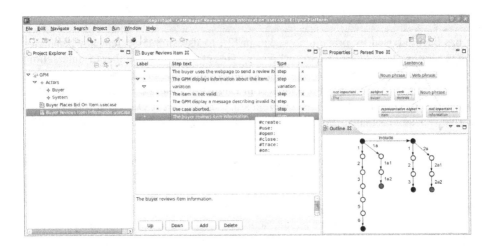

Fig. 2. Screenshot from the REPROTOOL application

In the first phase, the user creates several use-cases with steps written as sentences in plain English. Each sentence (step) is automatically parsed and transformed into a linguistic parse tree. Depending on the sentence structure, the type of the action is derived automatically or set manually by the user. This way, REPROTOOL derives LTS from the use-cases and renders a graphical representation of the LTS as depicted in Figure 2.

In the next phase, the user can assign annotations to individual steps to define precedence relations determining temporal dependencies among use-cases and their steps. These will be verified in the next phase.

When looking at the motivation example, the temporal dependency between U_1 and U_2 can be captured using a pair of annotations – *use:item* and *create:item* (for illustration see Figure 3 providing annotated use-cases and capturing their creation in iterations). The semantics of them is that in each trace containing a step with the *use:item* annotation, any other step with a *create:item* annotation has to precede the former (pairwise).

At some point, during the iterative process of writing use-cases, the user initiates the verification procedure performed within the REPROTOOL application.

If a verification error is detected, the model-checker shows a trace that violates the temporal properties determined by annotations. After the verification is finished, the user can adjust the textual specification to fix the reported error by:

– Adding precedence relationships among use-cases, which fix the missing *create* annotation that the preceded use-case might have provided.
– Adding an abort-handling branch as seen in the motivation example (Fig. 3).
– Adjusting annotations of steps or rewriting/reorganizing them.

In the motivation example, after introducing the abort branch (variation $2a$ of U_2), the model-checker detected an error trace (Figure 3, *Iteration #2*). The user fixed the error

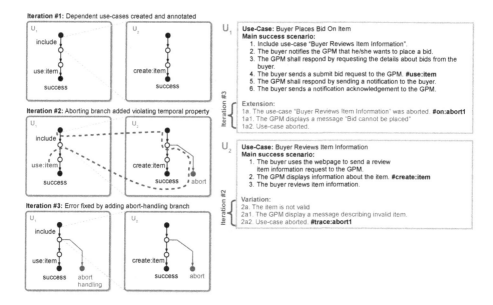

Fig. 3. Verification of dependent use-cases with aborts using temporal annotations

by adding an extension $1a$ into U_1 (Figure 3, *Iteration #3* and Figure 1, "Necessary correction").

In addition to the *create-use* annotation pair, we have also described the *open-close* annotation pair in the text below. These annotations cover the majority of dependencies among use-cases that we encountered in our survey [17]. However, since the UCTV method internally uses LTL formulae to capture desired temporal properties, our approach is also applicable for other annotations, the semantics of which can be described by LTL or other temporal logic formlae.

4   Verification of Use-Cases

In this section, we describe all the annotations and the REPROTOOL verification algorithm in detail.

4.1   Annotations in Use-case Steps

There are two types of annotations: (a) annotations expressing temporal dependencies (technically translated to LTL), and (b) annotations constraining the set of traces to be inspected by the model-checker.

(a) Annotations expressing temporal dependencies ("temporal annotations") :
The create-use annotation pair: In all traces it must hold that for any step annotated by *use:x* there must previously appear a step annotated by *create:x* (as above, x is a

user-chosen identifier). That is, if x is used, it must be created before. Next, it must hold that for each step annotated by *create:x*, there must be a trace reaching this step and then eventually reaching another step annotated by *use:x*. In other words, if x is created then it must be somewhere used in the future [3]. An example is shown in Figure 4.

The open-close annotation pair: For any trace that with a step annotated by *open:x*, there must eventually appear a step annotated by *close:x*. Obviously, another *open:x* step is not allowed in between. In a similar vein, *close:x* cannot appear without a preceding *open:x*.

(b) Annotations constraining traces :

The trace-on annotation pair: These annotations serve to control application of use-case variations.

Technically, the *trace:x* annotation marks with a flag x all the traces going through the step where this annotation appears. This flag may be later tested and used as a guard in branching via the annotation *on:x*. That is, a trace that goes through a step marked with *trace:x* annotation and reaches this branching state must continue using the step marked with an *on:x* annotation and a trace that does not go through a step marked with a *trace:x* annotation and reaches this branching state must continue using any other step going from this state.

Typically, this annotation pair is used when detecting unhandled aborts in use-cases. Figures 3 and 4 show examples.

4.2   The Verification Strategy

Verification of textual use-cases is done in two phases. First the precedences and includes are statically checked for presence of cyclic dependencies. Second, a dedicated type of LTS (use-case automaton) is built from the textual use-cases and further model-checking is employed to verify temporal dependencies expressed by annotations.

Before the actual verification starts, the textual use-cases are parsed using the method described in [4] into an internal form where the sequence of steps, variations and extensions of steps, actions in use-case steps, and annotations of use-case steps are specifically represented. After the internal form has been created, the verification proceeds as described below.

Static Check of Precedences and Includes. In this phase, precedence and include use-case relationships are checked statically. The cyclic dependencies among use-cases represented in the internal form are detected by creating an oriented precedence and include graphs.

Model-Checking of Temporal Dependencies. In this phase, the internal form is used to build LTS-like structure (based on use-case automata). The annotations expressing temporal dependencies are converted into an LTL formula. Finally, a modified LTL

---

[3] Strictly speaking, creating something without its usage is not an error. Nevertheless, since it is not a good practice, we consider such a trace to be erroneous.

model-checking algorithm (Use Case Model Checking – UCMC)[4] is applied to verify the LTL properties. This phase comprises three steps:

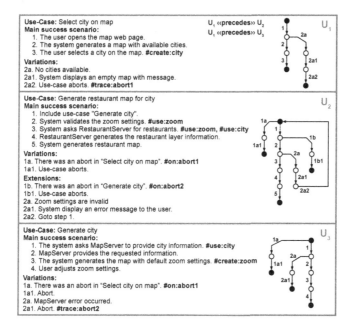

Fig. 4. Fragment of a use-case specification of a web portal providing information about restaurants. For clarity reasons, the annotations (prefixed by the "#" character) are visible only in the textual specification and hidden in the corresponding label transition system (use-case automaton with includes).

- **A use-case automaton with includes (UCAI)** is built for each use-case. Basically, UCAI is an LTS with transitions corresponding to steps of a use-case. Specifically, it contains *include transitions*, which correspond to include steps in the use-case. Figure 4 shows an example of three textual use-cases and the corresponding UCAIs.
- By creating **resolved use-case automata (RUCAs)**, includes in UCAIs are inlined. RUCA is obtained from UCAI by replacing each of the *include* transitions by inlining the reference automaton. See Figure 5a for an example of resolution of the automaton U_2 from Figure 4.
  Moreover the annotations constraining the traces are converted into guards (controlled by dedicated variables) on the automata transitions (Figure 5c shows an automaton with guards).
- The annotations expressing **temporal dependencies are converted to LTL formulae**[5]. Figure 5b shows the automaton with annotations on transitions.

---

[4] The model-checking algorithm cannot be used in its standard form since we consider also finite traces and LTS with guards – discussed in detail in Section 5.5

[5] In this paper, we only consider LTL formulae corresponding to the *create-use* and *open-close* annotation pairs.

- A **set of automata which captures overall behavior of the system** (**OB**) is created. Because the precedes relations define only a partial ordering of use-case applications, the overall behavior *OB* is determined by a set of all possible sequences of the use-case applications.

  Technically, each such a sequence is represented by a RUCA created by a concatenations of the RUCAs representing the individual members of the sequence. Figure 5d shows an example of concatenation of the use-case automata U_1 and U_2 from Figure 4.

- In the final step, the UCMC algorithm is used to verify each RUCA in OB against the extracted LTL formulae.

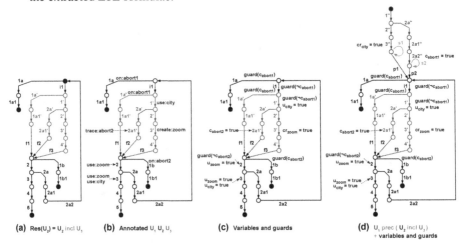

(a) Res(U_2) = U_2 incl U_3 (b) Annotated $U_1 U_2 U_3$ (c) Variables and guards   (d) U_1 prec (U_2 incl U_3) + variables and guards

Fig. 5. Visual representation of the construction of the verifying LTS: (a) Included LTS is inlined to the base LTS, (b)+(c) annotations are initialized either as LTL variables or control variables with guards, (d) all final states of the preceded LTS are connected to the initial state of the base LTS. Note: These LTS automata correspond to use-cases from the Figure 4

5   Theoretical Background

In this section, we provide a formal definition of the key abstraction used by the UCTV method, specifically this includes UCAI, RUCA and a proof of the correctness of the UCMC algorithm.

5.1   Use-case Automaton with Includes

We define *use-case automaton with includes (UCAI)* and the way it corresponds to a textual use-case. The correspondence is straightforward – steps of a textual use-case correspond to transitions of a *use-case automaton with includes*.

Definition 1 (Use-case automaton with includes–UCAI).

   A use-case automaton with includes (UCAI) $P = \langle V_P, V_P^{init}, V_P^{abort}, V_P^{succ}, A_P, \tau_P \rangle$ *consists of the following elements:*

- V_P is a set of states.
- $V_P^{init} \subseteq V_P$ is a set of initial states. We require that V_P^{init} contains at most one state. If $V_P^{init} = \emptyset$, then P is called empty.
- $V_P^{abort} \subseteq V_P$ is a set of abort states.
- $V_P^{succ} \subseteq V_P$ is a set of succeeded states. We require that V_P^{succ} contains at most one state.
- $A_P = A_P^I \cup A_P^{include} \cup \{\epsilon\}$ is a set of all actions. A_P^I, $A_P^{include}$ are mutually disjoint sets of internal and include actions, ϵ is the empty action.
- $\tau_P \subseteq V_P \times A_P \times V_P$ is a set of transitions.

Definition 2 (Annotation function). *Let A_P be a set of actions of UCAI P and N a set of annotations. Annotation function Af : $\tau_P \mapsto 2^N$ maps a transition of P to a set of annotations.*

Note that that two instances of an annotation with an identical name – i.e. two *on* : *x* annotations annotating different steps of use-case – are not considered as equal. Hence, there is no annotation that annotates two different steps.

Definition 3 (Correspondence of a use-case to UCAI). *Let U be a use-case, let $P = \langle V_P, V_P^{init}, V_P^{abort}, V_P^{succ}, A_P, \tau_P \rangle$ be UCAI. We say that P corresponds to U if for each step st_i of U there is the corresponding transition $t_i = (s_i, a_i, s_i') \in \tau_P, s_i, s_i' \in V_P, a_i \in A_P$ of P such that:*
    If st_i is:

- *an include step then $a_i \in A_P^{include}$, if st_i is an abort or a goto step $a_i = \epsilon$, otherwise $a_i \in A_P^I$.*

$V_P, V_P^{init}, V_P^{abort}, V_P^{succ}$, and τ_P are defined as:

- *is a transition such that there exists another transition $st_j \neq st_i$ with the same target state, then either st_j or st_i is a goto step, the last step of a variation, or the last step of an extension,*
- *not the first step of the main success scenario, the first step of a variation, or the first step of an extension, let $st_{i-1} \in U$ be a step preceding the step st_i and $(s_{i-1}, a_{i-1}, s_{i-1}') \in \tau_P$ a corresponding transition of P. It holds that $s_{i-1}' = s_i$,*
- *the first step of the main success scenario of U then $s_i \in V_P^{init}$,*
- *the last step of the main success scenario of U then $s_i' \in V_P^{succ}$,*
- *the first step of a variation of the step $st_j \in U$ and let $(s_j, a_j, s_j') \in \tau_P$ be the transition of P corresponding to the step st_j, then it holds that $s_i = s_j$,*
- *the first step of an extension of the step $st_j \in U$ and let $(s_j, a_j, s_j') \in \tau_P$ be the transition of P corresponding to the step st_j and $st_{j+1} \in U$ be the step following the step st_j and $(s_{j+1}, a_{j+1}, s_{j+1}') \in \tau_P$ corresponding transition, it holds that $s_i = s_j'$,*
- *the last step of a variation or an extension and it is an abort step, then $a_i = \epsilon$ and $s_i' \in V^{abort}$,*
- *the last step of a variation or an extension and it is not an abort or goto step, then let st_j be the step that st_i extends or variates and $(s_j, a_j, s_j') \in \tau_P$ be the corresponding transition, it holds that $s_i' = s_j'$,*

– a goto step and $st_j \in U$ is the target step and let (s_j, a_j, s'_j) be the transition of P corresponding to the step st_j, it holds that $s'_i = s_j$.

The annotation function Af is defined as: if st_i is annotated by a set of annotations N, then $\text{Af}(t_i) = N$.

Example 1. Figure 4 shows three textual use-cases U_1, U_2, and U_3 and the corresponding UCAIs.

5.2 Resolution of the Include Relationship

We define the operation of resolution of includes – a transformation of *UCAI* to *RUCA*. This operation replaces include transitions with transitions of the included automata.

Definition 4 (Resolved use-case automaton–RUCA). Resolved use-case automaton *(RUCA) is UCAI that does not contain any include action.*

Definition 5 (Resolution of includes). *Let P be UCAI. Let I be the set of use-case automata included in automaton P. The operation of resolution of includes (Res) transforms $P = \langle V_P, V_P^{init}, V_P^{abort}, V_P^{succ}, A_P, \tau_P \rangle$ to RUCA $Q = \langle V_Q, V_Q^{init}, V_Q^{abort}, V_Q^{succ}, A_Q, \tau_Q \rangle$ in the following way:*

- $V_Q = V_P \bigcup_{U \in I} V_{\text{Res}(U)}$,
- $V_Q^{init} = V_P^{init}$,
- $V_Q^{abort} = V_P^{abort}$,
- $V_Q^{succ} = V_P^{succ}$,
- $A_Q = A_P \setminus A_P^{include} \bigcup_{U \in I} A_{\text{Res}(U)}$,
- $\tau_Q = \tau_P \cup \tau_A \setminus \{\tau_I\}, \tau_I = (s, inc, s') \in \tau_P, inc \in A_P^{inc}, s, s' \in V_P$.

τ_A is defined as follows. Let $t_i = (s_i, inc, s'_i) \in \tau_P, s_i, s'_i \in V_P$ be a transition of the automaton P that contains an include action, let Q_{inc} be UCAI associated with the include action inc and $R = \text{Res}(Q_{inc})$ be the corresponding resolved use-case automaton. For every such a transition t_i, τ_A contains:

- $(s_i, \epsilon, s_0), s_0 \in V_R^{init}$
- $(s_{final}, \epsilon, s'_i) s_{final} \in V_R^{succ} \cup V_R^{abort}$

Example 2. Figure 5a shows an example of UCAI U_2 from Figure 4 after the operation of resolution of includes.

5.3 Resolution of Annotations

In textual use-cases, additional behavioral restrictions and consistence constraints are captured using annotations. Additional behavioral restrictions are captured using trace-on annotation pair and additional consistency properties are captured by create-use and open-close annotation pairs. We describe how these annotations define valuation of variables in transitions of the automaton, guard functions, and LTL formulae. Guard functions restrict sequences of transitions that the automaton captures and LTL formulae describe consistency requirements on the automaton.

Definition 6 (Valuation of states of RUCA). *Let P be RUCA and X a set of variables. Valuation of transitions of P over the set of variables X is a function* $\text{Val}_P : \tau_P \mapsto 2^X$ *that maps each transition of P to a set of variables. We denote each variable* $v \in \text{Val}_P(s)$ *as* satisfied *in a transition* $s \in V_P$.

The set of variables X_P *is called* variables of P *if* $\forall x \in X_P : \exists v \in V_P$ *such that* $x \in \text{Val}_P(v)$. *By* $X_P^s = X_P \setminus \text{Val}(s)$ *we denote the set of variables that are* not *satisfied in the transition* s.

Definition 7 (Guard functions). *Let P be RUCA and* X_P *a set of variables of P. Guard functions* $\text{Guard}^+ : \tau_p \mapsto (2^{X_P})$ *and* $\text{Guard}^- : \tau_p \mapsto (2^{X_P})$ *map each transition of P to a set of variables.*

The concept of guard functions is important for defining enabled transitions (Definition 13); how a guard function is constructed expresses the Definition 8.

Definition 8 (Correspondence of annotations to valuation of a use-case automaton). *Let P be a RUCA, N the set of all annotations of the transitions of P. We define* Val *(valuation function),* Guard^+ *and* Guard^- *(guard functions) as follows:*
If the annotation $an \in N$ *attached to a transition* $t = \{s_i, a, s_j\}$ *is of the form:*

- *trace:id, there is a variable* c_{id} *such that* $c_{id} \in \text{Val}(t)$,
- *on:id, there is a variable* $c_{id} \in \text{Guard}^+(t)$ *and for all transitions* $t_u = (s_i, a_k, s_n), s_n \neq s_j,$ *it holds that* $c_{id} \in \text{Guard}^-(t_u)$,
- *create:id, there is a variable* cr_{id} *such that* $cr_{id} \in \text{Val}(t)$,
- *use:id, there is a variable* u_{id} *such that* $u_{id} \in \text{Val}(t)$,
- *open:id, there is a variable* o_{id} *such that* $o_{id} \in \text{Val}(t)$,
- *close:id, there is a variable* cl_{id} *such that* $cl_{id} \in \text{Val}(t)$.

Consequently, for $t_i \in \tau_p$ is $\text{Guard}^+(t_i) \cap \text{Guard}^-(t_i) = \emptyset$.

Example 3. Figure 5b shows RUCA with annotated transitions and Figure 5c shows this RUCA with valuations of transitions and guards. The transition $1a$ is annotated by a set of annotations $\{on : abort1\}$ and the other transition $i1$ from the input state of the transition $1a$ has no $on : id$ annotation. Hence, values of guard functions on these transitions are defined as follows: $Guard^+(1a) = \{c_{abort1}\}, Guard^-(1a) = \{\},$ $Guard^+(i1) = \{\},$ and $Guard^-(i1) = \{c_{abort1}\}$.

Definition 9 (Consistency properties). *Let P be RUCA, N the set of all annotations of the states of P. The set of* consistency properties LTL_P *associated with the automaton P is defined as follows:*
If N contains:

- *open:id or close:id then* LTL_P *contains the LTL formulae depicted in Figure 6a,*
- *create:id or open:id then* LTL_P *contains the LTL formulae depicted in Figure 6b.*

Example 4. For RUCA P in Figure 5c we define the following LTL formulae: $LTL_P = \{G(cr_{city} \rightarrow X(G(\neg cr_{city}))), \neg u_{city} U cr_{city}, \neg G(cr_{city} \rightarrow G(\neg u_{city})), G(cr_{zoom} \rightarrow X(G(\neg cr_{zoom}))), \neg u_{zoom} U cr_{zoom}, \neg G(cr_{zoom} \rightarrow G(\neg u_{zoom}))\}$.

(a)	$G(op_{id} \rightarrow F(cl_{id}))$	After 'open' there should always be 'close'
	$\neg cl_{id} \; U \; op_{id}$	First 'open' then 'close'
	$G(cl_{id} \rightarrow X(\neg cl_{id} \; U \; op_{id}))$	No multi-close without open
	$G(op_{id} \rightarrow X(\neg op_{id} \; U \; cl_{id}))$	No multi-open without close
(b)	$G(cr_{id} \rightarrow X(G(\neg cr_{id})))$	Only one 'create'
	$\neg u_{id} \; U \; cr_{id}$	No 'use' before 'create'
	$\neg G(cr_{id} \rightarrow G(\neg u_{id}))$	After 'create' there must be a branch with 'use'

Fig. 6. LTL formulae generated from temporal annotations

5.4   Resolution of Precedence Relationship

Now, we define how automata capturing behavior of individual use-cases are serialized according to the precedence relationship.

Definition 10 (Concatenated RUCA). *Let* $s = (R_1, R_2, ..., R_k)$ *be an sequence of RUCAs. Concatenated RUCA* Q *corresponding to* s *is defined as follows:*

- $V_Q = \bigcup_{R \in s} V_R$
- $V_Q^{init} = V_{R_1}^{init}$
- $V_Q^{abort} = V_{R_k}^{abort}$
- $V_Q^{succ} = V_{R_k}^{succ}$
- $A_Q = \bigcup_{R \in s} A_R$
- $\tau_Q = \bigcup_{R \in s} \tau_R \cup \tau_A$

τ_A *is defined as follows. Let* (R_i, R_{i+1}) *be a pair of subsequent resolved use-case automata in the sequence* s. *Let* $init_{i+1}$ *be the initial state of the automaton* R_{i+1}. *For every such a pair and every final state* $final_i \in V_i^{succ} \cup V_i^{abort}$ *of the automaton* R_i, *there are transitions* $(succ_i, \epsilon, init_{i+1})$ *and* $(final_i, \epsilon, final_i) \in \tau_A$.

Obviously, this definition stems from classical automata concatenation; the key enhancement here is the introduction of the transitions of the form $(final_i, \epsilon, final_i)$, which corresponds to the semantics of Prec. That is, U_i must occur before U_{i+1}, hence all traces that reach U_{i+1} must go through U_i. However, it is not required that U_{i+1} is executed after U_i. There exist infinite traces that go through U_i and loop using the transition $(final_i, \epsilon, final_i)$ thus never reaching U_{i+1}.

Example 5. Figure 5d shows an example of concatenation of RUCA U_1 from Figure 4 and $Res(U_2)$ from Figure 5a. The initial state of the resulting automaton is the initial state of U_1, abort and succeeded states of the resulting automaton are the same as abort and succeeded states of the automaton $Res(U_2)$. The two automata are connected using transitions $p1$ and $p2$ going from the final states of the automaton U_1 to the initial state of the automaton $Res(U_2)$. Then, there are looping transitions $s1$ and $s2$ going from each final state of U_1 back to this state. All these transitions contain the ϵ action.

Definition 11 (Precedence Relation). Precedence relation *defined on a set of RUCA U* Prec : $U \times U$ *is an antisymmetric and irreflexive relation, whose transitive closure* Prec* *is antisymmetric and irreflexive as well. We say that* U_i^R *precedes* U_j^R *if* $(U_i^R, U_j^R) \in$ Prec. *We say that* U_k^R *must be executed before* U_l^R *if* $(U_k^R, U_l^R) \in$ Prec*.

Definition 12 (Overall-behavior–OB). *Let U be a set of RUCAs, let* Prec *be a precedence relation, and let S be the set of all permutations of RUCAs from U ordered according to* Prec. *The* overall-behavior OB *set with respect to U and* Prec *is the set of concatenated RUCAs corresponding to members of S.*

Example 6. There are two permutations of use-cases in use-case specification in Figure 4 ordered according to specified precedences. That is, (U_1, U_2, U_3) and (U_1, U_3, U_2). Hence, the set OB for this specification consists of two automata.

It should be noted that our approach does not tackle the problem of parallel execution of use-case steps. Instead, it focuses on verification of temporal properties of all use-case sequences which could be defined by the *precede* relation (these sequences are captured in the OB set).

5.5   Verification Algorithm

In this section, we define the verification algorithm and related concepts.

Definition 13 (Enabled transition). *Let P be RUCA. Let* $tr = v_0, a_0, v_1, a_1, ..., v_n$ *be an alternating sequence of states and actions such that* $t_i = (v_i, a_i, v_{i+1}) \in \tau_P$. *The transition* t_i *is enabled on* tr *if all the transitions* $t_j, j < i$ *are enabled, for all* $v^+ \in$ Guard$^+(t_i)$ *there exists* $t_k, k \leq i$ *such that* $v^+ \in$ Val(t_k), *and there is no* $t_l, l \leq i$ *such that for some* $v^- \in$ Guard$^-(t_i)$ *it holds* $v^- \in$ Val(t_l). *If the transition is not enabled on* tr, *we say that it is* disabled *on* tr.

Example 7. Consider the use-case automaton in Figure 5d and the sequence of transitions $(p1, i1, 1', 2a', 2a1', f2, 1b, 1b1)$. For the transition $p1$ both guard functions return the empty set and this transition is trivially enabled on sq_1. Next, $Guard^+(i1) = \{\}$ and $Guard^-(i1) = \{c_{abort1}\}$ and there is no predecessor t_j of a transition $i1$ in the sequence sq_1 such that $c_{abort1} \in$ Val(t_j). Hence, the transition $i1$ is enabled on sq_1. Values of guard functions on transition $1'$ are the same and therefore this transition is also enabled on sq_1. Transitions $2a'$, $2a1'$, and $f2$ are trivially enabled on sq_1. Transition $1b$ is enabled on sq_1 because $Guard^+(1b) = \{c_{abort2}\}$ and $Guard^-(1b) = \{\}$ and for the transition $2a1'$ it holds Val$(2a1') = \{c_{abort2}\}$.

Now, consider a sequence of transitions $(p1, 1a, 1a1)$. Similar to the previous example, the transition $p1$ is trivially enabled on sq_2. $Guard^+(1a) = \{c_{abort1}\}$ and there is no predecessor s_j of the transition $1a$ in the sequence sq_2 for that $c_{abort1} \in$ Val(s_j). Hence, a transition $1a$ is disabled on sq_2. Both guard functions for a transition $1a1$ return the empty set, however, because a transition $1a$, which precedes the transition $1a1$, is disabled on sq_2; the transition $1a1$ is also disabled on sq_2.

Definition 14 (Execution fragment). *An* execution fragment *of RUCA P is an alternating sequence of states and actions* $v_0, a_0, v_1, a_1, ...$ *such that all transitions in the sequence* $t_i = (v_i, a_i, v_{i+1}) \in \tau_P$ *are enabled on P.*

Definition 15 (Execution trace). *An* execution trace *of RUCA P is an execution frag-ment of use-case automaton P that starts in the initial state of P and is infinite or end in some final state* $v^{final} \in V_C^{succ} \cup V_C^{abort}$ *of the automaton P.*

Definition 16 (Consistent use-case). *A resolved use-case automaton P is* consistent *if for all execution traces of the automaton P all formulae from LTL_P are satisfied.*

Verification Algorithm. The verification algorithm takes a set U of use-cases (already parsed textual use-cases encoded in an internal form). and a precedence relation $Prec$ describing the precedence relationship among use-cases in U as input. First, a static check of precedences and includes is done. If a cyclic dependency is found, the algorithm stops and returns *not consistent*.

Second, model-checking of temporal properties (using UCMC algorithm) is performed: UCAI is built for each use-case in U (Definition 3); the set of RUCAs is created by resolving all UCAIs (Definition 5), then valuation of variables, guard functions (Definition 8), and consistency properties (Definition 9) are generated from annotations of RUCAs, the set OB is built (Definition 12) and then each RUCA in OB is model checked for consistency with generated LTL formulae (Definition 16). If all such automata are consistent, the algorithm returns *consistent*. If there is an inconsistent RUCA in OB, there is an execution trace for which the LTL formula corresponding to a consistency property of the RUCA does not hold. In this case, the algorithm returns *not consistent* and provides further details comprising (1) the steps of use-cases from U that correspond to this execution trace, and (2) the ordering of use-cases corresponding to the inconsistent RUCA.

RUCA defines formal behavior of use-cases. We are able to model RUCA using the SMV system and then use the SMV system to check all the generated LTL formulae. In the future work, we consider to let a user to specify an arbitrary temporal dependencies by defining new annotations and mapping of these annotations to valuation of variables and LTL formulae.

Theorem 1 (Correctness of the verification algorithm). *Let U be the set of textual use-cases, G_{prec} be the graph describing a precedence relationship, and G_{incl} be the graph describing an include relationship. Assume that G_{prec} and G_{incl} do not contain cycles. Then, the algorithm returns* consistent *iff all the sequences of the use-cases corresponding to the specification consisting of U and complying with G_{prec} does not contain any incorrectly used* create, use, open *or* close *annotation.*

Proof. The proof is based on the fact that the standard algorithm for checking LTL formula in a Kripke structure returns *consistent* iff the Kripke structure satisfies the given LTL formula.

Because RUCA (an element of the OB set) corresponds to a Kripke structure, it is sufficient to show that the semantics of annotated textual specification corresponds to semantics of the generated OB set and LTL formulae.

This can be done in three steps proving that:

1. traces[6] of transitions captured by the elements of OB (RUCAs) exactly correspond to the sequences of steps captured by U with G_{prec} when the annotations are not considered,
2. execution traces of RUCAs in OB correspond to the sequences of steps captured by U with G_{prec} when the *trace-on* annotations are considered.
3. based on (1) and (2), from the Definition 9, it follows that LTL formulae generated from the *create-use* and *open-close* annotations correspond to semantics of these annotations. Specifically from this fact and the step (2), it follows that the sequences of steps captured by U and G_{prec} with correctly used annotations exactly correspond to the execution traces where all the generated LTL formulae are satisfied. Since there are no cyclic include dependencies and the number of variables is finite, the number of traces to explore is also finite and the algorithm eventually terminates. And thus the algorithm is correct.

Let us prove now the step (1). From the Definition 3 and the Definition 5 it follows that there is a sequence of steps that a use-case $u \in U$ describes iff there is a trace in RUCA corresponding to u. From the Definition 10 it follows that the semantics of concatenation of RUCA corresponds to the semantics of G_{prec}. From the Definition 12 it follows that for each possible order of executions of the use-cases in U determined by G_{prec} there is a RUCA in OB such that it consists of the RUCAs concatenated in compliance with G_{prec}.

Finally, let us prove the step (2). From the Definition 3 it follows that the annotations of steps of a use-case $u \in U$ correspond to the annotations of traces of the RUCA corresponding to u. The *trace-on* annotations restrict the sequences of steps captured by the specification. From this fact and (1), it follows that for each sequence of steps captured by U and G_{prec} when the *trace-on* annotations are considered, there is a trace of a RUCA from OB. The trace is the execution trace if for each transition annotated with *on:id* there is a transition annotated with *trace:id* before this transition. That is, there is no execution fragment which would not correspond to a sequence of steps captured by U and G_{prec}.

6   Summary and Future Work

We have developed means for verifying consistency of textual use-cases useful especially when use-cases are written iteratively by multiple authors. By introducing annotations to use-case steps, we can capture temporal dependencies among use-cases which is a foundation for further verification of temporal properties (based on LTL). As a key contribution, we have defined a formal behavior model (based on LTS) and defined its correspondence to textual use-case specification. A formal behavior model satisfying LTL formulae inferred from user annotations corresponds to a consistent use-case specification. Even though we have considered just two annotation pairs, the *create-use* and

---

[6] The term *trace* in this context is defined in the same way as the *execution trace* (see Definition 15) with the modification that all the possible transitions are considered (not just the enabled ones).

open-close pairs, our approach is applicable for other annotations as well, the semantics of which can be described by LTL. This is because we internally use LTL formulae to capture desired temporal properties. It should be noted that most of the examples in the text were taken from case studies of real-life use-cases [5].

Currently, we continue the development of REPROTOOL which integrates the verification method with analysis of natural language. As a future work we plan to tackle the following challenges:

- We plan to extend the palette of annotations in future and potentially to let users define their own annotations using arbitrary LTL-formulae.
- We could also implement asynchronous events in use-case specification. As pointed out by Larman [9] these events can be attached to multiple steps, e.g. "at any time" or "within a range of steps".
- Our method would work even if we did not use any tools for processing natural language. Users could manually mark sentences as *goto-*, *abort-* or *include-actions*. However, due to the restrictions of the natural language in use-case specifications [3,9,19], we can benefit from NLP tools and thus automate this process. It should be also possible to infer the use-case step annotations from the text automatically. We intend to improve the currently employed NLP tools in REPROTOOL.

Acknowledgements. This work was partially supported by the Grant Agency of the Czech Republic project P103/11/1489, by the Ministry of Education of the Czech Republic (grant MSM0021620838) and by the grant SVV-2011-263312.

References

1. de Alfaro, L., Henzinger, T.A.: Interface Automata. SIGSOFT Softw. Eng. Notes 26(5), 109–120 (2001)
2. Boehm, B.: Software Engineering Economics. Prentice-Hall, Englewood Cliffs (1981)
3. Cockburn, A.: Writing Effective Use Cases. Addison-Wesley, Boston (2000)
4. Drazan, J., Mencl, V.: Improved Processing of Textual Use Cases: Deriving Behavior Specifications. In: van Leeuwen, J., Italiano, G.F., van der Hoek, W., Meinel, C., Sack, H., Plášil, F. (eds.) SOFSEM 2007. LNCS, vol. 4362, pp. 856–868. Springer, Heidelberg (2007)
5. Firesmith, D.: Global personal marketplace system requirements specification (2003), http://www.it.uu.se/edu/course/homepage/pvt/SRS.pdf
6. Hoare, C.A.R.: Communicating Sequential Processes. Prentice Hall Int. (UK) Ltd. (1985)
7. Kof, L.: From textual scenarios to message sequence charts: Inclusion of condition generation and actor extraction. In: Proc. RE 2008, pp. 331–332. IEEE CS (2008)
8. Kofron, J., Poch, T., Sery, O.: TBP: Code-Oriented Component Behavior Specification. In: SEW 2008: Proceedings of the 2008 32nd Annual IEEE Software Engineering Workshop, pp. 75–83. IEEE CS, Washington, DC (2008)
9. Larman, C.: Applying UML and Patterns: An Introduction to Object-Oriented Analysis and Design and Iterative Development. Prentice Hall PTR, Upper Saddle River (2004)
10. Luisa, M., Mariangela, F., Pierluigi, I.: Market research for requirements analysis using linguistic tools. Requir. Eng. 9, 40–56 (2004)

11. Magee, J., Dulay, N., Eisenbach, S., Kramer, J.: Specifying Distributed Software Architectures. In: Botella, P., Schäfer, W. (eds.) ESEC 1995. LNCS, vol. 989, pp. 137–153. Springer, Heidelberg (1995),
    `http://pubs.doc.ic.ac.uk/SpecifyDistributedArchitectures/`
12. Mencl, V.: Deriving behavior specifications from textual use cases. In: Proc. of WITSE 2004 (September 2004)
13. Milner, R.: Communication and Concurrency. Prentice Hall International (UK) Ltd., Hertfordshire (1995)
14. OMG: Unified Modeling Language (2008), `http://www.uml.org`
15. Plasil, F., Mencl, V.: Getting 'Whole Picture' Behavior In A Use Case Model. Journ. of Integrated Design and Process Sci. 7(4), 63–79 (2003)
16. Pow-Sang, J.A., Nakasone, A., Imbert, R., Moreno, A.M.: An approach to determine software requirement construction sequences based on use cases. In: Proc. of ASEA 2008, pp. 17–22. IEEE CS, Washington, DC (2008)
17. Simko, V.: Patterns in specification documents. Tech. Rep. 2011/6, Charles Uni. (2011),
    `http://d3s.mff.cuni.cz/publications/download/tr2011-6.pdf`
18. Yue, T., Briand, L., Labiche, Y.: An Automated Approach to Transform Use Cases into Activity Diagrams. In: Kühne, T., Selic, B., Gervais, M.-P., Terrier, F. (eds.) ECMFA 2010. LNCS, vol. 6138, pp. 337–353. Springer, Heidelberg (2010)
19. Yue, T., Briand, L.C., Labiche, Y.: A Use Case Modeling Approach to Facilitate the Transition Towards Analysis Models: Concepts and Empirical Evaluation. In: Schürr, A., Selic, B. (eds.) MODELS 2009. LNCS, vol. 5795, pp. 484–498. Springer, Heidelberg (2009)

Author Index